NORTH AMERICA

ARCTIC OCEAN

New Siberian Islands

North Magnetic Pole ★
North Pole ★

ASIA

GREENLAND

ARCTIC CIRCLE

QUEEN ELIZABETH ISLANDS

GREENLAND

Iceland

Hudson Bay

NORTH AMERICA

NORTH PACIFIC OCEAN

NORTH ATLANTIC OCEAN

TROPIC OF CANCER

Hawaii

CENTRAL AMERICA

GULF OF MEXICO

EQUATOR

A N D E S

SOUTH AMERICA

MID-ATLANTIC RIDGE

SOUTH PACIFIC OCEAN

TROPIC OF CAPRICORN

SOUTH ATLANTIC OCEAN

Falkland Islands

ANTARCTIC CIRCLE

ANTARCTIC PENINSULA

Alexander Island

WEDDELL

Marie Byrd Land

Ellsworth Land

Vinson Massif

A N T A

GLOBAL SATELLITE MOSAIC

The beauty and complexity of Earth's landscape—relative and below the oceans—is revealed with the Global Satellite Mosaic. This mosaic was created for the National Geographic Society by NASA's Jet Propulsion Laboratory using more than 500 satellite images from the National Oceanic and Atmospheric Administration. The cloud-free images show Earth in its natural colors as it would be seen from space. One can easily identify the world's major glaciers, deserts, mountain ranges, and rain forests. For example, follow the green ribbon of lush vegetation of the Nile into the stark, dry Sahara. The mountain ranges seem to rise off the map thanks to digital elevation databases from the Department of Defense. The deepest areas of the ocean realm are colored dark blue in contrast to the light blue areas highlighting continental shelves, submarine ridges, and underwater mountains.

BIOSPHERE

Thousands of satellite images were combined to show a picture of biological productivity. In oceans, red, yellow, and green indicate waters rich in phytoplankton. On land, dark green areas show high potential plant productivity; tan and yellow suffer from productivity limitations due to aridity and temperature.

THE W

SATEL

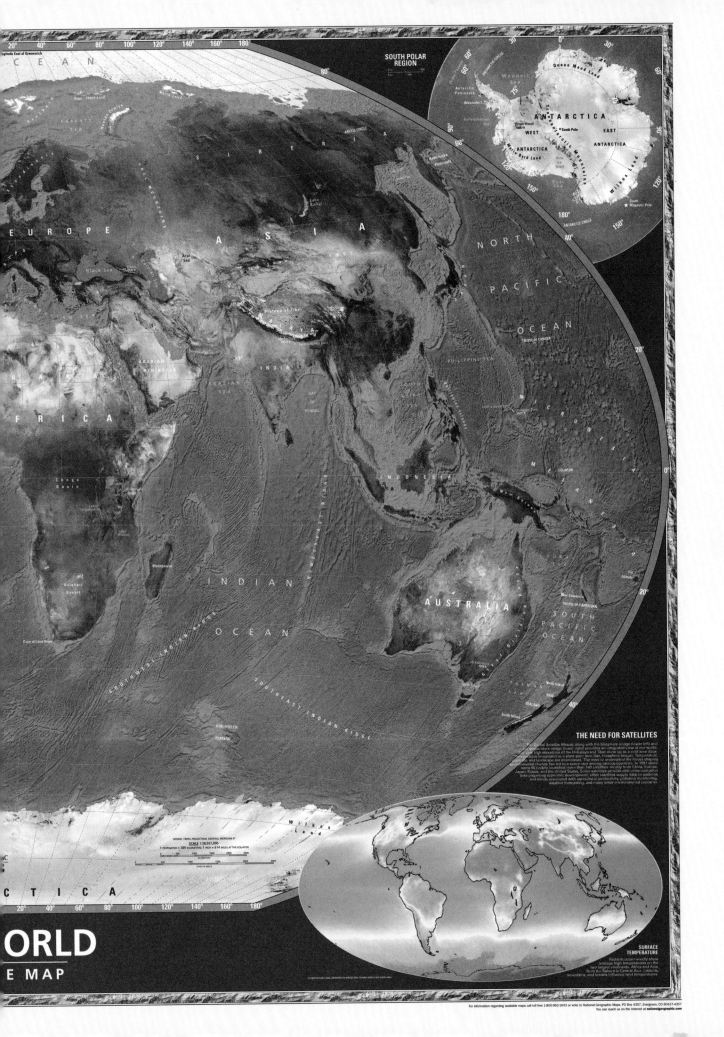

SOUTH POLAR REGION

THE NEED FOR SATELLITES

WINKEL TRIPEL PROJECTION, CENTRAL MERIDIAN 0°
SCALE 1:38,931,000
1 CENTIMETER = 389 KILOMETERS; 1 INCH = 614 MILES AT THE EQUATOR

WORLD
E MAP

SURFACE TEMPERATURE

For information regarding available maps call toll free 1-800-962-1643 or write to National Geographic Maps, PO Box 4357, Evergreen, CO 80437-4357
You can reach us on the Internet at nationalgeographic.com

This registration code provides access to documents

and other sources available at the

Worlds Together, Worlds Apart 3E StudySpace site:

wwnorton.com/studyspace

FMES-LKIC

THIRD EDITION
VOLUME A

Worlds Together, WORLDS APART

ROBERT TIGNOR

JEREMY ADELMAN

PETER BROWN

BENJAMIN ELMAN

XINRU LIU

HOLLY PITTMAN

BRENT SHAW

THIRD EDITION
VOLUME A
BEGINNINGS TO 1200

Worlds Together, WORLDS APART

W · W · NORTON & COMPANY
NEW YORK · LONDON

W. W. Norton & Company has been independent since its founding in 1923, when William Warder Norton and Mary D. Herter Norton first published lectures delivered at the People's Institute, the adult education division of New York City's Cooper Union. The firm soon expanded its program beyond the Institute, publishing books by celebrated academics from America and abroad. By mid-century, the two major pillars of Norton's publishing program—trade books and college texts—were firmly established. In the 1950s, the Norton family transferred control of the company to its employees, and today—with a staff of four hundred and a comparable number of trade, college, and professional titles published each year—W. W. Norton & Company stands as the largest and oldest publishing house owned wholly by its employees.

Editor: Jon Durbin
Developmental Editor: Alice Vigliani
Copy Editor: Ellen Lohman
Project Editor: Rebecca Homiski
Photo Editor: Stephanie Romeo
Production Manager: Benjamin Reynolds
Managing Editor, College: Marian Johnson
Marketing Manager: Tamara McNeill
Emedia Editor: Steve Hoge
Design Director: Rubina Yeh
Ancillary Editor: Lorraine Klimowich
Editorial Assistant: Jason Spears
Layout Artist: Brad Walrod
Composition: TexTech, Inc.
Cartographer: Carto-Graphics/Alice Thiede

The Library of Congress has cataloged the one-volume edition as follows:

Worlds together, worlds apart : a history of the world from the beginnings of humankind to the present / Robert Tignor ... [et al.]. — 3rd ed.
    p. cm.
  Includes bibliographical references and index.
  ISBN 978-0-393-93492-2 (hardcover)
1. World history. I. Tignor, Robert L.
  D21.W94 2011
  909—dc22

                        2010036837

This edition:
ISBN: 978-0-393-93495-3 (pbk.)

W. W. Norton & Company, Inc., 500 Fifth Avenue, New York, NY 10110
wwnorton.com

W. W. Norton & Company Ltd., Castle House, 75/76 Wells Street, London W1T 3QT

4 5 6 7 8 9

Contents in Brief

Contents

CHAPTER 1   BECOMING HUMAN   3

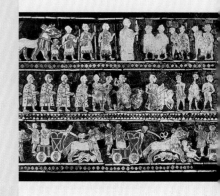

CHAPTER 4   FIRST EMPIRES AND COMMON CULTURES IN AFRO-EURASIA, 1250–325 BCE   125

CHAPTER 9   NEW EMPIRES AND COMMON CULTURES, 600–1000 CE   321

CHAPTER 10   BECOMING "THE WORLD," 1000–1300 CE   363

Global Connections & Disconnections Features

Primary Sources

Maps

The New Edition

Worlds Together, Worlds Apart has set the standard for two editions for those instructors who want to teach a globally integrated world history survey course. Just as the dynamic field of world history evolves, so has *Worlds Together, Worlds Apart* with each edition. With the Third Edition, *Worlds Together, Worlds Apart* continues to offer a highly coherent, cutting-edge survey of the field, while becoming more streamlined and accessible for a wider range of students. The Third Edition offers a number of improvements over the first two. First, the chapters are shorter. We cut the narrative by 50,000 words, reducing its length by nearly 20 percent. We shrank the text to highlight even more clearly the distinctive world history stories and themes that each chapter is built around. Readers should be in little doubt now about what truly counted globally in each of the time periods that the chapters cover. The new edition should also be a good page turner for students for while we reduced the length of the book to just over 840 pages, we did not dramatically cut back on the map, illustration, and primary-source programs. By shortening the text, we also wanted to allow instructors to make greater use of outside reading materials, especially primary sources, which are so vital to understanding the life and thought of people living in different time periods and locations. Second, pedagogically, we have re-written the chapter introductions to emphasize the themes even more strongly. We have also added a new pedagogy feature called "Storylines," which is designed to provide the reader with a snapshot of the main chapter themes and show how they relate to each major region of the world. We also went through all the pedagogical features with great care to make sure that the prose and questions were pitched at a good level for a wide range of students. Third, we are pleased to announce the publication of *Worlds Together, Worlds Apart: A Companion Reader*. Long-time users of the book have been asking for a primary-source reader designed to accompany *Worlds Together, Worlds Apart* since its First Edition. The new companion reader has been carefully assembled by Ken Pomeranz, Laura Mitchell, and James Given, all of whom teach the world history survey course at the University of California, Irvine, and all of whom have been teaching with *Worlds Together, Worlds Apart* for many years. The companion reader contains nearly 150 primary sources (both visual and textual) and will greatly enhance an instructor's ability to teach students how to analyze primary sources, while building off the key themes and topics of *Worlds Together, Worlds Apart*. Finally, Norton StudySpace offers an exciting new feature called World History Tours powered by Google Maps. These digitally based tours trace global developments over time, touching down on locations to launch documents and images for analysis. For example, the Silk Road tour follows the bubonic plague from its eastern origins to Europe, chronicling this movement through journals and images from the Muslim world, Italy, and England.

Since work began on *Worlds Together, Worlds Apart*, world history has gained even more prominence in college classrooms and historical studies. Courses in the history of the world now abound, often replacing the standard surveys of European history and western civilization overviews. Graduate history students receive training in world history, and journals routinely publish studies in this field. A new generation of textbooks was needed to help students and instructors make sense of this vast, complex, and rapidly evolving field.

We believe that *Worlds Together, Worlds Apart* remains the most cutting-edge, engaging, readable, and useful text available for all students of world history. We also believe that this text, one that has advanced the teaching of this field, could have only grown out of the highly collaborative effort of a team of scholars and teachers rather than the more typical single- or two-author efforts. Indeed, the idea to build each chapter around stories of world history significance and the execution of this model grew out of our monthly team meetings and our joint writing efforts during the development stage. As a team-driven text, *Worlds Together, Worlds Apart* also has the advantage of area experts to make sure the material is presented accurately, which is always a challenge for the single- or two-author texts, especially in world history. Finally, our book also reads with a single voice due to the extraordinary efforts of our general editor, and leader, Robert Tignor, who with every edition makes the final major sweep through the text to make sure that the voice, style, and level of detail are consistent throughout. Building on these distinctive strengths, we have worked hard and thoughtfully to make the Third Edition of *Worlds Together, Worlds Apart* the best one so far. While there are many exciting additions to the main text and support package, we have made every effort to remain true to our original vision.

OUR GUIDING PRINCIPLES

Five principles inform this book, guiding its framework and the organization of its individual chapters. The first is that **world history is global history**. There are many fine histories of the individual regions of the world, which we have endeavored to make good use of. But unlike the authors of many other so-called world histories, we have chosen not to deal with the great regions and cultures of the world as separate units, reserving individual chapters to East Asia, South Asia, Southwest Asia, Europe, Africa, and the Americas. Our goal is to place each of these regions in its largest geographical context. Accordingly, we have written chapters that are truly global in that most major regions of the world are discussed in each. We achieved these globally integrated chapters by building each around a significant world history story or theme. There are a number of wonderful examples throughout the book, including the peopling of the earth (Chapter 1), the building of the Silk Road (Chapter 6), the rise of universal religions (Chapters 8 and 9), the Black Death (Chapter 11), the effects of New World silver on the economies of the world (Chapter 13), alternative visions to nineteenth-century capitalism (Chapter 15), the rise of nation states and empires (Chapter 16), and so on. It would be misleading, of course, to say that the context is the world, because none of these regions, even the most highly developed commercially, enjoyed commercial or cultural contact with peoples all over the globe before Columbus's voyage to the Americas and the sixteenth century. But the peoples living in the Afro-Eurasian landmass, probably the single most important building block for our study, were deeply influenced by one another, as were the more scattered peoples living in the Americas and in Africa below the Sahara. Products, ideas, and persons traveled widely across the large land units of Eurasia, Africa, and the Americas. Indeed, Afro-Eurasia was not divided or thought of as divided into separate landmasses until recent times. It is in this sense that our world history is global.

The second principle informing this work is **the importance of chronology in framing world history**. Rather than telling the story of world history by analyzing separate geographical areas, we have elected to frame the chapters around significant world history themes and periods that transcended regional and cultural boundaries—moments or periods of meaningful change in the way that human beings organized their lives. Some of these changes were dramatic and affected many people. Environments changed; the earth became drier and warmer; humans learned to domesticate plants and animals; technological innovations in warfare, political organization, and commercial activities occurred; and new religious and cultural beliefs spread far and wide. These changes swept across large landmasses, paying scant heed to preexisting cultural and geographical unity. They affected peoples living in widely dispersed societies. In other cases, changes occurred in only one locality while other places retained their traditions or took alternative routes. Chronology helps us understand the ways in which the world has, and has not, shared a common history.

The third principle is **historical and geographical balance**. Ours is not a history focused on the rise of the West. We seek to pay attention to the global histories of all peoples and not to privilege those developments that led directly into European history as if the rest of the history of the world was but a prelude to the rise of western civilization. We deal with peoples living outside Europe on their own terms and try to see world history from their perspective. Even more significantly, while we describe societies that obviously influenced Europe's historical development, we do so in a context very different from that which western historians have stressed. Rather than simply viewing these cultures in terms of their role in western development, we seek to understand them in their own terms and to illuminate the ways they influenced other parts of the world. From our perspective, it is historically inaccurate to annex Mesopotamia and Egypt to western civilization, because these territories lay well outside Europe and had a large influence on Africa, South Asia, and East Asia as well as on Europe. Indeed, our presentation of Europe in the period leading up to and including the founding of the Roman Empire is different from many of the standard treatments. The Europeans we describe are rather rough, wild-living, warring peoples living on the fringes of the settled parts of the world and looked down on by more politically stable communities. They hardly seem to be made of the stuff that will catapult Europeans to world leadership a millennium later—indeed, they were very different people from those who, as the result of myriad intervening and contingent events, founded the nineteenth- and twentieth-century empires whose ruins are still all around us.

Our fourth principle is **an emphasis on connections and what we call disconnections across societal and cultural boundaries**. World history is not the history of separate regions of the world at different periods of time. It is the history of the connections among peoples living often at great distances from one another, and it is also the history of the resistances of peoples living within and outside societies to connections that threatened to put them in subordinate positions or to rob them of their independence.

A stress on connections inevitably foregrounds those elements within societies that promoted long-distance ties. Merchants are important, as are military men and political potentates seeking to expand their polities. So are scholars and religious leaders, particularly those who believed that they had universalistic messages with which to convert others to their visions. Perhaps most important of all in pre-modern world history, certainly the most understudied, are the nomadic pastoral peoples, who were often the agents for the transmission of products, peoples, and ideas across long and harsh distances. They exploded onto the scene of settled societies at critical junctures, erasing old cultural and geographical barriers and producing new unities, as the Arabs did in the seventh century CE and the Mongols in the thirteenth century. *Worlds Together, Worlds Apart* is not intended to convey the message that the history of the world is a story of increasing integration. What for one ruling group brought benefits in the form of increased workforces, material prosperity, and political stability often meant enslavement, political subordination, and loss of territory for other groups. The historian's task, then, is not only to represent the different experiences of increased connectedness, describing worlds that came together, but also to be attentive to the opposite trends, describing peoples and communities that remained apart.

The fifth and final principle is that **world history is a narrative of big themes and high-level comparisons**. *Worlds Together, Worlds Apart* is not a book of record. Indeed, in a work that covers the whole of the historical record of humankind from the beginnings of history to the present, the notion that no event or individual worthy of attention would be excluded is the height of folly. We have sought to offer clear themes and interpretations in order to synthesize the vast body of data that often overwhelms histories of the world. Our aspiration is to identify the main historical forces that have moved history, to highlight those monumental innovations that have changed the way humans lived, and to describe the creation and evolution of those bedrock institutions, many of which, of course, endure. In this regard, self-conscious cross-cultural comparisons of developments, institutions, and even founding figures receive attention to make students aware that some common institutions, such as slavery, did not have the same features in every society. Or, in the opposite fashion, the seemingly diverse terms that were used, say, to describe learned and religious men in different parts of the world—monks in Europe, ulama in Islam, Brahmans in India, and scholar-gentries in China—often meant much the same thing in very different settings. We have constructed *Worlds Together, Worlds Apart* around big ideas, stories, and themes rather than filling the book with names and dates that encourage students only to memorize rather than understand world history concepts.

OUR MAJOR THEMES

The primary organizing framework of *Worlds Together, Worlds Apart*—one that runs through the chapters and connects the different parts of the volume—is the theme of **interconnection and divergence**. While describing movements that facilitated global connectedness, this book also shows how different regions developed their own ways of handling or resisting connections and change. Throughout history, different regions and different population groups often stood apart from the rest of the world until touched by traders or explorers or missionaries or soldiers. Some of these regions welcomed global connections. Others sought to change the nature of their connections with the outside world, and yet others resisted efforts to bring them into the larger world. All, however, were somehow affected by their experience of connection. Yet, the history of the world is not simply one of increasing globalization, in which all societies eventually join a common path to the present. Rather, it is a history of the ways in which, as people became linked, their experience of these global connections diverged.

Besides the central theme of interconnection and divergence, other themes also stand out in *Worlds Together, Worlds Apart*. First, the book discusses **how the recurring efforts of people to cross religious, political, and cultural borders brought the world together**. Merchants and educated men and women traded goods and ideas. Whole communities, in addition to select groups, moved to safer or more promising environments. **The transregional crossings of ideas, goods, and peoples produced transformations and conflicts**—a second important theme. Finally, the movement of ideas, peoples, products, and germs over long distances upset the balance of power across the world and within individual societies. Such movements changed the relationship of different population groups with other peoples and areas of the world and led over time to dramatic shifts in the ascendancy of regions. **Changes in power arrangements within and between regions explain which parts of the world and regional groups benefited from integration and which resisted it.** These three themes (exchange and migration, conflict and resistance, and alterations in the balance of power) weave themselves through every chapter of this work. While we highlight major themes throughout, we tell the stories of the people caught in these currents of exchange, conflict, and changing power relations, paying particular attention to the role that gender and the environment play in shaping the evolution of societies.

The history of the world is not a single, sweeping narrative. On the contrary, the last 5,000 years have produced multiple histories, moving along many paths and trajectories. Sometimes these histories merge, intertwining themselves in substantial ways. Sometimes they disentangle themselves and simply stand apart. Much of the time, however, they are simultaneously together and apart. In place of a single narrative, the usual one being the rise of the West, this book maps the many forks in the road that confronted the world's societies at different times and the surprising turns and unintended consequences that marked the choices that peoples and societies made, including the unanticipated and dramatic rise of the West in the nineteenth century. Formulated in this way, world history is the unfolding of many possible histories, and readers of this book should come away with a reinforced sense of the unpredictability of the past, the instability of the present, and the uncertainty of the future.

OVERVIEW OF VOLUME ONE

Volume One of *Worlds Together, Worlds Apart* deals with the period from the beginnings of human history through the Mongol invasions of the thirteenth century and the spread of the Black Death across Afro-Eurasia. It is divided into eleven chapters, each of which marks a distinct historical period. Hence, each chapter has an overarching theme or small set of themes that hold otherwise highly diverse material together.

Chapter 1, "Becoming Human," presents biological and cultural perspectives on the way that early hominoids became truly human. We believe that this chapter is important in establishing the global context of world history. We believe too that our chapter is unique in its focus on how humans became humans, so we discuss how early humans became bipedal and how they developed complex cognitive processes such as language and artistic abilities. Recent research indicates that *Homo sapiens* originated in Africa, probably no more than 200,000 years ago. These early men and women walked out of the African landmass sometime between 120,000 and 50,000 years ago, gradually populating all regions of the world. What is significant in this story is that the different population groups around the world, the so-called races of humankind, have only recently broken off from one another. Also in this chapter, we describe the domestication of plants and animals and the founding of the first village settlements around the globe.

NEW: Discussions of the role that dogs played in human evolution and the latest findings on the origins of humans.

Chapter 2, "Rivers, Cities, and First States, 4000–2000 BCE," covers the period during which five of the great river basins experienced extraordinary breakthroughs in human activity. On the flood plains of the Tigris and Euphrates in Mesopotamia, the Nile in Egypt, the Indus valley in modern-day northern India and Pakistan, and the Yellow and Yangzi rivers in China, men and women mastered annual floods and became expert in seeding and cultivating foodstuffs. In these areas, populations became dense. Riverine cultures had much in common. They had highly developed hierarchical political, social, and cultural systems, priestly and bureaucratic classes, and organized religious and cultural systems. But they also differed greatly, and these differences were passed from generation to generation. The development of these major complex societies certainly is a turning point in world history.

Extensive climatic and technological changes serve as major turning points for **Chapter 3, "Nomads, Territorial States, and Microsocieties, 2000–1200 BCE."** Drought, environmental degradation, and political instability brought the first riverine societies to a crashing end around 2000 BCE. When aridity forced tribal and nomadic peoples living on the fringes of the settled populations to move closer to settled areas, they brought with them an insurmountable military advantage. They had become adept at yoking horses to war chariots, and hence they were in a position to subjugate or intermarry with the peoples in the settled polities in the river basins. Around 2000 BCE these peoples established new territorial kingdoms in Mesopotamia, Egypt, the Indus valley, and China, which gave way a millennium later (1000 BCE) to even larger, militarily and politically more powerful states. In the Americas, the Mediterranean, sub-Saharan Africa, and the

Pacific worlds, microsocieties arose as an alternative form of polity in which peoples lived in much smaller-scale societies that showcased their own unique and compelling features.

NEW: Expanded discussions of how the Egyptian pyramids were built and their role in Egyptian cosmology and fuller integration of material on the environmental catastrophe that shaped the third millennium BCE.

Chapter 4, "First Empires and Common Cultures in Afro-Eurasia, 1200–350 BCE," describes the different ways in which larger-scale societies grew and became unified. In the case of the world's first empires, the neo-Assyrian and Persian, political power was the main unifying element. Both states established different models that future empires would emulate. The Assyrians used brutal force to intimidate and subjugate different groups within their societies and neighboring states. The Persians followed a pattern that relied less on coercion and more on tributary relationships, while reveling in cultural diversity. The Zhou state in China offered yet a third way of political unity, basing its rule on the doctrine of the mandate of heaven, which legitimated its rulers' succession as long as they were able to maintain stability and order. Vedic society in South Asia offers a dramatically different model in which religion and culture were the main unifying forces. Religion moves to the forefront of the narrative in other ways in this chapter. The birth of monotheism occurred in the Zoroastrian and Hebrew faiths and the beginnings of Buddhism. All three religions endure today.

NEW: Revised and expanded discussion of the origins of Judaism.

The last millennium before the common era witnessed some of the most monumental developments in human history. In the six and half centuries discussed in **Chapter 5, "Worlds Turned Inside Out, 1000–350 BCE,"** teachers and thinkers, rather than kings, priests, and warriors, came to the fore. Men like Confucius, the Buddha, Plato, and Aristotle, to name only the best known of this brilliant group, offered new insights into the natural world and provided new guidelines for how to govern justly and live ethically. In this era, small-scale societies, benefiting from more intimate relationships, took the place of the first great empires, now in decline. These highly individualistic cultures developed new strategies for political organization, even including experimenting with a democratic polity. In Africa, the Bantu peoples spread across sub-Saharan Africa, and the Sudanic peoples of Meroe created a society that blended Egyptian and sub-Saharan influences. These were all dynamic hybrid societies building on existing knowledge. Equally dramatic transformations occurred in the Americas, where the Olmec and Chavín peoples were creating hierarchical societies of the like never before seen in their part of the world.

NEW: Increased discussion of the first millennium as an "axial age."

Chapter 6, "Shrinking the Afro-Eurasian World, 350 BCE–250 CE," describes three major forces that simultaneously integrated large segments of the Afro-Eurasian landmass culturally and economically. First, Alexander and his armies changed the political and cultural landscape of North Africa and Southwest and South Asia. Culturally, Alexander spread Hellenism through North Africa and Southwest and central Asia, making it the first cultural system to achieve a transregional scope. Second, it was in the post-Alexander world that these commercial roads were stabilized and intensified. For the first time, a trading network, known as the Silk Road, stretching from Palmyra in the West to central Asia in the East, came into being. Buddhism was the first religion to seize on the Silk Road's more formal existence as its followers moved quickly with the support of the Mauryan Empire to spread their ideas into central Asia. Finally, we witness the growth of a "silk road of the seas" as new technologies and bigger ships allowed for a dramatic expansion in maritime trade from South Asia all the way to Egypt and East Africa.

Chapter 7, "Han Dynasty China and Imperial Rome, 300 BCE–300 CE," compares Han China and the Roman Empire, the two political, economic, and cultural systems that dominated much of the Afro-Eurasian landmass from 200 BCE to 200 CE. Both the Han Dynasty and the Roman Empire ruled effectively in their own way, providing an instructive comparative case study. Both left their imprint on Afro-Eurasia, and rulers for centuries afterward tried to revive these glorious polities and use them as models of greatness. This chapter also discusses the effect of state sponsorship on religion, as Christianity came into existence in the context of the late Roman Empire and Buddhism was introduced to China during the decline of the Han.

Out of the crumbling Roman Empire new polities and a new religion emerged, the major topic of **Chapter 8, "The Rise of Universal Religions, 300–600 CE."** The Byzantine Empire, claiming to be the successor state to the Roman Empire, embraced Christianity as its state religion. The Tang rulers patronized Buddhism to such a degree that Confucian statesmen feared it had become the state religion. Both Buddhism and Christianity enjoyed spectacular success in the politically fragmented post-Han era in China and in the feudal world of western Europe. These dynamic religions represent a decisive transformation in world history. Christianity enjoyed its eventual successes through state sponsorship via the Roman and Byzantine empires and by providing spiritual comfort and hope during the chaotic years of Rome's decline. Buddhism grew through imperial sponsorship and significant changes to its fundamental beliefs, when adherents to the faith deified Buddha and created notions of an afterlife. In Africa a wide range of significant developments and a myriad of cultural practices existed; yet large common cultures also arose. The Bantu peoples spread throughout the southern half of the landmass, spoke closely related languages, and developed similar political institutions based on the prestige of individuals of high achievement. In the Americas the Olmecs established their own form of the city-state, while the Mayans owed their success to a decentralized common culture built around a strong religious belief system and a series of spiritual centers.

NEW: Revised discussions of what enables a religion to become "universal."

In **Chapter 9, "New Empires and Common Cultures, 600–1000 CE,"** in a relatively remote corner of the Arabian Peninsula another world religion, Islam, exploded with world-changing consequences. The rise of Islam provides a contrast to the way in which universalizing religions and political empires interacted. Islam and empire arose in a fashion quite different from Christianity and the Roman Empire. Christianity took over an already existing empire—the Roman—after suffering persecution at its hands for several centuries. In contrast, Islam created an empire almost at the moment of its emergence. By the time the Abbasid Empire came into being in the middle of the eighth century, Islamic armies, political leaders, and clerics exercised power over much of the Afro-Eurasian landmass from southern Spain, across North Africa, all the way to Central Asia. The Tang Empire in China, however, served as a counterweight to Islam's power both politically and intellectually. Confucianism enjoyed a spectacular recovery in this period. With the Tang rulers, Confucianism slowed the spread of Buddhism and further reinforced China's development along different, more secular pathways. Japan and Korea also enter world history at this time, as tributary states to Tang China and as hybrid cultures that mixed Chinese customs and practices with their own. The Christian world split in this period between the western Latin church and the eastern Byzantine church. Both branches of Christianity played a role in unifying societies, especially in western Europe, which lacked strong political rule.

NEW: Reorganized to integrate material on the agricultural revolutions that spread across Afro-Eurasia as a result of the rise of Islam between 600 and 1000 BCE.

In the three centuries from 1000 to 1300 (**Chapter 10, "Becoming 'the World,' 1000–1300 CE"**) Afro-Eurasia experienced an unprecedented rise in prosperity and population that even spread into West and East Africa. Just as importantly, the world in this period divided into regional zones that are recognizable today. And trade grew rapidly.

A view of the major trading cities of this time demonstrates how commerce transformed cultures. Sub-Saharan Africa also underwent intense regional integration via the spread of the Mande-speaking peoples and the Mali Empire.

The Americas witnessed their first empire in the form of the Chimu peoples in the Andes. This chapter ends with the Mongol conquests of the twelfth and thirteenth centuries, which brought massive destruction. The Mongol Empire, however, once in place, promoted long-distance commerce, scholarly exchange, and travel on an unprecedented scale. The Mongols brought Eurasia, North Africa, and many parts of sub-Saharan Africa into a new connectedness. The Mongol story also underscores the important role that nomads played throughout the history of the early world.

NEW: Expanded discussion of the Crusades.

The Black Death brought Afro-Eurasia's prosperity and population growth to a catastrophic end as discussed in **Chapter 11, "Crises and Recovery in Afro-Eurasia, 1300s–1500s."** The dying and destruction of the fourteenth century saw traditional institutions give way and forced peoples to rebuild their cultures. The polities that came into being at this time and the intense religious experimentation that took place effected a sharp break with the past. The bubonic plague wiped out as much as two-thirds of the population in many of the densely settled locations of Afro-Eurasia. Societies were brought to their knees by the Mongols' depredations as well as by biological pathogens. In the face of one of humanity's grimmest periods, peoples and societies demonstrated tremendous resilience as they looked for new ways to rebuild their communities, some turning inward and others seeking inspiration, conquests, and riches elsewhere. Volume One concludes on the eve of the "Columbian Exchange," the moment when "old" worlds discovered "new" ones and a vast series of global interconnections and divergences commenced.

NEW: Expanded discussion of the Renaissance.

OVERVIEW OF VOLUME TWO

The organizational structure for Volume Two reaffirms the commitment to write a decentered, global history of the world. Christopher Columbus is not the starting point, as he is in so many modern world histories. Rather, we begin in the eleventh and twelfth centuries with two major developments in world history: the Mongols and the Black Death. The first, set forth in **Chapter 10, "Becoming 'the World,' 1000–1300 CE,"** describes a world that was divided for the first time into regions that are recognizable today. This world experienced rapid population growth, as is shown by a simple look at the major trading cities from Asia in the East to the Mediterranean in the West. Yet nomadic peoples remain a force as revealed in the Mongol invasions of Afro-Eurasia.

NEW: Expanded discussion of the Crusades.

Chapter 11, "Crises and Recovery in Afro-Eurasia, 1300s–1500s," describes how the Mongol warriors, through their conquests and the integration of the Afro-Eurasian world, spread the bubonic plague, which brought death and depopulation to much of Afro-Eurasia. Both these stories set the stage for the modern world and are clear-cut turning points in world history. The primary agents of world connection described in this chapter were dynasts, soldiers, clerics, merchants, and adventurers who rebuilt the societies that disease and political collapse had destroyed.

NEW: Expanded discussion of the Renaissance.

The Mongols joined the two hemispheres, as we describe in **Chapter 12, "Contact, Commerce, and Colonization, 1450s–1600,"** bringing the peoples and products of the Western Hemisphere into contact and conflict with Eurasia and Africa. It is the collision between the Eastern and Western Hemispheres that sets in motion modern world history and marks a distinct divide or turning point between the premodern and the modern. Here, too, disease and increasing trade linkages were vital. Unprepared for the advanced military technology and the disease pool of European and African peoples, the Amerindian population experienced a population decline even more devastating than that caused by the Black Death.

NEW: Expanded discussion of the Protestant Reformation.

Europeans sailed across the Atlantic Ocean to find a more direct, less encumbered route to Asia and came upon lands, peoples, and products that they had not expected. One item, however, that they had sought in every part of the world and that they found in abundance in the Americas was precious metal. In **Chapter 13, "Worlds Entangled, 1600–1750,"** we discuss how New World silver from Mexico and Peru became the major currency of global commerce, oiling the long-distance trading networks that had been revived after the Black Death. The effect of New World silver on the world economy was so great that it, even more than the Iberian explorations of the New World, brought the hemispheres together and marks the true genesis of modern world history. Sugar also linked the economies and polities of western Europe, Africa, and the Americas and was a powerful force in a triangular trade centered on the Atlantic Ocean. This trade involved the shipment of vast numbers of African captives to the Americas, where they toiled on sugar, tobacco, cotton, and rice slave plantations.

Chapter 14, "Cultures of Splendor and Power, 1500–1780," discusses the Ottoman scientists, Safavid and Mughal artists, and Chinese literati, as well as European thinkers, whose notable achievements were rooted in their own cultures but tempered by awareness of the intellectual activities of others. In this chapter, we look closely at how culture is created as a historical process and describe how the massive increase in wealth during this period, growing out of global trade, led to one of the great periods of cultural flourishing in world history.

NEW: Discussions of the Seven Years' War as the first global war.

Around 1800, transformations reverberated outward from the Atlantic world and altered economic and political relationships in the rest of the world. In **Chapter 15, "Reordering the World, 1750–1850,"** we discuss how political revolutions in the Americas and Europe, new ideas about how to trade and organize labor, and a powerful rhetoric of freedom and universal rights underlay the beginning of "a great divide" between peoples of European descent and those who were not. These forces of laissez-faire capitalism, industrialization, the nation-state, and republicanism not only attracted diverse groups around the world; they also threatened groups that put forth alternative visions. Ideas of freedom, as manifested in trading relations, labor, and political activities, clashed with a traditional world based on inherited rights and statuses and further challenged the way men and women had lived in earlier times. These political, intellectual, and economic reorderings changed the way people around the world saw themselves and thus represent something quite novel in world history.

NEW: Discussions of "industriousness" and how the work habits of westerners were changing in the period before the Industrial Revolution.

These new ways of envisioning the world did not go unchallenged, as **Chapter 16, "Alternative Visions of the Nineteenth Century,"** makes clear. Here, intense resistance to evolving modernity reflected the diversity of peoples and their hopes for the future. Wahabbism in Islam, the strongman movement in Africa, Indian resistance in America and Mexico, socialism and communism in Europe, the Taiping Rebellion in China, and the Indian Mutiny in South Asia catapulted to historical prominence prophets and leaders whose visions often drew on earlier traditions and led these individuals to resist rapid change.

NEW: Streamlined discussions comparing the alternative visions of the nineteenth century.

Chapter 17, "Nations and Empires, 1850–1914," discusses the political, economic, military, and ideological power that thrust Europe and North America to the fore of global events and led to an era of nationalism and modern imperialism, new forces in world history. Yet this period of seeming European supremacy was to prove short-lived.

As **Chapter 18, "An Unsettled World, 1890–1914,"** demonstrates, even before World War I shattered Europe's moral certitude, many groups at home (feminists, Marxists, and unfulfilled nationalists) and abroad (anti-colonial nationalists) had raised a chorus of complaints about European and North American dominance. As in Chapter 14, we look at the processes by which specific cultural movements rose and reflected the concerns of individual societies. Yet here, too, syncretistic movements emerged in many cultures and reflected the sway of global imperialism, which by then had become a dominant force.

NEW: Revised discussions of cultural modernism.

Chapter 19, "Of Masses and Visions of the Modern, 1910–1939," briefly covers World War I and then discusses how, from the end of World War I until World War II, different visions of being modern competed around the world. It is the development of modernism and its effects on multiple cultures that integrate the diverse developments discussed in this chapter. In the decades between the world wars, proponents of liberal democracy struggled to defend their views and often to impose their will on authoritarian rulers and anticolonial nationalists.

NEW: Discussions of the Spanish Civil War as a global phenomenon.

Chapter 20, "The Three-World Order, 1940–1975," presents World War II and describes how new adversaries arose after the war. A three-world order came into being—the First World, led by the United States and extolling capitalism, the nation-state, and democratic government; the Second World, led by the Soviet Union and favoring authoritarian polities and economies; and the Third World, made up of former colonies seeking an independent status for themselves in world affairs. The rise of this three-world order dominates the second half of the twentieth century and constitutes another major theme of world history.

NEW: Expanded discussions of the Holocaust.

In **Chapter 21, "Globalization, 1970–2000,"** we explain that, at the end of the cold war, the modern world, while clearly more unified than before, still had profound cultural differences and political divisions. At the beginning of the twenty-first century, capital, commodities, peoples, and ideas move rapidly over long distances. But cultural tensions and political impasses continue to exist. It is the rise of this form of globalism that represents a vital new element as humankind heads into a new century and millennium.

We close with an **Epilogue**, which tracks developments since the turn of the millennium. These last few years have brought profound changes to the world order, yet we hope readers of *Worlds Together, Worlds Apart* will see more clearly how this most recent history is, in fact, entwined with trends of much longer duration that are the chief focus of this book.

NEW: Fully up-to-date on the global financial collapse, wars in the Middle East, and the Obama presidency.

INNOVATIVE PEDAGOGICAL PROGRAM, MADE BETTER

Worlds Together, Worlds Apart is designed for maximum readability. The crisp, clear, and succinct narrative, built around memorable world history stories and themes, is reinforced through a highly innovative pedagogical program designed to help students think critically and master the core content. All the pedagogical elements have been carefully revised for the Third Edition to ensure that students will find them highly useful. Highlights of this innovative program are described below.

NEW "STORYLINES" FEATURE

New "Storylines" features provide a thematic snapshot of the chapter and appear right after the chapter introduction. Each "Storylines" feature highlights the chapter themes and shows how they apply to each region of the world.

STELLAR MAP PROGRAM WITH NEW GUIDING QUESTIONS

The book's more than 120 beautiful maps are designed to reinforce the main stories and themes in each chapter. Most chapters open with a beautiful two-page map of the world to highlight the main storyline of the chapter. Within the chapter are four to five more maps that focus on the regions covered. Enhanced captions with new guiding questions help students learn how to read historical maps and to understand the relationship between geography and history.

REVISED FOCUS-QUESTION SYSTEM

The focus-question system has been fully revised and now contains more manageable questions in order to help the reader remain alert to key concepts and questions on every page of the text. Focus questions guide students' reading in three ways: (1) a focus question box at the beginning of the chapter previews the chapter's contents, (2) relevant questions reappear at the start of the section where they are discussed, and (3) running heads on right-hand pages keep these questions in view throughout the chapter.

PRIMARY-SOURCE DOCUMENTS WITH NEW QUESTIONS FOR ANALYSIS

The authors have selected three to five primary-source documents for each chapter that reinforce the chapter's main themes and help students learn how to analyze primary sources. Many of them challenge students to see world history through the eyes of others and from different perspectives. The questions for analysis after each document have been carefully revised to draw students into the document, moving from simpler to more complex. Additional primary sources are available in *Worlds Together, Worlds Apart: A Companion Reader* and in the Digital History Reader, which is part of the Norton StudySpace website.

GLOBAL CONNECTIONS & DISCONNECTIONS

Each chapter contains one thematic feature built around key individuals or phenomena that exemplify the main emphasis of the text. Among the many topics are how historians use technology to date bones and objects from early history, the use of ritual funeral objects in the contexts of religion and trade, the role of libraries in early world history, the travels of Marco Polo and Ibn Battuta, coffee drinking and coffeehouses in different parts of the world, cartography and maps as expressions of different worldviews, the growth of universities around the world, and Che Guevera as a radical visionary who tried to export revolution throughout the Third World.

STREAMLINED CHAPTER CHRONOLOGIES

Chapter chronologies appear at the end of each chapter, and they are organized regionally rather than temporally. The chapter chronologies have been streamlined for the Third Edition to make it easier for students to identify the most important events, to track unifying concepts, and to see influences across cultures and societies within a given time period.

REVISED STUDY QUESTIONS

New Study Questions appear at the end of each chapter. Each question has been carefully crafted to ensure that students can identify chapter themes, master core content, and identify the most important comparisons and connections from the reading.

FURTHER READINGS

A section at the back of the book includes an ample list of up-to-date suggestions for further reading, broken down by chapter and annotated so that students can see what each work covers.

RESOURCES FOR INSTRUCTORS

INSTRUCTOR'S MANUAL

Amy Hudnall and Neva Specht
Appalachian State University
Includes chapter outlines, lecture ideas, classroom activities, recommended books, recommended film lists with annotations, and recommended websites.

TEST BANK/COMPUTERIZED TEST BANK

Sara Jorgensen and Andrea Becksvoort
University of Tennessee, Chattanooga
The Test Bank has been revised in accordance with the Norton Assessment Guidelines. Questions are organized around a Concept Map and are ranked by knowledge type, difficulty, and section reference.

All Norton test banks are available with Exam View Test Generator software, allowing instructors to effortlessly create, administer, and manage assessments. The convenient and intuitive testmaking wizard makes it easy to create customized exams with no software learning curve. Other key features include the ability to create paper exams with algorithmically generated variables and to export files directly to Blackboard, WebCT, and Angel.

INSTRUCTOR'S RESOURCE DISC

This helpful classroom presentation tool features:
- Lecture PowerPoint slides that include a suggested classroom-lecture script in the notes field. These are particularly helpful to first-time teachers of the course.
- A separate set of art PowerPoints featuring photographs and maps, retouched for in-class projection.

DOWNLOADABLE INSTRUCTOR'S RESOURCES

wwnorton.com/instructors
Instructional content for use in lecture and distance education, including coursepacks, test banks, PowerPoint lecture slides, images, figures, and more.

COURSEPACKS

Available at no cost to professors or students, Norton coursepacks for online or hybrid courses are available in a variety of formats, including all versions of Blackboard and WebCT. With just a simple download from our instructor's website, an instructor can bring high-quality Norton digital media into a new or existing online course (no extra student passwords required), and it's theirs to keep forever. Content includes chapter-based assignments, test banks and quizzes, interactive learning tools, and selected content from the StudySpace website.

NORTON GRADEBOOK

With the free, easy-to-use Norton Gradebook, instructors can easily access StudySpace student quiz results and avoid email inbox clutter. No course setup required. For more information and an audio tour of the Gradebook, visit wwnorton.com/college/nrl/gradebook.

NORTON ONLINE

Norton Online provides a seamless and flexible online learning environment featuring proven resources that help students succeed. By integrating Norton's market-leading textbooks with interactive tools in an easy-to-use learning-management system, Norton Online provides a high-quality online course that can be used right away or customized to suit an instructor's specific needs.

RESOURCES FOR STUDENTS

STUDYSPACE: YOUR PLACE FOR A BETTER GRADE

StudySpace tells students what they know, shows them what they need to review, and then gives them an organized study plan to master the material.

Students rely on effective and well-designed online resources to help them succeed in their courses—StudySpace is unmatched in providing a one-stop solution that's closely aligned with their textbook. This free and easy-to-navigate website offers students an impressive range of exercises, interactive-learning tools, assessment, and review materials, including:

Quiz+ Quiz+ doesn't just tell students how they did; it shows them how they can do better. With Quiz+, students are presented with a targeted study plan that offers specific page references and links to the ebook and other online learning tools.

NEW: World History Tours powered by Google Maps. These tours trace global developments over time, touching down on locations to launch documents and images for analysis.

NEW: Nearly 100 new documents increase the collection of readings to 350 sources. Each source is accompanied by a media analysis worksheet that offers students a simple guided method to *Observe* a document's primary themes, *Express* an opinion or respond to the author's objective, and *Connect* the document to broader historical relevance.

Engaging Review Materials include chapter summaries and outlines, focus questions, flashcards with audio pronunciations, and diagnostic quizzes.

More Help with Geography: iMaps offer students tools to view maps one layer of information at a time, focusing on specific geographic sections.

Map Review Worksheets provide each map in the textbook as a label-less image; students are given a list of labels to connect to the map. These worksheets can be printed out so that the exercises can be completed off line.

Chrono-Sequencers: These interactive chapter chronologies challenge students to reassemble sequences of events and reinforce their understanding of the flow of history.

Research Topics and Documents: Each chapter clusters primary sources around a topic, complete with an opening question and introduction to help students focus on the connections between the documents.

EBOOK AND CUSTOM VERSIONS

Ebook: Same great book, *one-third* the price!

An affordable and convenient alternative, Norton ebooks retain the content and design of the print book and allow students to highlight and take notes with ease, print chapters as needed, and search the text. Norton ebooks are available online and as downloadable PDFs. They can be purchased directly from our website or with a registration folder that can be sold in the bookstore.

Chapter Select

With Chapter Select instructors can create a custom ebook that contains only the chapters they want to assign. For more information, go to norton**ebooks**.com: includes pricing and purchasing details as well as instructions about how to create a custom ebook using Chapter Select.

ACKNOWLEDGMENTS

Worlds Together, Worlds Apart would never have happened without the full support of Princeton University. In a highly unusual move, and one for which we are truly grateful, the university helped underwrite this project with financial support from its 250th Anniversary Fund for undergraduate teaching and by allowing release time for the authors from campus commitments.

The history department's support of the effort over many years has been exceptional. Four chairs made funds and departmental support available, including the department's incomparable administrative talents. We would be remiss if we did not single out the department manager, Judith Hanson, who provided us with assistance whenever we needed it. We also thank Eileen Kane, who provided help in tracking down references and illustrations and in integrating changes into the manuscript. We also would like to thank Pamela Long, who made all of the complicated arrangements for ensuring that we were able to discuss matters in a leisurely and attractive setting. Sometimes that meant arranging for long-distance conference calls. She went even further and proofread the entire manuscript, finding many errors that we had all overlooked.

We drew shamelessly on the expertise of the departmental faculty, and although it might be wise simply to include a roster of the Princeton history department, that would do an injustice to those of whom we took most advantage. So here they are: Mariana Candido, Robert Darnton, Sheldon Garon, Anthony Grafton, Molly Greene, David Howell, Harold James, William Jordan, Emmanuel Kreike, Michael Mahoney, Arno Mayer, Kenneth Mills, John Murrin, Susan Naquin,

Willard Peterson, Theodore Rabb, Bhavani Raman, Stanley Stein, and Richard Turits. When necessary, we went outside the history department, getting help from L. Carl Brown, Michael Cook, Norman Itzkowitz, Martin Kern, Thomas Leisten, Heath Lowry, and Peter Schaefer. Two departmental colleagues—Natalie Z. Davis and Elizabeth Lunbeck—were part of the original team but had to withdraw because of other commitments. Their contributions were vital, and we want to express our thanks to them. David Gordon, now at Bowdoin College, used portions of the text while teaching an undergraduate course at the University of Durban in South Africa and shared comments with us. Shamil Jeppie, like David Gordon a graduate of the Princeton history department, now teaching at the University of Cape Town in South Africa, read and commented on various chapters.

Beyond Princeton, we have also benefited from exceptionally gifted and giving colleagues who have assisted this book in many ways. Colleagues at Louisiana State University, the University of Florida, the University of North Carolina, the University of Pennsylvania, and the University of California at Los Angeles, where Suzanne Marchand, Michael Tsin, Holly Pittman, and Stephen Aron, respectively, are now teaching, pitched in whenever we turned to them. Especially helpful have been the contributions of James Gelvin, Naomi Lamoreaux, Gary Nash, and Joyce Appleby at UCLA; Michael Bernstein at Tulane University; and Maribel Dietz, John Henderson, Christine Kooi, David Lindenfeld, Reza Pirbhai, and Victor Stater at Louisiana State University. It goes without saying that none of these individuals bears any responsibility for factual or interpretive errors that the text may contain. Xinru Liu would like to thank her Indian mentor, Romila Thapar, who changed the way we think about Indian history.

The quality and range of reviews on this project were truly exceptional. The final version of the manuscript was greatly influenced by the thoughts and ideas of numerous instructors. We wish to particularly thank our consulting reviewers, who read multiple versions of the manuscript from start to finish.

First Edition Consultants
Hugh Clark, Ursinus College
Jonathan Lee, San Antonio College
Pamela McVay, Ursuline College
Tom Sanders, United States Naval Academy

Second Edition Consultants
Jonathan Lee, San Antonio College
Pamela McVay, Ursuline College
Steve Rapp, Georgia State University
Cliff Rosenberg, City University of New York

First Edition Reviewers
Lauren Benton, New Jersey Institute of Technology
Ida Blom, University of Bergen, Norway

Ricardo Duchesne, University of New Brunswick
Major Bradley T. Gericke, United States Military Academy
John Gillis, Rutgers University
David Kenley, Marshall University
John Kicza, Washington State University
Matthew Levinger, Lewis and Clark College
James Long, Colorado State University
Adam McKeown, Columbia University
Mark McLeod, University of Delaware
John Mears, Southern Methodist University
Michael Murdock, Brigham Young University
David Newberry, University of North Carolina, Chapel Hill
Tom Pearcy, Slippery Rock State University
Oliver B. Pollak, University of Nebraska, Omaha
Ken Pomeranz, University of California, Irvine
Major David L. Ruffley, United States Air Force Academy
William Schell, Murray State University
Major Deborah Schmitt, United States Air Force Academy
Sarah Shields, University of North Carolina, Chapel Hill
Mary Watrous-Schlesinger, Washington State University

Second Edition Reviewers
William Atwell, Hobart and William Smith Colleges
Susan Besse, City University of New York
Tithi Bhattacharya, Purdue University
Mauricio Borrerero, St. John's University
Charlie Briggs, Georgia Southern University
Antoinne Burton, University of Illinois, Urbana-Champaign
Jim Cameron, St. Francis Xavier University
Kathleen Comerford, Georgia Southern University
Duane Corpis, Georgia State University
Denise Davidson, Georgia State University
Ross Doughty, Ursinus College
Alison Fletcher, Kent State University
Phillip Gavitt, Saint Louis University
Brent Geary, Ohio University
Henda Gilli-Elewy, California State Polytechnic University, Pomona
Fritz Gumbach, John Jay College
William Hagen, University of California, Davis
Laura Hilton, Muskingum College
Jeff Johnson, Villanova University
David Kammerling-Smith, Eastern Illinois University
Jonathan Lee, San Antonio College
Dorothea Martin, Appalachian State University
Don McGuire, State University of New York, Buffalo
Pamela McVay, Ursuline College
Joel Migdal, University of Washington
Anthony Parent, Wake Forest University
Sandra Peacock, Georgia Southern University
David Pietz, Washington State University
Jared Poley, Georgia State University

John Quist, Shippensburg State University
Steve Rapp, Georgia State University
Paul Rodell, Georgia Southern University
Ariel Salzman, Queen's University
Bill Schell, Murray State University
Claire Schen, State University of New York, Buffalo
Jonathan Skaff, Shippensburg State University
David Smith, California State Polytechnic University,
    Pomona
Neva Specht, Appalachian State University
Ramya Sreeniva, State University of New York, Buffalo
Charles Stewart, University of Illinois,
    Urbana-Champaign
Rachel Stocking, Southern Illinois University,
    Carbondale
Heather Streets, Washington State University
Tim Teeter, Georgia Southern University
Charlie Wheeler, University of California, Irvine
Owen White, University of Delaware
James Wilson, Wake Forest University

Third Edition Reviewers
Henry Antkiewicz, Eastern Tennessee State University
Anthony Barbieri-Low, University of California,
    Santa Barbara
Andrea Becksvoort, University of Tennessee, Chattanooga
Hayden Bellonoit, United States Naval Academy
John Bloom, Shippensburg University
Kathryn Braund, Auburn University
Catherine Candy, University of New Orleans
Karen Carter, Brigham Young University
Stephen Chappell, James Madison University
Jessey Choo, University of Missouri, Kansas City
Timothy Coates, College of Charleston
Gregory Crider, Wingate University
Denise Davidson, Georgia State University
Jessica Davidson, James Madison University
Sal Diaz, Santa Rosa Junior College
Todd Dozier, Baton Rouge Community College
Richard Eaton, University of Arizona
Lee Farrow, Auburn University, Montgomery
Bei Gao, College of Charleston
Behrooz Ghamari-Tabrizi, University of Illinois,
    Urbana-Champaign
Steven Gish, Auburn University, Montgomery
Jeffrey Hamilton, Baylor University
Barry Hankins, Baylor University
Brian Harding, Mott Community College
Tim Henderson, Auburn University, Montgomery
Marjorie Hilton, University of Redlands
Richard Hines, Washington State University
Lisa Holliday, Appalachian State University
Jonathan Lee, San Antonio College
David Kalivas, University of Massachusetts, Lowell

Christopher Kelley, Miami University, Ohio
Kenneth Koons, Virginia Military Institute
Michael Kulikowski, Pennsylvania State University
Benjamin Lawrence, University of California, Davis
Lu Liu, University of Tennessee, Knoxville
David Longfellow, Baylor University
Harold Marcuse, University of California,
    Santa Barbara
Dorothea Martin, Appalachian State University
David Mayes, Sam Houston State University
James Mokhiber, University of New Orleans
Mark Munzinger, Radford College
David Murphree, Virginia Tech University
Joshua Nadel, North Carolina Central University
Wing Chung Nq, University of Texas, San Antonio
Robert Norrell, University of Tennessee, Knoxville
Chandrika Paul, Shippensburg University
Beth Pollard, San Diego State University
Timothy Pytell, California State University,
    San Bernardino
Stephen Rapp, Professional Historian
Alice Roberti, Santa Rosa Junior College
Aviel Roshwald, Georgetown University
James Sanders, Utah State University
Lynn Sargeant, California State University, Fullerton
William Schell, Murray State University
Michael Seth, James Madison University
Barry Stentiford, Grambling State University
Gabrielle Sutherland, Baylor University
Lisa Tran, California State University, Fullerton
Michael Vann, California State University, Sacramento
Peter Von Sivers, University of Utah
Andrew Wackerfuss, Georgetown University
Ted Weeks, Southern Illinois University, Carbondale
Angela White, Indiana University of Pennsylvania
Jennifer Williams, Nichols State University
Andrew Wise, State University of New York, Buffalo
Eloy Zarate, Pasadena City College
William Zogby, Mohawk Valley Community College

We also want to thank Nancy Khalek (Ph.D. Princeton University), who now teaches at Brown University. Nancy was our jack-of-all-trades who helped in any way she could. She attended all the monthly meetings during the development of the early volume. She provided critiques of the manuscript, helped with primary research, worked on the photo program and the Global Connections & Disconnections features, and contributed content to the student website. She was invaluable. For the Third Edition, Nancy has authored a number of the new digital World History Tours powered by Google Maps. We would also like to thank Neva Specht and Amy Hudnall (both from Appalachian State University), who have authored the Instructor's Manual for the last two editions. They have filled the manual with many wonderful classroom exercises and a highly useful annotated suggested films list. Finally, we'd like to thank our two newcomers, Sara Jorgensen and Andrea Becksvoort (both from the University of Tennessee, Chattanooga) for thoroughly revising the test bank.

Our association with the publisher of this volume, W. W. Norton & Company, has been everything we could have asked for. Jon Durbin took us under the wing of the Norton firm. He attended all of our monthly meetings for the first two editions spanning the better part of four years across the creation of both volumes. How he put up with some of our interminable discussions will always be a mystery, but his enthusiasm for the endeavor never flagged, even when we seemed to grow weary. He has brought the same energy and determination to the Third Edition. Sandy Lifland was the ever-watchful and ever-careful development editor for each volume for the First Edition and a good portion of the Second Edition. She let us know when we were making sense and when we needed to explain ourselves more fully. Alice Falk was our talented and insightful co-developmental editor for the Second Edition. Between the efforts of Sandy and Alice, our vision became a reality. For the Third Edition, Alice Vigliani was an unimaginably superb development editor. She took a book that we were all very proud of, and she has helped bring it closest to our original vision. She responded immediately to all queries, kept everyone on an even keel, shrank the text where it was too wordy, and demanded that we add color and vitality where the writing flagged. If the Third Edition showcases the big world history stories better than ever, and it is easier to read and more accessible than the first two (and we believe that this is the case), we owe these improvements to her. Rebecca Homiski did a fabulous job as our project editor on the Second and Third editions, coordinating the responses of up to twelve authors on both volumes combined and locking down all the details on the project. We also want to thank Ellen Lohman for copyediting the manuscript ably and with just the right touch for the Second and Third Editions. Stephanie Romeo led the charge again, finding all the new photos we requested, and Rubina Yeh integrated the new "Storylines" features and the new chapter chronologies into her already gorgeous design. Debra Morton-Hoyt has provided us again with what have to be the most distinctive and appealing world history book covers in the field. Ben Reynolds guided the manuscript through the production process, and Jason Spears capably pulled together all the important loose ends to get the manuscript ready for copyediting, working on the photo captions, glossary, and art manuscript, among other tasks. On the media front, we want to thank Steve Hoge for creating the Norton StudySpace website, which includes the impressive Norton Digital History Reader and the exciting new Norton World History Tours powered by Google Maps. On the print ancillary front, we'd like to thank Lorraine Klimowich and Rachel Comerford for finding an excellent group of authors to create the instructor's manual and test bank. Carla Zimowsk, the information officer for the history department at Princeton University, simplified the multiple transmission of revised chapters among all twelve of the authors, no easy task. She made what is a very complicated set of procedures easy to understand and workable.

Finally, we must recognize that while this project often kept us apart from family members, their support held our personal worlds together.

About the Authors

ROBERT TIGNOR (Ph.D. Yale University) is Professor Emeritus and the Rosengarten Professor of Modern and Contemporary History at Princeton University and the three-time chair of the history department. With Gyan Prakash, he introduced Princeton's first course in world history nearly twenty years ago. Professor Tignor has taught graduate and undergraduate courses in African history and world history and written extensively on the history of twentieth-century Egypt, Nigeria, and Kenya. Besides his many research trips to Africa, Professor Tignor has taught at the University of Ibadan in Nigeria and the University of Nairobi in Kenya.

JEREMY ADELMAN (D.Phil. Oxford University) is currently the Director of the Council for International Teaching and Research at Princeton University and the Walter S. Carpenter III Professor of Spanish Civilization and Culture. He has written and edited five books, including *Republic of Capital: Buenos Aires and the Legal Transformation of the Atlantic World*, which won the best book prize in Atlantic history from the American Historical Association, and most recently *Sovereignty and Revolution in the Iberian Atlantic*. Professor Adelman is the recent recipient of a Guggenheim Memorial Foundation Fellowship and the Frederick Burkhardt Award from the American Council of Learned Societies.

STEPHEN ARON (Ph.D. University of California, Berkeley) is professor of history at the University of California, Los Angeles, and executive director of the Institute for the Study of the American West, Autry National Center. A specialist in frontier and Western American history, Aron is the author of *How the West Was Lost: The Transformation of Kentucky from Daniel Boone to Henry Clay* and *American Confluence: The Missouri Frontier from Borderland to Border State*. He is currently editing the multi-volume *Autry History of the American West* and writing a book with the tentative title *Can We All Just Get Along: An Alternative History of the American West*.

PETER BROWN (Ph.D. Oxford University) is the Rollins Professor of History at Princeton University. He previously taught at London University and the University of California, Berkeley. He has written on the rise of Christianity and the end of the Roman Empire. His works include *Augustine of Hippo, The World of Late Antiquity, The Cult of the Saints, Body and Society, The Rise of Western Christendom*, and *Poverty and Leadership in the Later Roman Empire*. He is presently working on issues of wealth and poverty in the late Roman and early medieval Christian worlds.

BENJAMIN ELMAN (Ph.D. University of Pennsylvania) is professor of East Asian studies and history at Princeton University. He is currently serving as the chair of the Princeton East Asian Studies Department. He taught at the University of California, Los Angeles, for over fifteen years. His teaching and research fields include Chinese intellectual and cultural history, 1000–1900; the history of science in China, 1600–1930; the history of education in late imperial China; and Sino-Japanese cultural history, 1600–1850. He is the author of five books: *From Philosophy to Philology: Intellectual and Social Aspects of Change in Late Imperial China; Classicism, Politics, and Kinship: The Ch'ang-chou School of New Text Confucianism in Late Imperial China; A Cultural History of Civil Examinations in Late Imperial China; On Their Own Terms: Science in China, 1550–1900*; and *A Cultural History of Modern Science in China*. He is the creator of Classical Historiography for Chinese History at www.princeton.edu/~classbib/, a bibliography and teaching website published since 1996.

STEPHEN KOTKIN (Ph.D. University of California, Berkeley) is professor of European and Asian history as well as international affairs at Princeton University. He formerly directed Princeton's program in Russian and Eurasian studies (1996–2009). He is the author of *Magnetic Mountain: Stalinism as a Civilization, Uncivil Society: 1989 and the Implosion of the Communist Establishment*, and *Armageddon Averted: The Soviet Collapse, 1970–2000*. He is a coeditor of *Mongolia in the Twentieth Century: Landlocked Cosmopolitan*. Professor Kotkin has twice been a visiting professor in Japan.

XINRU LIU (Ph.D. University of Pennsylvania) is associate professor of early Indian history and world history at the College of New Jersey. She is associated with the Institute of World History and the Chinese Academy of Social Sciences. She is the author of *Ancient India and Ancient China, Trade and Religious Exchanges*, AD *1–600; Silk and Religion, an Exploration of Material Life and the Thought of People*, AD *600–1200; Connections across Eurasia, Transportation, Communication, and Cultural Exchange on the Silk Roads*, co-authored with Lynda Norene Shaffer; and *A Social History of Ancient India* (in Chinese). Professor Liu promotes South Asian studies and world history studies in both the United States and the People's Republic of China.

SUZANNE MARCHAND (Ph.D. University of Chicago) is professor of European and intellectual history at Louisiana State University, Baton Rouge. Professor Marchand also spent a number of years teaching at Princeton University. She is the author of *Down from Olympus: Archaeology and Philhellenism in Germany, 1750–1970* and *German Orientalism in the Age of Empire: Religion, Race and Scholarship*.

HOLLY PITTMAN (Ph.D. Columbia University) is professor of art history at the University of Pennsylvania, where she teaches art and archaeology of Mesopotamia and the Iranian Plateau. She also serves as curator in the Near East Section of the University of Pennsylvania Museum of Archaeology and Anthropology. Previously she served as a curator in the Ancient Near Eastern Art Department of the Metropolitan Museum of Art. She has written extensively on the art and culture of the Bronze Age in the Middle East and has participated in excavations in Cyprus, Turkey, Syria, Iraq, and Iran, where she currently works. Her research investigates works of art as media through which patterns of thought, cultural development, and historical interactions of ancient cultures of the Near East are reconstructed.

GYAN PRAKASH (Ph.D. University of Pennsylvania) is professor of modern Indian history at Princeton University and a member of the Subaltern Studies Editorial Collective. He is the author of *Bonded Histories: Genealogies of Labor Servitude in Colonial India, Another Reason: Science and the Imagination of Modern India*, and *Mumbai Fables*. Professor Prakash edited *After Colonialism: Imperial Histories and Postcolonial Displacements* and *Noir Urbanisms*, coedited *The Space of the Modern City* and *Utopia/Dystopia*, and has written a number of articles on colonialism and history writing. He is currently working on a history of the city of Bombay. With Robert Tignor, he introduced the modern world history course at Princeton University.

BRENT SHAW (Ph.D. Cambridge University) is the Andrew Fleming West Professor of Classics at Princeton University, where he is director of the Program in the Ancient World. He was previously at the University of Pennsylvania, where he chaired the Graduate Group in Ancient History. His principal areas of specialization as a Roman historian are Roman family history and demography, sectarian violence and conflict in Late Antiquity, and the regional history of Africa as part of the Roman Empire. He has published *Spartacus and the Slaves Wars*; edited the papers of Sir Moses Finley, *Economy and Society in Ancient Greece*; and published in a variety of books and journals, including the *Journal of Roman Studies*, the *American Historical Review*, the *Journal of Early Christian Studies*, and *Past & Present*.

MICHAEL TSIN (Ph.D. Princeton) is associate professor of history and international studies at the University of North Carolina at Chapel Hill. He previously taught at the University of Illinois at Chicago, Princeton University, Columbia University, and the University of Florida. Professor Tsin's primary interests include the histories of modern China and colonialism. He is the author of *Nation, Governance, and Modernity in China: Canton, 1900–1927*. He is currently writing a social history of the reconfiguration of Chinese identity in the twentieth century.

PACIFIC
OCEAN

NORTH
AMERICA

ATLANTIC
OCEAN

SAHARA

Niger R.

SOUTH
AMERICA

0   1000   2000 Miles

0   1000   2000 Kilometers

THE GEOGRAPHY OF THE ANCIENT AND MODERN WORLDS

Today, we believe the world to be divided into continents, and most of us think that it was always so. Geographers usually identify six inhabited continents: Africa, North America, South America, Europe, Asia, and Australia. Inside these continents they locate a vast number of subcontinental units, such as East Asia, South Asia, Southeast Asia, the Middle East, North Africa, and sub-Saharan Africa. Yet this geographical understanding would have been completely alien to premodern men and women, who did not think that they inhabited continents bounded by large bodies of water. Lacking a firm command of the seas,

they saw themselves living on contiguous landmasses, and they thought these territorial bodies were the main geographical units of their lives. Hence, in this volume we have chosen to use a set of geographical terms, the main one being *Afro-Eurasia*, that more accurately reflect the world that the premoderns believed that they inhabited.

The most interconnected and populous landmass of premodern times was Afro-Eurasia. The term *Eurasia* is widely used in general histories, but we think it is in its own ways inadequate. The preferred term from our perspective must be *Afro-Eurasia*, for the interconnected

ARCTIC OCEAN

AFRO-EURASIA

EUROPE

INNER EURASIA

Danube R.

BLACK SEA

CASPIAN SEA

ARAL SEA

CENTRAL ASIA

TAKLAMAKAN DESERT

AEGEAN SEA

MEDITERRANEAN SEA

TAURUS MTS.

Tigris R.

IRANIAN PLATEAU

Indus R.

HIMALAYA MTS

Yellow R.

YELLOW SEA

DESERT

Euphrates R.

SOUTHWEST ASIA

Yangzi R.

EAST ASIA

RED SEA

ARABIAN SEA

SOUTH ASIA

Pearl R.

PACIFIC OCEAN

Lake Chad

Nile R.

SOUTHEAST ASIA

SOUTH CHINA SEA

Congo R.

SUB-SAHARAN AFRICA

Lake Victoria

INDIAN OCEAN

AUSTRALIA

landmass of premodern and indeed much of modern times included large parts of Europe and Asia and significant regions in Africa. The major African territories that were regularly joined to Europe and Asia were Egypt, North Africa, and even parts of sub-Saharan Africa.

Only gradually and fitfully did the divisions of the world that we take for granted today take shape. The peoples inhabiting the northwestern part of the Afro-Eurasian landmass did not see themselves as European Christians, and hence as a distinctive cultural entity, until the Middle Ages drew to a close in the twelfth and thirteenth centuries. Islam did not arise and extend its influence throughout the middle zone of the Afro-Eurasian landmass until the eighth and ninth

centuries. And, finally, the peoples living in what we today term the *Indian subcontinent* did not feel a strong sense of their own cultural and political unity until the Delhi Sultanate of the thirteenth and fourteenth centuries and the Mughal Empire, which emerged at the beginning of the sixteenth century, brought political unity to that vast region. As a result, we use the terms *South Asia*, *Vedic society*, and *India* in place of *Indian subcontinent* for the premodern part of our narrative, and we use *Southwest Asia* and *North Africa* to refer to what today is designated as the *Middle East*. In fact, it is only in the period from 1000 to 1300 that some of the major cultural areas that are familiar to us today truly crystallized.

Chapter

1

BECOMING HUMAN

n 2003, in a remote corner of the Ethiopian highlands of Africa, a team of evolutionary biologists
came upon a remarkable cache of fossil remains
lodged in volcanic rock. Identifying and reassembling these remains took six years, but the researchers eventually reconstructed
one of the most revealing sets of human fossils ever found: a
nearly complete skeleton of an adult male, and the partial remains
of another adult and a juvenile. By dating the volcanic rock, the
team determined that the bones were about 160,000 years old. Although the skeletal remains were not identical to those of modern men and women (who are technically *Homo sapiens sapiens*,
the sole surviving subspecies of *Homo sapiens*), they were close
enough to form part of the family of modern humans. In short,
the bones represented the oldest record of *Homo sapiens*. The fossil finds confirmed what earlier studies had suggested: *Homo sapiens*, or modern humans, originated in a small region of Africa
about 200,000 years ago and migrated out of Africa about
100,000 years ago. As the team leader proclaimed, "We are all
Africans."

3

Not everyone agrees with the "Out of Africa" thesis, which contends that modern human beings are all descendants of recent migrants out of Africa. Doubters claim that the world's "races" evolved separately in different regions for up to one million years after migrating out of Africa. These doubters argue that as the early descendants of modern men and women evolved in widely dispersed geographical settings, they took on diverse personality traits and distinctive physical appearances, with the result that they appear today as different "races." In this view, the story of humanity was about fundamental differences. Now the opposite is becoming clear: all humans share a common heritage, and our differences are not genetic or crudely physical, but mainly cultural. We are also much newer than scholars once imagined.

As a species we have been living apart for a comparatively short amount of time, and as a result the world's "races" have much in common. Most of the common traits of human beings—the abilities to make tools, engage in family life, use language, and refine cognitive abilities—evolved over many millennia and crystallized on the eve of the exodus from Africa. Only with the advent of settled agriculture did significant cultural divergences occur, as artifacts such as tools, cooking devices, and storage containers reveal. The differences in humankind's cultures are less than 15,000 or 20,000 years old.

This chapter lays out the origins of humanity from its common source. It shows how many different hominids (erect bipedal mammals, represented today by humans, chimpanzees, gorillas, and orangutans) preceded modern humans, and that humans came from only one—very recent—stock of migrants out of Africa. Fanning out across the world, our ancestors adapted to environmental constraints and opportunities. They created languages, families, and clan systems, often innovating to defend themselves against predators. One of the biggest breakthroughs was the domestication of animals and plants—the creation of agrarian settlements. With this development,

humans could cease following food and begin producing it in their own backyards.

Before we begin our exploration, it will be useful to clarify two terms that occur frequently in this chapter's discussion: *evolution*, and *modern humans*. **Evolution** is the process by which the different species of the world—its plants and animals—made changes in response to their environment that enabled them to survive and increase in numbers. Biological evolution does not imply progress to higher and more exalted forms of life, only adaptation to environmental surroundings. The term *modern humans* refers to members of the *Homo sapiens* subspecies that evolved about 200,000 years ago. So when we say "modern" (and "recent") we are speaking in relative terms; compared to the life of the universe and even to the earliest hominids, the ancient creatures we call modern humans were indeed "modern." This chapter's discussion will show that as modern humans evolved, they passed through successive waves of migration, adaptation, and innovation.

PRECURSORS TO MODERN HUMANS

> ✦ *What traits made early hominids different from other animal species?*

To understand the origins of modern humans (*Homo sapiens*), we must consider what is common to all humans and what distinguishes them from one another. We must also come to terms with time. Though the hominids that evolved into modern humans lived millions of years ago, our tools for analyzing them are relatively new. What we now know about the origins of human existence and the evolution into modern humans would have been unimaginable a century ago.

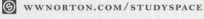

Focus Questions

✦ *What traits made early hominids different from other animal species?*

✦ *How did* Homo sapiens *become the only hominid species?*

✦ *How did art and language increase* Homo sapiens' *chances of survival?*

✦ *What factors contributed to the domestication of plants and animals?*

✦ *What factors contributed to innovation, as opposed to borrowing, in agriculture?*

✦ *How did agricultural revolutions change human relations?*

CREATION MYTHS AND BELIEFS

Only 350 years ago, English clerics claimed on the basis of biblical calculations and Christian tradition that the first day of creation was Sunday, October 23, 4004 BCE. One scholar even specified that creation happened at 9:00 A.M. on the morning of that day. Now we see things differently. The origin of the universe dates back some 15 billion years, and the hominid separation from African pongids (members of the ape family) began some 6 or 7 million years ago. These discoveries have proved as mind-boggling to Hindus and Muslims as to Christians and Jews—all of whom believed, in different ways, in a creationist account of humanity's origins. (See Primary Source: A Hindu Creation Myth.) The Judaic-Christian belief in creation was based on the first book of the Old Testament, Genesis, which portrayed God creating the universe from nothingness, all of its plants and animals and the first set of human beings (Adam and Eve), over a period of seven days. This story became foundational for Western societies and also for the Islamic world, which accepted the Old and New Testaments—though not the divinity of Jesus—as the word of God.

Modern discoveries about humanity's origins have also challenged other major cultural traditions, because no tradition conceived that creatures evolved into new kinds of life, that humans were related to apes, and that all of humanity originated in a remote corner of Africa. The Yoruba peoples of West Africa, whose creation story is centuries old and is representative of many African creation accounts, believed that God descended from the heavens in human form. He became the godlike king Oduduwa, who established the Yoruba kingdom and the rules by which his subjects were to live. According to the Brahmanical Vedas and the Upanishads, which date to the seventh or sixth century BCE and remain fundamental to Hindu faith today, the world is millions, not billions, of years old. The Chinese from East Asia, who do not appear to have their own creation story, and the Buddhists believed in a continuous reappearance of human and animal souls. Chinese Han dynasty (202 BCE–220 CE) astronomers also believed that at the world's beginning the planets were conjoined and that they would merge again at the end of time. The Buddhists' cosmos comprised millions of worlds, each consisting of a mountain encircled by four continents, its seas surrounded by a wall of iron.

Even the million-year time frames and multiple planetary systems that ancient Asian thinkers endorsed did not prepare their communities for the idea that humans are related to apes. In all traditional cosmologies, humans came into existence fully formed, at a single moment, as did the other beings that populated the world.

Primary Source

A HINDU CREATION MYTH

Around 1500 BCE *a migrant people speaking an Indo-European language settled in South Asia. These Vedic people sang hymns while making sacrifices to their gods, and the hymns were later collected in the Rig-Veda—the earliest Hindu sacred text. This hymn describes the creation of the universe by the gods' sacrifice ("oblation") of a creature—Purusha, or "Man." From Purusha's body come four different kinds of people: the Brahman, the Rajanya, the Vaishya, and the Shudra. They represent the forefathers of the four castes, or hereditary social classes, of India.*

Thousand-headed Purusha, thousand-eyed, thousand-footed—he, having pervaded the earth on all sides, extends ten fingers beyond it.

Purusha alone is all this—whatever has been and whatever is going to be. Further, he is the lord of immortality and also of what grows on account of food.

Such is his greatness; greater, indeed than this is Purusha. All creatures constitute but one-quarter of him, his three-quarters are the immortal in the heaven.

With his three-quarters did Purusha rise up; one-quarter of him again remains here. With it did he variously spread out on all sides over what eats and what eats not. . . . When the gods performed the sacrifice with Purusha as the oblation, then the spring was its clarified butter, the summer the sacrificial fuel, and the autumn the oblation.

The sacrificial victim, namely, Purusha born at the very beginning, they sprinkled with sacred water upon the sacrificial grass. With him as oblation, the gods performed the sacrifice, and also the Sādhyas [a class of semidivine beings] and the rishis [ancient seers].

From that wholly offered sacrificial oblation were born the verses and the sacred chants; from it were born the meters [*chandas*]; the sacrificial formula was born from it.

From it horses were born and also those animals who have double rows [i.e., upper and lower] of teeth; cows were born from it, from it were born goats and sheep.

When they divided Purusha, in how many different portions did they arrange him? What became of his mouth, what of his two arms? What were his two thighs and his two feet called?

His mouth became the brāhman; his two arms were made into the rājanya; his two thighs the vaishyas; from his two feet the shūdra was born.

The moon was born from the mind, from the eye the sun was born; from the mouth Indra and Agni, from the breath [*prāna*] the wind [*vāyu*] was born.

From the navel was the atmosphere created, from the head the heaven issued forth; from two feet was born the earth and the quarters (the cardinal directions) from the ear. Thus did they fashion the worlds.

- *In early Vedic society the Brahman (priest) was the highest caste, and the Shudra (outsider/laborer) was the lowest. What parts of Purusha's body did these two castes come from, and what is the significance of each?*
- *According to this myth, what other beings came into existence fully formed?*

Source: *Sources of Indian Tradition,* vol. 1, *From the Beginning to 1800,* edited and revised by Ainslie T. Embree, 2nd ed. (New York: Columbia University Press, 1988), pp. 18–19.

Evolutionary Findings and Research Methods

Revisions in the time frame of the universe and human existence have occurred over a long period of time. Geologists made early breakthroughs in the eighteenth century when their research into the layers of the earth's surface revealed a world much older than biblical time implied. Evolutionary biologists, most notably Charles Darwin (1809–1882), concluded that all life had evolved over long periods from simple forms of matter. In the twentieth century astronomers, evolutionary biologists, and archaeologists (scholars of ancient cultures whose information comes mainly from nonliterary sources such as fossils, monuments, and artifacts) have employed sophisticated dating techniques to pinpoint the chronology of the universe's creation and the evolution of all forms of life on earth. (See Global Connections & Disconnections: Determining the Age of Fossils and Sediments.) Their discoveries have radically transformed humanity's understanding of its own history, a shift comparable to the

DETERMINING THE AGE OF FOSSILS AND SEDIMENTS

Our knowledge of human origins has been the result of several remarkable scientific breakthroughs. Only recently have scholars been able to date fossil remains and to use biological research to understand the relationships among the world's early peoples.

The first major advance in the study of prehistory (the time before written historical records) occurred after World War II, and it involved the use of *radiocarbon dating*. All living things contain the radiocarbon isotope C^{14}, which plants acquire directly from the atmosphere and animals acquire indirectly when they consume plants or other animals. When these living things die, the C^{14} isotope begins to decay into a stable nonradioactive element, C^{12}. Because the rate of decay is regular and measurable, it is possible to determine the age of fossils that leave organic remains for up to 40,000 years.

A second major dating technique, the *potassium-argon method*, also involves analysis of the changing chemical structure of objects over time. Scientists can calculate the age of nonliving objects by measuring the ratio of potassium to argon in them, since potassium decays into argon. This method allows scientists to calculate the age of objects up to a million years old. It also enables them to date the sediments in which researchers find fossils—as a gauge of the age of the fossils themselves.

DNA (deoxyribonucleic acid) analysis is a third crucial tool for unraveling the beginnings of modern humans. DNA, which determines biological inheritances, exists in two places within the cells of all living organisms—including the human body. *Nuclear DNA* occurs in the nucleus of every cell, where it controls most aspects of physical appearance and makeup. *Mitochondrial DNA* occurs outside the nucleus of cells, where its structures within cell bodies convert the energy from food into a form that cells can use. While nuclear DNA exists in males and females, mitochondrial DNA exists only in females and passes from mothers to female offspring. By examining mitochondrial DNA, researchers can measure the genetic variation among living objects—including human beings. Such analysis has enabled researchers to pinpoint human descent from an original African population to other, genetically related populations that lived approximately 100,000 years ago.

The genetic similarity of modern humans suggests that the population from which all *Homo sapiens* descended originated in Africa about 200,000 years ago. When these humans moved out of Africa around 100,000 years ago, they spread eastward into Southwest Asia and then throughout the rest of Afro-Eurasia. One group migrated to Australia about 50,000 years ago. Another group moved into the area of Europe about 40,000 years ago. When the scientific journal *Nature* published these findings in 1987, it inspired a groundswell of public interest—and a contentious scientific debate that continues today.

Neanderthal DNA Extraction. This sample of fossilized Neanderthal bone will have its genetic material extracted and sequenced as part of the Neanderthal Genome Project.

sixteenth-century realization that the earth rotates around the sun. Understanding the sweep of human history, calculated in millions of years, requires us to revise our sense of time. Moreover, the scientists' findings have important, if unsettling, implications concerning who we are as human beings.

A mere century ago, who would have accepted the fact that the universe came into being 15 billion years ago, that the earth appeared about 4.5 billion years ago, and that the earliest life forms began to exist about 3.8 billion years ago? The great cultural traditions would not have considered that human beings are part of a long evolutionary chain stretching from microscopic bacteria to African apes that appeared about 23 million years ago. And they would not have accepted the findings that Africa's ape population separated into three distinct groups: one becoming present-day gorillas; the second becoming chimpanzees; and the third group, **hominids**, becoming modern-day humans only after following a long and complicated evolutionary process.

At what stage did the first hominids appear? What traits distinguished them from other animals? No single variable separated these humanlike beings from other creatures; instead, a combination of distinguishing traits evolved over several million years. These include (1) lifting the torso and walking on two legs (bipedalism), thereby freeing hands and arms to carry objects and hurl weapons; (2) controlling and then making fire; (3) fashioning and using tools; (4) developing cognitive skills and an enlarged brain and therefore the capacity for language; and (5) acquiring a consciousness of "self." Together, these traits began to differentiate hominids from other animal species and in the long (long!) run enabled humans to become the dominant species on the globe. All these traits were in place at least 150,000 years ago.

Yet this was just a beginning in human development. It was only about 12,000 years ago that modern humans were ready to make another spectacular advance: domesticating plants and animals, and living in village communities.

EARLY HOMINIDS AND ADAPTATION

What was it like to be a hominid in the millions of years before the emergence of modern humans? The first clue came from a discovery made in 1924 at Taung, not far from the present-day city of Johannesburg, South Africa. A scientist named Raymond Dart happened upon a skull and bones that appeared to be partly human and partly ape. Believing the creature to be "an extinct race of apes intermediate between living anthropoids (apes) and man," Dart labeled the creature the "Southern Ape of Africa," or *Australopithecus africanus*. This individual had a brain capacity of approximately one pint, or a little less than one-third that of a modern man and about the same as that of modern-day African apes. Yet these **australopithecines** were different from other animals, for they walked on two legs. Because Dart also found animal bones in the same vicinity, he mistakenly concluded that our early ancestors were bloodthirsty creatures who carried their prey to slaughtering grounds. It turns out that early hominids were only about five feet tall and weighed at most 110 pounds, so they were no match for big, muscular, and swift animal predators; the hominids were the hunted, not the hunters.

The fact that the hominids survived at all in such a hostile environment is a miracle. But they did, and over the first million years of their existence in Africa the australopithecines developed into more than six species. (A **species** is a group of animals or plants possessing one or more distinctive characteristics.) It is important to emphasize that these australopithecines were not humans but that they carried the genetic and biological material out of which modern humans would later emerge. These precursors to modern humans had a key trait for evolutionary survival: they were remarkably good adapters. They could deal with dynamic environmental shifts, and they were intelligent.

LUCY   Australopithecines existed not only in southern Africa but in the north as well. In 1974, an archaeological team working at a site in present-day Ethiopia unearthed a relatively intact skeleton of a young adult female australopithecine in the valley of the Awash River. The researchers gave the skeleton a nickname, Lucy, based on the popular Beatles song "Lucy in the Sky with Diamonds."

Lucy was remarkable. She stood a little over three feet tall, she walked upright, her skull contained a brain within the ape size range, and her jaw and teeth were humanlike. Her arms were long, hanging halfway from her hips to her knees—suggesting that she might not have been bipedal at all

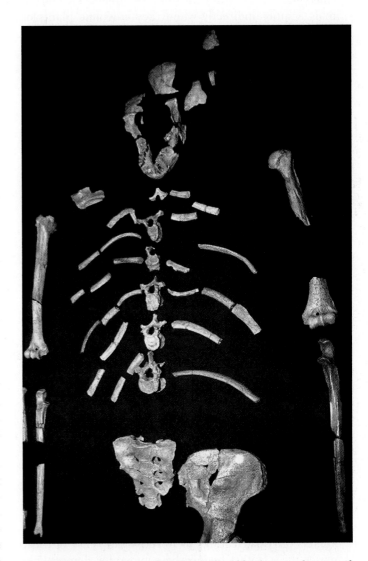

Fossil Bones of Lucy. Archaeologist Donald Johanson discovered the fossilized bones of this young female in the Afar region of Ethiopia. They are believed to date from approximately 3.2 million years ago and provide evidence of some of the first hominids to appear in Africa. This find was of great importance because the bones were so fully and completely preserved.

TABLE 1-1   **Human Evolution**

Australopithecus anamensis	4.2 million years ago
Australopithecus afarensis (including Lucy)	3.4 million years ago
Australopithecus africanus	3.0 million years ago
Homo habilis (including Dear Boy)	2.5 million years ago
Homo erectus (including Java and Peking Man)	1.8 million years ago
Neanderthals	200,000 years ago
Homo sapiens	200,000 years ago
Homo sapiens sapiens (modern humans)	35,000 years ago

times and sometimes resorted to arms for locomotion, in the fashion of a modern baboon. Above all, Lucy's skeleton was relatively complete and was very, very old—half a million years older than any other complete hominid skeleton found up to that time. Lucy showed us that human precursors were walking around as early as 3 million years ago. (See Table 1-1.) But it also raised some significant questions: Was Lucy a precursor to modern-day humans? If so, what kind of a precursor? What species did she represent? Or was she a modern human?

ADAPTATION   To survive, hominids had to adapt and evolve as their environments altered. During the first millions of years of hominid existence, these changes were slow. They involved far more physical adaptations to the environment than cultural transformations. Hominids, like the rest of the plant and animal world, had to keep pace with rapidly changing physical environments—for if they did not, they would die out. Many of the early hominid groups did just that. In fact, no straight-line descent tree exists from the first hominids to modern men and women. The places where researchers have found early hominid remains in southern and eastern Africa had environments that changed from being heavily forested and well watered to being arid and desert-like, and then back again. (See Map 1-1.) Survival required constant **adaptation** (the ability to alter behavior and to innovate, finding new ways of doing things), and some of the hominid groups were better at it than others.

In adapting, early hominids began to distinguish themselves from other mammals that were physically similar to themselves. It was not their hunting prowess that made the hominids stand out, because plenty of other species chased their prey with skill and dexterity. The single trait that gave early hominids a real advantage for survival was **bipedalism**: they became "two-footed" creatures that stood upright. At some point, the first hominids were able to remain upright and move about, leaving their arms and hands free for other useful tasks, like carrying food over long distances. Once they ventured into open savannas (grassy plains with a few scattered trees), about 1.7 million years ago, hominids had a tremendous advantage. They were the only primates (an order of mammals consisting of man, apes, and monkeys) to move consistently on two legs. Because they could move continuously and over great distances, they were able to migrate out of hostile environments and into more hospitable locations as needed.

Explaining why and how hominids began to walk on two legs is critical to understanding our human origins. Along with the other primates, the first hominids enjoyed the advantages of being long-limbed, tree-loving animals with good vision and dexterous digits. Why did these primates, in contrast to their closest relatives (gorillas and chimpanzees), leave the shelter of trees and venture out into the open grasslands, where they were vulnerable to attack? The answer is not self-evident. Explaining how and why some apes took these first steps also sheds light on why humanity's origins lie in Africa. Fifteen million years ago there were apes all over the world, so why did a small number of them evolve new traits in Africa?

ENVIRONMENTAL CHANGES   What eastern and southern Africa offered was a climate conducive to the development of diverse plant and animal species. At a critical moment, the environment in this region changed dramatically. The world had entered its fourth great ice age approximately 40 million years ago, during which the earth's temperatures diminished and its continental ice sheets, polar ice sheets, and mountain glaciers increased. This ice age lasted until 10,000 years ago. Like all ice ages, it had alternating warming and cooling phases that lasted between 40,000 and 100,000 years each. Between 10 and 15 million years ago, the climate in Africa went through one such cooling and drying phase. To the east of Africa's Rift Valley, stretching from South Africa north to the Ethiopian highlands, the cooling and drying forced forests to contract and savannas to spread. It was in this region that some apes came down from trees, stood up, and learned to walk, to run, and to live in savanna lands—thus becoming the precursors to humans, and distinctive as a new species.

Using two feet for locomotion did more than augment the means of survival for creatures whose environments were changing. It also increased their options for subsistence and led to the acquisition of **cognitive skills** (such as thought, memory, problem-solving, and—ultimately—language) to obtain food and avoid predators. Cognition itself became the basis for further developments. Thus, as hands no longer had to pull bodies around, they were free for carrying other things

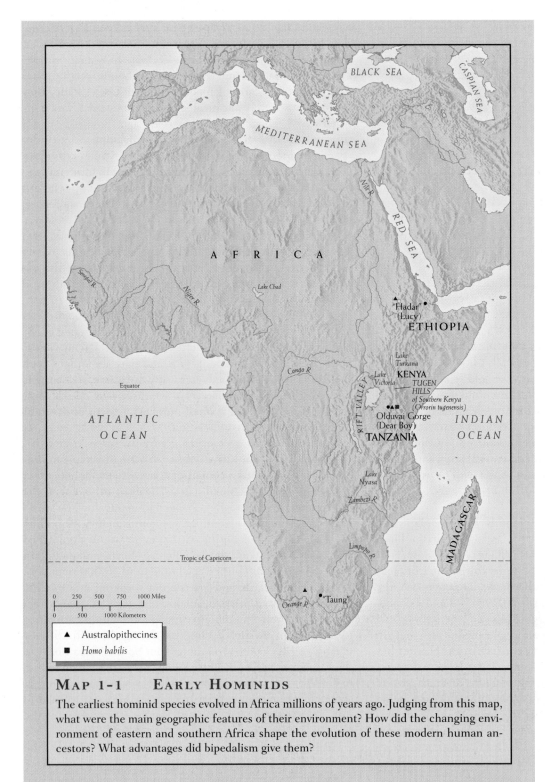

MAP 1-1   EARLY HOMINIDS

The earliest hominid species evolved in Africa millions of years ago. Judging from this map, what were the main geographic features of their environment? How did the changing environment of eastern and southern Africa shape the evolution of these modern human ancestors? What advantages did bipedalism give them?

alter materials found in nature. Manual dexterity and standing upright also enabled them to carry young family members if they needed to relocate, or to throw missiles (such as rocks and sticks) with deadly accuracy to protect themselves or to obtain food. They used their increased powers of observation and memory to gather wild berries and grains and to scavenge the meat and marrow of animals that had died of natural causes or as the prey of predators. All primates are good at these activities, but hominids came to excel at them.

The early hominids were highly social. They lived in bands of about twenty-five individuals, trying to survive by hunting small game and gathering wild plants. Not yet a match for large predators, they had to find safe hiding places. They also sought ecological niches where a diverse supply of wild grains and fruits and abundant wildlife ensured a secure, comfortable existence. In such locations, small hunting bands of twenty-five could swell through alliances with others to as many as 500 individuals. Like other primates, hominids communicated through gestures, but they also may have developed an early form of spoken language that led (among other things) to the establishment of cultural codes such as common rules and customs.

The early hominids lived in this manner for up to 3

and, eventually, making the first tools. A free hand could hold a spear or the ever-useful digging stick.

In addition to being bipedal, hominids had another trait that helped them to survive and create and use tools—opposable thumbs. This trait, shared with other primates, gave hominids great physical dexterity, enhancing their ability to explore and to

million years, changing their way of life very little except for moving around the African landmass in their never-ending search for more favorable environments. Even so, their survival is surprising. There were not many of them, and they struggled in hostile environments surrounded by a diversity of large mammals, including predators such as lions.

→ *What traits made early hominids different from other animal species?*

As the environment changed over the millennia, these early hominids gradually altered in appearance. Fossils from 3 million years ago reveal that their brains almost doubled in size; their foreheads became more elongated; their jaws became less massive; and they took on a much more modern look. Adaptation to environmental changes also created new skills and aptitudes, which expanded the ability to store and analyze information. With larger brains, hominids could form mental maps of their worlds—they could learn, remember what they learned, and convey these lessons to their neighbors and offspring. In this fashion, larger groups of hominids created communities with shared understandings of their environments. This process enhanced the advantages of those with larger brains as they underwent natural selection—the process whereby offspring inherit traits that improve the probability of survival and reproduction.

DIVERSITY We know that hominids were much older than we thought, but it turns out that they were also much more diverse. Consider some startling finds from Ethiopia and Kenya. In southern Kenya, researchers have discovered bone remains, at least 6 million years old, of a chimpanzee-sized hominid (named *Orrorin tugenensis*) that walked upright on two feet. This discovery indicates that bipedalism must be millions of years older than we used to think. Moreover, these hominids' teeth indicate that they were closer to modern humans than to australopithecines. In their arms and hands, though, which show characteristics needed for tree climbing, the *Orrorin* hominids seemed more apelike than the australopithecines. So *Orrorin* hominids were still somewhat tied to an environment in the trees. Also, recent discoveries of the bones of five individuals in the Afar depression in Ethiopia (an area just south of Lucy's discovery) have revealed a different kind of bipedal hominid dating back at least 5 million years. Yet another recent discovery, this one in northern Kenya, has revealed yet another species of early hominid.

The fact that different kinds of early hominids were living side by side in the same environment in eastern Africa between 3 and 4 million years ago indicates much greater diversity and development among their populations than scholars previously imagined. The environment in eastern Africa was generating a fair number of different hominid populations, a few of which would provide our genetic base, but most of which would not survive in the long run. In fact, the survival of any of these hominid lines was no certain thing.

THE FIRST HUMANS: *HOMO HABILIS*

One million years after Lucy, the first examples of human beings, to whom we give the name *homo,* or "true human," appeared. They, too, were bipedal, possessing a smooth walk based on upright posture. And they had an even more important advantage over other hominids: large brains. Big brains were like little motors of **innovation**: learning and storing lessons so that humans could pass those lessons on to later generations, especially in the making of tools and the

Searching for Hominid Fossils. Olorgasalie in Kenya has proved to be one of the most important archaeological sites for uncovering evidence of early hominid development. Rick Potts, a leader in the field, is shown here on-site. Among his discoveries were hand axes and indications that hominids in this area had learned to use fire.

The Leakeys. Louis Leakey and his wife, Mary, were dedicated archaeologists whose work in East Africa established the area as one of the starting points of human development. Mary Leakey (*right*) was among the most successful archaeologists studying hominids in Africa. Her finds, including the one in this photograph from Laetoli, Tanzania, highlight the activities of early men and women in Africa. The footprints, believed to be those of an *Australopithecus afarensis*, date from 3.7 to 3 million years ago.

Olduvai Gorge, Tanzania. Olduvai Gorge is arguably the most famous archaeological site containing hominid finds. Mary and Louis Leakey, convinced that early human beings originated in Africa, discovered the fossil remains of *Homo habilis* ("Skillful Man") in this area between 1960 and 1963. They argued that these findings represent a direct link to *Homo erectus*.

efficient use of resources (and, we suspect, in defending themselves). Mary and Louis Leakey, who made astonishing fossil discoveries in the 1950s at Olduvai Gorge (part of the Great Rift Valley) in present-day northeastern Tanzania, identified these important traits. The Leakeys' finds are the most significant discoveries of early humans in Africa—in particular, an intact skull that was 1.8 million years old.

The Olduvai Gorge is a thirty-mile-long canyon in which a winding stream has exposed many layers of volcanic rock containing abundant fossil remains. Louis S. B. Leakey was a paleontologist (a scientist studying fossil remains from past geological periods) educated at the University of Cambridge. In 1931, Leakey began a research project in Olduvai along with his wife, Mary Nicol Leakey, an archaeologist. Although their Cambridge mentors had rejected the notion of humanity's African origins, the Leakeys' work would ultimately prove them wrong. After decades of frustrating work and financial troubles, Mary Leakey could hardly believe her good fortune when she stumbled upon an almost totally intact skull. The Leakeys nicknamed it Dear Boy.

Other objects discovered with Dear Boy demonstrated that by this time early humans had begun to make tools for butchering animals and, possibly, for hunting and killing smaller animals. The tools were flaked stones with sharpened edges for cutting apart animal flesh and scooping out the marrow from bones. To mimic the slicing teeth of lions, leopards, and other carnivores, the Oldowans had devised these tools through careful chipping. Dear Boy and his companions had carried usable rocks to distant places where they made their implements with special hammer stones—tools to make tools. Unlike other tool-using animals (for example, chimpanzees), early humans were now intentionally fashioning implements, not simply finding them when needed. More important, they were passing on knowledge of these tools to their offspring and, in the process, gradually improving the tools. Because the Leakeys believed that making and using tools represented a new stage in the evolution of human beings, they gave these creatures a new name: **Homo habilis**, or "Skillful Man." Their tool-making ability made them the forerunners, though very distant, of modern men and women.

EARLY HUMANS ON THE MOVE: MIGRATIONS OF *HOMO ERECTUS*

All the different species of hominids flourished together in Africa between 1 and 2.5 million years ago. By 1 million years ago, however, many had died out. One surviving species, which emerged about 1.8 million years ago, had a large brain capacity and walked truly upright; it therefore gained the name **Homo erectus,** or "Standing Man." Even though this species was more able to cope with environmental changes than other hominids had been, its story was not a predictable triumph. Only with the hindsight of millions of years can we

understand the decisive advantage of intelligence over brawn—larger brains over larger teeth. Indeed, there were many more failures than successes in the gradual changes that led *Homo erectus* to be one of the few hominid species that would survive until the arrival of *Homo sapiens.*

One of the traits that contributed to the survival of *Homo erectus* was the development of extended periods of caring for their young. Although their enlarged brain gave these hominids advantages over the rest of the animal world, it also brought one significant problem: their heads were too large to pass through the females' pelvises at birth. Their pelvises were only big enough to deliver an infant with a cranial capacity that was about a third an adult's size. As a result, offspring required a long period of protection by adults as they matured and their brain size tripled.

This difference from other species also affected family dynamics. For example, the long maturing process gave adult members of hunting and gathering bands time to train their children in those activities. In addition, maturation and brain growth required mothers to spend years attending to their infants, via lactation as well as food preparation for children after weaning. This investment of time and energy was so critical to survival that mothers devised means to share the burden of childrearing. They figured out how to reduce the risks of accidents or attacks, sometimes even fending off assaults by predatory fathers and other males. Mothers relied on other women (their own mothers, sisters, and friends) and girls (often their own daughters) to help in the nurturing and protecting, a process known as allomothering (literally, "other mothering").

Two main features of *Homo erectus* distinguished them from their competitors: bipedalism and their attempts to control the environment. Being bipedal, they could move with a smooth and rapid gait, so they could cover large distances quickly. They were the world's first long-distance travelers, forming the first mobile human communities. In addition, they began to make rudimentary attempts to control their environment. Not only did these early human ancestors make stone tools for hunting and food preparation, but they also began to control fire—another significant marker in the development of human culture. It is hard to tell from fossils when humans learned to use fire. The most reliable evidence comes from cave sites, less than 250,000 years old, where early humans apparently cooked some of their food. Less conservative estimates suggest that human mastery of fire occurred as early as 500,000 years ago. Fire provided heat, protection, a gathering point for small communities, and a way to cook food. It was also symbolically powerful: here was a source of energy that humans could extinguish and revive at will. The uses of fire had enormous long-term effects on human evolution. Because they were able to boil, steam, and fry wild plants, as well as otherwise undigestible foods (especially raw muscle fiber), early humans could expand their diets and their potential food base. Mastery of fire also enabled early humans to survive in colder regions. Without fire, hominids might not have ventured out of Africa.

The populating of the world by hominids proceeded in waves. Around 1 or 2 million years ago, *Homo erectus* individuals migrated first into the lands of Southwest Asia. From there, according to some scholars, they traveled along the Indian Ocean shoreline, moving into South Asia and Southeast Asia and later northward into what is now China. Their **migration** was a response in part to the environmental changes that were transforming the world. The Northern Hemisphere experienced thirty major cold phases during this period, marked by glaciers (huge sheets of ice) spreading over vast expanses of the northern parts of Eurasia and the Americas. The glaciers formed as a result of intense cold that froze much of the world's oceans, lowering them some 325 feet below present-day levels. So it was possible for the migrants to travel across land bridges into Southeast Asia and from East Asia to Japan, as well as from New Guinea to Australia. The last parts of the Afro-Eurasian landmass to be occupied were in Europe. The geological record indicates that ice mantles blanketed the areas of present-day Scotland, Ireland, Wales, Scandinavia, and the whole of northern Europe (including the areas of present-day Berlin, Warsaw, Moscow, and Kiev). Here, too, a lowered ocean level enabled human predecessors to cross by foot from areas in Europe into what is now England.

It is astonishing how far *Homo erectus* hominids traveled. Discoveries of the bone remains of "Java Man" and "Peking Man" (named according to the places where archaeologists first unearthed their remains) confirmed early settlements of *Homo erectus* in Southeast and Eastern Asia. The remains of Java Man, found in 1891 in central Java, turned out to be those of an early *Homo erectus* that had dispersed into Asia

nearly 2 million years ago. In 1969, at Sangiran (also on the island of Java), archaeologists uncovered remains with a fuller cranium that was very thick, indicating that the individual's brain was about half the size of a modern human's. Because this discovery dates from about 800,000 years ago, scientists realized that African hominids were moving northward and eastward into Asia at least a million years ago and had reached Java, which was then connected by land to the rest of the Afro-Eurasian landmass.

Similar twentieth-century finds in China give a clearer picture of the daily lives of these pioneering hominids. Peking Man was a cave dweller, toolmaker, and hunter and gatherer who settled in the warmer climate in northern China perhaps 400,000 years ago. Peking Man's brain was larger than that of his Javan cousins, and there is evidence that he controlled fire and cooked meat in addition to hunting large animals. He made tools of vein quartz, quartz crystals, flint, and sandstone. These *Homo erectus* hominids were more adept at toolmaking than their predecessors. Their major innovation was the double-faced axe, a stone instrument whittled down to sharp edges on both sides to serve as a hand axe, a cleaver, a pick, and probably a weapon to hurl against foes or animals. Even so, and in spite of their enlarged brains, these early predecessors still had a long way to go before becoming modern humans.

Rather than seeing human evolution as a single, gradual development, increasingly scientists view our origins as shaped by a series of progressions and regressions as hominids adapted or failed to adapt and went extinct (died out). As the climate changed, especially with the cyclical warming and cooling of the ice ages, weather conditions altered the course of *speciation*, or species formation. Several species could exist simultaneously, but some were more suited to changing environmental

Skulls of Ancestors of *Homo sapiens*. Shown here are seven skulls of ancestors of modern-day men and women, arranged to highlight brain growth over time. The skulls represent (left to right): *Adapis*, a lemur-like animal that lived 50 million years ago; *Proconsul,* a primate that lived about 23 million years ago; *Australopithecus africanus*; *Homo habilis*; *Homo erectus*; *Homo sapiens* from the Qafzeh site in Israel, about 90,000 years old; and Cro-Magnon *Homo sapiens sapiens* from France, about 22,000 years old.

conditions—and thus more likely to survive—than others. Although those in the *Homo habilis* and *Homo erectus* species were among some of the world's first humanlike inhabitants, they probably were not direct ancestors of modern man and woman. The early settlers of Afro-Eurasia from the *Homo erectus* group went extinct. Later waves of hominids followed them, walking out of the African landmass just as their predecessors had done. By 500,000 years ago, caves in many areas of Afro-Eurasia housed residents who made fire, flaked stones into implements, and formed settlements. Yet we are not their descendants. Although the existence of *Homo erectus* may have been necessary for the evolution into *Homo sapiens*, it was not, in itself, sufficient.

THE FIRST MODERN HUMANS

> → *How did* Homo sapiens *become the only hominid species?*

Homo sapiens moved out of Africa sometime between 120,000 and 50,000 years ago. If we consider the 5 million years of hominid life as a single hour of our time today, then the history of *Homo sapiens* is slightly less than two minutes.

The early hominids could not form large communities, as they had limited communication skills. They could utter simple commands and communicate with hand signals, but complex linguistic expression eluded them. This achievement was one of the last in the evolutionary process of becoming human; it did not occur until between 100,000 and 50,000 years ago. Many scholars view it as the critical ingredient in distinguishing human beings from other animals. It is this skill that made *Homo sapiens* "sapiens," which is to say "wise" or "intelligent"—humans who could create culture. Creating language enabled humans to become modern humans.

HOMO SAPIENS AND THEIR MIGRATION

About 200,000 years ago, large-scale shifts in Africa's climate and environment put huge pressures on all types of mammals, including hominids. In these extremely warm and dry environments, the smaller, quicker, and more adaptable mammals survived. What counted now was no longer large size and brute strength, but the ability to respond quickly, with agility, and with great speed.

Caught up in these environmental transformations, early humans were no different from other mammals. It is therefore no surprise that a bigger-brained, more dexterous, and more agile species of humans appeared in the highlands of eastern Africa. Referred to as **Homo sapiens**, they differed notably from their precursors. The eclipse of *Homo erectus* by *Homo sapiens* was not inevitable. After all, *Homo erectus* was already scattered around Africa and Eurasia; in contrast, current thinking suggests that even as late as 100,000 years ago there were only about 10,000 *Homo sapiens* adults living in a small part of the African landmass. But when *Homo sapiens* moved out of Africa and the two species encountered each other in the same places across the globe, *Homo sapiens* individuals were better suited to survive—in part because of their greater cognitive and language skills.

The *Homo sapiens* newcomers followed the trails blazed by earlier migrants from Africa. (See Map 1-2.) In many places, they moved into the same areas as their genetic cousins, migrating by way of the Levant (the area encompassing modern-day Lebanon, Israel, Palestine, Jordan, and Syria), moving across Southwest Asia and from there into central Asia—but not into the area of Europe. They flourished and reproduced. By 30,000 years ago, the population of *Homo sapiens* had grown to about 300,000. Between 60,000

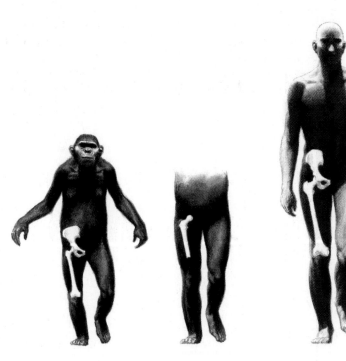

The Physical Evolution of Hominids. These three figures show the femur bones of Lucy, *Orronin tugenensis* (one of the earliest of the hominids, who may have existed as many as 6 million years ago), and *Homo sapiens*. *Homo sapiens* has a larger femur bone and was bigger than Lucy—a representative of the hominid species *Australopithecus afarensis*—but has the same bone structure.

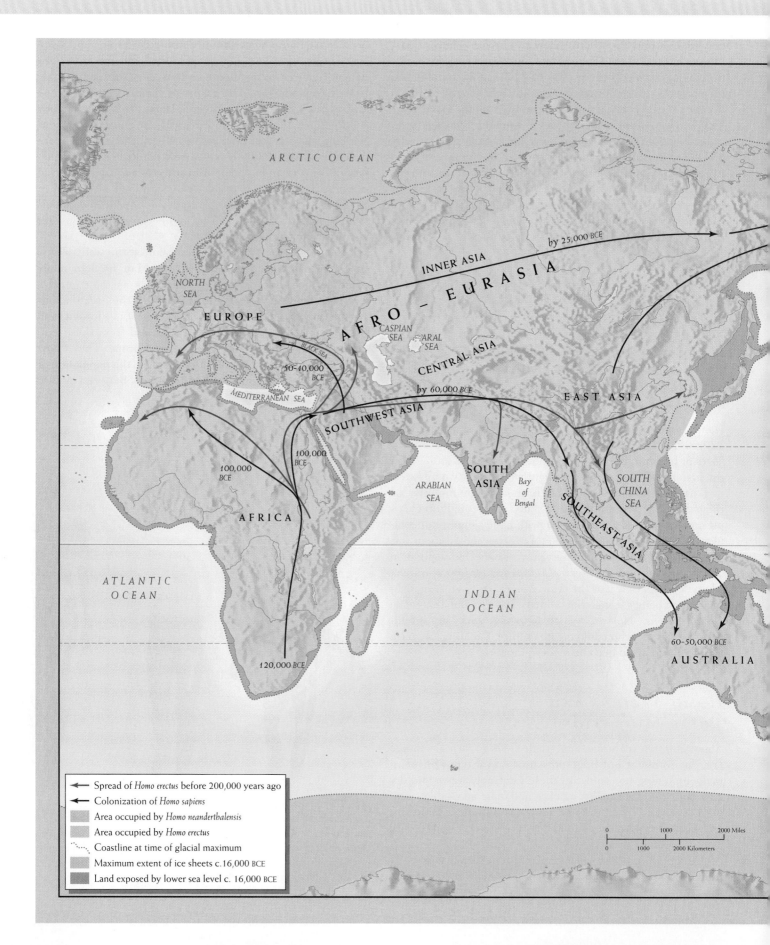

ARCTIC OCEAN

NORTH
SEA

EUROPE

INNER ASIA

by 25,000 BCE

AFRO – EURASIA

CASPIAN
SEA

ARAL
SEA

BLACK SEA

50–40,000
BCE

CENTRAL ASIA

MEDITERRANEAN SEA

by 60,000 BCE

EAST ASIA

SOUTHWEST ASIA

100,000
BCE

100,000
BCE

SOUTH
ASIA

Bay
of
Bengal

SOUTH
CHINA
SEA

ARABIAN
SEA

SOUTHEAST ASIA

AFRICA

ATLANTIC
OCEAN

INDIAN
OCEAN

60–50,000 BCE

AUSTRALIA

120,000 BCE

Spread of *Homo erectus* before 200,000 years ago
Colonization of *Homo sapiens*
Area occupied by *Homo neanderthalensis*
Area occupied by *Homo erectus*
Coastline at time of glacial maximum
Maximum extent of ice sheets c.16,000 BCE
Land exposed by lower sea level c. 16,000 BCE

0   1000   2000 Miles
0   1000   2000 Kilometers

→ *How did* Homo sapiens *become the only hominid species?*

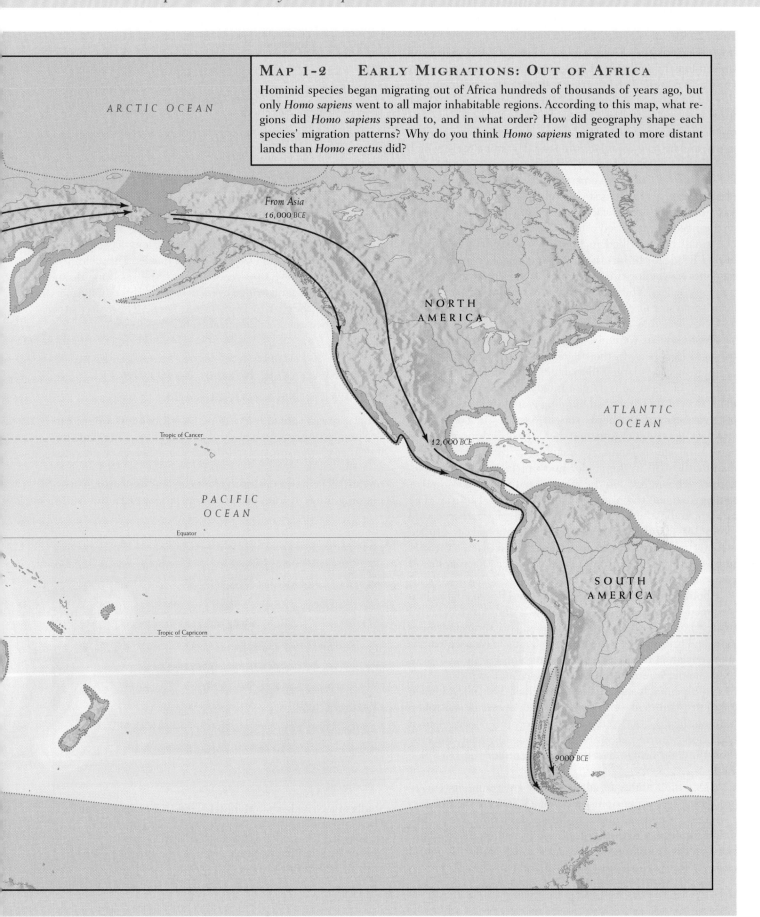

MAP 1-2 EARLY MIGRATIONS: OUT OF AFRICA

Hominid species began migrating out of Africa hundreds of thousands of years ago, but only *Homo sapiens* went to all major inhabitable regions. According to this map, what regions did *Homo sapiens* spread to, and in what order? How did geography shape each species' migration patterns? Why do you think *Homo sapiens* migrated to more distant lands than *Homo erectus* did?

ARCTIC OCEAN

From Asia
16,000 BCE

NORTH
AMERICA

ATLANTIC
OCEAN

Tropic of Cancer

12,000 BCE

PACIFIC
OCEAN

Equator

SOUTH
AMERICA

Tropic of Capricorn

9000 BCE

and 12,000 years ago, these modern humans were surging into areas tens of thousands of miles from the Rift Valley and the Ethiopian highlands of Africa. In the area of present-day China, they were thriving and creating distinct regional cultures. Consider Shandingdong Man, a *Homo sapiens* whose fossil remains and relics date to about 18,000 years ago. His physical characteristics were closer to those of modern humans, and he had a similar brain size. His stone tools, which included choppers and scrapers for preparing food, were similar to those of the *Homo erectus* Peking Man. His bone needles, however, were the first stitching tools of their kind found in China, and they indicated the making of garments. Some of the needles measured a little over an inch in length and had small holes drilled in them. Shandingdong Man also buried his dead. In fact, a tomb of grave goods includes ornaments suggesting the development of aesthetic tastes and religious beliefs. The social unit of these hominids may have been some sort of clan descended from a common ancestor and thus linked by genealogy.

Homo sapiens were also migrating into the northeastern fringe of East Asia. In the frigid climate there, they learned to follow herds of large Siberian grazing animals. The bones and dung of Mastodons, large-tusked mammals, for instance, made decent fuel and good building material. Pursuing their prey eastward as the herds sought pastures in the steppes (treeless grasslands) and marshes, these groups migrated across the ice to Japan. Archaeologists have discovered a mammoth fossil in the colder north of Japan, for example, and an elephant fossil in the warmer south. Elephants in particular roamed the warmer parts of inner Eurasia. The hunters and gatherers who moved into Japan gathered wild plants for sustenance, and they dried, smoked, or broiled meat by using fire. They refined these practices once the seas separated the islands from Asia and limited the supplies of game and plants.

About 16,000 years ago, *Homo sapiens* began edging into the weedy landmass that linked Siberia and North America (which hominids had not populated). This thousand-mile-long land bridge, later called Beringia, must have seemed like an extension of familiar steppeland terrain. For thousands of years, modern humans poured eastward and southward into the uninhabited terrain of North America. The oldest known location of human settlement in the Americas is Broken Mammoth, a 14,000-year-old site in central Alaska. A final migration occurred about 8,000 years ago by boat, since by then the land bridge had disappeared under the sea. (See Table 1-2.)

Using their ability to adapt to new environments and to innovate, these expansionist migrants, who were the first discoverers of America, began to fill up the landmasses. They found ample prey in the herds of woolly mammoths, caribou, giant sloths (weighing nearly three tons), and 200-pound beavers. But the explorers could also themselves be prey—

TABLE 1-2 Migrations of *Homo sapiens*

Homo erectus leave Africa	c. 1.5 million years ago
Homo sapiens leave Africa	c. 100,000 years ago
Homo sapiens migrate into Asia	c. 60,000 years ago
migrate into Europe	c. 40–50,000 years ago
migrate into Australia	c. 40,000 years ago
migrate into the Americas	c. 11–16,000 years ago

for they encountered saber-toothed tigers, long-legged eagles, and giant bears that moved faster than horses. The melting of the glaciers about 8,000 years ago and the resulting disappearance of the land bridge eventually cut off the first Americans from their Afro-Eurasian origins. Thereafter, the Americas became a world apart from Afro-Eurasia.

CRO-MAGNON *HOMO SAPIENS* REPLACE NEANDERTHALS

Homo sapiens spread out and occupied habitats where earlier hominid migrants had dwelled. From the time that they left Africa, approximately 100,000 years ago, they migrated over the whole globe. By 25,000 years ago, as DNA analysis reveals, all genetic cousins to *Homo sapiens* were extinct, leaving only modern humans' ancestors to populate the world.

Skulls of a Neanderthal Man (left) and Cro-Magnon (right). These two skulls show that Neanderthals had a large brain capacity and a larger head than modern man. However, Neanderthals lost out to *Homo sapiens* in the struggle to survive as *Homo sapiens* spread across the globe.

Neanderthals, members of an early wave of hominids from Africa, had settled in western Afro-Eurasia (ranging from present-day Uzbekistan and Iraq to Spain) perhaps 150,000 years ago. They were there well before *Homo sapiens*. Therein lies a tale, for Western scholars have had a long fascination with these hominids.

For a long time, many scholars believed that Neanderthals were the primary precursors of modern-day Europeans. We now know that this is not true. The first knowledge of Neanderthals came with the discovery in 1856 of a skull in the Neander Valley of present-day Germany (the *thal* or *tal* in their name is the German word for "valley"). Some authorities wondered if the skull represented the so-called missing link between apes and humans. Not only did Neanderthals have big brains, but they also used tools, buried their dead, hunted, and lived in caves. To judge from their behavior, their brain structure was not as complex as that of modern humans, so their cognitive abilities were far more limited than those of *Homo sapiens*, especially in their perception and creation of symbols.

Neanderthals eventually gave way to Cro-Magnon peoples, a group of *Homo sapiens* named after fossil discoveries from 1868 in Cro-Magnon, France. Although Neanderthal and Cro-Magnon communities overlapped in Europe for thousands of years, the Neanderthals were not as well equipped to survive as the Cro-Magnons, who were truly modern humans. The Neanderthals' short arms and legs and bulky torso may have made them stronger than Cro-Magnon men and women, but the Neanderthals were awkward and clumsy. The Cro-Magnons had the advantages of physical dexterity and high intelligence; the latter attribute gave them cognitive and language abilities not available to Neanderthals to the same degree.

Neanderthals and other advanced hominids in China and Java represented the culmination of a long evolutionary process that made individuals more specialized and better adapted to specific environmental conditions. When the environment began to change, these descendants from Africa had difficulty coping. They lacked the range and adaptive fluidity of *Homo sapiens*. In the scramble for food and shelter, *Homo sapiens* had an edge. From their last refuge around Zafarraya in Spain, the Neanderthals vanished, leaving only a small trace in the gene pool that evolved into modern humanity somewhere between 1 and 4 percent. Like the *Homo erectus* species in Java and China, this particular trajectory of hominid development came to a dead end.

EARLY *HOMO SAPIENS* AS HUNTERS AND GATHERERS

Like their hominid predecessors, modern humans were hunters and gatherers, and they subsisted in this way until

The San Hunters and Gatherers of Southern Africa. The San, who live in the Kalahari Desert in present-day Botswana, continue to follow a hunting and gathering existence that has died out in many parts of the world. Hunting and gathering was the way that most humans lived for millennia.

around 12,000 years ago. They hunted animals, fished, and foraged for wild berries, nuts, fruit, and grains, rather than planting crops, vines, or trees. Even today hunting and gathering societies endure, although only in the most marginal locations—often at the edge of deserts. For example, researchers consider the present-day San peoples of southern Africa as an isolated remnant continuing their traditional hunting and gathering modes of life. On the basis of analogy, modern scholars use the San to reveal how men and women must have lived hundreds of thousands of years ago. (See Primary Source: Problems in the Study of Hunters and Gatherers.) As late as 1500 CE, as much as 15 percent of the world's population still lived by **hunting and gathering**.

The fact that hominid men and women survived as hunters and gatherers for millions of years, that early *Homo sapiens* also lived this way, and that a few contemporary communities still forage for food suggests the powerful attractions of this way of life. Hunters and gatherers could find enough food in about three hours of foraging each day, thus affording time for other pursuits such as relaxation, interaction, and friendly competitions with other members of their

PROBLEMS IN THE STUDY OF HUNTERS AND GATHERERS

One of the challenges in studying the origins of humanity is that the evidence is incomplete. Archaeologists and anthropologists have to theorize on the basis of what they can lay their hands on. In the case of archaeologists, these include fossil records. In the case of anthropologists, their subjects are tribal peoples—such as the San of southern Africa—whose lifeways today may resemble those of their ancestors tens of thousands of years ago.

To date, the hunting way of life has been the most successful and persistent adaptation man has ever achieved.

. . . It is appropriate that anthropologists take stock of the much older way of life of the hunters. This is not simply a study of biological evolution, since zoologists have come to regard behavior as central to the adaptation and evolution of all species. The emergence of economic, social, and ideological forms are as much a part of human evolution as are the developments in human anatomy and physiology. . . .

. . . Ever since the origin of agriculture, Neolithic (new stone age) peoples have been steadily expanding at the expense of the hunters. Today the latter are often found in unattractive environments, in lands which are of no use to their neighbors and which pose difficult and dramatic problems of survival. The more favorable habitats have long ago been appropriated by peoples with stronger, more aggressive social systems.

. . . Taking hunters as they are found, anthropologists have naturally been led to the conclusion that their life (and by implication the life of our ancestors) was a constant struggle for survival.

At the dawn of agriculture 12,000 years ago, hunters covered most of the habitable globe, and appeared to be generally most successful in those areas which later supported the densest populations of agricultural peoples. By 1500 CE the area left to hunters had shrunk drastically and their distribution fell largely at the peripheries of the continents and in the inaccessible interiors. However, even at this late date, hunting peoples occupied all of Australia, most of western and northern North America, and large portions of South America and Africa. This situation rapidly changed with the era of colonial expansion, and by 1900, when serious ethnographic research got under way,

much of this way of life had been destroyed. As a result, our notion of unacculturated hunter-gatherer life has been largely drawn from peoples no longer living in the optimum portion of their traditional range.

To mention a few examples, the Netsilik Eskimos, the Arunta, and the Kung Bushmen are now classic cases in ethnography. However, the majority of the precontact Eskimos, Australian aborigines, and Bushmen lived in much better environments. Two-thirds of the Eskimos, according to Laughlin, lived *south* of the Arctic circle, and the populations in the Australian and Kalahari deserts were but a fraction of the populations living in the well-watered regions of southeast Australia and the Cape Province of Africa. Thus, within a given region the "classic cases" may, in fact, be precisely the opposite: namely, the most isolated peoples who managed to avoid contact until the arrival of the ethnographers. In order to understand hunters better it may be more profitable to consider the few hunters in rich environments, since it is likely that these peoples will be more representative of the ecological conditions under which man evolved than are the dramatic and unusual cases that illustrate extreme environmental pressure. Such a perspective may better help us to understand the extraordinary persistence and success of the human adaptation.

→ *Why is it important to study hunting and gathering communities?*

→ *Why are the "classic cases" not necessarily the most representative of this early lifeway?*

SOURCE: Richard B. Lee and Irven De Vore, "Problems in the Study of Hunters and Gatherers" from *Man the Hunter*, pp. 3 and 5. Copyright © 1968 by Aldine Publishers. Reprinted by permission of Aldine Transaction, a division of Transaction Publishers.

bands. Scholars believe that these small bands were relatively egalitarian. They speculate that men specialized in hunting and women specialized in gathering and child rearing but that men and women contributed equally to the bands' welfare.

Scholars also believe that women made a larger contribution and had high status because the dietary staples were cereals and fruits, whose harvesting and preparation were likely women's responsibility.

ART AND LANGUAGE

→ *How did art and language increase* Homo sapiens' *chances of survival?*

Despite the remorselessly nature-bound quality of life for early humans, the first *Homo sapiens* made an evolutionary breakthrough. They developed cultural forms that reflected a consciousness of self, a drive to survive, an appreciation of beauty, and an ability to engage dynamically with their environments.

ART

Few of the cultural achievements of early *Homo sapiens* communities have engaged modern-day observers more than their artistic endeavors. Accomplished drawings have come to light in areas in Europe, probably as a response to the harsher environment there and also because of intense competition with the Neanderthals. The ability to draw allowed *Homo sapiens* to understand their environment, to bond among their kin groups (groups related by blood ties), and to articulate important mythologies. In times of stress, such behaviors gave these individuals an adaptive advantage to survive in extremely challenging circumstances.

"Look, Daddy, oxen!" That is what the daughter of Marcelino Sanz de Sauruola cried to her father as she looked at the ceiling of a deep cave on his property at Altamira, Spain, that he was exploring one summer afternoon. As he looked up, Sauruola could not believe what he saw. Arranged across the ceiling of the huge chamber were more than two dozen life-size figures of bison, horses, and wild bulls, all painted in vivid red, black, yellow, and brown. He did not think that anyone would believe these fabulous images were tens of thousands of years old, but he knew in his heart that they were. That was in 1879. Only in 1906 did the world accept that the Altamira paintings, and those later discovered in other caves, were the work of early humans. Even today, with researchers having found more than 50,000 works of art by early humans in Europe, these paintings compel wonder and awe at the innate artistic abilities unique to humans. (See Primary Source: The Art of Chauvet Cave.)

The images on cave walls accumulated over a period of 25,000 years, and they changed very little in that time. The subjects are most often large game—animals that early humans would have considered powerful symbols. The artists rendered these animals with a striking economy of line, frequently painted in such a way that the natural contours of the cave wall defined a bulging belly or an eye socket. Many appear more than once, suggesting that they are the works from several occasions or by several artists. The remarkably few human images show naked females or dancing males.

There are also many handprints made by blowing paint around a hand placed on the cave wall, or by dipping hands in paint and then pressing them to the wall. There are even abstract symbols such as circles, wavy lines, and checkerboards; often these appear at places of transition in the caves.

We can only speculate what the images meant to ancient humans. Scholars have rejected an initial explanation that they were decorative, for the deep caves were not the ancients' homes and had no natural light to render the images visible. Perhaps the images had a social function, helping the early humans to define themselves as separate from other parts of nature. Among other interpretations is a theory that they were the work of powerful shamans, individuals believed to hold special powers to understand and control the tremendous forces of the cosmos. The subjects and the style of the paintings are similar to images engraved or painted on rocks by some hunter and gatherer societies living today, especially the San and the !Kung peoples of southern Africa. In those societies, paintings mark important places of ritual: shamans make them during trances while interceding with the spirit world on behalf of their communities.

Paintings were not the only form of artistic expression for early humans. Archaeologists also have unearthed small sculptures of animals shaped out of bone and stone that are even older than the paintings. Most famous are figurines of enormously fat and pregnant females. Statuettes like the so-called Venus of Willendorf, found in Austria, demonstrate that successful reproduction was a very important theme. Among the most exquisite sculptures are those of animals carved in postures of movement or at rest.

The caves of early men and women also resounded to the strains of music. In 2008 archaeologists working in southwestern Germany discovered a hollowed-out bone flute with five openings that they dated to approximately 35,000 years ago, roughly the same time that humans began to occupy this

Willendorf Venus. This squat limestone statuette—only about six inches in height—was discovered in 1908 near the village of Willendorf, Austria, and dates back about 25,000 years. As one of the earliest representations of a female figure found in Europe, it is a famous icon of prehistoric art. The emphasis on the woman's breasts and reproductive organs—to the exclusion, for example, of her facial features— and the presence of a red ochre dye on her genitalia suggest the maker's concern with the woman's fertility and procreative functions.

THE ART OF CHAUVET CAVE

A spectacular discovery at Chauvet Cave in southwestern France in 1994 overturned all previous ideas about the development of prehistoric art. Dating to about 35,000 years ago (much older than the 20,000-year-old paintings from Lascaux in southeastern France, or the 17,000-year-old paintings from Altamira in northwestern Spain), they are the oldest prehistoric cave paintings known in Europe. The hundreds of representations found at Chauvet Cave are more detailed and more brilliant than the ones at Altamira and Lascaux. There are drawings of mammoths, musk oxen, horses, lions, bears, and even rhinoceroses, as well as human palm prints (and footprints on the cave's floor) and "Venus" figures with exaggerated female genitalia—

the latter apparently signifying a preoccupation with human fertility. These amazing engravings and paintings shocked scholars because they were produced only a few thousand years after the first modern humans appeared in Europe.

→ *These drawings show horses, a musk ox, and a rhinoceros. What characteristics of these animals might have inspired the early* Homo sapiens *artists, and why?*

→ *What does their decision to portray certain animals but not others tell us?*

Almost as soon as their first appearance in western Europe, modern humans seemed to have rapidly developed a sense, ability, and desire to portray other living beings in their environment. This brilliant drawing shows the detail in a depiction of horses' heads.

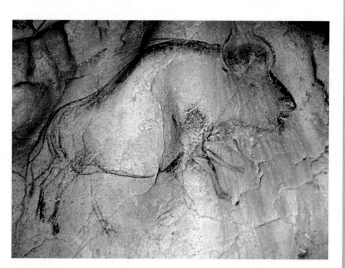

This image uses a doubling effect—drawing additional hindquarters and legs—to give the bison the appearance of motion and speed. The ability to portray dynamic movement was once thought to be a skill that humans developed much later.

region. When researchers put the flute to musical tests, they also concluded that this seemingly primitive instrument was capable of making harmonic sounds comparable to those of modern-day flutes, no small achievement for these early humans whose artistic prowess must have provided much enjoyment to listeners and viewers.

Sculpture and drawing are the oldest forms of visual representation, which was a fundamental part of early human life; yet with the possible exception of the Neanderthals, hominid lines produced very few extant examples. Only members of *Homo sapiens* developed and used this cognitive capacity for symbolic expression by leaving a permanent mark

on the landscape. Such visual expressions marked the dawn of human culture and of a consciousness of men and women's place in the world. Symbolic activity of this sort helped early humans to make sense of themselves, nature, and the relationships between humanity and nature.

LANGUAGE

Few things set humans off from the rest of the animal world more starkly than their use of language, whose genesis and evolution spark heated controversies. Scholars do agree, however, that the cognitive abilities involved in language development marked an evolutionary milestone.

It is important to distinguish between vocal-utterance speech, possessed by many precursor hominids (such as the Neanderthals), and natural **language** (the use of sounds to make words that convey meaning to others), which is unique to modern humans. The development of language necessitated a large brain and complex cognitive organization to create word groups that would convey symbolic meaning. Verbal communication thus required an ability to think abstractly and to communicate abstractions. Language was a huge breakthrough, because individuals could teach words to neighbors and offspring and could use them to integrate communities for survival. Language also enhanced the ability to accumulate knowledge that could be transmitted across both space and time.

Biological research has demonstrated that humans can make and process many more primary and distinctive sounds, called phonemes, than other animals can. Whereas a human being can utter fifty phonemes, an ape can form only twelve. Also, humans can process sounds more quickly than other primates can. With fifty phonemes it is possible to create more than 100,000 words; by arranging those words in different sequences and developing syntax in language, individuals can express countless subtle and complex meanings. Recent research suggests that use of complex languages occurred about 100,000 years ago and that the nearest approximation to humanity's proto-language (earliest language) existing today belongs to two African peoples, the !Kung of southern Africa and the Hadza of Tanzania. These peoples make a clicking sound by dropping the tongue down from the roof of the mouth and exhaling—a sound similar to vervet monkeys' warnings of impending danger. As humans moved out of Africa and dispersed around the globe, they expanded their original language into nineteen language families, from which all of the world's languages then evolved. (See Map 1-3.) It was the development of cultural forms and language that allowed *Homo sapiens* to engage dynamically with their environments.

MAP 1-3   ORIGINAL LANGUAGE FAMILY GROUPS

The use of complex language developed 100,000 years ago among *Homo sapiens* in Africa. As humans dispersed throughout the globe, nineteen language families evolved from which all modern languages originate. How many different landmasses did language evolve on? On the basis of this map, what geographic features kept emerging language families distinct from one another? Why do you think separate languages emerged over time?

THE BEGINNINGS OF FOOD PRODUCTION

> → *What factors contributed to the domestication of plants and animals?*

About 12,000 years ago, a fundamental change occurred in human behavior. It involved a shift in the way humans controlled and produced food for themselves—what some scholars have called a revolution in agriculture and ecology. In this era of major change, humans established greater control over nature, especially over plants and animals. This new wave of innovation and adaptation changed human modes of life. The transformation consisted of the cultivation of wild grasses and cereals and the **domestication** (the bringing under human control) of wild animals. For the first time, human intelligence refashioned nature to meet human needs. Five locations that scholars acknowledge to be independent centers of this agricultural revolution were Southwest Asia, East Asia, Southeast Asia, Mesoamerica, and northeastern America. (See Map 1-4.) Four others may also have been independent regions for this revolution, although the evidence suggests some borrowing. These were East Africa, inland West Africa, southeastern Europe, and South America.

Many factors triggered the move to settled agriculture. Population pressure was a precipitant, as hunting and gathering alone could not sustain the growth in numbers of people. Some regions may have hit the ceiling of natural food supply without the cultivation of crops or the domestication of animals. An agricultural revolution shattered this ceiling—and led to a vast population expansion because men and women could now produce more calories per unit of land than in the past. To be sure, learning to control environments and domesticate resources did not liberate humans from the risks of natural disasters. Without food storage systems, for example, a sharp drought could wipe out or uproot entire communities.

EARLY DOMESTICATION OF PLANTS AND ANIMALS

Settled agriculture, the application of human labor and tools to a fixed plot of land for more than one growing cycle, entails the changeover from a hunting and gathering lifestyle to one based on agriculture, which requires staying in one place until the soil has been exhausted. Around 9000 BCE, abundant rainfall and mild winters created optimal conditions in Southwest Asia for settled life. Once hunters and gatherers could meet their subsistence needs in one diverse ecological

niche, they could afford to settle in a single location. They did so throughout Southwest Asia in greater numbers than before, learning to exploit mountainous areas covered with forest vegetation and home to wild sheep, wild goats, and long-horned wild oxen. In attractive locations such as the valleys of the Taurus Mountains in Upper Mesopotamia (present-day Iraq) and the Anatolian plateau (in modern-day Turkey), the early humans established permanent settlements.

The formation of settled communities enabled humans to take advantage of favorable regions and to take risks, spurring agricultural innovation. In areas with abundant wild game and edible plants, people began to observe and experiment with the most adaptable plants. For ages, people gathered grains by collecting seeds that fell freely from their stalks. At some point, observant collectors perceived that they could obtain larger harvests if they pulled grain seeds directly from plants. The process of plant domestication probably began when people noticed that certain edible plants retained their nutritious grains longer than others, so they collected these seeds and scattered them across fertile soils. When ripe, these plants produced bigger and more concentrated crops. It took time to understand this process, but ultimately a community supporting this kind of innovation realized that it could sustain a larger population than its neighbors. Plant domestication occurred when the plant retained its ripe, mature seeds, allowing an easy harvest. People used most seeds for food but saved some for planting in the next growing cycle, to ensure a food supply for the next year. The gradual domestication of plants began in the southern Levant and spread from there into the rest of Southwest Asia.

DOMESTICATION OF ANIMALS If dogs are a man's best friend, we are now beginning to learn how long and important that friendship has been. Dogs were the first animals to be domesticated (although in fact they may have adopted humans, rather than the other way around). About 12,000 years ago in the area of present-day Iraq, dogs became an essential part of human society. They did more than comfort humans, however, for they provided a vital example of how to achieve the domestication of other animals. Moreover, dogs with herding instincts aided humans in controlling sheep once they had been domesticated.

Wild sheep and wild goats were the next animals to come under human control. This process took place in the central Zagros Mountains region, where wild sheep and wild goats were abundant. A favored explanation is that hunters returned home with young wild sheep, which then grew up within the human community. They reproduced, and their offspring never returned to the wild. The animals accepted their dependence because the humans fed them. As it became clear that controlling animal reproduction was more reliable than hunting, domesticated herds became the primary source of protein in the early humans' diet. This shift probably happened first with the wild sheep living in herds on the mountain slopes.

When the number of animals under human control and living close to the settlement outstripped the supply of food needed to feed them, community members could move the animals to grassy steppes for grazing. Later this lifestyle, called **pastoralism** (the herding of domesticated animals), became an important subsistence strategy that complemented settled farming. Pastoralists herded domesticated animals, moving them to new pastures on a seasonal basis. Goats, the other main domesticated animal of Southwest Asia, are smarter than sheep but more difficult to control. The pastoralists may have introduced goats into herds of sheep to better control herd movement. Pigs and cattle also came under human control at this time.

PASTORALISTS AND AGRICULTURALISTS

The domestication of plants and animals offered new and powerful subsistence strategies that at first augmented and then replaced hunting, gathering, and foraging. Both of these new sources of food and raw materials required radically different ways to use the land which in turn led to different modes of social, political, and economic organization.

Pastoralism, which involved the herding of sheep and goats but also cattle, appeared as a way of life around 5500 BCE, essentially at the same time that full-time farmers appeared. The first pastoralists were closely affiliated with agricultural villages whose inhabitants grew grains, especially wheat and barley, which required large parcels of land. Pastoralists produced both meat and dairy products, as well as wool for textiles, and exchanged these products with the agriculturalists for grain, pottery, and other staples. In the fertile crescent surrounding the Mesopotamian alluvium, many extended families farmed and herded at the same time, growing crops on large estates and grazing their herds in the foothills and mountains nearby. These herders moved their livestock seasonally, usually pasturing their flocks in higher lands during summer and in valleys in winter. This movement over short distances is called transhumance and did not require herders to vacate their primary locations, which were generally in the mountain valleys.

A quite different form of pastoralism, often called nomadic pastoralism, also based on the herding of cattle and other livestock, came to flourish in other settings, notably in the steppe lands north of the agricultural zone of southern Eurasia. This way of life was characterized by horse-riding herders of livestock. These herders often had no fixed home, unlike the transhumant herders of Southwestern Asia, though they often returned to their traditional locations, but moved in response to the size and needs of their herds. The

northern areas of the Eurasian landmass stretching from present-day Ukraine across Siberia and Mongolia to the Pacific Ocean became the preserve of these horse-riding pastoral peoples in a region unable to support the extensive agriculture necessary for large settled populations.

Historians know much less about these horse-riding pastoral peoples than about the agriculturalists and their transhumant cousins, as their numbers were small and they left fewer archaeological traces or historical records. Their role in world history, however, is as important as that of the settled societies. In Afro-Eurasia, they domesticated horses and developed weapons and techniques that at certain points in history enabled them to conquer sedentary societies. They also transmitted ideas, products, and people across long distances, maintaining the linkages that connected east and west.

The archaeological record indicates that full-fledged pastoralism had crystallized in the steppe lands of northern Eurasia by 3000 BCE. By this time, the peoples living there had learned to yoke and ride animals, to milk them, and to use their hair for clothing, as well as to slaughter them for food. Of all the domesticated animals in the steppe lands, the horse became the most important. Because horses provided decisive advantages in transportation and warfare, they gained more value than other domesticated animals. Thus, horses soon became the measure of household wealth and prestige. The domestication of plants and animals and the move to settled agriculture led to a global agricultural revolution.

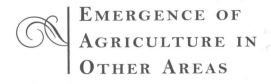

EMERGENCE OF AGRICULTURE IN OTHER AREAS

> → *What factors contributed to innovation, as opposed to borrowing, in agriculture?*

Agricultural revolutions occurred worldwide between 9000 and 2000 BCE. They had much in common: the same factors of climatic change; increased knowledge about plants and animals; and the need for more efficient ways to feed, house, and promote the survival of larger numbers. These concerns led peoples in Eurasia, Africa, and the Americas to see the advantages of cultivating plants and domesticating wildlife.

The following sections examine early agriculture in five key regions: (1) Southwest Asia; (2) the southern part of China in East Asia, where water and rice were critical; (3) western Europe, where the new cultivators borrowed from Southwest Asia; (4) the Americas, which had the disadvantage of offering few animals that humans could domesticate; and (5) Africa,

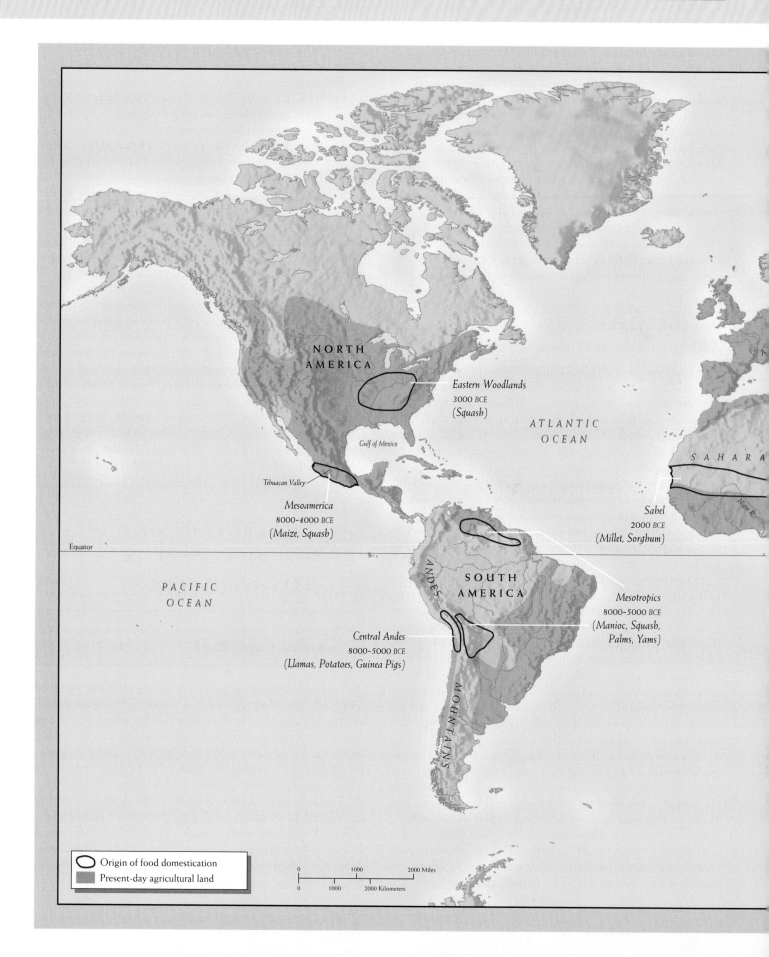

Eastern Woodlands
3000 BCE
(Squash)

NORTH AMERICA

ATLANTIC OCEAN

Gulf of Mexico

SAHARA

Tehuacan Valley

Mesoamerica
8000–4000 BCE
(Maize, Squash)

Sahel
2000 BCE
(Millet, Sorghum)

Niger R.

Equator

PACIFIC OCEAN

ANDES

SOUTH AMERICA

Mesotropics
8000–5000 BCE
(Manioc, Squash, Palms, Yams)

Central Andes
8000–5000 BCE
(Llamas, Potatoes, Guinea Pigs)

MOUNTAINS

Origin of food domestication
Present-day agricultural land

0   1000   2000 Miles
0   1000   2000 Kilometers

→ *What factors contributed to innovation, as opposed to borrowing, in agriculture?*

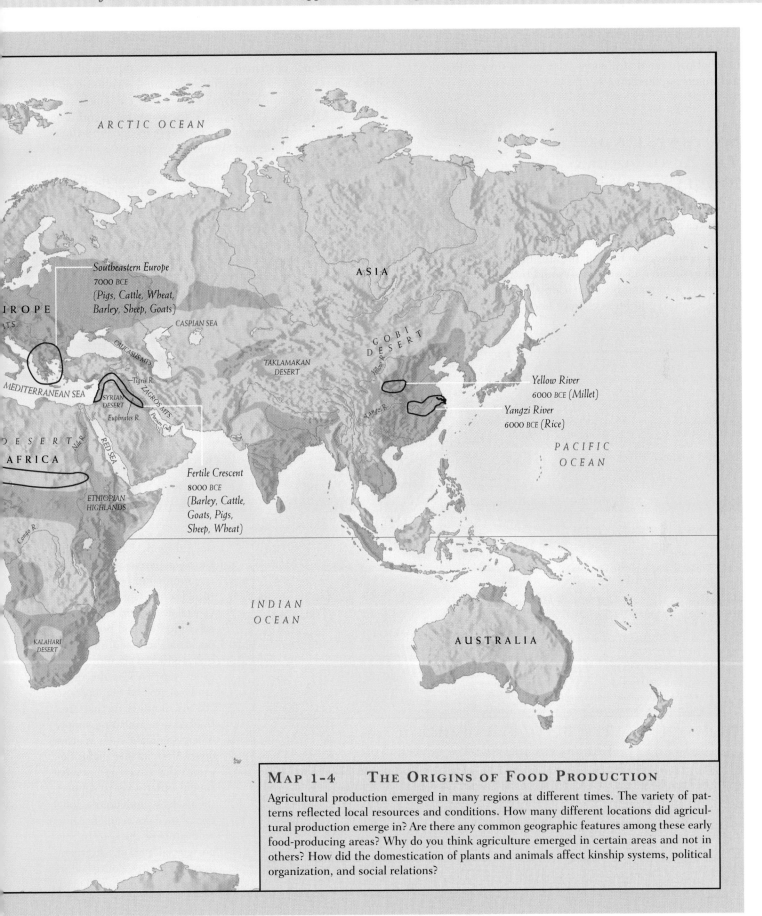

Southeastern Europe
7000 BCE
(Pigs, Cattle, Wheat,
Barley, Sheep, Goats)

CASPIAN SEA

ARCTIC OCEAN

ASIA

GOBI DESERT

TAKLAMAKAN
DESERT

Tigris R.

MEDITERRANEAN SEA

CAUCASUS MTS.

SYRIAN
DESERT

ZAGROS MTS.

Euphrates R.

Persian Gulf

Yellow R.

Yangzi R.

Yellow River
6000 BCE *(Millet)*

Yangzi River
6000 BCE *(Rice)*

PACIFIC
OCEAN

DESERT

AFRICA

Nile R.

RED SEA

Fertile Crescent
8000 BCE
(Barley, Cattle,
Goats, Pigs,
Sheep, Wheat)

ETHIOPIAN
HIGHLANDS

Congo R.

INDIAN
OCEAN

AUSTRALIA

KALAHARI
DESERT

MAP 1-4   THE ORIGINS OF FOOD PRODUCTION

Agricultural production emerged in many regions at different times. The variety of patterns reflected local resources and conditions. How many different locations did agricultural production emerge in? Are there any common geographic features among these early food-producing areas? Why do you think agriculture emerged in certain areas and not in others? How did the domestication of plants and animals affect kinship systems, political organization, and social relations?

where a fishing culture resembled the agricultural revolutions occurring elsewhere. Our discussion highlights the broad array of patterns that humans tried out as they settled down as farmers and herders.

SOUTHWEST ASIA: THE AGRICULTURAL REVOLUTION BEGINS

The first agricultural revolution occurred in Southwest Asia in an area bounded by the Mediterranean Sea and the Zagros Mountains. Known today as the Fertile Crescent because of its rich soils and regular rainfall, the area played a leading role in the domestication of wild grasses and the taming of animals important to humans. Six large mammals—goats, sheep, pigs, cattle, camels, and horses—have been vital for meat, milk, skins (including hair), and transportation. Humans domesticated all of these except horses in Southwest Asia.

The presence of so many valuable plants and animals enabled Southwest Asia to lead the agricultural revolution and to give rise to many of the world's first major city-states (see Chapter 2). An event that prepared the way was a significant warming trend that began about 13,000 years ago; it resulted in a profusion of plants and animals, large numbers of which began to live closer to humans.

Around 9000 BCE, in the southern corridor of the Jordan River valley, humans began to domesticate the wild ancestors of barley and wheat. (See Map 1-5.) Various wild grasses were abundant in this region, and barley and wheat were the easiest to adapt to settled agriculture and the easiest to transport. Although the changeover from gathering wild cereals to regular cultivation took several centuries and saw failures as well as successes, by the end of the ninth millennium BCE, cultivators were selecting and storing seeds and then sowing them in prepared seedbeds. Moreover, in the valleys of the Zagros Mountains on the eastern side of the Fertile Crescent, similar experimentation was occurring with animals around the same time.

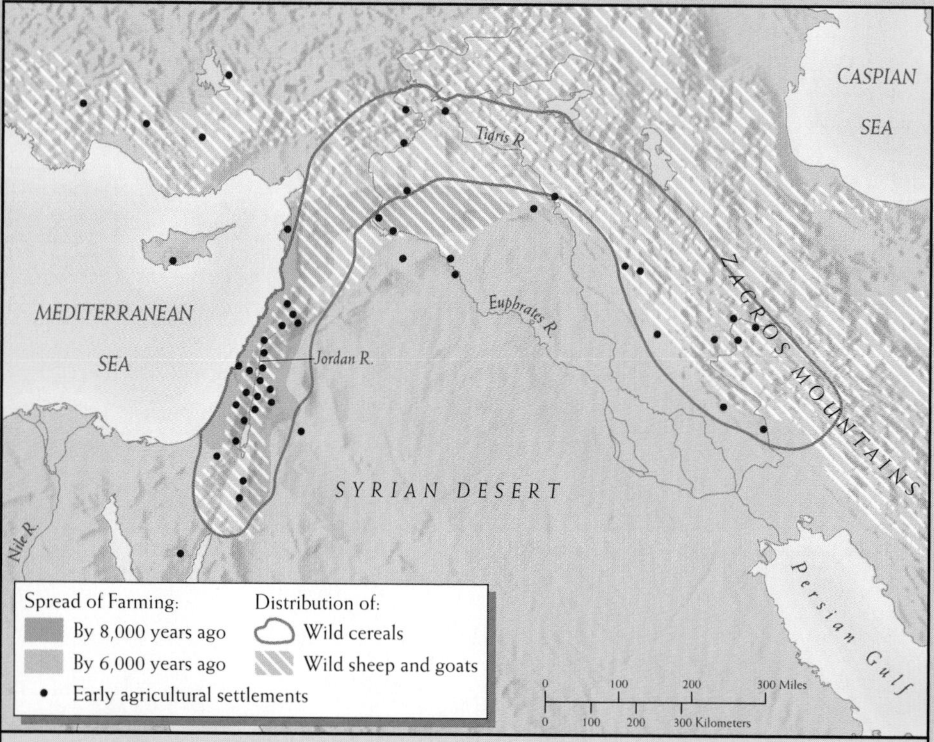

EAST ASIA: RICE AND WATER

When the glaciers began to melt around 13,000 BCE and the ocean levels began to rise, environmental changes affected subsistence patterns for coastal dwellers in East Asia. A revolution in food production occurred here too, although under different circumstances. (See Map 1-6.) As the rising sea level created the Japanese islands, hunters in that area tracked a diminishing supply of large animals, such as giant deer. After all big game became extinct, men and women sought other ways to support themselves, and before long they settled down and became cultivators of the soil. In this postglacial period, divergent human cultures flourished in northern and southern Japan.

MAP 1-5   THE BIRTH OF FARMING IN THE FERTILE CRESCENT

Agricultural production occurred in the Fertile Crescent starting roughly at 9000 BCE. Though the process was slow, farmers and herders domesticated a variety of plants and animals, which led to the rise of large-scale, permanent settlements. What does the map reveal about the environment and natural resources in the Fertile Crescent? Why was agriculture absent in the region of the southern Tigris and Euphrates rivers during this period? What relationship existed between cereal cultivators and herders of goats and sheep?

⇢ *What factors contributed to innovation, as opposed to borrowing, in agriculture?*

Hunters in the south created primitive pebble and flake tools, whereas those on the northern-most island, Hokkaido, used sharper blades about a third of an inch wide. Earthenware pottery production also may have begun in this period in the south. Converting mud into pottery—a hard, lightweight substance—was a breakthrough that enabled people to store food more easily.

Throughout the rest of East Asia, the spread of lakes, marshes, and rivers created habitats for population concentrations and agricultural cultivation. Two newly formed river basins became densely populated areas that were focal points for intensive agricultural development. These were the Yellow River, which flowed through the arid North China plain, and the Yangzi River, which traversed a land of streams and lakes in central China.

Rice in the south and millet in the north were for East Asia what barley and wheat were for western Asia—staples adapted to local environments that humans could domesticate to support a large, sedentary population. Archaeologists have found evidence of rice cultivation in the Yangzi River valley in 6500 BCE, and of millet cultivation in the Yellow River valley in 5500 BCE. Innovations in grain production spread through internal migration and wider contacts. When farmers migrated east and south, they carried domesticated millet and rice. In the south, they encountered strains of faster-ripening rice (originally from Southeast Asia), which they adopted. Rice was a staple, but millet and wheat (which spread to China from Southwest Asia) were also fundamental to the food-producing revolution in East Asia. There is even evidence of early plow cultivation. Ox plows and water buffalo plowshares were

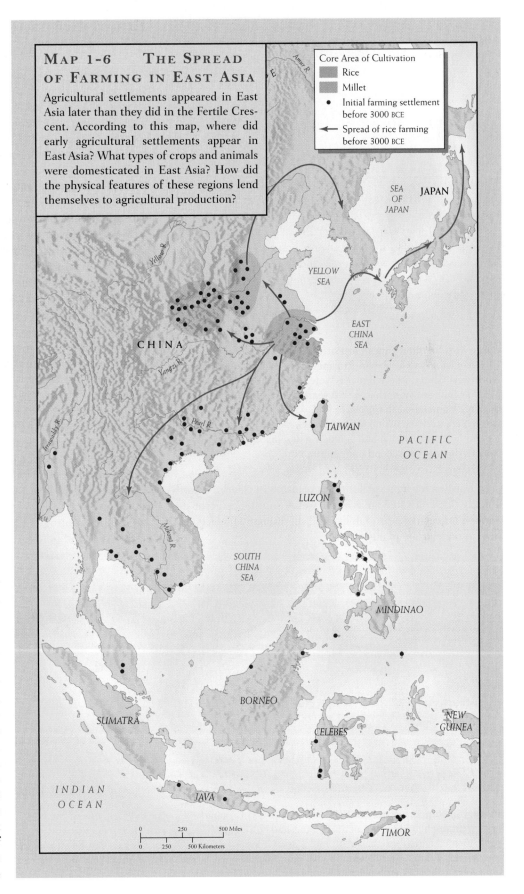

MAP 1-6   THE SPREAD OF FARMING IN EAST ASIA
Agricultural settlements appeared in East Asia later than they did in the Fertile Crescent. According to this map, where did early agricultural settlements appear in East Asia? What types of crops and animals were domesticated in East Asia? How did the physical features of these regions lend themselves to agricultural production?

Core Area of Cultivation
- Rice
- Millet
- • Initial farming settlement before 3000 BCE
- ← Spread of rice farming before 3000 BCE

Large Two-handled Yangshao Pot. This pot comes from the village of Yangshao in Henan Province, along the Yellow River in Northwest China, where remains were first found in 1921 of a people who lived more than 6,000 years ago. The Yangshao lived in small, rammed-earth fortresses and, without the use of pottery wheels, created fine white, red, and black painted pottery with human faces and animal and geometric designs. This jar dates back to the third or second millennium BCE.

prerequisites for large-scale millet planting in the drier north and the rice-cultivated areas of the wetter south. Each crop depended on ecological suitability and the human knowledge of how to manipulate plants.

EUROPE: BORROWING ALONG TWO PATHWAYS

At the western fringe of Afro-Eurasia, in Europe, domestication occurred through the diffusion of ideas and peoples from centers elsewhere. As in East Asia, once the new techniques arrived, they spread rapidly. By 6000–5000 BCE, people in regions of Europe close to the societies of Southwest Asia, such as Greece and the Balkans, were abandoning their hunting and gathering lifeways to become agriculturists who exerted control over plants and animals. (See Map 1-7.) Places like the Franchthi Cave in Greece reveal that around 6000 BCE the inhabitants borrowed innovations from their neighbors in Southwest Asia, such as how to herd domesticated animals and to plant wheat and barley. From the Aegean and Greece, settled agriculture and domesticated animals expanded westward throughout Europe, accompanied by the development of settled communities.

The emergence of agriculture and village life occurred in Europe along two separate paths. The first and most rapid trajectory followed the northern rim of the Mediterranean Sea. Domestication of crops and animals moved westward, following the prevailing currents of the Mediterranean, from what is now Turkey through the islands of the Aegean Sea to mainland Greece, and from there to southern and central Italy and Sicily. Whether the process involved the actual migration of individuals or the abstract spread of ideas, connections by sea quickened the pace of the transition. Once the basic elements of domestication had arrived in the Mediterranean region from Southwest Asia, the speed and ease of seaborne communications aided astonishingly rapid changes. Almost overnight, hunting and gathering gave way to domesticated agriculture and herding.

Pottery in Banpo Village (c. 4800–4200 BCE). This remarkable, intact village, one of the best-known ditch-enclosed settlements of Yangshao culture, provides us with clear evidence of a sophisticated agriculture based on millet and Chinese cabbage. One of China's first farming cultures, the people of Banpo interacted directly with other villages on the North China Plain and were indirectly in contact with peoples from as far away as Southeast Asia.

→ *What factors contributed to innovation, as opposed to borrowing, in agriculture?*

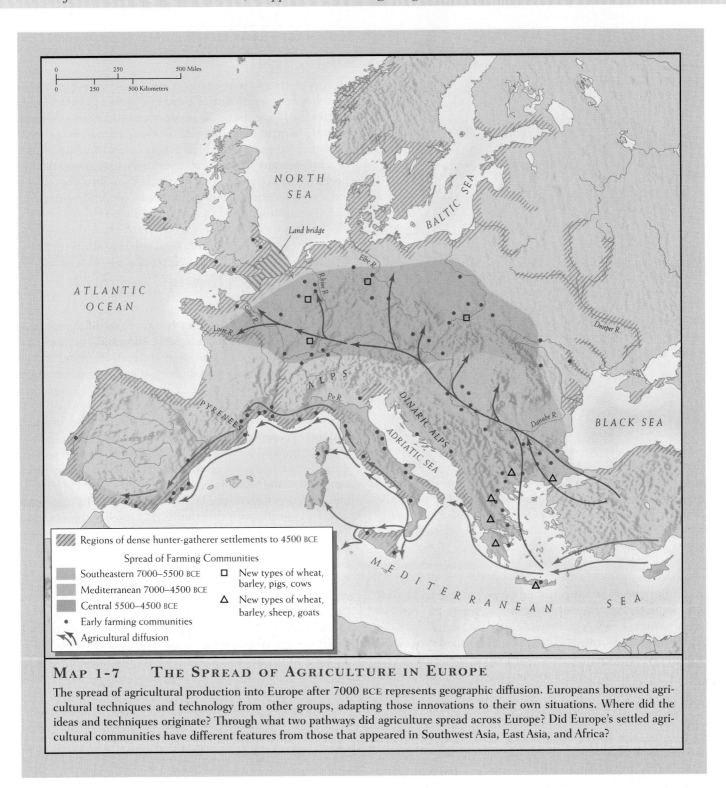

MAP 1-7   THE SPREAD OF AGRICULTURE IN EUROPE

The spread of agricultural production into Europe after 7000 BCE represents geographic diffusion. Europeans borrowed agricultural techniques and technology from other groups, adapting those innovations to their own situations. Where did the ideas and techniques originate? Through what two pathways did agriculture spread across Europe? Did Europe's settled agricultural communities have different features from those that appeared in Southwest Asia, East Asia, and Africa?

The second trajectory took an overland route: from Anatolia, across northern Greece into the Balkans, then northwestward along the Danube River into the Hungarian plain, and from there farther north and west into the Rhine River valley in modern-day Germany. Change here likely resulted from the transmission of ideas rather than from population migrations, for community after community adopted domesticated plants and animals and the new mode of life. This route of agricultural development was slower than the Mediterranean route for two reasons. First, domesticated crops, or individuals who

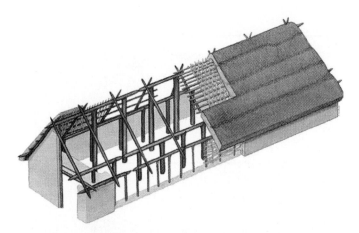

"Long House." The people who opened up the whole of central Europe to agriculture typically lived in communities of six to twelve "long houses." Although large in size (varying between 60 and 120 feet in length), long houses were built on simple principles: a framework of wooden beams and posts with walls made of mud and woven branches beneath a thatched roof. These dwellings probably sheltered large extended family or kinship units that cooperated to provide the hard work needed to carve out pioneer farming settlements along river valleys. This cutaway reconstruction of a long house shows the placement of wall timbers and internal support posts.

knew about them, had to travel by land, as there were few large rivers like the Danube. Second, it was necessary to find new groups of domesticated plants and animals that could flourish in the colder and more forested lands of central Europe. Agriculturalists here had to plant their crops in the spring and harvest in the autumn, rather than the other way around. Cattle rather than sheep became the dominant herd animals.

In Europe, the main cereal crops were wheat and barley, and the main herd animals were sheep, goats, and cattle—all of which had been domesticated in Southwest Asia. (Residents domesticated additional plants, such as olives and grape-producing vines, later.) These fundamental changes did not bring dramatic material progress, however. The normal settlement in Europe at this time consisted of a few dozen mud huts. These settlements, although few, often comprised large "long houses" built of timber and mud, designed to store produce and to shelter animals during the long winters. Some settlements had sixty to seventy huts—in rare cases, up to a hundred. Hunting, gathering, and fishing still supplemented the new settled agriculture and the herding of domesticated animals. The innovators were dynamic in blending the new ways with the old. Consider that around 6000 BCE, hunter-gatherers in southern France adopted the herding of domesticated sheep, but not the planting of domesticated crops—*that* would have conflicted with their

preference for a life of hunting, which was a traditional part of their economy.

By about 5000–4000 BCE, communities living in areas around rivers and in the large plains had embraced the new food-producing economy. Elsewhere (notably in the rugged mountain lands that still predominate in Europe's landscape), hunting and foraging remained humans' primary way of relating to nature. The transition to settled farming and herding brought an enormous rise in population, however. As agricultural communities supported more and more people, such communities became the dominant social organization.

THE AMERICAS: A SLOWER TRANSITION TO AGRICULTURE

When people crossed Beringia and trekked southward through the Americas, they set off an ecological transformation but also adapted to unfamiliar habitats. The flora and fauna of the Americas were different enough to induce the early settlers to devise ways of living that distinguished them from their ancestors in Afro-Eurasia. Then, when the glaciers began to melt around 12,500 BCE and water began to cover the land bridge between East Asia and America, the Americas and their peoples truly became a whole world apart.

Early humans in America used chipped blades and pointed spears to pursue their prey, which included mastodons, woolly mammoths, and bison. In doing so, they extended the hunting traditions they had learned in Afro-Eurasia, establishing campsites and moving with their herds. Researchers have named these hunters "Clovis people" because a site near Clovis, New Mexico, first yielded their typical arrowhead point. Their archaeological sites located all over North America contain the remains of their weaponry.

CLIMATIC CHANGE AND ADAPTATION For many years, scientists thought that the Clovis communities had wiped out the large Ice Age mammals they found in America. Recent research suggests, though, that climatic change destroyed the indigenous plants and trees—the feeding grounds of large prehistoric mammals—and that abundant forage became scarce. The vast spruce forests that had fed the great mastodons, for instance, shrank into isolated pockets, leaving undernourished mastodons vulnerable to human and animal predators until they vanished. The tall grassland prairies gave way to areas with short grass; where short grass once flourished, cacti took over. As in Afro-Eurasia, the arrival of a long warming cycle compelled those living in the Americas to adapt to different ecological niches and to create new subsistence strategies. Thus, in the woodland area of the present-day northeastern United States, hunters learned to trap smaller wild animals for food and furs. To supplement the protein from meat and fish, these people also dug for roots and gathered berries. What is important is that even as most communities adapted to the settled agricultural economy, they did not abandon basic survival strategies of hunting and gathering.

Food-producing changes in the Americas were different from those in Afro-Eurasia because this area did not undergo the sudden cluster of innovations that revolutionized agriculture in Southwest Asia and elsewhere. Tools ground from stone, rather than chipped implements, appeared in the Tehuacán Valley by 6700 BCE, and evidence of plant domestication there dates back to 5000 BCE. But villages, pottery making, and sustained population growth came later. For many early American inhabitants, the life of hunting, trapping, and fishing went on as it had for millennia. Indeed, researchers have found the remains of ancient shellfishing throughout the coastal Americas from Alaska to Chile on the Pacific Ocean side. Along the Pacific coast, communities formed around fishing cultures, many relying on dugout canoes and spears to obtain food.

On the coast of what is now Peru, people found food by fishing and gathering shellfish from the Pacific. Archaeological remains include the remnants of fishnets, bags, baskets, and textile implements; gourds for carrying water; and stone knives, choppers, scrapers, bone awls, and thorn needles. Oddly enough, there is no evidence of watercraft even though thousands of villages likely dotted the seashores and riverbanks of the Americas. Some made breakthroughs in the management of fire that enabled them to manufacture pottery; others devised irrigation and water sluices in floodplains. And some even began to send their fish catches inland in return for agricultural produce.

DOMESTICATION OF PLANTS AND ANIMALS The earliest evidence of plant experimentation in Mesoamerica dates from around 7000 BCE, and it went on for a long time. Maize, squash, and beans (first found in what is now central Mexico) became dietary staples. The early settlers foraged small seeds of maize, peeled them from ears only a few inches long, and planted them. Maize offered real advantages because it was easy to store, relatively imperishable, nutritious, and easy to cultivate alongside other plants. Nonetheless, it took 5,000 years for farmers to complete its domestication—that is, to settle in one place, live there year-round, plant maize, and stay beyond a single growing and harvesting cycle. Over the years, farmers had to mix and breed different strains of maize for it to evolve from thin spikes of seeds to cobs rich with kernels, with a single plant yielding big, thick ears to feed a growing permanent population. (See Primary Source: A Mesoamerican Creation Myth.) Thus the agricultural changes afoot in Mesoamerica were slow and late in maturing. The pace was even more gradual in South America, where early settlers clung to their hunting and gathering traditions.

Head of Mayan Corn God. Corn, or maize, was a revered crop in Mesoamerica, where people ritually prayed to their deities for good harvests. Notice the crown made not of precious metals and stones but of corn husks as an example of the cultural emphasis on maize.

Across the Americas, the settled, agrarian communities found that legumes (beans), grains (maize), and tubers (potatoes) complemented one another in keeping the soil fertile and offering a balanced diet. Unlike the Afro-Eurasians, however, the settlers did not use domesticated animals as an alternative source of protein. In only a few pockets of the Andean highlands is there evidence of the domestication of tiny guinea pigs, which may have been tasty but unfulfilling meals. Nor did people in the Americas tame animals that could protect villages (as dogs did in Afro-Eurasia) or carry heavy loads over long distances (as camels did in Afro-Eurasia). Although llamas could haul heavy loads, their patience and cooperation were limited. Considered at best semidomesticates, llamas were mainly useful for clothing.

Nonetheless, the domestication of plants and animals in the Americas, as well as the presence of villages and clans, suggests significant diversification and refinement of technique. At the same time, the centers of such activity were

A MESOAMERICAN CREATION MYTH

There are very few extant texts from indigenous peoples of the Americas before the time of European conquest and colonization. The Popol Vuh *is an extraordinary exception. Representing a whole body of mythological and historical narratives, it explained the elements of Mayan cosmology and established the Mayan right to rule by virtue of their descent from gods—although some scholars dispute this interpretation.*

Here, then, is the beginning of when it was decided to make man, and when what must enter into the flesh of man was sought.

And the Forefathers, the Creators and Makers, who were called Tepeu and Gucumatz said: "The time of dawn has come, let the work be finished, and let those who are to nourish and sustain us appear, the noble sons, the civilized vassals: let man appear, humanity, on the face of the earth." Thus they spoke.

They assembled, came together and held council in the darkness and in the night; then they sought and discussed, and here they reflected and thought. In this way their decisions came clearly to light and they found and discovered what must enter into the flesh of man.

It was just before the sun, the moon, and the stars appeared over the Creators and Makers.

From Paxil, from Cayalá, as they were called, came the yellow ears of corn and the white ears of corn.

These are the names of the animals which brought the food: *yac* [the mountain cat], *utiú* [the coyote], *quel* [a small parrot], and *hob* [the crow]. These four animals gave tidings of the yellow ears of corn and the white ears of corn, they told them that they should go to Paxil and they showed them the road to Paxil.

And thus they found the food, and this was what went into the flesh of created man, the made man; this was his blood; of this the blood of man was made. So the corn entered [into the formation of man] by the work of the Forefathers.

* * *

The animals showed them the road. And then grinding the yellow corn and the white corn, Xmucané made nine drinks, and from this food came the strength and the flesh, and with it they created the muscles and the strength of man. This the Forefathers did, Tepeu and Gucumatz, as they were called.

After that they began to talk about the creation and the making of our first mother and father; of yellow corn and of white corn they made their flesh; of corn meal dough they made the arms and the legs of man. Only dough of corn meal went into the flesh of our first fathers, the four men, who were created.

* * *

It is said that they only were made and formed, they had no mother, they had no father. They were only called men. They were not born of woman, nor were they begotten by the Creator nor by the Maker, nor by the Forefathers. Only by a miracle, by means of incantation were they created and made by the Creator, the Maker, the Forefathers, Tepeu and Gucumatz. And as they had the appearance of men, they were men; they talked, conversed, saw and heard, walked, grasped things; they were good and handsome men, and their figure was the figure of a man.

They were endowed with intelligence; they saw and instantly they could see far, they succeeded in seeing, they succeeded in knowing all that there is in the world. When they looked, instantly they saw all around them, and they contemplated in turn the arch of heaven and the round face of the earth.

The things hidden [in the distance] they saw all, without first having to move; at once they saw the world, and so, too, from where they were, they saw it.

Great was their wisdom; their sight reached to the forests, the rocks, the lakes, the seas, the mountains, and the valleys. In truth, they were admirable men, Balam-Quitzé, Balam-Acab, Mahucutah, and Iqui-Balam.

Then the Creator and the Maker asked them: "What do you think of your condition? Do you not see? Do you not hear? Are not your speech and manner of walking good? Look, then! Contemplate the world, look [and see] if the mountains and the valleys appear! Try, then, to see!" they said to [the four first men].

And immediately they [the four first men] began to see all that was in the world. Then they gave thanks to the Creator and the Maker: "We really give you thanks, two and three times! . . ."

→ *From what material did the creators make living creatures?*
→ *Why do you think they chose this material?*
→ *What commands did the Creator and the Maker convey to the first men? Why do you think this is significant?*

SOURCE: Adrian Recinos, from *Popol Vuh: The Sacred Book of the Ancient Quiché Maya,* trans. Delia Goetz and Sylvanus G. Morley, pp. 165–68. Copyright © 1950 by the University of Oklahoma Press. Reprinted with permission of University of Oklahoma Press.

many, scattered, and more isolated than those in Afro-Eurasia—and thus more narrowly adapted to local geographical climatic conditions, with little exchange among them. This fragmentation in migration and communication was a distinguishing force in the gradual pace of change in the Americas, and it contributed to their taking a path of development separate from Afro-Eurasia's.

AFRICA: THE RACE WITH THE SAHARA

Some societies, like those in Southwest Asia and East Asia, were innovators, while others, like those in Europe, were borrowers. What about Africa, where the story began? The evidence for settled agriculture in different regions there is uncertain. Most scholars think that the Sahel area (spanning the African landmass just south of the Sahara Desert) was most likely where hunters and gatherers became settled farmers and herders without any borrowing. In this area, an apparent move to settled agriculture, including the domes-

tication of large herd animals, occurred two millennia before it did along the Mediterranean coast in North Africa. In fact, the Sahel agricultural revolution was so early that it cannot serve as an example of diffusion from Southwest Asia via the Nile River valley. From this innovative heartland, Africans carried their agricultural breakthroughs across the landmass.

It was in the wetter and more temperate locations of the vast Sahel, particularly in mountainous areas and their foothills, that villages and towns developed. These regions were lush with grassland vegetation and teeming with animals. Before long, the inhabitants had made sorghum, a cereal grass, their principal food crop. Residents constructed stone dwellings, underground wells, and grain storage areas. In one such population center, fourteen circular houses faced each other to form a main thoroughfare, or a street. Recent archaeological investigations have unearthed remarkable rock engravings and paintings, one often composed on top of another, filling the cave dwellings' walls. Many images portray in fascinating detail the changeover from hunting and gathering to pastoralism. Caves abound with pictures of cattle,

North African Cave Painting. This cave painting comes from Tassili n'Ajjer, highlands in the Sahara Desert, and dates from the second millennium BCE. In this illustration, early men and women covered the walls with pictures of daily life: children tending calves tethered to a rope. The white ovals to the left represent huts.

which were a mainstay of these early men and women. The cave illustrations also depict daily activities of men and women living in conical huts, doing household chores, crushing grain on stone, and riding bareback on oxen (with women always sitting behind the men).

The Sahel was colder and moister 10,000 years ago than it is today. As the world became warmer and the Sahara Desert expanded, around 4,000 years ago this region's inhabitants had to disperse and take their agricultural and herding skills into other parts of Africa. (See Map 1-8.) Some went south to the tropical rainforests of West Africa, while others trekked eastward into the Ethiopian highlands. In their new environments, farmers searched for new crops to domesticate. The rainforests of West Africa yielded root crops, particularly the yam and cocoyam, both of which became the principal life-sustaining foodstuffs. The enset plant, similar to the banana, played the same role in the Ethiopian highlands.

REVOLUTIONS IN SOCIAL ORGANIZATION

> ⇥ *How did agricultural revolutions change human relations?*

With the domestication of plants and animals came settlement in agricultural villages. These villages were near fields for accessible sowing and cultivating, and near pastures for herding livestock. Villagers collaborated to clear fields, plant crops, and celebrate rituals in which they sang, danced, and sacrificed to nature and the spirit world for fertility, rain, and successful harvests. They also produced stone tools to work the fields, and clay and stone pots or woven baskets to collect and store the crops. As populations grew and lands yielded surplus food, some villagers became craftworkers, devoting their time to producing pottery, baskets, textiles, or tools, which they could trade to farmers and pastoralists for food. Craft specialization and the buildup of surpluses contributed to early social stratification, as some people accumulated more land and wealth while others led the rituals and sacrifices.

SETTLEMENT IN VILLAGES

The earliest dwelling places of the first settled communities were simple structures: circular pits with stones piled on top to form walls, with a cover stretched above that rested on poles. Social structures were equally simple, being clanlike and based on kinship networks. With time, however, population growth enabled clans to expand. As the use of natural resources intensified, specialized tasks evolved and divisions of labor arose. Some community members procured and prepared food; others built terraces and defended the settlement. Later, residents built walls with stones or mud bricks and clamped them together with wooden fittings.

As construction techniques changed, houses changed from the traditional circular plan to a rectangular one. Because the rectangular shape does not exist in nature, it is a truly human mark on the landscape. This new shape reflected new attitudes and social behaviors: in rectangular houses, walls did more than support and protect—they also divided and separated. The introduction of interior walls meant that family members gained separate spaces and that privacy improved. Human relations would never be the same as they had been in the relatively egalitarian arrangements of the mobile hunters and gatherers.

Although the food-producing changes were gradual and dispersed, a few communities stand out as pioneers in the long transition from hunting and gathering to agrarian and pastoral life. Around Wadi en-Natuf, located about ten miles from present-day Jerusalem, a group of people known historically as Natufians began to dig sunken pit shelters and to chip stone tools around 12,500 BCE. Over the next two millennia these bands stayed in one place, improving their tool-making techniques, building circular shelters, and developing various ways to preserve and prepare food. They dwelled in solid structures, buried their dead, and harvested grains. Although they did not plant seeds and did not give up hunting, their increasing knowledge of wild plants paved the way for later breakthroughs.

It was only a matter of time before the full transition to settled agriculture and full-scale pastoralism took place. As noted above, the agricultural revolution spread in all directions. In the highlands of eastern Anatolia (the area encompassing modern-day Turkey), large settlements clustered around monumental public buildings with impressive stone carvings that reflect a complex social organization. In central Anatolia, at the site of Çatal Höyük, a dense honeycomb settlement featured rooms covered with wall paintings and sculptures of wild bulls, hunters, and pregnant women. The use of art and imagery to express consciousness of self, to provide identity, and to master the powerful forces of the cosmos is a human characteristic originating with the early cave artists. The difference now was that men and women made their own structures where they worshipped the forces of nature and the spirit world, interacting with one another according to rituals that defined their place in society.

After 5500 BCE, people moved into the river valley in Mesopotamia (in present-day Iraq) along the Tigris and Euphrates rivers, and small villages began to appear. They collaborated to build simple irrigation systems to water their

→ *How did agricultural revolutions change human relations?*

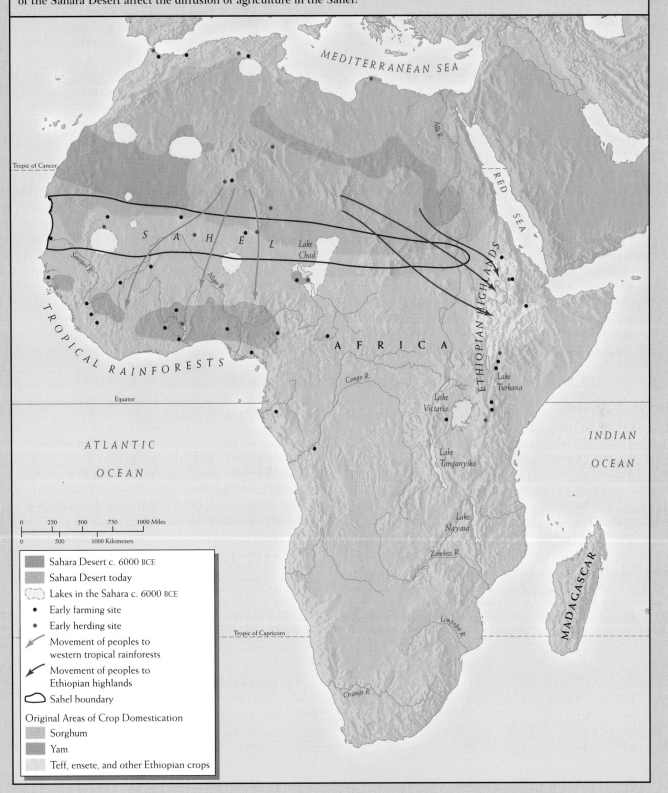

MAP 1-8   THE SPREAD OF FARMING IN AFRICA

Societies living in the Sahel (the region south of the Sahara Desert) developed their own version of agricultural production after 6000 BCE. Where is the Sahel on this map? Why did farming spread in the directions that it did? How did the expansion of the Sahara Desert affect the diffusion of agriculture in the Sahel?

MEDITERRANEAN SEA

Nile R.

RED SEA

Tropic of Cancer

S A H E L

Senegal R.

Lake Chad

ETHIOPIAN HIGHLANDS

Niger R.

TROPICAL RAINFORESTS

AFRICA

Congo R.

Lake Victoria

Lake Turkana

Equator

ATLANTIC OCEAN

INDIAN OCEAN

Lake Tanganyika

Lake Nyasa

Zambezi R.

MADAGASCAR

| 0 | 250 | 500 | 750 | 1000 Miles |
| 0 | 500 | 1000 Kilometers |

Tropic of Capricorn

Limpopo R.

Orange R.

Legend:

- Sahara Desert c. 6000 BCE
- Sahara Desert today
- Lakes in the Sahara c. 6000 BCE
- • Early farming site
- • Early herding site
- ↙ Movement of peoples to western tropical rainforests
- ↘ Movement of peoples to Ethiopian highlands
- ◯ Sahel boundary

Original Areas of Crop Domestication
- Sorghum
- Yam
- Teff, ensete, and other Ethiopian crops

Primary Source

MOTHERING AND LACTATION

One of the dividing lines among all animals, humans included, involves child rearing and the division of labor between mothers and fathers. This text argues that lactation (milk production) became a major factor shaping the social roles of primate mothers.

"Is sex destiny?" When this question is posed, it's a safe bet that the underlying agenda has to do with what women *should* be doing. Should they be home caring for their children or off pursuing other interests? A comparative look at other creatures that (like humans) breed cooperatively and share responsibilities for rearing young with other group members reveals that sex *per se* is not the issue. Lactation is.

Caretakers of both sexes, wet-nurses, even "daycare"—none of these are uniquely human, nor particularly new. They are standard features of many cooperatively breeding species. As we saw, cooperative breeding is exquisitely well developed in insects such as honeybees and wasps. Shared provisioning is also common among birds such as acorn woodpeckers, bee-eaters, dunnocks, and scrub jays. Although cooperative breeding is uncommon among mammals generally, it is richly developed in species such as wolves, wild dogs, dwarf mongooses, elephants, tamarins, marmosets, and humans. In all these animals, individuals other than the mother ("allomothers") help her provision or otherwise care for her young. Typically, allomothers will include the mother's mate (often but not necessarily the genetic progenitor). Individuals other than either parent ("alloparents") also help. These helpers are most often recruited from kin who are not yet ready to reproduce themselves, or from subordinates who do not currently—or may never have—better options. In the human case, the most important alloparents are often older, post-reproductive relatives who have already reproduced.

Among mammals, the trend toward having young who require costly long-term care began modestly enough. It probably began with an egg-laying brooding reptile that started to secrete something milklike. Such egg-layers gradually developed glands especially equipped for milk production. Only among mammals did one sex come to specialize in manufacturing custom-made baby formula, to provide something critical for infant survival that the other sex could not. This peculiarity has had many ramifications, especially as infants became dependent for longer periods in the primate line.

The ante was upped substantially when primate mothers, instead of bearing litters, began focusing care on one baby at a time. These singletons were born mature enough to cling to their mother's fur, to be carried by her right from birth and for months thereafter. Whether or not this intimate and prolonged association is the mother's destiny, *sex* is not the issue. Lactation is.

➤ *How does lactation affect mothers' child-rearing roles differently from fathers'?*
➤ *Why is the difference more marked among humans than among other species?*

SOURCE: From *Mother Nature* by Sarah Blaffer Hrdy, copyright © 1999 by Sarah Blaffer Hrdy. Used by permission of Pantheon Books, a division of Random House, Inc.

fields. Perhaps because of the increased demands for community work to maintain the irrigation systems, the communities in southern Mesopotamia became stratified, with some people having more power than others. We can see from the burial sites and myriad public buildings uncovered by archaeologists that for the first time, some people had higher status derived from birth rather than through the merits of their work. A class of people who had access to more luxury goods, and who lived in bigger and better houses, now became part of the social organization.

It is important to emphasize that changes arising from agriculture enabled larger numbers of people to live in denser concentrations, and the household with its dominant male replaced the small, relatively egalitarian band as the primary social unit.

MEN, WOMEN, AND EVOLVING GENDER RELATIONS

One of the fundamental divisions evident in the fossil remains of early hominids and humans is the division between males and females. This observation raises questions about the relationships between the sexes in prehistoric times.

For millions of years, biological differences—the fact that females give birth to offspring and that males do not—determined female and male behaviors and attitudes toward each other. Thus it is incorrect to think of these biologically based sexual relations as "gender" (social and cultural) relations. One can speak of the emergence of "gender" relations and roles only with the appearance of modern humans (*Homo sapiens*) and, perhaps, Neanderthals. Only when humans began to think in complex symbolic ways and give voice to these perceptions in a spoken language did true gender categories as *man* and *woman* crystallize. As these cultural aspects of human life took shape, the distinction between "men" and "women," rather than between "males" and "females," arose. At that point, around 150,000 years ago, culture joined biology in governing human interactions. (See Primary Source: Mothering and Lactation.)

Gender roles became more pronounced during the gradual transition to an agriculturally based way of life. As human communities became larger, more hierarchical, and more powerful, the rough gender egalitarianism of hunting and gathering societies eroded. However, an enhanced

human power over the environment did not bring equal power to everyone, and it is possible to say that women were the net losers of the agricultural revolution. Although their knowledge of wild plants had contributed to early settled agriculture, they did not necessarily benefit from that transition. One observer of primate behavior, Sarah Hrdy, has called the settled agricultural transformation a "Great Leap Sideways" because advances for some people meant losses for others.

Advances in agrarian tools introduced a harsh working life that undermined women's traditional status as farmers. Men, no longer so involved in hunting and gathering, now took on the heavy work of yoking animals to plows. This left to women the backbreaking and repetitive tasks of planting, weeding, harvesting, and grinding the grain into flour. Thus, although agricultural innovations increased productivity, they also increased the drudgery of work, especially for women. Consider the evidence from fossils found in Abu Hureyra, Syria: damage to the vertebrae, osteoarthritis in the toes, and curved and arched femurs suggest that the work of bending over and kneeling in the fields took its toll on female agriculturalists. These maladies do not usually appear among the bone remains of (male) hunters and gatherers.

The increasing differentiation of the roles of men and women also affected power relations within households and communities. The senior male figure became dominant in these households, and males became dominant over females in leadership positions. The agricultural revolution marked a greater division among men, and particularly between men and women. Where the agricultural transformation was most widespread, and where population densities began to grow, the social and political differences created inequalities. As these inequalities affected gender relations, patriarchy (the rule of senior males within households) began to spread around the globe.

 CONCLUSION

Over thousands of generations, African hominids evolved from other primates into *Homo erectus* hominids, who migrated far from their native habitats to fill other landmasses. They did so in waves, responding to worldwide cycles of glaciation and melting. These human predecessors had some features in common with modern humans (*Homo sapiens*): they stood erect on two feet, made stone tools, lived in extended families, and, to a certain extent, communicated with one another (by means other than language).

What separated humans from other animal species was their ability to adapt to environmental change, to innovate, and to accumulate their breakthroughs. *Homo sapiens*, who had greater cognitive skills than other hominids had, also emerged in Africa and migrated out of Africa about 100,000 years ago. Since *Homo sapiens* had greater adaptive skills, they were better prepared to face the elements when a cooling cycle returned, and eventually they eclipsed their genetic cousins. One critical variable was their ability to use language—to engage in abstract, representational thought, and to convey the lessons of experience to their neighbors and descendants. As modern humans stored and shared knowledge, their adaptive abilities increased. Another remarkable development was the use of art to portray the world around them and to locate themselves within it.

Although modern men and women shared an African heritage, these individuals adapted over many millennia to the environments they encountered as they began to fill the earth's corners. Some settled near lakes and took to fishing, while others roamed the northern steppes hunting large mammals. No matter where they went, their dependence on nature yielded broadly similar social and cultural structures.

It took another warming cycle for people ranging from Africa to the Americas to begin putting down their hunting weapons and start domesticating animals and plants.

The changeover to settled agriculture was not uniform worldwide, although there were some common features. These included reliance on wood, stone, and natural fibers to make tools, shelter, and cultural items; and increasing social hierarchies—especially an unequal status between men and women. As communities became more settled, though, the world's regions began to vary as humans learned to modify nature to fit their needs. The varieties of animals that they could domesticate and the differing climatic conditions and topography that they encountered shaped the ways in which people drifted apart in spite of their common origins.

One important commonality remained: there was a limit to the scale and complexity of settlements and communities. As a result, most people continued a life of foraging for food. Villages grew—but they did not become cities. Peoples moved across mountains or deserts to find fresh pastures for their animals, richer lands for their crops, or new waters where fish were spawning. The remains of rudimentary pottery, tools, and dwellings reflect worlds that were rural, socially egalitarian, and dependent on the natural flow of fresh water and the natural fertility of soils. As we will see in Chapter 2, another round of technical advances was necessary before humans could further change their relationship to nature and create the foundations for complex societies.

Chronology

5 mya*		1 mya

◆ *3 mya Australopithecus africanus hominid species appears*

2.5 mya Homo habilus *appears* ◆

2.5–1 mya Homo erectus appears and migrates ◆-------------------------------◆

Beginnings of Ice Age across the Northern Hemisphere ◆

Review and research materials are available
at StudySpace: Ⓢ WWNORTON.COM/STUDYSPACE

KEY TERMS

adaptation (p. 9)
australopithecines (p. 8)
bipedalism (p. 9)
cognitive skills (p. 9)
domestication (p. 24)
evolution (p. 4)
hominid (p. 7)
Homo erectus (p. 13)
Homo habilis (p. 13)

Homo sapiens (p. 15)
hunting and gathering (p. 19)
innovation (p. 11)
language (p. 23)
migration (p. 14)
pastoralism (p. 25)
settled agriculture (p. 24)
species (p. 8)

STUDY QUESTIONS

1. Explain how evolutionary biologists and archaeologists working in recent decades have transformed our understanding of human origins. What tools and discoveries led them to their conclusions?
2. Describe the evolutionary process through which *Homo sapiens* emerged. Was it a linear progression?
3. Identify the advantages that language and symbolic art gave *Homo sapiens* over other species. What can modern observers learn about early humans by studying their artistic expressions?
4. List the nine regions where agricultural production first emerged. What common factors in all these places facilitated the domestication of plants and animals?
5. Why did the first agricultural breakthrough occur in Southwest Asia?
6. Analyze the advantages and disadvantages of agricultural production versus nomadic foraging. How were agricultural or pastoral communities different from those of hunters and gatherers?

200,000 ya**	150,000 ya	100,000 ya	50,000 ya		10,000 ya	1 CE

30,000 ya Cave art develops in Europe ✦

200,000 ya Neanderthal evident in Europe
18,000 ya Human migration from Afro-Eurasia to Americas begins ✦

16,000–10,000 BCE Ice age ✦------✦

200,000–50,000 ya Homo sapiens *emerges in Africa and migrates*
✦-------------✦

9000 BCE Beginnings of agricultural revolution in Southwest Asia ✦

6500 BCE Millet cultivation in Yellow River valley develops ✦

5500 BCE Rice cultivation in Yangzi River valley develops ✦

6700–2000 BCE Domestication of plants and animals begins ✦-----✦

6000–5000 BCE Agricultural settlements using Southwest Asian domesticants emerges ✦

3000 BCE Pastoralism begins in Inner Asia ✦

2000 BCE Maize cultivation emerges in central Mexico ✦

years ago

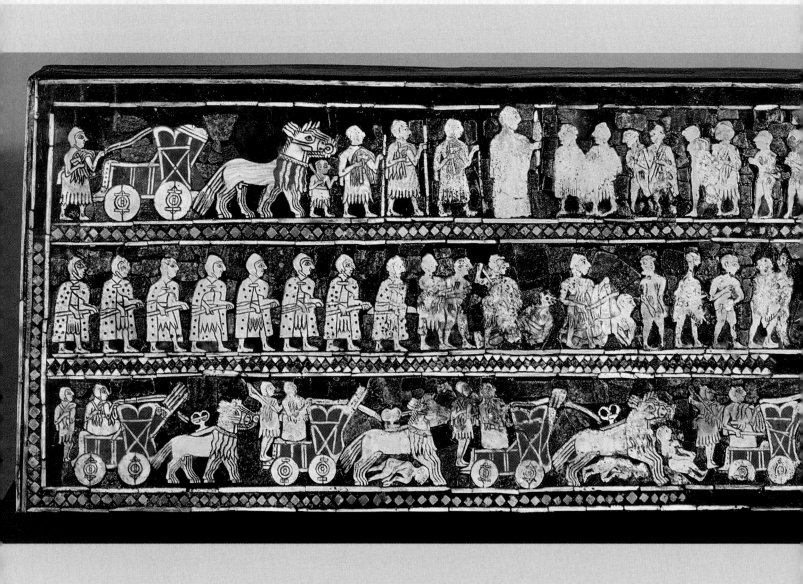

2

RIVERS, CITIES, AND FIRST STATES, 4000–2000 BCE

One of the first urban centers in the world was the ancient city of Uruk. Located in southern Mesopotamia on a branch of the Euphrates River, it was home to more than 10,000 people by the late fourth millennium BCE and boasted many large public structures and temples. One temple had stood there since before 3000 BCE; with a lime-plastered surface of niched mud-brick walls that formed stepped indentations, it perched high above the plain. In another sacred precinct, administrative buildings and temples adorned with elaborate façades stood in courtyards defined by tall columns. Colored stone cones arranged in elaborate geometric patterns covered parts of these buildings, making Uruk the "shining city" of the epic devoted to its later king, Gilgamesh.

Over the years Uruk became an immense commercial and administrative center. A huge wall with seven massive gates surrounded the metropolis, and down the middle ran a canal carrying water from the Euphrates. On one side of the city were gardens, kilns, and textile workshops. On the other was the temple quarter where priests lived, scribes kept records, and lu-gal ("the big man") conferred with the elders. As Uruk grew, many small industries became centralized in response to the increasing sophistication of construction and manufacturing. Potters, metalsmiths, stone bowl makers, and brickmakers all worked under the city administration.

Uruk was the first city of its kind in world history, marking a new phase in human development. Earlier humans had settled in small communities scattered over the landscape; gradually, however, some communities became focal points for trade. Then a few hubs grew into cities—concentrations with large populations and institutions of economic, religious, and political power. Most inhabitants no longer produced their own food, working instead in specialized professions.

Between 4000 and 2000 BCE, a handful of remarkable societies clustered in a few river basins on the Afro-Eurasian landmass. These regions, located on the shores or in the deltas of five rivers with regular annual floods (in Mesopotamia, northwest India, Egypt, Northern China, and Central China), became the heartlands for densely populated settlements with complex cultures. Here the world saw the birth of the first large cities and territorial states. One of these settings (Mesopotamia) brought forth humankind's first writing system, and all laid the foundations for kingdoms radiating out of opulent cities. This chapter describes how each society evolved, and it explores their similarities and differences. It is important to note how exceptional these places were—and thus we cannot ignore the many smaller societies that prevailed elsewhere, far from urbanizing locales. The Aegean, Anatolia, and Western Europe serve as reminders that most of the world's people continued to dwell in small communities, far removed culturally from the monumental architecture and accomplishments of the big new states.

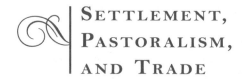

SETTLEMENT, PASTORALISM, AND TRADE

> → **What strategies did people develop to live in their environments?**

Over many millennia, people had developed strategies to make the best of their environments. The remarkable cultural changes, demographic leaps, and technological innovations that occurred around 3500 BCE yielded complex hierarchical societies, clustered in cities and reinforced by new urban institutions. City life transformed the human experience.

Reliable water sources determined where and how people settled, because predictable flows of water allowed them to sow crops adequate to feed large populations. Abundant rainfall allowed the world's first villages to emerge, but the breakthroughs into big cities occurred in drier zones where large rivers formed beds of rich alluvial soils (created by deposits from rivers when in flood). With irrigation innovations, soils became arable. Equally important, a worldwide warming cycle caused growing seasons to expand. These environmental and technical shifts profoundly affected who lived where and how.

As rivers sliced through mountains, steppe lands (vast treeless grasslands), and deserts before reaching the sea, their waters carried topsoils and deposited them around the deltas. The combination of fertile soils, water for irrigation, and availability of domesticated plants and animals made each **river basin** (an area drained by a river, including all its

Focus Questions

 WWNORTON.COM/STUDYSPACE

→ *What strategies did people develop to live in their environments?*

→ *What role did cities play in Mesopotamian society?*

→ *Why do we know less about Harappan culture than about others in Afro-Eurasia?*

→ *How did the Nile River shape early Egyptian society?*

→ *What hallmarks of urban life emerged in China during this period?*

→ *How did the growth of urban societies in river basins affect people living in the Aegean region, Anatolia, and Europe?*

tributaries) attractive for human habitation. Here, cultivators began to produce agricultural surpluses to feed the city dwellers.

With cities came greater divisions of labor, as dense settlement enabled people to specialize in making goods for the consumption of others: weavers made textiles, potters made ceramics, and jewelers made precious ornaments. Soon these goods found additional uses in trade with outlying areas. And as trade expanded over longer distances, raw materials such as wool, metal, timber, and precious stones arrived in the cities. These materials served in the construction and decoration of city walls, temples, and palaces, as well as in the fashioning of tools and weapons. One of the most coveted metals was copper: easily smelted and shaped (not to mention shiny and alluring), it became the metal of choice for charms, sculptures, and valued commodities. When combined with arsenic or tin, copper hardens and becomes **bronze**, which is useful for tools and weapons. For this reason the new age is often called a Bronze Age, though the term simplifies the breadth of the breakthroughs.

EARLY CITIES ALONG RIVER BASINS

The material and social advances of the early cities occurred in a remarkably short period—from 4000 to 2000 BCE—in three locations: the basin of the Tigris and Euphrates rivers in central Southwest Asia; the Indus River basin in northwestern South Asia; and the northern parts of the Nile River flowing toward the Mediterranean Sea. (See Map 2-1.) In these regions humans farmed and fed themselves by relying on intensive irrigation agriculture. Gathering in cities inhabited by rulers, administrators, priests, and craftworkers, they changed their methods of organizing communities by obeying divinely inspired monarchs and elaborate bureaucracies. They also transformed what and how they worshipped, by praying to zoomorphic and anthropomorphic gods (taking the form and personality of animals and humans) who communicated through kings and priests living in palace complexes and temples.

The same advances occurred at the same time on a smaller scale along the river valleys of the Iranian plateau and in central Southwest Asia. About a millennium later a similar process began along the Yellow River in North China, laying the foundations for a culture that has flourished unbroken until this day.

As people congregated in cities, new technologies appeared. The wheel, for example, served both as a tool for mass-producing pottery and as a key component of vehicles used for transportation. At first vehicles were heavy, using four solid wooden wheels drawn by oxen or onagers (Asian wild asses). Two other technologies, metallurgy and stoneworking, provided luxury objects and utilitarian tools.

The emergence of cities as population centers created one of history's most durable worldwide distinctions: the **urban-rural divide**. Where cities appeared alongside rivers, people adopted lifestyles based on specialized labor and the mass production of goods. In contrast, residents of the countryside remained on their lands, cultivating the land or tending livestock; but they exchanged their grains and animal products for goods from the urban centers. Therefore the new distinction never implied isolation, because the two lifeways were interdependent. Despite the urban-rural divide, both worlds remained linked through family ties, trade, politics, and religion.

As the dynamic urban enclaves evolved, they made intellectual advances. One significant advance was the invention of writing systems, which enabled people to record and transmit sounds and words through visual signs. An unprecedented cultural breakthrough, the technology of writing used the symbolic storage of words and meanings to extend human communication and memory: scribes figured out ways to record oral compositions as written texts and, eventually, epics recounting life in these river settlements.

SMALLER SETTLEMENTS AROUND 3500 BCE

Around 3500 BCE, most people worldwide were living in small villages close to the animals and plants they used for food. As they hunted, gathered, fished, and cultivated plants, they formed small, egalitarian communities organized on the basis of clan and family allegiances. They used tools made of wood and/or stone, and carried gourds to transport food and water. In some locations, artisans formed and fired clay to make vessels for storing and preparing food. In other locations, craftworkers pounded native copper into small items of personal adornment. As the population in certain areas increased, divisions between artisans and manual laborers emerged, community life became more hierarchical, and villages grew into towns.

THE AMERICAS In certain places, environmental factors limited the size of human settlements. Here the techniques of food production and storage, transportation, and communication restricted the surpluses for feeding those who did not work the land. Thus these communities did not grow in size and complexity. For example, in the Chicama Valley of Peru, which opens onto the Pacific Ocean, people still nestled in small coastal villages to fish, gather shellfish, hunt, and grow beans, chili peppers, and cotton (to make twined textiles, which they dyed with wild indigo). By around 3500 BCE, these fishermen abandoned their cane and adobe homes for sturdier houses, half underground, on streets lined with cobblestones.

Hundreds if not thousands of such villages dotted the seashores and riverbanks of the Americas. Some made the

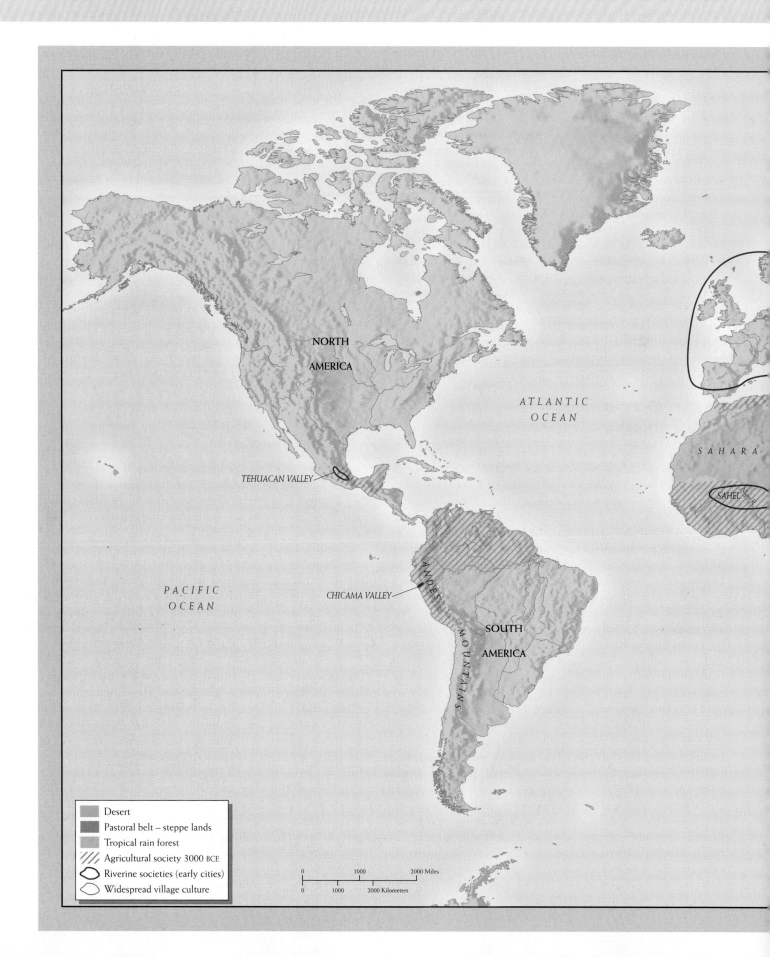

NORTH
AMERICA

ATLANTIC
OCEAN

TEHUACAN VALLEY

SAHARA

SAHEL

PACIFIC
OCEAN

CHICAMA VALLEY

SOUTH
AMERICA

ANDES MOUNTAINS

Desert

Pastoral belt – steppe lands

Tropical rain forest

Agricultural society 3000 BCE

Riverine societies (early cities)

Widespread village culture

0   1000   2000 Miles

0   1000   2000 Kilometers

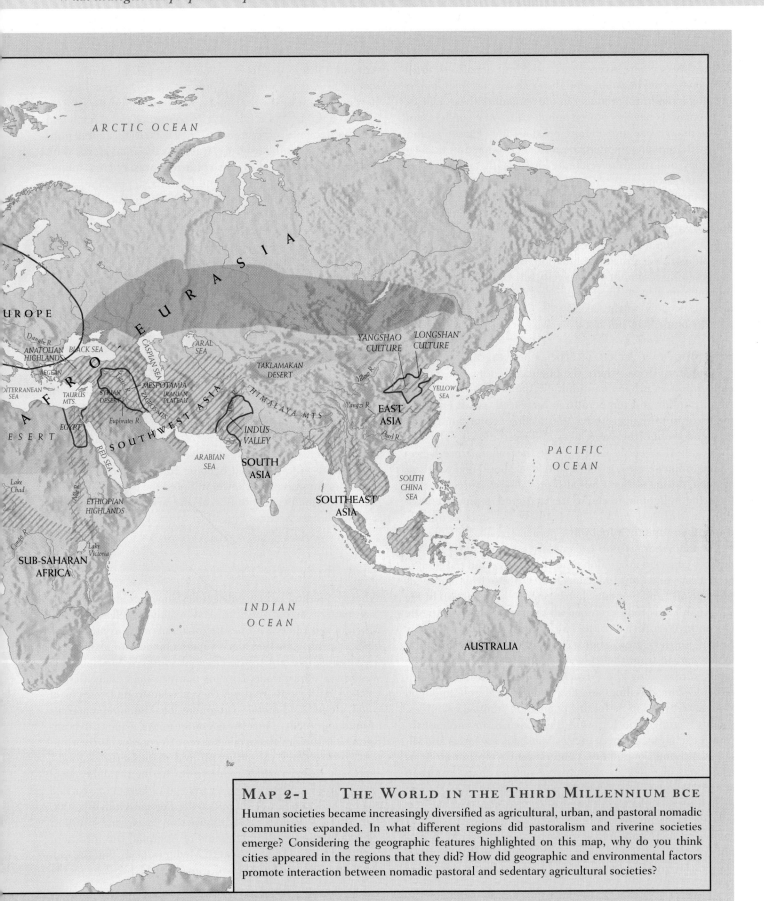

MAP 2-1 THE WORLD IN THE THIRD MILLENNIUM BCE

Human societies became increasingly diversified as agricultural, urban, and pastoral nomadic communities expanded. In what different regions did pastoralism and riverine societies emerge? Considering the geographic features highlighted on this map, why do you think cities appeared in the regions that they did? How did geographic and environmental factors promote interaction between nomadic pastoral and sedentary agricultural societies?

technological breakthroughs required to produce pottery; others devised irrigation systems and water sluices in flood-plains (areas where rivers overflowed and deposited fertile soil). Some even began to send their fish catches inland in return for agricultural produce. In the remains of these villages, archaeologists have recovered temples, fire-pit chambers, and tombs that reveal an elaborate religious life. These ceremonial structures highlighted communal devotion and homage to deities, and rituals to celebrate birth, death, and the memory of ancestors.

In the Americas, the largest population center was in the valley of Tehuacán (near modern-day Mexico City). Here the domestication of corn created a subsistence base that enabled people to migrate from caves to a cluster of pit-house villages that supported a growing population. By 3500 BCE the valley held nothing resembling a large city, although it teemed with inhabitants. People lived in clusters of interdependent villages, especially on the lakeshores: here was a case of high population density, but not urbanization.

SUB-SAHARAN AFRICA   The same pattern occurred in sub-Saharan Africa, where the population grew but did not concentrate in urban communities. About 12,000 years ago, when rainfall and temperatures increased, small encampments of hunting, gathering, and fishing communities congregated around the large lakes and rivers flowing through the region that would later become the Sahara Desert. Elephants, rhinoceroses, gazelles, antelopes, lions, and panthers roamed, posing a threat but also providing a source of food. Over the millennia, in the wetter and more temperate locations of this vast region—particularly the upland massifs (mountains) and their foothills—permanent villages emerged.

As the Sahara region became drier, people moved to the desert's edges, to areas along the Niger River and the Sudan. Here they grew yams, oil palms (a tree whose fruit and seeds produce oil), and plantains (a fruit similar to bananas). In the savannah lands that stretched all the way from the Atlantic Ocean in West Africa to the Nile River basin in present-day Sudan, settlers grew grains such as millet and sorghum, which spread from their places of origin to areas along the lands surrounding the Niger River basin. Residents constructed stone dwellings and dug underground wells and food storage areas. As an increasing population strained resources, groups migrated south toward the Congo River and east toward Lake Nyanza, where they established new farms and villages. Although population centers were often hundreds or thousands of miles apart and were smaller than the urban centers in Egypt and Mesopotamia, they maintained trading and cultural contacts. We know of their connection because villagers from the area spanning present-day Mali in the west to present-day Kenya in the southeast used the same style of pottery, characterized by bowls with rounded bottoms and wavy decorations.

PASTORAL NOMADIC COMMUNITIES

Around 3500 BCE, Afro-Eurasia witnessed the growth and spread of pastoral nomadic communities. The transhumant herder communities that had appeared in Southwest Asia around 5500 BCE (see Chapter 1) continued to be small and their settlements impermanent. They lacked substantial public buildings or infrastructure, but their seasonal moves were stable. Across the vast expanse of Afro-Eurasia's great mountains and its desert barriers, and from its steppe lands ranging across inner and central Eurasia to the Pacific Ocean, these transhumant herders lived alongside settled agrarian people, especially when occupying their lowland pastures. They traded meat and animal products for grains, pottery, and tools produced in the agrarian communities.

In the arid environments of Inner Mongolia and central Asia transhumant herding and agrarian communities initially followed the same combination of herding animals and cultivating crops that had proved so successful in Southwest Asia. However, because the steppe environment could not support large-scale farming, these communities came to focus on animal breeding and herding. As secondary pursuits they continued to fish, hunt, and farm small plots in their winter pastures. Their economy centered on domesticated cattle, sheep, and horses. As their herds increased, these horse-riding nomads had to move often to new pastures, driving their herds across vast expanses of land. By the second millennium BCE, they had become full-scale nomadic pastoral communities, and they dominated the steppes. In these pastoral nomadic economies of the arid zones of central Eurasia, horses became crucial to survival.

THE RISE OF TRADE

When the earliest farming villages developed around 7000 BCE, trade patterns across Afro-Eurasia were already well established. Much of this trade was in exotic materials such as obsidian, a black volcanic glass that made superb chipped-stone tools.

Vitally important to the cities of southern Mesopotamia was long-distance trade. Lacking many raw materials that developed settlements require, they needed to find sources of wood, stones, and metal to augment local building materials of mud and reeds. Thus these communities established outposts near the raw materials' sources to coordinate their import. In exchange the cities offered manufactured goods, especially luxury textiles made from the finest quality wool and embroidery. This trade began around 5000 BCE, carried out by boats along the shores of the Persian Gulf. By 3000 BCE there was extensive interaction between southern Mesopotamia and the highlands of Anatolia, the forests of the Levant bordering the eastern Mediterranean, and the rich mountains and vast plateau of Iran. (See Map 2-2.)

MAIN THEMES

→ *Complex societies form around five great river basins.*
→ *The world's first cities arise from the river-basin societies, transforming human life.*
→ *Most people around the globe still live in interdependent villages.*
→ *Pastoral nomadic peoples appear, herding animals and trading animal products for grains, pottery, and tools.*

FOCUS ON *Societies in the Great River Basins*

Mesopotamia

◆ Peoples living along the **Tigris River** and **Euphrates River** control floodwaters and refine irrigation techniques.
◆ Mesopotamians establish the world's first large cities, featuring powerful rulers, social hierarchies, and monumental architecture.
◆ Mesopotamia is the birthplace of writing.

Indus Valley

◆ South Asian peoples harness the **Indus River** and create cities like Harappa and Mohenjo Daro.

Egypt

◆ Peoples of Egypt use **Nile River** waters to irrigate their lands and create a bountiful agriculture.
◆ Egyptian rulers known as pharaohs unify their territory, establish a powerful state, and develop a vibrant economy.
◆ Egyptians build magnificent burial chambers (pyramids) and worship a pantheon of gods.

East Asia

◆ Peoples dwelling in the basins of the **Yellow River** and the **Yangzi River** control the waters' flow and expand agriculture.
◆ These people develop an elaborate culture, which scholars later label Yangshao and Longshan.

Over thousands of years, trade increased. By the mid-third millennium BCE, flourishing communities populated the oases (fertile areas with water in the midst of arid regions) dotting the deserts of western Syria, the Iranian plateau, northern Afghanistan, and Turkmenistan. As these communities actively traded with their neighbors, trading stations at the borders facilitated exchanges among many partners. Here in these "borderlands," although far from big cities, the urbanites exchanged cultural information. Their caravans of pack animals—first donkeys and wild asses; much later, camels—transported goods through deserts, steppes, and forests. Stopping at oasis communities to exchange their wares for water and supplies, these caravans carried ideas across Afro-Eurasia. In this way, borderlands and borderlanders—along with the cities they connected—played a vital role in world history.

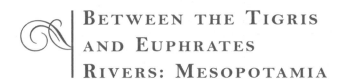

BETWEEN THE TIGRIS AND EUPHRATES RIVERS: MESOPOTAMIA

> → *What role did cities play in Mesopotamian society?*

In 3500 BCE, in a world where people had been living close to the land in small clans and settlements, a radical breakthrough occurred in one place: the Mesopotamian river basin. Here the world's first complex society arose. Here the city and the river changed how people lived.

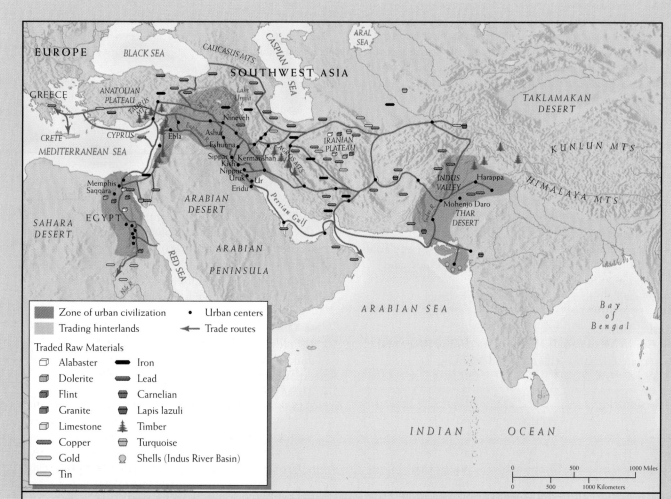

MAP 2-2   TRADE AND EXCHANGE IN SOUTHWEST ASIA AND THE EASTERN MEDITERRANEAN—THIRD MILLENNIUM BCE

Extensive commercial networks linked the urban cores of Southwest Asia. Of the traded raw materials shown on the map, which ones were used for building materials, and which ones for luxury items? Why were there more extensive trade connections between Mesopotamians and people to their northwest and east than with Egypt to the west? According to the map, in what ways did Mesopotamia become the crossroads of Afro-Eurasia?

TAPPING THE WATERS

Mesopotamia, whose name is a Greek word meaning "[country] between two rivers," is not at first glance a hospitable place. From their headwaters in the mountains to the north and east to their destination in the Persian Gulf, the Tigris and Euphrates rivers are wild and unpredictable, flooding in periods of heavy rainfall and snow, and drying up during the parched summer months. Thus water was both scourge and blessing for those who migrated to the Tigris and Euphrates river basin. Unpredictable floodwaters could wipe out years of hard work, but when managed properly they could

transform the landscape into verdant and productive fields. In retrospect, the irrigation systems that the earliest Mesopotamians created were revolutionary. A landmass that includes all of modern-day Iraq and parts of Syria and southeastern Turkey, Mesopotamia embraces a rich variety of topography and cultures—all unified by natural drainage basins. Both rivers provided water for irrigation and, although hardly navigable, were important routes for transportation and communication by pack animal and by foot.

The first advances occurred in the foothills of the Zagros Mountains along the banks of the smaller rivers that feed the Tigris. Here, settlers discovered that rudimentary irrigation techniques enabled them to achieve higher agricultural yields and greater surpluses than the rain-fed areas to the north could provide. Over time they ventured out of the foothills onto the southern alluvial plain of the Tigris and Euphrates basin. (An **alluvium** is an area of land created by river deposits.) Although floods were more severe there and the water harder to harness, the land held greater promise of abundant harvests.

Converting the floodplain of the Euphrates River into a breadbasket required mastering the unpredictable waters. Both the Euphrates and the Tigris, unless controlled by waterworks, were profoundly unfavorable to cultivators because the annual floods and low-water seasons came at the wrong times in the farming sequence. Floods occurred at the height of the growing season, when crops were most vulnerable. Low water levels occurred when crops required abundant irrigation. To prevent the river from overflowing during its flood stage, farmers built levees (barriers to the waters) along the banks and dug ditches and canals to drain away the floodwaters. Their solution was ingenious. Since the bed of the Euphrates is higher than that of the Tigris, and the Euphrates floods sometimes drained toward the Tigris, engineers devised extensive irrigation systems contoured to the shallow gradient between the rivers. Under this scheme the Euphrates served as the supply and the Tigris as the drain of the southern alluvium. Storing and channeling water year after year required constant maintenance and innovation by a corps of engineers.

The Mesopotamians' technological breakthrough was in irrigation, not in agrarian methods. Because the soils were fine, rich, and constantly replenished by the floodwaters' silt,

Early Mesopotamian Waterworks. From the sixth millennium BCE, irrigation was necessary for successful farming in southern Mesopotamia. By the first millennium BCE, sophisticated feats of engineering allowed the Assyrians to redirect water through constructed aqueducts, like the one illustrated here on a relief from the palace of the Assyrian king Sennacherib at Nineveh.

soil tillage was light work. Farmers sowed a combination of wheat, millet, sesame, and barley (the basis for beer, a staple of their diet). Their yields may have been as high as those afforded by modern-day wheat fields in Canada.

CROSSROADS OF SOUTHWEST ASIA

Though its soil was rich and water was abundant, southern Mesopotamia had few other natural resources apart from the mud, marsh reeds, spindly trees, and low-quality limestone that served as basic building materials. To obtain high-quality, dense wood, stone, metal, and other materials for constructing and embellishing their cities (notably their temples and palaces), Mesopotamians had to interact with the inhabitants of surrounding regions. In return for textiles, oils, and other commodities, they imported cedar wood from Lebanon, copper and stones from Oman, more copper from Turkey and Iran, and the precious blue gemstone called lapis lazuli, as well as the ever-useful tin, from faraway Afghanistan. Maintaining trading contacts was easy, given Mesopotamia's open boundaries on all sides. (In this crucial respect Mesopotamia contrasted with Egypt, whose land was cut off by impassable deserts to the east and west, and by the Nile River rapids to the south.)

Mesopotamia's natural advantages—its rich agricultural land and water, combined with easy access to neighboring regions—favored the growth of cities. The area became a magnet for waves of newcomers from the deserts and the mountains (an early version of migration from the countryside to cities), and thus a crossroads for the peoples of Southwest Asia, the meeting grounds for distinct cultural and linguistic groups. Among the dominant groups were Sumerians, who concentrated in the south; Hurrians, who lived in the north; and Akkadians, who populated western and central Mesopotamia.

THE WORLD'S FIRST CITIES

During the first half of the fourth millennium BCE, a demographic transformation occurred in the Tigris-Euphrates river basin. The population expanded as a result of the region's agricultural bounty, and swelling ranks of Mesopotamians migrated from country villages to centers that eventually became cities. (A **city** is a large, well-defined urban area with a dense population.) The earliest cities—Eridu, Nippur, and Uruk—developed over about 1,000 years, dominating the southern part of the floodplain by 3500 BCE. Here archaeologists have found buildings of mud brick marking successive layers of urban development. Consider Eridu, a village dating back to 6000 BCE. Home to the Sumerian water god, Ea, Eridu was a sacred site where temples piled up on top of one another for over 4,000 years. Throughout more than twenty

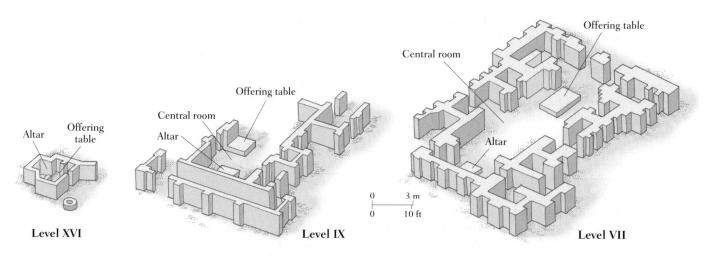

Layout of Eridu. Over several millennia, temples of increasing size and complexity were built atop each other at Eridu in southern Iraq. The culmination came with the elaborate structure of level VII.

reconstructions the temples became increasingly elaborate, standing on an ever-higher base. The final temple rose from a platform like a mountain, visible for miles in all directions.

As the temple grew skyward, the village expanded outward and became a city. Gods oversaw the sprawl. From their homes in temples located at the center of cities, they broadcast their powers. In return, urbanites provided finery, clothes, and enhanced lodgings for the gods and their priestly envoys. In Sumerian cosmology, man was created solely to serve the gods, so the urban landscape reflected this fact: with a temple at the core, with goods and services flowing to the center, and with divine protection and justice flowing outward.

Some thirty-five cities with divine sanctuaries dotted the southern plain of Mesopotamia. Sumerian ideology glorified a way of life and a territory composed of politically equal city-states, each with a guardian deity and sanctuary supported by its inhabitants. (A **city-state** is a political organization based on the authority of a single, large city that controls outlying territories.) Local communities in these urban hubs expressed homage to individual city gods and took pride in the temple, the god's home.

Because early Mesopotamian cities served as meeting places for peoples and their deities, they gained status as religious and economic centers. Whether enormous (like Uruk and Nippur) or modest (like Ur and Abu Salabikh), all cities were spiritual, economic, and cultural homes for Mesopotamian subjects.

Simply making a city was therefore not enough: it had to be made great. Urban design reflected the city's role as a wondrous place to pay homage to the gods and their human intermediary, the king. The early cities contained enormous spaces within their walls, with large houses separated by date palm plantations. The city limits also encompassed extensive sheepfolds (which became a frequent metaphor for the city). As populations grew, the Mesopotamian cities became denser

and the houses smaller. Some urbanites established new suburbs, spilling out beyond old walls and creating neighborhoods in what used to be the countryside.

The typical layout of Mesopotamian cities reflected a common pattern: a central canal surrounded by neighborhoods of specialized occupational groups. The temple marked the city center, while the palace and other official buildings graced the periphery. In separate quarters for craft production, families passed down their trades across generations. In this sense, the landscape of the city mirrored the growing **social hierarchies** (distinctions between the privileged and the less privileged).

GODS AND TEMPLES

The worldview of the Sumerians and, later, the Akkadians included a belief in a group of gods that shaped their political institutions and controlled everything—including the weather, fertility, harvests, and the underworld. As depicted in the *Epic of Gilgamesh* (a second-millennium BCE composition based on oral tales about Gilgamesh, a historical but mythologized king of Uruk), the gods could give but could also take away—with searing droughts, unmerciful floods, and violent death. Gods, and the natural forces they controlled, had to be revered and feared. Faithful subjects imagined their gods as immortal beings whose habits were capricious, contentious, and gloriously work-free. Each major god of the Sumerian pantheon (an officially recognized group of gods) dwelled in a particular city that he or she had created, giving rise to each city's character, institutions, and relationships with its urban neighbors.

Temples served as the gods' home and as the symbol of urban identity. (A **temple** is a building where believers worshipped their gods and goddesses and where some peoples believed the deities had earthly residence.) Rulers lavished resources on temple construction and adornment to demonstrate their cities' power. Inside the temple was an altar displaying the cult image. (A **cult** is a religious movement, often based on the worship of a particular god or goddess.) Benches lined the walls, with statues of humans standing in perpetual worship of the deity's images. By the end of the third millennium BCE, the temple's platform base had changed to a stepped platform called a *ziggurat*. On top of the temple tower stood the main temple. Surrounding the ziggurat were buildings that housed priests, officials, laborers, and servants—all bustling about to serve the city's god.

While the temple was the god's home, it was also the god's estate. As such, temples functioned like large households engaging in all sorts of productive and commercial activities. Their dependents cultivated cereals, fruits, and vegetables by using extensive irrigation. The temples owned vast flocks of sheep, goats, cows, and donkeys. Those located close to the river employed workers to collect reeds, to fish, and to hunt. Enormous labor forces were involved in maintaining this high level of production. Other temples operated huge workshops for manufacturing textiles and leather goods, employing craftworkers, metalworkers, masons, and stoneworkers.

THE PALACE AND ROYAL POWER

The palace, as both an institution and a set of buildings, appeared around 2500 BCE—about two millennia later than the Mesopotamian temple. It joined the temple as a landmark of city life, upholding order and a sense of shared membership in city affairs. Over time, the palace became a source of power rivaling that of the temple. (A **palace** is the official residence of a ruler, his family, and his entourage.) While palaces were off limits to most citizens unless they were connected to the royal court, elite members of the Sumerian community did enjoy access to the cult chamber. As time went on, the god, like the king, became inaccessible to all but the most elite.

Although located at the edge of cities, palaces soon became the symbols of permanent secular, military, and administrative authority distinct from the temples' spiritual and economic power. As the population grew in the southern alluvium, competition among the city-states increased over scarce arable land and access to water for irrigation. Gradually the more powerful city-states came to dominate their weaker neighbors, thereby upsetting the balance of power within and among Mesopotamian cities.

Rulers tied their status to their gods through elaborate burial arrangements. The Royal Cemetery at Ur offers spectacular archaeological evidence of how Sumerian rulers dealt with death. Housed in a mud-brick structure, the royal burials held not only the primary remains but also the bodies of people who had been sacrificed—in one case, more than 80 men and women. Artifacts including huge vats for cooked food, bones of animals, drinking vessels, and musical instruments enable scholars to reconstruct the lifestyle of those

Ziggurat. The first ziggurat of Mesopotamia, dedicated to the moon god Nanna, was built by the founder of the Neo-Sumerian dynasty, Ur-Nammu (2112–2095 BCE). Although temples had been raised on platforms since early times, the distinctive stepped form of the ziggurat was initially borrowed from the Iranian plateau. It became the most important sacred structure in Mesopotamia.

The Royal Tombs of Ur. The Royal Tombs of Ur, excavated in the 1930s, contained thousands of objects in gold, silver, lapis lazuli, and shell that were buried along with elites of the First Dynasty of Ur. In one grave, along with the skeletons of more than sixty members of a royal household, were musical instruments, including this large harp with a golden bull's head. Such instruments would have been played at the ritual meal associated with these fabulously rich burials. Pu-Abi, identified as a queen by the cylinder near her body, was buried in a separate chamber. She was interred in full regalia, including the elaborate headdress shown here.

who joined their masters in the graves. Honoring the royal dead by including their followers and possessions in their tombs reinforced the social hierarchies—including the vertical ties between humans and gods—that were the cornerstone of these early city-states.

SOCIAL HIERARCHY AND FAMILIES

Social hierarchies were an important part of the fabric of Sumerian city-states. Mesopotamia's city-states at first had assemblies of elders and young men who made collective decisions for the community. At times, certain effective individuals took charge of emergencies, and over time these people surrounding the leaders acquired more durable political power. The social hierarchy set off the rulers from the ruled. Ruling groups secured their privileged access to economic and political resources by erecting systems of bureaucracies, priesthoods, and laws. Priests and bureaucrats served their rulers well, championing rules and norms that legitimized the political leadership.

Occupations within the cities were highly specialized, and a list of professions circulated across the land so that everyone could know his or her place in the social order. The king and priest in Sumer were at the top of the list, followed by bureaucrats (scribes and household accountants), supervisors, and craftworkers. The latter included cooks, jewelers, gardeners, potters, metalsmiths, and traders. The biggest group, which was at the bottom of the hierarchy, comprised workers who were not slaves but who were dependent on their employers' households. Movement among economic classes was not impossible but, as in many traditional societies, it was

rare. There were also independent merchants who risked long-distance trading ventures, hoping for a generous return on their investment.

The family and the household provided the bedrock for Sumerian society, and its organization reflected the balance between women and men, children and parents. The Sumerian family was hierarchical, so the senior male dominated as the patriarch. Most households were composed of a single extended family, all of whose members lived under the same roof. The family consisted of the husband and wife bound by a contract: she would provide children, preferably male, while he provided support and protection. Monogamy was the norm unless there was no son, in which case a second wife or a slave girl would bear male children to serve as the married couple's offspring. Adoption was another way to gain a male heir. Sons would inherit the family's property in equal shares, while daughters would receive dowries necessary for successful marriage into other families. Most women lived inside the contract of marriage, but a special class of women joined the temple staff as priestesses. By the second millennium BCE, they gained economic autonomy that included ownership of estates and productive enterprises. Even in this case, though, their fathers and brothers remained responsible for their well-being.

FIRST WRITING AND EARLY TEXTS

Mesopotamia was the birthplace of the first recorded words of history, inscribed to promote the power of the temples and kings in the expanding city-states. Small-scale hunter-gatherer societies and village-farming communities had

Cylinder Seal of Adad Carved from Green Stone. Many people in Mesopotamia involved with administration and public life had one or more cylinder seals. Cylinder seals were carved with imagery and inscriptions and were impressed into clay tablets and other documents while they were still malleable in order to guarantee the authenticity of a transaction. The cylinder seal shown here carries the inscription of the scribe Adda. The imagery includes representations of important gods of the Akkadian pantheon. The sun god Shamash rises from between the mountains in the center. Ishtar as a warrior goddess stands to the left. To the right is Ea, the god of wisdom, who is associated with flowing water and fish. Behind him is the servant Usmu, whose double face allows him to see everything. At the far left is a god of hunting.

developed rituals of oral celebrations based on collective memories transmitted by families across generations. But as societies grew larger and more complex, and their members more anonymous, oral traditions provided inadequate "glue" to hold the centers together.

Those who wielded new writing tools were **scribes**; from the very beginning they were at the top of the social ladder, under the major power brokers—the big man and the priests. As the writing of texts became more important to the social fabric of cities, and facilitated information sharing across wider spans of distance and time, scribes consolidated their grip on the upper rungs of the social ladder.

Mesopotamians became the world's first record keepers and readers. The precursors to writing appeared in Mesopotamian societies when farming peoples and officials who had been using clay tokens and images carved on stones to seal off storage areas began to use them to convey messages. These images, when combined with numbers drawn on clay tablets, could record the distribution of goods and services.

In a flash of human genius, someone, probably in Uruk, understood that the marks (most were pictures of objects) could also represent words or sounds. A representation that transfers meaning from the name of a thing to the sound of that name is a *rebus*. Before long, scribes connected visual symbols with sounds, and sounds with meanings. As people combined rebus symbols with other visual marks, they discovered they could record messages by using abstract symbols or signs to denote concepts. Such signs later came to represent syllables, the building blocks of words. (See Primary Source: The Origins of Writing According to the Sumerians.)

By impressing signs into wet clay with the cut end of a reed, scribes pioneered a form of wedge-shaped writing that we call *cuneiform*; it filled tablets with information that was intelligible to anyone who could decipher it, even in faraway locations or in future generations. This Sumerian innovation enhanced the urban elites' ability to produce and trade goods, to control property, and to transmit ideas through literature, historical records, and sacred texts. The result was a profound change in human experience, because representing symbols of spoken language facilitated an extension of communication and memory. Although these gradual steps toward literacy were fundamental to the innovative process occurring in cities, only a tiny but influential scribal elite mastered writing at first.

Much of what we know about Mesopotamia rests on our ability to decipher cuneiform script. Rebus writing appeared around 3200 BCE, but not until 700 years later could the script record spoken utterances completely. By around 2400 BCE, texts began to describe the political makeup of southern Mesopotamia, giving details of its history and economy. Northern cities borrowed cuneiform to record economic transactions and political events, but in their own Semitic tongue. In fact, cuneiform's adaptability to different languages was a main reason its use spread widely.

As city life and literacy expanded, they gave rise not only to documents but also to written narratives, the stories of a "people" and their origins. One famous set of texts written around 2100 BCE, "The Temple Hymns," describes thirty-five divine sanctuaries. The magnificent Sumerian King List, known from texts written around 2000 BCE, recounts the reigns of kings by dynasty, one city at a time. It narrates the fabulously long reigns of legendary kings before the so-called Great Flood, which, in turn, is one of many traditional stories that people transmitted orally for generations (and it later evolved into the book of Genesis as part of the Bible's creation story). The Great Flood, a crucial event in Sumerian identity, explained Uruk's demise as the gods' doing. Flooding was the most riveting of natural forces in the lives of a riverine folk, and it helped shape the material and symbolic foundations of Mesopotamian societies.

Primary Source

THE ORIGINS OF WRITING ACCORDING TO THE SUMERIANS

One Sumerian myth records the invention of writing by the Lord of Kulaba, Enmerkar. He wanted to transmit complex messages across vast distances to the Land of Aratta, where his rival for the love of the goddess Inanna lived. Normally messengers would memorize messages and responses and deliver them orally after making an arduous journey across the mountains. Enmerkar felt he could not trust his messenger's memory to deliver one particularly complicated message, so he invented writing in the form of cuneiform script.

His speech was substantial, and its contents extensive. The messenger, whose mouth was heavy, was not able to repeat it. Because the messenger, whose mouth was tired, was not able to repeat it, the lord of Kulaba patted some clay and wrote the message as if on a tablet. Formerly, the writing of messages on clay was not established. Now, under that sun and on that day, it was indeed so. The lord of Kulaba inscribed the message like a tablet. It was just like that. The messenger was like a bird, flapping its wings; he raged forth like a wolf following a kid. He traversed five mountains, six mountains, seven mountains. He lifted his eyes as he approached Aratta. He stepped joyfully into the courtyard of Aratta, he made known the authority of his king. Openly he spoke out the words in his heart. The messenger transmitted the message to the lord of Aratta:

"Your father, my master, has sent me to you; the lord of Unug, the lord of Kulaba, has sent me to you." "What is it to me what your master has spoken? What is it to me what he has said?"

"This is what my master has spoken, this is what he has said. My king is like a huge *meš* tree, . . . son of Enlil; this tree has grown high, uniting heaven and earth; its crown reaches heaven, its trunk is set upon the earth. He who is made to shine forth in lordship and kingship, Enmerkar, the son of Utu, has given me a clay tablet. O lord of Aratta, after you have examined the clay tablet, after you have learned the content of the message, say whatever you will say to me, and I shall announce that message in the shrine E-ana as glad tidings to the scion of him with the glistening beard, whom his stalwart cow gave birth to in the mountains of the shining *me*, who was reared on the soil of Aratta, who was given suck at the udder of the good cow, who is suited for office in Kulaba, the mountain of great *me*, to Enmerkar, the son of Utu; I shall repeat it in his *ĝipar*, fruitful as a flourishing *meš* tree, to my king, the lord of Kulaba."

After he had spoken thus to him, the lord of Aratta received his kiln-fired tablet from the messenger. The lord of Aratta looked at the tablet. The transmitted message was just nails, and his brow expressed anger. The lord of Aratta looked at his kiln-fired tablet. At that moment, the lord worthy of the crown of lordship, the son of Enlil, the god I_kur, thundering in heaven and earth, caused a raging storm, a great lion, in . . . He was making the mountains quake . . . , he was convulsing the mountain range . . . ; the awesome radiance . . . of his breast; he caused the mountain range to raise its voice in joy. (lines 500–551)

→ *What passages in this reading reveal the Sumerians' familiarity with pastoralism?*
→ *What aspects of Sumerian history and geography does this mythic story preserve and transmit?*

SOURCE: J. A. Black, G. Cunningham, E. Fluckiger-Hawker, E. Robson, and G. Zólyomi, *The Electronic Text Corpus of Sumerian Literature* (Oxford, 1998–2006), www-etcsl.orient.ox.ac.uk/.

Cuneiform version of the myth "Enmerkar and the Lord of Aratta."

SPREADING CITIES AND FIRST TERRITORIAL STATES

Although no single state dominated the history of fourth- and third-millennium BCE Mesopotamia, a few stand out. The most powerful and influential were the Sumerian city-states of the Early Dynastic Age (2850–2334 BCE) and their successor, the Akkadian territorial state (2334–2193 BCE).

While the city-states of southern Mesopotamia flourished and competed, giving rise to the land of Sumer, the rich agricultural zones to the north inhabited by the Hurrians also became urbanized. (See Map 2-3.) Beginning around 2600 BCE, northern cities were comparable in size to those in the south. Though their inhabitants were culturally related to the Sumerians and Akkadians, the northern cities had economic, political, and social organizations that were distinct and independent.

As Mesopotamia swelled with cities, it became unstable. The Sumerian city-states with expanding populations soon found themselves competing for agrarian lands, scarce water, and lucrative trade routes. And as pastoralists far and wide learned of the region's bounty, they journeyed in greater numbers to the cities, fueling urbanization and competition.

Cities also spawned rivalry and struggles for supremacy. In fact, the world's first great conqueror emerged from one of these cities, and by the end of his long reign he had united (by force) the independent Mesopotamian cities south of modern-day Baghdad. The legendary Sargon the Great (r. 2334–2279 BCE), king of Akkad, brought the era of competitive independent city-states to an end. His most remarkable achievement was unification of the southern cities through an alliance. Although this unity lasted only three generations, it represented the first multiethnic collection of urban centers—the **territorial state**. (A territorial state is a form of political organization that

holds authority over a large population and landmass; its power extends over a wider area than that of city-states.)

The most obvious legacy of Sargon's dynasty was sponsorship of monumental architecture, artworks, and literary works. These cultural achievements stood for centuries, inspiring generations of builders, architects, artists, and scribes. And by encouraging contact with distant neighbors, many of whom adopted aspects of Mesopotamian culture, the Akkadian kings increased the geographic reach of Mesopotamian influence.

The riches and competition among cities also lured invaders, with the result that Sargon's "empire" was short-lived. Foreign tribesmen from the Zagros Mountains infiltrated the heartland of Akkad, conquering the capital city around 2190 BCE. This cycle of urban magnificence punctuated by disintegration triggered by outside forces gave rise to epic history writing, and its myth of urban civility and rural backwardness still captivates readers today. The fall of Sargon's "empire"

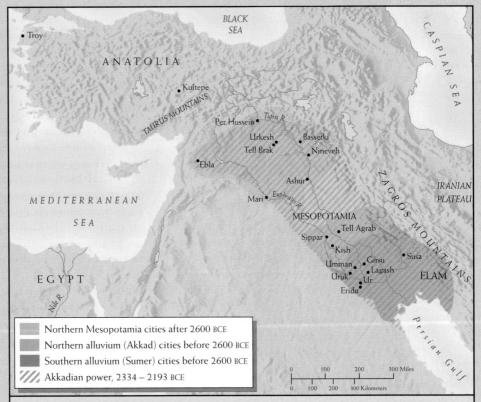

Northern Mesopotamia cities after 2600 BCE
Northern alluvium (Akkad) cities before 2600 BCE
Southern alluvium (Sumer) cities before 2600 BCE
Akkadian power, 2334 – 2193 BCE

MAP 2-3   **THE SPREAD OF CITIES IN MESOPOTAMIA AND THE AKKADIAN STATE, 2600–2200 BCE**

Urbanization began in the southern alluvium of Mesopotamia and spread northward. Eventually, the region achieved unification under one territorial state. According to this map, what were the natural boundaries of the Mesopotamian cities? How did proximity to the Zagros Mountains affect the new urban centers? How did the expansion northward reflect the continued influence of geographic and environmental factors on urbanization?

Naram Sin. This life-size head of a ruler cast of almost pure copper was found at Nineveh in northern Iraq in the destruction levels of the Assyrian Empire. The style and imagery of this sculptural masterpiece identify it as a ruler of Old Akkadian dynasty. While sometimes identified as Sargon, it is most likely a portrait of his grandson, Naram Sin, who consolidated and transformed the Akkadian state. It must have stood for over fifteen hundred years in the courtyard of a temple at Nineveh before it was defaced by the Medes and Elamites, whose savage attack on Nineveh cause the Assyrian Empire to fall.

underscores a fundamental but often neglected reality of the ancient world: living side by side with the city-state dwellers were peoples who followed a simpler way of life. They often did not enter the historical record except when they intruded on the lives of their more powerful and prosperous neighbors.

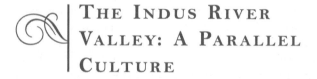

THE INDUS RIVER VALLEY: A PARALLEL CULTURE

> → *Why do we know less about Harappan culture than about others in Afro-Eurasia?*

We call the urban culture of the Indus area "Harappan" after the urban site of Harappa that arose in the third millennium BCE on the banks of the Ravi River, a tributary of the Indus.

Developments in the Indus basin reflected an indigenous (local) tradition combined with strong influences from Iranian plateau peoples, as well as indirect influences from distant cities on the Tigris and Euphrates rivers. Villages appeared around 5000 BCE on the Iranian plateau along the Baluchistan Mountain foothills, to the west of the Indus. By the early third millennium BCE, frontier villages had spread eastward to the fertile banks of the Indus River and its tributaries. (See Map 2-4.) The riverine settlements soon yielded agrarian surpluses that supported greater wealth, more trade with neighbors, and public works. In due course, urbanites of the Indus region and the Harappan peoples began to fortify their cities and to undertake public works similar in scale to those in Mesopotamia, but strikingly different in function.

The Indus Valley ecology boasted many advantages—especially compared to the area near the Ganges River, the other great waterway of the South Asian landmass. The semi-tropical Indus Valley had plentiful water from melting snows in the Himalayas that ensured flourishing vegetation, and the region did not suffer the yearly monsoon downpours that flooded the Ganges plain. The expansion of agriculture in the Indus basin depended on the river's annual floods to replenish the soil and avert droughts (as in Mesopotamia, Egypt, and China). From June to September, the rivers inundated the plain. Once the waters receded, farmers planted wheat and barley. They harvested crops the next spring as temperatures rose. At the same time, the villagers improved their tools of cultivation. Researchers have found evidence of furrows, probably made by plowing, that date to around 2600 BCE. Farmers were soon achieving harvests like those of Mesopotamia, yielding a surplus that freed many inhabitants from producing food and allowed them to specialize in other activities.

In time, rural wealth produced urban splendor. More abundant harvests, now stored in large granaries, brought migrants into the area and supported expanding populations. By 2500 BCE cities began to replace villages throughout the Indus River valley, and within a few generations towering granaries marked the urban skyline. Harappa and Mohenjo Daro, the two largest cities, each covered a little less than half a square mile and may have housed 35,000 residents. As in Mesopotamia, such population densities were unprecedented departures from the more common agrarian villages or nomadic communities, which remained self-sufficient.

Harappan cities sprawled across a vast floodplain covering 500,000 square miles—two or three times the Mesopotamian cultural zone. At the height of their development, the Harappan peoples reached the edge of the Indus ecological system and encountered the cultures of northern Afghanistan, the inhabitants of the desert frontier, the nomadic hunter-gatherers to the east, and the traders to the west.

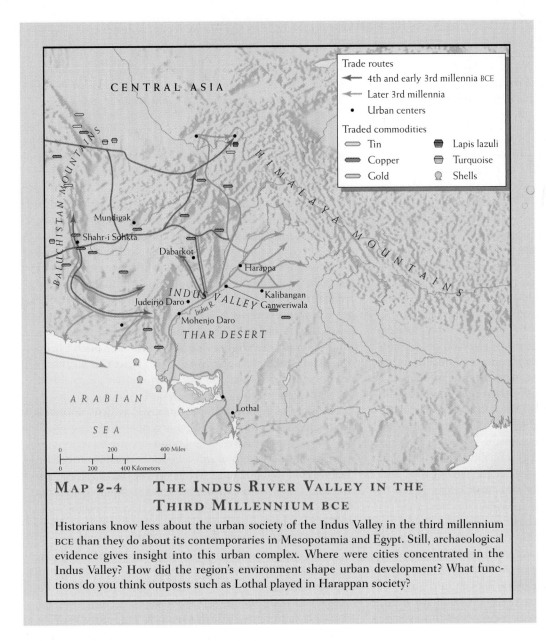

MAP 2-4   THE INDUS RIVER VALLEY IN THE THIRD MILLENNIUM BCE

Historians know less about the urban society of the Indus Valley in the third millennium BCE than they do about its contemporaries in Mesopotamia and Egypt. Still, archaeological evidence gives insight into this urban complex. Where were cities concentrated in the Indus Valley? How did the region's environment shape urban development? What functions do you think outposts such as Lothal played in Harappan society?

Mesopotamians and Egyptians did)—and may not even have had kings—scholars cannot chart a Harappan political history by tracing the rise and fall of dynasties and kingdoms.

We base our knowledge about Harappa on archaeological reconstructions, and these are sketchy. The sketchiness reminds us that "history" is not what happened but only *what we know about what happened*. Relying only on fragmentary archaeological evidence, scholars have been unable to draw the rich portraits of Harappan life that they have supplied for the Mesopotamians and the Egyptians.

What we know is impressive nonetheless. The layout of Harappan cities and towns followed a well-planned pattern: a fortified citadel housing public facilities, alongside a large residential area. The main street running through the city had covered drainage on both sides, with house gates and doors opening onto back alleys. Citadels were likely centers of political and ritual activities. At the center of the citadel of Mohenjo Daro was the famous great bath, a brick structure 39.3 feet by 23 feet and 9.8 feet deep. Flights of steps led to the bottom of the bath, while other stairs went up to a level of rooms surrounding it. The bath was sealed with mortar and bitumen (a sticky, tar-like form of petroleum), and its water came from a large well nearby. The water drained out through a channel leading to lower land. The location, size, and quality of the structures all suggest that the bath was for public bathing rituals.

The Harappans used brick extensively—in houses for notables, city walls, and underground water drainage systems. Workers used large ovens to manufacture the durable construction materials, which the Harappans laid so skillfully that basic structures remain intact to this day. A well-built house had private bathrooms, showers, and toilets that

HARAPPAN CITY LIFE

We know less about Harappan culture than about other contemporary cultures of Afro-Eurasia, because many of its remains lie buried under deep silt deposits accumulated over thousands of years of heavy flooding. Further, scholars have been unable to identify the Indus peoples' language or decipher the script of about 400 symbols. The script might not represent a spoken language; instead, it might be a nonlinguistic symbol system. (See Primary Source: The Mystery of Harappan Writing.) Most of what remains is visible on a thousand or more stamp seals and small plaques excavated from the region, which may represent the names and titles of individuals rather than complete sentences. Moreover, because the Harappans did not produce King Lists (as the

Primary Source

THE MYSTERY OF HARAPPAN WRITING

No one has deciphered the writing system of the Harappa culture in the Indus Valley. The Indus script appeared on seals and tablets—and in a recently discovered site, on a board for public display. Although no one is sure which language it represents, some of its characteristics provide scholars with fuel for speculation.

As for verbal communication through writing, it needs to be understood that no one has as yet succeeded in deciphering the Harappan script and that this will remain an unlikely eventuality unless a bilingual inscription—in Harappan and a known form of writing—is found, that incorporates the names of people or places. The Harappan script is logographic: there are 375 to 400 signs, which rules out an alphabet (where one sign stands for one vowel or consonant) because alphabets usually have no more than thirty-six signs. Often Harappan bangles or metal tools are inscribed with just one sign. Harappan writing goes from right to left, as can be made out from close examination of overlapping signs scratched on pots. Short strokes indicate numbers, and numerals precede other signs, which could mean that in the Harappan language adjectives preceded the nouns they qualified. Certain signs, computer concordances reveal, tend to occur frequently at the end of inscriptions, which points to a language using a set of phonetic suffixes.

The Harappan language was probably agglutinative, or a language which added suffixes to an unchanging root. This feature is characteristic of the Dravidian language family rather than the Indo-Aryan languages. This, and the fact that the earliest Indo-Aryan text, the *Rigveda*, shows Dravidian influence (indicating that the early Indo-Aryans in the northwest had some contact with Dravidian speakers), make it likely that the language of the Harappans was a Dravidian one. (Note, also, that Brahui, spoken in the hills of southern Baluchistan today, is a Dravidian language.)

The inscriptions on the seals being brief, on average five to six signs long, they probably gave little more than the owner's name and designation. Perhaps it was the pictorial (often solo animal) emblem, rendered with great skill, that indicated the lineage, ancestry or social origins of the owner. There is no geographic pattern to the occurrence of the various seal animals (unicorn, bull, rhinoceros, antelope, tiger or elephant), so the animal could not possibly have signified the place of origin of the seal owner. Perhaps it was this pictorial image that lent authority to any spoken message that accompanied a seal or an object stamped with one. It may be noted that so far it is Harappa and Mohenjo-daro—and mound E rather than

the 'citadel mound' AB at Harappa—that have yielded the evidence for the most intensive writing activity. These were probably centres of administration.

Harappan writing occurs on pots, seals, terracotta (stoneware) and shell bangles, copper tablets and tools, and ivory rods. Large numbers of scored goblets with pointed bases that occur at Harappa and Mohenjo-daro are important as they are one of the very few pottery forms that can occasionally carry seal impressions (as distinct from scratched signs)—their use remains a mystery. We get the impression that writing was for humdrum purposes. A striking exception to this is the occurrence of a huge "public" inscription that seems to have been set up on a street at Dholavira in Kutch, with letters about thirty-seven centimetres high cut out of stones and, R. S. Bisht suggests, fastened on a wooden board.

The most important point, however, is the enormous intellectual advance that the emergence of writing signifies. When we speak we utter sounds in one or other language using a series of sound sequences that carry specific meanings in that language. What writing does is to encode in visual form, that is, through a set of distinct symbols or signs, those sounds and sound sequences—thereby conveying meaning or information. Further, writing makes possible the storage of information or the maintenance of records for future reference. It makes communication at a distance possible. It requires of the writer knowledge of the signs and some amount of manual dexterity, and of the reader, knowledge of how the visual signs are vocalized and of course familiarity with the relevant language. Writing has been termed the most momentous invention human beings have ever made.

→ *Even though we cannot read Harappan script, why is the knowledge that the Harappans wrote in script important?*

→ *Judging from the information above about Harappan writing, what language do you think the script most likely represents?*

Source: Shereen Ratnagar, "The Mystery of Harappan Writing" from *Understanding Harappa Civilization in the Greater Indus Valley* (New Delhi: Tulika Publishers, 2001), pp. 60–62.

Mohenjo Daro. Mohenjo Daro, the "mound of dead," is a large urban site of the Harappan culture. The view of the city demonstrates a neat layout of houses and civic facilities such as sewer draining.

drained into municipal sewers, also made of bricks. Houses in small towns and villages were made of less durable and less costly sun-baked bricks, which are used throughout southern Eurasia even today.

TRADE

The Harappans engaged in trade along the Indus River, through the mountain passes to the Iranian plateau, and along the coast of the Arabian Sea as far as the Persian Gulf and Mesopotamia. They traded copper, flint, shells, and ivory, as well as pottery, flint blades, and jewelry created by their craftworkers, in exchange for gold, silver, gemstones, and textiles.

Some of the Harappan trading towns nestled in remote but strategically important places. Consider Lothal, a well-fortified port at the head of the Gulf of Khambhat (Cambay). Although distant from the center of Harappan society, it provided vital access to the sea and to valuable raw materials. Its many workshops processed precious stones, both local and foreign. Because the demand for gemstones was high on the Iranian plateau and in Mesopotamia, the Harappans knew that controlling their extraction and trade was essential to maintaining economic power. Carnelian, a precious red stone, was a local resource, but lapis lazuli had to come from what is now northern Afghanistan. So the Harappans built fortifications and settlements near its sources. Extending their frontier did not stop at gemstones, however. Because metals such as copper and silver also had strategic commercial

Harappan Gemstone Necklace. Beadmakers perforated lapis lazuli and other semi-precious stones using a bow drill to make tiny holes for suspension.

Harappan Seal Stamps. The stamp seals of the Indus Valley culture are distinctive. Cut from the soft stone steatite and fired to a white color to make them hard, they have a rounded boss pierced for suspension on the back. The images carved on their surface are usually animals: elephants, tigers, bulls. Occasionally human figures, perhaps deities, perhaps rulers, are depicted seated on a platform, or dancing, or surrounded by animals. Many of the stamp seals have inscriptions across the top edge. The script of the Harappan people has not been deciphered, nor has its underlying language been identified.

importance, the Harappans established settlements near their copper mines as well.

Through a complex and vibrant trading system, the Harappans maintained access to mineral and agrarian resources. To facilitate trade, rulers relied not just on Harappan script but also on a system of weights and measures that they devised and standardized. Archaeologists have found Harappan seals, used to stamp commodities with the names of their owners or the nature of the goods, at sites as far away as the Persian Gulf, Mesopotamia, and the Iranian plateau (see Global Connections & Disconnections on p. 78).

The general uniformity in Harappan sites suggests a centralized and structured state. Unlike the Mesopotamians and the Egyptians, however, the Harappans apparently built neither palaces, nor grand royal tombs, nor impressive monumental structures. The elites expressed their elaborate urban culture in ways that did not proclaim their high standing. The Harappans were as unassuming as the Egyptians and Mesopotamians were boastful. This quality has puzzled scholars, but it underscores the profound differences in ancient societies: they did not all value the same things. The advent of writing, urban culture, long-distance trade, and large cities did not always produce the same social hierarchies and the

same ethos (a set of principles governing social and political relations). What the Indus River people show us is how much the urbanized parts of the world were diverging from one another, even as they borrowed from and imitated their neighbors.

"THE GIFT OF THE NILE": EGYPT

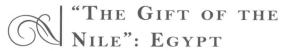

> → *How did the Nile River shape early Egyptian society?*

The earliest inhabitants along the banks of the Nile River were a mixed people. Some had migrated from the eastern and western deserts in Sinai and Libya as these areas grew barren from climate change. Others came from the Mediterranean. Equally important were peoples who trekked northward from Nubia and central Africa. Ancient Egypt was a melting pot where immigrants blended cultural practices and technologies.

Egypt had much in common with Mesopotamia and the Indus Valley. Like them, it had densely populated areas whose inhabitants depended on irrigation, built monumental architecture, gave their rulers immense authority, and created a complex social order. Tapping the Nile waters gave rise to agrarian wealth, commercial and devotional centers, early states, and new techniques of communication.

Yet the ancient Egyptian culture was profoundly distinct from its contemporaries in Mesopotamia and the Indus Valley. To understand its unique qualities, we must begin with its geography. The environment and the natural boundaries of deserts, river rapids, and sea dominated the country and its inhabitants. The core area of ancient Egypt covered 386,560 square miles, of which only 11,720 square miles (7.5 million acres) were cultivable. Of this total, roughly 6 million acres were in the Nile delta—the rich alluvial land lying between the river's two main branches as it flows north of modern-day Cairo into the Mediterranean Sea.

THE NILE RIVER AND ITS FLOODWATERS

Knowing Egypt requires appreciating the pulses of the Nile. The world's longest river, it stretches 4,238 miles from its sources in the highlands of central Africa to its destination in the Mediterranean Sea. In this way (and many others), Egypt was deeply attached to sub-Saharan Africa. Not only did its life-giving irrigation waters and rich silt deposits come from the African highlands, but much of its original population had migrated into the Nile valley from the west and the south many millennia earlier.

The Upper Nile is a sluggish river that cuts through the Sahara Desert. Rising out of central Africa and Ethiopia, its two main branches—the White and Blue Niles—meet at present-day Khartoum and then scour out a single riverbed 1,500 miles long to the Mediterranean. The annual floods gave the basin regular moisture and alluvial richness. Although the Nile's floodwaters did not fertilize or irrigate fields as broad as those in Mesopotamia or Harappa, they created green belts flanking the broad waterway. These gave rise to a society whose culture stretched along the navigable river and its carefully preserved banks. Away from the riverbanks, on both sides, lay a desert rich in raw materials but largely uninhabited. Egypt had no fertile hinterland like the sprawling plains of Mesopotamia and the Indus Valley. In a sense, Egypt was the most "riverine" of the riverine cultures.

The Nile's predictability as the source of life and abundance shaped the character of the people and their culture. In contrast to the wild and uncertain Euphrates and Tigris rivers, the Nile was gentle and bountiful, leading Egyptians to view the world as beneficent. During the summer as the Nile swelled, local villagers built earthen walls that divided the floodplain into basins. By trapping the floodwaters, these basins captured the rich silt washing down from the Ethiopian highlands. Annual flooding meant that the land received a new layer of topsoil every year.

The light, fertile soils made planting simple. Peasants cast seeds into the alluvial soil and then had their livestock trample them to the proper depth. The never-failing sun, which the Egyptians worshipped, ensured an abundant harvest. In the early spring, when the Nile's waters were at their lowest and no crops were under cultivation, the sun dried out the soil.

EGYPT'S UNIQUE RIVERINE CULTURE

The peculiarities of the Nile region distinguished it from Mesopotamia and the Indus Valley. Some 2,500 years ago, the Greek historian and geographer Herodotus noted that Egypt was the gift of the Nile and that the entire length of its basin was one of the world's most self-contained geographical entities. Bounded on the north by the Mediterranean Sea, on the east and west by deserts, and on the south by cataracts (large waterfalls), Egypt was destined to achieve a common culture. The region was far less open to outsiders than were Mesopotamia and the Indus River basin.

Like the other pioneering societies, Egypt created a common culture by balancing regional tensions and reconciling regional rivalries. Ancient Egyptian history is a struggle of opposing forces: the north or Lower Egypt versus the south or

Nile Agriculture. The Nile is fed by the Blue Nile, which has its source in the Ethiopian highlands, and the White Nile in southern Sudan. It rises and falls according to a regular pattern that was the basis for the ancient Egyptian agricultural cycle. Flooding the valley in August and September, the Nile recedes, depositing a rich layer of silt in which the crops were planted in the fall and harvested in April and May.

Upper Egypt; the sand, the so-called red part of the earth, versus the rich soil, described as black; life versus death; heaven versus earth; order versus disorder. For Egypt's ruling groups—notably the kings—the primary task was to bring stability or order, known as *ma'at*, out of these antagonistic impulses. The Egyptians believed that keeping chaos, personified by the desert and its marauders, at bay through attention to *ma'at* would allow all that was good and right to occur.

THE RISE OF THE EGYPTIAN STATE AND DYNASTIES

Once the early Egyptians harnessed the Nile to agriculture, the area changed from being scarcely inhabited to socially complex. Whereas Mesopotamia and Harappa developed gradually, Egypt seemed to grow overnight. It quickly became a powerhouse state, projecting its splendor along the full length of the river valley.

A king, called pharaoh, was at the center of Egyptian life. His primary responsibility was to ensure that the forces of nature, in particular the regular flooding of the Nile, continued without interruption. This task had more to do with appeasing the gods than with running a complex hydraulic system—hence, Egypt's large clerical class. The king also had to protect his people from invaders from the eastern desert, as well as from Nubians on the southern borders. These groups threatened Egypt with social chaos. As guarantors of the social and political order, the early kings depicted themselves as shepherds. In wall carvings, artists portrayed them carrying the crook and the flail, indicating their responsibility for the welfare of their flocks (the people) and of the land. Moreover, under the king an elaborate bureaucracy organized labor and produced public works, sustaining both his vast holdings and general order throughout the realm.

The narrative of ancient Egyptian history follows its dynasties—a structure that gives a sense of deep continuity. According to a third-century BCE Egyptian cleric named Manetho, Egypt saw no fewer than thirty-one dynasties, spanning three millennia from 3100 BCE down to its conquest by Alexander the Great in 332 BCE. (See Table 2-1.) Since the nineteenth century, however, scholars have recast the story around three periods of dynastic achievement: the Old Kingdom, the Middle Kingdom, and the New Kingdom. At the end of each era, cultural flourishing suffered a breakdown in central authority, known respectively as the First, Second, and Third Intermediate Periods. No other region of the world has charted a history of such extraordinary length and durability.

TABLE 2-1 **Dynasties of Ancient Egypt**	
Pre-dynastic Period	
dynasties I and II	3100–2686 BCE
Old Kingdom	
dynasties III–VI	2686–2181 BCE
First Intermediate Period	
dynasties VII–X	2181–2055 BCE
Middle Kingdom	
dynasties XI–XIII	2055–1650 BCE
Second Intermediate Period	
dynasties XIV–XVII	1650–1550 BCE
New Kingdom	
dynasties XVIII–XX	1550–1069 BCE
Third Intermediate Period	
dynasties XXI–XXV	1069–747 BCE
Late Period	
dynasties XXVI–XXXI	747–332 BCE

SOURCE: Compiled from Ian Shaw and Paul Nicholson, eds., *The Dictionary of Ancient Egypt* (1995), pp. 310–11.

RITUALS, PYRAMIDS, AND COSMIC ORDER

The Third Dynasty (2686–2613 BCE) launched the foundational period known as the Old Kingdom, the golden age of ancient Egypt. (See Map 2-5.) By the time it began, the basic institutions of the Egyptian state were in place, as were the ideology and ritual life that legitimized the dynastic rulers.

The king as god presented himself to the population by means of impressive architectural spaces, and the priestly class performed rituals reinforcing his supreme status within the universe's natural order. The most important ceremony was the Sed festival, which renewed the king's vitality after he had ruled for thirty years. Although it focused on the king's vitality, its origins lay in ensuring the perpetual presence of water.

King Djoser, the second king of the Third Dynasty, celebrated the Sed festival in his tomb complex at Saqqara. This magnificent complex, the world's oldest stone structure (rather than the mud-brick temples and palaces of Mesopotamia), took shape during his reign. It began as a huge flat structure identical to earlier royal tombs. However, the architect, Imhotep, was not satisfied with the modest shape of earlier burial chambers. Throughout six renovations he transformed the structure into a step pyramid that ultimately rose some 200 feet above the plain, dominating the landscape like the later Mesopotamian ziggurats did (see p. 53). This mountainlike

→ *How did the Nile River shape early Egyptian society?*

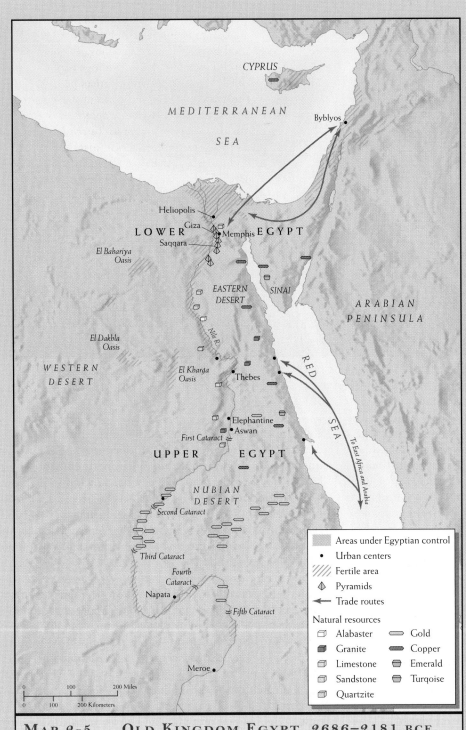

MAP 2-5   OLD KINGDOM EGYPT, 2686–2181 BCE

Old Kingdom Egyptian society reflected a strong influence from its unique geographical location. What geographical features contributed to Egypt's isolation from the outside world and the people's sense of their unity? What natural resource enabled the Egyptians to build the Great Pyramids? Based on the map, why do you think it was important for upper and lower Egypt to be united?

structure stood at the center of an enormous walled precinct housing five courts where the king performed rituals emphasizing the divinity of kingship and the unity of Upper and Lower Egypt. Because most of the structures were facades, the whole complex became a stage for state rituals. The symbolism of the unity of Upper and Lower Egypt was pervasive, embodied in the entwined lotus and papyrus—symbols of each region. The step pyramid complex incorporated artistic and architectural forms that would characterize Egyptian culture for millennia.

The Egyptian pharaoh—the king as god—used the royal tomb to embody the state's ideology and the principles of the Egyptian cosmos. The ritual of death, leading to everlasting life, became part of the cultural myth. So did a common ideology stressing the unity of the long river valley's distinct regions. The pharaoh also employed symbols (for example, the dual crown representing Upper and Lower Egypt), throne names, and descriptive titles for himself and his advisers to represent his own power and that of his administrators, the priests, and the landed elite. The Egyptian cosmic order was one of inequality and stark hierarchy. Established at the time of creation, the universe was the king's responsibility to maintain for eternity. The belief that the king was a god compelled him to behave like one: serene, orderly, merciful, and perfect. He always had to wear an expression of divine peace, not the angry snarl of mere human power.

Pyramid building evolved rapidly from the step version of Djoser to the grand pyramids of the Fourth Dynasty (2613–2494 BCE). These kings erected their

The Pyramids of Giza. The Pyramid Fields of Giza lie on the western side of the Nile just south of the modern city of Cairo. The Old Kingdom pharaohs built their eternal resting places there, surrounded by the smaller pyramids and bench tombs of their relatives and courtiers. The largest pyramid of Khufu is to the north. Khafra's is linked to the Nile by a causeway flanked by the famous Sphinx. The smallest is that of Menkaure, the penultimate king of the glorious Fourth Dynasty.

magnificent structures at Giza, just outside modern-day Cairo and not far from the early royal cemetery site of Saqqara. The pyramid of Khufu, rising 481 feet above ground, is the largest stone structure in the world, and its corners are almost perfectly aligned to due north, west, south, and east. Khafra's pyramid, though smaller, is even more alluring because it retains some of its original limestone casing and because it enjoys the protective presence of the sphinx. Surrounding these royal tombs were those of high officials, almost all members of the royal family. The enormous amount of labor involved in constructing these monuments provides another measure of the degree of centralization and the surpluses in Egyptian society at this time. The manpower came from peasants and workers who labored for the state at certain times of year, slaves brought from Nubia, and captured Mediterranean peoples.

Through their majesty and architectural complexity, the Giza pyramids reflect the peak of Old Kingdom culture and the remarkable feats that its bureaucracy could accomplish. Construction of these monuments entailed the back-breaking work of quarrying the massive stones (some weighed over two tons), digging a canal so barges could bring them from the Nile to the base of the Giza plateau, building a harbor there, and then constructing sturdy brick ramps that could withstand the stones' weight as workers hauled them ever higher along the pyramids' faces. Most likely a permanent work force of up to 21,000 laborers endured 10-hour workdays, 300 days per year, for approximately 14 years just to complete the great pyramid of Khufu.

RELIGION

Religion stood at the center of this ancient world, so all aspects of the culture reflected spiritual expression. Egyptians understood their world as inhabited by three groups: gods, kings, and the rest of humanity. Official records only showed representations of gods and kings. Yet the people did not confuse their kings with gods—at least during the kings' lifetimes. Mortality was the bar between rulers and deities; after death, kings joined the gods whom they had represented while alive.

CULTS OF THE GODS   As in Mesopotamia, every region in Egypt had its resident god. The fate of each deity found expression in the history of its region. Some gods, such as Amun (believed to be physically present in Thebes, the political center of Upper Egypt), transcended regional status because of the importance of their hometown. Over the centuries the Egyptian gods evolved, combining often-contradictory aspects into single deities represented by symbols: animals and human figures that often had animal as well as divine attributes. They included Horus, the hawk god; Osiris, the god of regeneration and the underworld; Hathor, the goddess of childbirth and love; Ra, the sun god; and Amun, a creator considered to be the hidden god.

Official religious practices took place in the main temples, the heart of ceremonial events. The king and his agents cared for the gods in their temples, giving them respect, adoration, and thanks. In return the gods, embodied

Egyptian Gods. Osiris (*top left*) is the dying god who rules over the netherworld. Most frequently he is depicted as a mummy wearing a white crown with plumes and holding the scepter across his chest. The god Horus (*top right and bottom*), who was also rendered as Ra-Horakhty, is the falcon-headed Egyptian sky god. Horus is the earliest state god of Egypt and is always closely associated with the king. Horus is a member of the nine deities of Heliopolis and is the son of Osiris and Isis.

in sculptured images, maintained order and nurtured the king and—through him—all humanity. In this contractual relationship, the gods were passive and serene while the kings were active, a difference that reflected their unequal relationship. The practice of religious rituals and communication with the gods formed the cult, whose constant and correct performance was the foundation of Egyptian religion. Its goal was to preserve cosmic order fundamental to creation and prosperity.

One of the most enduring cults was that of the goddess Isis, who represented ideals of sisterhood and motherhood. According to Egyptian mythology, Isis, the wife of the murdered and dismembered Osiris, commanded her son, Horus, to reassemble all of the parts of Osiris so that he might reclaim his rightful place as king of Egypt, taken from him by his assassin, his evil brother Seth. Osiris was seen as the god of rebirth, while Isis was renowned for her medicinal skills and knowledge of magic. For millennia her principal place of worship was a magnificent temple on the island of Philae. Well after the Greeks and Romans had conquered Egypt, the people continued to pay homage to Isis at her Philae temple.

THE PRIESTHOOD The responsibility for upholding cults fell to the king. However, the task of upholding the cult, regulating rituals according to a cosmic calendar, and mediating among gods, kings, and society fell to one specialist class: the priesthood. Creating this class required elaborate rules for selecting and training the priests to project the organized power of spiritual authority. The fact that only the priests could enter the temple's inner sanctum demonstrated their exalted status. The god, embodied in the cult statue, left the temple only at great festivals. Even then the divine image remained hidden in a portable shrine. This arrangement ensured that priests monopolized communication between spiritual powers and their subjects—and that Egyptians understood their own subservience to the priesthood.

Although the priesthood helped unify the Egyptians and focused their attention on the central role of temple life, unofficial religion was equally important. Ordinary ancient Egyptians matched their elite rulers in faithfulness to the gods, but their distance from temple life caused them to find different ways to fulfill their religious needs and duties. Thus they visited local shrines, just as those of higher status visited the temples. There they prayed, made requests, and left offerings to the gods.

MAGICAL POWERS Magic had a special importance for commoners, who believed that amulets (ornaments worn to bring good fortune and to protect against evil forces) held extraordinary powers—for example, preventing illness and guaranteeing safe childbirth. To deal with profound questions, commoners looked to omens and divination (a practice that

residents of Mesopotamia and ancient China also used to predict and control future events). Like the elites, commoners attributed supernatural powers to animals. Chosen animals received special treatment in life and after death: for example, the Egyptians adored cats, whom they kept as pets and whose image they used to represent certain deities. Apis bulls, sacred to the god Ptah, merited special cemeteries and mourning rituals. Ibises, dogs, jackals, baboons, lizards, fish, snakes, crocodiles, and other beasts associated with deities enjoyed similar privileges.

WRITING AND SCRIBES

Egypt, like Mesopotamia, was a scribal culture. Egyptians often said that peasants toiled so that scribes could live in comfort; in other words, literacy sharpened the divisions between rural and urban worlds. By the middle of the third millennium BCE, literacy was well established among small circles of experts in Egypt and Mesopotamia. The fact that few individuals were literate heightened the scribes' social status. Although in both cultures writing emerged in response to economic needs, people soon grasped its utility for commemorative and religious purposes. As soon as literacy took hold, Mesopotamians and Egyptians were drafting historical records and literary compositions.

Both the early Mesopotamian and Egyptian scripts were complex. In fact, one feature of all writing systems is that over time they became simpler and more efficient at representing the full range of spoken utterances. Only when the first alphabet appeared (in Southwest Asia, to record Aramaic around 1500 BCE) did the potential for wider literacy surface. To judge from remaining records, it seems that more Egyptians than Mesopotamians were literate. Most high-ranking Egyptians were also trained as scribes working in the king's court, the army, or the priesthood. Some kings and members of the royal family learned to write as well.

Egyptians used two basic forms of writing throughout antiquity. *Hieroglyphs* (from the Greek "sacred carving") served in temple, royal, or divine contexts. First Dynasty tombs yield records in a cursive script written with ink on papyrus, pottery, or other absorbent media. This *demotic writing* (from the Greek *demotika*, meaning "popular" or "in common use") was more common. Used for record keeping, it also found uses in letters and works of literature—including narrative fiction, manuals of instruction and philosophy, cult and religious hymns, love poems, medical and mathematical texts, collections of rituals, and mortuary books.

Becoming literate involved taking lessons from scribes, and these skills clustered in extended families. Most students started training when they were young, before entering the bureaucracy. After mastering the copying of standard texts in demotic cursive or hieroglyphs, students moved on to literary

Egyptian Hieroglyphs and "Cursive Script." The Egyptians wrote in two distinctive types of scripts. The more formal is hieroglyphs, which is based on pictorial images that carry values of either ideas (idiograms) or sounds (phonemes). All royal and funerary inscriptions, such as this funerary relief from the Old Kingdom, are rendered in hieroglyphic script. Daily documents, accountings, literary texts, and the like were most often written in a cursive script called demotic, which was written with ink on papyrus. The form of the cursive signs is based on the hieroglyphs but is more abstract and can be formed more quickly.

works. The upper classes prized the ability to read and write, regarding it as proof of high intellectual achievement. When they died, they had their student textbooks placed alongside their corpses as evidence of their talents. The literati produced texts mainly in temples, where these works were also preserved. Writing in hieroglyphs and transmitting texts continued without break in ancient Egypt for almost 3,000 years.

THE PROSPERITY OF EGYPT

The agrarian surpluses, urbanization, elaborate belief systems, population growth, and splendor that characterized Mesopotamian, Harappan, and Egyptian societies led to heightened standards of living and rising populations. Under pharaonic rule, Egypt enjoyed spectacular prosperity. Its population grew at an unprecedented rate, swelling from 350,000 in 4000 BCE to 1 million in 2500 BCE and nearly 5 million by 1500 BCE.

The state's success depended on administering resources skillfully, especially agricultural production and labor. Everyone, from the most powerful elite to the workers in the field, was part of the system. In principle, no one possessed private property; in practice, Egyptians treated land and tools as their own—but submitted to the intrusions of the state. No one challenged the state's control, especially over taxation, prices, and the distribution of goods. Such control required a large bureaucracy that maintained records, taxed the population,

appeased the gods, organized a strong military, and aided local officials in regulating the Nile's floodwaters.

LATER DYNASTIES AND THEIR DEMISE

As the Old Kingdom expanded without a uniting or dominating city like those of Mesopotamia or Harappa, the Egyptian state became more dispersed and the dynasties began to look increasingly outward. Expansion and decentralization eventually exposed the dynasties' weaknesses. The shakeup resulted not from external invasion (as in the Indus Valley) or bickering between rival city-states (as in Mesopotamia), but from feuding among elite political factions. In addition, an extended drought strained Egypt's extensive irrigation system, which could no longer water the lands that fed the region's million inhabitants. Imagery of great suffering filled the royal tombs' walls. The long reign of Pepy II (2278–2184 BCE) marked the end of the Old Kingdom. Upon his death, royal power collapsed. (See Primary Source: The Admonitions of Ipuwer.) For the next hundred years, rivals jostled for the throne. Local magnates assumed hereditary control of the government in the provinces and treated lands previously controlled by the royal family as their personal property. And local leaders plunged into bloody regional struggles to keep the irrigation works functioning for their own communities. This so-called First Intermediate Period lasted roughly from 2181 to 2055 BCE until the century-long drought ended.

Primary Source

THE ADMONITIONS OF IPUWER

In order to maintain power during a period of increasing drought, Pepy II (r. 2278–2184 BCE) gave many advantages and tax exemptions to provincial nobles. At the end of his long reign, no successors were capable of maintaining centralized power. The collapse of the central state was traumatic, and Egyptian society fell into chaos. A number of poignant texts written by prophets and wise men captured this situation. One of the most moving was the text known as the Ipuwer Papyrus, written by an Egyptian sage.

Behold, the fire has gone up on high, and its burning goes forth against the enemies of the land.

Behold, things have been done which have not happened for a long time past; the king has been deposed by the rabble.

Behold, he who was buried as a falcon [is devoid] of biers, and what the pyramid concealed has become empty.

Behold, it has befallen that the land has been deprived of the kingship by a few lawless men.

Behold, men have fallen into rebellion against the Uraeus, the [. . .] of Re, even she who makes the Two Lands content.

Behold, the secret of the land whose limits were unknown is divulged, and the Residence is thrown down in a moment.

Behold, Egypt is fallen to pouring of water, and he who poured water on the ground has carried off the strong man in misery.

Behold, the Serpent is taken from its hole, and the secrets of the Kings of Upper and Lower Egypt are divulged.

Behold, the Residence is afraid because of want, and [men go about] unopposed to stir up strife.

Behold, the land has knotted itself up with confederacies, and the coward takes the brave man's property.

Behold, the Serpent [. . .] the dead: he who could not make a sarcophagus for himself is now the possessor of a tomb.

Behold, the possessors of tombs are ejected on to the high ground, while he who could not make a coffin for himself is now [the possessor] of a treasury.

Behold, this has happened [to] men; he who could not build a room for himself is now a possessor of walls.

Behold, the magistrates of the land are driven out throughout the land: [. . .] are driven out from the palaces.

Behold, noble ladies are now on rafts, and magnates are in the labor establishment, while he who could not sleep even on walls is now the possessor of a bed.

Behold, the possessor of wealth now spends the night thirsty, while he who once begged his dregs for himself is now the possessor of overflowing bowls.

Behold, the possessors of robes are now in rags, while he who could not weave for himself is now a possessor of fine linen.

Behold, he who could not build a boat for himself is now the possessor of a fleet; their erstwhile owner looks at them, but they are not his.

Behold, he who had no shade is now the possessor of shade, while the erstwhile possessors of shade are now in the full blast of the storm.

Behold, he who was ignorant of the lyre is now the possessor of a harp, while he who never sang for himself now vaunts the Songstress-goddess.

➤ *In this reading, the "Residence" is the palace and the "Two Lands" are Upper and Lower Egypt. Who do you think "he who was buried as a falcon" is?*

➤ *What were the effects of the collapse of Egypt's Old Kingdom?*

➤ *How can we use such a document as "The Admonitions of Ipuwer" to understand conditions in Egypt at this time?*

SOURCE: James B. Pritchard, ed., "The Admonitions of Ipuwer" from *Ancient Near Eastern Texts Relating to the Old Testament,* Third Edition with Supplement. Copyright © 1950, 1955, 1969, renewed 1978 by Princeton University Press. Reprinted by permission of Princeton University Press.

THE YELLOW AND YANGZI RIVER BASINS: EAST ASIA

> → *What hallmarks of urban life emerged in China during this period?*

Like the Mesopotamians and Egyptians, East Asian peoples clustered in river basins. Their settlements along the Yellow River in the north and the Yangzi River in the south became the foundation of the future Chinese state. By 5000 BCE, both millet in the north and rice in the south were under widespread cultivation.

Yet in the following three millennia (when Mesopotamia, Egypt, and the Indus Valley were creating complex, city-based cultures) the Chinese moved slowly. China's great riverine cultures did not arise until the second millennium BCE. (See Map 2-6.) Like the other regions' waterways, the Yellow and Yangzi rivers had annual floods and extensive floodplains suitable for producing high agricultural yields and supporting dense populations. In China, however, the evolution of hydraulic works, big cities, priestly and bureaucratic classes, and a new writing system took longer.

Living conditions and the environment played a key role in ancient Chinese society, just as they did in the riverine cultures of Mesopotamia, Harappa, and Egypt. In the river basins of China, abundant food and the fact that communities were widely dispersed encouraged the development of localized agrarian cultures. Complex cities would come later. Also contributing to their different development were a lack of easily domesticated animals and plants and an abundance of geographic barriers. Geography isolated China, for the Himalayan Mountains and the Taklamakan and Gobi deserts prevented large-scale migrations between East Asia and central Asia and hindered the diffusion of cultural breakthroughs occurring elsewhere in Afro-Eurasia.

FROM YANGSHAO TO LONGSHAN CULTURE

China's classical histories place the beginnings of Chinese culture at the Xia dynasty, dating from 2200 BCE. Archaeological studies of riverine environments in East Asia tell a different story. Whether or not the Xia existed as a historical dynasty, archaeological evidence suggests our study of the Yellow River basin and Yangzi delta should begin earlier—in the two millennia from 4000 to 2000 BCE.

China was never completely free of outside influences. Unlike the Americas, East Asia was not separated from the rest of Afro-Eurasia by great oceans. Some travelers did arrive via the ocean, but more came via the Mongolian steppe, through which nomads introduced important technologies such as metalworks. Nomads were drawn to the agricultural settlements (as they were in Mesopotamia), and they brought innovations, bronze (an alloy of copper and tin), and other goods from afar. Through trade and migration, nomadic cultures and technologies filtered from the steppes to settled communities on the rivers.

The combination of agrarian settlements and increasing contact with neighbors promoted greater cultural complexity. The evidence includes breakthroughs in communication. Although the Chinese did not create a graphic writing system until the middle of the second millennium BCE, archaeologists have found preliterate signs and marks on pottery at Jiahu, on the Yellow River. These date as early as the seventh millennium BCE—long before similar signs appeared in Mesopotamia and Egypt.

Markings on red pottery, found near the village of Yangshao along the Yellow River in northwestern China, are another pioneering system of signs and symbols from as early as 5000 BCE. Archaeologists have also discovered analogous signs on early pottery in southern China. A complex society that required writing (such as that of the Sumerians) did not develop until much later. Nevertheless, shamans in the emerging villages of the fourth and third millennia BCE may have used signs in performing rituals, music, and healing, as well as in divination.

China's early riverine societies produced stone and pottery storage vessels that reflected increasingly urban settlements. Near the village of Longshan in Shandong province on the North China plain, for example, archaeologists discovered

Yangshao Bowl with Dancing Figures, c. 5000–1700 BCE. The Yangshao, also referred to as the "painted pottery" culture, produced gray or red pottery painted with black geometric designs and occasionally with pictures of fish or human faces and figures. Because the potter's wheel was unknown at the time, the vessels were probably fashioned with strips of clay.

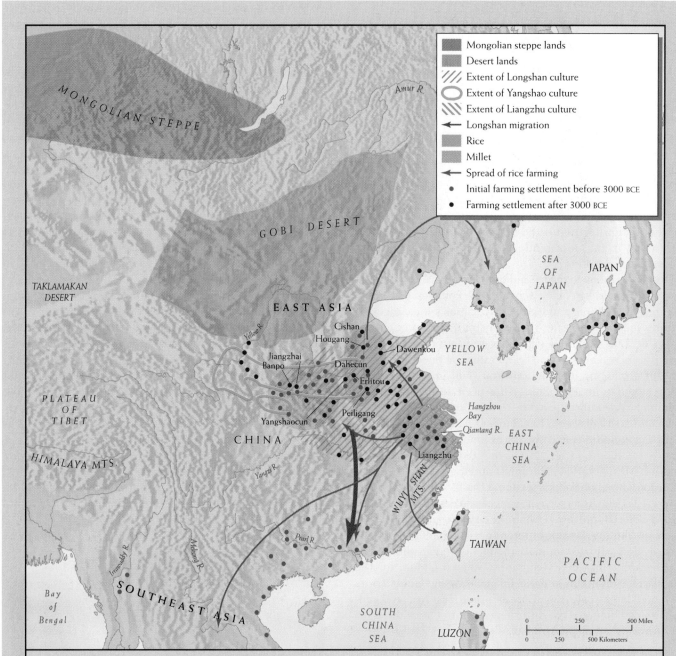

Map Legend:
- Mongolian steppe lands
- Desert lands
- Extent of Longshan culture
- Extent of Yangshao culture
- Extent of Liangzhu culture
- Longshan migration
- Rice
- Millet
- Spread of rice farming
- Initial farming settlement before 3000 BCE
- Farming settlement after 3000 BCE

MAP 2-6   RIVERINE PEOPLES IN EAST ASIA, 5000–2000 BCE

Complex agricultural societies emerged in East Asia during the third millennium BCE. What were the regional cultures that flourished here during this time? What are the major geographic differences between the northern and southern regions of China in this period? Based on geographic differences among the areas, how were these cultures different, and how were they similar?

polished black pottery and a complete town enclosure of compacted earth. Such finds contrast with the simpler artifacts of the Yangshao sites. Furthermore, Longshan residents burned deer scapulas (shoulder blades) so that diviners could interpret the cracks that formed. This ritual probably gave rise to the inscribed oracle bones introduced later during the Shang dynasty (1600–1045 BCE), which diviners consulted for advice from ancestors when making important decisions.

Longshan Beaker, c. 2500 BCE. Longshan has been called the "black pottery" culture, and its exquisite black pottery was not painted but rather decorated with rings, either raised or grooved. Longshan culture was more advanced than the Yangshao culture, and its distinctive pottery was likely formed on a potter's wheel.

The Longshan people likely migrated in waves from the peripheries of East Asia to the eastern China seashore. Their achievements, compared to those of the Yangshao, suggest marked development between 5000 and 2000 BCE. Several independent regional cultures in northern and southern China began to produce similar pottery and tools and to plant the same crops, probably reflecting contact. They did not yet produce city-states, but agriculture and small settlements flourished in the increasingly populated Yellow River valley.

Some of the hallmarks of early urban life are evident. For example, the Longshan buried their dead in cemeteries outside their villages. Of several thousand graves uncovered in southern Shanxi province, the largest ones contain ritual pottery vessels, wooden musical instruments, copper bells, and painted murals. Shamans performed rituals using jade axes. Jade quarrying in particular indicated technical sophistication, as skilled craftworkers incised jade tablets with powerful expressions of ritual and military authority. The recent discovery of a Longshan household whose members were scalped demonstrates the danger of organized violence. Attackers filled the water wells with five layers of human skeletons, some decapitated. Clearly, the villages' defensive walls were essential.

As communities became more centralized, contact between regions increased. Links between northern and southern China arose when Longshan peoples began to migrate along the East Asian coast to Taiwan and the Pearl River delta in the far south. Similarities in artifacts found along the coast and at Longshan sites in northern China, such as the form and decoration of pottery and jade items, also point to a shared sphere of culture and trade. (See Primary Source: Archaeological Evidence for Longshan Culture.)

Archaeologists also have found evidence of short-lived political organizations. Although they were nothing like the dynastic systems in Egypt, Mesopotamia, and the Indus Valley, they were wealthy—if localized—polities. They constituted what scholars call the era of Ten Thousand States (*Wan'guo*). One of them, the Liangzhu, has drawn particular interest for its remarkable jade objects.

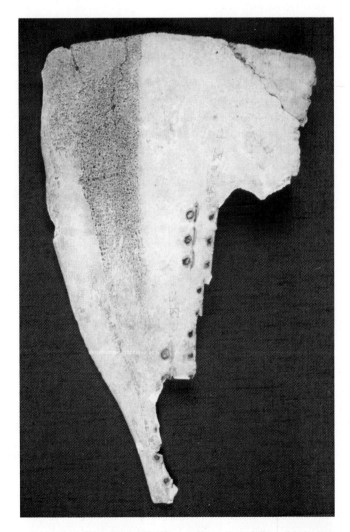

Oracle Bone Artifact. The Shang dynasty use of oracle bones (such as the one above) may have grown out of the Longshan people's ritual of interpreting the cracks in burned deer scapulas.

ARCHAEOLOGICAL EVIDENCE FOR LONGSHAN CULTURE

Over the course of a millennium, multiple cultures with strong similarities emerged in north and northwest China. Some scholars argue that a single Longshan culture grew out of these close-knit groups. While these were not fully integrated spheres interacting with one another, the changes that Longshan represented were remarkable.

Let us take a quick look at the kind of innovations that sprouted everywhere and that, because of the similarities of style, must be interrelated:

1. Archaeologically acceptable evidence of copper objects, mostly trinkets and small tools of no agricultural value, has been unearthed in Shantung, western Honan, southern Shansi, and Ch'i-chia from archaeological horizons comparable in age. The finds do not suffice to point to a major metal industry as yet, but in light of what happened later on one must regard the Lung-shan metallurgy as worthy of note. . . .

2. Industrially much more important is the extremely widespread use of potter's wheels for the manufacture of ceramics. There was tremendous variation in the pottery wares of the various Lung-shan Cultures, but the overwhelming change from red to gray and the general decline of painted decoration must have been the result of a conscious choice on the part of the potters, who, armed with improved kilns and the wheel, must have represented a specialized profession in the Lung-shan society.

3. The stamped-earth construction technology and the construction of town walls using that technology are separate issues, but the town walls in Shantung, east Honan, north Honan, and west Honan indicate both the transmission of a technology and the rise of the necessity for defensive public works.

4. Related to the rise of defensive ramparts is the archaeological evidence of institutionalized violence. This takes two forms—evidence of raids or wars, such as the Chien-kou-ts'un finds of skulls and bodies in the water well; and burials of possible ritual victims relating to the construction of chiefly or royal monuments.

5. There are several manifestations of rituals, especially ones closely tied to persons of high political status. The first is the role of some animals and birds in ritual art, such as those found or identified recently in Liang-ch'eng, Shantung; the Liang-chu sites, in Kiangsu and Chekiang; and T'ao-ssu, Shansi.

6. The *ts'ung* tube, especially if associated with animals and birds, is a very distinctive ritual object manifesting a unique cosmology. Its discovery in Liang-chu on the coast and T'ao-ssu in the interior cannot be accidental; it indicates without question an interregional transmission of cosmology or even a spherewide substratum featuring that cosmology. If we include jade rings (*pi*) in this cosmological bag, the Ch'i-chia Culture also becomes involved.

7. The virtually universal occurrence of scapulimancy among the Lung-shan Cultures is another manifestation of the spherewide communication or substratum of cosmology.

8. The archaeological evidence for violence and for ritual on an institutional basis almost inevitably means a society featuring sharp political and economic divisions, and that is exactly what we find in the mortuary remains of many of the Lung-shan Cultures. We have already seen archaeological indications of social ranking in the mortuary remains of the Neolithic sites of the fifth and fourth centuries B.C. . . . These trends accelerated and further intensified in the Lung-shan cemeteries. Furthermore, as the Ch'eng-tzu (Shantung) and T'ao-ssu (Shansi) cemeteries show, the economic and political polarization appears to have taken place within the framework of the unilinear clans and lineages.

All of the above happenings are plainly indicated by archaeological evidence, but they do not point to a single Lung-shan Culture. Instead, they indicate a series of interrelated changes in culture and society that took place within each of the regional cultures in the Chinese interaction sphere. From the point of view of each of the regional sequences, both the external interaction network and internal changes during a period of two thousand years were essential for its readiness, toward the end of the third millennium B.C., to step over the next threshold into the state society, urbanism, and civilization.

→ *What were the key features of Longshan culture?*

→ *What does* scapulimancy *mean, and how widespread was its use?*

→ *What does the evidence of violence reveal about Longshan society?*

SOURCE: Kwang-chih Chang, *The Archaeology of Ancient China*, 4th ed. (New Haven: Yale University Press, 1986), pp. 287–88.

LIANGZHU CULTURE

The Liangzhu people were sophisticated agriculturalists, growing rice and fruits along the Qiantang River where it flows into Hangzhou Bay. Among their implements were flat and perforated spades, as well as rectangular and curved sickle-like knives with holes. They raised domesticated water buffalo, pigs, dogs, and sheep. Archaeologists have discovered the remains of net sinkers, wooden floats, and wooden paddles, which demonstrate a familiarity with watercraft and fishing. Other wood artifacts are pieces of boats, house foundations, tools, and utensils. Stone and bone artifacts were sophisticated as well. Liangzhu artisans produced a black pottery from soft paste thrown on a wheel, and like the Longshan they created ritual objects from several varieties of jade. They mined it in the Great Lake (Taihu) area of the Yangzi delta, close to the Liangzhu tombs. Animal masks and bird designs adorned many pieces, revealing a shared cosmology that informed the rituals of the Liangzhu elite.

In the late third millennium BCE, a long drought hit China (as it did Egypt, Mesopotamia, and India). Although the climate change limited progress and forced migrations to more dependable habitats, the Chinese recovered early in the second millennium BCE. Now they created elaborate agrarian systems along the Yellow and Yangzi rivers that were similar to earlier irrigation systems along the Euphrates, Indus, and Nile. Extensive trading networks and a stratified social hierarchy emerged; like the other river basin complexes of Asia and North Africa, China became a centralized polity. Here, too, a powerful monarchy eventually united the independent communities. But what developed in China was a social and political system that emphasized an idealized past and a tradition represented by sage-kings. In this and other ways, China diverged from the rest of Afro-Eurasia.

LIFE ON THE MARGINS OF AFRO-EURASIA

→ *How did the growth of urban societies in river basins affect people living in the Aegean region, Anatolia, and Europe?*

Those dwelling in river basins and established cities with hierarchies, bureaucracies, and strong militaries were inclined to see outsiders—particularly nomads—as "barbarians." Actually, the city people's imagery and narratives that depict nomads as uncivilized are not objective, because they were more concerned with promoting themselves than with portraying the nomads accurately. The nomads surely would not have recognized themselves as savages lacking culture, faith, and organized life. In fact, they had frequent contact with the urbanites and became skilled users of their technologies. (See Map 2-7.) Despite being less urbanized and stratified than city dwellers, they fashioned institutions and belief systems that were as durable as those of the metropolitan centers.

The people living outside the river basins had a distinctive warrior-based ethos, such that the top tiers of the social ladder held chiefs and military men instead of priests and scribes. This feature was especially evident in Europe and Anatolia, where weaponry rather than writing, palisades (defensive walls and turrets) rather than palaces, and conquest rather than commerce dominated everyday life. Here, too, the inhabitants moved beyond stone implements and hunting and gathering, but they remained more egalitarian than riverine folk and did not evolve much beyond small societies led by chiefs.

Liangzhu Jade Axe Blade, c. 3400–2250 BCE. The Liangzhu represented the last new Stone Age culture in the Yangzi River delta. Their culture was highly stratified, and jade, silk, ivory, and lacquer artifacts were found exclusively in elite burial sites.

AEGEAN WORLDS

Contact with Egypt and Mesopotamia affected the Aegean worlds, but it did not transform them. Geography stood in the way of significant urban development on the mountainous islands, on the Anatolian plateau, and in Europe. Even though people from Anatolia, Greece, and the Levant had

MAP 2-7   SETTLEMENTS ON THE MARGINS: THE EASTERN MEDITERRANEAN AND EUROPE, 5000–2000 BCE

Urban societies in Southwest Asia had profound influences on peripheral societies. What three peripheral worlds did the urban societies of Southwest Asia influence? In what ways did the spread of flint and copper tools and weapons transform Aegean and European societies? How did agriculture spread from Southwest Asia to these worlds?

populated the Aegean islands in the sixth millennium BCE, their small villages endured for 2,000 years before becoming more complex.

On mainland Greece and on the Cycladic islands in the Aegean, fortified settlements housed local rulers who controlled a small area of agriculturally productive countryside. Metallurgy developed in both Crete and the Cyclades. There

is evidence of more formal administration and organizations in some communities by 2500 BCE, but the norm was scattered settlements separated by natural obstacles. Consider rocky and mountainous Crete, the largest island in the Aegean, where seafaring peoples occupied settlements sprinkled throughout its rugged interior. By the early third millennium BCE, Crete had made occasional contact with Egypt and the coastal towns of the Levant, encountering new ideas, technologies, and materials as foreigners arrived on its shores. People coming by ship from the coasts of Anatolia and the Levant, as well as from Egypt, traded stone vessels and other luxury objects for the island's abundant copper.

Lacking a rich agrarian base, most communities remained small at fewer than 100 inhabitants, and only a few grew over time. By the middle of the third millennium BCE, a more complex society was emerging in eastern Crete. During the second millennium BCE, Knossos, located in a rich agricultural plain, became the primary palace-town in an extended network of palaces. Evidence from burial sites suggests that some households belonged to an elite class, for they took gold jewelry and other exotic objects with them to their graves. (For a discussion of objects buried with the dead in several cultures, see Global Connections & Disconnections: Ritual Objects in the Iranian Plateau, China, and Egypt.) Aegean elites did not reject the niceties of cultured life, but they knew that their power rested as much on their rugged landscape's resources as on self-defense and trade with others.

ANATOLIA

The highland plateau of Anatolia shows clear evidence of regional cultures focused on the control of trade routes and mining outposts. This area had been populated almost from the time that humans walked out of Africa, and the pace of change was slow because people clung to their village ways and stone tools. True cities did not develop here until the third millennium BCE, and even then they were not the sprawling population centers typical of the Mesopotamian plain. Instead, small communities emerged around fortified citadels housing local rulers who competed with one another. Two impressively fortified centers were Horoz Tepe and Alaça Hüyük, which have yielded more than a dozen graves—apparently royal—full of gold jewelry, ceremonial standards, and elaborate weapons.

Another important site in Anatolia was Troy to the far west. It is legendary as the place of the famous war launched by the Greeks (the Achaeans) and recounted by Homer in the *Iliad*. Troy developed around 3000 BCE on the Mediterranean coast in a fertile plain. In the 1870s the German archaeologist Heinrich Schliemann identified Troy level I as a third-millennium BCE fortified settlement with monumental stone gateways and stone-paved ramps. The extremely rich Troy level II had five large buildings called *megarons*, forerunners of the classic Greek temple. Here, Schliemann found gold and silver objects, vessels, jewelry, and other artifacts. Many are similar to the ones found in graves at Alaça Hüyük. Moreover, since they parallel finds on Crete and on the Greek mainland, they indicate that Troy participated in the trading system linking the Aegean and Southwest Asian worlds. At the same time, Troy faced predatory neighbors and pirates who attacked from the sea—an observation that explains its impressive fortifications.

EUROPE: THE WESTERN FRONTIER

At the western reaches of the Eurasian landmass was a region featuring more temperate and also more frigid climates with smaller population densities. Its peoples—forerunners of present-day Europeans—began to make objects out of metal, formed permanent settlements, and started to create complex societies. Here, too, hierarchies replaced egalitarian ways. Yet, as in the Aegean worlds, population density and social complexity had limits.

More than in the Mediterranean or Anatolia, warfare dominated social development in Europe. Two contributing factors were the persistent fragmentation of the region's peoples and the type of agrarian development they pursued. The introduction of the plow and the clearing of woodlands expanded agriculture. Agrarian development here was not the result of city-states or dynasties organizing irrigation and settlement (as in Mesopotamia and Egypt), but rather the result of households and communities wielding axes for defense and for cutting down trees. Compared to the riverine societies, Europe was a wild frontier where violent conflicts over resources were common.

The gradual expansion of agricultural communities eventually reached a critical point. The growth of flint mining to an industrial level (as evident in the thousand shafts sunk at Krzemionki in Poland and the flint-mining complex of Grimes Graves in England) indicates a social and economic transformation. Most important, mining output slashed the cost and increased the availability of raw materials needed to make tools for clearing forested lands and tilling them into arable fields. As agricultural communities proliferated, some became villages that dominated their regions. But nowhere did these folk create large cities and corresponding states.

By 4000 BCE the more developed agrarian peoples had coalesced into large communities, constructing impressive monuments that remain visible today. In western Europe, large ceremonial centers shared the same model: enormous shaped stones, some weighing several tons each, set in common patterns—in alleyways, troughs, or circles—known as *megalithic* ("great stone") constructions. These daunting projects required cooperative planning and work. In the British Isles, where such developments occurred later, the famous megalithic complexes at Avebury and Stonehenge probably reached their highest stages of development just before 2000 BCE. No matter how forbidding the ecology of Europe was in this period, in the centuries after 3000 BCE, culminating in new developments around 2000 BCE, the whole of the northern European plain came to share a common

Global Connections & Disconnections

RITUAL OBJECTS IN THE IRANIAN PLATEAU, CHINA, AND EGYPT

An important aspect of religious practice is the interaction between the worldly and the divine, between the living and the dead. Thousands of years ago ritual objects, such as amulets, statues, or carved objects representing the gods, were tangible representations of the connection between the earthly and the sacred. Other objects carrying images of important myths and stories were useful in ceremonies marking major events, such as birth or death. They may also have acted as more permanent signs of the divine, in shrines or temples. In both cases, ritual objects represented the sacred in everyday life.

IRANIAN PLATEAU Ancient humans deposited symbolic objects with the dead to ease the journey to the world beyond and to provide necessities in the afterlife. Excavated graves in the Jiroft region of south-central Iran contain thousands of symbolic objects as well as utilitarian vessels. Most numerous are cylindrical vessels made of soft green stone (locally available steatite or chlorite) carved with elaborate designs that carried symbolic meaning. Also carved from the green stone and featuring similar designs are furniture inlays and rectangular slabs with handles.

While many of the designs show a repeating grid pattern or curls or scorpions, some represent gods in human form wearing bull horns on their heads as a sign of divinity. A common motif portrays a bird of prey grasping a snake in its talons; a leopard confronts the snake. Both the body of the bird and the snake have holes for holding multihued stones, making the overall pattern colorful and lively. The confrontation of the snake and the leopard represents the struggle between forces of nature. Neither wins; rather, they are always in equilibrium.

Vessels from Jiroft have come to light in the Persian Gulf and in Mesopotamia. Some historians argue that they were objects of trade, just like semiprecious lapis lazuli and carnelian were. However, the centrality of these

Jiroft Vase. Persians looked to the distant past for universal imagery. Bull icons appear on a chlorite vase from near Jiroft, where such items were crafted in about 2500 BCE.

vessels to the home society's funerary customs suggests that they were personal effects carried by traders and craftsmen who traveled to the large cities of the distant river valleys. There is no evidence that the objects were exchanged in trade.

CHINA   The Liangzhu people of ancient China crafted ritual objects from several varieties of jade that they mined in the Yangzi delta. The Liangzhu decorated many of these pieces with animal masks or bird designs. Especially important were circular jade objects called *bi* discs (found in tomb sites) and square *cong* tubes. The *cong* jades, used in divination practices, were round in their hollow interior. The rounded portion represented heaven and the square portion the earth; the jade tubes thus signified interaction between heaven and earth, the dead and the living. Both heaven and earth were penetrated by a central axis running through the jade's shaft, which symbolized the sacred mountains dividing the land of the living from the place of the dead.

Jade was the most important precious substance in East Asia. Associated with qualities of goodness, purity, luck, and virtue, it was carved into ceremonial knives, blade handles, religious objects, and elaborate jewelry. Because jade is extremely hard, its intricate carving required much time and great skill. Smaller objects, such as blades and amulets, could also serve a ceremonial purpose. Jade objects used in burials might sit in the mouths and on the eyes of the deceased, or jade ornaments, jewelry, and ritual objects might accompany them. Men and women had different ornaments, including necklaces and headdresses, swords and seals.

EGYPT   In ancient Egypt, precious stones and metals shaped into jewelry and ritual objects were important, especially in burying the dead. Archaeologists often find amulets and funerary jewelry placed in specific positions on the bodies of mummies. The system of preparing a body for mummification was so specialized that it required special jewelry distinct from what ordinary people wore during their lives. Scholars think that funerary amulets served to protect mummies from suffering in the afterlife. The Egyptian *Book of the Dead* contains

Egyptian Funeral Amulet. This winged scarab is a symbol of rebirth and would have been placed in the wrapping of the mummy along with other amulets to assure the successful passage of the deceased into the afterlife. The Egyptians understood the dung-beetle that pushes a ball of dung as Khepri, the divine protector of the daily solar cycle.

drawings, paintings, and spells explaining how to use certain amulets.

Nearly every mummy that archaeologists have discovered has had one such amulet, made of stone, glass, or wood in the shape of a pillar with cross bars at its top, perhaps mimicking the form of a tree (see Carol Andrews, *Egyptian Mummies*). Other types of amulets resemble parts of the body, particularly an arm or a foot, indicating that the person had suffered in that body part or that a limb was missing, and the amulet could serve as its substitute. In either case, embalmers apparently desired to make the deceased person as whole as possible for the journey into the afterlife. Amulets of this sort often complemented the features of the person whom they accompanied.

Whether they expressed religious or social status in this world or fended off evil spirits in the next, ritual objects were key in the practice of religion. Amulets and ritual jewelry personalized the divine, representing a connection to heaven that could belong to an individual. In this way, ritual objects stressed the interconnectedness of worldly and spiritual life.

Stonehenge. This spectacular site, located in the Salisbury Plain in Wiltshire in southwestern England, is one of several such megalithic structures found in the region. Constructed by many generations of builders, the arrangement of the large stone uprights enabled people to determine precise times in the year through the position of the sun. Events such as the spring and autumn equinoxes were connected with agricultural and religious activities.

material culture based on agriculture, the herding of cattle for meat and milk, the use of the plough, and the use of wheeled vehicles and metal tools and weapons, mainly of copper. The most characteristic objects associated with this shared culture are the Corded Ware pots—so-called from the cords used to impress lines on their surfaces (see Map 2-7). The fact that this new economy was found from Ukraine in the east to the Low Countries in the west is evidence of the much improved communications that linked and united previous disparate and widely separated regions.

Increasing communication, exchange, and mobility among the European communities led to increasing wealth but also sparked organized warfare over frontier lands and valuable resources. In an ironic twist, the integration of local communities led to greater friction and produced regional social stratification. The first sign of an emerging warrior culture was the appearance of drinking cups. (See Primary Source: The Male Warrior Burials of Varna and Nett Down.) The violent men who now protected their communities received ceremonial burials complete with their own drinking cups and weapons. Archaeologists have found these warrior burials in a swath of European lands extending from present-day France and Switzerland to present-day central Russia. Because the agricultural communities now were producing surpluses that they could store, residents had to defend their land and resources from encroaching neighbors.

An aggressive culture was taking shape based on violent confrontations between adult males organized in "tribal" groups. War cultures arose in all western European societies,

THE MALE WARRIOR BURIALS OF VARNA AND NETT DOWN

Burials of elite individuals across the region stretching from the Black Sea to the Atlantic reveal precious objects and weapons associated with a competitive warrior culture. At Varna, on the Black Sea coast of Bulgaria, the lifestyle of the "big men" associated with a farming village from around 4000 BCE came to light in 1972 when a farmer driving a tractor uncovered an ancient cemetery. The burials at Varna may represent a powerful and well-connected settlement, since most other contemporary sites do not display such high levels of wealth. The grave of a man who died at about age forty-five (pictured here), large pots used for drinking and storage were found. More striking were the 990 gold objects: most were decorative devices sewn onto his clothing, but others included bracelets on both arms, a necklace, and small gold-handled axe. The weapons buried with him—daggers, axes, and spearheads, and points—were made of flint.

Another burial—from Nett Down in Wiltshire, England, and dating to around 2500 BCE—reveals a less developed culture. In this case, a small tomb cut into the chalk ground and covered with a small mound of earth contained a young male warrior. He was buried with the two most significant objects connected with his life: a bronze dagger and, by his hands, a large bell beaker. No gold or precious metal ornaments accompanied the man, who was clearly part of a poorer society than Varna's. As one scholar has remarked, "the grave neatly encapsulates the ideal male image of drinking and fighting."

→ *Most individual burials contain male bodies. What does this fact tell us about men's roles in these evolving patriarchal societies?*

→ *When we compare these sites to those in Egypt and China, what can we learn about the importance of burying the dead across these societies?*

marked by the universal presence of a new drinking instrument, the "bell beaker"—so named by archaeologists because it resembled an inverted bell. Armed groups carried these cups across Europe, using them to swig beer and mead distilled from grains, honey, herbs, and nuts. As beer drinking spread, many local variations on beer mugs appeared, again illustrating the constant interplay between external communication and local forces.

As new tools and weapons spread across Europe, the region adopted similar cultural practices. The twin pillars of agriculture and metalworking, initially in copper, became the supports of daily life almost everywhere. At the same time, though, a split between Europe's eastern and western flanks occurred: in the millennium following 2500 BCE, warriors in western Europe became more combative in battling for territory and resources.

Warfare had the ironic effect of accentuating the borrowing among the region's competing peoples. After all, the violent struggles and emerging kinship groups fueled a massive demand for weapons, alcohol, and horses. Warrior elites borrowed from Anatolia the technique of combining copper with tin to produce harder-edged weapons made of the alloy bronze. Soon smiths were producing them in bulk—as evidenced by hoards of copper and bronze tools and weapons from the period found in central Europe. Traders used the rivers of central and northern Europe to exchange their prized metal products, creating one of the first commercial networks that covered the landmass.

Constant warfare propelled Europe to become an innovative frontier society. The culture of violence and conflict that now drove a basic agricultural economy had two significant effects: it integrated European kinship-based oral societies in a realm of their own, and it separated them from the Mediterranean societies—an ordered world of palaces, scribes, and well-disciplined commoners.

CONCLUSION

Over the fourth and third millennia BCE, the world's social landscape changed in significant ways. In a few key locations, where giant rivers irrigated fertile lands, complex human cultures began to emerge. These areas experienced all the advantages and difficulties of expanding populations: occupational specialization; social hierarchy; rising standards of living; sophisticated systems of art and science; and centralized production and distribution of food, clothing, and other goods. Ceremonial sites and trading crossroads became cities that developed centralized religious and political systems. As scribes, priests, and rulers labored to keep complex societies together, the differences between country folk and city dwellers sharpened. In effect, urbanization was an example of the many ways in which societies were becoming more complex and stratified. Social distinctions also affected the roles of men and women, as urban families began to differ from kinship groups in the countryside.

Although the riverine cultures shared basic features, each one's evolution followed a distinctive path. Where there was a single river—the Nile or the Indus—the agrarian hinterlands that fed the cities lay along the banks of the mighty waterway. In these areas cities were small; thus the Egyptian and Harappan worlds enjoyed more political stability and less rivalry. In contrast, cities in the immense floodplain of the Tigris and Euphrates needed large hinterlands to sustain their populations. Because of their growing power and need for resources, Mesopotamian cities vied for preeminence, and their competition often became violent. (As we will see in Chapter 3, a similar pattern emerged after 1500 BCE in China, where the Yellow and Yangzi river environments facilitated the rapid expansion of Chinese settlements into cities.)

Cities stood at one end of the spectrum of social complexity. At the other end, in most areas of the world, people still lived in simple, egalitarian societies based on hunting, gathering, and basic agriculture—as in the Americas and sub-Saharan Africa. In between were worlds such as Anatolia, Europe, and large parts of China, where towns emerged and agriculture advanced—but not with the leaps and bounds of the great riverine cultures. Beyond these frontiers, farmers and nomads survived as they had for many centuries. Some of them, as in the Aegean, forged warrior societies. Elsewhere, as in the borderlands between Mesopotamian city-states, people created thriving trading networks.

In spite of these global differences, changes in climate affected everyone and could slow or even reverse development.

Chronology

	5000 BCE	4000 BCE
		3500 BCE Earliest Sumerian cities in southern Mesopotamia appear ✦
SOUTHWEST ASIA AND NORTH AFRICA		
SOUTH ASIA		
EAST ASIA	✦ 5000 BCE Yangshao culture thrives in northwest China along Yellow River 5000–2000 BCE Longshan culture emerges in northeast Yellow River valley 5000–2500 BCE Jomon culture in Japan ✦	
THE EASTERN MEDITERRANEAN AND EUROPE	4000 BCE Megalithic stone constructions begin in western Europe ✦	
THE AMERICAS	3500 BCE Chicama Valley along Pacific Ocean coast in modern-day Peru thrives ✦ 3500 BCE Tehuacán Valley in modern-day Mexico thrives ✦	
SUB-SAHARAN AFRICA	3500 BCE Dense village life by Lake Chad and Niger River, Congo River, and Lake Victoria ✦	
INNER AND CENTRAL EURASIA	3500 BCE Growth and spread of nomadic pastoralism begins ✦	

How—and whether—cultures adapted depended on local circumstances. As the next chapter will show, the human agents of change often came from the fringes of larger settlements and urban areas.

KEY TERMS

alluvium (p. 51)
bronze (p. 45)
city (p. 51)
city-state (p. 52)
cult (p. 53)
palace (p. 53)

river basin (p. 44)
scribes (p. 55)
social hierarchies (p. 52)
temple (p. 52)
territorial state (p. 57)
urban-rural divide (p. 45)

STUDY QUESTIONS

1. Describe how cities in Mesopotamia, the Indus Valley, and Egypt differed from small village communities across the globe. Why did cities emerge in relatively few places between 4000 and 2000 BCE?
2. Define *pastoralism*. Where in Afro-Eurasia did this form of social organization develop and thrive?
3. Identify shared characteristics among urbanites in Mesopotamia, the Indus Valley, and Egypt. What features distinguished each from the others?
4. Compare and contrast city-state structures in Egypt and Mesopotamia. Why was Egypt more politically unified than Mesopotamia?
5. Analyze the influence of long-distance trade on the political and economic development of urban societies in Egypt, Mesopotamia, and the Indus Valley. How did contacts with other people influence each society?
6. Compare and contrast the ways in which early writing emerged in the urban societies between 4000 and 2000 BCE. How did each use this new technology? How common was literacy?
7. Explain how the rise of cities represented a leap forward in complexity in human history. How did urban dwellers shape political, economic, and cultural developments in their region?
8. Explain East Asia's relative physical isolation from other Afro-Eurasian societies during this period. To what extent did this isolation shape social development in this region between 4000 and 2000 BCE?
9. Identify shared characteristics of European, Anatolian, and Aegean settlements between 5000 and 2000 BCE. How did settlements in these regions on the margins differ from urban settlements in river basins?

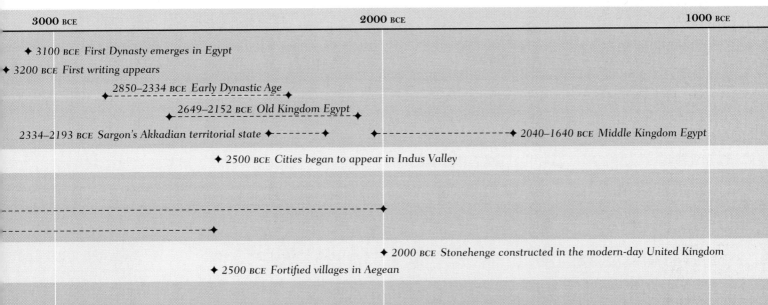

| 3000 BCE | 2000 BCE | 1000 BCE |

◆ 3100 BCE First Dynasty emerges in Egypt
◆ 3200 BCE First writing appears
2850–2334 BCE Early Dynastic Age
2649–2152 BCE Old Kingdom Egypt
2334–2193 BCE Sargon's Akkadian territorial state ◆-------◆   ◆---------------◆ 2040–1640 BCE Middle Kingdom Egypt
◆ 2500 BCE Cities began to appear in Indus Valley
◆ 2000 BCE Stonehenge constructed in the modern-day United Kingdom
◆ 2500 BCE Fortified villages in Aegean

殷代车马坑
编号：(AGM5146)
坑内葬1车、2
马、1人、2000
车发现于孝民屯
东地。

Chariot Pit of the Shang Dynasty
(No: AGM5146)
One chariot, 2
horses and one per-
son were buried in
this pit, which were
discovered and un-
earthed in the east-
ern land of Xiaomi-
otun Village in 2000.

3

Nomads, Territorial States, and Microsocieties, 2000–1200 BCE

Around 2200 BCE, the Old Kingdom of Egypt collapsed. Evidence for its ruin includes a history of numerous ineffective rulers in Memphis, imprecise workmanship on pyramids, and many incomplete funerary and temple structures. Yet the collapse did not occur because of incompetent rulers or a decline in the arts and sciences. The Old Kingdom fell because of radical changes in climate—namely, a powerful warming and drying trend that blanketed Afro-Eurasia between 2200 and 2150. The Mesopotamians and Harappans were as hard hit as the Egyptians. In Egypt the environmental disaster yielded a series of low Niles because the usual monsoon rains did not arrive to feed the river's upper regions, particularly the Blue Nile arising in the mountains of Ethiopia.

Documents from this period reveal widespread suffering and despair. Indeed, people who had enjoyed prosperity and good government for centuries now lived in utter disbelief that the world had been turned upside down and that the wicked triumphed over the virtuous. Consider the following tomb inscription: "All of Egypt was dying of hunger to such a degree that everyone had come to eating his children." Or another: "The tribes of the desert have become Egyptians everywhere. . . . The plunderer is everywhere, and the servant takes what he finds."

Settled societies were not alone in their losses. Herders and pastoral nomads also felt the pinch. As these outsiders pressed upon permanent settlements in search of sustenance, the governing structures in Egypt, Mesopotamia, and the Indus Valley collapsed. The pioneering city-states may have created unprecedented differences between elites and commoners, between urbanites and rural folk, but everyone felt the effects of this disaster.

This chapter focuses on the impact of climate change on the peoples of Afro-Eurasia. At first, the consequences were decisively negative: famines occurred, followed by political and economic turmoil; the old order gave way; river-basin states in Egypt, Mesopotamia, and the Indus Valley collapsed. Herders and pastoral nomads, driven from grazing areas that were drying up, forced their way into the heartlands of these great states in pursuit of better-watered lands. Once there, they challenged the traditional ruling elites. They also brought with them an awesome new military weapon—the horse-drawn chariot, which would dominate warfare for a half a millennium. Yet the nomads' advantage was temporary. Soon the Egyptians, Mesopotamians, Chinese, and many others learned from their conquerors: they assimilated some of their foes into their own societies and drove others away, adopting the invaders' most useful techniques.

We must note that the rise of highly centralized polities does not tell the entire story of this period; thus the chapter also examines worlds apart from the expanding centers of population and politics. The islanders of the Pacific and the Aegean, as well as peoples living in the Americas, did not interact with one another with such intensity—and therefore their political systems evolved differently. In these locales, microsocieties were the norm.

NOMADIC MOVEMENT AND THE EMERGENCE OF TERRITORIAL STATES

> → *How did nomadic groups change the cultural landscape of Afro-Eurasia during the second millennium BCE?*

At the end of the third millennium BCE, drought and food shortages led to the overthrow of ruling elites throughout central and western Afro-Eurasia. Walled cities could not defend their hinterlands. Trade routes lay open to predators, and pillaging became a lucrative enterprise. Clans of pastoral nomads from the Inner Eurasian steppes swept across vast distances on horseback. Later, they threatened settled people in the mighty cities. More immediately threatening were the **transhumant migrants** from the borderlands of the Iranian plateau and the Arabian Desert who advanced on the populated areas, searching for food and resources. Similar migratory patterns occurred in the Indus River valley and the Yellow River valley. (See Map 3-1.)

Environmental changes compelled humans across Afro-Eurasia to adapt or perish. When and where the pastoral

Focus Questions

→ *How did nomadic groups change the cultural landscape of Afro-Eurasia during the second millennium BCE?*

→ *What were the direct and indirect effects of drought on the organization of societies?*

→ *How did Vedic migrations influence South Asia?*

→ *What methods did the Shang state use to maintain its rule?*

→ *How did Austronesian migrations affect the emergence of microsocieties in the South Pacific?*

→ *How did long-distance trade influence the Aegean world?*

→ *Why did polities remain small-scale in Europe?*

→ *How did the environment influence early state systems in the Central Andes?*

NOMADIC MOVEMENT AND THE EMERGENCE OF TERRITORIAL STATES | **87**

→ *How did nomadic groups change the cultural landscape of Afro-Eurasia during the second millennium* BCE?

nomads and transhumant herders managed to adjust to the dry conditions, they prompted the rise of new territorial states from pharaonic Egypt and Mesopotamia to Vedic South Asia and Shang China. Using **chariots** (a two-wheeled horse-drawn vehicle used in warfare and later in processions and races), the horse-mounted nomads introduced technologies that led to new forms of warfare whose spread transformed the Afro-Eurasian world. Moreover, the new rulers' efforts at state building altered society and government so that people could survive and flourish in the changed climate.

NOMADIC AND TRANSHUMANT MIGRATIONS

Desperate for secure water sources and pastures, many transhumant herders and pastoralists migrated onto the highland plateaus bordering the Inner Eurasian steppes. From there, some continued into the more populated river valleys and soon were competing with the farming communities over space and resources. They also streamed in from the western and southern deserts in Southwest Asia in modern-day Turkey.

These migrants settled in the agrarian heartlands of Mesopotamia, the Indus River valley, the highlands of Anatolia, Iran, China, and Europe. After the first wave of newcomers, more migrants arrived by foot or in wagons pulled by draft animals. Some sought temporary work; others settled permanently. They brought horses and new technologies that were useful in warfare; religious practices and languages; and new pressures to feed, house, and clothe an ever-growing population.

HORSES AND CHARIOTS Although the hard-riding pastoral nomads contributed much to settled societies (they

War Chariots. *Bottom left:* A large vase typical of Mycenaean art on the mainland areas of Greece. The regular banding and presentation of scenes reflect a society that is more formally ordered and rigidly hierarchical than that on Minoan Crete. Note the presence of the horse-drawn chariot. Possessing this more elaborate means of transport and warfare characterized the warrior elites of Mycenaean society and linked them to developments over wide expanses of Afro-Eurasia at the time. *Upper left:* This wooden chest covered with stucco and painted on all sides with images of the Egyptian pharoah in his war chariot was found in the fabulously wealthy tomb of Tutankhamun in the Valley of the Kings in Egypt. The war chariot was introduced into Egypt by the Hyksos. By the reign of Tutankhamun in the New Kingdom, depictions of the pharaoh single-handedly smiting the enemy from a war chariot drawn by two powerful horses were common. *Upper right:* The Shang fought with neighboring pastoral nomads from the central Asian steppes. To do this, they imported horses from central Asia and copied the chariots of nomads they had encountered. This gave Shang warriors devastating range and speed for further conquest.

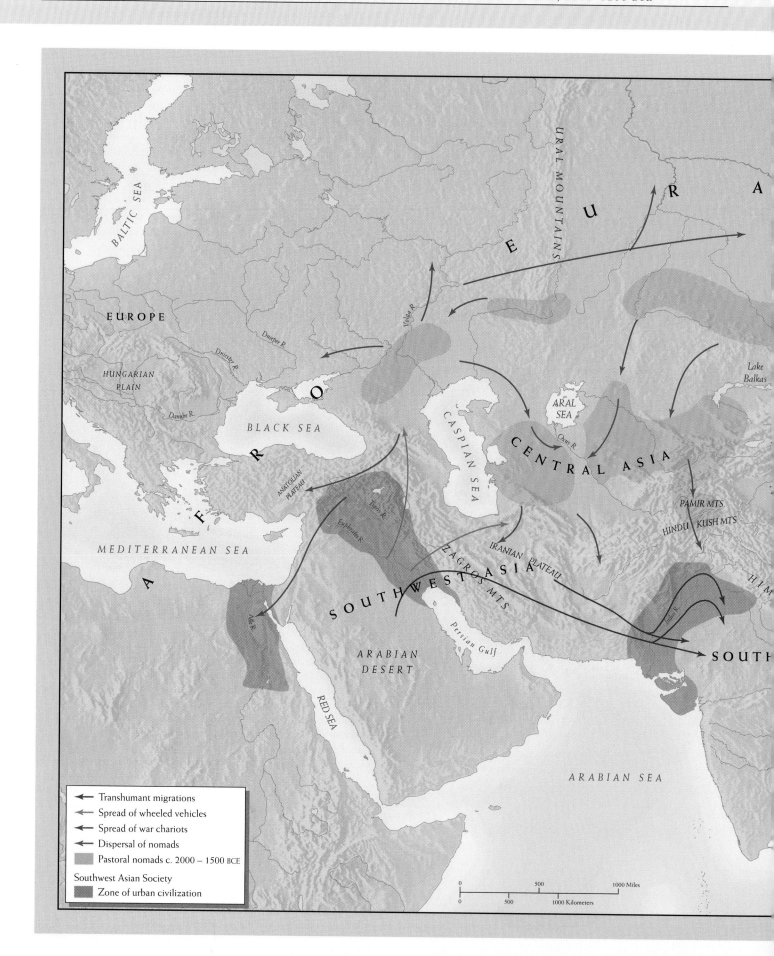

BALTIC SEA

URAL MOUNTAINS

E U R A

EUROPE

Dnieper R.

Dniester R.

Volga R.

HUNGARIAN
PLAIN

Danube R.

BLACK SEA

R   O

CASPIAN
SEA

ARAL
SEA

Oxus R.

C E N T R A L   A S I A

Lake
Balkas

ANATOLIAN
PLATEAU

Tigris R.

Euphrates R.

PAMIR MTS.

HINDU KUSH MTS.

A   F   R

MEDITERRANEAN SEA

IRANIAN   PLATEAU

S O U T H W E S T   A S I A

ZAGROS MTS.

HIM

Nile R.

Indus R.

A

ARABIAN
DESERT

Persian Gulf

S O U T H

RED SEA

ARABIAN SEA

Transhumant migrations
Spread of wheeled vehicles
Spread of war chariots
Dispersal of nomads
Pastoral nomads c. 2000 – 1500 BCE

Southwest Asian Society
Zone of urban civilization

0   500   1000 Miles

0   500   1000 Kilometers

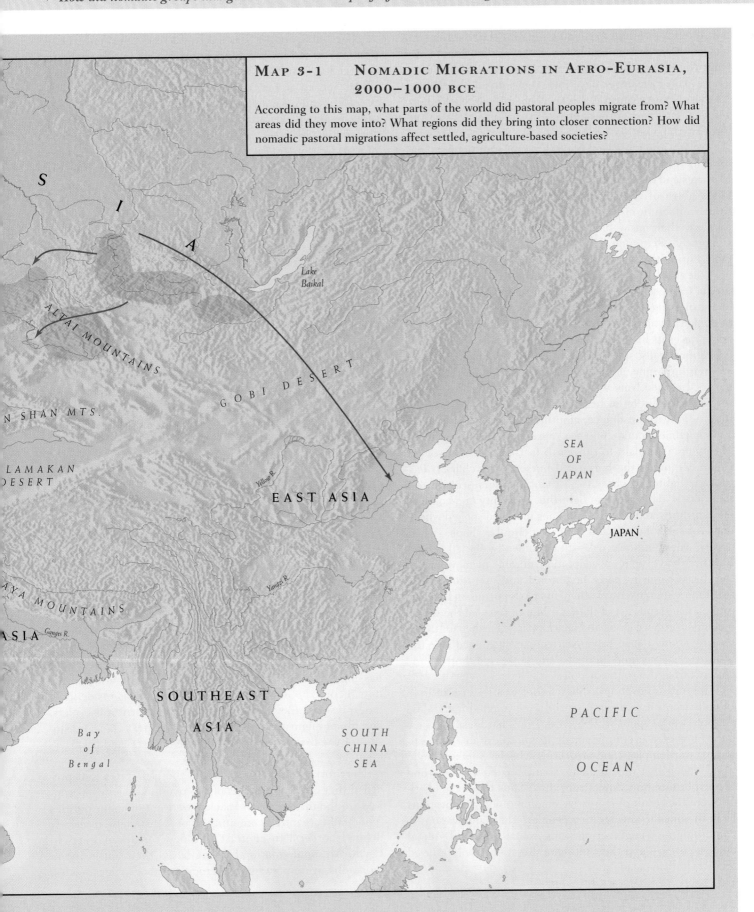

MAP 3-1   NOMADIC MIGRATIONS IN AFRO-EURASIA, 2000–1000 BCE

According to this map, what parts of the world did pastoral peoples migrate from? What areas did they move into? What regions did they bring into closer connection? How did nomadic pastoral migrations affect settled, agriculture-based societies?

Lake Baikal

S I A

ALTAI MOUNTAINS

N SHAN MTS.

LAMAKAN DESERT

GOBI DESERT

Yellow R.

EAST ASIA

SEA OF JAPAN

JAPAN

AYA MOUNTAINS

ASIA

Ganges R.

Yangzi R.

SOUTHEAST ASIA

Bay of Bengal

SOUTH CHINA SEA

PACIFIC OCEAN

linked cities in South Asia and China for the first time, enhanced trade, and maintained peace), they could not control what the elites whom they conquered wrote about them. Those who lost power described the nomadic warriors as "barbaric," portraying them as cruel enemies of "civilization." Yet what we know of these nomads today suggests that they were anything but barbaric.

Perhaps the most vital breakthroughs that nomadic pastoralists transmitted to settled societies were the harnessing of horses and the invention of the chariot. On the vast steppe lands north of the Caucasus Mountains, during the late fourth millennium BCE, settled people had domesticated horses in their native habitat. Elsewhere, as on the northern steppes of what is now Russia, horses were a food source. Only during the late third millennium BCE did people harness them with cheek pieces and mouth bits, signaling their use for transportation. Horses can outrun other draft animals, but harnessing them for pulling is complicated. Unlike cattle or donkeys, which stretch their necks ahead when walking, a horse raises its head. So the drivers needed headgear to control their steeds' speed and direction. In tombs scattered around the steppe, archaeologists have found parts of horse harnesses made from wood, bone, bronze, and iron. These reveal the evolution of headgear from simple mouth bits to full bridles with headpiece, mouthpiece, and reins.

Sometime around 2000 BCE, pastoral nomads beyond the Mesopotamian plain to the north in the mountains of the Caucasus joined the harnessed horse to the chariot. Pastoralists lightened chariots so their war horses could pull them faster. They were so light that an empty one could be lifted by one hand. Such techniques included spoked wheels made of special wood and bent into circular shapes, wheel covers, axles, and bearings—all produced by settled people. But there was even more adaptation: durable metal went into the chariot's moving parts, first bronze and later iron. A cluster of more than twenty settlements of steppe nomads, based in the area to the east of the Ural Mountains, led the way in making bronze weapons and chariot parts. Farther south, artisans working out of urban settlements fashioned true tin-bronze weapons and utensils and imported horses and chariots from the steppe peoples.

The next innovation in the chariot was the use of iron. Initially iron was a decorative and experimental metal, and all tools and weapons were bronze. Iron's hardness and flexibility, however, eventually made it more desirable for reinforcing moving parts and protecting wheels. Similarly, solid wood wheels that were prone to shatter ceded to spokes and hooped bronze (and, later, iron) rims. Thus the horse chariots were the result of a creative combination of innovations by both nomadic and agrarian peoples. These innovations—combining new engineering skills, metallurgy, and animal domestication—and their ultimate diffusion revolutionized the way humans made war.

The horse chariot slashed travel time between capitals and overturned the machinery of war. Slow-moving infantry now ceded to battalions of chariots. Each vehicle carried a driver and an archer, and it charged into battle with lethal precision and ravaging speed. In fact, the mobility, accuracy, and shooting power of warriors in horse-drawn chariots tilted the political balance. For after the nomads perfected this type of warfare (by 1600 BCE), they challenged the political systems of Mesopotamia and Egypt and soon were affecting war-making in distant regions such as present-day Greece, India, China, and Sweden. Only with the arrival of cheaper armor made of iron (after 1000 BCE) could foot soldiers (in China, armed with crossbows) recover their military importance. For much of the second millennium BCE, then, charioteer elites prevailed in Afro-Eurasia.

For city dwellers in the river basins the first sight of horse-drawn chariots must have been terrifying, but they knew that war-making had changed and they scrambled to adapt. The Shang kings of China and the pharaohs in Egypt probably copied chariots from nomads or neighbors, and they came to value them highly. For example, the young pharaoh Tutankhamun (c. 1350) was a chariot archer who made sure his war vehicle and other gear accompanied him in his tomb. A century later the Shang kings of the Yellow River valley, in the heartland of agricultural China, likewise were entombed with their horse chariots.

THE EMERGENCE OF TERRITORIAL STATES

While nomad and transhumant populations toppled the riverine cities in Mesopotamia, Egypt, and China, the turmoil that ensued sowed seeds for a new type of regime: the territorial state. (See Map 3-2.) Breaking out of the urban confines of its predecessors, the **territorial state** exerted power over distant hinterlands. In this way, it represented the chief political innovation of this new era. Centralized kingdoms, organized around charismatic rulers, now emerged. In so doing they stabilized political systems, by devising rituals for passing the torch of command from one generation to the next. People no longer identified themselves as residents of cities; instead, they felt allegiance to large territories, rulers, and broad linguistic and ethnic communities. These territories for the first time had identifiable borders, and their residents felt a shared identity.

Territorial states differed from the city-states that preceded them. The city-states of the riverine societies, organized around the temple and palace, were autonomous **polities** (politically organized communities or states) without clearly defined borders. In contrast, the new territorial states in Egypt, Mesopotamia, and China based their authority on monarchs, widespread bureaucracies, elaborate legal codes,

MAIN THEMES

→ *Dramatic warming and drying of the world's climate leads to the collapse of river-basin societies.*
→ *Herders and pastoral nomads migrate into riverine societies, utilizing horse-drawn chariot warfare to challenge traditional ruling elites and conquer surrounding states.*
→ *Large territorial states arise, led by charismatic rulers who expand boundaries, create more competition and trade, and wage warfare.*
→ *Microsocieties emerge in other parts of the world based on expanding populations and increased trade.*

FOCUS ON *The Emergence of Territorial States*

Egypt and Southwest Asia

◆ Invasions by nomads and transhumant herders lead to the creation of larger territorial states: New Kingdom Egypt, Hittites, Babylonia, and Kassites.
◆ A centuries-long peaceful era, "The Community of Major Powers," emerges among the major states as the result of shrewd statecraft and diplomacy.

Indus River Valley

◆ Migratory Vedic peoples from the steppes of inner Eurasia use charioteer technology and rely on domesticated animals to spread out and begin integrating the northern half of South Asia.

Shang State (China)

◆ Shang dynasts promote improvements in metalworking, agriculture, and the development of writing, leading to the growth of China's first major state.

Microsocieties

◆ Substantial increases in population, migrations, and trade lead to the emergence of microsocieties among peoples in the South Pacific (Austronesians), the Aegean world (Minoans and Mycenaeans), and the Americas, while Europe remains a land of warmaking small chieftanships.

---

large territorial expanses, definable borders, and ambitions for continuous expansion. Although power still emanated from central cities, some new ruling groups had appeared: the once-marginalized peoples of the Syrian Desert (the Amorites) and of the northern steppe lands and Anatolia (the Hittites) now held power. Their drive to conquer and expand replaced the earlier models of competition and coexistence. Territorial states also emerged in Greece and the Aegean where the newcomers who took power adopted local ways more completely. Other regions went through similar processes, but more slowly; they would not see state formation for a few more centuries. In one fundamental way, the South Pacific, the Aegean, Europe, and the Americas were different from the lands stretching from North Africa to South Asia: because they were less densely populated, they experienced less rivalry and less conflict over borders.

THE RISE OF TERRITORIAL STATES IN EGYPT AND SOUTHWEST ASIA

> → *What were the direct and indirect effects of drought on the organization of societies?*

Climatic change, invasions by pastoral nomads, and the use of war chariots transformed the city-states of Egypt and Southwest Asia. They brought an end to regimes like Old Kingdom Egypt and the many states occupying the

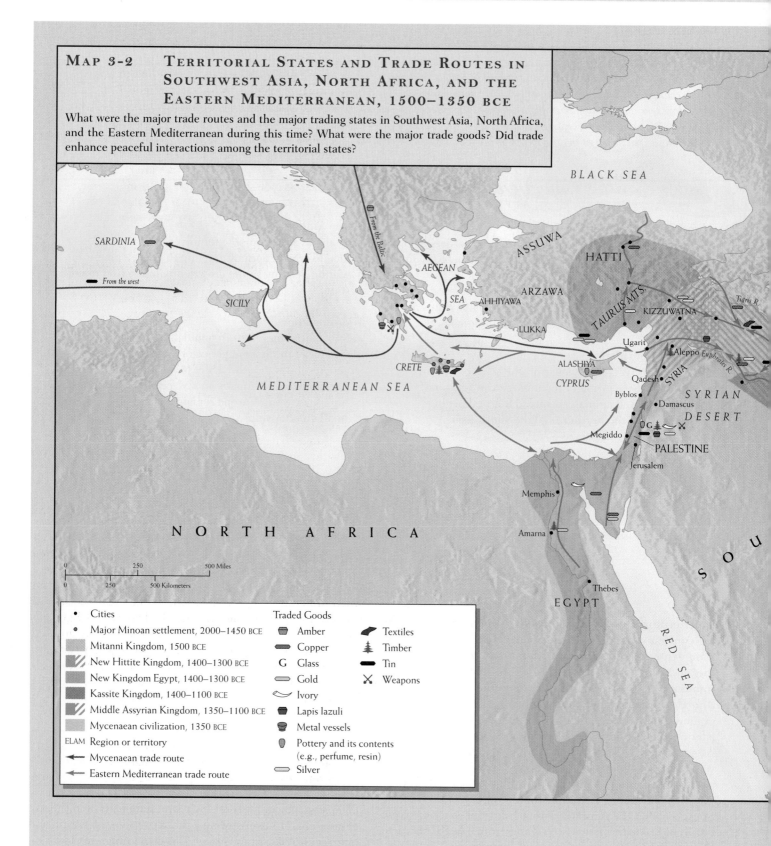

MAP 3-2 TERRITORIAL STATES AND TRADE ROUTES IN SOUTHWEST ASIA, NORTH AFRICA, AND THE EASTERN MEDITERRANEAN, 1500–1350 BCE

What were the major trade routes and the major trading states in Southwest Asia, North Africa, and the Eastern Mediterranean during this time? What were the major trade goods? Did trade enhance peaceful interactions among the territorial states?

BLACK SEA

SARDINIA

From the Baltic

ASSUWA

HATTI

From the west

SICILY

AEGEAN

ARZAWA

TAURUS MTS.

Tigris R.

KIZZUWATNA

SEA

AHHIYAWA

LUKKA

Ugarit

Aleppo Euphrates R.

CRETE

ALASHIYA

SYRIA

MEDITERRANEAN SEA

CYPRUS

Qadesh

SYRIAN

Byblos

Damascus

DESERT

Megiddo

G

PALESTINE

Jerusalem

NORTH AFRICA

Memphis

Amarna

SOU

RED SEA

Thebes

EGYPT

0   250   500 Miles
0   250   500 Kilometers

Cities
- Cities
- Major Minoan settlement, 2000–1450 BCE

Mitanni Kingdom, 1500 BCE

New Hittite Kingdom, 1400–1300 BCE

New Kingdom Egypt, 1400–1300 BCE

Kassite Kingdom, 1400–1100 BCE

Middle Assyrian Kingdom, 1350–1100 BCE

Mycenaean civilization, 1350 BCE

ELAM Region or territory

← Mycenaean trade route

← Eastern Mediterranean trade route

Traded Goods
- Amber
- Copper
- G Glass
- Gold
- Ivory
- Lapis lazuli
- Metal vessels
- Pottery and its contents (e.g., perfume, resin)
- Silver
- Textiles
- Timber
- Tin
- Weapons

→ *What were the direct and indirect effects of drought on the organization of societies?*

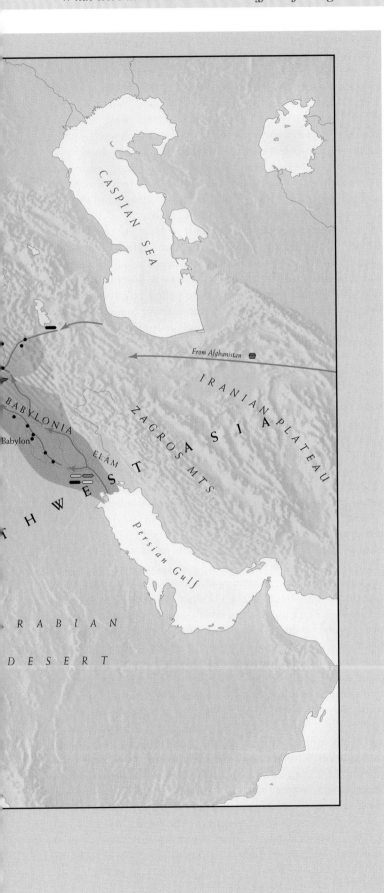

Mesopotamian floodplain. But, as inhabitants of these areas assimilated the newcomers or drove out those who resisted assimilation, new states came to the fore. Thus the second millennium BCE divides into two distinct phases. The first phase, roughly 2000 to 1600 BCE, resembled what had gone before: small kingdoms, organized by territorial and ethnic identities, dominated the landscape from the Aegean Sea through Mesopotamia and Iran. The most powerful kingdoms were Babylonia in Mesopotamia and the Middle Kingdom in Egypt. A more radical phase occurred after 1600 BCE, when a renewed wave of nomadic migrations and conquests undermined these earlier fledgling but unstable territorial kingdoms. After an agonizing century of turmoil, the balance of power shifted and a new group of expansionist, territorial states emerged. From their urban capitals, these new states commanded vast hinterlands, claimed definable boundaries, and consolidated common cultures. The most powerful states of the second period were New Kingdom Egypt, the Hittites of Anatolia, and Babylonia and the Kassites of Mesopotamia.

In this second period the entire region was marked by competition between well-balanced military kingdoms. Although there was much quarreling and some warfare, shrewd statecraft and international diplomacy kept the peace for many centuries. Not so fortunate were the smaller kingdoms, such as the Syro-Palestinian states, squeezed between the major powers. They served as buffer zones between the regions that the territorial powers dominated.

EGYPT

The first of the great territorial kingdoms of this era arose from the ashes of chaos in Egypt. There the pharaohs of the Middle Kingdom and, later, the New Kingdom reunified the river valley and expanded south and north. The long era of prosperity associated with the Old Kingdom had ended when drought brought catastrophe to the area. For several decades the Nile did not overflow its banks, and Egyptian harvests withered. As the pharaohs lost legitimacy and fell prey to feuding among rivals for the throne, regional notables replaced the authority of the centralized state. Egypt, which had been one of the most stable corners of Afro-Eurasia, would endure more than a century of tumult before a new order emerged.

MIDDLE KINGDOM EGYPT (2040–1640 BCE) Around 2050 BCE, after a century of drought, the Nile's floodwaters returned to normal. Crops grew again. But who would restore order and reunite the kingdom? From about 2061 to 1991 BCE, two rulers at Thebes (far south of the Old Kingdom's seat of power in Memphis) both named Mentuhotep consolidated power in Upper Egypt and began new state-building activity. They ushered in a new phase of stability that historians call the Middle Kingdom. For 350 years, the new pharaonic line built on earlier foundations to increase the

Amun. This sculpture of the head of the god Amun was carved from quartzite during the Eighteenth Dynasty, around 1335 BCE. At Thebes in Upper Egypt, a huge temple complex was dedicated to the combined god Amun-Re. The powerful kings of the Middle and New Kingdoms each added a courtyard or a pylon, making this one of the largest religious structures in the ancient world.

state's power and to develop religious and political institutions far beyond their original forms.

GODS AND KINGS Spiritual and worldly powers reinforced each other in Egypt. Just as rulers of this new phase came from the margins, so did its gods. The Twelfth Dynasty (1985–1795 BCE), with its long list of kings, dominated the Middle Kingdom partly because its sacred order replaced the chaos that people believed had brought drought and despair. Amenemhet I (1985–1955 BCE) elevated a formerly insignificant god, Amun, to prominence. The king capitalized on the god's name, which means "hidden," to convey a sense of his own invisible omnipresence throughout the realm.

Because Amun's attributes were largely hidden, believers in other gods were able to embrace his cult. Amun's cosmic power appealed to those in areas that had recently been impoverished. As the pharaoh elevated the cult of Amun he unified the disparate parts of his kingdom, further empowering Amun—as well as his worldly sponsor, the pharaoh. In this way Amun eclipsed all the other gods of Thebes. Merging with the formerly omnipotent sun god Re, the deity now was called Amun-Re: the king of the gods. Because the power of the gods and kings was intertwined, Amun's earthly champion (the king) enjoyed enhanced legitimacy as the supreme ruler. The cult was more than a tool of political power, however: it also had a strong spiritual impact on the pharaoh and on Egyptian society.

ROYAL SPLENDOR AND ROYAL CARE While gods and kings allied, Middle Kingdom rulers tapped into their kingdom's bounty, their subjects' loyalty, and the work of untold slaves and commoners to build the largest, longest-lasting public works project ever undertaken. For 2,000 years, Egyptians and slaves toiled to erect monumental gates, enormous courtyards, and other structures in a massive temple complex at Thebes. Dedicated to Amun-Re, it demonstrated the glorious power of the pharaohs and the gods.

Unlike the spiritually perfect and remote rulers of the Old Kingdom, the Middle Kingdom rulers nurtured a cult of the pharaoh as the good shepherd whose prime responsibility was to fulfill the needs of his human flock. By instituting charities, offering homage to gods at the palace to ensure regular floodwaters, and performing ceremonies to honor their own generosity, the pharaohs portrayed themselves as the stewards of their people.

MERCHANTS AND TRADE NETWORKS Prosperity gave rise to an urban class of merchants and professionals who used their wealth and skills to carve out places for their own leisure and pastimes. Indoors they indulged in formal banquets with professional dancers and singers, and outdoors they honed their skills in hunting, fowling, and fishing. What was new was that they did not depend on the kings for such benefits. In a sign of their upward mobility and autonomy, some members of the middle class constructed tombs filled with representations of the material goods they would use in the afterlife as well as the occupations that would engage them for eternity. During the Old Kingdom, this privilege had been the exclusive right of the royal family and a few powerful nobles.

Centralized and reforming kingdoms also expanded their trade networks. Because the floodplains had long since been deforested, the Egyptians needed to import massive quantities of wood by ship. Most prized were the cedars from Byblos (a city in the land soon known as Phoenicia, roughly present-day Lebanon), which artisans crafted into furniture for the living and coffins for the dead. Superb examples remain from the tombs of nobles and pharaohs. Commercial networks extended south through the Red Sea as far as present-day Ethiopia; traders brought back precious metals, ivory, livestock, slaves, and exotic animals such as panthers and monkeys to enhance the pharaoh's palace. Expeditions to the Sinai Peninsula searched for copper and turquoise. Egyptians looked south for gold, which they prized for personal and architectural ornamentation. To acquire it they crossed into Nubia, where they met stiff resistance; eventually the Egyptians colonized Nubia to broaden their trade routes and secure these coveted resources. As part of their colonization, a series of forts extended as far south as the second cataract of the Nile River. (See Map 2-5 in Chapter 2.)

HYKSOS INVADERS AND NEW FOUNDATIONS Pharaonic peace brought prosperity, but it did not ensure uninterrupted pharaonic rule. Now Egypt found itself open to migration and foreign invasion, coming once again from the margins. First, the very success of the new commercial networks lured pastoral nomads who were searching for work. Later, a new people from Southwest Asia attacked Egypt, initially destabilizing the kingdom but ultimately putting it on stronger foundations.

Sometime around 1640 BCE a western Semitic-speaking people, whom the Egyptians called the Hyksos ("Rulers of Foreign Lands"), overthrew the unstable Thirteenth Dynasty. The Hyksos had mastered the art of horse chariots. Thundering into battle with their war chariots and their superior bronze axes and composite bows (made of wood, horn, and sinew), they easily defeated the pharaoh's foot soldiers. Yet the victors did not destroy the conquered land; instead, they ruled over it. By adopting Egyptian ways, they also reinforced them. The Hyksos settled down and ruled as the Fifteenth Dynasty, asserting control over the northern part of the country and transforming the Egyptian military force.

After a century of political conflict, an Egyptian who ruled the southern part of the country, Ahmosis (r. 1550–1525 BCE), successfully used the Hyksos weaponry—horse chariots—against the invaders themselves and became pharaoh. The Egyptian rulers had learned an important lesson from the invasion: they had to vigilantly monitor their frontiers, for they could no longer rely on deserts as buffers. Ahmosis assembled large, mobile armies and drove the "foreigners" back. Diplomats followed in the army's path, as the pharaoh initiated a strategy of interference in the affairs of southwest Asian states. Such policies laid the groundwork for statecraft and an international diplomatic system that future Egyptian kings would use to dominate the eastern Mediterranean world.

The migrants and invaders from the west introduced new techniques that the Egyptians adopted to consolidate their power. These included bronze working (which the Egyptians had not perfected), an improved potter's wheel, and a vertical loom. In addition, South Asian animals such as humped zebu cattle, as well as vegetable and fruit crops, now appeared on the banks of the Nile for the first time.

Of course, the most significant innovations pertained to war: the horse and chariot, the composite bow, the scimitar (a sword with a curved blade), and other weapons from western Eurasia. These weapons transformed the Egyptian army from a standing infantry to a high-speed, mobile, and deadly fighting force. As Egyptian troops extended the military frontier as far south as the fourth cataract of the Nile River, the kingdom now stretched from the Mediterranean shores to Ethiopia.

NEW KINGDOM EGYPT By the beginning of the New Kingdom (1550–1069 BCE), Egypt was projecting its interests outward: it defined itself as a superior, cosmopolitan society with an efficient bureaucracy run by competent and socially mobile individuals. For 100 years Egypt expanded its control southward into Nubia, a source of gold, exotic raw materials, and manpower. Historians identify this expansion most strongly with the reign of Egypt's most powerful woman ruler, Hatshepsut. She served as regent for her young son, Thutmosis III, who came to the throne in 1479 BCE. When he was seven years old she proclaimed herself "king," ruling as co-regent until she died. During her reign there was little military activity, but trade contacts into the Levant and Mediterranean and southward into Nubia flourished.

Thutmosis III (r. 1479–1425 BCE) launched another expansionary phase that lasted for 200 years. Spreading northeastward into the Levant, under his rule the Egyptians collided with the Mitanni and the Hittite kingdoms. At the Battle of Megiddo (1469 BCE), the first recorded chariot battle in history, Thutmosis III defeated vassals of the Mitanni and established an Egyptian presence in Palestine. Egypt was now poised to engage in commercial, political, and cultural exchanges with the rest of the region (see "The Community of Major Powers" on p. 100).

Hatshepsut. The only powerful queen of Egyptian pharaonic history was Hatshepsut, seen here in a portrait head created during her reign. Because a woman on the throne of Egypt would offend the basic principles of order (*ma'at*), Hatshepsut usually portrayed herself as a man, especially late in her reign. This was reinforced by the use of male determinatives in the hieroglyphic renditions of her name.

ANATOLIA AND THE RISE OF THE HITTITES

Anatolia was an overland crossroads that linked the Black and Mediterranean seas. Like other plateaus of Afro-Eurasia it had high tablelands, was easy to traverse, and was hospitable to large herding communities. Thus during the third millennium BCE Anatolia had become home to numerous polities run by indigenous elites. These societies combined pastoral lifeways, agriculture, and urban commercial centers. Before 2000 BCE, peoples speaking Indo-European languages began to enter the plateau, probably coming from the steppe lands north and west of the Black Sea. The newcomers lived in fortified settlements and often engaged in regional warfare, and their numbers grew. Splintered into competing clans, they fought for regional supremacy. They also borrowed extensively from the cultural developments of the Southwest Asian urban cultures, especially those of Mesopotamia.

THE OLD AND NEW HITTITE KINGDOMS (1800–1200 BCE)

In the early second millennium BCE chariot warrior groups, which were the most powerful of the competing communities in Anatolia, grew even more powerful on the commercial activity that passed through Anatolia. Chief among them were the Hittites. Their chariots carried lancers and archers across vast expanses to plunder their neighbors and demand taxes and tribute. The chariot aristocracies finally became unified during the seventeenth century BCE under Hattusilis I.

After securing his base in Anatolia, Hattusilis turned his attention to the east, crossed the Taurus Mountains, and defeated the kingdom that controlled all of northern Syria. In 1595 BCE, Hattusilis and his son Mursilis I marched even farther, campaigning along the Euphrates River as far as the city of Babylon, which they sacked. The Hittites enjoyed another period of political and military success two centuries later under the great king Suppilulimua I (r. 1380–1345 BCE), who restored Hittite glory in Southwest Asia from the Euphrates in the east to Syria in the south. At Qadesh they met the Egyptians in what some experts regard as the greatest battle in ancient times, one that involved a vast number of chariots. Because the Hittites controlled much of the territory between Mesopotamia and the Nile, their rulers were crucial in maintaining the region's balance of power.

MESOPOTAMIA

In Mesopotamia, as in Egypt and Anatolia, the intervention of pastoral peoples led to the emergence of new states. Here, too, drought was devastating. Harvests shrank, the price of basic goods rose, and the social order broke down. Already short of agricultural produce, the towns of southern Mesopotamia suffered invasions by transhumant migrants from two directions: the Zagros Mountains and the Syrian Desert. These herders, who did not use horses or chariots, were seeking grazing lands to replace those swallowed up by the expanding deserts. As elsewhere in Afro-Eurasia, environmental changes were altering the human landscape.

A millennium of intense cultivation, combined with severe drought, had ruined the land's productivity. The rich alluvial soil lost more and more nutrients, while at the same time salt water from the Persian Gulf seeped into the marshy deltas and contaminated the water table (the underground level at which water can reliably be found). As the main branch of the Euphrates River shifted to the west, large areas of previously arable land no longer received sufficient water for cultivation. As a result, many of the ancient cities lost access to their fertile agrarian hinterlands and withered away. All these alterations pushed Mesopotamia's center of political and economic gravity northward, away from the silted, marshy deltas of the southern heartland.

NOMADIC AND TRANSHUMANT MIGRATION TO MESOPOTAMIAN CITIES

The conquerors of Mesopotamian cities were the Amorites, a name given them by their vanquished urban dwellers and taken from the Akkadian word for "west," *Amurru*. City dwellers were scornful of these rustic folk, as the following poetry makes clear. It states that the Amorite is

> a tent-dweller, [buffeted] by wind and rain, [who offers no] prayer,
> He who dwells in the mountains, [knows not] the places [of the gods];
> A man who digs up mushrooms at the foot of the mountain, who knows no submission,
> He eats uncooked meat,
> In his lifetime has no house,
> When he dies, he will not be buried;
> My girlfriend—why would you marry Martu?!
> (Klein, "The Marriage of Martu," 89)

Transhumant herders may have been "foreigners" in the cities of Mesopotamia, but they were not strangers to them. They had always played an important role in Mesopotamian urban life and knew the culture of its city-states. These rural folk wintered in villages close to the river to water their animals, which grazed on fallow fields. In the scorching summer, they retreated to the cooler highlands. Their flocks provided wools for the vast textile industries of Mesopotamia, as well as leather, bones, and tendons for other crafted products. In return, the herders purchased crafted products and agricultural goods. They also paid taxes, served as warriors, and labored on public works projects. Yet despite being part of the urban fabric, they had few political rights within city-states.

As scarcities mounted, transhumant peoples began to press in upon settled communities more closely. Finally, in

2004 BCE, Amorites from the western desert joined allies from the Iranian plateau to bring down the Third Dynasty of Ur (which had controlled all of Mesopotamia and southwestern Iran for more than a century). As in Egypt, a century of political instability followed the demise of the old city-state models. Here, too, it was pastoral folk who finally restored order, taking the wealth of the regions they conquered and helping the cultural realm to flourish. They founded the Old Babylonian kingdom around 2000 BCE; they also expanded trade and founded new kinds of political communities: territorial states with dynastic ruling families and well-defined frontiers. This was yet another example of the contribution of mobile communities to settled societies.

RESTORED ORDER AND CULTURE   Restored order and prosperity enabled the new kings of Babylonia to nourish a vibrant intellectual and cultural milieu. They commissioned public art and works projects, and institutions of learning thrived. The court supported workshops for skilled artisans such as jewelers and sculptors, and it established schools for scribes, the transmitters of an expanding literary culture.

Now the Babylonians and their successors, the Kassites (1475–1125 BCE), reproduced the cultural achievements of earlier Mesopotamia. To dispel their image as rustic foreigners and to demonstrate their familiarity with the region's core values, they studied the oral tales and written records of the earlier Sumerians and Akkadians. Scribes copied the ancient texts and preserved their tradition. Royal hymns, for instance, continued the Sumerian language that had not been spoken for centuries. These hymns portrayed the king as a legendary hero of quasi-divine status.

Heroic narratives about legendary founders, based on traditional stories about the rulers of ancient Uruk, served to legitimize the new rulers. These great poems constituted the first epic narratives of human—as opposed to godly—achievement. Written in the Old Babylonian dialect of the Semitic Akkadian language, they identified the history of a people with their king, and their wide circulation helped to unify the kingdom. The most famous was the *Epic of Gilgamesh* (see Primary Source: *The Epic of Gilgamesh*). This story (composed more than a millennium earlier in the Sumerian language) narrated the heroism of the legendary king of early Uruk, Gilgamesh. Throughout the ages, scribes of royal courts preserved the tradition for future generations to venerate the idea of the benevolent king. It stands out as an example of how the Mesopotamian kings continually invested in cultural production in order to explain important political relations, unify their people, and distinguish their subjects from those of other kingdoms.

TRADE AND THE RISE OF A PRIVATE ECONOMY With restored prosperity came a shift away from economic activity dominated by the city-state and toward independent private ventures. The new rulers designated private entrepreneurs rather than state bureaucrats to collect taxes. People paid taxes in the form of commodities such as grain, vegetables, and wool, which the entrepreneurs exchanged for silver. They, in turn, passed on the silver to the state after pocketing a percentage for their profit. This process generated more private activity and wealth, and more revenues for the state.

Mesopotamia at this time was a crossroads for caravans leading east and west. When the region was peaceful and well

Gilgamesh. This terra-cotta plaque in the Berlin Museum is one of the very few depictions of Gilgamesh (on the left wielding the knife) and his sidekick, Enkidu. It illustrates one of the episodes in their shared adventures, the killing of Ḥumwawa, the monster of the Cedar Forest. The style of the plaque indicates that it was made during the Old Babylonian period, between 2000 and 1600 BCE.

THE EPIC OF GILGAMESH

Gilgamesh, an early ruler of ancient Uruk, was the supreme hero of Mesopotamian legend. He was a successful ruler, boastful and vain, as well as a courageous adventurer and a devoted friend to his companion Enkidu. The Gilgamesh epic, constructed in the early second millennium BCE from numerous stories, is the oldest piece of world literature. It portrays a tragic hero who is obsessed with glory and whose quest for immortality ends in failure. The following excerpt tells of his anguish on his fruitless journey to gain immortal life. He is speaking to an alewife (a woman who keeps an alehouse) as he continues to deny his humanity and the inevitability of death.

The alewife spoke to him, to Gilgamesh,
"If you are truly Gilgamesh, that struck down the
　Guardian,
Destroyed Humbaba, who lived in the Pine Forest,
Killed lions at the mountain passes,
Seized the Bull of Heaven who came down from the sky,
　struck him down,
Why are your cheeks wasted, your face dejected,
Your heart so wretched, your appearance worn out,
And grief in your innermost being?
Your face is like that of a long-distance traveler,
Your face is weathered by cold and heat . . .
Clad only in a lion skin you roam open country."
Gilgamesh spoke to her, to Siduri the alewife,
"How could my cheeks not be wasted, my face not
　dejected.
Nor my heart wretched, nor my appearance worn out,
Nor grief in my innermost being,
Nor my face like that of a long-distance traveler,
My friend whom I love so much, who
Experienced every hardship with me,
Enkidu, whom I love so much, who experienced every
　hardship with me—
The fate of mortals conquered him! Six days and seven
　nights I wept over him,

I did not allow him to be buried, until a worm fell out of
　his nose.
I was frightened and . . .
I am afraid of Death, and so I roam open country.
The words of my friend weigh upon me.
I roam open country for long distances; the words of my
　friend
Enkidu weigh upon me.
I roam open country on long journeys.
How, O how, could I stay silent, how O how could I keep
　quiet
My friend whom I love has turned to clay:
Enkidu my friend whom I love has turned to clay.
Am I not like him? Must I lie down too,
Never to rise, ever again?"

❖ *What lines of the passage reveal how Gilgamesh feels about
the death of Enkidu? Why does he feel that way?*
❖ *What does this passage tell us about human relationships
and human nature during this period? What does it tell us
about rulers and their relationship with their gods?*

SOURCE: "The Epic of Gilgamesh" from *Myths from Mesopotamia: Creation, The Flood, Gilgamesh and Others*, pp. 100–101, trans. Stephanie Dalley. © Stephanie Dalley 1989. Reprinted with permission of Oxford University Press.

governed, the trading community flourished. The ability to move exotic foodstuffs, valuable minerals, textiles, and luxury goods across Southwest Asia won Mesopotamian merchants and entrepreneurs a privileged position as they connected producers with distant consumers. Merchants also used sea routes for trade with the Indus Valley. Before 2000 BCE, mariners had charted the waters of the Red Sea, the Gulf of Aden, the Persian Gulf, and much of the Arabian Sea. Now, during the second millennium BCE, shipbuilders figured out how to construct larger vessels and to rig them with towering masts and woven sails—creating truly seaworthy craft that could carry bulkier loads. Of course, shipbuilding required wood (particularly cedar from Phoenicia) as well as wool and other fibers (from the pastoral hinterlands) for sails. Such reliance on imported materials reflected a growing regional economic specialization and an expanding sphere of interaction across western Afro-Eurasia.

Doing business in Mesopotamia was profitable but also risky. If harvests were poor, cultivators and merchants could not meet their tax obligations and thus incurred heavy debts. The frequency of such misfortune is evident from the many royal edicts that annulled certain debts as a gesture of tax relief. Moreover, traders and goods had to pass through lands where some hostile rulers refused to protect the caravans. Thus taxes, duties, and bribes flowed out along the entire route. If goods reached their final destination, they yielded large profits; if disaster struck, investors and traders had nothing to show for their efforts. As a result, merchant households sought to lower their risks by formalizing commercial rules, establishing insurance schemes, and cultivating extended kinship networks in cities along trade routes to ensure strong commercial alliances and to gather intelligence. They also cemented their ties with local political authorities. Indeed, the merchants who dominated the ancient city of Assur on the Tigris pumped revenues into the coffers of the local kingdom in the hope that its wealthy dynasts would protect their interests.

MESOPOTAMIAN KINGDOMS The new rulers of Mesopotamia also changed the organization of the state. Where city-states had once prevailed, rulers from nomadic stock now fashioned kingdoms that covered large territories. These herders-turned-urbanites mixed their own social organization with that of the city-states to create the structures necessary to support territorial states.

The basic social organization of the Amorites was tribal, dominated by a ruling chief. Tribal polities, even those extending over wide areas, comprised clans; each claimed descent from a common ancestor and thus drew a line between itself and all who were not kin. (However, the clans did allow intermarriage and adoption.) Even the many Amorites who had given up their nomadic ways and settled in the cities remained conscious of their genealogical roots. The new territorial polities honored identification with the clan and tribe.

The emergence of ruling cliques from among the nomadic chieftains led to a new model of statecraft. This process occurred in three stages. First, chieftains became kings. Second, the new kings turned their authority—which in the tribe had depended on personal charisma and battlefield prowess—into an alliance with wealthy merchants in exchange for revenues and political support. Third, royal status became hereditary. This practice of hereditary succession replaced the tribal system under which influential community leaders had elected the leaders. Even in the new system, though, kings could not rule without the support of nobles and merchants.

Over the centuries, powerful Mesopotamian kings continued to expand their territories. They subdued weaker neighbors, coaxing or forcing them to become **vassal states**—that is, allies who had to pay tribute in luxury goods, raw materials, and manpower as part of a broad confederation of polities under the kings' protection. Control over military resources (access to metals for weaponry and, later, to herds of horses for pulling chariots) was necessary to gain dominance, but it was no guarantee of success. The ruler's charisma also mattered. This emphasis on personality explains why Mesopotamian kingdoms were strong for certain periods under certain rulers, but vulnerable to rivals and neighbors under other rulers. It also distinguished them from Middle Kingdom Egypt and Hittite Anatolia, territorial states where power was more institutionalized and durable.

The most famous Mesopotamian ruler of this period was Hammurapi (or Hammurabi) (r. 1792–1750), who ascended the throne as the sixth king of Old Babylonia's First Dynasty. Continuously struggling with powerful neighbors, he sought to centralize state authority and to create a new legal order. Using diplomatic and military skills to become the strongest king in Mesopotamia, he made Babylon his capital and declared himself "the king who made the four quarters of the earth obedient." He implemented a new system to secure his power, appointing regional governors to manage outlying provinces and to deal with local elites.

Hammurapi's image as ruler imitated that of the Egyptian pharaohs of the Middle Kingdom. The king was shepherd and patriarch of his people, responsible for proper preparation of the fields and irrigation canals and for his followers' well-being. Such an ideal recognized that being king was a delicate balancing act. While he had to curry favor among powerful merchants and elites, he also had to meet the needs of the poor and disadvantaged—in part to avoid a reputation for cruelty, and in part to gain a key base of support should the elites become dissatisfied with his rule.

Hammurapi elevated this balancing act into an art form, encapsulated in a grand legal code—**Hammurapi's Code**. It began and concluded with the rhetoric of paternal justice. For example, he concluded by describing himself as "the shepherd who brings peace, whose scepter is just. My benevolent shade was spread over my city, I held the people of the lands of Sumer and Akkad safely on my lap."

Hammurapi's Code was in fact a compilation of more than 300 edicts addressing crimes and their punishments. One theme rings loud and clear: governing public matters was man's work, and upholding a just order was the supreme charge of rulers. Whereas the gods' role in ordering the world was distant, the king was directly in command of ordering relations among people. Accordingly, the code elaborated in exhaustive detail the social rules that would ensure the kingdom's peace through its primary instrument—the family. The code outlined the rights and privileges of fathers, wives, and children. The father's duty was to treat his kin as the ruler would treat his subjects, with strict authority and care. Adultery, which represented the supreme violation of this moral code, was a female crime. Any woman found with a man who

Hammurapi's Code. The inscription on the shaft of Hammurapi's Code is carved in a beautiful rendition of the cuneiform script. Because none of the laws on the code were recorded in the thousands of judicial texts of the period, it is uncertain if Hammurapi's Code presented actual laws or only norms for the proper behavior of Babylonian citizens.

was not her husband would be bound and thrown into the river, and likewise her lover.

Hammurapi's Code also divided the Babylonian kingdom into three classes: each member was a free person (*awilum*), a dependent (*mushkenum*), or a slave (*wardum*). Each had an assigned value and distinct rights and responsibilities. In this way, Hammurapi's order stratified society while also pacifying the region. By the end of his reign, Hammurapi had established Babylon as the single great power in Mesopotamia and had reduced competitor kingdoms to mere vassals. Following his death, his sons and successors struggled to maintain control over a shrinking domain for another 155 years in the face of internal rebellions and foreign invasions. In 1595 BCE, Babylon fell to the Hittite king Hattusilis I.

KASSITE RULE   As a crossroads for Afro-Eurasia, Mesopotamia continued both to benefit from and be threatened by the arrival of nomadic and transhumant migrants. The

Kassites, for instance, who came from the Zagros Mountains, had entered southern Mesopotamia from the Iranian plateau. Arriving in the river valley as agricultural laborers as early as 2000 BCE, they integrated themselves into Babylonian society by becoming bureaucrats associated with the temple. Once entrenched, they were well placed to fill the power vacuum when the Hittites destroyed the First Dynasty of Babylon. By 1475 BCE, Kassite rulers had reestablished order in the region. Over the next 350 years they brought all of southern Mesopotamia under their control, creating one of the great territorial states within an emerging network of states from North Africa to Southwest Asia.

The Kassites presided over a golden age based on trade in such precious commodities as horses, chariots, and lapis lazuli, which they exchanged for gold, wood, and ivory. Like earlier immigrant communities to this ancient land, the Kassites absorbed the traditions and institutions of Mesopotamia. Even more than their predecessors, they strove to preserve the past and transmit its institutions to posterity. Although very little remains of their own language and customs (apart from their personal names), with thoroughness and dedication the Kassite scribes translated much of the older Sumerian literature into Akkadian. They revised and compiled texts into standard editions, from which scholars have recovered a Babylonian creation myth called the Enuma Elish. In their determination to become even more Babylonian than the Babylonians, the Kassites saved a treasure trove of historical literature and artifacts for later generations. During the subsequent period of the Community of Major Powers the Kassites served as the crucial link between Egypt, Anatolia, and southwestern Iran.

THE COMMUNITY OF MAJOR POWERS (1400–1200 BCE)

Between 1400 and 1200 BCE, the major territorial states of Southwest Asia and Egypt perfected instruments of international diplomacy that have stood the test of time and inspired later leaders. The leaders of these powers learned to settle their differences through treaties and diplomatic negotiations rather than on the battlefield. Each state knew its place in the political pecking order. It was an order that depended on constant communication—the foundation of what we now call diplomacy. In fact, a remarkable cache of 300 letters discovered at the present-day village of Amarna, beneath which Egyptologists discovered the remains of the capital city of the New Kingdom pharaoh Akhenaten, offers intimate views of these complex interactions. Most are letters from the Egyptian king to his subordinates in the vassal states of Palestine, but others are from Akhenaten and his father to the Babylonian, Mitanni, Middle Assyrian, Kassite, and Hittite kings. Many of these letters are in a dialect of Akkadian (used by the Babylonian bureaucrats) that served as the diplomatic

Akhenaten. The pharaoh Amenhotep IV changed his name to Akhenaten to reflect his deep devotion to Aten, the god of the sun disk. The art of the period of his reign, like his religion, challenged conventions. In it, the faces of the king and queen, as well as their bodies, were extremely elongated and distorted. Some scholars think that this distortion reflects a condition that the king himself suffered from.

language of the era. This correspondence reveals a delicate balance, constantly shifting, among competing kings who were intent on maintaining their status and who knew that winning the loyalty of the small buffer kingdoms was crucial to political success.

Formal treaties brought an end to military eruptions and replaced them with diplomatic contacts. In its more common form, diplomacy involved strategic marriages and the exchange of specialized personnel to reside at the court of foreign territorial states. Gifts also strengthened relations among the major powers and signaled a ruler's respect for his neighbors. Rulers had to acknowledge the gesture by reciprocating with gifts of equal value.

The foundations of power were not always durable, however. Building the state system was ultimately the task of those at the bottom of the social pyramid, and the ruling classes' reliance on them for power and political authority was a weakness of these regimes. Commoners remained tied to the land, which sometimes belonged to communities or institutions, not individual families. They paid taxes to the state, performed labor required by the state for public works (such as irrigation or building projects), and served as foot soldiers. The collapse of the international age had many

causes, but one factor was the disintegration of the social fabric as workers could not pay their taxes or fled their communities rather than fight in the rulers' armies.

NOMADS AND THE INDUS RIVER VALLEY

Late in the third millennium BCE, drought ravaged the Indus River valley as it did other regions. By 1700 BCE, the population of the old Harappan heartland had plummeted. Here, too, around 1500 BCE, yet another group of nomadic peoples calling themselves Aryans ("respected ones") wandered out of their homelands in the steppes of inner Eurasia. But in contrast to Egypt, Anatolia, and Mesopotamia, these pastoral nomads did not immediately establish large territorial states. Crossing the northern highlands of central Asia through the Hindu Kush, they were a sight to behold. They descended into the fertile Indus River basin (see Map 3-3) with large flocks of cattle and horses, singing chants called Rig Veda as they sacrificed some of their livestock to their gods. Known collectively as the Veda ("knowledge"), these hymns served as the most sacred texts for the newcomers, who have been known ever since as the **Vedic people**. They also arrived with an extraordinary language, Sanskrit (perhaps prophetically labeled "perfectly made"). It was one of the earliest known Indo-European languages and a source for virtually all of the European languages, including Greek, Latin, English, French, and German. (See Global Connections & Disconnections: How Languages Spread—The Case of Nomadic Indo-European Languages.)

Like other nomads from the northern steppe, they brought domesticated animals—especially horses, which pulled their chariots and established their military superiority. Not only were the Vedic people superb horse charioteers, but they were also masters of copper and bronze metallurgy and wheel making. Their expertise in these areas allowed them to produce the very chariots that transported them into their new lands.

Like other Indo-European-speaking groups, the Vedic peoples were deeply religious. They worshipped a host of natural and supernatural deities, the most powerful of which were the sky god and the gods that represented horses. They were confident that their chief god, Indra (the deity of war), was on their side. The Vedic people also brought elaborate rituals of worship, which set them apart from the indigenous populations. (See Primary Source: Vedic Hymns to the Chariot Race of the Gods.) But, as with many Afro-Eurasian migrations, the outsiders' arrival led to fusion as well as to conflict. While the native-born peoples eventually adopted

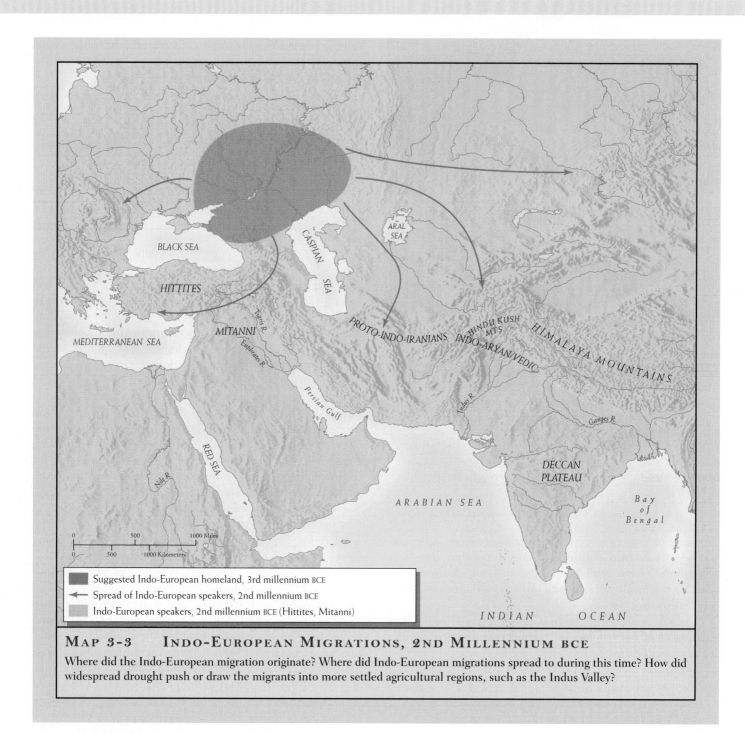

MAP 3-3   INDO-EUROPEAN MIGRATIONS, 2ND MILLENNIUM BCE

Where did the Indo-European migration originate? Where did Indo-European migrations spread to during this time? How did widespread drought push or draw the migrants into more settled agricultural regions, such as the Indus Valley?

the newcomers' language, the newcomers themselves took up the techniques and rhythms of agrarian life.

The Vedic people used the Indus Valley as a staging area for migrations throughout the northern plain of South Asia. As they mixed agrarian and pastoral ways and borrowed technologies (such as ironworking) from farther west, their population expanded and they began to look for new resources. With horses, chariots, and iron tools and weapons, they

marched south and east. By 1000 BCE, they reached the southern foothills of the Himalayas and began to settle in the Ganges River valley. Five hundred years later, they had settlements as far south as the Deccan plateau.

Each wave of occupation involved violence, but the invaders did not simply dominate the indigenous peoples. Instead, the confrontations led them to embrace many of the ways of the vanquished. Although the Vedic people despised

VEDIC HYMNS TO THE CHARIOT RACE OF THE GODS

There are no extant accounts of the Vedic people's chariot races and festivals, despite the centrality of these events to their culture. However, scholars have translated Vedic hymns praising the chariot races of gods. The following hymn portrays the Maruts—the storm gods under the direction of Indra—as skilled charioteers.

1. The Maruts charged with rain, endowed with fierce force, terrible like wild beasts, blazing in their strength, brilliant like fires, and impetuous, have uncovered the (rain-giving) cows by blowing away the cloud.

2. The [Maruts] with their rings appeared like the heavens with their stars, they shone wide like streams from clouds as soon as Rudra, the strong man, was born for you, O golden-breasted Maruts, in the bright lap of Prisni.

3. They wash their horses like racers in the courses, they hasten with the points of the reed on their quick steeds. O golden-jawed Maruts, violently shaking [your jaws], you go quick with your spotted deer, being friends of one mind.

4. Those Maruts have grown to feed all these beings, or, it may be, [they have come] hither for the sake of a friend, they who always bring quickening rain. They have spotted horses, their bounties cannot be taken away, they are like headlong charioteers on their ways.

5. O Maruts, wielding your brilliant spears, come hither on smooth roads with your fiery cows [clouds] whose udders are swelling; [come hither], being of one mind, like swans toward their nests, to enjoy the sweet offering.

6. O one-minded Maruts, come to our prayers, come to our libations like [Indra] praised by men! Fulfil [our prayer] like the udder of a barren cow, and make the prayer glorious by booty to the singer.

7. Grant us this strong horse for our chariot, a draught that rouses our prayers, from day to day, food to the singers, and to the poet in our homesteads luck, wisdom, inviolable and invincible strength.

8. When the gold-breasted Maruts harness the horses to their chariots, bounteous in wealth, then it is as if a cow in the folds poured out to her calf copious food, to every man who has offered libations.

→ *What parts of the hymn give clues about how the charioteers' horses looked and were cared for?*

→ *How do the images relating rain-filled clouds to cows reflect the pastoral roots of the Vedic nomads?*

→ *What kinds of gods were the Maruts, and what was their heavenly job when racing on horse chariots?*

SOURCE: Mandala II, Hymn 34, in Vedic Hymns, translated by Hermann Oldenberg, in vol. 32 of *Sacred Books of the East*, edited by F. Max Müller (1897; reprint, New Delhi: Motilal Banarsidass, 1979), pp. 295–96.

the local rituals, they were in awe of the inhabitants' farming skills and knowledge of seasonal weather. So they adapted even as they continued to expand their territory. They moved into huts constructed from mud, bamboo, and reeds. They refined the already sophisticated production of beautiful carnelian stone beads, and they further aided commerce by devising standardized weights. In addition to raising domesticated animals, they sowed wheat and rye on the Indus plain, and they learned to plant rice in the marshy lands of the Ganges River valley. Later they mastered the use of plows with iron blades, an innovation that transformed the agrarian base of South Asia.

The turn to settled agriculture was a major shift for the pastoral Vedic people. After all, their staple foods had always been dairy products and meat, and they were used to measuring their wealth in livestock (horses were most valuable, and cows were more valuable than sheep). Moreover, because they could not breed their prized horses in South Asia's semitropical climate, they initiated a brisk import trade from central and Southwestern Asia.

As the Vedic people adapted to their new environment and fanned out across uncharted agrarian frontiers, their initial political organization took a somewhat different course from those of Southwest Asia. Whereas competitive kingdoms dominated the landscape there, in South Asia competitive, balanced regimes were slower to emerge. The result was a slower process of political integration.

Global Connections & Disconnections

HOW LANGUAGES SPREAD: THE CASE OF NOMADIC INDO-EUROPEAN LANGUAGES

Language arose independently in a number of places around the world. All languages change with time, and scholars call related tongues with a common origin "language families." Even though members of the same language family diverged over time, they all share grammatical features and root vocabularies.

While technically there are more than a hundred language families, a much smaller number have influenced vast geographic areas. For example, the *Altaic* languages spread from Europe to central Asia. The *Sino-Tibetan* language family includes Mandarin, the most widely spoken language in the world. The *Uralic* family, which includes Hungarian and Finnish, occurs mainly in Europe. The *Afro-Asiatic* language family contains several hundred languages spoken in North Africa, sub-Saharan Africa, and Southeast Asia, Hebrew and Arabic among them.

One language family that linguists have studied extensively, and the one with the largest number of speakers, is *Indo-European*. It was identified by scholars who recognized similarities in grammar and vocabulary among classical Sanskrit, Persian, Greek, and Latin. Living languages in this family include English, Irish, German, Norwegian, Portuguese, French, Russian, Persian, Hindi, and Bengali. For the past 200 years, comparative linguists have sought to reconstruct Proto-Indo-European, the parent of all the languages in the family. They have drawn conclusions about its grammar, hypothesizing a highly inflected language with different endings on nouns and verbs according to their use. They have also made suggestions about its vocabulary. For example, after analyzing patterns of linguistic change, scholars have proposed that the basic Indo-European root that means "horse"—in Sanskrit, *aśva;* Persian, *aspa*; Latin, *equus*; and Greek, *hippos* (ἱππος)—is *ekwo-.

Table 3-1 demonstrates the similarity of words in some of the major Indo-European languages. We have emphasized numbers, which are especially stable in language systems because people do not like to change the way they count. We have also provided the equivalents in two Semitic languages (Arabic and Hebrew) to show how different these basic words are in another language family (the Afro-Asiatic).

Attempts to locate the homeland of the original speakers of Proto-Indo-European involve mapping the reconstructed vocabulary onto a matching geography. For example, some of the vocabulary contains words for "snow," "mountain," and "swift river," as well as for animals that are not native to Europe, such as "lion," "monkey," and "elephant." Other words describe agricultural practices and farming tools that date back as far as 5000 BCE. Many linguists believe that nomadic and pastoral peoples of the Eurasian steppes took this language—along with their precious horses and chariots—as far as the borderlands of what is now Afghanistan and eastern Iran.

We know that the early speakers of Indo-European languages used chariots and had words for "wheel," "yoke," and "axle." In fact, the earliest pictures of horse-drawn chariots, used in battle, came from the steppe region east of the Ural Mountains. Indo-European-speaking nomads inhabited this area and subsequently migrated to South Asia and the Iranian plateau. Thus the chariot was literally the vehicle for cultural mingling and, ultimately, the spread of the people's language.

Migration is only one of the possible reasons that languages move and change over vast areas and periods of time. Other influential factors are invasions, climatic conditions, natural resources, and ways of life. Even within one language, words can change through generations of

TABLE 3-1   Similarity of Words in Some Major Indo-European Languages

| | WORDS OF COMMON ORIGIN IN INDO-EUROPEAN LANGUAGES | | | | | | | SEMITIC LANGUAGES | |
	Sanskrit	Hindi	Greek	Latin	French	German	Spanish	Arabic	Hebrew
Numbers									
one	eka	ek	hen	unus	un	ein	uno	wahid	ehad
two	dva	do	duo	duo	deux	zwei	dos	ithnin	shnayim
three	tri	teen	treis	tres	trois	drei	tres	thalatha	shlasha
four	catur	chār	tessara	quattuor	quatre	vier	cuatro	arba'a	arba'a
five	pañca	pānch	penta	quinque	cinq	fünf	cinco	khamsa	hamisha
ten	daśa	das	deka	decem	dix	zehn	diez	ashra	asara
hundred	śata	sau	hekaton	centum	cent	hundert	cien	mi'a	me'a
Other common words									
father	pitṛ	pitā	pater	pater	père	vater	padre	abu	aba
mother	mātṛ	mātā	mêter	mater	mère	mutter	madre	umm	em
son	sūnu	betā	huios	filius	fils	sohn	hijo	ibn	ben
heart	hṛdaya	dil	kardia	cor	coeur	herz	corazón	qalb	lev
foot	pada	pair	pous	pes	pied	fuss	pie	qadam	regel
god	deva	dev	theos	deus	dieu	gott	dios	Allah	yahweh

use. And words from a common root can sometimes take on very different meanings while remaining similar phonetically. (To use an Indo-European root as an example, the Sanskrit *asura* means "demonic creature" whereas the Persian *ahura* means "Supreme God.")

Linguistic analysis sheds light on the geographic and demographic details of language penetration into different regions. Part of its allure is the fact that some issues defy resolution (for example, in some cases whether a given language was the dialect of the conquerors or the conquered). Nonetheless, the study of language families and their history underscores the key role of language in the intermingling of cultures throughout time.

Indra with Buddha. The Vedic people worshipped their gods by sacrificing and burning cows and horses and by singing hymns and songs, but they never built temples or sculptured idols. Therefore we do not know how they envisioned Indra and their other gods. However, when Buddhists started to make images of Buddha in the early centuries CE, they also sculpted Indra and Brahma as attendants of the Buddha. Indra in Buddhist iconography evolved into Vajrapani, the Diamond Lord. In this plate, the one on the left holding a stick with diamond-shaped heads is Indra/Vajrapani.

RISE OF THE SHANG STATE (1600–1045 BCE)

> → *What methods did the Shang state use to maintain its rule?*

Climatic change affected East Asia much as it had central and Southwestern Asia. As Chapter 2 detailed, this was a time of cultural integration among agricultural communities along the Yellow and Yangzi rivers. Chinese lore says that during

this era a mythological Yu the Great founded the Xia dynasty. While evidence for such a kingdom is sketchy, archaeological and other evidence confirms the emergence, around 1600 BCE, of a territorial state called Shang, located in northeastern China. (See Map 3-4.)

Like the ruling families in Southwest Asian societies, the Shang handed down their own foundation myths to unify the state. Stories supposedly written on bamboo strips and later collected into what historians call the "Bamboo Annals" tell of a time at the end of the Xia dynasty when the sun dimmed, frost and ice appeared in summer, and a long drought followed heavy rainfall and flooding. According to Chinese mythology, Tang, the first ruler of the Shang dynasty, defeated a despotic Xia king and then offered to sacrifice himself so that the drought would end. Tang survived, however, and proved to be a just and moral ruler who strengthened his state and unified his people.

As in South Asia, the Shang political system did not become highly centralized. The Shang state did not have clearly established borders like those of the territorial kingdoms of Southwest Asia. To be sure, it faced threats—but not in the form of rival territorial states encroaching on its peripheries. Thus it had little need for a strongly defended permanent capital, though its heartland was called Zhong Shang, or "center Shang." Its capital moved as its frontier expanded and contracted. This relative security is evident in the Shang kings' personalized style of rule, as they made regular trips around the country to meet, hunt, and conduct military campaigns with those who owed allegiance to them. Yet, like the territorial kingdoms of Southwest Asia, the Shang state had a ruling lineage (a line of male sovereigns descended from a common ancestor) that was eventually set down in a written record. (See Primary Source: Sima Qian on the Ruler's Mandate from Heaven to Rule.)

Shang rulers used metallurgy and writing to reinforce their rule, as well as ancestor worship, divination, and other rituals. At the heart of their power was their keen awareness of the importance of promoting agricultural growth and controlling the precious metals used to finance war.

STATE FORMATION

The Shang state built on the agricultural and riverine village cultures of the Longshan peoples, who had set the stage for a centralized state, urban life, and a cohesive culture (see Chapter 2). The Shang territorial state did not evolve out of city-states as occurred in Mesopotamia and Egypt. Rather, as the population increased and the number of village conflicts grew, it became necessary to have larger and more centralized forms of control. The Shang state emerged to play that governmental role.

The Longshan peoples had already introduced four elements that were instrumental in forming the Shang state: a

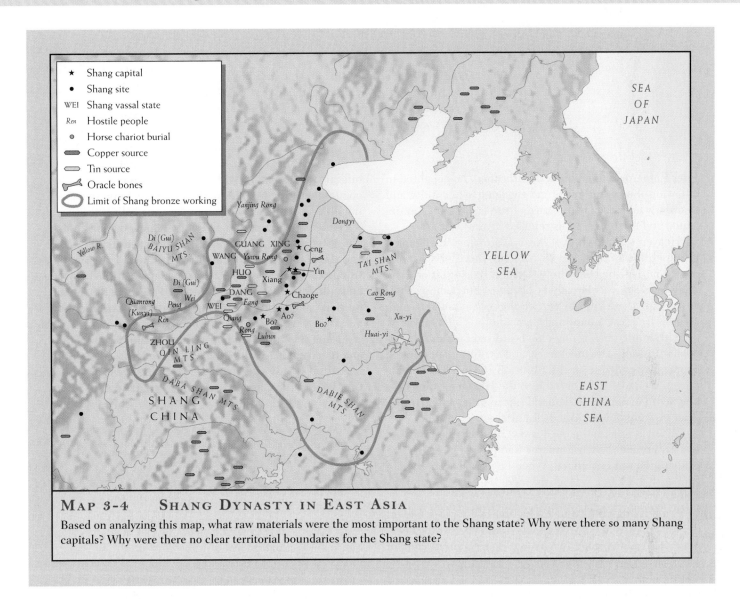

MAP 3-4   SHANG DYNASTY IN EAST ASIA
Based on analyzing this map, what raw materials were the most important to the Shang state? Why were there so many Shang capitals? Why were there no clear territorial boundaries for the Shang state?

metal industry based on copper; pottery making; walled towns; and divination using animal bones. To these foundations the Shang dynasty added a lineage of hereditary rulers whose power derived from their relation to ancestors and gods; written records; tribute; and rituals that enabled them to commune with ancestors and foretell the future. In particular, the Shang promoted large-scale metallurgy and the development of writing. These were major elements in the advance of Chinese society in the second millennium BCE.

To expand and protect their borders, the Shang fought with neighboring states and with pastoral nomads from the central Asian steppes. Horses imported from central Asia helped the Shang dominate northern and central China. Moreover, the Shang copied the chariots of the nomads they

encountered, improving them by adding bronze fittings and harnesses; this new technology gave the warriors devastating range and speed. Here too, as in Southwest Asia, chariot aristocracies emerged. But here, it is important to recall, chariot aristocracies did not produce centralized kingdoms.

Instead, East Asia became a patchwork of regimes that did not rise to the level of military-diplomatic jostling of Southwest Asia. Several other large states also developed in East Asia at this time. These included relatively urban and wealthy peoples in the southeast and more rustic peoples bordering the Shang. The latter traded with the former, whom they knew as the Fang—their label for those who lived in non-Shang areas. Other kingdoms in the south and southwest also had independent bronze industries, with casting technologies comparable to those of the Shang.

Primary Source

SIMA QIAN ON THE RULER'S MANDATE FROM HEAVEN TO RULE

Sima Qian was the first great historian in ancient China. He later had as much influence in East Asia as Herodotus, the first Greek historian, had in Greece and Rome. The excerpt below presents the transition from Xia ("Hsia") dynasty to Shang ("T'ang") dynasty as an example of the transfer of the ruler's heavenly mandate.

After Emperor K'ung-chia was enthroned, he delighted in following ghosts and spirits and engaging in licentious and disorderly actions. The prestige of the Hsia-hou Clan declined and the feudal lords rebelled against him.

Heaven sent down two dragons, a male and a female. K'ung-chia was not able to care for them and he lost the support of the Huan-lung (Dragon Raising) Clan. The Yao-t'ang Clan was already in decline, [but] among their descendants one Liu Lei learned the technique of taming dragons from the Huan-lung Clan and thus obtained service with K'ung-chia. K'ung-chia bestowed on him the *cognomen* Yü-lung (Dragon Tamer) and conferred on him the people descended from the Shih-wei [Clan]. The female dragon died and Liu Lei fed it to the Hsia-hou, the Hsia-hou sent [someone] to demand [more of it], and, fearing [that he would be punished], Liu Lei moved on.

When K'ung-chia passed away, his son Emperor Kao was enthroned. When Emperor Kao passed away his son Emperor Fa was enthroned. When Fa passed away, his son Emperor Lu-k'uei was enthroned. He was known as Chieh.

From K'ung-chia's time to the time of Emperor Chieh, the feudal lords had revolted many times against the Hsia. Chieh did not engage in virtuous [government] but in military power and [this] hurt the families of the hundred cognomens. The families of the hundred cognomens were not able to bear him.

Chieh then summoned T'ang and jailed him in Hsia-t'ai. After a while he freed him. T'ang cultivated his virtue and the feudal lords all submitted to T'ang. T'ang then led troops to attack Chieh of Hsia. Chieh fled to Ming-t'iao and subsequently was exiled and died there. Before he died he said to someone, "I regret failing to kill T'ang in Hsia-t'ai; that is what has brought me to this."

T'ang then ascended the throne of the Son of Heaven and received the world's homage in the Hsia's place. T'ang enfeoffed [made vassals or subjects] the descendants of the Hsia. In the Chou dynasty they were enfeoffed at Ch'i.

> → *What role did morality play in Sima Qian's description of the transfer of the Xia ruler's mandate from heaven to the Shang dynasty?*
> → *How do the references to feuding illustrate the type of society that China had at this time?*

SOURCE: Ssu-ma Ch'ien, "Sima Qian on the Ruler's Mandate," from *The Grand Scribe's Records*, ed. William H. Nienhauser Jr. Reprinted with permission of Indiana University Press.

The Shang state reached its peak around 1200 BCE. At Yin, the Shang erected massive palaces, royal neighborhoods, and bronze foundries. In workshops surrounding the palace, craftworkers decorated jade, stone, and ivory objects; wove silk on special looms; and produced bronze weapons as well as bronze ritual objects and ceremonial drinking vessels. Taking advantage of the local abundance of metal ores, artisans organized workshops to mass-produce the large bronze vessels. The levels of urbanization reached at Yin indicate that the Shang also collected tribute from the agrarian heartlands to support the city's nobles, priests, and dependent artisans and metalworkers. The Shang state simultaneously promoted the writings of elite scribes and the productions of common artisans.

METALWORKING, AGRICULTURE, AND TRIBUTE

Small-scale metalworking, which first emerged in northwestern China, was a critical element in the power of the Shang state. Pre-Shang sites reveal that casting techniques were in use as early as 1800 BCE. Because copper and tin were available from the North China plain, only short-distance trade was necessary to obtain the resources that a bronze culture needed. Access to copper and tin, and to new metallurgy technology, gave the Shang a huge advantage and unprecedented power over their neighbors.

The Shang used copper, lead, and tin to produce bronze, from which they made weapons, fittings for chariots, and

Bronze. At the height of the Shang state, circa 1200 BCE, its rulers erected massive palaces at the capital of Yin, which required bronze foundries for its wine and food vessels. In these foundries, skilled workers produced bronze weapons and ritual objects and elaborate ceremonial drinking and eating vessels, like the one pictured.

ritual vessels. They created hollow clay molds to hold the molten metal alloy, and then they removed the bronze objects after the liquid had cooled and solidified. The casting of modular components that artisans could assemble later promoted increased production and fueled the elites' extravagant uses of bronze vessels for burials. For example, archaeologists have unearthed a tomb at Anyang containing an enormous 1,925-pound bronze vessel; the Shang workshops had produced it around 1200 BCE. Another Anyang tomb from the same period contained 3,500 pounds of cast bronze.

The bronze industry of this period shows the high level not only of material culture (the physical objects produced) but also of cultural development. The Shang metalworking required extensive mining (and thus a large labor force), efficient casting, and a reproducible artistic style. The extraction of the resources was distinct from their conversion into goods: although the Shang state highly valued its artisans, it treated its copper miners as lowly tribute laborers.

By controlling access to tin and copper and to the production of bronze, the Shang kings prevented their rivals from forging bronze weapons and thus increased their own power and legitimacy. With their superior weapons, Shang armies could easily destroy armies wielding wooden clubs and stone-tipped spears. Moreover, the ruler enhanced his power by hiring artisans to record his feats for posterity. Shang workers produced large and small bronze vessels on which they delicately inscribed images of important events—particularly those showing the ruler in a significant role, such as a battle, a wedding, the birth of an heir, or an astrological sighting.

The Shang dynasts also understood the importance of agriculture for winning and maintaining power, so they did much to promote its development. In fact, the activities of local governors and the masses revolved around agriculture. The rulers controlled their own farms, which supplied food to the royal family, craftworkers, and army. New technologies led to increased food production. Farmers drained low-lying fields and cleared forested areas to expand the cultivation of millet, wheat, barley, and possibly rice. Their implements included stone plows, spades, and sickles. In addition, farmers cultivated silkworms and raised pigs, dogs, sheep, and oxen. To best use the land and increase production, they tracked the growing season. And to record the seasons, the Shang developed a twelve-month, 360-day lunar calendar; it contained leap months to maintain the proper relationship between months and seasons. The calendar also relieved fears about events such as solar and lunar eclipses by making them predictable.

As in other Afro-Eurasian states, the ruler's wealth and power depended on tribute from elites and allies. Elites supplied warriors and laborers, horses and cattle. Allies sent foodstuffs, soldiers, and workers and "assisted in the king's affairs"—perhaps by hunting, burning brush, or clearing land—in return for his help in defending against invaders and making predictions about the harvest. Commoners sent their tribute to the elites, who held the land as fiefs from the king. (Fiefs were grants, usually of land and occasionally of office, by kings and lords to subordinates.) Farmers transferred their surplus crops to the elite landholders (or to the ruler if they worked on his personal landholdings) on a regular schedule. Commoners also made payments in labor: some worked in the royal workshops producing bronze ritual vessels and armaments, such as dagger-axes, arrowheads, spearheads, helmets, shields, and chariot fittings; others labored to drain fields, clear land, build palaces, excavate tombs, or construct walls to protect towns or the capital.

Tribute could also take the form of turtle shells and cattle scapulas (shoulder blades), which the Shang used for divination (see below). Divining the future was a powerful way to legitimate royal power—and then to justify the right to collect more tribute. By placing themselves symbolically and literally at the center of all exchanges, the Shang kings reinforced their power over others.

SHANG SOCIETY AND BELIEFS

Both metalworking and agriculture contributed to the state's wealth and supported a complex society. The organizing principle of Shang society was a patrilineal ideal that traced descent back through the generations to a common male ancestor. Grandparents, parents, sons, and daughters lived and worked together. They held property in common, and male family elders took precedence. Women from other patrilines married into the family and won honor when they became mothers, particularly of sons.

The death ritual, which involved sacrificing humans to accompany the deceased in the next life, also reflected the social hierarchy. A member of the royal elite was often buried with his full entourage, including his wife, consorts, servants, chariots, horses, and drivers. The inclusion of personal slaves and servants indicates a belief that the familiar social hierarchy would continue in the afterlife. Modern Chinese historians have described the Shang as a "slave society," but the basis of its economy was not slave labor. Instead, the driving force was the tribute labor (in particular, metalworking and farming) of the commoners who constituted most of society.

The Shang state was a patrimonial theocracy: it claimed that the ruler at the top of the hierarchy derived his authority through guidance from ancestors and gods. Rulers therefore had to find ways to communicate with ancestors and foretell the future, and they relied on **divination**, much as did the rulers in Greece and Mesopotamia at this time. When diviners applied intense heat to the shoulder bones of cattle or to turtle shells, the bones or shells cracked. Diviners would interpret those cracks as an auspicious or inauspicious sign from the ancestors regarding royal plans and actions. (See Primary Source: The Oracle Bone.) On these bones, scribes subsequently inscribed the queries asked of the ancestors to confirm the diviners' interpretations. Thus, Shang writing began as a dramatic ritual performance in which the living responded to their ancestors' oracular signs.

In Shang theocracy, the ruler was also the head of a unified clergy. Because the ruler embodied both religious and political power, no independent priesthood emerged to challenge the royal family. Diviners and scribes were subordinate to the ruler and the royal pantheon of ancestors he represented. (Unlike in Mesopotamia and Egypt, rulers never entrusted diviners with independent action.) Ancestor worship sanctified Shang control and legitimized the rulers' lineage, ensuring that the ruling family kept all political and religious power.

Because the Shang gods were ancestral deities, all the rulers were deified when they died and ranked in descending chronological order. Thus, the primary Shang deity was Di, the High God (Shangdi), who was the founding ancestor of the Shang royal family. The Shang ruler who became a god was closer to the world of humans than the supreme Egyptian and Mesopotamian gods were, and he served to unite the world of the living with the world of the dead. Much as the Egyptians believed their pharaohs (supposedly born of human mothers and godlike fathers) ascended into heaven after their deaths, so the Shang believed their kings moved into a parallel other world when they died.

THE DEVELOPMENT OF WRITING IN CHINA

Although Shang scholars did not invent writing in East Asia, they perfected it. Oracle bones, so central to political and religious authority, are the primary evidence of early writing in China. Other written records may have been on materials that did not survive. Thus accidents of preservation may explain the major differences between the ancient texts in China (primarily divinations on bones) and in the Southwest Asian societies that impressed cuneiform on clay tablets (primarily for economic transactions, literary and religious documents, and historical records).

The inscriptions on oracle bones and bronzes leave no doubt that the Shang surpassed other peoples in northwestern China in their determination to leave records. After all, their governmental institutions and religious rituals were more complex than those of the peoples living nearby. However, in comparison with Mesopotamia and Egypt, the transformation of Shang record keeping (for example, questions to ancestors, lineages of rulers, or economic transactions) to literature (for example, myths about the founding of states) was slower.

As noted, Shang kings used writing to reinforce their position at the top of the hierarchy of royal families. And priests used it on oracle bones to address the other world and gain information about the future. Because the North China climate entered a warmer and wetter phase in the twelfth and eleventh centuries BCE, many divinations aimed at predicting rainfall for the sustenance of crops—in particular the staple crop, millet. Priests presented the living Shang ruler as the religious pivot among Di, the High God (who controlled the ever-important rain cycles), the ancestors, and their royal descendants.

In addition, like the Babylonian dynasts, later Shang rulers used an enlarged and increasingly powerful bureaucracy to promote their authority over tributary states and peoples. Imperial records of foods, wines, bronze vessels, and livestock are evidence of a centralized "royal household." During this period, the original archaic script evolved into the preclassical script seen on many bronze vessels. The preclassical script preceded the formal character-based system that has endured among elites to the present. The latter system sets apart the later Chinese, Japanese, Korean, and Vietnamese societies from the cultures in Mesopotamia and the Mediterranean that rely on syllable- and alphabet-based writing. (See Global Connections & Disconnections on p. 104.)

THE ORACLE BONE

About 3,000 years old, the oracle bone below dates from the Shang dynasty reign of King Wu Ding (c. 1200 BCE). Oracle bones enabled diviners to access the other world and provided the ruler with important information about the future. Shang kings often used divination to make political or military decisions and to predict the weather.

A partial translation of the left-hand side of this oracle bone reads

[Preface:] Crack making on *gui-si* day, Que divined:

[Charge:] In the next ten days there will be no disaster.

[Prognostication:] The king, reading the cracks, said, "There will be no harm; there will perhaps be the coming of alarming news."

[Verification:] When it came to the fifth day, *ding-you*, there really was the coming of alarming news from the west. Zhi Guo, reporting, said, "The Du Fang [a border people] are besieging in our eastern borders and have harmed two settlements." The Gong-fang also raided the fields of our western borders.

→ *What political or military decision do you think King Wu Ding might have made in response to the "alarming news"?*

→ *Why did Shang kings rely on oracle bones?*

SOURCE: This translation follows, with slight modifications by Bryan W. Van Norden, David N. Keightley, *Sources of Shang History* (Berkeley: University of California Press, 1978), p. 44.

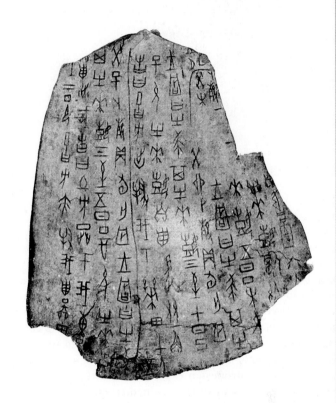

THE SOUTH PACIFIC (2500 BCE–400 CE)

→ *How did Austronesian migrations affect the emergence of microsocieties in the South Pacific?*

As Afro-Eurasian populations grew, and migration and trade brought cultures together, some peoples took to the waters in search of opportunities or refuge. By comparing the vocabularies and grammatical similarities of languages spoken today by the tribal peoples in Taiwan, the Philippines, and Indonesia, we can trace the ancient Austronesian-speaking peoples back to coastal South China in the fourth millennium BCE. Their first wave of migrants reached the islands of Polynesia. A second wave from Taiwan around 2500 BCE again reached Polynesia and then went beyond into the South Pacific. By 2000 BCE these peoples had replaced the earlier inhabitants of the East Asian coastal islands, the hunter-gatherers known as the Negritos. They had migrated south from the Asian landmass around 28,000 BCE, during an ice age when the coastal Pacific islands were connected to the Asian mainland.

Austronesian Canoe. Early Austronesians crossed the Taiwan Straits and colonized key islands in the Pacific using double-outrigger canoes from sixty to one hundred feet long equipped with triangular sails. In good weather, such canoes could cover more than 120 miles in a day.

SEAFARING SKILLS

Using their remarkable double-outrigger canoes, which were 60 to 100 feet long and bore huge triangular sails, the early Austronesians crossed the Taiwan Straits and colonized key islands in the Pacific. Their vessels were much more advanced than the simple dugout canoes used in inland waterways. In good weather, double-outrigger canoes could cover more than 120 miles in a day. The invention of a stabilization device for deep-sea sailing sometime after 2500 BCE triggered further Austronesian expansion into the Pacific. By 400 CE, these nomads of the sea had reached most of the South Pacific except for Australia and New Zealand.

Their seafaring skills enabled the Austronesians to monopolize trade wherever they went (as the Phoenicians did during the first half of the first millennium BCE). Among their craftworkers were potters, who produced distinctive Lapita ware (bowls and vessels) on offshore islets or in coastal villages. Archaeological finds reveal that these canoe-building people also conducted inter-island trade in New Guinea after 1600 BCE. By four hundred years later they had reached Fiji, Samoa, and Tonga, according to the evidence from pottery fragments and the remains of domesticated animals.

ENVIRONMENT AND CULTURE

Pottery, stone tools, and domesticated crops and pigs characterized Austronesian settlements throughout the coastal islands and in the South Pacific. These cultural markers reached the Philippines from Taiwan. By 2500 BCE, according to archaeologists, the same cultural features had spread to the islands of Java, Sumatra, Celebes, Borneo, and Timor.

Austronesians arrived in Java and Sumatra in 2000 BCE; by 1600 BCE they were in Australia and New Guinea, although they failed to penetrate the interior, where descendants of the indigenous peoples still live. The Austronesians then ventured farther eastward into the South Pacific, apparently arriving in Samoa and Fiji in 1200 BCE and on mainland Southeast Asia in 1000 BCE. (See Map 3-5.)

Equatorial lands in the South Pacific have a tropical or subtropical climate and, in many places, fertile soils containing nutrient-rich volcanic ash. In this environment the Austronesians cultivated dry-land crops (yams and sweet potatoes), irrigated crops (more yams, which grew better in paddy fields or in rainy areas), and tree crops (breadfruit, bananas, and coconuts). In addition, colonized areas beyond the landmass, such as the islands of Indonesia, had labyrinthine coastlines rich in maritime resources, including coral reefs and mangrove swamps teeming with wildlife. Island hopping led the adventurers to encounter new food sources, but the shallow waters and reefs offered sufficient fish and shellfish for their needs.

In the South Pacific, the Polynesian descendants of the early Austronesians shared a common culture, language, technology, and stores of domesticated plants and animals. These later seafarers came from many different island communities (hence the name *Polynesian*, "belonging to many islands"), and after they settled down, their numbers grew. Their crop surpluses allowed more densely populated communities to support craft specialists and soldiers. Most settlements boasted ceremonial buildings to promote local solidarity and forts to provide defense. On larger islands, communities often cooperated and organized workforces to enclose ponds for fish production and to build and maintain large irrigation works for agriculture. In terms of

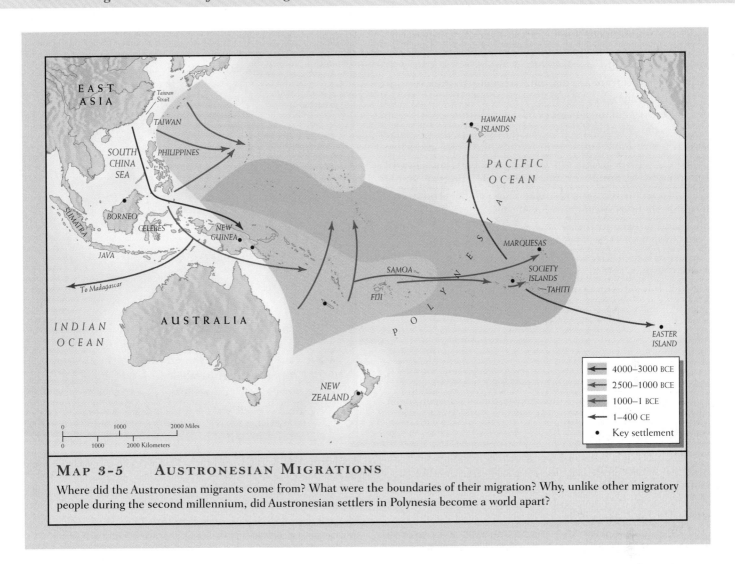

MAP 3-5 AUSTRONESIAN MIGRATIONS

Where did the Austronesian migrants come from? What were the boundaries of their migration? Why, unlike other migratory people during the second millennium, did Austronesian settlers in Polynesia become a world apart?

political structure, Polynesian communities ranged from tribal or village units to multi-island alliances that sometimes invaded other areas.

The Austronesians reached the Marquesas Islands, strategically located for northern and southern exploration, in the central Pacific around 200 CE. Over the next few centuries, some moved on to Easter Island to the south and Hawaii to the north. The immense thirty-ton stone structures on Easter Island represent the monumental Polynesian architecture produced after their arrival. In separate migrations they traversed the Indian Ocean westward and arrived at the island of Madagascar by the sixth century CE. Along the way, they transmitted crops such as the banana to East Africa.

The expansion of East Asian peoples throughout the South Pacific and their trade back and forth did not, however, integrate the islands into the mainland culture. Expansion could not overcome the tendency of these **microsocieties**, dispersed across a huge ocean, toward fragmentation and isolation.

MICROSOCIETIES IN THE AEGEAN WORLD

⟶ *How did long-distance trade influence the Aegean world?*

In the region around the Aegean Sea, the islands and the mainland of present-day Greece, no single power emerged before the second millennium BCE. Settled agrarian communities developed into local polities linked only by trade and culture. Fragmentation was the norm—in part because the landscape had no great riverine systems or large common plain. In terms of its fragmentation, the island world of the eastern Mediterranean initially resembled that of the South Pacific.

As an unintended benefit of the lack of centralization, there was no single regime to collapse when the droughts arrived. Thus, in the second millennium BCE, peoples of the eastern Mediterranean did not struggle to recover lost grandeur. Rather, they enjoyed a remarkable though gradual development, making advances based on influences they absorbed from Southwest Asia, Egypt, and Europe. It was a time when residents of Aegean islands like Crete and Thera enjoyed extensive trade with the Greek mainland, Egypt, Anatolia, Syria, and Palestine. It was also a time of population movements from the Danube region and central Europe into the Mediterranean. Groups of these migrants settled in mainland Greece in the centuries after 1900 BCE; modern archaeologists have named them Mycenaeans after the famous palace at Mycenae that dates to this era. Soon after settling in their new environment, the Mycenaeans turned to the sea to look for resources and interaction with their neighbors.

Seaborne Trade. The size of the seaborne trade is revealed most spectacularly in the shipwrecks recovered by underwater archaeologists. One of these ships, sunk off the southern coast of Anatolia around 1325 BCE, was transporting ten tons of copper in 354 oxhide-shaped ingots, as well as more than a hundred amphorae (large, two-handled jars) containing all kinds of high-value commodities.

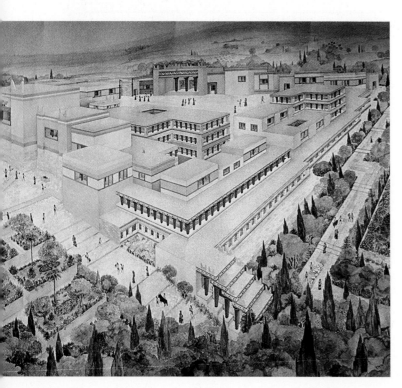

Palace at Knossos. An artist's reconstruction of the Minoan palace at Knossos on Crete. This complex, the largest such center on the island, covered more than six acres and contained more than thirteen hundred rooms. Its main feature was a large, open-air central courtyard, around which were arranged the storage, archive, ritual, and ceremonial rooms. Rather than the complex cities that would emerge later, the urbanized centers on Crete were represented by these large complexes, similar to palace complexes in contemporary Levantine sites.

SEABORNE TRADE AND COMMUNICATION

At the outset, the main influence on the Aegean world came from the east by sea. As the institutions and ideas that had developed in Southwest Asia moved westward, they found a ready reception along the coasts and on the islands of the Mediterranean. These innovations followed the sea currents, moving counterclockwise up the eastern seaboard of the Levant, then to the island of Cyprus and along the southern coast of Anatolia, and then westward to the islands of the Aegean Sea and to Crete. Trade was the main source of eastern influences, with vessels carrying cargoes from island to island and up and down the commercial centers along the coast. (See Map 3-6.)

The Mediterranean islands were important hubs that linked the mainland peoples of western Asia and Europe

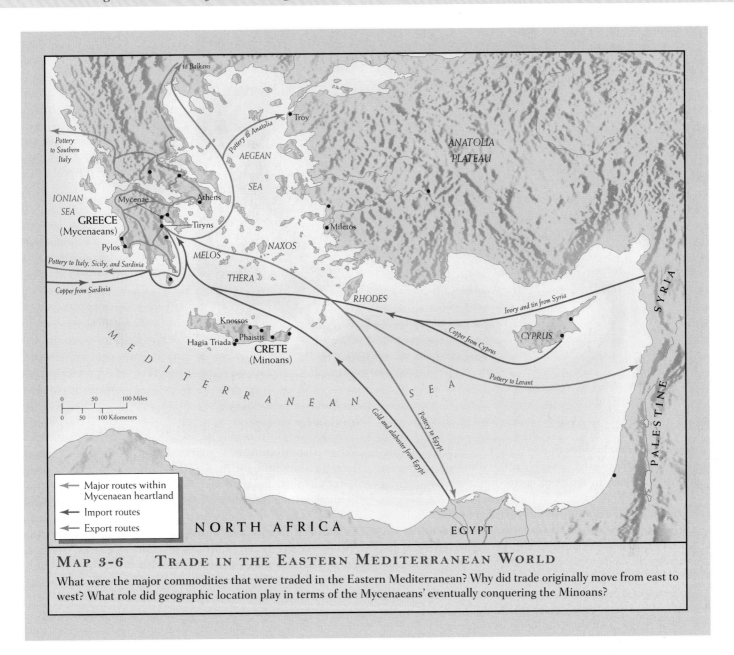

MAP 3-6   TRADE IN THE EASTERN MEDITERRANEAN WORLD
What were the major commodities that were traded in the Eastern Mediterranean? Why did trade originally move from east to west? What role did geographic location play in terms of the Mycenaeans' eventually conquering the Minoans?

with the islanders. They also served as a springboard from which eastern influences shot northward into Europe. By 1500 BCE, the islands were booming. Trade centered on tin from the east and readily available copper, both essential for making bronze (the primary metal in tools and weapons). Islands located in the midst of the active sea-lanes flourished. Because Cyprus straddled the main sea-lane, it was a focal point of trade. It also had large reserves of copper ore, which started to generate intense activity around 2300 BCE. By 2000 BCE, harbors on the southern and eastern sides of the island were shipping and transshipping goods, along with copper ingots, as far west as Crete, east to the Euphrates River, and south to Egypt. So identified was this island with

the metal that the English word *copper* is derived from "Cyprus."

Crete, too, was an active trading node in the Mediterranean, with networks reaching as far east as Mesopotamia. Around 2000 BCE, a large number of independent palace centers began to emerge on Crete, at Knossos and elsewhere. Scholars have named the people who built these elaborate centers the Minoans, after the legendary King Minos who may have ruled Crete at this time. The Minoans sailed back and forth across the Mediterranean, and by 1600 they were colonizing other Aegean islands as trading and mining centers. The Minoans' wealth soon became a magnet for the Mycenaeans, their mainland competitors, who took over Crete around 1400 BCE.

Aegean Fresco. This is one of the more striking wall paintings, or frescoes, discovered by archaeologists in the 1970s and 1980s at Akrotiri on the island of Thera (Santorini) in the Aegean Sea. Its brilliant colors, especially the blue of the sea, evoke the lively essence of Minoan life on the island. Note the houses of the wealthy along the port and the flotilla of ships that reflects the seaborne commerce that was beginning to flourish in the Mediterranean in this period.

MINOAN CULTURE

As the island communities traded with the peoples of Southwest Asia, they borrowed some ideas but also kept their own cultural traditions. In terms of borrowing, the monumental architecture of Southwest Asia found small-scale echoes in the Aegean world—notably in the palace complexes built on Crete between 1900 and 1600 BCE (the most impressive was at Knossos). Unlike in Mesopotamia or Egypt, however, microsocieties or small-scale insular communities remained the norm for human organization on these Aegean islands.

In terms of a distinctive cultural element, worship on the islands focused on a female deity, the "Lady," but there are no traces of large temple complexes similar to those in Mesopotamia, Anatolia, and Egypt. Nor, apparently, was there any priestly class of the type that managed the temple complexes of Southwest Asian societies. Moreover, it is unclear whether these societies had full-time scribes.

There was significant regional diversity within this small Aegean world. On Thera, a small island to the north of Crete, archaeologists have uncovered a splendid trading city—one that was not centered on a major palace complex—in which private houses had bathrooms with toilets and running water and rooms decorated with exotic wall paintings. One painting depicted a flotilla of pleasure, trading, and naval vessels. On Crete, the large palace-centered communities controlled centrally organized societies of a high order of refinement. Confident in their wealth and power, the sprawling palaces had no fortifications and no natural defenses. They were light, airy, and open to their surrounding landscapes.

MYCENAEAN CULTURE

When the Mycenaeans migrated to Greece from central Europe, they brought their Indo-European language, their horse chariots, and their metalworking skills. Their move was gradual, lasting from about 1850 to 1600 BCE, but ultimately they dominated the indigenous population. Known for their exceptional height, they maintained their dominance with their powerful weapon, the chariot, until 1200 BCE. Indeed, horse chariots were important in their mythology and cultural tradition. The battle chariots and festivities of chariot racing described in the epic poetry of Homer (which date from after the collapse of Mycenaean societies) express memories of glorious chariot feats that echo Vedic legends from South Asia (see p. 103).

The Mycenaeans were more war oriented than the Minoans, and they possessed a less refined material culture: it emphasized displays of weaponry, portraits of armed soldiers, and illustrations of violent conflicts. The main palace centers at Tiryns and Mycenae were the hulking fortresses of warlords surrounded by rough-hewn stone walls and strategically located atop large rock outcroppings. The Mycenaeans amassed an amazing amount of wealth and carried some of it to their graves. Their tombs contain many gold vessels and decorations; most ostentatious were the gold masks. The many amber beads indicate that the warriors had contacts with inhabitants of the coniferous forest regions in northern Europe.

Southwest Asian economic and political structures shaped the coastal sites where the Mycenaeans settled, such as

Tiryns and Pylos. Massive stone fortresses and fortified palaces dominated these urban hubs. A preeminent ruler (*wanax*) stood atop a complex bureaucratic hierarchy; numerous subordinates aided him, including slaves. At the heart of the palace society were scribes, who recorded the goods and services allotted to local farmers, shepherds, and metalworkers, among others. (See Primary Source: Linear A and B—Writing in the Early Mediterranean Worlds.)

Mycenaean expansion eventually overwhelmed the Minoans on Crete. The Mycenaeans also created colonies and trading settlements, reaching as far as Sicily and southern Italy. In this fashion, the trade and language of the early Greek-speaking peoples created a veneer of unity linking the dispersed worlds of the Aegean Sea.

At the close of the second millennium BCE, the eastern Mediterranean faced internal and external convulsions that ended the heyday of these microsocieties. Most notable was

Mycenaean Sword. The hilt and engraved gold pommel of a sword from the regal burials at the site of Mycenae. The presence of this weaponry, both depicted in the art of the period and preserved in artifacts buried with the dead, was typical of a violent society with a warrior elite. The riveted hilt and the bronze sword blade are of a kind found widely distributed in the Mediterranean, following the patterns of Mycenaean trade routes.

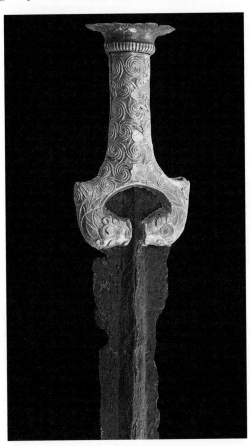

a series of migrations of peoples from central Europe who moved through southeastern Europe, Anatolia, and the eastern Mediterranean (see Chapter 4). The invasions, although often destructive, did not extinguish but rather reinforced the creative potential of this frontier area. Following the upheaval at the close of the millennium, a new social order emerged that was destined to have an even greater brilliance and influence. Because theirs was a closed maritime world—in comparison with the wide-open Pacific—the Greek-speaking peoples around the Aegean quickly reasserted dominance in the eastern Mediterranean that the Austronesians did not match in Southeast Asia or Polynesia.

EUROPE—THE NORTHERN FRONTIER

→ *Why did polities remain small-scale in Europe?*

The transition to settled agriculture and the raising of domesticated animals took longer in western Afro-Eurasia than in the rest of the landmass. Two millennia passed, from 5000 to 3000 BCE, before settled agriculture became the dominant economic form in Europe. In many broad areas, hunters and gatherers clung to their traditional ways. Even this frontier, however, saw occasional visits from peoples driving horse chariots during the second millennium BCE.

Forbidding evergreen forests dominated the northern area of the far western stretches of Europe, and the area's sparse population was slow to implement the new ways. The first agricultural communities were frontier settlements where pioneers broke new land. Surrounded by hunting and foraging communities, these innovators lived hard lives in harsh environments, overcoming their isolation only by creating regional alliances. Such arrangements were too unstable to initiate or sustain long-distance trade. These were not fertile grounds for creating powerful kingdoms.

The early European cultivators adopted the techniques for controlling plants and animals that Southwest Asian peoples had developed. But rather than establishing large, hierarchical, and centralized societies, the Europeans used these techniques to create self-sufficient communities. They did not incorporate the other cultural and political features that characterized the societies of Egypt, Mesopotamia, and the eastern Mediterranean. Occasional innovations such as the working of metal (initially, copper), the manufacture of pottery, and the use of the plow had little impact on local conditions. Throughout this period, Europe was hardly a developed cultural center. Instead, it was a wild frontier.

LINEAR A AND B—WRITING IN THE EARLY MEDITERRANEAN WORLDS

On the island of Crete and on the mainland of Greece, scribes working in the palace-centered societies kept records on clay tablets in two scripts that were linear. Linear A script, apparently written in Minoan, has not yet been deciphered. Linear B was deciphered in the 1950s and proved that, contrary to what almost all classical scholars had assumed, the Linear B tablets were the work of speakers of Mycenaean—an early form of Greek.

Massive numbers of these clay tablets have survived. Noting every detail of the goods and services that the palace bureaucracy managed, they contain lists short and long of persons or things—about as interesting as modern grocery lists. The following tablet from Pylos on the Greek mainland notes how much seed grain the bureaucrats were distributing to rural landholders who were dependent on the ruler:

The plot of Qelequhontas: this much seed: 276 l. of wheat

R. slave of the god, holds a lease: so much seed: 12 l. of wheat

W. the priest holds a lease: so much seed: 12 l. of wheat

Thuriatis, female slave of the god, dependant of P. the old man: so much seed: 108 l. of wheat

The plot of Admaos, so much seed: 216 l. of wheat. . . .

T. slave of the god, holds a lease: so much seed: 32 l. of wheat

The plot of A . . . eus, so much seed: 144 l. of wheat. . . .

The plot of T. slave of the god, holds a lease: 18 l. of wheat

The plot of R., so much seed: 138 l. of wheat. . . .

The plot of Aktaios, so much seed: 384 l. of wheat. . . .

➢ *Notice that all the people identified in this passage are going to plant wheat. How does this underscore the blending of agriculture with war-making in the aggressive Mycenaean society?*

➢ *What does this document suggest is the function of writing in these societies?*

SOURCE: M. Ventris and J. Chadwick, *Documents in Mycenaean Greek*, 2nd ed. (Cambridge: Cambridge University Press, 1973), doc. 116.

This is a typical Linear B document inscribed on clay with linear marks representing syllables and signs. The clay tablet was stored in a palace archive. This tablet came from the excavated Mycenaean palace at Pylos on the mainland of Greece.

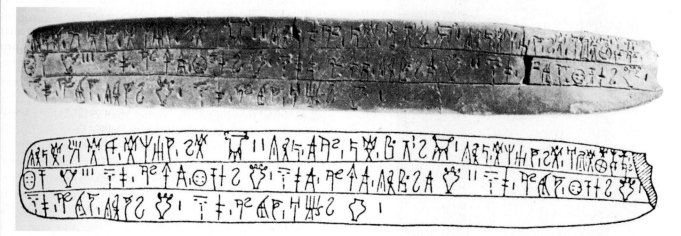

This is an example of the earlier Linear A script, used to write the non-Greek language of the Minoans. Because evidence of the script has appeared only on the island of Crete, scholars believe the early Minoan palace centers were its sole users (probably for keeping records). This example came from the small palace site at Hagia Triada.

Two significant changes affected the northern frontier: the domestication of the horse, and the emergence of wheeled chariots and wagons. Both became instruments of war, and both promoted adaptation to the steppe lands of inner and central Europe where pasturing animals in large herds proved profitable. The success of this horse culture led to the creation of several new frontiers, including those of agriculturally self-sustaining communities.

The new agriculturalists faced constant challenges not just within Europe but also to the east, as they entered the rolling grasslands of central Eurasia. Their attempts to enter this zone usually met overpowering resistance by fierce men on horseback. The inhabitants of the steppe lands north of the Black Sea gradually shifted from a primitive agriculture to an economy based on the herding of animals. In this zone, the domestication of the horse fostered a highly mobile culture in which whole communities moved on horseback or by means of large wheeled wagons. Because these pastoral nomads regularly sought out the richer agricultural lands in

Steppe Horse Culture. This gold comb from the early fourth century BCE is decorated with a battle scene from a Scythian heroic epic and illustrates the fascination of these European peoples with horses, weapons, and warfare.

central Europe, there was constant hostility between the two worlds.

These struggles among settlers, hunter-gatherers, and nomadic horse riders bred cultures with a strong warrior ethos. The fullest development of this mounted horse culture occurred in the centuries after 1000 BCE, when the steppe land Scythian peoples engaged in rituals (such as drinking blood) that forged bonds of blood brotherhood among warriors and heightened their aggressive behavior. This rough-and-tumble frontier gave its people an appetite to borrow more effective means of waging war. Europeans desired the nomadic people's weaponry, and over time their interactions with the horsemen included trade as well as violence. As a result of the trading contacts, Europeans adopted horses and finer metalworking technologies from the Caucasus. Of course, such trade made their battles even more lethal. And while the connections between this frontier zone and other parts of the Afro-Eurasian world began to multiply, it was still too dispersed and unruly to develop integrated kingdoms. At a time when the rest of Afro-Eurasia was developing an interrelated network of large territorial states, Europe remained a land of war-making, small chieftainships.

EARLY STATES IN THE AMERICAS

→ *How did the ecology of the Central Andes influence early state systems?*

Across all the Americas, river valleys and coasts sheltered villages and towns drawing sustenance from the rich resources in their hinterlands. Hunting and gathering was still the main lifeway here. But without beasts of burden or domesticated animals to carry loads or plow fields, local communities produced limited surpluses. Local trade involved only luxuries and symbolic trade goods, such as shells, feathers, hides, and precious metals and gems.

In the Central Andes, however, archaeologists have found evidence of early state systems that transcended local communities to function as confederations, or alliances of towns. These were not as well integrated as many of the territorial states of Southwest Asia, the Indus Valley, and China; they were more like settlements in Europe and the eastern Mediterranean, where towns traded basic goods and in some cases cooperated to resist aggressors.

The region's varied ecology promoted the development of such confederations. Along the arid coast of what is now Peru, fishermen harvested the currents teeming with large and small

Cerro Sechin Artifact. This stela of a warrior brandishing a club was discovered in the Casma Valley in present-day Peru and is a good example of the many striking stone sculptures found in this area.

fish; this was a staple that, when dried, was hardly perishable and easy to transport. The rivers flowing down from the Andean mountains fanned out through the desert, often carving out basins suitable for agriculture. And where the mountains rose from the Pacific, rainfall and higher altitudes favored extensive pasturelands. Here roamed wild llamas and alpacas—difficult as beasts of burden, but valued for their wool in textile production. Such ecological diversity within a limited area promoted greater trade among subregions and towns. Indeed, the interchange of manioc (root of the cassava plant), chili peppers, dried fish, and wool gave rise to the commercial networks that could support political ones.

Communities on the coast, in the riverbeds, or in the mountain valleys were small but numerous. They took shape around central plazas, most of which had large platforms with special burial chambers for elders and persons of importance. Clusters of dwellings surrounded these centers. Much of what we know about political and economic transactions among these communities—as well as long-distance trade and statecraft—comes from the offerings and ornaments left in the burial chambers. Painted gourds, pottery, and fine textiles illustrate the increasing contact among cultures, often bound in alliances. For instance, marriage between noble families could strengthen a pact or confederation.

One early site known as Aspero reveals how a local community evolved into a form of chiefship, with a political elite and diplomatic and trading ties with neighbors. Temples straddled the top of the central platform, and the large structure at the center boasted lavish ornamentation. Also, there is evidence that smaller communities around Aspero sent

Chronology

	MAJOR TRENDS	2000 BCE	1500 BCE
NORTHERN AFRICA	Global warming and drying cycle beginning 2000 BCE	✦ 2010–1640 BCE *Middle Kingdom in Egypt* ✦ ✦ 2000 BCE *Development of chariot technology* ✦- - - -	✦- - - - -
SOUTHWEST ASIA		✦ 1800–1600 BCE *Old Hittite Kingdom in Anatolia* ✦ ✦- - -✦ 1792–1750 BCE *Hammurapi's Babylonia*	✦- - - - ✦- -
SOUTH ASIA		1500 BCE *Vedic migration into Indus River valley begins* ✦	
EAST ASIA		1600 BCE *Shang State emerges* ✦	
THE AEGEAN		✦- - 2000–1600 BCE *Minoan culture* - -✦ ✦ 1850–1200 BCE *Mycenaean culture* - - -	
SOUTH PACIFIC		✦- - 2500–1000 BCE *Austronesian migration to East Asian coastal islands* - - -	- - -
EUROPE		*Rise of small chieftains* ✦	
CENTRAL ANDES		*Emergence of small-scale political confederations* 1700 BCE ✦	

crops (fruits) and fish (anchovies) as part of an intercommunity system of mutual dependence.

Not all politics among the valley peoples of Peru consisted of trade and diplomacy, however. In the Casma Valley near the Pacific coast, a clay and stone architectural complex at Cerro Sechín has revealed a much larger sprawl of dwellings and plazas dating back to 1700 BCE. Around the community's central structure stood a wall composed of hundreds of massive stone tablets, carved with ornate etchings of warriors, battles, prisoners, executions, and human body parts. The warriors' clothing is simple and rustic, and the main weapon resembles a club. Clearly, warfare accompanied the first expressions of statecraft in the Americas.

CONCLUSION

The second millennium BCE was an era of migrations, warfare, and kingdom building in Afro-Eurasia. Whereas riverine societies had flourished in the fourth and third millennia BCE in Mesopotamia, Egypt, and the Indus Valley, now droughts and deserts shook the agrarian foundations of their economies. Old states crumbled; from the steppes and plateaus nomadic pastoralists and transhumant herders descended in search of food, grazing lands, and plunder. As transhumant herders pressed into the riverine societies, the social and political fabric of these communities changed. Likewise, horse-riding nomads from steppe communities in inner Eurasia conquered and settled in the agrarian states, bringing key innovations. Foremost were the horse chariots, which became a military catalyst sparking the evolution from smaller states to large kingdoms encompassing crowded cities and vast hinterlands. The nomads and herders also adopted many of the settled peoples' beliefs and customs. On land and sea, migrating peoples created zones of long-distance trade that linked agrarian societies.

The Nile Delta, the basin of the Tigris and Euphrates rivers, the Indus Valley, and the Yellow River basin were worlds apart before 2000 BCE. Now trade and conquest brought many of these societies into closer contact, especially those in Southwest Asia and the Nile River basin. Here, the interaction even led to an elaborate system of diplomatic relations. The first territorial states appeared in this millennium, composed of communities living under common laws and customs. An alliance of farmers and warriors united agrarian wealth and production with political power to create and defend territorial boundaries. The new arrangements overshadowed the nomads' historic role as predators and enabled them to become military elites. Through taxes and drafted labor, villagers repaid their rulers for local security and state-run diplomacy.

The rhythms of state formation differed where regimes were not closely packed together. In East Asia, the absence of strong rivals allowed the emerging Shang dynasty to develop more gradually. Where landscapes had sharper divisions—as in the island archipelagos of the South China Sea, or in Europe—small-scale, decentralized microsocieties emerged. This was true above all in the Americas, where the lack of

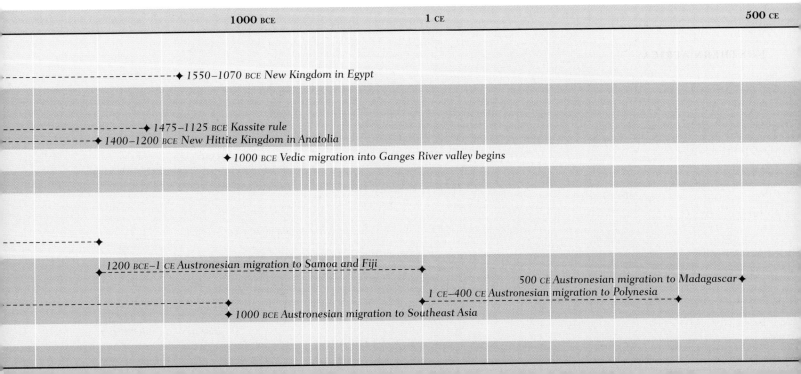

1000 BCE   1 CE   500 CE

◆ 1550–1070 BCE *New Kingdom in Egypt*

◆ 1475–1125 BCE *Kassite rule*
◆ 1400–1200 BCE *New Hittite Kingdom in Anatolia*
◆ 1000 BCE *Vedic migration into Ganges River valley begins*

1200 BCE–1 CE *Austronesian migration to Samoa and Fiji*
500 CE *Austronesian migration to Madagascar* ◆
1 CE–400 CE *Austronesian migration to Polynesia*
◆ 1000 BCE *Austronesian migration to Southeast Asia*

wheeled vehicles and horses made long-distance communication much more challenging—and inhibited rulers' territorial ambitions. Here, too, microsocieties were the norm. But fragmentation is not the same as isolation. Even peoples on the fringes and the subjects of microsocieties were not entirely secluded from the increasing flows of technologies, languages, goods, and migrants.

Review and research materials are available at StudySpace: ⓖ WWNORTON.COM/STUDYSPACE

KEY TERMS

chariots (p. 87)

divination (p. 110)

Hammurapi's Code (p. 99)

microsocieties (p. 113)

polities (p. 90)

territorial state (p. 90)

transhumant migrants (p. 86)

vassal states (p. 99)

Vedic people (p. 101)

STUDY QUESTIONS

1. Explain the differences between nomadic pastoral and transhumant migrations. How did each shape Afro-Eurasian history during the second millennium BCE?

2. Analyze the impact of the domestication of horses on Afro-Eurasia during this period. How did this development affect both nomadic and settled societies?

3. Define the term *territorial state*. In what areas of Afro-Eurasia did this new form of political organization emerge and thrive?

4. Compare and contrast political developments in Mesopotamia and Egypt during this period. To what extent did outside groups influence each region?

5. Identify the great territorial states of western Asia and North Africa during the second half of the second millennium BCE, and describe their relationships with one another. How did they pioneer international diplomacy?

6. Compare and contrast Austronesian and Indo-European migrations. What impact did each people have on the regions it settled?

7. Describe the Shang state in East Asia. How was it similar to and different from the territorial states of western Afro-Eurasia?

8. Compare and contrast the islands of the South Pacific to those in the eastern Mediterranean. Why were societies in the South Pacific more fragmented and isolated than those in the eastern Mediterranean?

9. Explain why early state structures were smaller and less integrated in Europe and the Central Andes than the territorial states that arose elsewhere. How similar and different were the early state structures in Europe and the Central Andes?

4

FIRST EMPIRES AND COMMON CULTURES IN AFRO-EURASIA, 1250–325 BCE

Sennacherib—ruler of the Assyrian Empire, which spanned much of Southwest Asia early in the seventh century BCE—writes that at the end of one successful campaign he took "200,150 people, great and small, male and female, horses, mules, asses, camels, and sheep without number. I brought away from them and counted them my spoil." Those who resisted were dragged back to Assyria and forced to labor on Sennacherib's expanding, magnificent capital, Nineveh, and toiled on the immense irrigation works to open up new agricultural frontiers.

The booty that Sennacherib took away was unheard of in earlier ages, even within the great territorial states of ancient Egypt and Mesopotamia. The immensity of the conquest highlights the arrival of a new era that involved states with even larger geographical, political, economic, and cultural ambitions and achievements. In fact, the prosperity and bounty of the first millennium BCE were the fruits of a spasm of disorder across Afro-Eurasia. As the states of the previous millennium collapsed, their successors were replacements—not descendants. The key factor shaping human development now was warfare spurred by military innovation.

Some of the warrior/political leaders of this era came from the fringes of formerly powerful empires and city-states, driven to challenge these centers of power when radical changes in climate made their home territories less viable. They established hybrid societies in Assyria, Persia, Vedic parts of South Asia, and Zhou China where new imperial ideologies and religious beliefs were elaborated in support of the new states. Under the protection of fierce warriors, cities and hinterlands came together under a single ruler. Farming yields again increased, and populations grew. The expansion of territorial power via conquest contributed to the integration of increasingly larger states, some of which became the first empires. Also, on the fringes of formerly great empires microsocieties arose and made significant contributions to human development: the seafaring Phoenicians provided Afro-Eurasia a simplified alphabet, the Israelites espoused a strict monotheism, and Greek city-states came to the fore and even began to challenge the power of the Persian Empire.

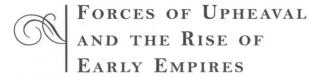

FORCES OF UPHEAVAL AND THE RISE OF EARLY EMPIRES

> → *What were the factors that led to the rise of early empires?*

Although the new, bigger states built on the existing achievements of earlier complex societies, they also developed in response to new forces. The first factor was *climate change*. Beginning around 1200 BCE another warming phase gripped Afro-Eurasia, with varying effects across the landmass. In some areas prolonged drought caused social upheavals and migrations: it led nomadic and seminomadic populations that had lived at the edge of settled societies to leave their home territories and move into the lands of the settled communities. In other regions the warming produced rapid population growth and led to soil depletion, forcing peoples to leave their homes in search of food and fertile land. (See Map 4-1.) Renewed migrations overturned urban societies and destroyed the administrative centers of kings, priests, and dynasties, leaving the way open for new states to develop.

A second factor was the large-scale and violent *movement of peoples*, often connected with climate change. Invaders moved out of loosely organized peripheral societies and assaulted the urban centers and territorial kingdoms of mainland Greece, Crete, Anatolia, Mesopotamia, and Egypt. Marauders from the Mediterranean basin and the Syrian desert upset the diplomatic relations and the elaborate system of international trade that had linked Southwestern Asia and North Africa. In East Asia, nomads from the steppes of Inner Eurasia tangled with the Shang authorities in the Yellow River valley and eventually overwhelmed the regime. In the Indus Valley, waves of nomads pressed down from the northwest, lured by fertile lands to the south. Once there, they became an agrarian folk. The process of settling down took centuries, but by the time of Alexander the Great (see Chapter 6) the splendor of India had become legendary.

The mingling of nomadic and settled societies provided opportunities for ambitious men to expand the old territorial kingdoms or to create new states that went on to conquer other kingdoms. Gradually, a new political organization came into being: the empire. (An **empire** is a group of states or different ethnic groups under a single sovereign power.)

Focus Questions

WWNORTON.COM/STUDYSPACE

> → *What were the factors that led to the rise of early empires?*
> → *How was the Neo-Assyrian Empire different from earlier territorial kingdoms?*
> → *In what ways was the Persian Empire similar to the Neo-Assyrian Empire, and in what ways was it different?*
> → *How did the growth of the first empires in Southwest Asia affect the broader region?*
> → *How did South Asia become more integrated despite the absence of an imperial state?*
> → *To what extent was the Zhou state similar to contemporary Southwest Asian empires?*

Empires connected distant regions through common languages (or through individuals fluent in multiple languages), unifying political systems, and shared religious beliefs. Some regions did not experience the rise of empire. The peoples of South Asia were united less through shared political systems than through shared cultures and religious beliefs. Trade also united regions. For example, the commercial activities of coastal cities such as Byblos and Tyre reached as far as—and sometimes farther than—the empires' military conquests. There were great variations within and across Afro-Eurasia.

A third factor was *technological change*. Pack camels, seaworthy vessels, iron tools for cultivation, and iron weapons for warfare were vital new ingredients in the rise of imperial institutions. The first-millennium empires were centralized and militarized states that used force to expand their boundaries, and the role of changing technology was significant in this process.

PACK CAMELS

The camel became the chief overland agent of change during this period, helping to open up trade routes across the Syrian and Arabian deserts. The fat stored in camels' humps allows them to survive long journeys and harsh desert conditions, and thick pads under their hoofs enable them to walk smoothly over sand. First to be domesticated was the one-humped camel called the *dromedary,* or Arab camel native to the Sahara Desert. Other peoples, probably in central Asia, later domesticated the bigger, two-humped Bactrian camel. A stockier and hardier animal, it was better able than the dromedary to survive the scorching heat of northern Iran and the frozen winters along the route from China that later

became the Silk Road (so named because silk was a major product carried along this route).

NEW SHIPS

New shipbuilding technologies had been developing rapidly since 1600 BCE and now were making a significant impact. Boats that had once been designed for limited transport on rivers and lakes and along shorelines could now be built stronger and bigger for sailing on seas. These new, truly seafaring ships boasted larger and better-reinforced hulls, and stronger masts and rigging that allowed billowing sails to harness wind power effectively. These innovations, along with smaller ones in steering and ballast (among others), propelled bold mariners to venture out across large bodies of open water like the Mediterranean Sea.

IRON

Although far more abundant than the tin and copper used to make bronze, iron is a harder substance to mold and hammer into shape. (**Iron** is a malleable metal found in combined forms almost everywhere in the world; it became the most important and widely used metal in world history after the Bronze Age.) To make iron implements, metalworkers learned to apply intense heat to soften the ore and remove its impurities. Subsequently they discovered that by adding carbon to the iron they could make an early form of steel. When the technology to smelt and harden iron advanced, iron tools and weapons replaced those made of bronze. The ability to use iron was a staggering breakthrough that leaped across territorial and cultural borders.

Camels. Dromedary camels (*left*) are good draft animals for travel and domestic work in the deserts of Arabia, Afghanistan, and India. Two-hump camels (*right*) are much bigger than dromedary camels. They are more suited to the extreme dry and cold weather in Iran and central Asia.

URAL MOUNTAINS

NORTH SEA

BALTIC SEA

EUROPE

Danube R.

Dnieper R.

Dniester R.

Volga R.

ARAL SEA

BLACK SEA

CASPIAN SEA

CENTRAL

MYCENAEANS
Troy
AEGEAN SEA
ANATOLIA
Tiryns
CRETE
CYPRUS
MEDITERRANEAN SEA

HITTITES   Nineveh
MITANNI   Ashur
ELAMITES   ZAGROS MTS.
IRANIAN PLATEAU

Tigris R.
Euphrates R.

SYRIAN DESERT
LEVANT
Tyre
Jericho
Jerusalem
Babylon

SOUTHWEST ASIA

Persian Gulf

NORTH AFRICA

A F R I C A

S A H A R A

Amarna
EGYPT
Thebes

Nile R.

ARABIAN PENINSULA

RED SEA

Sub-Saharan periphery:
Increased population
and gradual adoption
of agriculture

NUBIA

Niger R.

S U B - S A H A R A N   A F R I C A

Tropical woodlands:
Yams and palm nuts
cultivated

ATLANTIC OCEAN

Congo R.

Lake Victoria

Urban cores

Vedic settlement by 900 BCE

← Nomadic incursions (sea peoples)

← Nomadic incursions (pastoralists)

■ Destroyed site

• City

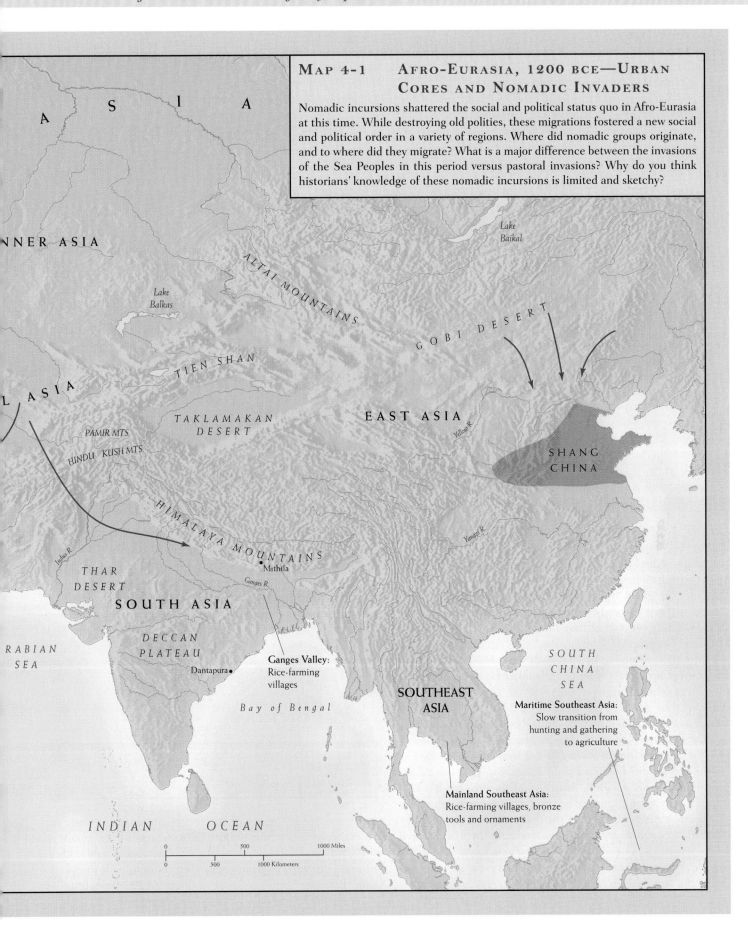

MAP 4-1   AFRO-EURASIA, 1200 BCE—URBAN CORES AND NOMADIC INVADERS

Nomadic incursions shattered the social and political status quo in Afro-Eurasia at this time. While destroying old polities, these migrations fostered a new social and political order in a variety of regions. Where did nomadic groups originate, and to where did they migrate? What is a major difference between the invasions of the Sea Peoples in this period versus pastoral invasions? Why do you think historians' knowledge of these nomadic incursions is limited and sketchy?

Ganges Valley: Rice-farming villages

Maritime Southeast Asia: Slow transition from hunting and gathering to agriculture

Mainland Southeast Asia: Rice-farming villages, bronze tools and ornaments

MAIN THEMES

→ *Climate change, nomadic migrations, and invasions from neighboring states lead to the collapse of territorial states across Afro-Eurasia.*

→ *The first great empires emerge, based on innovations in warfare, administration, commerce, metallurgy (iron), and agricultural production.*

→ *South Asia and smaller borderland states like the Greeks, Phoenicians, and Israelites innovate and build common cultures in nonpolitical ways.*

FOCUS ON *First Empires and Smaller States*

Ancient Near East

◆ Neo-Assyrians use raw military power and massive population relocations to build and maintain the world's first empire.

◆ Persians rely on persuasion and tolerance to build a cosmopolitan empire.

Mediterranean World

◆ Greeks, Phoenicians, and Israelites show the advantages of small-scale states with innovations in writing, trading, and religious thought.

South Asia

◆ Vedic peoples build a unified common culture through religious and economic ties.

China

◆ Zhou dynasty constructs a powerful tributary state and legitimates its rule via the mandate of heaven doctrine (good governance and upright behavior = legitimate rule).

Iron also helped cause a revolutionary shift in agrarian techniques. Innovators learned to tip their plowshares with forged-iron edges that they could easily shape and resharpen. With the iron-tipped plow, for instance, cultivators could clear the dense jungle of the Ganges plain and repeatedly till the topsoil to keep it weed-free and to enhance its quality. Increasingly, farmers did not have to rely on floods to restore layers of rich soil to their fields; instead, they could break the sod and turn it over to bring up fertile subsoils. The effects of this transformation drove the agrarian frontier far beyond the traditional floodplains of riverbank settings. Agricultural developments thus provided the technological basis for supporting larger, more integrated societies linked by roads and canals.

The final developments driving change were *innovations in military and administrative control*. Indeed, the expansion of the first empires depended on military might. For example, with an army wielding the most advanced weapons and armor, the Assyrian king led annual campaigns to establish and reinforce his control over the countryside. Deportations were another strategy to break resisters' unity, to provide slave labor in parts of the empire that needed manpower, and to integrate the realm. Throughout the 300 years of their rule, the Assyrians constructed an infrastructure of roads, garrisons,

and relay stations throughout the entire territory, making it easier to transfer information and move troops. Moreover, they made subject peoples send tribute in the form of grains, animals, raw materials and people, which they used to build imperial cities and to enrich the royal coffers. In later centuries these practices would become common among empires, with varying degrees of brutality as a method of control.

 THE NEO-ASSYRIAN EMPIRE

→ *How was the Neo-Assyrian Empire different from earlier territorial kingdoms?*

The narrative of the rise of empires begins in Southwest Asia with the Neo-Assyrian Empire (911–612 BCE), successor to the "Old" and "Middle" Assyrian states of the second millennium. The Neo-Assyrians perfected techniques of imperial rule that others imitated (not only their successors but also

Greeks and Romans) and that ultimately became standard in many ancient and modern empires. In particular the Neo-Assyrian state revealed the raw military side of imperial rule: constant and harsh warfare, brutal exploitation of subjects, and an ideology that glorified imperial masters and justified the subjugation and harsh treatment of subjects. In this regard the Neo-Assyrians were legendary for their ruthless efficiency, reliance on terror (such as cutting off ears, lips, and fingers; castration; and mass executions), deportations, and intimidation to crush their adversaries.

Neo-Assyrian rulers had ambitions beyond governing their own people: they also wanted to subordinate peoples in distant lands and control those areas' resources, trading cities, and trade routes. By the time that the state's full-scale expansion was under way, all institutions of the Neo-Assyrian state were focused on becoming an empire. They succeeded by the mid-seventh century BCE with the conquest of Southwest Asia and parts of North Africa, including Egypt (see Map 4-2).

EXPANSION INTO AN EMPIRE

The heartland of Assyria cradled the ancient cities of Ashur and Nineveh on the upper reaches of the Tigris River. By the ninth century BCE the Assyrian state had become strong enough to expand westward; by 824 BCE it dominated the lands and peoples all the way to the Mediterranean, controlling trade and tribute from the entire area.

The Assyrians had several advantages. First, their armies were hardened and disciplined professional troops led by officers who rose high in the ranks because of their merit, not their birth. In addition, they perfected the combined deployment of infantry and cavalry (horse-mounted

warriors equipped with iron weapons) together with horse-drawn chariots armored with iron plates and carrying expert archers. The Assyrians were also skilled siege warriors, using iron to build massive wheeled siege towers and to cap their battering rams. No city walls could stand against them for long. Finally, the Assyrian armies were massive. At the height of their power in the ninth century BCE, the rulers sent 120,000 soldiers on the annual campaign to the west. (In contrast, Chinese armies would not reach this scale for another 500 years.)

Assyrian expansion provoked fierce but ultimately futile opposition, particularly from the small independent states in the west. Resisting populations were devastated—they were

MAP 4-2   THE NEO-ASSYRIAN EMPIRE
The Neo-Assyrians built the first strong regional empire in Afro-Eurasia. In the process, they faced the challenge of promoting order and stability throughout their diverse realm. Where did the Neo-Assyrian Empire expand? Which parts of the empire were "the Land of Ashur," and which were "the Land under the Yoke of Ashur"? Why do you think expansion after 720 BCE led to the empire's destruction?

Map legend:
- Assyrian Heartland (911 BCE)
- 824 BCE
- 720 BCE
- 680 BCE

Tiglath Pileser III. The walls of the Assyrian palaces were lined with stone slabs carved with images of the victories of the king. This fragmentary slab from the palace of Tiglath Pileser III originally decorated the wall of his palace at Nimrud. It shows the inhabitants and their herds being forced to leave after the defeat of their town by the Assyrians. Below is Tiglath Pileser III, shaded by his royal umbrella, in his war chariot.

relocated through forced deportations, and their lands were annexed. The Assyrian state grew even more ambitious when a talented military leader usurped the throne. Naming himself Tiglath Pileser III (r. 745–728 BCE) after an earlier reform-minded Assyrian king, he reorganized the Assyrian state to centralize power in royal hands and thus prepare for a second phase of imperial expansion and consolidation. He took away the nobles' rights to own and inherit land and other wealth, and he replaced hereditary provincial governors with appointed officials whom the center of the empire controlled. He also reinstated aggressive, expansionary annual military campaigns. But the destruction and mass deportations carried out by his armies intensified the conquered peoples' hatred of the Assyrians.

INTEGRATION AND CONTROL OF THE EMPIRE

A unique imperial structure, deportations, and the labors of subjugated peoples, and an imperial ideology were the defining features of the Neo-Assyrian Empire. While they were hugely important to the success of the empire, they also contributed to its ultimate failure.

STRUCTURE OF THE EMPIRE The Assyrian rulers divided their empire into two parts and ruled them in different ways. The core, which the Assyrians called the "Land of Ashur," included the lands between the Zagros Mountains and the Euphrates River. The king's appointees governed these interior lands, whose inhabitants had to supply food for the temple of the national god Ashur, manpower for the god's residence in the city of Ashur, and officials to carry out the state's business.

The other area, known as "the Land under the Yoke of Ashur," lay outside of Assyria proper. Its inhabitants were not considered Assyrians; rather, their local rulers held power as vassals of Assyria. Instead of supplying agricultural goods and manpower, these vassal states had the greater burden of delivering massive amounts of tribute in the form of gold and silver. This wealth went directly to the king, who used it to pay for his extravagant court and ever-increasing military costs. After the reforms of Tiglath Pileser III, even more lands came into the Land of Ashur proper. While such incorporation eliminated the oppressive need to pay tribute, the empire continued to harshly administer its programs of forced Assyrianization. (Many empires in later centuries, including the Persian, Roman, and even the modern-day British and French empires, would use this strategy as well.)

DEPORTATION AND FORCED LABOR In the empire's early years, the army comprised Assyrians who went to war on annual summer campaigns. Later, when campaigning became year-round, the army grew to several hundred thousand men mobilized to protect and extend the imperial holdings. These forces included not only Assyrians but also men from the conquered peoples. By the seventh century BCE, the Assyrians

Capture of an Egyptian City. This stone panel from the palace in Nineveh shows warriors scaling walls with ladders during Ashurbanipal's campaign against Egypt (mid-seventh century BCE).

assigned different ethnic groups to specialized military functions: Phoenicians from the Levant provided ships and sailors for battle in the Mediterranean, Medes from the Iranian plateau served as the king's bodyguards, and charioteers from Israel subdued rebellious western provinces.

To accomplish its goals, the Assyrian state needed huge labor forces for agricultural work and for enormous building projects. Since so many Assyrians served in the army, the state recruited most agricultural and construction workers from conquered peoples. Over three centuries the Neo-Assyrian state relocated more than 4 million people—a practice that not only supported its stupendous work projects but also undermined local resistance efforts.

ASSYRIAN IDEOLOGY AND PROPAGANDA The Neo-Assyrian Empire put forth an imperial ideology to support and justify its system of expansion, exploitation, and inequality. (An **ideology** is the dominant set of ideas of a widespread culture or movement.) Even in the early stages of expansion, Assyrian inscriptions and art expressed a divinely determined destiny that drove the regime to expand westward toward the Mediterranean Sea. According to the ideology, the national god Ashur commanded all Assyrians to support the forcible growth of the empire, whose goal was to establish and maintain order and keep an ever-threatening cosmic chaos at bay. Only the god Ashur and his agent, the king, could bring universal order. The king conducted holy war to transform the known world into the well-regulated Land of Ashur, intensifying his campaign of terror and expansion with elaborate propaganda. This propaganda, based on a detailed historical record of countless military and political victories, proclaimed that Assyria's triumph was inevitable. Its main focus was the nobles, whom the king and the empire relied on for support.

The rulers devised three mutually reinforcing types of propaganda campaigns. First, they used elaborate architectural complexes to stage ceremonial displays of pomp and power (as in Egypt and China). Second, they made sure that different types of texts glorified the king and the empire. These texts were recited at state occasions, inscribed on monuments, written in annals about the kings' military campaigns and achievements, and buried at propitious places in public buildings, where only the eyes of Ashur could view them. (See Primary Source: The Banquet Stele of Assurnasirpal II.) Third, state officials placed images glorifying the king and the Assyrian army on palace walls. These images depicted the army's force, showing all who resisted being smashed into submission—their towns burned; their men killed, impaled on stakes, or flayed; and their women and children deported along with any male survivors.

The commitment to "accurately" depict the regime's triumphal events was evident not only on palace walls but also in a uniquely Assyrian literary form called **annals** (historical records, usually arranged chronologically). Constituting a milestone in human history, these documents illustrate how communication and writing promoted the formation of organized

The Annals of Ashurbanipal. This baked clay faceted cylinder carries a portion of the annals of Ashurbanipal. It was found at Nineveh along with thousands of other tablets preserved in his famous library. The annals of Ashurbanipal were detailed, almost novelistic accounts of his military and civic achievements. Unlike earlier annals, there is first-person discourse, indirect discourse, flashbacks, and lively description of events and places.

states. Court scribes inscribed the annals in cuneiform on stone slabs, tablets, and clay cylinders, detailing each campaign in the yearly report of the king's achievements. These written compositions, like the images, never gave any indication that the Assyrians did or could lose a battle.

ASSYRIAN SOCIAL STRUCTURE AND POPULATION

The Assyrians' iron-fisted rule rested on a rigid social hierarchy. Alone at the top was the king, who as the sole agent of the god Ashur conducted war to expand the Land of Ashur. Below were the state's military elites, handsomely rewarded through gifts of land, silver, and exemptions from royal taxes. Over time, they became the noble class and intimates of the king, replacing the older landed elites who lost their resources after Tiglath Pileser III reorganized the empire's landholdings. Elites often controlled vast estates that included both the land and the local people who worked it. The throne and the elites owned the most populous part of the society, the peasantry, in which various

Primary Source

THE BANQUET STELE OF ASSURNASIRPAL II

Starting in the third millennium BCE, the rulers of Mesopotamia used architecture to signal their power to their subjects. When a change of dynasty or other reorganization of power occurred, rulers would build new palaces or even move their capital city. In the ninth century, Assurnasirpal II established Assyria as an imperial power that intended to expand and consolidate its economic and political control of surrounding peoples. After moving the capital and building a new palace and royal precinct, he called all of the empire's peoples to a ten-day celebration. This remarkable event was commemorated by an inscribed stele (an inscribed stone pillar) that he erected next to the throne room.

(102) When Ashur-nasir-apli, king of Assyria, consecrated the joyful palace, the palace full of wisdom, in Kalach [and] invited inside Ashur, the great lord, and the gods of the entire land; 1,000 fat oxen, 1,000 calves [and] sheep of the stable, 14,000 . . . -sheep which belonged to the goddess Ishtar my mistress, 200 oxen which belonged to the goddess Ishtar my mistress, 1,000 . . . -sheep, 1,000 spring lambs, 500 *ayalu*-deer, 500 deer, 1,000 ducks [*iṣṣū rū rabûtu*], 500 ducks [*usū*], 500 geese, 1,000 wild geese, 1,000 *qaribu*-birds, 10,000 pigeons, 10,000 wild pigeons, 10,000 small birds, 10,000 fish, 10,000 jerboa, 10,000 eggs, 10,000 loaves of bread, 10,000 jugs of beer, 10,000 skins of wine, 10,000 containers of grain [and] sesame, 10,000 pots of hot . . . , 1,000 boxes of greens, 300 [containers of] oil, 300 [containers of] malt, 300 [containers of] mixed *raqqatu*-plants, 100 [containers of] *kudimmus*, 100 [containers of] . . . , 100 [containers of] parched barley, 100 [containers of] *ubuḫšennu*-grain, 100 [containers of] fine *billatu*, 100 [containers of] pomegranates, 100 [containers of] grapes, 100 [containers of] mixed *zamrus*, 100 [containers of] pistachios, 100 [containers of] . . . , 100 [containers of] ionions, 100 [containers of] garlic, 100 [containers of] *kuniphus*, 100 *bunches* of turnips, 100 [containers of] *ḫinḫinu*-seeds, 100 [containers of] *giddū*, 100 [containers of] honey, 100 [containers of] ghee, 100 [containers of] roasted *abšu*-seeds, 100 [containers of] roasted *šu'u*-seeds, 100 [containers of] *karkartu*-plants, 100 [containers of] *tiatu*-plants, 100 [containers of] mustard, 100 [containers of] milk, 100 [containers of] cheese, 100 bowls of *mīzu*-drink, 100 stuffed oxen, 10 homers of shelled *dukdu*-nuts, 10 homers of shelled pistachios, 10 homers of . . . , 10 homers of *ḫabbaququ*, 10 homers of dates, 10 homers of *titip*, 10 homers of cumin, 10 homers of *saḫūnu*, 10 homers of . . . , 10 homers of *andaḫšu*, 10 homers of *šišanibu*, 10 homers of *simberu*-fruit, 10 homers of *ḫašú*, 10 homers of fine oil, 10 homers of fine aromatics, 10 homers of . . . , 10 homers of *naṣṣabu*-gourds, 10 homers of *zinzimmu*-onions, 10 homers of olives; when I consecrated the palace of Kalach, 47,074 men [and] women who were invited from every part of my land, 5,000 dignitaries [and] envoys of the people of the lands Suhu, Hindanu, Patinu, Hatti, Tyre, Sidon, Gurgumu, Malidu, Hubushkia, Gilzanu, Kumu, [and] Musasiru, 16,000 people of Kalach, [and] 1,500 *zarīqū* of my palace, all of them—altogether 69,574 [including] those summoned from all lands and the people of Kalach—for ten days I gave them food, I gave them drink, I had them bathed, I had them anointed. [Thus] did I honour them [and] send them back to their lands in peace and joy.

→ *What does the extensive list of food and drink listed in the text tell the reader about the size and geographical reach of the empire and the role of trade in it?*

→ *What techniques, as reflected in the text of the Banquet Stele, did Assurnasirpal use to build loyalty among his subjects?*

SOURCE: *Assyrian Royal Inscriptions, Part 2: From Tiglath-pileser I to Ashur-nasir-apli II,* compiled and translated by Albert Kirk Grayson, vol. 2 of *Records of the Ancient Near East,* edited by Hans Goedicke (Wiesbaden: Otto Harrassowitz, 1976), pp. 175–76.

categories of workers had differing privileges. Those who were enslaved because they could not pay their debts were allowed to marry nonslave partners, conduct financial transactions, and even own property with other slaves attached. In contrast, foreigners who were enslaved after being captured had no rights—they were forced to do hard manual labor on the state's monumental building projects. Those who were forcibly relocated were not slaves but became attached to the lands that they had to work. Families were small and lived on modest plots of land, where they raised vegetables and planted vineyards.

Women in Assyria were far more restricted than their counterparts in the earlier periods of Sumerian and Old Babylonian Mesopotamia (see Chapter 3). Under the Assyrians' patriarchal social system, women had almost no control over their lives. Because all inheritance passed through the male line, it was crucial that a man be certain of the paternity of the children borne by his wives. As a result, all interactions between men and women outside of the family were highly restricted. The Middle Assyrians introduced the practice of veiling in the thirteenth century BCE, requiring it of all respectable women. Indeed, prostitutes who serviced the men of the army and worked in the taverns were forbidden to wear the veil, so that their revealed faces and hair could signal their disreputable status. Any prostitute found wearing the veil would be dragged to the top of the city wall, stripped of her clothing, flogged, and sometimes even killed.

The queens of Assyria obeyed the same social norms, but their lives were more comfortable and varied than the commoners'. They lived in a separate part of the palace with servants who were either women slaves or eunuchs (castrated males). Though Assyrian queens rarely wielded genuine power, they enjoyed respect and recognition, especially in the role of mother of the king. In fact, a queen could serve as regent for her son if the king died while his heir was still a child. Such was the case of Sammuramat, who served as regent from 810 to 806 BCE, successfully ruling the empire until her son came of age.

THE INSTABILITY OF THE ASSYRIAN EMPIRE

At their peak, the Assyrians controlled most of the lands stretching from Persia to Egypt. This was an awesome feat, but the empire was unstable nonetheless. Assyrian commanders had to position occupying armies far and wide to keep subjects in line; and as the propaganda machine ramped up, so did discontent among the nobility. When subject peoples rose up, they often used the same types of iron weapons on which their tormentors had relied. Once a successful rebellion challenged the Assyrian worldview of invincibility, the empire's fall was inevitable. Although successor states temporarily filled the Assyrian political vacuum, the three-millennia-long culture of Mesopotamia was dead. In 612 BCE, the Neo-Assyrian Empire collapsed as Nineveh was conquered.

THE PERSIAN EMPIRE

→ *In what ways was the Persian Empire similar to the Neo-Assyrian Empire, and in what ways was it different?*

The Persians were successors to the Neo-Assyrians. They created a gentler form of imperial rule, based more on persuasion and mutual benefit than on raw power. A nomadic group speaking an Indo-Iranian language, the Persians had arrived on the Iranian plateau from central Asia during the second millennium and gradually spread to the plateau's southwestern part. These expert horsemen shot arrows with deadly

Cyrus the Great. This great Genius with four wings was preserved in the doorjamb of Gate R at the palace of Cyrus the Great at Pasargadae. When Cyrus forged the Persian Empire from Media, Assyria, Babylonia, and Egypt, there was no coherent imperial imagery to represent the new political entity. His court artists borrowed freely from the realms that he had brought into his empire. The image is a combination of features borrowed from Egypt (the headdress), Assyria (low-relief representation on a stone slab and the four wings), and Babylonia (the long garment).

accuracy while whirling on horseback in the midst of battle. After Cyrus the Great (r. 559–529 BCE) united the Persian tribes, his armies defeated the Lydians in southwestern Anatolia and took over their gold mines, land, and trading routes. He next overpowered the Greek city-states on the Aegean coast of Anatolia.

Further conquests set the stage for a vast multicultural empire that spread from Europe to South Asia. Because their ancestors were pastoralists, the Persians had no urban tradition to draw on. Instead, they adapted the ideologies and institutions of the Babylonians (see Chapter 3) and the Assyrians, modifying them to fit their own customs and political aims. This process gave rise to uniquely Persian institutions that undergirded the new empire, which would last until the arrival of Alexander the Great in 331 BCE.

THE INTEGRATION OF A MULTICULTURAL EMPIRE

Cyrus, the founder of the Persian Empire, traced his ancestry back to a legendary king and used that heritage to legitimate his empire-building. From their base on the Iranian plateau, over the next 200 years the Persian rulers developed an enormous empire that reached from the Indus Valley to northern Greece and from central Asia to the south of Egypt. (See Map 4-3.)

Cyrus presented himself as a benevolent ruler who claimed to have liberated his subjects from the oppression of their own kings. He pointed to his victory in Babylon as a sign that the city's gods had turned against its king as a heretic. According to the cuneiform text known as the Cyrus cylinder, the Babylonians greeted him "with shining faces." At the same

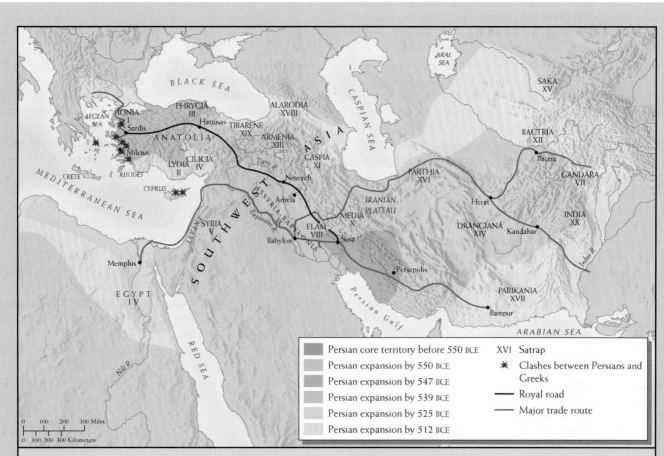

MAP 4-3 THE PERSIAN EMPIRE, 550–479 BCE

Starting in the sixth century BCE, the Persians succeeded the Assyrians as rulers of the large regional empire of Southwest Asia and North Africa. Compare the Persian Empire's territorial domains to those of the Neo-Assyrian Empire in Map 4-2. Geographically, how did the Persian Empire differ from the Neo-Assyrian state? Analyzing the map, how many Persian satrapies existed, and what role do you think they played in the success of the Persian Empire? How does geography help explain why the Greeks were able to defeat the Persians twice?

time, Cyrus released the Jews from their fifty-year captivity in Babylon. They, too, considered him a savior who, having freed them on the orders of their God, allowed them to return to Jerusalem and rebuild their temple. Even the Greeks, who later defeated the Persians, saw Cyrus as a model ruler.

Following Cyrus's death on the battlefield, Darius I (r. 521–486 BCE) put the nascent empire on a solid footing. First he suppressed revolts across the lands, recording this feat on a monumental rock relief overhanging the road to his capital, Persepolis. (See Primary Source: Beisitun Inscription.) Then he conquered territories held by seventy different ethnic groups, stretching from the Indus River in the east to the Aegean and Mediterranean seas in the west, and from the Black, Caspian, and Aral seas in the north to the Nile River in the south. To manage this huge domain, Darius introduced dynamic administrative systems that enabled the empire to flourish for another two centuries. Its new bureaucracy combined central and local administration to make best use of the strengths of local tradition, economy, and rule—rather than forcing Persian customs on subject people via rigid central control (as the Assyrians had done).

This empire was both centralized and multicultural. The Persians believed that all subject peoples were equal; the only requirement was to give the king their loyalty and pay tribute—which was considered an honor, not a burden. Although local Persian administrators used local languages, in time Aramaic (a dialect of a Semitic language long spoken in Southwest Asia) became the empire's official language because many of its literate scribes came from Mesopotamia. They wrote Aramaic on parchment or papyrus in an alphabetic script, and its use spread quickly.

Much like Tiglath Pileser III of Assyria, Darius understood that he could not expand the empire without reorganizing and centralizing. To bring the wealth of the provinces to the imperial center he established a system of provinces, or satrapies, each ruled by a satrap (a governor) who was a relative or a close associate of the king. The local bureaucrats and officials who administered the government worked under close monitoring by military officers, central tax collectors, and spies (the so-called eyes of the king) who enforced the satraps' loyalty. Further, Darius established a system of fixed taxation and formal tribute allocations; when needed, he also instituted economic reforms. Moreover, he promoted trade throughout the empire by building roads, establishing a standardized currency including coinage, and introducing standard weights and measures.

ZOROASTRIANISM, IDEOLOGY, AND SOCIAL STRUCTURE

Like the Assyrians, the Persians established their ideology of kingship on religious foundations. They believed that the supreme god, Ahura Mazda, appointed the monarch as ruler over all people and lands of the earth and charged him with maintaining a perfect order from which all would benefit. Unlike their Mesopotamian neighbors, the Persians drew their religious ideas from their pastoral and tribal roots (which reflected the same traditions of warrior and priestly classes as those preserved in the Vedic texts of the Indus Valley; see Chapter 3).

Zoroaster (also known as Zarathustra), who most likely taught sometime after 1000 BCE in eastern Iran, was responsible for crystallizing the region's traditional beliefs into a formal religious system. The eastern tribes of the Iranian plateau spread the ideas of **Zoroastrianism** to the Iranian peoples living in the west, and Zoroastrianism ultimately became the religion of the entire empire. The main source for the teachings of Zoroaster is the Avesta, a collection of holy works initially transmitted orally by priests and then written down in the sixth century CE. (It has much in common linguistically with the Vedic texts of the people of the Indus Valley.)

Zoroaster's teachings tried to wean the Iranian faithful away from their earlier animistic beliefs that led them to see all objects, alive and dead, as possessing life and vitality. In a radical change, Zoroaster promoted belief in the god Ahura Mazda, who had created the world and all that was good. (Though rare, monotheism also existed during this time in Judah; it had briefly been the official religion of Egypt, when Akhenaten imposed worship of Aten, the sun.) Persians came to believe that the universe was dualistic: Ahura Mazda was good and capable only of good, whereas his adversary, Ahiram, was deceitful and wicked. The Persians saw these two forces as engaging in a cosmic struggle for control of the universe.

Unlike the fatalistic religions of Mesopotamia, Zoroastrianism treated humans as capable of choosing between good and evil. Their choices had consequences—rewards or punishments in the afterlife. Strict rules of behavior determined the fate of each individual. For example, because animals were good, they deserved to be treated well. Intoxicants, widely used in tribal religions, were forbidden. Also, there were strict rules for treatment of the dead. For example, to prevent death from contaminating the sacred elements of earth, fire, and water, it was forbidden to bury, burn, or drown the deceased. Instead, people left corpses out for beasts and birds of prey to devour.

Persian kings enjoyed absolute authority. In return, they were expected to follow moral and political guidelines that reflected Zoroastrian notions of ethical behavior. As the embodiment of the positive virtues that made them fit to hold power, they were to display insight and the ability to distinguish right from wrong so that they could preserve justice and maintain social order. In addition, kings had to show physical superiority that matched their moral standing. They had to be awe-inspiring horsemen and peerless in wielding bows and spears—qualities valued by all Persian nobles, who revered the virtues of their nomadic ancestors. Indeed, the ancient Greek historian Herodotus tells us that Persian boys were taught three things only: "to ride, to shoot with the bow, and to tell the truth."

The Persian social order included four diverse groups: a ruling class of priests, nobles, and warriors; an administrative

BEISITUN INSCRIPTION

To commemorate his consolidation of power over the Persian state, Darius I commissioned a pictorial relief of himself as victor high above the main road leading from Mesopotamia to Ecbatana (the modern city of Hamadan) in western Iran. The images are surrounded by a long text inscribed in three languages—Old Persian, Akkadian, and Elamite. This is the earliest Old Persian inscription; it is a version of cuneiform script that Darius devised especially for this occasion.

4.31–2. Saith Darius the King: These IX kings I took prisoner within these battles.

4.33–6. Saith Darius the King: These are the provinces which became rebellious. The Lie made them rebellious, so that these [men] deceived the people. Afterwards Ahuramazda put them into my hand; as was my desire, so I did unto them.

4.36–40. Saith Darius the King: Thou who shalt be king hereafter, protect thyself vigorously from the Lie; the man who shall be a Lie-follower, him do thou punish well, if thus thou shalt think, "May my country be secure!"

4.40–3. Saith Darius the King: This is what I did; by the favor of Ahuramazda, in one and the same year I did [it]. Thou who shalt hereafter read this inscription, let that which has been done by me convince thee; do not thou think it a lie.

Darius's Relief at Beisitun. At Beisitun, high above the Royal Road through the Zagros Mountains, Darius carved a relief commemorating his victories over Gaumata (the false Smerdis) and nine rebel kings. The kings are roped together at the neck, and Gaumata lies under Darius's feet. Above the rebels is a winged disk, probably representing the god Ahura Mazda. Darius had his scribes develop a version of cuneiform script to represent Old Persian. In a trilingual inscription (Old Persian, Elamite, and Akkadian) he recorded this victory, which consolidated and expanded the empire founded by Cyrus. This inscription provided the key for deciphering Babylonian cuneiform.

4.43–5. Saith Darius the King: I turn myself quickly to Ahuramazda, that this [is] true, not false, [which] I did in one and the same year. . . .

4.52–6. Saith Darius the King: Now let that which has been done by me convince thee; thus to the people impart, do not conceal it: if this record thou shalt not conceal, [but] tell it to the people, may Ahuramazda be a friend unto thee, and may family be unto thee in abundance, and may thou live long!

4.57–9. Saith Darius the King: If this record thou shalt conceal, [and] not tell it to the people, may Ahuramazda be a smiter unto thee, and may family not be to thee!

4.59–61. Saith Darius the King: This which I did, in one and the same year by the favor of Ahuramazda I did; Ahuramazda bore me aid, and the other gods who are.

4.61–7. Saith Darius the King: For this reason Ahuramazda bore aid, and the other gods who are, because I was not hostile, I was not a Lie-follower, I was not a doer of wrong—neither I nor my family. According to righteousness I conducted myself. Neither to the weak nor to the powerful did I do wrong. The man who cooperated with my house, him I rewarded well; whoso did injury, him I punished well.

4.67–9. Saith Darius the King: Thou who shalt be king hereafter, the man who shall be a Lie-follower or who shall be a doer of wrong—unto them do thou not be a friend, [but] punish them well.

4.69–72. Saith Darius the King: Thou who shalt hereafter behold this inscription which I have inscribed, or these sculptures, do thou not destroy them, [but] thence onward protect them; as long as thou shalt be in good strength!

→ *Throughout the millennia, local and imperial rulers on the Iranian plateau used rock reliefs such as the Beisitun inscription to project their power and to mark boundaries. Who would see these monuments, and what messages would they receive?*

SOURCE: Roland G. Kent, *Old Persian: Grammar, Texts, Lexicon,* 2nd rev. ed. (New Haven: American Oriental Society, 1953), pp. 131–32.

Panel from the Palace of Darius. The Palace of Darius at Susa was elaborately decorated with glazed bricks. This panel shows human-headed winged lions in a heraldic seated posture. Above them is a winged disk with tendrils and a human bust. This symbol, which borrows from Assyrian and Egyptian imagery, is thought to represent the Zoroastrian god Ahura Mazda.

and commercial class consisting of scribes, bureaucrats, and merchants; and two laboring groups of artisans and peasants. Each group had a well-defined role. Priests maintained the ritual fire in temples, nobles administered the state by paying taxes and performing appropriate duties, warriors protected and expanded the empire, bureaucrats kept records, merchants secured goods from distant lands, artisans rendered raw materials into symbolic form, and peasants grew the crops and tended the flocks that fed the imperial machine.

Surrounding the king was the powerful Persian hereditary nobility, whose support was crucial. These men had vast landholdings and often served the king as satraps or advisers. Also close to the king were wealthy merchants who directed trade across the vast empire. The king's obligations to them involved taking his wives only from their families and exempting them from certain taxes. To consolidate his hold on the throne, though, Darius reduced the aristocrats' political power. By controlling all appointments, he essentially made the nobles his puppets. However, he let them keep their high status in a society in which birth and royal favor counted for everything.

Royal gifts solidified the relations between king and nobles, reinforcing the king's place at the top of the political pyramid. In public ceremonies he presented gold vessels, elaborate textiles, and jewelry to reward each recipient's loyalty and demonstrate dependence on the crown. Most gifts were made from gold and silver obtained through tribute, and they reminded the recipients of their continual obligation to the ruler. Any kind of failure would result in the withdrawal of royal favor. Should such failures be serious or treasonous, the offenders faced torture and death.

PUBLIC WORKS AND IMPERIAL IDENTITY

Persian power begat large-scale road building and a system of rapid and dependable communication. A key unifying element was the Royal Road, which followed age-old trade

Persian Water-Moving Technique. The Persians perfected the channeling of water over long distances through underground channels called *qanats.* This technique, an efficient way to move water without evaporation, is still used today in hot, arid regions. In this example near Yazd, in central Iran, the domed structure leading to the underground tunnel is flanked by two brick towers called "badgir," an ancient form of air conditioning that cools the water using wind (*bad* in Persian).

Persepolis. In the highland valley of Fars, the homeland of the Persians, Darius and his successors built a capital city and ceremonial center at the site of Persepolis. On top of a huge platform, there were audience halls, a massive treasury, the harem, and residential spaces. The building was constructed of mudbrick. The roof was supported by enormous columns projecting the images of bulls.

The King and His Courtiers. Leading to the Apadana (reception hall) are two monumental staircases that are faced with low-relief representations of the king and his courtiers, as well as all of the delegations bringing tribute to the center of the empire. The lion attacking the bull is a symbolic rendering of the forces of nature. Above the central plane is the winged disk of Ahura Mazda and the human-headed lion griffins.

routes some 1,600 miles from western Anatolia to the heart of the empire in southwestern Iran, continuing eastward across the northern Iranian plateau and into central Asia. Traders used the Royal Road, as did the Persian army (and, later, other warriors); subjects took tribute to the king, and royal couriers carried messages to the satraps and imperial armies. As the Assyrians had done, the Persians placed way stations with fresh mounts and provisions along the route.

In addition to the Royal Road, the Persians devised other ways to connect the far reaches of the empire with its center. Darius oversaw the construction of a canal more than 50 miles long linking the Red Sea to the Nile River. One of the Persians' most ingenious contributions was the invention of *qanats*, underground tunnels through which water flowed over long distances without evaporating or being contaminated. (Later adopted by many cultures, this type of system moves water across arid lands even today.) Laborers from the local populations toiled to build these feats of engineering as part of their civic obligation.

Until Cyrus's time, the Persians had been pastoral nomads who lacked traditions of monumental architecture, visual arts, or written literature or history. Cyrus began to define a Persian court style, but Darius was most responsible for promoting visual and physical expressions that were uniquely Persian. The vast capital at Persepolis expressed this new imperial identity. On the highland plain near Cyrus's capital at Pasargadae, Darius built an immense complex that complemented the administrative center at Susa in the lowlands. Skilled craftsmen from all over the empire labored on the complex, blending their distinct cultural influences into a new Persian architectural style. Darius erected his city, designed for celebrations and ceremonies, on a monumental terrace covering more than thirty acres. Into the cliffs behind it, he and his successors cut their eternal resting places from the rock. Persepolis was also an important administrative hub, where archaeologists have found more than 30,000 cuneiform tablets detailing the workings of the bureaucracy of the great empire.

The Persians used monumental architecture with grand columned halls and huge open spaces to provide reception rooms for thousands of representatives bringing tribute from all over the empire and as a way to help integrate subject peoples by connecting them to one central, imperial authority. In the royal palace, three of the columned halls stood on raised platforms accessed via processional stairways that were lined with elaborate images of subjects bringing gifts and tribute to the king. This was a highly refined program of visual propaganda, with the carved images showing the Persian Empire as a diverse society of obedient peoples. The carvings on the great stairway of Persepolis offer a veritable ethnographic museum frozen in stone. Each group brings distinctive tribute—the Armenians present precious metal vessels, the Lydians from Anatolia carry gold

armlets and bowls, the Egyptians offer exotic animals, and the Sogdians from central Asia lead proud horses. Gateway figures and protective relief images copied from the palaces of Assyria represent the grandeur of the occasion and the power of the king.

IMPERIAL FRINGES IN WESTERN AFRO-EURASIA

> → *How did the growth of the first empires in Southwest Asia affect the broader region?*

A very different world emerged on Afro-Eurasia's western edges, well beyond the reach of the Neo-Assyrian and Persian empires. Although their powerful neighbors affected them, these western people retained their own languages, beliefs, and systems of rule. Their communities were smaller than those in Southwest Asia, and their compactness and intimacy enabled them to project a unique kind of power and influence.

MIGRATIONS AND UPHEAVAL

Beginning around 1200 BCE, demographic upheavals and migrations propelled new waves of Indo-European-speaking peoples inhabiting the Danube River basin in Central Europe to become dynamic historical actors. Previously this area's dynamism had come from the outside (from the imperial centers of Southwest Asia and Egypt), but two key factors reversed this trend. These were a rapid rise in population and the development of local natural resources—including metallurgy in a new metal, iron. By the end of the second millennium BCE, this surplus population, armed with its new metal weapons, moved in large groups back down the Danube into southeastern Europe, the Aegean, and the eastern Mediterranean. Advancing even into Southwest Asia, the invaders brought turmoil to the peoples living there. These huge movements weakened the power of empires and regimes in the region, increased the value of mobility and communication as peoples vied for resources, and opened new frontiers for the development of smaller, more innovative communities.

The ultimate blow to imperial states from the fringe was military: armed invasions caused the collapse of even the most highly developed societies in the region. The first to fall were the Hittites, who had once dominated the central lands of what is today Turkey (see Chapter 3), because they could not retain power in the face of violence and social chaos. The

Mycenaean Arms and Armor. A Mycenaean vase that illustrates the central role of arms and war to the societies on mainland Greece in the period down to 1200 BCE. The men bear common suits of armor and weapons—helmets, corsets, spears, and shields—most likely supplied to them by the palace-centered organizations to which they belonged. Despite these advantages, they were not able to mount a successful defense against the land incursions that destroyed the Mycenaean palaces toward the end of the thirteenth century BCE.

result was general upheaval as the center of political, military, and technological power moved to the fringes.

Once the invaders reached the Mediterranean, they mainly used boats for transportation. These dynamic communities are sometimes known as the Sea Peoples. The Egyptians knew them as the Peleset, and only by marshalling all the resources of their land did the pharaohs manage to repel them. Outside Egypt, states and kingdoms suffered heavily from their ravages. The Sea Peoples settled along the southern coast of the Levant, where they became known as the Philistines.

From 1100 to 900 BCE, a long economic downturn further unsettled the major kingdoms as well as the coastal cities of the eastern Mediterranean and the Aegean islands. During this time societies began to decline: artistic representation and large-scale construction declined, urban centers ceased to develop, trading and shipping ebbed, and writing, record keeping, and much else disappeared. Societies now comprised smaller, technically simpler, impoverished, illiterate, and more violent rural communities.

In the Mediterranean, the Sea Peoples' intrusion shook the social order of the Minoans on the island of Crete and of the Mycenaeans in mainland Greece (see Chapter 3). Agricultural production declined, and local populations moved to other islands in the Aegean and to southwestern Anatolia. As the palace-centered bureaucracies and priesthoods of the second millennium BCE vanished, more violent societies

emerged that relied on the newcomers' iron weapons. This was the culture of warrior-heroes described in the *Iliad*, an epic poem about the Trojan War composed centuries after the events it relates. It was based on oral tales passed down and embellished for generations. The Greeks told these stories about a hazily recalled war that may have occurred around 1200 BCE at Troy, a city in Anatolia, during a time of seismic political and social upheaval. (See Primary Source: War in Homer's *Iliad*.)

For the long-established kingdoms and states of Southwest Asia and the Mediterranean, these rapid transformations were destructive and traumatic. But they were also creative because they shattered traditional ways of doing things, wiping the social slate clean. In fact, violent change and the emergence of new powers at the margins were the first steps toward completely new patterns of human relations.

PERSIA AND THE GREEKS

Of the different small-scale societies that emerged in Persia's shadow, the Greeks offer the best example of the energy and dynamism of these communities. In areas of contact with the Persian Empire, Greek-speaking people in different cities sometimes cooperated with the Persians, even borrowing their ideas, but sometimes strongly resisted them.

In 499 BCE, some Greek city-states and others in the eastern Mediterranean revolted against the Persians, who claimed control over the Greek islands and mainland from their base in Anatolia. During the five-year struggle, some Greek communities sided with the Persians and suffered condemnation by other Greeks for doing so. On the mainland, farther away from the contact zone, most Greek cities resisted the Persian king's authority. So, in 492 BCE, Darius sent his fleet to subdue Athens and Sparta on the mainland, but the ships were destroyed in a storm. Two years later, Darius and his vast army invaded mainland Greece but suffered a humiliating defeat at the hands of the much smaller force of Athenians at Marathon, near Athens. The Persians retreated and waited another decade before challenging their western foe again. Meanwhile, however, Athens was becoming a major sea power.

Under the leadership of Themistocles in the 480s BCE and exploiting newfound silver mines, Athens became a naval power whose strength was its fleet of triremes (battleships). This shift in power had a significant effect on the subsequent relationship between Greeks and Persians. When the two forces met again in 480 BCE, the Persians lost the pivotal naval battle at Salamis. A year later, they suffered a decisive defeat on land and eventually lost the war. (But in a way that was typical of the intertwined relationships between the two cultures, Themistocles, the hero of Salamis, later finished his career in the service of the Persian king.)

Persian military defeats changed the balance of power. For the next 150 years Persia lost ground to the Greeks,

Primary Source

WAR IN HOMER'S *ILIAD*

The great epic poem called the Iliad—*about the war that took place at Ilium, a Greek name for the city of Troy—was attributed by the later Greeks to a poet named Homer. However, the written text is actually the result of generations of oral singers who composed different versions of this story in the ninth and eighth centuries* BCE. *The story takes place on the plains in front of Troy, and it focuses on a few prominent warriors—such as Achilles and Odysseus on the side of the Achaeans (the Greeks, also called Akhaians), and Hector and Paris (the son of Priam, king of Troy) on the Trojans' side. Historians debate the historical reality of the story, but almost all agree on the site of the ancient city it describes.*

The son of Priam wearing a gleaming breastplate
let fly through the lines but his sharp spear missed
and he hit Leucus instead, Odysseus' loyal comrade,
gouging his groin as the man hauled off a corpse—
it dropped from his hands and Leucus sprawled across it.
Enraged at his friend's death Odysseus sprang in fury,
helmed in fiery bronze he plowed through the front
and charging the enemy, glaring left and right
he hurled his spear—a glinting brazen streak—
and the Trojans gave ground, scattering back,
panicking there before his whirling shaft—
a direct hit! Odysseus struck Democoon,
. . . speared him straight through one temple
and out the other punched the sharp bronze point
and the dark came swirling thick across his eyes—
down he crashed, armor clanging against his chest.
And the Trojan front shrank back, glorious Hector too
as the Argives yelled and dragged away the corpses,
pushing on, breakneck on. But lord god Apollo,
gazing down now from the heights of Pergamus,
rose in outrage, crying down at the Trojans,
"Up and at them, you stallion-breaking Trojans!
Never give up your lust for war against these Argives!
What are their bodies made of, rock or iron to block
your tearing bronze? Stab them, slash their flesh!

* * *

Now Amarinceus' son
Diores . . . . a jagged rock
struck him against his right shin, beside the ankle.
Pirous son of Imbrasus winged it hard and true,
the Thracian chief who had sailed across from Aenus . . .
the ruthless rock striking the bones and tendons

crushed them to pulp—he landed flat on his back,
slamming the dust, both arms flung out to his comrades,
gasping out his life. Pirous who heaved the rock
came rushing in and speared him up the navel—
his bowels uncoiled, spilling loose on the ground
and the dark came swirling down across his eyes.

But Pirous—
Aetolian Thoas speared *him* as he swerved and sprang away,
the lancehead piercing his chest above the nipple
plunged deep in his lung, and Thoas, running up,
wrenched the heavy spear from the man's chest,
drew his blade, ripped him across the belly,
took his life but he could not strip his armor.

And now . . .
no man who waded into that work could scorn it any longer,
anyone still not speared or stabbed by tearing bronze
who whirled into the heart of all that slaughter—
not even if great Athena led him by the hand,
flicking away the weapons hailing down against him.
That day ranks of Trojans, ranks of Achaean fighters
sprawled there side-by-side, facedown in the dust.

→ *What does this selection reveal about the style of combat and the weapons used in this period?*
→ *More important, what do the poet's words tell us about how violence connects gods, humans, social identity, and personal relationships?*
→ *What can we surmise about the cultures from which these soldiers come?*

SOURCE: "The Truce Erupts in War" from *The Iliad* by Homer, translated by Robert Fagles, copyright © 1990 by Robert Fagles. Used by permission of Viking Penguin, a division of Penguin Group (USA), Inc.

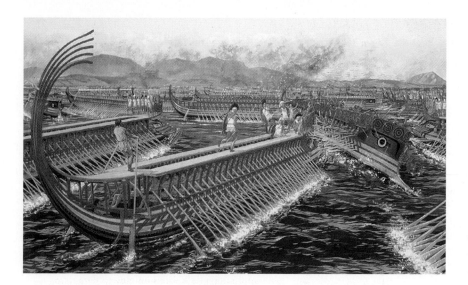

The Sea Battle at Salamis. A modern artist's reconstruction of the sea battle at Salamis in which the Greek ships led by Athens defeated a large invading fleet commanded by King Xerxes of Persia. The trireme—so-called because of its three banks of oars—was the state-of-the-art battleship of the time. Drawing on their long experience of sailing on the Mediterranean and using the fleet of triremes built under Themistocles, the Athenians gained a critical victory over the Persians and asserted ascendancy over the eastern Mediterranean.

who gradually regained territory in southeastern Europe and western Anatolia. During this time, palace intrigues and rebellions throughout the empire preoccupied the Persian court. The Greek historian Xenophon wrote that "whereas the king's empire was strong in that it covered a vast territory with large numbers of people, it also was weak because of the need to travel great distances and the wide distribution of its forces, making it vulnerable to a swift attack." In the end, the fatal blow against Persian rule came from the most remote Greek outpost in the eastern Mediterranean—Macedonia. Its armies, led by Alexander the Great, later ranged as far as India in their own quest for empire (see Chapter 6).

THE PHOENICIANS

Certain peoples living on the borderlands of empire, such as the Phoenicians, coexisted with and flourished under imperial rule—and also created autonomous spheres of action. Particularly successful were those on the western edges of the emerging Assyrian and later Persian empires. (See Map 4-4.)

Living in the region of modern-day Lebanon were the Chanani (called "Canaanites" in the Bible). We know these entrepreneurial people by the name that the Greeks gave them—Phoenicians ("Purple People")—because of an expensive purple dye that they manufactured and traded. A mixture of the local population and the Sea Peoples from recent centuries, these traders preferred opening up new markets and new ports to subduing frontiers. Their coastal cities were ideally situated to develop trade throughout the entire Mediterranean basin. Inland stood an extraordinary forest of massive cedars—perfect timber for making large, seaworthy craft, and a highly desirable export to the treeless heartlands of Egypt and Mesopotamia.

The innovations in shipbuilding and seafaring outlined earlier enabled the Phoenicians to sail as far west as present-day Morocco and Spain, carrying huge cargoes of such goods as timber, dyed cloth, glassware, wines, textiles, metal ingots,

and carved ivory. Their trading colonies all around the southern and western rims of the Mediterranean (including Carthage in modern-day Tunisia on the North African coast) became full-scale ports that shipped goods from interior regions throughout the Mediterranean.

During the eighth and seventh centuries BCE, the Assyrians expected the Phoenicians to supply the empire with special commercial services and, in return, allowed them autonomy in their business activities. The Assyrian kings signed treaties requiring the Phoenicians to pay tribute with luxury goods in return for their relative political autonomy. As the Phoenician merchants sent out waves of ships to other ports full of goods from the east, they brought back exotic luxuries for the Assyrian elites to enjoy. At the same time, Greek merchants established colonies on the northern rim of the Mediterranean. The competition and interaction of the two groups facilitated the transmission across the Mediterranean of many ideas from the advanced cultures of Southwest Asia.

The Phoenicians absorbed Mesopotamian religious and cultural elements such as gods, laws, units of measurement, and science, but the Phoenicians themselves developed an innovation that revolutionized communication and commerce: the alphabet. Introduced in the second millennium BCE in the western Levant, this new method of writing arrived in the west in 800 BCE, probably through Greek traders working in Phoenician centers. The alphabet allowed educated men to communicate directly with one another, dramatically reducing the need for professional scribes.

THE ISRAELITES AND JUDAH

To the south of the mountains of Lebanon, the homeland of the Phoenicians, another minor region extended to the borderlands of Egypt. In this narrow strip of land between the Mediterranean Sea to the west and the desert to the east, an important microsociety emerged, one that was to have an

| PHŒNICIAN | ANCIENT GREEK | LATER GREEK | ROMAN |

The Phoenician Alphabet. *Left*: The first alphabet was written on clay tablets using the cuneiform script. It was developed by Phoenician traders who needed a script that was easy to learn and could represent their form of west Semitic language. This tablet was found at the port town of Ugarit (Ras Shamra) in Syria and is dated to the fourteenth century BCE. *Right*: The forms of the letters in the Phoenician alphabet of the first millennium BCE are based on signs used to represent the Aramaic language. These Phoenician letters were then borrowed by the ancient Greeks. Our alphabet is based on that used by the Romans, who borrowed their letter forms from the later Greek inscriptions.

impact on world history that was out of proportion to its population and the geographic size of its homeland. The impact of the Phoenicians, to the north, was to spread the new form of the city-state, seaborne commerce based on markets and trade, and efficient means of communication attached to these, above all the alphabet. The Israelites, to the south, were less oriented to the Mediterranean and to seafaring. Their hybrid society mixed their local culture with social, economic, and religious forms typical of southwest Asia and Egypt.

THE ISRAELITES   We do not know much that is certain about Israelite origins. Their own later stories emphasized primal origins in Mesopotamia to the east, and origins of the patriarch Abraham from Ur on the Euphrates. Later stories emphasized connections with Egypt of the pharaohs to the west and the mass movement of a captive Israelite population out of Egypt under Moses. All that scholars can state with reasonable certainty is that material signs of a local regional culture began to emerge in the area of present-day Israel between 1200 and 1000 BCE, culminating with the emergence of a state in the form of a kingdom centered at Jerusalem under King David (ca. 1000–960 BCE). The kingdom that David and

his successor Solomon (ca. 960–930 BCE) established around Jerusalem, centered on the great temple that Solomon built in the city, did not last long. Because of internal disputes, it fragmented immediately after Solomon's reign into a tiny northern kingdom, Israel, and a small southern one, Judah.

MONOTHEISM AND PROPHETS   Within the microstate founded by David and Solomon, profound religious and cultural changes took place. A single great temple in Jerusalem now outranked all other shrines in the land. Especially among the educated upper classes linked to the temple, an absolute priority focused on one god, YHWH, over other regional deities. For a long time, however, this emphasis was relative, what modern scholars call *henotheism*: the ascendancy and power of one god over other spirits and deities that still exist. Gradually, however, there was a move to true *monotheism*: the acceptance of only one god to the exclusion of all others. What little evidence there is indicates that this process was in place by the 700s and 600s BCE, when YHWH was so dominant compared to the few remnant deities that he was mostly unchallenged. This road to monotheism, however, did not take place without quarrels and resistance, because it was a

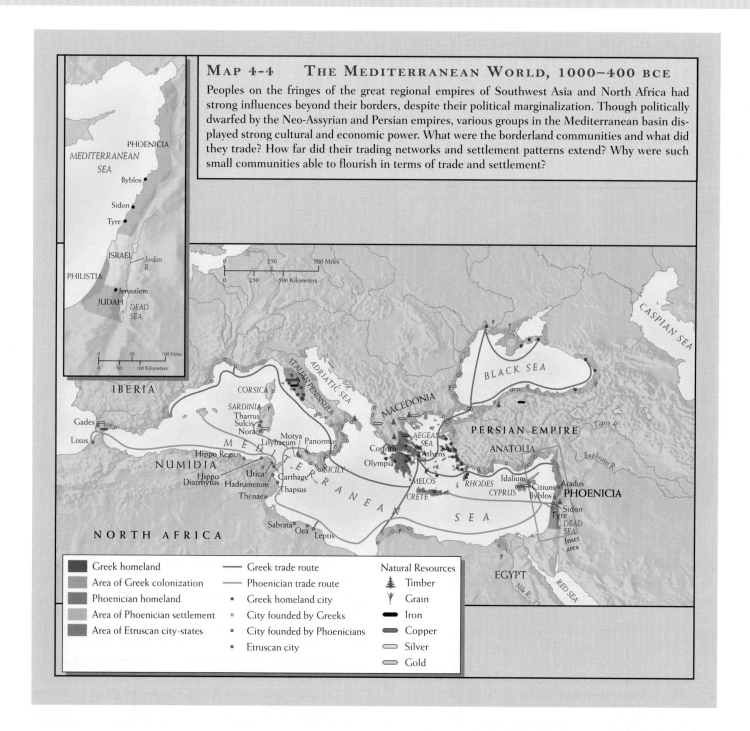

MAP 4-4   THE MEDITERRANEAN WORLD, 1000–400 BCE

Peoples on the fringes of the great regional empires of Southwest Asia and North Africa had strong influences beyond their borders, despite their political marginalization. Though politically dwarfed by the Neo-Assyrian and Persian empires, various groups in the Mediterranean basin displayed strong cultural and economic power. What were the borderland communities and what did they trade? How far did their trading networks and settlement patterns extend? Why were such small communities able to flourish in terms of trade and settlement?

Legend:
- Greek homeland
- Area of Greek colonization
- Phoenician homeland
- Area of Phoenician settlement
- Area of Etruscan city-states
- Greek trade route
- Phoenician trade route
- Greek homeland city
- City founded by Greeks
- City founded by Phoenicians
- Etruscan city

Natural Resources
- Timber
- Grain
- Iron
- Copper
- Silver
- Gold

contentious process centered on prophetic figures. The **prophets** were freelance religious men of power who found themselves in opposition to the formal power of the kings and priests of the temple in Jerusalem.

The most ferocious of these charismatic religious figures, men like Isaiah (ca. 720s BCE), Ezra (ca. 600s BCE), and Jeremiah (ca. 590s BCE), were central to the formation of an exclusive monotheistic religion and culture. They did not shrink from threatening divine annihilation for groups that opposed the new idea of one temple, one god, and one moral system to the exclusion of all others. On one occasion, the prophet Ezra

thundered: "Whoever will not obey the law of your God and the law of the king, let judgment be rigorously executed upon him, be it death, banishment, confiscation of property, or imprisonment" (Ezra 7:26 New English Bible). The moral preaching, exhortations, and threats of these men marked the high point of a long and difficult battle to defeat the divine diversity to which many people were accustomed. But prevail they did. They were part of a movement to enforce belief in a single, all-powerful god and his strict social and moral codes that governed the daily lives of all members of the community. These laws came to be enshrined in the Torah, a series of books that encapsulated the laws governing all aspects of life, including family and marriage, food, clothing, sex, and worship. The whole of it was formulated as a "contract" between all these people and their one and only god. They alone were his people.

The monotheism of the Israelites was to have far-reaching and long-lasting historical consequences, in part because Jewish peoples scattered far and wide throughout Afro-Eurasia and in part because of its influence in Christianity and Islam.

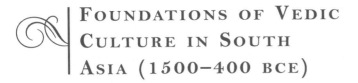

FOUNDATIONS OF VEDIC CULTURE IN SOUTH ASIA (1500–400 BCE)

> → *How did South Asia become more integrated despite the absence of an imperial state?*

In South Asia, it was language and belief systems that brought people together. As we have noted, people were on the move in greater numbers and covering longer distances in this era. In doing so, they created new mechanisms of integration, and not all were political. The Indo-European-speaking peoples who gradually entered South Asia through the passes in the Hindu Kush Mountains eventually occupied the whole of what are today Pakistan, Bangladesh, and northern India (see Chapter 3). Here their populations expanded and created a flourishing culture. Unlike societies in Mesopotamia and Egypt, the rulers in this region did not have previous polities to draw on. Floods and earthquakes had weakened the earlier Harappan urban centers in the Indus River valley (see Chapter 2), and its peoples had died out several centuries before the nomads streamed in from the northwest.

SOCIAL AND RELIGIOUS CULTURE

Like the Persians, the new migrants lacked an urban tradition. They did, however, bring many of the cultural traits of Indo-European communities from the Inner Eurasian steppe lands and central Asia. The rituals that the early Vedic Aryan settlers valued so much included sacrificing cattle, horses, and sheep to numerous gods and gathering together at festivities to sing hymns, make animal sacrifices, burn *ghee* (clarified butter) for the gods, and share a meal. Priests conducted these ceremonies, receiving payment in cows. Moreover, as part of their rituals they composed rhymes, hymns, and explanatory texts called **Vedas** ("wisdom," "knowledge"). The Vedas were initially passed on orally, and although the newcomers did not develop a writing system for at least 800 years, the Vedas became their most sacred religious works. They were eventually written down in Sanskrit.

The Indo-European-speaking migrants encountered indigenous people who either lived in agricultural settlements or were herders like themselves. The migrants allied with some of the inhabitants, who showed them how to live in their new environment. They made enemies of others, fighting with them for territory and dominance. In their interaction with people of different cultural practices and languages, the Vedic migrants kept their own language and religious rituals but also absorbed the local vocabulary and deities. Allies and defeated enemies who became part of their society had to accept Vedic culture—a culture that had originated in the steppes but changed in the South Asian environment. By the middle of the first century BCE, the Vedic peoples covered all of what is now northern India, and their language and rituals had become dominant.

Even though the Vedic migrants changed the social and cultural landscape of the region, they did not give it greater political coherence by creating a single, unified regional kingdom. (See Map 4-5.) This world grew more integrated only through a shared culture: its inhabitants followed basic principles expressed in the Vedas.

MATERIAL CULTURE

Initially, the material culture of Vedic society was rudimentary. Even chiefs and elite warriors enjoyed few luxuries. Early trade was not based on imported luxuries but on horses, which had to come in from the northwest beyond the Hindu Kush because local environmental factors prevented successful breeding or training. The ruling elite never gave up their preoccupation with fine horses, though. To make their trade in these coveted beauties easier, they created a long-distance route across the North Indian plain that stretched from the Khyber Pass to the lower Ganges.

Settlement and communication lifted Vedic communities from their rustic ways. As the Vedic people entered the fertile river basins they gradually gave up their roaming inclinations, settling down as cultivators of the land and herders of animals instead. Their turn to agriculture was fairly smooth because they learned plowing from local farmers and had access to excellent iron ore. In fact, the iron plow was crucial for tilling the Ganges plain and transforming the Deccan plateau into croplands. In the drier north, the Vedic people grew wheat, barley, millet, and cotton; in the wet lowlands, they cultivated rice paddies. Farmers also toiled to produce tropical crops such as sugarcane and spices (pepper, ginger, and cinnamon). Over time, the Vedic people transformed a sparsely populated region into a crowded domain.

As farming became the dominant way of life and urban settlements stretched out across the region, trade blossomed via river and land routes. Trade between settlements developed as the agricultural surpluses grew, and grain traveled to towns to feed their residents. Artisans pressed sugarcane into sugar in the cities, and merchants sold the finished product back to people in the agricultural villages.

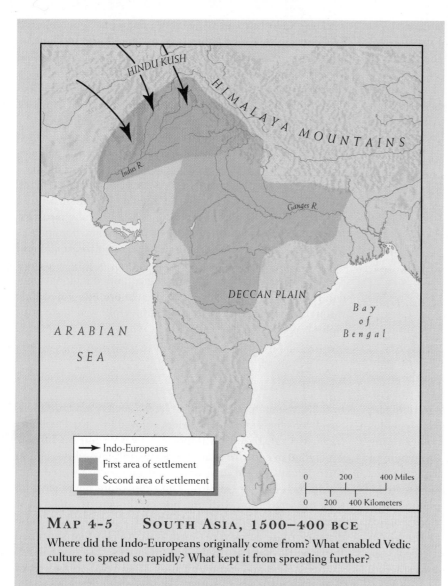

MAP 4-5   SOUTH ASIA, 1500–400 BCE

Where did the Indo-Europeans originally come from? What enabled Vedic culture to spread so rapidly? What kept it from spreading further?

Map legend:
→ Indo-Europeans
First area of settlement
Second area of settlement

lineage through blood ties, alliances via marriage, and, in many cases, invented family relations. The earliest Vedic society had two main lineages: the lunar lineage and the solar lineage. Each had its own creation myth, ancestors, language, and rituals. The lineages included many clans (a **clan** is a social group comprising many households, claiming descent from a common ancestor) in which seniority determined one's power and importance. The Vedic people absorbed many of the indigenous people's clans into their own lineages. Clans that adopted the Vedic culture became part of the lineage (through marriage or made-up ties) and were considered insiders. In contrast, clans that had other languages and rituals were considered uncivilized outsiders.

As the Vedic society expanded, the clans of the solar lineage usually stayed together in the same area. In contrast, the clans of the lunar lineage split into many branches; some migrated east to the Ganges River valley and others south to the northern Deccan plain. Though separated by distance, the clans maintained their relationship through marriage. Within kin-bound clan structures, each member had a well-defined place in the political and social order.

Once urban society and states arose, these lineages no longer underpinned the social structure, but they lived on in two major epics that recounted tales of the Vedic people. The *Mahabharata* relates the last phase of the lunar lineage, and the *Ramayana* focuses on a hero of the solar lineage. Later rulers continued to draw on the memory of these two ancient lineages, legitimizing their regimes by claiming blood links with them.

SPLINTERED STATES

The region's social and economic integration offered a stark contrast to its continuing political disintegration. In the process of fanning out from the Punjab (the region of the five tributaries of the Indus River) and settling along the Ganges River, the Vedic peoples created small regional governments and chieftainships. And as much as they fought with the indigenous peoples, they fought even more fiercely among themselves. Such aggression reinforced the importance of warriors and of the gods of war (Indra) and fire (Agni). The elite warriors battled one another and the farmers for land and other resources (just as in the Mycenaean societies, the tribal societies of the Iranian plateau, and Zhou China).

Their chieftainships eventually became small kingdoms with inhabitants bound to each other through lines of descent from a common ancestor. They traced their family descent or

CASTES IN A STRATIFIED SOCIETY

When the Vedic peoples first spread out across South Asia, their herding societies were all quite similar. But as they settled down and created state structures, they became more complex and varied. Thus, the rise of settled agriculture after 1000 BCE led to a greater divide between those who controlled land and those who worked it. As these divisions hardened, the Vedic peoples created a unique social system based on rigid class distinctions. Later, in the fourteenth century, the Portuguese called these rigid class differences **castes**—a term that has served ever since to describe the specific lineages representing social, political, and economic differences in South Asia. (See Chapter 5 for more discussion.) Dominant clan members became Kshatriyas. Originally the warrior class,

Primary Source

BECOMING A BRAHMAN PRIEST

When the Vedic people became farmers, many of them started to question the validity of sacrificing cows, the draft animals valued for their use in cultivation. Around the seventh century BCE, *some thinkers abandoned Vedic rituals and chose to live simply in forests as they debated the meaning of life and the structure of the universe. Those sages were Brahman rishi, highly respected priests. However, not every one of the famous Brahmans was born a Brahman.*

1. Satyakâma, the son of Gabâlâ, addressed his mother and said: 'I wish to become a Brahmakârin [religious student], mother. Of what family am I?'

2. She said to him: 'I do not know, my child, of what family thou art. In my youth when I had to move about much as a servant [waiting on the guests in my father's house] I conceived thee. I do not know of what family thou art. I am Gabâlâ by name, thou art Satyakâma [Philalethes]. Say that thou art Satyakâma Gâbâla.'

3. He going to Gautama Hâridrumata said to him, 'I wish to become a Brahmakârin with you, Sir. May I come to you, Sir?'

4. He said to him: 'Of what family are you, my friend?' He replied: 'I do not know, Sir, of what family I am. I asked my mother, and she answered: "In my youth when I had to move about much as a servant, I conceived thee. I do not know of what family thou art. I am Gabâlâ by name, thou art Satyakâma," I am therefore Satyakâma Gâbâla, Sir.'

5. He said to him: 'No one but a true Bráhmana would thus speak out. Go and fetch fuel, friend, I shall initiate you. You have not swerved from the truth.'

Having initiated him, he chose four hundred lean and weak cows, and said: 'Tend these friend.'

He drove them out and said to himself. 'I shall not return unless I bring back a thousand.' He dwelt a number of years [in the forest], until the cows became a thousand.

→ *Satyakama became a well-known Brahman teacher after his study. Judging from this story, was he born a Brahman?*

→ *At that time, how did the rishis and their disciples survive in the forest areas when thinking and studying?*

SOURCE: *The Upanishads,* translated by F. Max Müller, vol. 1 of *Sacred Books of the East,* edited by F. Max Müller (1900; reprint, New Delhi: Motilal Banarsidass, 1981), pp. 60–61.

they had power and controlled the land. Meanwhile, lesser clan members became Vaishya, householders who worked the land and tended livestock. As rice production expanded and labor-intensive paddy cultivation took hold, many households hired laborers and used slaves. These people came from outside the Vedic lineages and were known as Shudras ("the small ones"). They constituted the lowest caste.

In time, the Vedic social system gave rise to four castes, known as *varna.* The Kshatriyas controlled the land and were the ruling caste, the Vaishyas were agrarian commoners, and the Shudras were servants and laborers. A fourth caste, the priests or Brahmans who performed rituals and communicated with gods, was above the Kshatriyas. Some of them still functioned as priests for the chiefs, and some were sages who lived as ascetics (individuals who deny themselves comforts) in forests, where they discussed philosophical questions with

their students. Their ability to communicate with the heavens, the most coveted of skills, placed them at the top of the social pyramid. Indeed, the Brahmans guided a society in which the proper relationship with the forces of nature as represented by the deities constituted the basis of prosperity. As agriculture became ever more important, Brahmans acted as agents of Agni, the god of fire, to purify the new land for cultivation. (See Primary Source: Becoming a Brahman Priest.)

Thus, as the Vedic peoples settled down, they created stratified societies that bore little resemblance to those of their egalitarian, pastoral ancestors. In time, powerful monarchies arose around hereditary kings who ruled with councils of elders. Kings also had help from the Brahmans, who transformed social rules and practices into formal legal codes. Much later (c. 100 BCE–100 CE) one or several sages, using the name Manu (Sanskrit for "human being"),

Global Connections & Disconnections

FOUNDING TEXTS—
COMPARING JEWISH AND VEDIC SOURCES

One of the defining traits of religious movements is a reliance on sacred texts. Their stories, historical material, and parables contributed to belief systems that have become the backbone of religious identity. In many faiths we find one immutable core text, such as the Bible, for Jews and Christians; the Vedas, for Hindus; and the Koran, for Muslims. Additional supplementary texts clarify or expand on the core texts.

Like many religions, Judaism is based on a revealed scripture, thought to have been transmitted directly from God to his prophets. Rabbis argued for centuries over the interpretation of these works, and their students passed on the discussions orally. Judaism is thus built on a series of texts that include debates about the Bible by generations of scholars.

Biblical texts from a Hebrew Bible. Written around 3,000 years ago, these texts served as the primary source of the religion of the Israelites—Judaism.

The Jews did not originally use the name *Bible*; instead, a common term was *Tanakh,* an acronym derived from the Hebrew titles of the text's three major parts: (1) Torah (literally, "Instruction")—the law of the Jewish people whose authorship was traditionally ascribed to Moses; (2) Nevi'im (Prophets)—texts ascribed to prophets who preached about how to live in accordance with the law; (3) Ketuvim (Writings)—texts that include the Psalms and Proverbs.

According to Jewish tradition, the Tanakh consists of twenty-four books that took their canonical written form gradually, beginning with the Torah in the sixth century BCE. Determined to ensure their religion's survival, priests in exile in Babylon combined and finalized writings that others had begun to record in the tenth century BCE. The entire canon was not closed until the first or second century CE, when the Jewish religion was imperiled by social and religious upheaval following the Romans' destruction of the second temple in Jerusalem in 70 CE. The huge compilation of oral law, the Talmud, was finally written down (in two versions) around the fifth and sixth centuries BCE. Taken together, these texts express the Jewish community's ability to adapt and persevere when historical conditions changed.

We have already discussed the four foundational Vedic texts and their use in religious rituals. Brahmans, the priests and intellectuals of Vedic society, composed other works—the Brahmanas and Aranyakas—to explain how and when to recite the hymns and chants of the Vedas during ritual performances. However, as Vedic peoples embraced settled agriculture and abandoned their former nomadic lifeways, some thinkers doubted the validity of sacrificial rituals based on gods driving chariots and began to reflect on the meaning of life and the universe. Scholars then composed the Upanishads, mystic speculative works whose concepts of

gathered these laws into a single text (see Chapter 8). These legal books both guided the king and regulated the behavior of his subjects.

VEDIC WORLDS

A Vedic culture, transmitted from generation to generation by the Brahman caste, unified what political rivalries had divided. Belief in Indra and other gods, a common language (Sanskrit), and shared cultural symbols linked the dispersed communities and gave the Vedic peoples a collective sense of destiny. Though Sanskrit was a language imported from central Asia, the people used it to transmit the Vedas orally. By expressing the people's sacred knowledge in the beautiful rhythms and rhymes of Sanskrit, the Vedas effectively passed on their culture from one age to the next.

As the priests of Vedic society, the Brahmans were responsible for memorizing every syllable and tone of the Vedic

The Bodhisattva Manjusri. This text was written in 967 at one of the great monasteries of northeastern India. It is an example of how Buddhists copied foundational texts onto palm leaves.

life and death, time and space, geography and the cosmos laid the foundations for most, if not all, of South Asia's later schools of thought, including Buddhism and Jainism.

Vedic literature, both hymns and rules for rituals, long remained an oral tradition. Even after Buddhists started to write down texts in the late first millennium BCE, Brahmans resisted the temptation to make copies of the Vedas, fearing they would lose exclusive control of their sacred works. Sometime after the beginning of the Common Era, they may have started copying Vedic passages onto palm leaves to aid their memory. When Brahmanism was reborn as Hinduism during the first millennium CE, a host of new

deities became objects of cults of worship and gave rise to new genres of Sanskrit literature, such as Puranas (stories of the past) and epics. The Vedas are still the final authority of Hinduism, though most Hindus find their contents incomprehensible and of little relevance.

In both Jewish and Vedic traditions, the pressures of a changing world created a new relationship among oral culture, texts, and interpretation. Though they abandoned their old systems of religious practice, Jewish and Vedic worshippers continued to interpret sacred texts as they made sense of their lives, passing from religions of oral tradition to those of the written word.

works. These included commentaries on sacred works from early nomadic times, as well as new rules and rituals explaining the settled, farming way of life. The Vedas promoted cultural unity and pride through common ritual practices and support for hereditary *raja* kingdoms. The main body of Vedic literature includes the four Vedas: Rig-Veda, Sama-Veda, Yajur-Veda, and Atharva-Veda. The Rig-Veda, the earliest text, is a collection of hymns praising the gods, including Indra (god of war), Agni (god of fire), and Varuna (god of water).

Indra stands out as the most powerful and important, as he is the one who set the order of the universe and made life possible. The Sama-Veda is a textbook of songs for priests to perform when making ritual sacrifices; most of their stanzas also appear in the Rig-Veda. The Yajur-Veda is a prayerbook for the priest who conducted rituals for chariot races, horse sacrifices, or the king's coronation. The Atharva-Veda includes charms and remedies; many address problems related to agriculture, a central aspect of life.

Although the Vedic period left no impressive buildings and artifacts, it created a wealth of thinking about cosmology and human society. In this way, it laid the religious foundations for coming generations. (See Global Connections & Disconnections: Founding Texts—Comparing Jewish and Vedic Sources.)

During the middle of the first millennium BCE, thinkers (mostly Brahman ascetics dwelling in forests) felt that the Vedic rituals no longer provided satisfactory answers to the many questions of a rapidly changing society. The result was a collection of works known as the Upanishads, or the supreme knowledge, which expanded the Vedic cultural system. Taking the form of dialogues between disciples and a sage, the Upanishads explored questions of deep concern at that time. Out of these dialogues came a set of lessons that offered insights into the ideal social order, and a script and eventually a canon to be shared beyond local communities.

The Upanishads teach that people are not separate from each other but belong to a cosmic universe called Brahma. While the physical world is always changing and is filled with chaos and illusion, *atman*, the eternal being, exists in all people and all creatures. Atman's presence in each living being makes all creatures part of a universal soul. While all living beings must die, the atman guarantees eternal life, ensuring that souls are re-born and transmigrate into new lives. This cycle continues with humans as they are either reborn as humans or as other living creatures, like cows, insects, or plants. Only when humans reach a permanent union with Brahma, which is the highest level of achievement, are they able to break this cycle of birth and rebirth. Living an ascetic life, separated from the pleasures and comforts of this world, and engaging in meditation enable individuals to transcend the physical world, merge their souls with Brahma, and experience eternal life and happiness.

These unique Vedic views of life and the universe were passed along as principles of faith, bringing spiritual unity to the northern half of South Asia. Unlike the societies of Southwest Asia and North Africa, here in the kingdoms of the Indus Valley and the Ganges plain the common Vedic culture—rather than larger political units—was the unifying bond.

Zhou Chariots. After swearing allegiance to the Shang, the Zhou assembled superior military forces in the northwest, in part by emulating Shang chariots. The Zhou subsequently used their own chariots and archers to defeat the Shang in about 1045 BCE. The regional lords who owed allegiance to the Zhou king distinguished themselves in the aristocratic hierarchy by using chariots for travel and battle.

THE EARLY ZHOU EMPIRE IN EAST ASIA (1045–771 BCE)

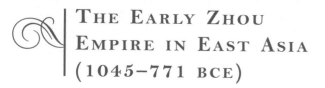

> → *To what extent was the Zhou state similar to contemporary Southwest Asian empires?*

Around the same time that western Afro-Eurasian societies experienced periods of upheaval and reconsolidation, the political and social map of East Asia featured invasion and warfare. The small Zhou state, based in the Shanxi region, initially swore allegiance to the Shang and allied with them in their fight against nomadic incursions on the western borderlands. But the Zhou eventually turned against the Shang, assembling superior military forces to defeat them in about 1045 BCE. (See Map 4-6.)

INTEGRATION THROUGH DYNASTIC INSTITUTIONS

When the Zhou took over from the Shang, China was not yet a fully integrated empire. Like Vedic South Asia, China under the Zhou dynasty was initially split into regional powers. As we will see, though, China's local administration, first developed in the Shang Dynasty, gave it greater unity. Moreover, the Zhou copied the Shang's unifying dynastic structure: a patrimonial state centered on ancestor worship in which the rulers' power passed down through genealogies of

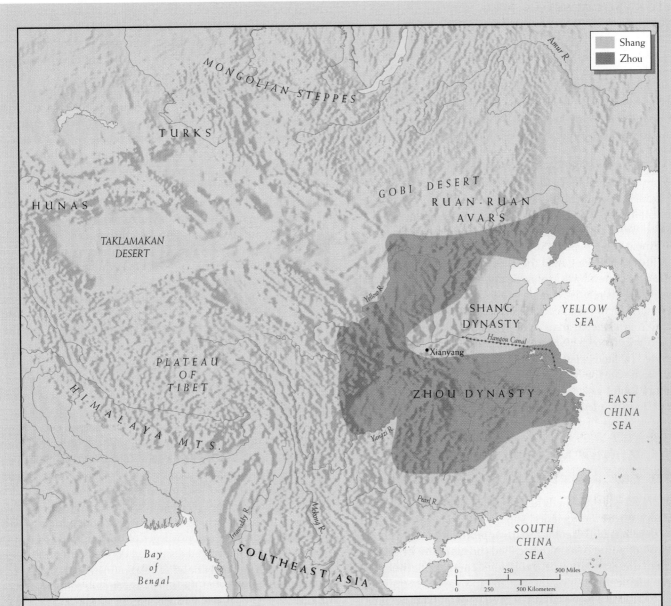

MAP 4-6   THE ZHOU DYNASTY, 2200–256 BCE

Toward the end of the second millennium BCE, the Zhou state supplanted the Shang dynasty as the most powerful political force in East Asia. Using the map above, compare and contrast the territorial reach of the Zhou state with that of the Shang. In what direction did the Zhou state expand the most dramatically? Why do you think this was the case? How did the Zhou integrate their geographically large and diverse state?

male ancestors reaching back to the gods. (A **genealogy** is a history of the descent of a person or family from a distant ancestor.) On such a foundation (notably absent in Vedic South Asia) an integrated and remarkably lasting dynasty structure developed.

As the Zhou adopted the local political organization of the Shang, they began an extended process of integration. Bit by

bit, regional aristocracies subordinated themselves to a single ruler. It was a balancing act between a dynastic central ruler and powerful local lords, however. Using cultural symbols and the art of statecraft rather than religion, the Zhou peoples established a dynasty that had broad geographic influence but limited power over its regional states. This was integration, but not quite unification.

ZHOU SUCCESSION AND POLITICAL FOUNDATIONS

The nature of early Chinese political successions differed from that of Southwest Asia, where outsiders invaded and took power. Instead, in China, the northwestern Zhou peoples gradually took over from the Shang. For many years, the Zhou and the Shang lived side by side, trading and often allying to fend off raiders from the far west. Though initially less advanced in writing and technology than the Shang, the Zhou learned and borrowed from them. And when the Zhou became strong enough, they overcame the Shang.

Evidence from this period indicates that a powerful King Wu established Zhou control in northwestern China and expanded north toward what is now Beijing and south toward the Yangzi River valley. (See Primary Source: Zhou Succession Story.) This king held the allegiance of the lords of older states and of new lords whom he appointed in annexed areas. Rewarding his relatives and key followers with lands that they could pass on to their descendants was an important means of controlling strategic areas. Often, the new colonies consisted of a garrison town (where the Zhou colonizers lived) surrounded by fields containing the local inhabitants (the farmers). As under the Shang, Zhou regional lords had to supply military forces as needed, pay tribute, and appear at the imperial court to pledge their continuing allegiance to the king.

THE ZHOU "MANDATE OF HEAVEN" AND THE JUSTIFICATION OF POWER

The Zhou rulers justified their takeover of Shang wealth and territories by claiming moral superiority. To accomplish this, they developed an ideology that supported a morally correct transfer of power, which they called the **mandate of heaven**. At first the mandate was a religious compact between the Zhou people and their supreme god in heaven (literally, the "sky god"), but it evolved into a fundamental Chinese political doctrine. The Zhou argued that since worldly affairs were supposed to align with those of the heavens, heavenly powers conferred legitimate rights to rule on their chosen representative. The ruler was then duty-bound to uphold heaven's principles of harmony and honor. Any ruler who failed in this duty, who let instability creep into earthly affairs, or who let his people suffer would lose his mandate. Under this system, it was the prerogative of spiritual authority to withdraw support from any wayward dynasts and find another, more worthy agent. Thus the Zhou sky god legitimated regime change.

In using this creed to justify their takeover, the Zhou rulers had to acknowledge that any group of rulers, themselves included, could be ousted if they lost the mandate of heaven because of improper practices. After the Zhou overturned the Shang line of succession, rulers were no longer considered gods. From that point on, dynastic legitimacy depended on ruling in accordance with the principles of good governance and upright behavior. China's rulers (unlike the theocracies of Southwest Asia and the later emperor system of Japan) created an empire based more on politics, military power, and morality than on religious legitimacy.

The early Zhou kings contended that heaven favored their triumph because the last Shang kings had been evil men whose policies brought pain to the people through waste and corruption. Thereafter, the mandate became a political tool. It was a compelling way to defend continuity of political institutions, if not rulers, in the name of preserving a natural order. It also helps explain why the change in power did not bring about an abrupt overhaul of political and cultural institutions.

The Shang had used writing to communicate with the divine world, and the Zhou continued this practice. But the Zhou also expanded its use, recording matters ranging from royal divinations (omens, predictions, and questions for the gods) to a variety of political practices, such as kingly speeches, grants of official offices, and rewards. Other texts described the organization and administration of government. These were reportedly the work of the Duke of Zhou, but they were actually from a much later period.

Writing became even more essential when King Mu (r. 956–918 BCE) established a more formal system of bureaucratic governance. He restructured the court and military by appointing officials, supervisors, and military captains who were not related to him, and he instituted a formal legal code. These changes created a need for bureaucratic records, including archives of appointments and legal verdicts. Increasingly, a pool of scribes and scholars joined the entourage of royal diviners, using their mastery of writing to find patrons at court and among regional powers. Through their powerful rhetoric, they tied many of the new changes to the early Zhou founding myth.

One of the duties and privileges of the king was to create a royal calendar. This official document defined times for undertaking agricultural activities and celebrating rituals, and it was an impartial measure of the ruler's success or failure. In fact, unexpected events such as solar eclipses or natural calamities threw into question the ruling house's authority. Since rulers claimed that their authority came from heaven, the Zhou made great efforts to gain accurate knowledge of the stars and to perfect the astronomical system on which they based their calendar. By creating a calendar that improved on the Shang's version, they enhanced their public legitimacy. Advances in astronomy and mathematics enabled Zhou astronomers to precisely calculate the length of a lunar month (29.53 days) and measure the length of the solar year (365.25 days). But a year of twelve lunar months is 354.36 days long, so to resolve the discrepancy the Zhou occasionally inserted a leap month. Scribes dated the reigns of kings by days and years within a repeating sixty-year cycle, which was said to match the cosmological interaction between heaven and earth.

Zhou legitimacy also derived indirectly from Shang material culture—that is, the use of bronze ritual vessels, statues,

Primary Source

ZHOU SUCCESSION STORY

Chinese lore often glamorized the early Zhou dynasty as an era of sage rulers such as King Wu and the Duke of Zhou (Chou). The Shangshu (Book of History) account, however, shows that the transition of power from the founder, King Wu, to the Duke of Zhou was fraught with difficulty—as was often the case in early states. It reveals how the Duke of Zhou tried simultaneously to protect his reputation as regent to King Wu's young son and to preserve Zhou rule. This document also represents one of the first major efforts in Chinese history to provide a historical narrative of events.

After he had completed the conquest of the Shang people, in the second year, King Wu fell ill and was despondent. The two lords, the duke of Shao and Tai-kung Wang, said, "For the king's sake let us solemnly consult the tortoise oracle." But the duke of Chou [King Wu's younger brother, named Tan] said, "We must not distress the ancestors, the former kings."

The duke of Chou then offered himself to the ancestors, constructing three altars within a single compound. . . . Then he made this announcement to the Great King, to King Chi, and to King Wen, his great grandfather, grandfather, and father, and the scribe copied down the words of his prayer on tablets:

"Your chief descendant So-and-so [King Wu's personal name is tabooed] has met with a fearful disease and is violently ill. If you three kings are obliged to render to Heaven the life of an illustrious son, then substitute me, Tan, for So-and-so's person. I am good and compliant, clever and capable. I have much talent and much skill and can serve the spirits. . . ."

Then he divined with three tortoises, and all were auspicious. He opened the bamboo receptacles and consulted the documents, and they too indicated an auspicious answer. The duke of Chou said to the king, "According to the indications of the oracle, you will suffer no harm."

[The king said,] "I, the little child, have obtained a new life from the three kings. I shall plan for a distant end. I hope that they will think of me, the solitary man."

After the duke of Chou returned, he placed the tablets containing the prayer in a metal-bound casket. The next day the king began to recover.

[Later, King Wu died and was succeeded by his infant son, King Ch'eng. The duke of Chou acted as regent and was slandered by King Wu's younger brothers, whom he was eventually forced to punish.]

In the autumn, when a plentiful crop had ripened but had not yet been harvested, Heaven sent great thunder and lightning accompanied by wind. The grain was completely flattened and even large trees were uprooted. The people of the land were in great fear. The king and his high ministers donned their ceremonial caps and opened the documents of the metal-bound casket and thus discovered the record of how the duke of Chou had offered himself as a substitute for King Wu. . . .

The king grasped the document and wept. "There is no need for us to make solemn divination about what has happened," he said. "In former times the duke of Chou toiled diligently for the royal house, but I, the youthful one, had no way of knowing it. Now Heaven has displayed its terror in order to make clear the virtue of the duke of Chou. I, the little child, will go in person to greet him, for the rites of our royal house approve such action."

When the king came out to the suburbs to meet the duke of Chou, Heaven sent down rain and reversed the wind, so that the grain all stood up once more. The two lords ordered the people of the land to right all the large trees that had been blown over and to earth them up. Then the year was plentiful. (*Chin t'eng.*)

→ *How does the passage demonstrate the Zhou's reliance on male ancestor worship?*
→ *What do the direct speeches tell us about the place of divination in Zhou politics?*

SOURCE: Translated in Burton Watson, *Early Chinese Literature* (New York: Columbia University Press, 1962), pp. 35–36.

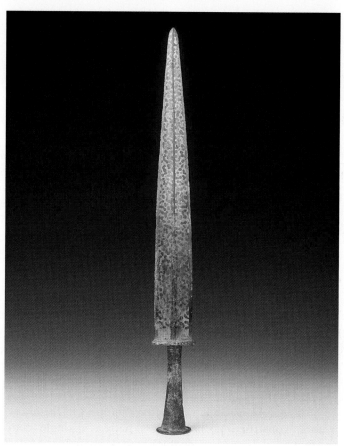

Zhou Wine Vessel and Sword. Under the Zhou, bronze metallurgy depended on a large labor force. Many workers initially came from Shang labor groups, who were superior to the Zhou in technology. The use of bronze, such as for this wine vessel and sword, exemplified dynastic continuity between the Shang and Zhou.

ornaments, and weapons. As the Zhou emulated the Shang's large-scale production of ceremonial bronzes, they developed an extensive system of bronze metalworking that required a large force of tribute labor. Many of its members were Shang, who were sometimes forcibly transported to new Zhou towns to produce the bronze ritual objects.

Such continuity with old ways was very useful to the Zhou, who revered their predecessors and conducted elaborate rituals to underscore the importance of inheritance and thereby justify their power. Ancestor worship was a critical component of political life, which celebrated the resilient influence of the past on the present.

SOCIAL AND ECONOMIC TRANSFORMATION

As the Chinese social order became more integrated, it also became more class-based. Directly under the Zhou ruler and his royal ministers were the hereditary nobles, divided into

five ranks. These regional lords had landholdings of different sizes. They all owed allegiance to the Zhou king, and they all supplied warriors to fight in the king's army and laborers to clear land, drain fields, and do other work. They periodically appeared at court and took part in complex rituals to reaffirm their allegiance to the king. Below the regional lords were high officers at the Zhou court, as well as ministers and administrators who supervised the people's work. A military caste of aristocratic warriors stood at the bottom of the noble hierarchy.

OCCUPATIONAL GROUPS AND FAMILY STRUCTURES

Initially, most of the population worked as farmers on fields owned by great landholding families. Some commoners were artisans, such as those who produced valuable bronze ritual vessels, or weavers who spun delicate silk textiles. Over time, an elaborate ladder of occupational strata arose. This system divided people by function: landholders who produced grain, growers of plants and fruit trees, woodsmen, breeders of cattle and chickens, artisans, merchants, weavers, servants, and those with no fixed occupation. The central government apparently controlled how each group did its work—for example, telling landholders what crops to plant, when to harvest, and when to irrigate. Although reports of these efforts may overstate the government's reach, the Chinese state clearly played a major role in uniting the region's diverse peoples—in ways that none of Eurasia's other great regimes did.

One important method of integration was the political and legal use of family structures. In their patrilineal society, the Zhou established strict hierarchies for both men and women. Both art and literature celebrated the son who honored his parents. Men and women had different roles in family and ceremonial life. On landholdings, men farmed and hunted, while women produced silk and other textiles and fashioned them into clothing. Wealth increasingly trumped gender and class distinctions, however. In particular, rich women high in the Zhou aristocracy enjoyed a greater range of actions than other women. And wealthy merchants in emerging cities challenged the authority of local lords.

TECHNOLOGICAL DEVELOPMENT What has been remarkable about China throughout history is how its integration progressed in small steps, not in a single, triumphal bound. Zhou achievements likewise were incremental, rooted in a transformation of the countryside as both princes and peasants began expanding the agrarian frontier inland. Wooden and, much later, iron plows enabled farmers to break the hard sod of lands beyond the river basins, and over time cultivators learned the practice of field rotation to prevent soil nutrients from being exhausted. A great advance occurred in the middle of the first millennium BCE as regional states organized local efforts to regulate the flow of the main rivers. They built long canals to promote communication and trade, and they dug impressive irrigation networks to convert arid lands into fertile belts. (Some of these systems remain in use today.) This slow agrarian revolution enabled the Chinese population to soar—reaching perhaps 20 million by the late Zhou era.

Under the Zhou dynasty, landowners and rulers organized the construction of dikes and irrigation systems to control the floodplain of the Yellow River and Wei River valley surrounding the capital at Xianyang (present-day Xi'an). For centuries, peasants labored over this floodplain and its tributaries—building dikes, digging canals, and raising levees as the waters flowed to the sea. When their work was done, the bottom of the floodplain was a latticework of rich, well-watered fields, with carefully manicured terraces rising in gradual steps to higher ground. This enormous undertaking was the work of many generations. Eventually, irrigation works grew to such a scale that they required management by powerful territorial rulers, the Zhou dynasts centered in the Wei River valley, and their skilled engineers. The engineers

also designed canals that connected rivers and supported commerce and other internal exchanges. Tens of thousands of workers spent countless days digging these canals, paying tribute in the form of labor. (As we have seen, other dynasties in Afro-Eurasia also produced massive building works through forced labor.)

Increasingly, the canals linked China's two breadbaskets: the wheat and millet fields in the north, and the rice fields in the south. And as with the Yellow River in the north, engineers controlled the Yangzi River in the south. So wealthy was China that its influence even reached the distant steppe lands to the north and west. Nomads in mountainous areas or on the Zhou frontiers, who often fought with the Zhou ruler and his regional lords, now depended on trade with the fertile heartlands. In return for their pastoral produce the Zhou received textiles, metal tools and weapons, and luxury items.

LIMITS AND DECLINE OF ZHOU POWER

At its center the Zhou state had great influence, but its power elsewhere was limited. Unlike Assyria and Persia, it never evolved into a regional power. The dynasty relied instead on culture (its bronzes) and statecraft (the mandate of heaven) to maintain its leadership among competing powers and lesser principalities. Rather than having absolute control of an empire, the Zhou state was first among many regional economic and political allies.

The Zhou dynasty ruled over a much larger territory than the Shang did, but it was not highly centralized. Instead, it expected regional lords (who in this regard resembled Persian satraps) to hold provinces in line. Military campaigns continued to press into new lands or to defend Zhou holdings from enemies. Rulers attempted to keep neighbors and allies in line by giving them power, protecting them from aggression, and continuing the tried-and-true method of intermarriage between dynastic family members and local nobles. However, as a result of the Zhou's ruling methods, their subordinates had more than autonomy; they also had genuine resources that they could turn against the dynasts at opportune moments.

The power of the Zhou royal house over its regional lords declined in the ninth and eighth centuries BCE. In response, the Zhou court at its impressive capital at Xianyang introduced ritual reforms with grandiose ceremonies featuring larger, standardized bronze vessels. Yet even this move could not reverse the regime's growing political weakness in dealing with its steppe neighbors and internal regional lords. For the most part, the Zhou court became a theater state, hoping that impressive rituals would conceal its lack of military might.

The facade began to crumble as wars, social dislocations, and changes in landholding shook the system's social and political foundations. The Zhou dynasts managed to cling to their authority until 771 BCE, when northern steppe invaders forced them to flee their western capital. The Zhou dynastic period, like the Shang, was later idealized by Chinese historians as a golden age of wise kings and officials. In fact, the Zhou model of government, culture, and society became the standard for later generations. As a result, a tradition emerged in China of upholding political continuity and social stability. The regime's legitimacy was seen as resting on the moral bonds between ruling families, who were at the top of a carefully managed social pyramid, and those in the orderly layers beneath them. Though the Mesopotamian and Persian superpowers were capable of greater expansion during this period, China was sowing the seeds of a more durable state.

CONCLUSION

Upheavals in the territorial states of Afro-Eurasia led to the emergence of more extensive political powers—in Mesopotamia, Persia, and China—during the first half of the first millennium BCE. For seven centuries, both the Assyrian Empire based in Mesopotamia and the Persian Empire based in Iran were superpowers whose reach continued to grow. These first empires expanded territorial states far beyond their "ethnic" or linguistic homelands and, in so doing, brought more extensive interactions and exchanges to parts of Afro-Eurasia. Driving these events were changes in climate, invasions by nomadic people, new weaponry, trade, and new administrative strategies and institutions.

The Assyrian and Persian empires differed in fundamental ways from the earlier city-states and territorial states of this area. Assyrians and Persians created ideologies, political institutions, economic ties, and cultural ways that extended their power across vast regions. Indeed, their strong imperial institutions enabled them to exploit human and material resources at great distances from the imperial centers.

But there were other models of expansion that did not yield political empires—at least at first. In the Vedic world of the Indus Valley and Ganges plain, shared values and revered texts did not lead even to a single state. The unparalleled degree of integration across northern South Asia was cultural and economic rather than political. Centuries would pass before a regime would layer a state over this shared cultural world.

In China as well, a core of cultural and political beliefs developed. As in Persia and the Indus Valley and Ganges plain, shared ideas and values spanned a wide geographic area. But unlike in Vedic South Asia, a powerful dynastic political system emerged in China when the Zhou rulers began integrating diverse peoples and territories. Their rule could not last, however. Although the Zhou transformed China, they could not overcome the power of local nobles or fully protect the western frontier from nomadic attacks. Thus the regime never developed military and fiscal powers as great as those of the Southwest Asian empires. Nevertheless, Zhou efforts did implant the foundations of a political and ruling culture that enabled later imperial rulers to achieve success.

Empire building did not occur everywhere; the majority of the world's people still lived in smaller political groupings. Even within Afro-Eurasia, some areas were completely untouched. And even where the Assyrian and Persian rulers,

Chronology

	1100 BCE	1000 BCE	900 BCE
SOUTHWEST ASIA AND NORTH AFRICA			◆ 950–612 BCE Neo-Assyrian Empire
THE MEDITERRANEAN			
SOUTH ASIA		◆ 1000 BCE New Vedic migrations into the Ganges River valley begin ◆ 1000 BCE Development of settled agriculture ◆ 1000 BCE Emergence of caste system	
EAST ASIA		◆ 1045–771 BCE Zhou state	

soldiers, and traders came into contact with certain groups, they did not necessarily crush them. For example, the nomadic peoples of the northern steppes and the southern desert locations throughout Eurasia continued to be autonomous. But fewer and fewer were untouched by the technological, cultural, and political pulses of empires.

The peoples living on the eastern Mediterranean shore, in the Vedic society of South Asia, and in the Zhou kingdom of China made lasting contributions to the cultural and religious history of humanity. The Phoenician Sea Peoples traversed the whole of the Mediterranean basin and spread their simplified alphabet. From the land of Judah, a budding monotheism sprouted. Late Vedic South Asia spun out the concept of cyclic universal time in the form of reincarnation. And in late Zhou China, an ideal of statecraft and social order took shape. All evolved into powerful cultural forms that in time spread their influences far beyond their sites of origin.

Review and research materials are available at StudySpace: ⓢ WWNORTON.COM/STUDYSPACE

KEY TERMS

annals (p. 133)
caste (p. 148)
clan (p. 148)
empire (p. 126)
genealogy (p. 153)
ideology (p. 133)

iron (p. 127)
mandate of heaven (p. 154)
prophets (p. 146)
Vedas (p. 147)
Zoroastrianism (p. 137)

STUDY QUESTIONS

1. Migrating populations paved the way for greater cultural integration across Afro-Eurasia after 1200 BCE. Where did the migrants come from, and where did they invade? In South Asia, for example, how much of the original culture did the migrants incorporate into their own way of life?

2. Compare and contrast the statecraft of the Neo-Assyrian and Persian empires. How did each try to integrate their multicultural empires?

3. Analyze the role of the fringe societies in the Aegean and Levant in western Afro-Eurasia during the first millennium BCE. How did they contribute to cultural integration and expansion during this time?

4. Explain the role of clans and castes in Vedic society in South Asia during the first millennium BCE. To what extent did they maintain a culturally integrated and distinct world in the absence of political unity?

5. Compare and contrast the Zhou state to the regional empires in western Afro-Eurasia in the second millennium BCE. What legacies did each leave?

6. Compare and contrast the role of the state in facilitating regional integration in East Asia, South Asia, and western Afro-Eurasia.

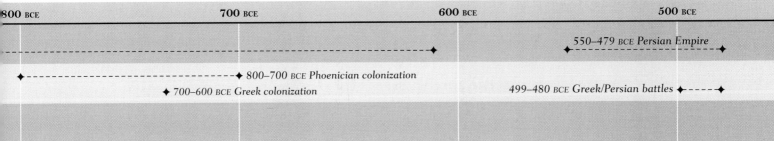

800 BCE | 700 BCE | 600 BCE | 500 BCE

550–479 BCE *Persian Empire*

800–700 BCE *Phoenician colonization*

700–600 BCE *Greek colonization*

499–480 BCE *Greek/Persian battles*

WORLDS TURNED INSIDE OUT, 1000–350 BCE

A struggle for power and territory gripped societies from China to Africa. It turned the sixth century BCE into an age of violent upheaval. In the midst of this mayhem, Master Kong Fuzi of China instructed his disciples on how to govern, saying: "Guide them by edicts, keep them in line with punishments, and the people will stay out of trouble but will have no sense of shame. Guide them by virtue, keep them in line with the rites, and they will, besides having a sense of shame, reform themselves" (Confucius, *The Analects*, II, 3).

Master Kong, also known as Confucius, represented a new breed of influential leaders—teachers and thinkers; not kings, priests, or warriors. Instead of fighting wars of conquest, they conducted wars of ideas. At the same time, it was the convulsions around them that motivated the search for new insights and solutions. By viewing the world in new ways, they sought to lead societies out of that turbulence. Their arsenal: words. Their strategy: instruction. These teachers strove to instruct rulers on how to govern justly, and to show ordinary individuals how to live ethically. In doing so, they began to integrate regional worlds with shared beliefs.

Teachers and prophets are a primary focus of this chapter, for the period's thinkers were some of the most influential in history. In China, Confucius elaborated a set of principles for ethical living that has guided the Chinese population up to modern times. In South Asia, Siddhartha Gautama (the Buddha) laid out social and spiritual tenets that challenged the traditional caste system and the privileged warrior and priestly classes. In Greece, Socrates, Plato, and Aristotle described a world that conformed to natural and intelligible laws. New thinking also led to new institutions, most notably in the city-states of the eastern Mediterranean where political, economic, and cultural innovations led to new political institutions, including experiments in democratic forms of government, and vigorous economic activity. Some modern thinkers call these centuries "the axial age," to emphasize it as a pivotal period between the declining empires of ancient Egypt, Northern India, and Zhou China, and the successor empires of Alexander the Great, Rome, and the Han Chinese (see Chapters 6 and 7). This intellectually and institutionally dynamic period gave rise to the ethical, philosophical, and religious foundations of cultures in India, China, and what later became western Europe. Even distant worlds saw major breakthroughs in belief systems that created more culturally integrated regions. In Mesoamerica, the Olmecs established the first complex, urban-based society, with artistic and religious reverberations well beyond their homelands. In Africa, distinct regional identities spread in the Upper Nile (in Nubia) and West Africa.

The philosophers, theologians, poets, political leaders, and merchants of the axial age founded literary traditions, articulated new belief systems, and established new political and economic institutions that spread well beyond the places that inspired them. While wars and havoc occurred within their societies and long-distance trade and travel linked societies,

these centuries were dominated by a search for order and an appetite for new thinking. This created opportunities for texts and their authors to create cultural systems that re-imagined entire regions integrated by more than trade or conquest, but by common values and shared beliefs. The axial age involved powerful impulses for cultural integration.

ALTERNATIVE PATHWAYS AND IDEAS

> → *How did "second-generation" cultures expand social, political, and cultural options?*

During the first millennium BCE, societies on the edges of regional empires or within declining empires started to follow innovative paths. (See Map 5-1.) They tinkered with new types of political and social organization, and new ways of fighting and expanding borders. Such innovation occurred, for example, in Eastern Zhou China, where nearly constant warfare and power struggles ultimately led to the formation of several large and powerful territorial states and led to ethical and political formulas for ordering human behavior. Radical changes also occurred in Greece and the Levant, where the chaos and economic decline caused by the Sea Peoples' onslaught culminated in the emergence of dynamic city-states and new ideas about good governance.

Along the great river valleys of East and South Asia, the Caribbean coast of Mexico, and the coasts of the Mediterranean, complex societies arose with cultural and political ideas that differed radically from those of the regional empires

Focus Questions

Ⓢ WWNORTON.COM/STUDYSPACE

→ *How did "second-generation" cultures expand social, political, and cultural options?*

→ *In what ways did scholars propose ending the warfare and chaos of China's Spring and Autumn and Warring States periods?*

→ *How did political and social transformations encourage new beliefs and dissident thinkers in South Asia?*

→ *How did cultural integration occur in the Andes and Mesoamerica in the absence of political unity?*

→ *How did the spread of iron smelting shape the social landscape of sub-Saharan Africa?*

→ *In what ways did city-states integrate the dispersed settlements of the Mediterranean?*

MAIN THEMES

→ *Age of violent warfare spreads across Afro-Eurasia.*
→ *Innovative societies arise worldwide.*
→ *Teachers and prophets reshape peoples' views of the world.*

FOCUS ON *Innovative Societies*

China

+ Multistate system emerges from warfare, revolutionizing society and thought.
+ Confucius and the hundred masters outline the ideals of governing and living.

South Asia

+ Small monarchies and urban oligarchies emerge after the Vedic peoples' migrations and rule over societies organized around the caste system.
+ Dissident thinkers like Mahavira and the Buddha challenge Brahman priests and the caste system.

The Americas

+ Olmecs and Chavín peoples produce increasingly hierarchical societies and connect villages via trade.
+ Large-scale common cultures emerge.

Sub-Saharan Africa

+ Expansion of the Sahara Desert and population explosion cause people to coalesce in a few locations.
+ Early signs of a Sudanic common culture appear across the region.

The Mediterranean World

+ Independent city-states emerge from social destruction and facilitate revolutionary principles in rulership, commerce, and thought.
+ Thinkers like Democritus, Plato, and Aristotle challenge conventions and encourage public discourse about the role of the individual in society and the way the universe works.

---

of Southwest Asia. In the Indus Valley, such societies emphasized sacred categories (especially caste, which determined every individual's status and occupation) and new religious experiences. These communities revolved around small-scale monarchies and urban oligarchies (societies led by small cliques) dominated by elite families. In China, small polities held by regional lords under the Zhou king gave way to increasingly centralized and belligerent states. In the Americas, the dispersed settlements of the Olmecs in Mesoamerica and the Chavín peoples of the Andes produced increasingly hierarchical social orders despite a continued reliance on simple agricultural technology. Around the Mediterranean Sea, new social forms were taking shape in independent cities. These communities borrowed some elements from older societies, but more often they developed in place to match their environments.

The new communities were not just extensions of old lifeways. In each, dramatic innovations in cultural and religious beliefs expanded people's social, political, and cultural options.

Although the cultures were clearly different from one another, we might call them all **second-generation societies**, simultaneously building on their predecessors and representing a departure from ancient legacies.

New ideas by no means bred consensus. In fact, the age of great ideas witnessed magnificent disputes over what was best for humanity, and over the very political and moral status of the individual. In Greece, philosophers questioned the possibility of gaining and transmitting true or reliable knowledge of the world. They began to doubt the permanence of the social order and pondered the relationship between humans and the cosmos. In Eastern Zhou China, beset by constant warfare, sages debated how best to restore order; some advocated engagement while others urged withdrawal from government. In the Ganges Valley, thinkers questioned the traditional Brahmanic rituals and sought new ways of behaving morally and attaining enlightenment. Whereas many Greek philosophers endorsed skepticism for its own sake, thinkers in Eastern Zhou China and in the Ganges Valley at

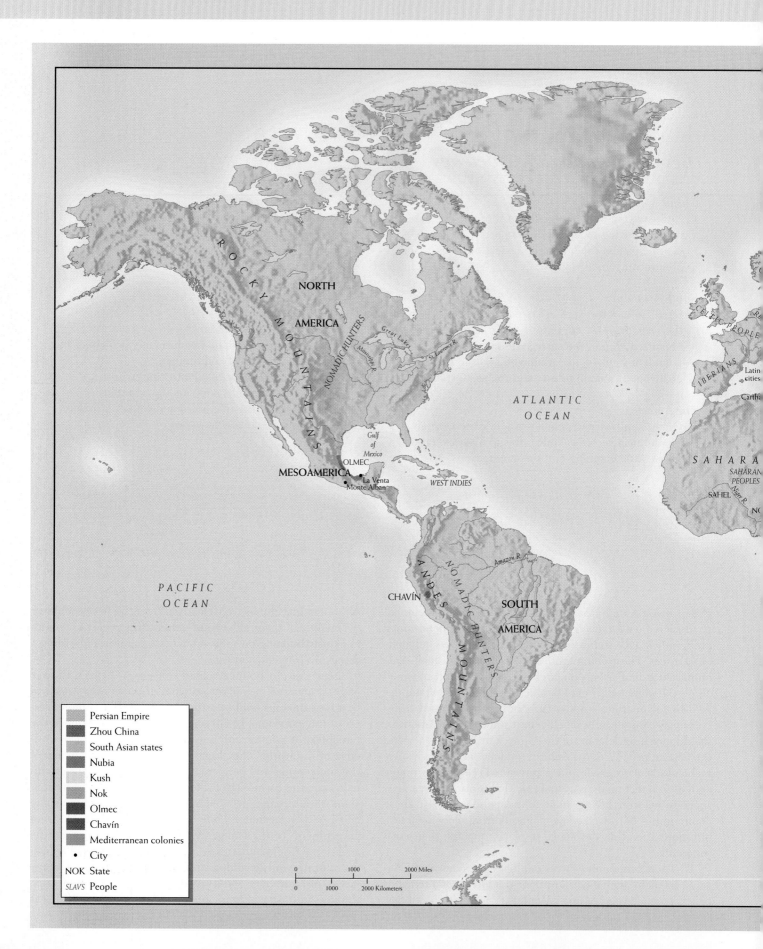

NORTH

AMERICA

ROCKY MOUNTAINS

NOMADIC HUNTERS

Great Lakes

Mississippi R.

St. Lawrence R.

ATLANTIC
OCEAN

*Gulf
of
Mexico*

OLMEC

MESOAMERICA

La Venta
Monte Alban

WEST INDIES

CELTIC PEOPLE

IBERIANS

Latin
cities

Carth

S A H A R A

*SAHARAN
PEOPLES*

SAHEL

Niger R.

PACIFIC
OCEAN

CHAVÍN

ANDES MOUNTAINS

NOMADIC HUNTERS

Amazon R.

SOUTH

AMERICA

	Persian Empire
	Zhou China
	South Asian states
	Nubia
	Kush
	Nok
	Olmec
	Chavín
	Mediterranean colonies
•	City
NOK	State
SLAVS	People

0   1000   2000 Miles

0   1000   2000 Kilometers

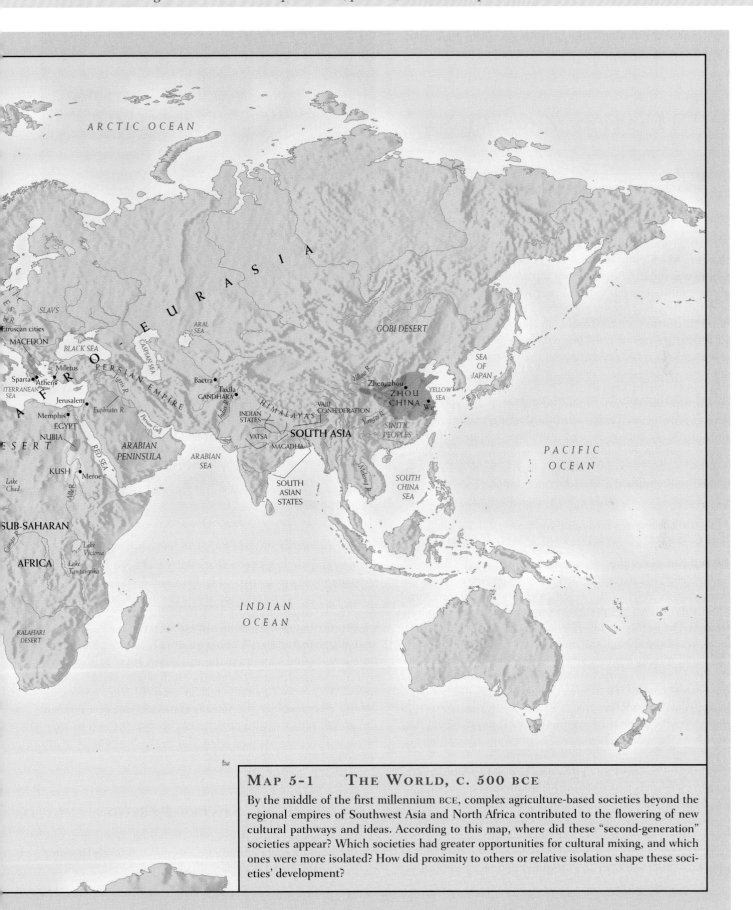

MAP 5-1   THE WORLD, C. 500 BCE

By the middle of the first millennium BCE, complex agriculture-based societies beyond the regional empires of Southwest Asia and North Africa contributed to the flowering of new cultural pathways and ideas. According to this map, where did these "second-generation" societies appear? Which societies had greater opportunities for cultural mixing, and which ones were more isolated? How did proximity to others or relative isolation shape these societies' development?

the time of the Buddha sought ultimate truths that would yield a unitary vision of state and society.

 EASTERN ZHOU CHINA

→ *In what ways did scholars propose ending the warfare and chaos of China's Spring and Autumn and Warring States periods?*

Altogether critical for the appearance of new ideas, radical thinkers like Confucius, and the notion of starting anew in China was the utter destruction of the old political order. In short, political degeneration preceded widespread political and intellectual innovation. Thus, to understand the circumstances that led to Confucian thought and China's cultural flourishing, one must begin with the political arena. The starting point is the emergence of the Eastern Zhou dynasty, centered on Luoyang, a period in Chinese history known as the Spring and Autumn period (722–481 BCE), which in turn ended with the Warring States period (403–221 BCE) when seven major regional states consolidated their power into territorial states. The result was a multistate system that fostered revolutionary developments in agriculture, government, politics, and society and during which scholar-officials assumed great political and social importance.

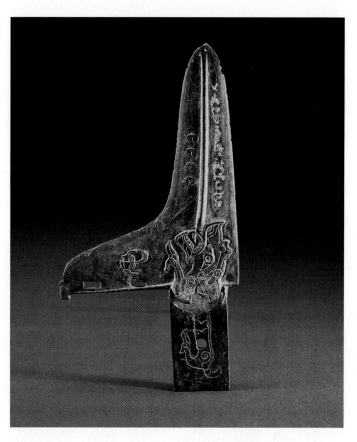

Bronze Spearhead. Although bronze weaponry gave way to stronger iron swords and armor during the Warring States era, stylized bronze spearheads were still prized by Zhou kings and regional lords.

THE SPRING AND AUTUMN PERIOD

From the outset of the Spring and Autumn period, China witnessed levels of anarchic violence previously unseen for centuries. Regional states possessed more power than the central Zhou ruler; they forged alliances and created new administrative units in the countryside to conscript men and to collect taxes. Even though the major states competed for power and land, they still nominally accepted the Zhou ruler's authority. In effect, China's fractured political system inverted the normal pattern. Here, strong central states did not dominate weaker satellites. Instead, the central states were a buffer zone between the large peripheral states to which they were forced to swear allegiance. They became the battlefields on which larger states fought for dominance.

Growing political anarchy coincided with technological breakthroughs. As new smelting techniques to remove impurities from iron spread across China, bronze weaponry gave way to stronger iron swords and armor. Zhou kings tried hard to monopolize iron production and stockpile weapons, but to no avail. The spread of cheaper and more lethal weaponry shifted influence from the central government to local authorities.

In fact, the regional states became so powerful that they undertook large-scale projects that earlier had been feasible only for empires. While constructing dikes and drainage and irrigation systems, they brought greater areas of land under cultivation. New canals linked rivers, and the networks spurred transformation. For example, in 486 BCE the lord of the Wu state began to build what would eventually become the 1,000-mile-long Grand Canal, linking the Yellow River in the north with the Yangzi River in the south. Stretching several hundred miles, Wu's canal functioned as an artificial Nile, promoting greater integration of the various states' economies. Like all the grand infrastructure projects of this era, it owed its existence to the back-breaking labor of peasants working off their tax obligations to regional lords.

THE WARRING STATES PERIOD

At the beginning of the Warring States period, seven large territorial states dominated the Zhou world, and several smaller states on the Central Plain remained within the major powers'

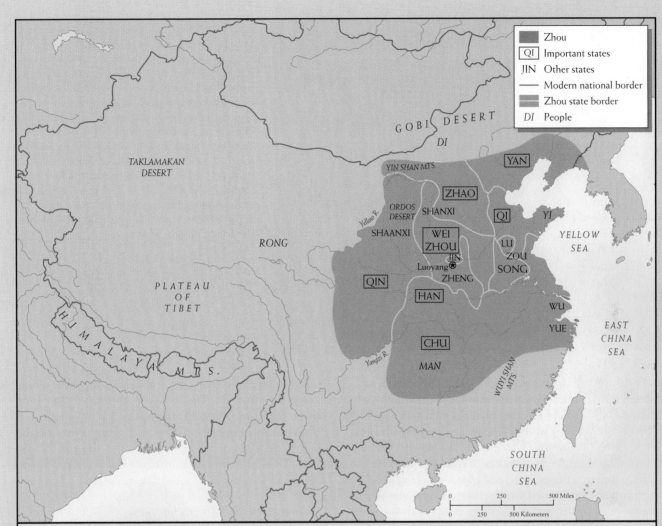

MAP 5-2   ZHOU CHINA IN THE WARRING STATES PERIOD

The Warring States period witnessed a fracturing of the Zhou dynasty into a myriad of states. Find the Zhou capital of Lu-oyang on the map. Where was it located relative to the other key states? What about this map tells us why diplomacy was so important during this period? What does this map tell us about the relationships between "civilized" and "barbarian" peoples in East Asia? How do you think so many smaller polities could survive when they were surrounded first by seven and then by three even larger and more powerful states (Qin, Qi, and Chu)?

sphere of influence. (See Map 5-2.) Their wars and shifting political alliances involved the mobilization of armies and resources on an unprecedented scale (far surpassing the Assyrian armies at the height of their power). Qin, the greatest state, ultimately replaced the Zhou dynasty in 221 BCE. Its armies in particular combined huge infantries in the tens of thousands with lethal cavalries and even more lethal legions of skilled archers using state-of-the-art crossbows. To ensure the Qin war machine could match all threats, the preparation

to defend the Chinese heartland even crossed into the other-world. Some 7,000 artisans and workers prepared thousands of ornate, carefully made terra-cotta warriors and horses, which the Qin buried in precise military formations within the tomb of the first Qin emperor to help him in the expected wars he would face in the next life.

The Warring States alternately engaged in diplomacy or battle, depending on which furthered their interests at the moment. Thus statecraft emerged (similar to that among

Qin Warriors. Terra-cotta warriors were buried with the Qin emperor in the expectation that they would join in his military campaigns in the next life. For such battles the emperor was to have at his disposal over 8,000 soldiers, 130 chariots with 520 horses, and 150 cavalry horses to accompany his soul as he passed from this world to the next, intimidating his rivals along the way. These reproduced warriors and horses were quite modest in number, but they symbolically evoked the massive scale of the Qin armies above ground. In the real world, the Qin mobilized millions of peasants in the northwest for their military campaigns and complemented them with hundreds of thousands of horses to produce the most devastating military force yet seen on earth before the famed Roman legions.

major Southwest Asian states in the second millennium BCE; see Chapter 3). Trained diplomats traveled on missions seeking alliances with rulers of other states, and if dismissed by their first employer they would offer their services to another. Always seeking to maintain a balance of power, the Warring States would re-form their coalitions if one state became too powerful. Moreover, impersonal legal codes, which established uniform punishments based on the crime rather than the perpetrator's social status, enhanced these rulers at the expense of the aristocratic elites.

Overall, the conception of central power changed dramatically during this era, as royal appointees replaced hereditary officeholders. By the middle of the fourth century BCE, power was so concentrated in the major states' rulers that each began to call himself "king." Despite the incessant warfare, scholars, soldiers, merchants, peasants, and artisans thrived in the midst of an expanding agrarian economy and interregional trade. At the same time, major innovations occurred in government, warfare, culture, and the economy.

NEW IDEAS AND THE "HUNDRED MASTERS"

Out of this political and social turmoil came bold new ideas that dominated Chinese thinking about man's (and, to a much lesser extent, woman's) place in society and the polity for many centuries. Often it was the losers among the political elites, seeking to replace their former advantages with status gained through new types of service, who sparked this intellectual creativity. Important teachers emerged, each with disciples. The most prominent of the "hundred masters" of the age was **Confucius** (551–479 BCE); others either expanded on Confucian thought or formulated opposing ideas about human nature and the role of government. Their philosophies constitute the Hundred Schools of Thought.

CONFUCIUS Confucius left no writings, but his followers compiled and transmitted his teachings after his death. *The Analects,* Confucius's ethical teachings and cultural ideals, had an extraordinary influence on many leading scholar-officials who came after him. In his effort to persuade society to reclaim the lost ideals of the early Zhou, Confucius proposed a moral framework stressing correct performance of ritual (*li*), responsibility and loyalty to the family (*xiao*), and perfection of moral character to become a "superior man" (*junzi*)—that is, a man defined by benevolence and goodness rather than by the pursuit of profit. Confucius believed that a society of such superior men would not need coercive laws and punishment to achieve order. He taught these concepts to anyone who was highly intelligent and willing to work, whether noble or humble; thus any man could gain the education to become a gentleman of the ruling class. This was a dramatic departure from past centuries, when only nobles were believed capable of ruling. Nonetheless, Confucius's distinctions between gentlemen-rulers and commoners continued to support a social hierarchy—although an individual's position in that hierarchy might rest now on education rather than on birth.

EASTERN ZHOU CHINA | **169**

→ *In what ways did scholars propose ending the warfare and chaos of China's Spring and Autumn and Warring States periods?*

MO DI   One competing school of thought, later called Mohism, derived from the teachings of Mozi, also known as Mo Di (c. 479–438 BCE). This writer and craftsman-builder believed that each man should feel obligated to all other people, not just to his own family and friends. Thus he emphasized practical concerns of good government: promoting social order, ensuring material benefits for its people, and supporting population growth. He opposed wars of conquest, arguing that they wasted life and resources and interfered with productivity and the fair distribution of wealth; but he recognized the need for strong urban defenses to keep out marauders. His utilitarian philosophy appealed mainly to city dwellers.

LAOZI AND ZHUANGZI   Another key philosophy was **Daoism**, which diverged sharply from Confucius and his followers by scorning rigid rituals and social hierarchies. Its ideas originated with a Master Lao (Laozi, "Old Master"), who—if he actually existed—may have been a contemporary of Confucius. His sayings were collected in *The Daodejing,* or *The Book of the Way and Its Power* (c. third century BCE). His book was then elaborated by Master Zhuang (Zhuangzi, c. 369–286 BCE). Daoism stressed the *dao* (the Way) of nature and the cosmos: the best way to live was to follow the natural order of things. Its main principle was *wuwei,* "doing nothing": what mattered was spontaneity, noninterference, and acceptance of the world as it is, rather than attempting to change it through politics and government. In Laozi's vision, the ruler who interfered least in the natural processes of change was the most successful. Zhuangzi focused on the enlightened individual living spontaneously and in harmony with nature, free of society's ethical rules and laws and viewing life and death simply as different stages of existence. (See Primary Source: Warring Ideas: Confucianism versus Daoism—On the Foundations of Government.)

XUNZI AND HAN FEI   Legalism, or Statism, another view of how best to live an orderly life, grew out of the writings of Master Xun (Xunzi, 310–237 BCE) toward the end of the Warring States period. He believed that men and women were innately bad and therefore required moral education and authoritarian control. In the decades before the Qin victory over the Zhou, the Legalist thinker Han Fei (280–233 BCE) agreed that human nature was primarily evil. He imagined a state with a ruler who followed the Daoist principle of *wuwei,* detaching himself from everyday governance—but only after setting an unbending standard (strict laws, accompanied by harsh punishments) for judging his officials and people. For Han Fei, the establishment and uniform application of these laws would keep people's evil nature in check. As we will see in Chapter 7, the Qin state, before it became the dominant state in China, systematically followed the Legalist philosophy.

SCHOLARS AND THE STATE

What emerged from all this activity was a foundational alliance of scholars and the state that was destined to become a vital feature of Chinese society through many centuries. Scholars became state functionaries dependent on the rulers' patronage. In return, rulers recognized the scholars' expertise in matters of punishment, ritual, astronomy, medicine, and divination. Philosophical deliberations, which tended to view the world as static, focused on the need to maintain order and stability by preserving the state. (In contrast, philosophers and priests in Greece and South Asia did not exclusively serve the state or a particular ruler, so they freely speculated on a far broader range of issues. Also, they viewed the world as constantly changing.) The bonds that rulers forged with their scholarly elites distinguished governments in Warring States China from the other Afro-Eurasian polities.

The growing importance of statecraft and philosophical discourse promoted the use of writing. In fact, even though the Chinese script was not standardized until 221 BCE, its use in the philosophical debates raging across states and regions helped foster cultural unity at a time of intellectual pluralism (diversity of thinking). As scholar-diplomats and scribes debated in forceful prose the best methods for creating stable and harmonious societies, some 9,000 to 10,000 graphs or signs became required for writing. The elevated influence that scholar-bureaucrats enjoyed in these debates set China apart from other societies of this period.

Over ensuing centuries, the ideas of Confucianism, Daoism, and Legalism merged into a unified story about the ancient sage-kings' crucial role in empire building. This account invoked the mandate of heaven (see Chapter 4), but scholars embellished the concept with details of how the dynastic cycle of history worked. The Qin imperial victors—Statists who achieved order through raw military power and strict Legalist approaches—drew on the unifying themes in their rivals' political and social discourses even as they scorned Daoists, who they said were naïve for "leaving things alone," and Confucians, who they said were overly concerned with ritual. This new formulation described the evolution of state power as a natural process (borrowing from the Daoists) as small states grew into a unified empire, and thus gave the chaotic Warring States period a virtuous, moral purpose (borrowing from the Confucians) aiming toward unity.

INNOVATIONS IN STATE ADMINISTRATION

Although the most durable new developments in China in this era occurred in the realm of ideas, important innovations also took place in politics and economics. To begin with the political arena, the Spring and Autumn period saw regional rulers enhance their ability to obtain natural resources, to

Primary Source

WARRING IDEAS: CONFUCIANISM VERSUS DAOISM—ON THE FOUNDATIONS OF GOVERNMENT

Though both Confucians and Daoists viewed the world of political power as perilous, their competing teachings offered regional Chinese rulers a choice in political philosophies.

Confucius wanted to end the chaos of the times and restore order by promoting education, moral behavior, and the performance of ritual. He thought that cooperation rather than conflict, ethical behavior rather than reckless actions, merit rather than heredity, and concern with the welfare of others rather than self-aggrandizement should be the basis of society and government. Not as interventionist as the Legalists, the Confucians opposed autocracy and appealed to the mandate of heaven as the "voice of the people." Not as laissez-faire as the Daoists, the Confucians prioritized strict ritual as a philosophy of behavior that would lead to cultural solidarity even in times of political chaos. The Daoists' rejoinder charged that the Confucians were, in effect, shutting the barn door after the horses had already escaped. A natural morality had once been the rule in small villages; a true morality was now the social exception, betrayed in practice by the moral hypocrisy of Confucian officials in the capital.

Initially, Confucius's call for moral rigor had little appeal to those in power. But some saw the attractions of his beliefs after they realized that a tyrannical government that punished its citizens harshly could be brought down by a peasant rebellion. In one exchange with a student, Confucius described the core foundations of government:

> Zigong asked about government. The Master said, "Sufficient food, sufficient military force, the confidence of the people." Zigong said, "If one had, unavoidably, to dispense with one of these, which of them should go first?" The Master said, "Get rid of the military." Zigong said, "If one had, unavoidably, to dispense with one of the remaining two, which should go first?" The Master said, "Dispense with food: Since ancient times there has always been death, but without confidence a people cannot stand." (*Analects* 12.7)

Many individuals who sought power were drawn more to Daoism, whose teachings warned that overly assertive rulers could ruin the state. Thus, the Daodejing (*The Book of the Way and Its Power*), a famous Daoist work attributed to Master Lao (Laozi), argued that political and social intervention was futile and that long-term rule should be based on "doing nothing" (*wuwei*); that is, letting everything take its natural course without premeditated human intervention:

> If one desires to take the empire and act on it,
> I say that he will not succeed.
> The empire is a sacred vessel,
> That cannot be acted upon.
> In being acted upon, it is harmed;
> And in being grasped, it is lost.
> Thus the sage rejects the excessive, the extravagant,
> the extreme.
> (*The Book of the Way and Its Power*, Vol. 1, p. 86)

→ *What elements of Confucius's teaching emphasized moral rigor and, when applied to government, would enable it to win "the confidence of the people"?*

→ *Why did Confucius believe that a cruel tyrant could not remain in power for very long?*

→ *Why did the Legalists find Daoism more appealing than Confucianism as a practical and moral philosophy?*

SOURCE: Excerpts from *Analects* and *The Book of the Way and Its Power* from *Sources of Chinese Tradition*, Volume 1, eds. William Theodore de Bary and Irene Bloom, © 1999 Columbia University Press. Reprinted with the permission of the publisher.

EASTERN ZHOU CHINA | **171**

→ *In what ways did scholars propose ending the warfare and chaos of China's Spring and Autumn and Warring States periods?*

recruit men for their armies, and to oversee conquered areas. This trend continued in the Warring States period, as the major states created administrative districts with stewards, sheriffs, and judges and a system of registering peasant households to facilitate tax collection and army conscription. The officials were drawn from the *shi,* who under the Western Zhou had been knights but were now bureaucrats in direct service to the ruler. Confucius and other classical masters called them "gentlemen" or "superior men" (*junzi*) and considered them partners of the ruler in state affairs. Officials were paid in grain and sometimes received gifts of gold and silver, as well as titles and seals of office, from the ruler.

Of all the ministers who sought to enhance the central government, none was more successful than Shang Yang of Qin. His reforms positioned the Qin domain to become the dominant state of its time. Dividing the state into administrative districts and appointing their magistrates, vice magistrates, military commanders, and overseers, he extended the ruler's authority into the hinterland and used the districts for universal military recruitment. He divided the land into blocks for individual households to farm, and he introduced a head tax, ensuring that households having two or more adult sons would pay more taxes than families with only one. Those who distinguished themselves in war (as determined by the number of enemy killed in battle) earned titles and land; conversely, nobles who failed to distinguish themselves in war were stripped of

Shang Yang of Qin. An important statesman of Qin during the Warring States period, Shang Yang introduced administrative reforms that enhanced the power of the central government.

status and honors. Shang Yang introduced a harsh penal code that stressed collective responsibility (for example, those who harbored criminals had their bodies cut in two). The legal code applied equally to government officials and peasants, with severe punishments for violent crimes, theft, use of nonstandard weights and measures, and wrongdoing in office.

INNOVATIONS IN WARFARE

The most successful states in China ruled over millions of people, and by 221 BCE they boasted million-man armies. (Contrast this with Athens, the most powerful city-state in the Mediterranean: with a population of 250,000, it could field an army of just 20,000 men. Only Rome, later to become a mega-state, could ultimately match China's scale.) With administrative reform came reforms in military recruitment and warfare. As noted above, one purpose of registering the rural population was to guarantee their military service. During the Spring and Autumn period, rulers relied on men from the countryside to expand their armies and to serve as personal bodyguards. During the Warring States period, as such practices persisted, the conscription of peasants guaranteed ever-larger military organizations.

In earlier battles, nobles had let fly their arrows from chariots while conscripted peasants fought beside them on the blood-stained ground. Now the Warring States relied on massed infantries of peasants bearing iron lances who fought fiercely and to the death, unconstrained by their relationships with nobles. War now involved huge state armies containing as many as 1,000,000 commoners in the infantry, supported by 1,000 chariots and 10,000 bow-wielding cavalrymen. During the Spring and Autumn period, one state's entire army would face another state's; now armies could divide into separate forces and wage several battles simultaneously.

Armies also boasted elite professional troops wearing heavy iron armor and helmets, brandishing iron weapons, and wielding the recently invented crossbow. The crossbow's tremendous power, range, and accuracy, with its ingenious trigger mechanism, enabled archers to easily kill lightly armored cavalrymen or charioteers at a distance. The technology of siege warfare also advanced in response to the growing presence of defensive walls along frontiers and around towns. Enemy armies used counterweighted siege ladders (the Chinese called them "cloud ladders") to scale urban walls or dug tunnels under them; defenders often pumped smoke into the tunnels to thwart the attackers. The rhythms of warfare also changed. Rather than lasting through an agricultural season, campaigns now stretched over a year or longer. As commanders strategized over which troops to place where, which terrain was best suited for battle, and how to outmaneuver opposing armies, military action and thought became increasingly sophisticated.

ECONOMIC, SOCIAL, AND CULTURAL CHANGES

Rather than draining the economy, the incessant warfare of both the Spring and Autumn period and the Warring States period spurred China's economic growth to remarkable heights. As an agricultural revolution on the North China plain along the Yellow River led to rapid population growth, the inhabitants of the Eastern Zhou reached approximately 20 million. Demographic changes also affected the environment. As more people required more fuel, deforestation—particularly on the North China plain—led to erosion of the fields. In addition, many animals were hunted to extinction; others, like the elephant, found their open range sharply curtailed. Many inhabitants migrated south to domesticate the marshes, lakes, and rivers of the Yangzi River delta; here they created new arable frontiers out of former wetlands, thus averting the ecological disaster that swept through northern China.

Eventually, such population pressures on arable land set in motion a vicious and tragic economic cycle for Chinese peasants. The shortage of cultivable land eventually pushed agricultural technology, based largely on peasant manual labor, to its limits. The agrarian methods of the time could produce only so much food. With historical hindsight, we know that population growth typically outpaces agricultural productivity—that is, until some kind of technological breakthrough raises productivity. Agricultural growth was the result of ever-attentive peasant farmers tilling the fields of North and South China. From the late Zhou forward, they produced more rice and wheat than anyone else on earth, but they also created families with an unprecedented number of mouths to feed. The long-term economic result was a declining standard of living for the massive numbers of Chinese peasants, unless new land or new "miracle" rice came under cultivation. In the meantime, the search for food propelled farmers into new frontiers at the expense of the wetlands, its flora and its fauna. When this frontier hit its limits—which it did, invariably—Chinese families faced terrible food shortages and famines.

Knife Coin. Zhou dynasty coins, like the later Han coin shown here, were made of bronze and produced in a variety of shapes, some resembling spades and knives, depending on the region. Each of the Warring States had its own currency.

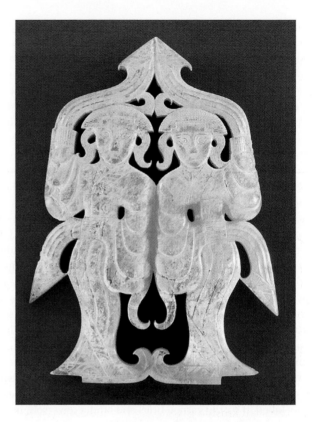

Pendant. Gender relations became more inflexible because of male-centered kinship groups. Relations between the sexes were increasingly ritualized and were marked by heavy moral and legal sanctions against any behavior that appeared to threaten the purity of powerful lineages. This pendant depicts two women who formed a close relationship with each other in the "inner chambers" of their homes.

Nevertheless, in the short term, economic changes began in the Spring and Autumn period when some rulers gave peasants the right to own their land in exchange for taxes and military service. Because the peasants now could enjoy the benefits of their own labor, their productivity increased. Innovations in agricultural technologies also raised productivity, through crop rotation (millet and wheat in the north, rice and millet in the south) and the use of iron plowshares harnessed to oxen to prepare fields.

With larger harvests and advances in bronze and iron casting came trade in surplus grain, pottery, and ritual objects—the beginning of a market economy. Grain and goods traveled along roads, rivers, and canals. Peasants continued to barter, but elites and rulers used minted coins. Early bronze coins had a variety of shapes, some resembling spades. Private traders and merchants also emerged during this time.

During the Warring States period, these changes continued. The new bargain with the peasants (private ownership of land in exchange for taxes and military service) undergirded the economies of all the Warring States, as did a strong emphasis on the military. Infrastructure benefited directly, as roads and walls, forts and towers rose to defend against invading armies. In addition, rulers and administrators applied their keen military organizational skills to public projects, undertaking irrigation projects, building canals and dikes, and draining low-lying lands to open more acreage for agriculture. Military conscripts worked on these municipal projects when they were not needed for fighting.

Economic growth helped the rulers attain a high level of cultural sophistication, as reflected in their magnificent palaces and burial sites. At the same time, social relations became more fluid as commoners gained power and aristocrats lost it. In Qin, for example, peasants who served in the ruler's army were rewarded for killing enemy soldiers; their military success could win them land, houses, slaves, and a change in status. Officials also received lands and gifts that enhanced their status and wealth. Officials, ministers, and diplomats traveled far and wide during this period, but peasants had to keep toiling in their fields and villages, leaving them only to fight in the ruler's army.

While class relations had a revolutionary fluidity, gender relations became more rigid for elites and nonelites alike as male-centered kinship groups grew. The resulting separation of the sexes and male domination within the family affected women's position. An emphasis on monogamy, or at least the primacy of the first wife over additional wives and concubines, also emerged. Relations between the sexes became increasingly ritualized and constrained by moral and legal sanctions against any behavior that appeared to threaten the purity of authoritarian male lineages.

Archaeological evidence reveals that commoners and elites alike tried to restore stability in their lives through religion, medicine, and statecraft. The elites' rites of divination to predict the future and medical recipes to heal the body found parallels in the commoners' use of ghost stories and astrological almanacs to understand the meaning of their lives and the significance of their deaths. Elites recorded their political discourses on wood and bamboo slips, tied together to form scrolls. They also prepared military treatises, arts of persuasion, ritual texts, geographic works, and poetry in this way. Social changes were evident as well, as in commoners purchasing bronze metalwork whereas previously only Zhou rulers and aristocrats could afford to do so.

Even with the endless cycles of warfare and chaos—or perhaps because of them—many foundational beliefs, values, and philosophies for later dynasties sprang forth during the Spring and Autumn and Warring States periods. By the middle of the first millennium BCE, China's political activities and innovations were affecting larger numbers of people, spread over a much broader area, than comparable developments in South Asia and the Mediterranean.

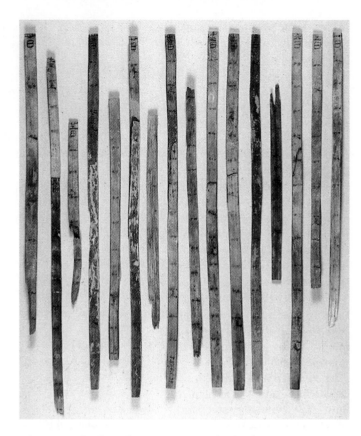

Chinese Calendar. This Han-period calendar for 63 BCE is formed from sixteen slips of wood with handwritten characters; each begins with day one, day two, and so on; the calendar is to be read from right to left.

THE NEW WORLDS OF SOUTH ASIA

→ *How did political and social transformations encourage new beliefs and dissident thinkers in South Asia?*

As in China, violence and warfare in South Asia provided the setting for vibrant cultural and intellectual insight. Following their migration into the Indus River Valley around 1500 BCE, the Vedic peoples fought with the indigenous population and with each other as they established and enlarged new states. Around 1000 BCE, they expanded eastward into the mid-Ganges plain, where they created new polities. At the same time that scholar-officials in Zhou China were theorizing about how to govern and make economic and social innovations, the Vedic peoples were also forging new political institutions, economic activities, and ways of viewing the natural and supernatural worlds. Vedic warriors and upper-class intellectuals drove these transformations.

THE RISE OF NEW POLITIES

Political and social transformations began around 600 BCE, after the Vedic peoples had spread into the mid-Ganges plain. This was a monsoon region where abundant rainfall made the land suitable for cultivating rice (whereas the best Indus Valley crops were wheat and barley). The migrants cleared land by setting fire to the forests and using iron tools—fashioned from ore mined locally—to remove what was left of the jungle.

Between 1000 and 600 BCE, settlements and towns evolved into small territorial states; as in China, it was a time of constant feuding. (See Map 5-3.) It was also a time of new thinking—especially Buddhism and its challenge to the authority of Vedic sacrifices and Brahmanical leadership.

Two major kinds of states appeared in the mid- and lower Ganges plain: those ruled by hereditary monarchs, and those ruled by an elected elite, or oligarchies. (An **oligarchy** is a clique of privileged rulers.) As described in Chapter 4, the South Asian oligarchies were led by warriors and officials called collectively as a class the Kshatriya. Both the rulers of the kingdoms and citizens of the Kshatriya republics assumed the title *raja*, usually translated as "king." But in the oligarchic communities, which were ruled collectively, each adult freeborn male head of a family was called a *raja*. Still, the Kshatriya oligarchy alone controlled the land and other resources. While there were ties between rulers and ruled, it was

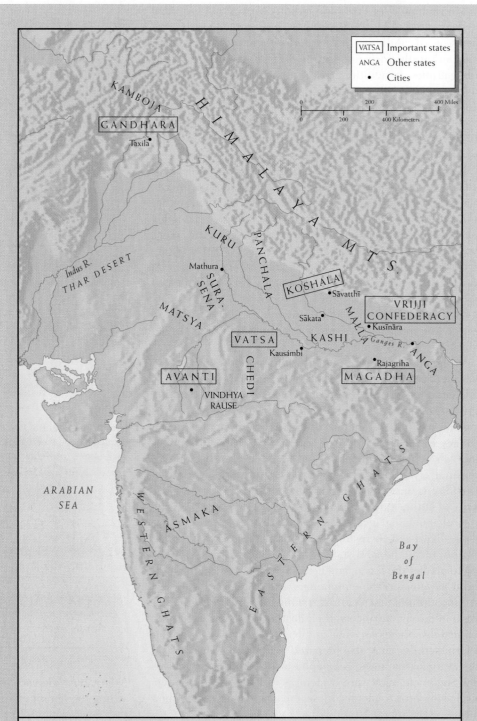

MAP 5-3 SIXTEEN STATES IN THE TIME OF THE BUDDHA IN SOUTH ASIA

South Asia underwent profound transformations in the first millennium BCE that reflected growing urbanization, increased commerce, and the emergence of two types of states: monarchies and oligarchies. Where did the new states and cities appear? What geographic and environmental features encouraged social and cultural integration? According to this map, what other regions had influence on South Asia, and where might South Asian culture spread?

clear that a small minority oversaw the large majority. How did the potentates get their power? There were a number of social ladders: upward through military ranks, marriage upward, and accumulation of land. Rulers often blended all three strategies, carefully sequencing them as they accumulated power. For instance, the *rajas* in kingdoms often came from low-status clans that gained power through military strength. Such *rajas* would elevate their status by marrying women from high-status clans.

EXPANSION OF THE CASTE SYSTEM

Though the kingdoms and oligarchic cities had different political structures, they shared many social features, including the caste system—one of increasing stratification in which each caste rank defined an individual's political power, economic activity, and social status. The traditional vertical scheme of Brahmans first (scholars and priests), followed by Kshatriyas second (warriors), Vaishyas third (commoners), and Shudras fourth (laborers and servants) expanded in an economy centered on farming by extended families. But the largest group to expand was the laboring caste, as agriculture flourished. Many more Shudras, from clans outside the Vedic lineages, joined the agricultural economy as subcastes or laborers of the farming households. (The Shudra laborers planted rice seedlings and harvested crops in the watery paddies.) Cows could not work in rice paddies and therefore were replaced by water buffaloes; some plows required six or eight of the well-muscled animals to pull them. Cultivating rice paddies was highly labor-intensive, since irrigation water had to flow in from distant rivers through elaborate irrigation canals that needed constant maintenance.

As households had to rely on hired workers and slaves, Shudra peasants became a distinct social group. While men in the other castes were "twice-born," having undergone a ritual rebirth around age twelve, this ceremony was denied to the Shudras, who remained outsiders—so they invented their own social hierarchy based on kinship and religious rituals. Even when they joined the Vedic landowners' farming economy as laborers, tenants, or cultivators, they maintained their communal structure by marrying inside their group. Called *jatis*, which signified being born into the group, they became the lower orders of an expanding caste system. The four-caste system, buttressed by Brahmanical ideals, seemed right and natural; its great success was measured by its ability to bring newcomers into existing ranks. In this fashion, the caste system combined hierarchical order with absorptive strength, making the South Asian social order stable yet dynamic.

Further expansion of the caste system occurred as the booming agricultural economy generated even more labor specialization. Carpenters and ironsmiths, traders and artisans, all fell within subcastes defined not only by profession but even by product. For example, a carpenter *jatis* was more prestigious than a tradesman such as a blacksmith, and all farmers viewed all leather tanners as literally untouchable. Social hierarchies layered cities as well as countryside. In the emerging urban centers, traders were "purer" than artisans, while those making gold utensils had higher status than those making copper or iron ones. Yet, members of each group colluded to contain internal competition, and they closed ranks to preserve their status. Even these subcastes monopolized skills and resources by banning intermarriage, thereby preventing other groups from accessing their knowledge. The increasingly elaborate caste system in part reflected the growing complexity of rural and urban worlds, and the resultant specialization of social roles. The guardians of this system contrived practices to make it harder and harder to move between ranks, even as the number of members swelled within them.

Brahman Recluse. When Buddhists started to tell stories in sculptures and paintings, Brahmans were included when appropriate. This character in Gandharan Buddhist art probably represents a Brahman who lived as a recluse, instead of as a priest. He is not shaved or dressed, but his expression is passionate.

NEW CITIES AND AN EXPANDING ECONOMY

Supported by rice agriculture, cities began to emerge on the Ganges plain around 500 BCE. These cities became centers of commercial exchange. Some, such as Shravasti and Rajagriha, also thrived as artisanal centers. Others in the northwest, like Taxila (on the border between present-day Pakistan and Afghanistan), engaged in trade with Afghanistan and the Iranian plateau.

LIFE IN THE NEW CITIES Cities in northern India grew as their commercial activities flourished, but they followed scant planning. Alleys leading from the main streets zigzagged between houses built with pebbles and clay. Although development was haphazard, civic authorities showed great interest in sanitation. The many squares dotting each city had garbage bins, and dirty water drained away in deep sink wells underground. Streets were graded so that rainfall would wash them clean. Because most cities of this period have been continuously inhabited, they are difficult sites for archaeologists to explore. Taxila, destroyed in the fifth century CE, is an exception: excavated in the twentieth century, it sheds light on urban life in early South Asia. Taxila did not have the well-planned streets and water drainage of a center like Mohenjo Daro, a rather opulent Indus city (see Chapter 2); Taxila's building materials were simpler. But civic consciousness produced a hygienic and healthy urban environment. City officials arranged to have garbage taken out of town and dirty water routed to sink wells. There is, moreover, archaeological evidence of deep ruts on the roads, from wagon wheels that plied the winding lanes and streets—revealing that bull and horse carts moved in and out of the city's open squares, which probably served as marketplaces.

The new cities offered exciting opportunities for those who were adventurous. Rural householders who moved into them prospered by importing rice and sugarcane from villages to sell in the markets; they then transported manufactured goods such as sugar, salt, and utensils back to their villages. Those who already possessed capital became bankers who financed trade and industry. The less affluent turned to craftwork, fashioning textiles, tools such as needles, fine pottery, copper plates, ivory decorations, and gold and silver utensils. Other professions included physicians, launderers, barbers, cooks, tailors, and entertainers. The elaborate division of labor suggests high degrees of specialization and commercialization in the urban hubs.

Traders and artisans formed guilds (associations of people with similar interests) to regulate competition, prices, and wages; to support destitute members and their families; and to set standards. To protect their monopolies, guilds required their members to marry within their organizations. As the guild leaders gained financial influence over the new urban communities, even kings heeded their advice on issues as important as war and peace.

Coins came into use in these cities at about the same time as they appeared in Greece and China. Traders and bankers established municipal bodies that issued the coins and vouched for their worth. Made of silver, the coins had irregular shapes but specific weights, which determined their value; they also were punch-marked, or stamped with symbols of authority on one side.

Taxila. (*Left*) Taxila became the capital of Gandhara, a kingdom located in what is today northern Pakistan and eastern Pakistan, at the time that it was occupied by the Persian Empire in the fifth century BCE. Dharmarajika was one of the most important monasteries. The walkway around the stupa, a mound-like structure containing Buddhist relics, was covered with glass tiles, and the stupa itself was decorated with jewels. (*Right*) This corner of a stupa exhibits a variety of the architectural styles that prevailed in Gandharan art at its height. Both square and round columns are covered by Corinthian capitals. The right arch gate shows the style of Sanchi, the famous stupa in central India.

UNEQUAL OPPORTUNITIES The new cities were melting pots of considerable social mobility—despite the rigid caste system. The story of the famous physician Jivika illustrates this combination of considerable mobility with persistent hierarchy. Jivika lived during the time of the Buddha, in the mid-sixth century BCE. His mother was a courtesan in the important city of Rajagriha in the lower Ganges Valley, beautiful and highly accomplished in dancing, singing, and playing the lute; her fame spread far and wide, attracting business to the city. When she discovered she was pregnant, she hid until the baby was born. Then, under cover of darkness, she had her maid carry the infant in a basket to a trash dump. The next morning, the baby's crying attracted the attention first of a crowd and then of a prince named Abhaya, who sent a servant to find out the reason for the disturbance. When he learned that the newborn boy was alive, he adopted the child as his own and named him Jivika, meaning "alive." Prince Abhaya raised the boy like a son, but after learning of his low birth Jivika decided to earn his own livelihood. From his hometown of Rajagriha, Jivika set out for Taxila. He traveled more than 800 miles along the Ganges River—a journey well worth the effort, for Taxila was an important center of learning. There, Jivika received the best training available in medicine, and after he returned to Rajagriha his knowledge and skill soon earned him a brilliant reputation throughout northern India.

The opportunities that the new cities provided for social mobility did not ensure success for everyone. Many who lost their land and livelihood entered cities in search of work, and some fared better than others. As a whole, people had more material wealth, but their lives were far more uncertain. In addition, urban life created a new social class: those who did the dirtiest jobs, such as removing garbage and sewage, and were therefore viewed as physically and ritually impure "untouchables." They were thought to be so polluting that a daughter of a decent householder was expected to wash her eyes after seeing one. Even though their work kept the cities clean, they were forced to live in shantytowns outside the city limits.

Some untouchables were dissatisfied with their fate. At a time when thinkers were questioning all types of authority, some of the outcastes joined dissident sects. As the turbulence in the new cities affected even the most abject of their inhabitants, they became receptive audiences for those challenging the Vedic rituals and Brahman priests.

BRAHMANS, THEIR CHALLENGERS, AND NEW BELIEFS

Wise men looked at the urban life around them and the increasing levels of social violence and decried what they saw. For Brahman priests, mingling was a problem: castes mixing indiscriminately, they felt, polluted society. Moreover, low-born persons grasped at higher status by acquiring wealth or skill. Even worse, as people learned to write they threatened the priests' inherited monopoly of oral traditions. When an alphabetic script appeared around 600 BCE, it undermined the Brahmans' ability to control the definition of right and wrong and thus weakened the moral legitimacy of the order they dominated. Formerly all of Vedic literature had been memorized, and only the brightest Brahmans could master the tradition. The newer, simpler writing made sacred knowledge more accessible. To the Brahmans, nothing about the cities seemed good.

Frightened by these conditions, Brahmans sought to strengthen their relationships with the *rajas* by establishing the idea of a king endowed with divine power. Kingship had been unnecessary according to Brahmanic scripts in a long-ago golden age; a moral code and priests to uphold it were enough to keep things in order. Over time, though, the world deteriorated and the pure mixed with the impure, until many inhabitants spoke of "fish eating fish" to refer to the practice of individuals killing each other for wealth. According to Brahmanic writings, the gods then decided that people on earth needed a king to maintain order. The gods selected Manu ("Man"), but Manu did not want to accept the difficult job. To win his consent, the gods promised him one-tenth of the grain harvest, one-fiftieth of the cattle, one-quarter of the merits earned by the good behavior of his subjects, and the most beautiful woman in his domain. In this Brahmanic account, royal power has a divine origin: the gods chose the king and protected him. Moreover, priests and Vedic rituals were essential to royal power, since kingly authority was validated through religious ceremonies carried out by Brahman priests. Another Brahmanic account conveys this point, relating a story in which the priests themselves magically create a king, whose "birth" wins divine celebration and approval. (See Primary Source: Warring Ideas: The Buddha versus the Brahmans—On the Origin of the King.)

This emphasis on divine kingship solved some problems but created new ones. The Brahmans' claim to moral authority caused resentment among the Kshatriyas—especially those in the oligarchic republics, whose leaders did not assert divine power. Merchants and artisans, as members of growing subcastes, also chafed at the Brahmans' claims to superiority. Such resentments provoked challenges to the Brahmans' domination. Some thinkers in South Asia (like those in China and in the Greek cities experiencing similar upheavals around this time) believed that they were in an age of acute crisis because their culture's ancient harmony had been lost. And like many scholars and philosophers elsewhere in this era, a new group of South Asian scholars and religious leaders developed their own answers to questions about human existence.

DISSIDENT THINKERS Dissident South Asian thinkers challenged the Brahmans' worldview by refusing to recognize the gods that populated the Vedic world. Some of these rebels sprang from inside the Vedic tradition; though Brahmans, they rejected the idea that sacrificial rituals pleased the gods. To them, God was a universal concept, not a superhuman

WARRING IDEAS: THE BUDDHA VERSUS THE BRAHMANS—ON THE ORIGIN OF THE KING

The Election of a King

This passage is from one of the earliest Buddhist texts, Dialogues of the Buddha. Here the Buddha explains to one of his disciples, Vāseṭṭha, how the state and king came into being. Early human beings were pure, but they became greedy and chaotic. As a result they elected one person as king to maintain order. They rewarded the chosen one, called the Great Elect, with a share of their rice. (Note that in this account the people themselves choose the king. Unlike the Brahmanic account that follows, there is no mention of priests or gods.)

When they had ceased rice appeared, ripening in open spaces, without powder, without husk, pure, fragrant and clean grained. Where we plucked and took away for the evening meal every evening, there next morning it had grown ripe again. Where we plucked and took away for the morning meal, there in the evening it had grown ripe again. There was no break visible. Enjoying this rice, feeding on it, nourished by it, we have so continued a long long while. But from evil and immoral customs becoming manifest among us, powder has enveloped the clean grain, husk too has enveloped the clean grain, and where we have reaped is no re-growth; a break has come, and the rice-stubble stands in clumps. Come now, let us divide off the rice fields and set boundaries thereto! And so they divided off the rice and set up boundaries round it.

Now some being, Vāseṭṭha, of greedy disposition, watching over his own plot, stole another plot and made use of it. They took him and holding him fast, said: Truly, good being, thou hast wrought evil in that, while watching thine own plot, thou hast stolen another plot and made use of it. See, good being, that thou do not such a thing again! Ay, sirs, he replied. And a second time he did so. And yet a third. And again they took him and admonished him. Some smote him with the hand, some with clods, some with sticks. With such a beginning, Vāseṭṭha, did stealing appear, and censure and lying and punishment became known.

Now those beings, Vāseṭṭha, gathered themselves together, and bewailed these things, saying: From our evil deeds, sirs, becoming manifest, inasmuch as stealing, censure, lying, punishment have become known, what if we were to select a certain being, who should be wrathful when indignation is right, who should censure that which should rightly be censured and should banish him who deserves to be banished? But we will give him in return a proportion of the rice.

Then, Vāseṭṭha, those beings went to the being among them who was the handsomest, the best favoured, the most attractive, the most capable and said to him: Come now, good being, be indignant at that whereat one should rightly be indignant, censure that which should rightly be censured, banish him who deserves to be banished. And we will contribute to thee a proportion of our rice.

And he consented, and did so, and they gave him a proportion of their rice.

---

creature. Also, they felt that the many cows that priests slaughtered for ritual sacrifices could serve more practical uses, such as plowing the land and producing milk. Their discussions and teachings about the universe and life were later collected in the Upanishads (see Chapter 4).

Other dissidents came from outside the Vedic tradition. Consider the Buddha and Mahavira (discussed below), who both came from the middle Ganges region where a pastoral economy and rituals of cattle sacrifice were nonexistent. Here people had never spoken Brahmanical Sanskrit and never had a Brahman caste in their communities. But they, too, challenged the Brahmans, though some adopted and developed ideas expressed in the Upanishads.

MAHAVIRA AND JAINISM Jainism and Buddhism were the two most influential schools outside the Vedic tradition

A King Selected by Brahmans and Endorsed by Gods

Several stories about the beginning of monarchy are preserved in Brahmanic Hindu literature. The story of Prithu tells of the mutual dependence of the king and Brahman priests, who selected the king and guaranteed the gods' endorsement of him. Initially a king named Vena refused to worship gods, so the Brahmans killed him. Then they created a new king, Prithu, who followed all the rituals.

Afterwards (after the Brahmans killed the vicious king Vena who refused to worship gods) the Munis (Brahmans) beheld a great dust arise, and they said to the people who were nigh, "What is this?" and the people answered and said, "Now that the kingdom is without a king, the dishonest men have begun to seize the property of their neighbors. The great dust that you behold, excellent Munis, is raised by troops of clustering robbers, hastening to fall upon their prey." The sages, hearing this, consulted, and together rubbed the thigh of the king, who had left no offspring, to produce a son. From the thigh, thus rubbed came forth a being of the complexion of a charred stake, with flattened features, and of dwarfish stature. "What am I to do?" cried he eagerly to the Munis. "Sit down" (Nishida), said they; and thence his name was Nishada. His descendants, the inhabitants of the Vindhya mountain, are still called Nishadas, and are characterized by the exterior tokens of depravity. By this means the wickedness of Vena was expelled; those Nishadas being born of his sins, and carrying them away. The Brahmans then proceeded to rub the right arm of the king, from which friction was engendered the illustrious son of Vena, named Prithu, resplendent in person, as if the blazing deity of Fire had been manifested.

There then fell from the sky the primitive bow (of Mahadeva) named Ajagava, and celestial arrows, and panoply from heaven. At the birth of Prithu all living creatures rejoiced; and Vena, delivered by his being born from the hell named Put, ascended to the realms above. The seas and rivers, bringing jewels from their depths, and water to perform the ablutions of his installation, appeared. The great parent of all, Brahma, with the gods and the descendants of Angiras (the fires), and with all things animate or inanimate, assembled and performed the ceremony of consecrating the son of Vena. Beholding in his right hand the (mark of the) discus of Vishnu, Brahma recognized a portion of that divinity in Prithu, and was much pleased; for the mark of Vishnu's discus is visible in the hand of one who is born to be universal emperor (chakravarti). One whose power is invincible even by the gods.

→ *After the Vedic peoples migrated into the mid-Ganges plain, rice cultivation and feuding characterized their society. How does the Buddha's story about the election of the first king reflect this social history?*

→ *How does the Brahmans' story underscore the role of the priests in upholding the monarchy? Why do you suppose the Brahman priests were so concerned that the king worship gods and follow traditional rituals?*

SOURCE: *Dialogues of the Buddha, Part iii*, vol. 4 of *Sacred Books of the Buddhists*, translated by T. W. Rhys David and C. A. F. Rhys David (London: Oxford University Press, 1921), pp. 87–88; *Vishnu Purana*, translated from Sanskrit by H. H. Wilson, 1st ed. 1840, 3rd ed. Calcutta: Punthi Pustak, 1961, pp. 83–84.

that set themselves against the Brahmans. In the sixth century BCE, Vardhamana Mahavira (c. 540–468 BCE) popularized the doctrines of **Jainism**, which had emerged in the seventh century BCE. Born a Kshatriya in an oligarchic republic, Mahavira left home at age thirty to seek the truth about life; he spent twelve years as an **ascetic** (one who rejects material possessions and physical pleasures) wandering throughout the Ganges Valley before reaching enlightenment. He taught that the universe obeys its own everlasting rules and cannot be affected by any god or other supernatural being. He also believed that the purpose of life is to purify one's soul through asceticism and to attain a state of permanent bliss. The Jains' religious doctrines emphasized asceticism over knowledge: strict self-denial enabled one to avoid harming other creatures and thereby purify the soul. Moreover, the doctrine of *ahimsa* ("no hurt") held that every living creature has a soul. Killing even an ant would lead one to an unfavorable rebirth and further away from permanent bliss. Therefore, believers had to watch every step to avoid inadvertently becoming a murderer.

Since land could not be cultivated without killing insects, the extreme nonviolence of Jainism excluded the peasants. Instead, it became a religion of traders and other city dwellers. Mahavira's followers originally transmitted his teachings orally; but a thousand years after his death they wrote them down. The strictly nonviolent doctrine, though originally intended only for followers of Jainism, has profoundly affected the inhabitants of South Asia down to modern times.

BUDDHA AND BUDDHISM The most direct challenge to traditional Brahmanic thinking came from Siddhartha Gautama (c. 563–483 BCE), usually called the **Buddha,** or the Enlightened One. He was a contemporary of Mahavira as well as of Confucius. The Buddha not only objected to

The Buddha's Footprints. Before his followers came to regard Buddha as a god, they were reluctant to make an idol of him—the footprints were an early representation of Buddha. They were carved in a limestone panel in a first-century BCE stupa in India.

Brahmanic rituals and sacrifices but also denied their elaborate **cosmology** (a branch of metaphysics devoted to understanding the order of the universe) and the preference for kingship that kept the priestly class in power. His teachings provided the peoples of South Asia and elsewhere with alternatives to established traditions. In this respect, Buddhism in South Asia functioned much like Confucianism in China. (See Global Connections & Disconnections: Prophets and the Founding Texts: Comparing Confucius and the Buddha.)

The Buddha came from a small Kshatriya, or warrior, community in the foothills of the Himalayas; in this oligarchic republic, his father was one of the *rajas*. Dismayed at the misery and political carnage of his age, Siddhartha left home at age twenty-nine in search of truth and enlightenment. Traveling through the Ganges region, he lived as a beggar and then as a hermit, and finally, according to legend, meditated for forty-nine days until he understood how to eliminate suffering from the world.

His wanderings and ascetic life led him to create a new credo, which his teachings expressed as the Four Truths: (1) life, from birth to death, is full of suffering; (2) all sufferings are caused by desires; (3) the only way to rise above suffering is to renounce desire; and (4) only through adherence to the Noble Eightfold Path can individuals rid themselves of desires and the illusion of separate identity and thus reach a state of contentment, or *nirvana*. The elements of the Eightfold Path represent wisdom (right views and right intentions), ethical behavior (right conduct, right speech, and right livelihood), and mental discipline (right effort, right thought, and right meditation). Because these principles were simple and clear, the Four Truths had a powerful appeal. This teaching also represented a dramatic shift in thinking about humanity and correct behavior. Like the teachings of Mahavira, the Buddha's doctrines left no space for the supernaturals to dictate human lives, a theme stressed in classical Brahmanic thinking. Buddha's logical explanation of human suffering and his guidelines for renouncing desire appealed to many people, for it set forth tenets by which its followers strove to live virtuously. Those who accumulated enough merits could be reborn in heaven. In contrast, wasting merits by indulging in desires could mean failing to reach heaven, or even sliding to hell.

Buddhism's appeal becomes more understandable in the context of reincarnation of the soul, a concept initiated in the Upanishads and widely accepted by the people of South Asia. If life itself is suffering, and if death leads simply to rebirth into another life, then the cycle of time brings endless suffering. Attaining nirvana, a state reached only after accumulating many merits, was the sole means of achieving liberation from life's troubles.

Like other dissident thinkers of this period, the Buddha delivered his message in a vernacular dialect of Sanskrit that all could understand. His many followers soon formed a community of monks called a *sangha* ("gathering"). The

PROPHETS AND THE FOUNDING TEXTS:
COMPARING CONFUCIUS AND THE BUDDHA

Throughout history, universalizing religions have been defined not just by their sacred texts but also by central figures whose lives inspired movements and long-lasting traditions. In Confucianism and Buddhism, we find key leaders who inspired the faiths that were subsequently named for them.

Confucius (551–479 BCE) was one of the ancient world's great innovators. Born in China, he elaborated a code of behavior that valued individual performance of traditional rituals and governmental morality based on correct social relationships, sincerity, and justice. Seeing division and war among rival states, he wished to restore order by promoting education, moral behavior, and the performance of ritual.

Over the centuries the method and substance of his teaching, with many revisions, became the mainstream value system of imperial China. His idea of modeling the state on the patriarchal family—that is, the ruler should respect the heaven as if it were his father and protect his subjects as if they were his children—became the foundation of Chinese political theory. One could summarize his philosophy of teaching in three statements: "I teach whoever wants to learn with no regard to his birth," "The best educated men should serve the government," and "Those who work with their minds should rule, and those who work with their hands should be ruled." Confucius wanted people to perform the rituals bequeathed by the early Zhou and to emulate the sages who had ordered the world according to principles of civility and culture.

Chinese philosophers did not always agree on how to interpret Confucius's ideas. Representing one school of Confucianists, Mencius (372–289 BCE) held that while recognizing the tendency of people to be led astray by worldly appetites and ambitions, Confucius believed in the inherent goodness of human nature. To recover that innate goodness required moral training. But according to Xunzi (310–237 BCE), Confucius saw humans as evil and lacking an innate moral sense. They therefore had to be controlled by education, ritual, and custom.

Nevertheless, both Mencius and Xunzi embraced Confucius's dictum that people were perfectible through education and the practice of proper conduct. All Confucians, whether pessimists or optimists, viewed moral cultivation through education as the heart of the civilizing process, and they ensured that his ideas remained a vital force throughout Chinese history.

The teachings of the **Buddha** (c. 563–483 BCE), like those of Confucius, had far-reaching influence. The two thinkers were roughly contemporary, and both formulated their ideas in response to social chaos and degeneration. The Buddha presented a vision of society that challenged the Brahmanic order. Buddhism shaped the views of life and death and the scheme of time and space of the universe in South Asia. It also had a profound impact on peoples outside the region and even replaced Confucianism as the dominant religion in China for a few hundred years.

The Buddha offered a logical approach in the form of a unified system underlying the universe, instead of invoking divine intervention, to understand the universe and social life at a time of rapid political development. He believed that the universe and individual lives go through eternal cycles of birth, death, and rebirth, and he elaborated the concept of *karma* ("fate" or "action"), a universal principle of cause and effect. The birth of every living being, human or animal, reflects actions taken in his or her past lives. Karma embodies the sins and merits of each individual, establishing his or her status in the current life. In turn, deeds in the current life affect that karma and thus determine suffering and happiness in the next life. Buddhist believers therefore focused on the consequences of their actions: through their own behavior, they could attain better future lives.

Confucianism and Buddhism, much like the Vedic, Brahmin, and Judaic faiths discussed in Chapter 4, emerged in times of great turmoil. All the faiths were first transmitted orally; later, adherents created a written record to spread them more widely. But Buddhism and Confucianism stand out in that they have founders whose identification with their belief systems remains their most defining characteristic: the Buddha as an enlightened one, and Confucius as a sage teacher. We will see this phenomenon again with the rise of Christianity (from the teachings of Jesus) and Islam (from the teachings of Muhammad) as we continue our discussion of universalizing religions.

Buddha and his followers wandered from one city to another on the Ganges plain, where they found large audiences as well as the alms needed to sustain the expanding *sangha*. In fact, the Buddha's most influential patrons were urban merchants. And in struggles between oligarchs and kings, the Buddha sided with the oligarchs—reflecting his upbringing in an oligarchic republic. He inevitably aroused opposition from the Brahmans, who favored monarchical government. While the Buddha himself did not seek to erase the caste hierarchy, the *sangha* provided an escape from its oppressive aspects and the prestige that it afforded the Brahmans. Although Mahavira and the Buddha did not erase the Brahmans' spiritual authority or dismantle the caste hierarchy, nevertheless they established independent enclaves that carried out religious, scholarly, and social activities based on their own doctrines.

COMMON CULTURES IN THE AMERICAS

> → *How did cultural integration occur in the Andes and Mesoamerica in the absence of political unity?*

Although peoples living in the Americas during what we have termed the axial age in Eurasia and North Africa did not have immense cities, elaborate written texts, domesticated animals, and the other ingredients that underlay the radical new ideas of this era elsewhere, political and intellectual leaders among the Chavín peoples of the Andes and the Olmecs of Mesoamerica provided answers to many of the same questions that were perplexing Eurasians and North Africans Their insights also left a profound imprint on their communities and on future generations. Of course, because we do not have the impressive documentary record that exists for Eurasian and North African written texts, our knowledge of their beliefs has to be based primarily on archaeological remains. These, however, provide clues to the cultural systems that these communities embraced.

THE CHAVÍN IN THE ANDES

In a world of extreme localization and diversity, the steep mountainsides and deep fertile valleys of the Andes Mountains became the home of a distinctive people called the Chavín. In what is now northern Peru, farmers and pastoralists began to share a common belief system around 1400 BCE.

With time, their artistic influence and spiritual principles touched a broad expanse of Andean folk. Like the peoples of South Asia, the Chavín were united by culture and faith more than by any political structure.

The Chavín peoples literally organized their societies vertically. Communities and households spread their trading systems up the mountainsides: valley floors yielded tropical and subtropical produce; the mountains supported maize and other crops; and in the highlands, potatoes became a staple and llamas produced wool and dung (as fertilizer and fuel) and, eventually, served as beasts of burden. Llamas could not transport humans, however, so the Chavín migratory and political reach remained limited. No empire would emerge in the Andes for another millennium.

The ecological diversity of the Chavín societies enabled them to find all necessities close at hand, but they did undertake some long-distance trade—mainly in dyes and precious stones, such as obsidian. By 900 BCE, the Chavín were erecting elaborate stone carvings, using advanced techniques to weave fine cotton textiles, and making gold, silver, and copper metal goods. Scholars have found evidence that by 400 BCE trade in painted textiles, ceramics, and gold objects spanned the Pacific coast, the Andean highlands, and the watershed eastward to the tropical rainforests of the Amazon basin. However, these networks were not extensive and only conveyed light precious goods.

What unified the fragmented Chavín communities was a shared artistic tradition reflecting devotion to powerful deities. Their spiritual capital was the central temple complex of Chavín de Huántar, in modern Peru's northeastern highlands. The temple boasted a U-shaped platform whose opening to the east surrounded a sunken, circular plaza; from its passageways and underground galleries, priests could make dramatic entrances during ceremonies. The priests took hallucinogenic drugs, which believers felt enabled them to become jaguars—the region's most dangerous predator—and to commune with the supernatural. Pilgrims brought tribute to Chavín de Huántar, where they worshipped and feasted together.

The Chavín drew on influences from as far away as the Amazon and the Pacific coast as they created devotional cults that revered wild animals as representatives of spiritual forces. Carved stone jaguars, serpents, and hawks, baring their large fangs and claws to remind believers of nature's powers, dominated the spiritual landscape. The "Smiling God" at Chavín de Huántar, El Lanzón, shaped from a slab of white granite fifteen feet high, had a human form but a fanged, catlike face, hair of writhing snakes, feet ending with talons, and hands bristling with claws. This supernatural image dominated an awe-inspiring stage: dimly lit from above so that his face would glow from the reflection of polished mirrors, the god stood over a canal, and the vibrations and deep rumbling sounds of the rushing water below conveyed a sense of spiritual forces. Though they borrowed from

El Lanzón. The Chavín excelled at elaborate stone carvings with complex images of their deities. This image of El Lanzón is a good example. At the center of one of the Chavín peoples' greatest temples is this massive gallery with a giant monument in the middle, etched with images of snakes, felines, and humans combined into one hybrid supernatural form. Observe the hands and feet with claws and the eyebrows that turn into serpents. The rendering on the right makes it easier to see the details on the actual object.

neighbors and refined existing sculptural techniques, the Chavín created the first great art style of the Andes. Their cult gave way around 400 BCE to local cultural heirs, but some elements of it survived in successor religions adopted by stronger states to the south.

THE OLMECS IN MESOAMERICA

Further to the north, in Mesoamerica, the first complex society emerged around 1500 BCE between the highland plateaus of central Mexico and the Gulf Coast around modern-day Veracruz. (See Map 5-4.) The Olmecs are an example of a first-generation community that created new political and economic institutions while contemplating profound questions about the nature of humanity and the world beyond.

Mesoamerican cultures sprang up from local village roots. The region's peoples formed a loose confederation of villages scattered from the coast to the highlands, mainly nestling in river valleys and along the shores of swampy lakes. Their residents traded with one another, shared a common language, and worshipped the same gods. These were the **Olmecs**, a name meaning "inhabitants in the land of rubber"—one of their staples. Around 1500 BCE, the residents of hundreds of hamlets began to develop a single culture and to spread their beliefs, artistic achievements, and social structure far beyond their heartland.

At the core of Olmec culture were its decentralized villages, which housed hundreds—possibly thousands—of households apiece. In these settlements productive subsistence farmers cultivated most of the foodstuffs their communities needed (especially maize, beans, squash, and cacao), while shipping lightweight products including ceramics and precious goods (such as jade, obsidian, or quetzal feathers, used to create masks and ritual figurines) to other villages. Most of the precious objects were for religious purposes rather than everyday consumption.

CITIES AS SACRED CENTERS Despite their dispersed social landscape, the Olmec peoples created shared belief systems, a single language, and a priestly class who ensured that villagers followed highly ritualized practices. Their primary cities, including San Lorenzo, La Venta, and Tres Zapotes, were not large compared to the urban centers of Afro-Eurasia, but they were religious and secular hubs. They were built around specialized buildings that featured massive earthen mounds, platforms, palaces, and capacious plazas.

The rulers of San Lorenzo, for instance, constructed a city of terraces and ridges on a plateau high above the Chiquito River. Their vassals used baskets to haul more than 2.3 million cubic feet of soil to lay out the enormous central platform, two football fields in length, upon which palaces and workshops rose. All around the courtyards and paths were massive stone monuments—colossal heads, jaguar sculptures, and

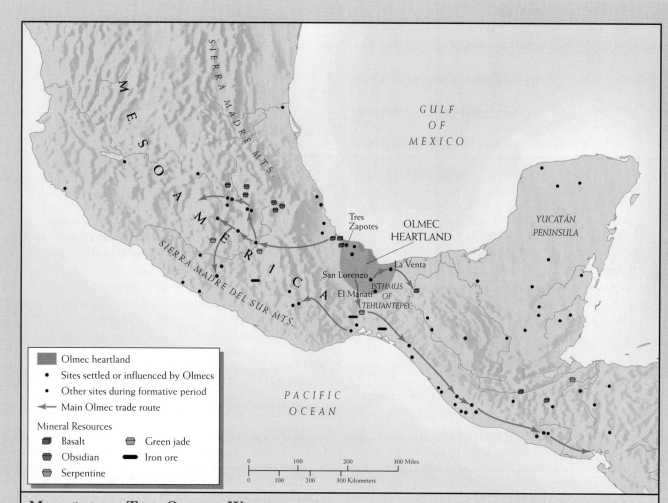

MAP 5-4 THE OLMEC WORLD

The Olmecs had a strong impact on Mesoamerica's early cultural integration. According to this map, how did they influence people living beyond the Olmec heartland? What factors limited the extent of Olmec influence? Why do you think the Olmecs never developed a politically unified regional empire?

basalt thrones—as well as clusters of large wooden busts. These vast sculpture gardens depicted the human rulers and deities to whom the Olmecs paid homage and offered sacrifice. Artificial lagoons and channels crisscrossed the precinct. Beneath these mounds archaeologists have found axes, knives of sharpened obsidian, other tools, and simple yet breathtaking figurines made most often of jade, buried as tokens for those who dwelled in the supernatural world. San Lorenzo was not a capital city with rulers and laws that controlled territorial domains. Rather, it was a devotional center whose monumental architecture and art had widespread influence reaching as far as the Olmec hinterlands.

Paying homage to their gods and rulers was part of the Olmecs' daily life. While devotional activity occurred on lakeshores, in caves, on mountaintops, and in other natural settings, it occurred above all in the primary cities. In La Venta, huge pits (one was 13 feet deep and 75 feet wide) contained massive offerings of hundreds of tons of serpentine carved blocks. Olmec art speaks to the powerful influence of devotion on creativity. (See Primary Source: Olmec Art as Ideology.) Many images featured representations of natural and supernatural entities—not just snakes, jaguars, and crocodiles, but also certain humans called **shamans**, whose powers supposedly enabled them to commune with the supernatural and to transform themselves wholly or partly into beasts (also evident in images at Chavín sites). A common figurine is the "were-jaguar," a being that was part man, part animal. Shamans representing jaguars invoked the

OLMEC ART AS IDEOLOGY

Olmec ideology emphasized ties among the natural, supernatural, and human worlds. It also sought to influence and possibly convert the Olmecs' neighbors. Known primarily for their monumental architecture and artwork, Olmec craftsworkers also made portable objects and miniature figures that unified their belief systems and could be transported over long distances to expand the spiritual frontier of Olmec belief throughout Mesoamerica.

One of the most famous surviving portable spiritual icons, called "Young Lord," combines many of the basic elements of Olmec belief into a single, beautiful jade figurine. Standing about two feet tall, Young Lord was a diplomatic artifact, intended to spread the influence of a complex belief system far and wide. His pose is rigid and tall, like that of a ruler who serves as the turning point to join earthly and supernatural worlds. Holding two scepters against his chest, and himself carved in the form of a scepter, he conveys power and influence. (A scepter is a staff or baton signifying authority.)

Young Lord is fierce. The delicate incisions around his body represent ceremonial practices—rituals that he oversees and that enable him to exercise shamanic powers over believers. His face, for instance, wears a mask that evokes classic Olmec shamanic images: a snarling mouth like a jaguar's, and a nose like an eagle's beak. The mask and its

carvings suggest that this lord is capable of transforming into a jaguar or a bird of prey to conduct sacrificial rites. Extensive incisions all over his body reinforce this point.

The incisions or scars emphasize bloodletting and human sacrifice, and they underscore the importance of the scepters, which can be used to draw blood. These sacrifices were intended to please the forces of the supernatural world, which would reward believers with rain. In fact, images of ritual performers and victims cover Young Lord's arms and hands. Adorning his legs are figures of serpentlike creatures, monsters with gaping jaws, fangs, and forked tongues.

The statue as a whole is divided horizontally into three, signifying the three layers of the cosmos—the supernatural, the terrestrial, and the underworld—which Young Lord has the power to travel among as he brings messages to believers and nonbelievers alike. This is a powerful image, one meant to drive home the authority of Olmec rulers to their subjects and neighbors.

→ *What wild beings do the carvings on Young Lord represent? What characteristics of each one would have led the Olmecs to use them as symbols?*

→ *What do the symbols reveal about spiritual aspects of Olmec society?*

Olmec Head. At La Venta, in Tabasco State in Mexico, four colossal heads rest on the ground, remnants of a field of monumental figures that once ornamented this Olmec site. Nine feet high and weighing up to twenty tons, the heads are the source of much speculation. Carved from single boulders, they are thought to be portraits of great kings or legendary ballplayers. Each head bears distinctive elements in homage to its subject.

Olmec rain god, a jaguarlike being, to bring rainfall and secure the land's fertility. Indeed, the Olmecs' ceremonial life revolved around agricultural and rainfall cycles. Evidence of a shared iconography throughout the heartland suggests an integrated culture that transcended ecological niches.

CITIES AS ATHLETIC HUBS The Olmecs' major cities were not just devotional centers but also athletic hubs, where victorious teams paid homage to their deities. Intricate ball courts had room on the sidelines for fans to applaud and jeer at the sweating contestants, who struggled to bounce hard rubber balls off parallel sidewalls and their bodies and into a goal. Noble players, bearing helmets and heavy padding, could touch the six-pound rubber ball only with their elbows, hips, knees, and buttocks, and they were honored when they knocked the ball through the stationary stone hoop. Massive sculptures of helmeted heads carved out of volcanic basalt suggest monuments to famous ballplayers. At La Venta, a huge mosaic made out of greenstone served as an elegant ball court;

at its center was a portal that was thought to open into the otherworld. Olmec archaeological sites are filled with the remains of game equipment and trophies, some of which were entombed with dead rulers so they could play ball with the gods in the otherworld. Ritual ball games, for all their entertainment value, were integral to Olmec devotional culture. It was in honor of the powerful rain god that players struggled to win.

What added to the thrill of the ball court was that they were dangerous places associated with water and agricultural fertility, for an equally important aspect of devotional culture was human sacrifice. Indeed, it is likely that athletics and sacrifice were blended in the same rituals. Many monuments depict a victorious and costumed ballplayer (sporting a jaguar headdress or a feathered serpent helmet) atop a defeated, bound human, though scholars are not sure whether the losers were literally executed. Rainmaking rites also included human sacrifice, which involved executing and dismembering captives. At El Manatí, offering sites alongside a spring and a boggy lakeshore have yielded the bones of children slaughtered for the gods. Across the Olmecs' artistic landscape are representations of human victims fed to the gods and to the rulers who embodied them.

MAN, NATURE, AND TIME The Olmec cosmology assumed a relationship between the natural and supernatural worlds, with the latter dictating the motions of the former. Olmec culture was saturated with belief in the power of supernatural forces and with tales of shamans controlling the supernatural. But the Olmecs were hardly a simple, superstitious folk; in fact, their conviction that the supernatural pervaded the natural world drove them to systematically observe the natural world so that they could discover godly meanings. There was no hard-and-fast line between what we now call "faith" and "science." The way that rulers reckoned time reflects this belief system, for they were convinced that the gods defined calendric passages—thus the seasons and crucial rainfall patterns. Priests, charting celestial movements, devised a complex calendar that marked the passage of seasons and generations. As in China and Mesopotamia, a cultural flowering encouraged priests and scholars to study and accurately chart the rhythms of the terrestrial and celestial worlds.

A WORLD OF SOCIAL DISTINCTIONS Daily labor kept Olmecs busy. The vast majority worked the fertile lands as part of household units, with children and parents toiling in the fields with wooden tools, fishing in streams with nets, and hunting turtles and other small animals. Most Olmecs had to juggle the needs of their immediate families, their village neighbors, and the taxes imposed by rulers.

Unlike many decentralized agrarian cultures that were simple and egalitarian, the Olmecs developed an elaborate cultural system marked by many tiers of social rankings. The priestly class, raised and trained in the palaces at La Venta, San Lorenzo, and Tres Zapotes, directed the exchanges of sacred ritual objects among farming communities. Because these exchanges involved immense resources, the wealthy ruling families had to be involved—an association that buttressed their claim to be the descendants of divine ancestors. At the same time, by controlling trade in precious secular goods they added to their fortunes. As ruling families blurred the line between the everyday and the religious, they legitimized their power and gained access to vast resources.

Alongside the priestly elite, a secular one emerged composed of chieftains who supervised agrarian transactions, oversaw artisans, and accepted villagers' tribute. They set up workshops, managed by foremen, where craftsworkers created pots, painted, sculpted, and wove. Some of their work featured stones and gems imported from surrounding villages. The highest-ranking chieftains commanded villages scattered over the approximate area of a territorial state (such as current-day Veracruz in Mexico).

The combination of an integrated culture and a complex social structure gave the Olmecs a degree of cohesion unprecedented in the Americas. Ultimately their influence radiated well beyond their heartland through trade. As the Olmecs' arts expanded, so did their demand for imported obsidian and jade, seashells, plumes, and other precious goods. The Olmecs themselves exported rubber (made by combining different latexes from trees and vines into a tough but pliable material—just right for a playing ball!), cacao, pottery, ceramics, figurines, jaguar pelts, and crocodile skins all throughout Mesoamerica. Importing and exporting were probably in the hands of a merchant class, about which scholars know little. The Olmecs also conveyed their belief system to neighbors—if not to convert them, at least to influence them and reinforce a sense of superiority. Without an urge to conquer or colonize, the Olmecs nonetheless shaped the social development of much of Mesoamerica.

THE LOSS OF CENTERS The breakdown of the Olmec culture is shrouded in mystery. The decline was abrupt in some centers and drawn out in others. At La Venta, the altars and massive basalt heads were defaced and buried, indicating a dramatic shift. Yet there is little evidence of a spasm of war, a peasant uprising, a population shift, or conflict within the ruling classes. Indeed, in many parts of the heartland, the religious centers that had been the hubs of the Olmec world were abandoned but not destroyed. Much of the Olmec hinterland remained heavily populated and highly productive.

Apparently the machinery for drawing resources into Olmec capitals eventually failed. As the bonds between rulers and subjects weakened, so did the exchange of ritual objects that had enlivened the Olmec centers and made them magnets for obedience and piety. Olmec hierarchies then collapsed. Without a sacred elite to transmit the belief system, it too faded. What was left of the Olmec heritage passed on to other Mesoamericans—especially those of the central plateaus and the tropical lowlands of the Yucatán peninsula.

The Las Limas Monument. The were-jaguar was an important figure in the pantheon of Olmec deities. This sculpture represents a youth holding a limp were-jaguar baby. We do not know what these figures represented exactly—most likely they refer to spiritual journeys. Some have argued that this monument harkens to child sacrifice.

COMMON CULTURES IN SUB-SAHARAN AFRICA

> → *How did the spread of iron smelting shape the social landscape of sub-Saharan Africa?*

In Africa, too, widespread common cultures emerged in this era in a number of favorable locations. Yet to understand these communities it is essential first of all to describe the climate and geography of Africa because these forces played a critical role in cultural formation. Climatically, Africa's most significant historical development at this time was the continued desiccation of the northern and central landmass, and the sprawl of the great Sahara Desert as its primary geographical and population barrier. (See Map 5-5.) Large areas that had once supported abundant plant and animal life, including human settlements, now became sparsely populated. As a result, the African peoples began to coalesce in a few locations. Most important was the Nile Valley, which may have held more than half of the entire population at this time.

THE FOUR ZONES

Climatic change divided Africa from the equator northward to the Sahara Desert into four zones. The first zone was the Sahara itself, which never completely emptied out despite its extreme heat and aridity. Its oases supported pastoral peoples, like the ancestors of the modern Tuareg tribal communities, who raised livestock and promoted contacts between the northern and western parts of the landmass. South of the Sahara was the Sahel, literally the "coast" (Arabic *sahil*) of the great ocean of sand. In time, some of Africa's great commercial cities, like Timbuktu, would arise here; but in the first millennium BCE no city of great size made an appearance.

The next zone was the Sudanic savanna, an area of high grasslands stretching from present-day Senegal along the Atlantic Ocean in the west to the Nile River and the Red Sea in the east. Many of West Africa's kingdoms emerged there because the area was free of the tsetse fly, which was as lethal to animals as to humans, killing off cattle, horses, and goats. The fourth zone comprised the western and central African rain forests, a sparsely populated region characterized by small-scale societies.

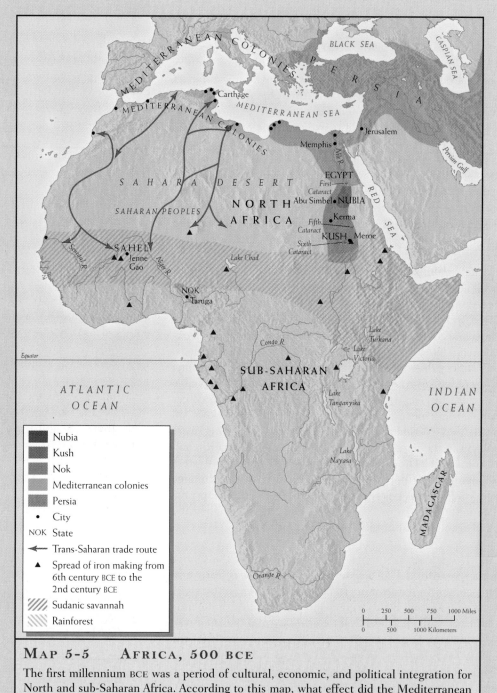

MAP 5-5   AFRICA, 500 BCE

The first millennium BCE was a period of cultural, economic, and political integration for North and sub-Saharan Africa. According to this map, what effect did the Mediterranean colonies have on Africa? What main factor integrated Kush, Nubia, and Egypt? Does the map reveal a relationship between the rise of Sudanic culture and the spread of ironworking? If so, what is it?

⟶ *How did the spread of iron smelting shape the social landscape of sub-Saharan Africa?*

Although there was contact across the Sahara, Africa below the Sahara differed markedly from North Africa and Eurasia. It did not develop a plow agriculture; instead, its farmers depended on hoes. Also, except in densely populated regions, land was held communally and never carried as much value as labor. African peoples could always move into new locations. They had more difficulty finding workers to turn the soil.

Distinctive and widespread common cultures that would characterize certain parts of sub-Saharan Africa from 1000 CE onward were only beginning to emerge during the first millennium BCE. In the savanna, millet and sorghum were the primary food crops; in the rain forests, yams and other root crops predominated. Relatively large populations inhabited the Sudanic savanna, the sole area for which substantial historical records exist. Here, in fact, a way of life that we can call Sudanic began to crystallize.

These peoples were not completely dependent on their feet to get around (as were their counterparts in the Americas). They had domesticated several animals, including cattle and goats, and even possessed small horses. Although their communities were scattered widely across Africa, they had much in common. For example, they all possessed a cosmology dominated by a high god, polities led by sacred kings, and burial customs of interring servants alongside dead rulers to serve them in the afterlife. These peoples were skilled cultivators and weavers of cotton, which they had domesticated. Archaeologists and historians used to believe that the Sudanic peoples borrowed their institutions, notably their sacred kingships, from their Egyptian neighbors; but linguistic evidence and their burial customs indicate that the Sudanic communities developed these practices independently.

NUBIA: BETWEEN SUDANIC AFRICA AND PHARAONIC EGYPT

One of the most highly developed locations of common culture in sub-Saharan Africa was Nubia, a region lying between the first Nile cataract (a large waterfall) and the last (near where the Blue and White Niles come together). From at least the fourth millennium BCE onward, peoples in this region had contact with both the northern and southern parts of the African landmass. It was one of the few parts of sub-Saharan Africa known to the outside world. The Greek poet Homer described its inhabitants as "the remotest nation, the most just of men; the favorites of the gods."

The first of the important Nubian states was Kush. It flourished between 1700 and 1500 BCE between the first and third cataracts and had its capital at Kerma. Because of its close proximity to Egypt it adopted many Egyptian cultural and political practices, even though it was under constant pressure from the northern powerhouse. Its successor states had to move farther south, up the Nile, to keep free from the powerful Egyptians; the kingdom's capitals were repeatedly uprooted and relocated upriver.

Nubia's historical connection to Egypt was obvious: it was Egypt's corridor to sub-Saharan Africa; a source of ivory, gold, and slaves; and an area that Egyptian monarchs wanted to dominate. The Egyptians called the region Kush, the name that later historians gave to the various regimes that flourished there. To the Egyptians, Kush was a land and the Kushites a people to be exploited. It was not a location that the Egyptians wished to reside in. Their chroniclers best described the Egyptian view of the territory and the people, referring to it repeatedly as "miserable Kush." The best known of the Egyptian conquerors was Ramses II, who left his

The Temple of Ramses II. The temple of Ramses II at Abu Simbel was constructed during the reign of Ramses II between 1304 and 1237 BCE. It was cut out of the rock and featured four colossal statues of the king, each of which was twenty meters high. When the Aswan High Dam was built in the 1960s, the monument had to be cut into large stone slabs and moved to higher ground so that it would not be submerged under the waters of Lake Nasser, which the High Dam formed.

imprint on Nubian culture with his magnificent monuments at Abu Simbel. Historians have long stressed such connections with Egypt, but only recently have scholars determined just how deeply the Nubian peoples were influenced by the cultures of sub-Saharan Africa.

Building on the foundations of earlier kings that had ruled Nubia, the Meroe kingdom arose in the fourth century BCE and flourished until 300 CE. Its rulers were influenced by the pharaonic culture, adapting hieroglyphs, erecting pyramids in which to bury their rulers, viewing their kings as divine, and worshipping the Egyptian god Amun. However, Meroe was equally a part of the Sudanic savanna lifeway—as evidenced by the distinctiveness of the language and the determination of its inhabitants to retain political autonomy from Egypt, including, if necessary, moving farther south out of the orbit of Egypt and more into the orbit of Sudanic polities. Although they called their kings pharaohs, the influential leaders of Meroe selected them from among the many members of the royal family, attempting to ensure that their rulers were men of proven talents. In addition, the Nubian states had close commercial contacts with other merchants and commercial hubs in Sudanic Africa.

Meroe soon became a thriving center of production and commerce. Its residents were especially skilled in iron smelting and the manufacture of textiles, and their products circulated widely throughout Africa. The capital city itself covered a square mile; at its center was a royal complex surrounded by a wall 300 yards long and half again as wide. The city featured monumental and highly decorated buildings that were constructed, according to local custom, not of stone but of mud bricks.

WEST AFRICAN KINGDOMS

Meroe was not the only sacred kingship in the Sudanic savanna lands. Similar polities thrived in West Africa, among peoples living in the Senegal River basin and among the Mande peoples living inland around the western branch of the Niger River. They established settlements at such places as Jenne and Gao, which eventually became large trading centers. Here, artisans smelted iron ore and wove textiles, and merchants engaged in long-distance trade.

Even more spectacular was the Nok culture, which arose in the sixth century BCE in an area that is today the geographical center of Nigeria. Though slightly south of the savanna lands of West Africa, it was (and still is) in regular contact with that region. At Taruga, near the present-day village of Nok, early iron smelting occurred in 600 BCE. Taruga may well have been the first place in western Africa where iron ores were smelted. Undeniably ironworking was significant for the Nok peoples, who moved from using

stone materials directly to iron, bypassing bronze and copper. They made iron axes and hoes, iron knives and spears, and luxury items for trade. Ironworking had spread east toward Egypt and Nubia and south to the Congo River by 300 BCE. This region in West Africa was also home to the Bantu-speaking peoples destined to play a major role in the history of the landmass. Around 300 BCE, small Bantu groups began to migrate southward into the equatorial rain forests, where they cleared land for farming; from there, some moved on to southern Africa. (See Chapter 8 for a discussion of the Bantu peoples.)

Nok has achieved its historical fame not for its iron-smelting prowess but for its magnificent terra-cotta figurines, discovered in the 1940s in the tin-mining region of central Nigeria. These naturalistic figures, whose features bear a striking resemblance to those of the region's modern inhabitants, date to at least 500 BCE. They were altarpieces for a cult associated with the land's fertility. Placed next to new lands that were coming into cultivation, they were believed to bless the soil and enhance its productivity. (See Primary Source: Reconstructing the History of Preliterate African Peoples.)

Although most sub-Saharan African communities lived in small-scale dispersed communities, in several locations, notably Nubia and West Africa, larger, common cultures based on shared beliefs and political institutions arose. The ability of these societies to produce more food and sustain larger settled communities ultimately caused the sub-Saharan population to triple in this period. As in the Americas, these lifeways proved durable.

WARRING IDEAS IN THE MEDITERRANEAN WORLD

> → *In what ways did city-states integrate the dispersed settlements of the Mediterranean?*

The widespread migrations that convulsed southern Europe and Southwest Asia around 1200 BCE (see Chapter 4) also brought marauding armed bands into the well-settled regions of the Mediterranean. The combined impact of large population movements and social destruction radically transformed social organizations and cultures throughout the region. Thus, the first millennium BCE in the Mediterranean was a time of political, economic, and social changes, all of which stimulated new thinking and saw the creation of new political and economic institutions (just as in Eastern Zhou China and Vedic South Asia, see Map 5-6).

Primary Source

RECONSTRUCTING THE HISTORY OF PRELITERATE AFRICAN PEOPLES

Traditionally, historians have relied on written records and thus have had difficulty reconstructing the history of pre-literate societies. Sources that now aid in understanding preliterate African groups include art, pottery, linguistic analysis, oral traditions, and many other elements. Here are two such vital historical sources.

The first is Nok terra-cottas. Discovered in the central region of modern-day Nigeria, the figurines probably were created in the Common Era but are part of a vibrant culture that dates back to the fifth century BCE.

The second source, Kush burial pyramids, comes from the sub-Saharan kingdom of Meroe, by no means a pre-literate society but one that has many important non-written sources. Meroe flourished for nearly a millennium from around the fourth century BCE to the fourth century CE. Its predecessor kingdoms, referred to as the kingdoms of Kush, were located between the first and third Nile cataracts. The first kingdom of Kush existed between 1700 and 1500 BCE. A second powerful Kushitic state arose around 1000 BCE, and its most dynamic dynasty even overpowered Egypt, creating Egypt's "black pharaohs" dynasty, Egypt's twenty-fifth dynasty. Later, when Egyptian power was again ascendant, the peoples of Nubia moved even farther south to establish the king-dom of Meroe. Although Meroe continued to be deeply influenced by the culture and political forms of Egypt, its peoples spoke a different language from the Egyptians, a Nilo-Saharan language.

Nubia's close contact with Egypt led to profound and obvious influences—for example, the use of the term *pharaoh* to refer to the king, borrowed religious beliefs, and

the use of hieroglyphs. Like the Egyptians, the Kushitic and Meroitic peoples buried their kings in pyramids and wrote texts on the walls of these burial chambers about what constituted an orderly and good life. The Meroitic peoples had a powerful priestly class, like the ancient Egyptians, but they retreated up the Nile to be independent of Egyptian rule. Scholars with the same archaeological and linguistic training as students of ancient Egypt (known as Egyptologists) have studied the Nubian cultures, but their studies have taken place more recently than those of ancient Egypt and have not yet yielded as much information.

Nok Figurine

→ *How do the Nok terra-cottas help scholars understand the very ancient culture of West Africa?*
→ *Do they provide insight into the artistic abilities of the people living in this region?*
→ *What can they tell us about how people dressed and how they looked?*
→ *Can you see the Egyptian influence in the photograph of the Kush burial pyramids?*

Burial Pyramids at the Royal Necropolis of the Ancient Kingdom of Kush

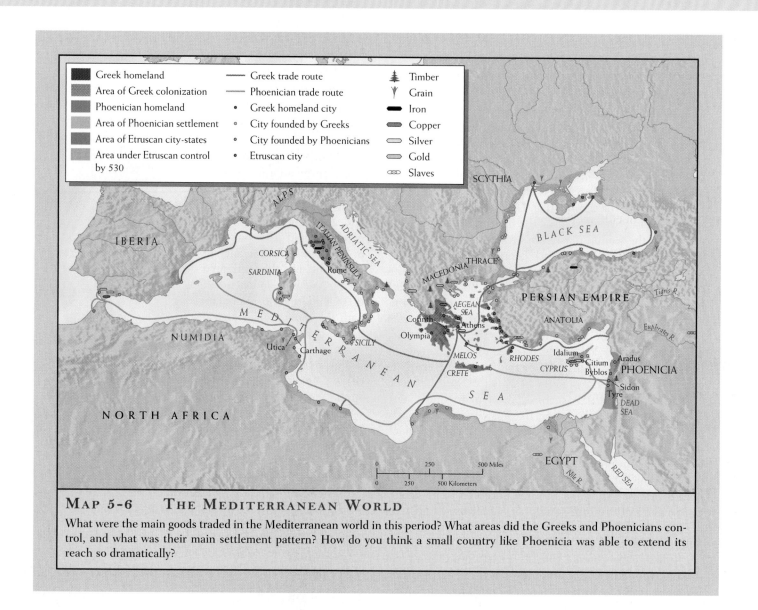

MAP 5-6   THE MEDITERRANEAN WORLD

What were the main goods traded in the Mediterranean world in this period? What areas did the Greeks and Phoenicians control, and what was their main settlement pattern? How do you think a small country like Phoenicia was able to extend its reach so dramatically?

NEW THINKING AND NEW SOCIETIES AT THE MARGINS

The violent upheavals that tore through the borderland areas of the northern Levant, the coastal lands of Anatolia, the islands of the Aegean and Mediterranean seas, and mainland Greece freed these peoples from the domination of Assyria and Persia. More on their own than ever before, these borderland communities could explore new cultural ideas and create new social and political organization. Thus, around 1000 BCE, these peoples, second-generation societies or hybrids that mixed the old and the new, devised new ways of organizing their societies.

Seaborne peoples from around the Mediterranean Sea basin—Phoenicians, Greeks, Cretans, Cypriots, Lydians, Etruscans, and many others—carried not just trade goods but also ideas about the virtues of self-sufficient cities whose inhabitants shared power more widely (even more democratically) than before. Inventions that proved valuable in one place, such as the use of money and the alphabet, spread rapidly; the result was an unprecedented degree of intercommunication among the region's diverse communities.

Increased knowledge and refinements in maritime technology were crucial during this period. In the ninth and eighth centuries BCE, improved design and construction of ships, better deployment of sail and rowing technology, and greater knowledge of winds, currents, and shorelines enabled sailing peoples to transform the seaborne world of the Mediterranean.

A NEW WORLD OF CITY-STATES

New ways of thinking about the world burst forth in the ninth and eighth centuries BCE, as order returned to the eastern Mediterranean and the population rebounded. The peoples who were clustered in more concentrated settlements at this time did not revive the old palace and temple organizations of the Mycenaeans and Minoans (see Chapter 3), however. Instead, they created something quite novel: city-states that, unlike those of earlier Mesopotamia, were governed not by semidivine monarchs but by their citizens. They also unleashed powerful waves of cultural innovation and economic activity.

SELF-GOVERNMENT AND DEMOCRACY The self-governing city-state was a new political form that profoundly influenced the Mediterranean region. First found among the Phoenicians (see Chapter 4) and in their settlements such as Carthage but ultimately associated with the Greeks, these new urban communities had multiplied throughout the Mediterranean by the sixth century BCE. The new urban entity was known by the Phoenicians as a *qart*, the Greeks as a *polis*, and the Romans as a *civitas*. Unlike the great urban centers in the Southwest Asian empires, the new city-states were not organized by an elite class of scribes or run by directives from high priests and monarchs.

The new principles of rulership were revolutionary. Ordinary residents, or "citizens," of these cities—such as Athens, Thebes, Sparta, or Corinth among the Greeks; Caere and Tarquinia among the Etruscans; Rome and Praeneste among the early Latins; Carthage and Gadir (modern-day Cádiz in Spain) among the western Phoenicians—governed themselves and selected their leaders. Their self-government took various forms. One kind was rule by a popularly approved political head of the city, whom the Greeks called a *tyrannis* ("tyrant"). Another was rule by a small number of wealthy and powerful citizens—the *oligoi,* meaning "the few" in Greek (hence "oligarchs" and "oligarchies"). The most inclusive type of government involved all free adult males in a city—in Greek, a *dēmokratia* ("democracy"). The wealthiest landowners often formed the power elite, but farmers, craftworkers, shopkeepers, merchants, soldiers, and traders were the backbone of the citizenry. They ran the city's affairs, set priorities for development, and decided when to go to war.

The new cities of the Mediterranean basin became communities of adult male citizens, other free persons (including women, who could not vote or hold office), foreign immigrants, and large numbers of unfree persons (including slaves and people tied to the land who could not vote or fight for the polis). Those enjoying full citizenship rights—the adult freeborn males—in each community decided what tasks the city-state would undertake and what kind of government and laws it would adopt. Consequently, the cities differed markedly from one another.

FAMILIES AS FOUNDATIONAL UNITS The small family unit, or household, was the most important social unit. In fact, thinkers like Aristotle regarded the state as a natural outgrowth of the household. To Aristotle, the household embodied the fundamental power relationships found in cities, where free men and citizens were lords over their wives and children, and masters of their slaves. The free adult male was fully entitled to engage in the city's public affairs.

In contrast, adult women of free birth remained enclosed within the private world of the family and had no standing to debate policy in public, vote, or hold office. Women who did carry on intelligent conversations with men in public about public matters were criticized. Spartan women were a partial exception to these rules, and their unusual behavior—such as exercising in the nude in public (as did men) or holding property in their own right—evoked humor and hostility from men in the other Greek city-states.

Hetaira. The painting on this vase by the artist Oitos is of a "companion" woman—called by the Greeks an *hetaira*—putting on a sandal. Proper Greek women were protected and kept within their households; they were modest and always fully clothed. Women who were so bold as to be out in public, talking and otherwise associating with men—like the woman portrayed here— were deemed immoral. The artist therefore had no problem portraying this *hetaira* in the nude.

COMPETITION AND ARMED WAR Because there were no centralized governments to control residents' actions and thoughts, the city-states were freewheeling and competitive places, sometimes bloodily so. Their histories relate violent rivalries between individuals, social classes, and other groups. Among the larger Greek city-states, only Sparta avoided most of this internal strife, achieving greater calm by means of rigorous social discipline and military organization that cut off the city from many external influences. The Spartans rejected coined money and chattel slavery (see below), thereby avoiding the "corruption" of cities with more mercantile interests. However successful it was as a military state, Sparta seemed to the other Greeks to be a very unusual polis.

Competition for honor and prestige was a value that shaped behavior in the city-states. This extreme competitive ethic found a benign outlet in organized sporting events. Almost from the moment that Greek city-states emerged, athletic contests sprang up—both on a small scale as an essential part of each city's life and in centralized events in which all Greeks could participate. The greatest competitions were the Olympic Games, which began in 776 BCE at Olympia in southern Greece.

The competitive spirit among communities took the destructive form of armed conflicts over borderlands, trade, valuable resources, religious shrines, and prestige. Wars of one sort or another were characteristic of city-state relations (as they were among states in Eastern Zhou China and Vedic South Asia during the same period). The incessant battles fueled new developments in military equipment, such as the heavy armor that gave its name to the hoplites, or infantrymen, and in tactics, such as the standard block-like configuration (which the Greeks called a *phalanx*) in which the regular rank and file fought. These wars were so destructive that they threatened to destabilize the city-states' world.

The bigger the states and the more resources they had, the more likely they were to engage in warfare, even to the detriment of their own people. The most famous conflict was the Peloponnesian War (431–404 BCE) between Athens and Sparta. It dragged on for decades, eating away the resources of the two great polities and their allies.

The story of the Peloponnesian War as told by the great historian Thucydides became a paradigm (an outstanding example) for the sheer destructiveness of these endless intercity conflicts. To protect itself against Spartan attacks, at the beginning of the war Athens barricaded its citizens within the city's walls. An immediate result was a disease epidemic brought to Athens' harbor by ships coming from Africa. Now known from DNA analysis to be typhoid fever, the epidemic wiped out a large part of the city's population and destroyed the basic humanity of its citizens toward each other. Every state was forced to take sides in the war. Sometimes, as in the case of the island of Corcyra, this led to savage internal wars in which the supporters of each side massacred each other, a terrible situation that led to a complete inversion of normal values—what was once called "cowardly," says Thucydides, was now called "brave." After three decades of this kind of war, Sparta finally "won," but only at the cost of destroying its own traditional social order. In the end, everyone lost.

ECONOMIC INNOVATIONS AND POPULATION MOVEMENT

Economic innovations (the alphabet, coins, and the central marketplace) facilitated trade among the fragmented Mediterranean communities. As a result, the city-states enjoyed accelerated economic growth in the ninth and eighth centuries BCE. Even more spectacular was the speed with

Hoplites. Most battles between Greek city-states took place on land between massed formations of infantrymen, or "hoplites" [*hoplon* meaning shield]. Serving the community in this way defined one's right to citizenship or membership in the city. Since hoplites wore the same armor and contributed equally to the battle line, the nature of hoplite warfare helped to define the democratic ethos of the individual citizen.

which they established colonies wherever they found resources and trade. The city-states' superior military technology, developed and tested in conflicts among themselves, enabled them to defeat local resistance. Moreover, through trade and colonization the Mediterranean peoples acquired as slaves the inhabitants of frontier communities to the north. The slaves' labor further contributed to the city-states' wealth and growth.

FREE MARKETS AND MONEY-BASED ECONOMIES
Without a top-down bureaucratic and administrative structure, residents of the new cities had to devise other ways to run their affairs. They developed open trading markets and a system of money that enabled buyers and sellers to know the precise value of commodities so that exchanges were efficient. The Greek historian Herodotus, who journeyed widely in the mid-fifth century BCE, observed that the new city-states had at their center a marketplace (*agora*), a large open area where individuals bought and sold commodities. He found no such great open public commercial spaces in Egypt or Babylonia.

Soon most transactions required money rather than barter or gift exchange. Coins also bought services, perhaps at first to hire mercenary soldiers. In the absence of large bureaucracies, the Mediterranean cities relied on money to connect the producers and buyers of goods and services. By the end

of the fifth century BCE the Greek city-states were issuing a striking variety of coins, and other peoples such as the Phoenicians, Etruscans, and Persians were also using them. (During the same period, money developed independently and saw common use in Vedic South Asia and Eastern Zhou China.)

TRADE AND COLONIZATION   The search for silver, iron, copper, and tin drove the first traders westward across the Mediterranean. By about 500 BCE the Phoenicians, Greeks, and others from the eastern Mediterranean had planted new city-states around the shores of the western Mediterranean and the Black Sea. Once established, these colonial communities became completely independent, and they transformed the coastal world. City-based life became common from southern Spain and western Italy to the Crimea on the Black Sea.

With amazing speed, seaborne communications spread a Mediterranean-wide urban culture that bolstered the region's wealthy and powerful elites. Found among the local elites of Tartessos in southern Spain, the Gallic chiefs in southern France, and the Etruscan and Roman nobles of central Italy, the new aristocratic culture featured similar public displays of wealth: richly decorated chariots, elaborate armor and weapons, high-class dining ware, elaborate houses, and public burials. From one end of the Mediterranean to the other,

The Agora. The agora, or central open marketplace, was one of the core defining features of Mediterranean city-states. At its center, each city had one of these open-air plazas, the heart of its commercial, religious, social, and political life. When a new city was founded, the agora was one of the first places that the colonists measured out. The large, rectangular, open area in this picture is the agora of the Greek colonial city of Cyrene (in modern-day Libya).

Mediterranean Coins. From the sixth century BCE onward, money in the form of precious metal coins began spreading through the city-states of the Mediterranean, beginning with the Greek city-states in the western parts of what is today Turkey, then spreading to the other Greek *poleis* and beyond. On the left here is the classic tetradrachm (four-drachma piece) coin of Athens with its owl of the goddess Athena; on the right is a silver coin of shekel weight produced by the city of Carthage in the western Mediterranean.

as well as to the Black Sea, the city-state communities developed a culture founded on alphabetic scripts, market-based economies, and private property.

CHATTEL SLAVERY The explosion of buying and selling produced an ethos in which everything that the city dwellers needed, even human beings, took on a monetary value. Treating men, women, and children as objects of commerce, to be bought and sold in markets, created something novel—a new form of slavery called **chattel slavery**. This commercial slavery spread quickly. Where dangerous and exhausting tasks such as mining required extra labor, the freeborn citizens purchased slave laborers. In Athens, the largest and most economically powerful Greek city-state, slaves may have constituted up to a quarter of the population. They were essential to every one of the new city-states, providing manual and technical labor of all kinds and producing the agricultural surpluses that supported the urban population.

The seaborne communication networks enhanced the slave trade. Supply lines furnished human chattels for the next 2,000 years, especially from lands around the Black Sea. This trade in humans was one of the most profitable businesses of the entire Mediterranean region.

ENCOUNTERS WITH FRONTIER COMMUNITIES The forces that transformed the Mediterranean region's mosaic of urban communities and surrounding rural areas also affected those in northern and central Europe. Whether they wished it or not, diverse tribes and ethnic groups, such as the Celts and Germans in western Europe and the Scythians to the north of the Black Sea, who were living in nomadic bands, isolated settlements, and small villages became integrated into the expanding cities' networks of violence, conquest, and trade.

Increasingly drawn to the city-states' manufactured goods—money, wine, ornate clothing, weapons—these tribal peoples became an armed threat to the region's core societies. Seeking to acquire the desired commodities through force rather than trade, frontier peoples convulsed the settled urban societies in wavelike incursions between 2200 and 2000 BCE,

1200 and 1000 BCE, and 400 and 200 BCE. Called "barbarians" (the Greeks' mocking name for foreigners unable to speak their language), the invaders actually were not much different from the Phoenicians or Greeks—who themselves had sought new homes and a better future by migrating. In colonizing the Mediterranean, they too had dispossessed the original inhabitants. The Celts, Gauls, Germans, Scythians, and other northerners came to the Mediterranean first as conquerors. Later, when Mediterranean empires grew more powerful and could keep them at bay, they were imported as slaves. Regarding these outsiders as uncivilized, the Greeks and western Phoenicians seized and colonized their lands—and sold the captives as commodities in their marketplaces.

NEW IDEAS

New ways of thinking about the world emerged from the competitive atmosphere that the Greek city-states fostered. Moreover, since there were very few top-down controls (as in the kingdoms of Southwest Asia), citizens had to devise methods for managing their own affairs. In the absence of monarchical or priestly rule, ideas were free to arise, circulate, and clash. Individuals argued publicly about the nature of the gods, the best state, what is good, and whether to wage war. There was no final authority to give any particular idea a final stamp of approval and force its acceptance.

NATURALISTIC SCIENCE AND REALISTIC ART In this atmosphere, some daring thinkers developed novel ways of perceiving the cosmos and representing the environment. Rather than seeing everything as the handiwork of all-powerful deities, they took a naturalistic view of humans and their place in the universe. Consider their art, which idealized the natural world. Artists increasingly represented humans, objects, and landscapes not in abstract or formal ways but in "natural" ways, as they appeared to the human eye. Even their portrayals of gods became more humanlike. Later, these objective and natural views of humans and nature turned into

→ *In what ways did city-states integrate the dispersed settlements of the Mediterranean?*

ideals, the highest of which was the unadorned human figure: the nude became the centerpiece of Greek art.

The public display of the uncovered human body, in both art and everyday life (notably in men's athletic training and competition), signaled the sharp break between the moral codes of the older, traditional societies of the East and those of the revolutionary cities of the Mediterranean. Vase painters such as Exekias signed their works and became known as individual artists. Sculptors like Praxiteles also became famous. No less assertive were creative writers, such as the poets Archilochus and Sappho, who wrote lyrics exploring their own emotions—a clear manifestation of the new sense of the individual being freed of the restraints of an autocratic state or a controlling religious system.

NEW THINKING AND GREEK PHILOSOPHERS Armed with their own ideas and this borrowed knowledge, thinkers in cities such as Miletus and Ephesus did not accept traditional explanations of how and why the universe worked. Rather than focusing on gods, they looked to nature as constituting some fundamental substance (usually one of the traditional elements: earth, air or breath, fire, or water). Thales (c. 636–546 BCE) believed that water was the primal substance from which all other things were created.

As each thinker competed to outdo his peers in offering persuasive and comprehensive explanations, theories became ever more radical. Men like Xenophanes (c. 570–480 BCE), from the city of Colophon, doubted the very existence of gods as they had been portrayed. He asserted instead that only one general divine aura suffused all creation. He pointed out that each ethnic group in fact produced images of gods that resembled themselves: Ethiopians represented their gods with dark skins and broad noses, while Thracians depicted theirs as blue-eyed redheads. Such variation in beliefs about divine attributes suggested that the gods existed only in the human imagination.

Some thinkers proposed that the real world had a physical, tangible basis. Among them was Democritus (c. 460–370 BCE), who claimed that everything comprised small and ultimately indivisible particles. Democritus called them *atoma* ("uncuttables"), or atoms. Even more radical were thinkers like Pythagoras, who devoted himself to the study of numbers (although the famous Pythagorean Theorem had already been discovered by Babylonian priests and mathematicians). Prefiguring the modern digital revolution, he held that a wide range of physical phenomena, like musical sounds, was in fact based in numbers.

The competition among ideas led to a more aggressive mode of public thinking. The Greeks called it *philosophia* ("love of wisdom"), and the professional thinkers who were good at it *philosophoi* ("philosophers"). Some of the earliest recorded debates addressed the nature of the cosmos, the environment, and the physical elements of human existence. By the fifth century BCE, philosophers were focusing on humans

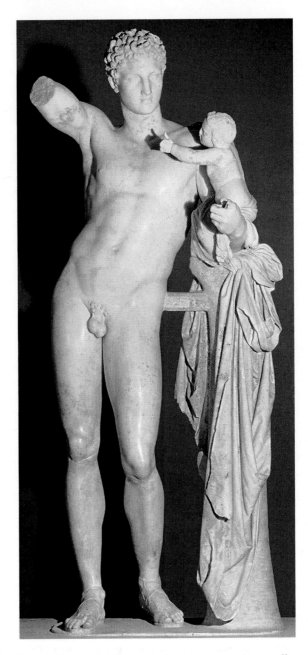

The Human Form. The human body as it appeared naturally, without any adornment, became the ideal set by Greek art. Even gods were portrayed in this same natural nude human form. This statue by Praxiteles is of the god Dionysus and the child Hermes. Such bold nude portraits of humans and gods were sometimes shocking to other peoples.

and their place in society. Finally, some thinkers tried to describe an ideal state, possessing harmonious relationships and being free from corruption and political decline.

Socrates (469–399 BCE), a philosopher in Athens, encouraged people to reflect on ethics and morality. He stressed the importance of honor and integrity as opposed to wealth and power (just as Confucius had done in Eastern Zhou China

WARRING IDEAS: PLATO VERSUS ARISTOTLE—ON GAINING KNOWLEDGE OF THE ESSENCE OF THE WORLD

Great debates raged among Greek thinkers during the fifth and fourth centuries BCE over the essence of the world and how humans can have knowledge of it. Rejecting the existence of creator gods and goddesses, they sought explanations elsewhere. Some looked to the material world (in primary substances like water), while others turned to abstractions.

The Greek philosopher and mathematician Pythagoras suggested that numbers were the basis of everything. Some later thinkers, notably Plato, took this argument further and argued that all existence—and therefore all human knowledge—is based on absolute concepts that are like numbers, existing independent of time and place. Each of them Plato called an idea, a word whose meanings in Greek include "shape," "form," and "appearance." In a number of Plato's dialogues, his teacher, Socrates, tries to explain this theory:

> **Socrates:** I am going to try to explain to you the theory of causes that I myself have thought out. . . . I assume that you admit the existence of absolutes like "beauty" and "good" and "size" and the rest. If you admit that these absolutes exist, then I can hope with their help to show you what causes are. . . . I remain obstinately committed . . . to the explanation that the one thing that causes a thing to be "beautiful," for example, is the existence in it of "the beautiful" or its sharing in "the beautiful"[;] . . . and so, is it not also the case that things that we call "big" are big because they share the idea of "bigness" and similarly that things that we call "small" are small because they share in the idea of "smallness"? [Socrates then dismisses the claim that in calling things "tall" or "small" we are simply describing them in relation to other things.]
>
> **Phaedo:** I believe that Socrates has persuaded us of these matters and that we have agreed that these different ideas do exist; and he has also persuaded us that the reason why specific things in our world are named after these ideas is that they share in the existence of the specific idea. (Phaedo 99d–102b)

Still other thinkers drew on some of the first Greek philosophers of the sixth century BCE to argue that the basis of all existing things was, quite simply, other things. They rejected the proposal that all things we perceive with our senses are poor copies of permanent ideas of them that exist in a separate, unchangeable realm. Human knowledge, they argued, was in fact acquired through careful observation of existing things and through meticulous collection of data about them. Thus in the following passage Aristotle rejects Plato's concept of ideas:

> As for the followers of Plato who claim that "ideas" (or "shapes") are the causes or origins of all things, this too is objectionable. First of all, in their struggle to find causes for things that exist in our world of sense perceptions, they simply introduce as many new things into the equation as they are attempting to explain[;] . . . so their "ideas" are as many . . . as the things whose causes they are seeking to explain and for which reason they were led to invent these ideas. They must do this because they must create an idea to match every substance that exists in our real everyday world . . . and also one in the realm of the eternal heavenly entities. Not one of the arguments by which they try to demonstrate that these ideas actually exist can demonstrate or prove their claim. From some of their arguments, indeed, no real conclusions follow. From other arguments of theirs it only follows that there must be ideas of things for which they themselves hold no such ideas can exist. (*Metaphysics* 1.9, 990a–b)

In other works Aristotle put forth his own views about how to gain reliable knowledge of the world:

> All teaching and learning by means of rational argument is based on our existing knowledge and observations; . . . and I think that we have reliable knowledge of each thing . . . when we think that we have found the cause because of which that thing exists—what is the cause of that thing and of nothing else, with the result that this thing or this fact cannot be other than it is. That this is real knowledge of something is very clear. . . . We know what we do by demonstration, by showing that it is true. By demonstration I mean an argument that produces real knowledge, . . . all of which is based on a knowledge and observation of facts and things. . . . But I also say that not all real knowledge can in fact be demonstrated or proved. (*Posterior Analytics* 1.1–3, 71a–72b)

→ *Can you think of ways in which our modern attitudes toward what we can know and how we know it reflect these two approaches?*

→ *What might have provoked Plato and Aristotle to advance such different concepts of knowledge?*

→ *Might such factors be linked to other major developments of the time, occurring not just in the Greek city-states but elsewhere (in South or East Asia, for example)?*

SOURCE: Plato, *Phaedo*, 99d–102b; Aristotle, *Metaphysics*, 1.9 = 990a–b; *Posterior Analytics*, 1.1–3 = 71a–72b. All translations are by Brent Shaw.

In the next generation, Plato's most famous pupil answered the same question differently. Deeply interested in the natural world, **Aristotle** (384–322 BCE) believed that by collecting all the facts one could about a given thing—no matter how imperfect—and studying them closely, one could achieve a better understanding. His main idea was that the interested inquirer can find out more about the world by collecting as much evidence as possible about a given thing and then making deductions from these data about general patterns. This was in stark contrast to Plato's claim that everything a person observes is in fact only a flawed copy of the "real" thing that exists in a thought-world of abstract patterns accessible only by pure mental meditation—completely the opposite of Aristotle's method. Following his approach, Aristotle collected evidence from more than 150 Greek city-states, and in *The Politics* he proposed institutional responses and codes of moral conduct that would allow urban communities to function better. But neither Plato nor Aristotle was able to preserve the city-state as the exemplary civilized society. During their lives the world of the independent city-state was to change dramatically, as new forms of bigger states emerged and became dominant.

CONCLUSION

Afro-Eurasia's great river-basin areas were still important in the first millennium BCE, but their time as centers of world cultures was passing. Now they yielded some of their leadership to regions that had been on the fringes, giving way to a generation of cultural and intellectual flourishing in search of alternative, new orders. As these borderland areas developed, the increased contacts fostered by city-states (in the Mediterranean world), smaller territorial states (in China), and smaller kingdoms and oligarchies (in Vedic South Asia) created great social dynamism.

During this period influential thinkers came to the fore with perspectives quite different from those of the river-basin civilizations. The Greek philosophers offered new views about nature, their political world, and human relations and values—all based on secular rather than religious ideas. In South Asia, dissident thinkers challenged the Brahmanic spiritual and political order, and the Buddha articulated a religious belief system that was much less hierarchical than its Vedic predecessor. In China, the political instability of the Warring States period propelled scholars such as Confucius to engage in political debate, where they stressed respect for social hierarchy.

Even where contacts with other societies were less intense, innovation occurred. In the Americas, the Olmecs developed a worldview in which mortals had to appease angry gods through human sacrifice and elaborate temples where many peoples could pay homage to the same deities. In sub-Saharan

Socrates

and the Buddha in Vedic South Asia). **Plato** (427–347 BCE), a student of Socrates, presented Socrates' philosophy in a series of dialogues (much as Confucius's students had written down his thoughts). In *The Republic*, Plato envisioned a perfect city that philosopher-kings would rule. He thought that if fallible humans could imitate this model city more closely, their polities would be less susceptible to the decline that was affecting the Greek city-states of his own day. This belief was an outgrowth of his more general theory of "ideas"—eternal and perfect models of abstract concepts and material objects—that are imperfectly copied in the real world. (See Primary Source: Warring Ideas: Plato versus Aristotle—On Gaining Knowledge of the Essence of the World.)

Africa, settled pockets devised complex cultural foundations for community life. The Mediterranean and Egyptian cultures continued to expand their influence up the Nile through Nubia and into sub-Saharan Africa. A spectacular example of sub-Saharan and Egyptian synthesis was the culture of Meroe. And in West Africa, the Nok peoples promoted interregional trade and cultural contact as they expanded their horizons.

As the world was coalescing into culturally distinct regions, all the ideas newly forged in Afro-Eurasia, the Americas, and sub-Saharan Africa would endure. No matter where they were created, they had a continuing impact on societies that followed.

Review and research materials are available at StudySpace: Ⓢ WWNORTON.COM/STUDYSPACE

KEY TERMS

Aristotle (p. 199)
ascetic (p. 179)
Buddha (p. 180)
chattel slavery (p. 196)
Confucius (p. 168)
cosmology (p. 180)
Daoism (p. 169)
Jainism (p. 179)

Legalism (p. 169)
oligarchy (p. 174)
Olmecs (p. 183)
Plato (p. 199)
second-generation
  societies (p. 163)
shamans (p. 184)
Socrates (p. 197)

Chronology

	1500 BCE		1000 BC
THE AMERICAS	◆ *1500–400 BCE Olmec culture emerges and diffuses throughout Mesoamerica*		
	◆ *1400–400 BCE Chavín culture flourishes in Central Andes of South America*		
SUB-SAHARAN AFRICA			
SOUTH ASIA		*1000–600 BCE Sixteen State period* ◆	
		1000–600 BCE Vedic migrations ◆	
THE MEDITERRANEAN			
		1000–900 BCE Migration of Sea Peoples ◆	
EAST ASIA			

STUDY QUESTIONS

1. Explain the "war of ideas" that occurred during the first millennium BCE in China.
   How did Legalism, Confucianism, and Daoism influence political developments during the Warring States period?

2. Analyze the impact of commerce and urbanization on the Vedic belief system in South Asia at this time. Why were urban audiences more receptive to Buddhist and other challenges than to Vedic concepts?

3. Compare and contrast Buddhist and Confucian philosophies. What problems and issues did they address, and what solutions did they propose?

4. Explain the broad cultural features that characterized Olmec and Chavín societies in the Americas in the first millennium BCE. To what extent did each cultural group leave an imprint on its region?

5. Analyze the extent to which diverse sub-Saharan peoples were connected to one another and to the larger world during this period. What processes brought groups together, and what kept them apart?

6. Describe the political and economic innovations in the Mediterranean world in the first millennium BCE. What impact did these ideas have on peoples living on the periphery of that world?

7. Analyze how the use of coins shaped economic systems in Afro-Eurasia. Which regions adopted this practice?

8. Compare and contrast the Greek philosophers Socrates, Plato, and Aristotle with Confucius in China and the Buddha in South Asia. What was similar and what was different in their proposals for creating a better world?

9. Explain how small states created new cultural and social pathways and ideas in Afro-Eurasia in the first millennium BCE. What alternative approaches to philosophy, economics, and religion emerged in East Asia, South Asia, and western Afro-Eurasia?

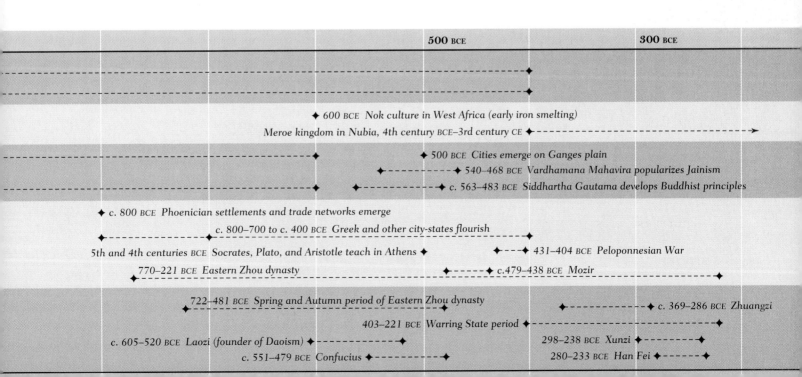

500 BCE   300 BCE

◆ 600 BCE Nok culture in West Africa (early iron smelting)

Meroe kingdom in Nubia, 4th century BCE–3rd century CE ◆- - - - - - - - - - - - - - - - →

◆ 500 BCE Cities emerge on Ganges plain

◆- - - - - - - - ◆ 540–468 BCE Vardhamana Mahavira popularizes Jainism

◆ c. 563–483 BCE Siddhartha Gautama develops Buddhist principles

◆ c. 800 BCE Phoenician settlements and trade networks emerge

c. 800–700 to c. 400 BCE Greek and other city-states flourish

5th and 4th centuries BCE Socrates, Plato, and Aristotle teach in Athens ◆   ◆- - ◆ 431–404 BCE Peloponnesian War

770–221 BCE Eastern Zhou dynasty   ◆- - - - - ◆ c.479–438 BCE Mozir

722–481 BCE Spring and Autumn period of Eastern Zhou dynasty   ◆- - - - - - ◆ c. 369–286 BCE Zhuangzi

403–221 BCE Warring State period ◆- -

c. 605–520 BCE Laozi (founder of Daoism) ◆- - - - - - - - ◆   298–238 BCE Xunzi ◆- - - - - - - - ◆

c. 551–479 BCE Confucius ◆- - - - - - - - ◆   280–233 BCE Han Fei ◆- - - - - - ◆

Shrinking the Afro-Eurasian World, 350 BCE–250 CE

In the blistering August heat of 324 BCE, at a town on the Euphrates River that the Greeks called Opis (not far from modern Baghdad), Alexander the Great's crack Macedonian troops declared that they had had enough. They had been fighting far from their homeland for more than a decade. They had marched eastward from the Mediterranean, forded wide rivers, traversed great deserts, trudged over high mountain passes, and slogged through rain-drenched forests. Along the way they had defeated massive armies, including those armed with fearsome war elephants. Some had taken wives from the cities and tribes they vanquished, so the army had become a giant swarm of ethnically mixed families. This was an army like no other. It did more than just defeat neighbors and rivals—it forcefully connected entire worlds, bringing together diverse peoples and lands.

Conquering in the name of building a new world, however, was not what the soldiers had bargained for. They loved their leader, but many thought he had gone too far. They had lost companions and grown weary of war. Some had mutinied at a tributary of the Indus, halting Alexander's advance into South Asia. Now they threatened to desert him altogether. Summoning up their courage, they voiced these resentments to their supreme commander. Alexander's response was immediate and inspired. In persuading his troops not to desert him, he evoked the astounding military triumphs and historic achievement they had accomplished: establishing his personal rule from Macedonia to the Indus Valley. This far-reaching political vision came to a sudden end with Alexander's death a year later, when he was thirty-two years old. Even in his short lifetime, though, he set in motion cultural and economic forces that would transform Afro-Eurasia.

During this period two broad cultural movements came to link diverse populations across wide expanses of the Afro-Eurasian landmass: Hellenism and Buddhism. They constitute the central subject of this chapter. In both cases new empires and broad trade routes created the circuits through which—and beyond which—new cultures flowed. Imperial conquests and long-distance trade laid the foundations for widespread cultural systems that were far more enduring than the empires themselves. Alexander's armies forged only a fleeting political regime, though an enormous one, extending all the way from the Greek homeland to northern India enabling a Greek-based culture that we call Hellenistic to stretch over the regions of conquests, and beyond. Although this movement did not eradicate local cultures, it provoked profound shifts in them. In the process, many of the world's regions, from China to Africa, became more integrated.

One region where Hellenism had a profound impact was South Asia, where it initiated a process of gradual political integration and religious change. The result: an equally powerful cultural movement, Buddhism, spread outward from its founding in South Asia (see Chapter 5) to become the world's most expansive religious system. It, too, had a political agent: the Mauryan dynasty of South Asia, indirectly influenced by Alexander's triumphs, whose powerful armies and legions of magistrates and monks spread the religion of the Buddha throughout South Asia, laying the groundwork for its expansion beyond. Dynastic empires, therefore, created the political latticework and institutions through which cultural influences grew and extended like vines spreading into regions far from their roots.

POLITICAL EXPANSION AND CULTURAL DIFFUSION

> → *How did political expansion facilitate exchanges among different parts of the Afro-Eurasian world?*

Alexander's bloody campaigns made for legendary drama. But from a long-term perspective, it was their cultural effects that were more dramatic. His armies trampled over their victims, but they also transformed Afro-Eurasia. They promoted the establishment of culturally Greek-oriented communities across Afro-Eurasia. For at least five centuries after Alexander's short-lived rule, Hellenistic culture reverberated from Rome in the west all the way to the Ganges in the east.

Hellenism (a term derived from the Greeks' name for themselves, *Hellēnes*) was a new phenomenon. It involved the process by which the individual cultures of the Greek city-states gave way to a uniform culture stressing the common identity of all who embraced Greek ways. This culture had common features of language, art, architecture, drama, politics, philosophy, and much more, to which anyone anywhere in the Afro-Eurasian world could have access. By diffusing well beyond its homeland, it brought worlds together: its influence spread from Greece to all shores of the Mediterranean, into parts of sub-Saharan Africa, across Southwest Asia, and through the Iranian plateau into central and South Asia. It even had echoes in China.

Alexander not only conquered but also laid the foundations for state systems and introduced institutional stability for (and protection and patronage of) trading systems. Instead of plundering, governments under his rule promoted trade. With their fear of attack reduced, cities could thrive.

Focus Questions

WWNORTON.COM/STUDYSPACE

→ *How did political expansion facilitate exchanges between different parts of the Afro-Eurasian world?*

→ *How did the spread of Hellenism reshape the Mediterranean world?*

→ *How did Hellenistic and pastoral nomadic cultures influence central and South Asia?*

→ *In what ways did the transformation of Buddhism represent cultural integration in South Asia?*

→ *How did long-distance exchanges affect the cultural geography of Afro-Eurasia?*

→ *What factors promoted sea trade on the Indian Ocean?*

MAIN THEMES

→ *Two broad cultural movements, Hellenism and Buddhism, link diverse populations across Afro-Eurasia.*
→ *Conquests by Alexander the Great and the influence of his successor states spread Hellenism across southwest Asia and into South Asia, where it begins the gradual process of cultural and political integration.*
→ *The Mauryan Empire accelerates the integration of South Asia and helps Buddhism spread throughout that region and into central and East Asia via the Silk Road.*

FOCUS ON *Forces That Unify Afro-Eurasia*

The Mediterranean World
✦ The spread of Hellenism around the Mediterranean via Alexander's conquests leads to a common language, cosmopolitan cities, new types of philosophy and religion, plantation slavery, and money-based economies.

Central and South Asia
✦ Alexander's withdrawal from the Indus Valley leads to the creation of the Mauryan Empire, which integrates the northern half of India.
✦ The Seleucid and Bactrian kingdoms further solidify the spread of Hellenism into central Asia.

Transformation of Buddhism
✦ The combined influences of Hellenism, nomadism, and Arab seafaring culture transform Buddhism into a world religion.

Formation of the Silk Road
✦ Nomadic warriors from central Asia complete the final links of the overland Silk Road, strengthening the ties that joined peoples across Afro-Eurasia.
✦ Overland traders use camels to carry spices, transport precious metals, and convey Buddhist thought along the Silk Road into China.
✦ Seafaring Arab traders use new navigation techniques and larger ships called dhows to expand the transport of Silk Road commodities to the Mediterranean world via the Indian Ocean.

Increasingly, states encouraged the use of money and a common language for contracts—innovations that aided commercial transactions. In effect, major commercial arteries replaced the early passageways that had carried small bands of traders. Political expansion facilitated all kinds of exchanges within the Afro-Eurasian world. One consequence was the emergence of the **Silk Road**, an artery that for nearly a thousand years was the primary commercial network linking East Asia and the Mediterranean world. This trade route extended over 5,000 miles and took its name from the huge quantities of precious silk that passed along it.

We cannot make sense of Alexander and the Hellenistic cultural movement or the spread of Buddhism without acknowledging the important ways in which distinct parts of the Afro-Eurasian world were already in contact. Indeed, political expansion driven by military conquest followed a period of extensive migration, trade, and technological diffusion. Alexander's conquests did not take arbitrary pathways, because earlier long-distance trade and cross-cultural exchanges had laid the trails for them. Similarly, Buddhism spread along preexisting trade routes. Slowly a new idea took hold: common cultures and shared commodities could integrate the Afro-Eurasian world.

These changes created grand opportunities for expanded trade, migration, and religious conversion. Regular trade routes now supported commercial centers that crisscrossed the landmass from China to the Mediterranean. Merchants joined with monks and administrators in connecting widespread parts of Afro-Eurasia, enabling busy sea-lanes and the Silk Road to flourish. Merely a few centuries after the conquests of Alexander and Mauryan kings, the world looked very different from the realms his armies had traversed.

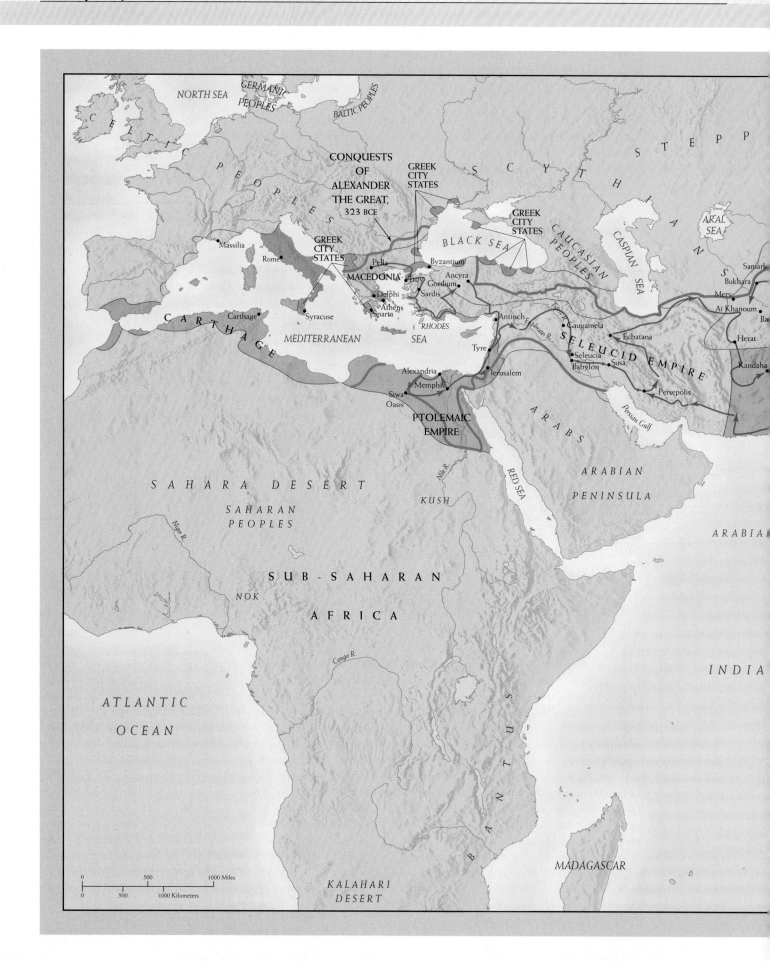

NORTH SEA

GERMANIC PEOPLES

BALTIC PEOPLES

CELTIC

PEOPLES

Massilia

Rome

CARTHAGE

Carthage

Syracuse

MEDITERRANEAN

CONQUESTS OF ALEXANDER THE GREAT, 323 BCE

GREEK CITY STATES

MACEDONIA

Pella

Delphi

Athens

Sparta

Troy

GREEK CITY STATES

Byzantium

GREEK CITY STATES

Ancyra

Gordium

Sardis

RHODES

SEA

SCYTHIANS

STEPP

ARAL SEA

CAUCASIAN PEOPLES

CASPIAN SEA

Samark

Bukhara

Merv

Aï Khanoum

Ba

Antioch

Tyre

Euphrates R.

Tigris R.

SELEUCID EMPIRE

Gaugamela

Seleucia

Babylon

Ecbatana

Susa

Herat

Kandaha

Alexandria

Memphis

Siwa Oasis

Jerusalem

Persepolis

Persian Gulf

PTOLEMAIC EMPIRE

ARABS

ARABIAN PENINSULA

SAHARA   DESERT

SAHARAN PEOPLES

Niger R.

Nile R.

KUSH

RED SEA

ARABIA

NOK

SUB-SAHARAN

AFRICA

Congo R.

ATLANTIC

OCEAN

BANTUS

INDIA

MADAGASCAR

KALAHARI DESERT

| 0 | 500 | 1000 Miles |
| 0 | 500 | 1000 Kilometers |

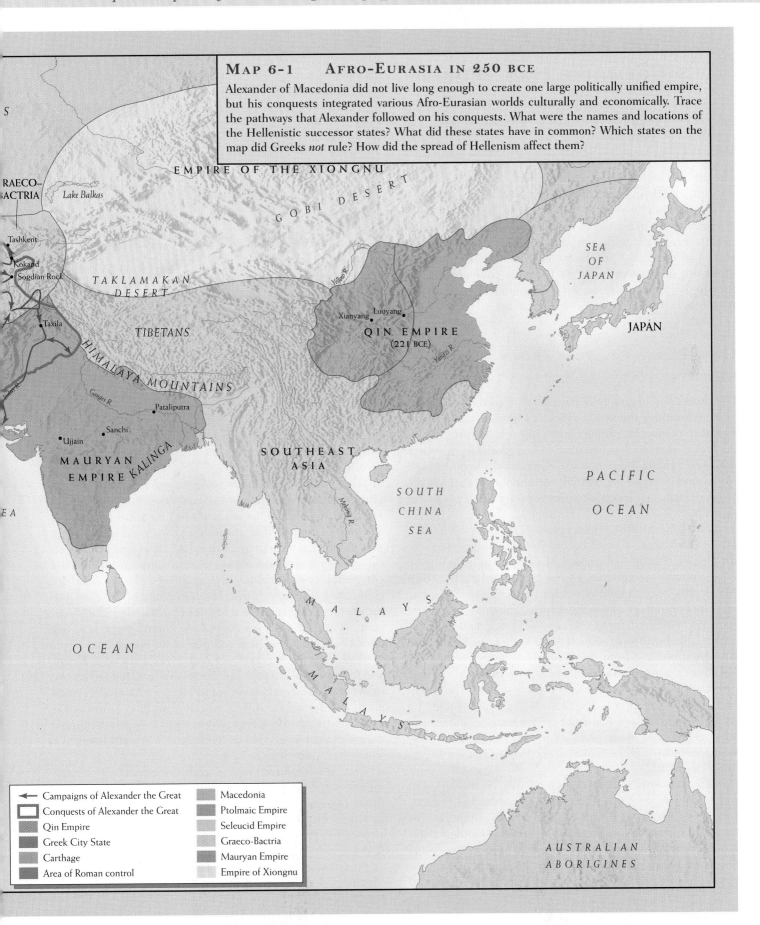

MAP 6-1   AFRO-EURASIA IN 250 BCE

Alexander of Macedonia did not live long enough to create one large politically unified empire, but his conquests integrated various Afro-Eurasian worlds culturally and economically. Trace the pathways that Alexander followed on his conquests. What were the names and locations of the Hellenistic successor states? What did these states have in common? Which states on the map did Greeks *not* rule? How did the spread of Hellenism affect them?

Legend:
- Campaigns of Alexander the Great
- Conquests of Alexander the Great
- Qin Empire
- Greek City State
- Carthage
- Area of Roman control
- Macedonia
- Ptolmaic Empire
- Seleucid Empire
- Graeco-Bactria
- Mauryan Empire
- Empire of Xiongnu

THE EMERGENCE OF A COSMOPOLITAN WORLD

> → *How did the spread of Hellenism reshape the Mediterranean world?*

The armed campaigns of a minor Greek people, the Macedonians, and their leader, Alexander the Great, began a drive for empire from the west. Alexander's novel use of new kinds of armed forces in a series of lightning attacks on the Persian Empire broke down barriers between the Mediterranean world and the rest of Southwest Asia. The massive transfers of wealth and power resulting from his conquests transformed the Mediterranean into a more unified world of economic and cultural exchange. (See Map 6-1.)

CONQUESTS OF ALEXANDER THE GREAT

Historians and biographers have filled libraries with books about **Alexander the Great** (356–323 BCE), yet he remains one of the most fascinating figures in world history. Alexander came from the frontier state of Macedonia to the north of Greece and for a dozen years commanded a highly mobile force armed with advanced military technologies that had developed during the incessant warfare among Greek city-states (see Chapter 5).

Under Alexander's predecessors—especially his father, Philip II—Macedonia had become a large ethnic and territorial state. Philip had unified Macedonia and then gone on to conquer neighboring states. Importantly, a region of Macedonia boasted gold mines that could finance his new military technology and a disciplined, full-time army. The costs of heavily armored infantry in closely arrayed phalanxes, allied with large-scale shock cavalry formations, were supported not just from the mines' substantial income but also from the enormous profits of a slave trade that passed directly through Macedonia. By the early 330s BCE, Philip had crushed the Greek city-states to the south, including Athens. After Philip's assassination, his son Alexander used this new military machine in a series of daring attacks on the apparently invincible power of the Persian Empire and its king, Darius III.

Like many other successful conquerors, Alexander owed much of his success to a readiness to take risks. In his initial forays into Southwest Asia he outpaced and outflanked his adversaries, repeatedly taking them by surprise. Through these rapid assaults he brought under the rule of his Greek-speaking elites all the lands of the former Persian Empire, which extended from Egypt and the shores of the Mediterranean to

Battle of Issus. Mosaic of the Battle of Issus between Alexander the Great of Macedon and Darius, the king of Persia (found as a wall decoration in a house at Pompeii in southern Italy). Alexander is the bareheaded figure to the far left; Darius is the figure to the right, gesturing with his right hand. The men represent two different types of warfare. On horseback, Alexander leads the cavalry-based shock forces of the Macedonian Greeks, while Darius directs his army from a chariot in the style of the great kings of Southwest Asia.

the interior of what is now Afghanistan as well as to the Indus River valley. (See Primary Source: Clash of Empires: The Battle of Gaugamela.)

The result of this violent rampage was hardly an empire, given that Alexander did not live long enough to establish institutions to hold the distant lands together. But his military campaigns continued a process that the Persians had set in motion of smashing barriers that had separated peoples on the eastern and western ends of Afro-Eurasia. Indeed, the conqueror saw himself as a new universal figure, a bridge connecting distant cultures. He demonstrated this vision in his choice of Roxana, the daughter of a Bactrian chief from central Asia, as a wife and in making Bactria, in present-day northern Afghanistan, into a center of his operations.

Alexander's conquests exposed Syria, Palestine, Egypt, and Mesopotamia to the commodities of the Mediterranean, to money-based economies (both Philip and Alexander issued gold coins to pay for their invasions), and to cultural ideas associated with the Greek city-states. Alexander founded dozens of new cities named after himself, the most famous of which was Alexandria in Egypt.

One of Alexander's most significant acts involved seizing the accumulated wealth that the Persian kings stored in their immense palaces, especially at Persepolis, and dispersing it into the money economies of the Mediterranean city-states. This massive redistribution of wealth (like the post-Columbian exploitation of the Americas; see Chapters 12 and 13) fueled a widespread economic expansion in the Mediterranean.

CLASH OF EMPIRES: THE BATTLE OF GAUGAMELA

The following passage, taken from the Greek historian Arrian, delineates the makeup of Darius's army as it prepared to confront Alexander and his forces in 331 BCE. In describing the size of the army—much larger than that of the largest Greek city-state, Athens—Arrian mentions the various ethnic groups of the Persian Empire that contributed troops. Contingents came from lands as far-flung as Bactria (near modern-day Afghanistan), Scythia (the broad area stretching from Ukraine to Kazakhstan), Armenia, Cappadocia (in east-central Turkey), and Caria (in southwestern Turkey), as well as from lands close to the Red Sea.

Darius's army was so large because it had been reinforced with Sogdians, with Bactrians, and with Indian peoples from the borderlands of Bactria, all under the command of Bessus, the satrap [i.e., the regional governor] of Bactria. There were also units of the Sakai—who were part of the Scythians who are found in Asia. They owed no loyalty to Bessus, but were still allies of Darius. These soldiers were mounted bowmen commanded by one Mauaces. The Arachotoi and the hillmen from India were commanded by Barsaentes, the satrap of Arachosia. The Areioi were commanded by their satrap, Satibarzanes; the Parthians, the Hyrcanians, and Tapeiroi, all cavalrymen, were commanded by Phratapherenes. The Medes, to whom were attached the Kadousioi, the Albanoi, and Sakesinai, were commanded by Atropates the Mede. All the units from the lands near the Red Sea were commanded by Orontobates, Ariobarzanes, and Orxines. The Ouxioi and Sousianoi were commanded by Oxathres, son of Aboultius. The men from Babylon, to whom were attached the Siracenioi and Carians, were commanded by Boupares—these Carians had been resettled in the empire by a mass transfer of their people. The Armenians were commanded by Orontes and Mithraustes; the Cappadocians, by Ariaces. The Syrians from Hollow Syria [i.e., the Bekáa Valley in modern Lebanon] and from Mesopotamia were commanded by Mazaeus. The total number of men in the army of Darius was reported to be 40,000 cavalry, 1,000,000 infantry, 200 scythed chariots [i.e., war chariots with blades mounted on both ends of the axle], and some war elephants—the Indians who came from this side of the Indus River had about fifteen of them.

→ *How many ethnic groups can you identify in this passage?*
→ *What does Darius's command of so many ethnic loyalties tell us about the nature of the Persian Empire?*
→ *How do you think Alexander was able to defeat such a large and talented army?*

SOURCE: Arrian, *The History of Alexander* 3.8; translated by Brent Shaw.

ALEXANDER'S SUCCESSORS AND THE TERRITORIAL KINGDOMS

Alexander died in Babylon at age thirty-two, struck down by overconsumption of alcohol and other excesses that matched his larger-than-life personality and reflected the war culture of Macedonian warriors. His death in 323 BCE brought on the collapse of the regime he had personally held together. The conquered lands fragmented into large territories over which his generals squabbled for control.

Alexander's generals became his successors. Seleucus, Ptolemy, Antigonus, Lysimachus, and others did not think of themselves as citizens, even very important ones, of a Greek city-state, but rather modeled themselves on the regional rulers they had defeated. As these men installed kingdoms in the eastern Mediterranean and Southwest and central Asia, they not only introduced Alexander's style of absolute rulership but also unified large blocks of territory under single, powerful rulers.

One effect of powerful families controlling whole kingdoms was that a few women could now hold great power, an unthinkable prospect in the democracies of the city-states. Queens in Macedonia, Syria, and Egypt—whether independent or as co-regents with their husbands—established new public roles for women. For example, Berenice of Egypt (c. 320–280 BCE) was the first in a series of powerful royal women who helped rule the kingdom of the Nile, a line that ended with the most famous of them all, Cleopatra, in the 30s BCE.

Berenice. Portrait head of Berenice, wife and consort of Ptolemy I, the first Macedonian king of Egypt after its conquest by Alexander the Great. Berenice was one of the women who, as queens of huge empires, wielded power and commanded wealth in their own right.

The old city-states of the Mediterranean, such as Athens and Corinth, still thrived, but now they functioned in a world dominated by much larger power blocs. Three large territorial states stood out in the new Hellenistic world: the Seleucid Empire (the dynasty established by Seleucus), stretching from Syria to present-day Afghanistan; Macedonia, ruled by the Antigonids (the dynasty established by Antigonus); and Egypt, ruled by the Ptolemies (the dynasty established by Ptolemy). In areas between these larger states, middle-sized kingdoms emerged. Elsewhere, polities banded together to survive; on mainland Greece, larger confederations forced previously independent city-states to join them.

In general, political states coalesced into larger units that displayed a uniformity unknown in the governments of the earlier city-states. Their impulse to standardization is evident not just in politics but in every aspect of daily life. Unlike the early empires described in Chapter 4, which subordinated neighbors as colonies or tribute states, these kingdoms integrated neighboring peoples as fellow subjects. They believed that their cultural assets merited dissemination across broader geographic areas.

Competition in war remained an unceasing fact of life, but the wars among the kingdoms of Alexander's successors were broader in scope and more complex in organization than ever before. At the same time, their relative parity in strength meant a near-constant state of wars between the new kings that never achieved very much. After all, every large state had access to essentially the same advanced military technology: rulers went into the marketplace and acquired the highly trained soldiers, mercenaries, generals, and military advisers required to run their armies. After battles that killed tens of thousands, and severely injured and wounded hundreds of thousands more, the three major kingdoms—and even the minor ones—remained largely unchanged.

The great powers therefore settled into a centuries-long game of watching one another and balancing threats with alliances. What emerged was a fierce competition that dominated international relations, in which diplomacy and treaty-making sometimes replaced actual fighting. This was an equilibrium reminiscent of the first age of international interstate relations in the second millennium BCE (see Chapter 3). Long periods of peace began to grace the intervals between the new kingdoms' violent and destructive wars.

HELLENISTIC CULTURE

Just as broad uniformity in politics and war trumped the small size and diversity of the old city-state, so the individual city-state cultures now gave way to a homogenized Hellenistic culture. Following the existing commercial networks, this uniform Greek culture spread rapidly through the entire Mediterranean basin and beyond. It was an alluring package, and ruling elites in all regions that encountered it fell under its powerful spell.

Hellenistic culture included philosophical and political thinking, secular disciplines ranging from history to biology, popular entertainment in theaters, competitive public games, and art for art's sake in all kinds of media. No other society at the time had such a complete package of high culture; hence its widespread appeal and diffusion. Archaeologists have found a Greek-style gymnasium and theater in the town of Aï Khanoum in modern Afghanistan, and adaptations of Greek sculptures made at the order of the Vedic king Sandrakottos (better known as Chandragupta; see below). We also know of Carthaginians in North Africa who became "Greek" philosophers, and Gallic and Berber chieftains, from the far west of France and North Africa, who had fine Greek-style drinking vessels buried with them.

COMMON LANGUAGE The core element of Hellenism was a common language, known as *koine*, or Greek. It replaced the city-states' numerous dialects with an everyday form that people anywhere could understand and quickly became the international language of its day.

Most peoples who came into contact with Hellenistic culture accepted the benefits that it afforded in expanding a network of communication and exchange. Peoples in Egypt, Judea, Syria, and Sicily, who all had distinct languages and cultures, could now communicate more easily with one another, and enjoy the same dramatic comedies and new forms of art and sculpture. Despite pockets of resistance, the Hellenizing movement was remarkably successful in spreading a shared Greek culture throughout the Mediterranean world and into Southwest Asia.

COSMOPOLITAN CITIES Much as Athens had been the model city of the age of the Greek city-state, Alexandria in Egypt became exemplary in the new age. Whereas fifth-century BCE Athens had zealously maintained an exclusive civic identity, Alexandria was a multiethnic city built from

Primary Source

THE COSMOPOLITAN CITY OF ALEXANDRIA

According to legend, Alexander selected the site of Alexandria and named the city after himself. As a result of his personal influence and its strategic location, Alexandria attracted an immense and diverse immigrant population from the entire Mediterranean world. In the following description, the Greek geographer Strabo—writing later during the time of the Roman Empire—emphasizes the city's function as an enormous entrepôt for trade and commerce across Afro-Eurasia. (Entrepôts are transshipment centers where seafaring vessels unload their cargoes and then send them elsewhere, by sea or by land.)

As for the Great Harbor at Alexandria, it is not only wonderfully well closed in and protected by artificial levees and by nature, it is also so deep that even the largest ships can be moored right at the stairs along its quayside. This Great Harbor is divided up into several minor harbors. . . . Even more exports are handled than imports. Anyone who might happen to be at Alexandria and at Dichaiarchia [the large Italian port on the Bay of Naples] would easily see for himself that the cargo ships sailing from here are bigger and more heavily laden. . . . The city itself is crisscrossed by streets that are wide enough for riding horses and driving chariots, and intersected by two main roads very much broader than the others. Its streets and avenues cut across each other at right angles. The city also boasts exceedingly beautiful public parks and its royal quarters take up a quarter, perhaps even a third of the whole city. . . . In earlier times, not even twenty ships would dare to go as far as the Arabian Gulf and manage to get a look outside its straits. But now large fleets of ships are sent out as far as India and to the furthest lands of the Ethiopians, from which the most valuable cargoes are brought to Egypt and then sent out again to other regions of the world. Double charges are collected on these shipments—both when they come in and when they go out—and the duties are especially high on luxury goods . . . for Alexandria alone does not just receive trade goods of this kind from all over the world, but it also furnishes supplies to the whole of the world outside.

→ *According to this passage, what features of the site made Alexandria well suited as a center for sea trade and a destination for immigrants?*

→ *By Strabo's time, Alexandria was the second-largest city in the Mediterranean, surpassed only by Rome. How does this passage reflect the role of trade in its development?*

→ *The passage indicates that Alexandria exported more than it imported. In what way does this indicate the city's role as a cosmopolitan entrepôt?*

SOURCE: Strabo, *Geography* 17.1.6, 7, 8, 13; translated by Brent Shaw.

---

scratch by immigrants, who rapidly totaled half a million as they streamed in from all over the Mediterranean and Southwest Asia seeking new opportunities. Members of its dynamic population, representing dozens of Greek and non-Greek peoples, communicated in the common language that supplanted their original dialects. Soon a new urban culture emerged to meet the needs of so diverse a population. (See Primary Source: The Cosmopolitan City of Alexandria.)

The culture of the Hellenistic movement took the place of local art forms. In the previous city-state world, comic playwrights had written plays for their individual cities and local cultures, highlighting familiar languages, foibles, problems, and politicians. In contrast, entertainment in the more widely connected world had to appeal to bigger audiences and a greater variety of people. Plays were now staged in any city touched by Greek influence, and they were understood in any environment. Distinctive regional humor and local characters gave way to dramas populated by stock characters of standard sit-coms that any audience could identify with: the miser, the old crone, the jilted lover, the golden-hearted whore, the boastful soldier, the befuddled father, the cheated husband, the rebellious son. At performances throughout the Mediterranean basin, laughter would be just as loud in Syracuse on the island of Sicily as in Scythopolis in the Jordan Valley of Judea.

Ways of thinking changed to match this unified world. The new ideas reflected the fact that individuals were no longer citizens of a particular city (*polis*); instead they were

The Theater at Syracuse. The great theater in the city-state of Syracuse in Sicily was considerably refurbished and enlarged under the Hellenistic kings. It could seat 15,000 to 20,000 persons. Here the people of Syracuse attended plays written by playwrights who lived on the far side of their world, but whose works they could understand as if the characters were from their own neighborhood. In the common culture of the Hellenistic period, plays deliberately featured typecast characters and situations, thereby broadening their audience.

the first "cosmopolitans," belonging to the whole world, or "universe" (*kosmos*). The new political style was relentlessly cosmopolitan, radiating out of cities not just into nearby hinterlands but also to distant (and often rivalrous) cities.

Kingdoms and states by now had become so enormous that individuals could relate to political style only through the personality of kings or rulers and their families. Rulership was personality, and personality and style united large numbers of subjects. For example, Demetrius Poliorcetes, the ruler of Macedonia, wore high-platform shoes and heavy makeup, and he decorated his elaborate, flowing cape with images of the sun, the stars, and the planets. In the presence of a powerful and solitary sun king like Demetrius, ordinary individuals felt small, inconsequential, and isolated. In response, an obsessive cult of the self arose, as Hellenistic religion and philosophy increasingly focused on the individual and his or her place in the larger world.

PHILOSOPHY AND RELIGION Growing concern with the individual self found expression in many ways. Consider the Athenian philosopher Diogenes (c. 412–323 BCE). He sought self-sufficiency and freedom from society's laws and customs, rejecting cultural norms as human-made inventions not in tune with nature and therefore false. He masturbated in public to "relieve himself" (it was, after all, a "natural need"), as well as to show disdain for what he considered to be the city's artificial sexual mores. He lived with no clothing in a wooden barrel in the public square, or *agora*, of Athens, with his female companion in her own barrel beside him. Other teachers also rejected the values of the city-state,

although with more finesse and less contentiousness than Diogenes. Nonetheless, all recognized the need for a new orientation now that the world of the city-state, with its face-to-face relationships, had vanished.

The teacher Epicurus (c. 341–279 BCE), founder of a school in Athens that he called The Garden, likewise emphasized the self. He envisioned an ideal community centered on The Garden and stressed the importance of sensation, saying that pleasurable sensations were good and painful sensations were bad. Epicurus taught his students to pursue a life of contemplation and ask themselves, "What is the good life?" Known as Epicureans, his followers struggled to develop a sense of "not caring" (*ataraxia*) about worries—like threats to personal health or the challenges of coping with excessive wealth—in order to find peace of mind. In Epicurus's cult, none of the social statuses of the old city-state had more value than any other: women, slaves, and others in the underclass were equally welcome in The Garden as worshippers.

Epicurus and his new ideas acquired followers throughout the Mediterranean, but they were hardly alone. Unrestrained by the controls of any one city-state, other cults and schools of philosophy emerged. Of these, Stoicism was perhaps the most widespread. A man named Zeno (c. 334–262 BCE), from the island of Cyprus, initiated it, and other cosmopolitan figures across the Hellenistic world—from Babylon in Mesopotamia to Sinope on the Black Sea—developed its beliefs. Their mission was to help individuals understand their place in the cosmos. Zeno put forth his ideas in the Stoa Poikilē, a decorated and roofed colonnade that opened onto the central marketplace in Athens and gave his followers their

→ *How did the spread of Hellenism reshape the Mediterranean world?*

The Painted Stoa. An artist's reconstruction of the Stoa Poikilē, or "Painted Stoa," in the city-state of Athens of the fourth century BCE. In the manner of a modern-day strip mall, this business and administrative center ran along the northern side of the agora, or central business and marketplace of the city. Philosophers and their students would hang out at the Stoa, lounging in the shaded areas under the colonnade as they debated the ideas flowing into Athens from all over the Hellenistic world. The painted wall decoration behind the columns (from which the Stoa received its name) depicts the Battle of Marathon.

name. For the Stoics, everything was grounded in nature itself, which they saw as the ultimate, permanent world. They regarded cities and kingdoms as human-made things, important but transient. Being in tune with nature and living a good life required understanding the rules of the natural order and being in control of one's passions, and thus indifferent to pleasure and pain.

Greek colonial control of other lands transformed long-established religions, and then re-exported them throughout the Mediterranean. For example, the Greeks in Egypt drew on the indigenous cult of Osiris and his consort, Isis (formerly a vital element in pharaonic temple rituals; see Chapter 2), to fashion a new narrative about Osiris's death and rebirth that represented personal salvation from death. Isis became a supreme goddess whose "excellencies" or "supreme virtues" encompassed the powers of dozens of other Mediterranean gods and goddesses. Believers experienced personal revelations and out-of-body experiences (*exstasis,* "ecstasy"). A ritual of dipping in water (*baptizein,* "to baptize") marked the transition of believers, "born again" into lives devoted to a "personal savior" who delivered an understanding of a new life by direct revelation. These new beliefs, like the worship of Isis, emphasized the spiritual concerns of humans as individuals, rather than the collective worries of towns or cities.

HELLENISM AND THE ELITES Once high Greek culture coalesced, its appeal to elites in widely dispersed communities along the major communication routes became almost irresistible. Social elites sought to enhance their position by adopting Hellenistic culture, the only one that had standing above the level of local values. Syrian, Jewish, and Egyptian elites in the eastern Mediterranean adopted this attitude, as well as Roman, Carthaginian, and African elites in the western Mediterranean. The later Roman high culture was itself a form of Greek culture. Of the Romans' extensive borrowings from the Greeks, not the least important was a belief in the value of a written history. The Romans, too, began writing about contemporary and past events. Secular plays, philosophy, poetry, competitive games, and art followed, all based on Greek forms or local imitations. North African kings similarly decked themselves out in Greek dress, built Greek-style theaters, imported Greek philosophers, and wrote history. Now they, too, had "culture."

The Hellenistic influences penetrated deeply into sub-Saharan Africa, where the kingdom of Meroe (see Chapter 5), already influenced by pharaonic forms, now absorbed characteristics of Greek culture as well. It is not surprising that Greek influences were extensive at Meroe, because continuous interaction with the Egyptians also exposed its people to the world of the Mediterranean. Both Meroe and its rival,

Axum, located in the Ethiopian highlands, used Greek stelae to boast of their military exploits. Moreover, the Greek historian Herodotus mentions that the citizens of Meroe "worshipped Zeus and Dionysus alone of the gods, holding them in great honor. There is an oracle of Zeus there, and they make war according to its pronouncements." The rulers of Meroe, understanding the advantages of the Greek language, employed Greek scribes to record their accomplishments on the walls of Greek-Egyptian temples. In this way, Meroe developed a remarkable mix of Greek, Egyptian, and African cultural and political elements.

JEWISH RESISTANCE TO HELLENISM

Not every community succumbed to the allure of Hellenism. The Jews in Judea, squeezed between Egypt and the super-states of Mesopotamia, offer a striking case of resistance to its universalizing forces. The Jews had a long schooling in surviving and resisting foreign rule, having been conquered by the Assyrians and the Babylonians (see Chapter 4). After the Persians defeated Babylon, a royal edict of restoration issued by the Persian monarch Cyrus led to the integration of Judea—now a province—into the Persian Empire. As the Jews who had once been forced to move to Babylon returned to Judea, the process of rebuilding Jerusalem began.

All this rebuilding of Jewish society occurred under the administration of another great Southwest Asian empire—that of the Persians, who tolerated local customs and beliefs. It took Alexander's lightning defeat of the Persian Empire in the 330s BCE to introduce a shocking new openness to the cultural innovations of the Mediterranean world. Hellenism came in the wake of Alexander's sweep through the region.

While some parts of the Jewish ruling elite began to adopt Greek ways—to wear Greek clothing, to introduce the culture of the gymnasium with its cult of male nudity, to produce images of gods as art, other rejected the push. Those who spurned assimilation rebelled against the common elements of Hellenism—its language, music, gymnasia, nudity, public art, and secularism—as being deeply immoral and threatening to their beliefs. Ultimately, this resistance led to a full-scale armed revolt, headed up by the family of the Maccabees, in 166 BCE, provoked when Syrian overlords, the Seleucids, forbade the practice of Judaism and profaned the Jews' temple. Though the Maccabees succeeded in establishing an independent Jewish state centered on the temple in Jerusalem, they did not entirely overcome the impact of the new universal culture. By the beginning of the first century BCE, descendants of the Maccabees were calling themselves kings, minting coins with Greek legends, and presiding over a largely secular kingdom. Moreover, a huge Jewish society in the Hellenistic city of Alexandria in Egypt embraced the new culture. Scholars there produced a Bible in koine Greek, and historians (such as Jason of Cyrene) and philosophers (such as Philo of Alexandria) wrote in Greek, imitating Greek models.

THE HELLENISTIC WORLD AND THE BEGINNINGS OF THE ROMAN EMPIRE

Other cities were less reluctant than Jerusalem to follow Hellenistic ways. Early on, the Romans saw the Greek model as offering opportunities to increase their own importance. In the 330s and 320s BCE, when Alexander was uniting the eastern Mediterranean, a city-state on the Tiber River in central Italy took the first critical military actions to unify Italy; eventually it would bring together the rest of the Mediterranean and parts of Southwest Asia. Rather than beginning as a kingdom like Macedonia, Rome went from being a city-state to flourishing as a large territorial state. During this transformation it adopted significant elements of Hellenistic culture: Greek-style temples, elaborately decorated Greek-style pottery and paintings, and an alphabet based on that of the Greeks.

The Roman elites saw immersion in Greek culture and language as a way to appear to the rest of the world as "civilized." Yet the Roman elites did not accept this notion without resistance, worry, and debate. Consider the Roman senator Cato the Elder (234–149 BCE), who struggled with the tensions that these changes involved. Although he was devoted to the Roman past, the Latin language, and the ideal of small-scale Roman peasant farmers and their families, he embraced many Hellenistic influences. For example, he wrote a standard manual for the new economy of slave plantation agriculture (see below), invested in shipping and trading, learned Greek rhetoric (both speaking and writing the language), added the genre of history to Latin literature, and much more. Indeed, Cato blended an extreme devotion to tradition, manifested in his public statements, with bold innovations in most aspects of his daily life.

CARTHAGE

In contrast to Rome, which assimilated Greek ways to elevate its status in the Mediterranean world, cities that were prosperous and already well integrated into the world economy welcomed Hellenistic culture because it facilitated communication and exchange. When Hellenism reached the great city of Carthage (in the area of present-day Tunisia), its residents adapted it without fanfare but with much success.

Not only did Carthaginian merchants trade with other Phoenician colonies in the western Mediterranean, but the city's ruling families took control over western Sicily and

→ *How did the spread of Hellenism reshape the Mediterranean world?*

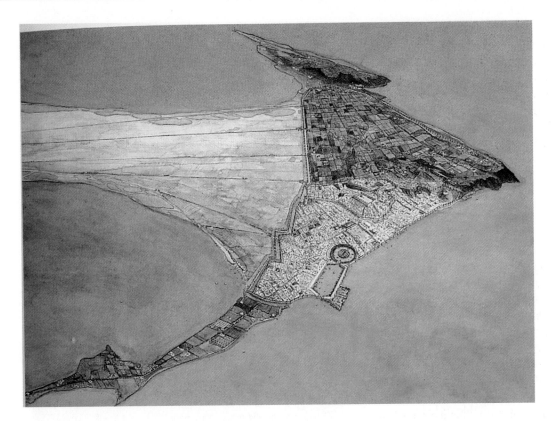

Aerial View of Punic Carthage. Carthage was located on a promontory in the Bay of Tunis. In the lower foreground of this artist's reconstruction is a rectangular area of water and above it a circular-shaped one. These were the two major harbors of Carthage—the rectangular one was the commercial port and the circular one was the military harbor. Above these harbors are the main market square and the high central point named the Byrsa. To the left is the twenty-mile-long wall that defended the city on its land side.

Sardinia. Remains of pottery and other materials demonstrate that the Carthaginians' trading contacts extended far beyond other Phoenician settlements to towns of the Etruscans and the Romans in Italy, to the Greek trading city of Massilia (modern Marseilles) in southern France, and to Athens in the eastern Mediterranean. In addition, the Carthaginians expanded their commercial interests into the Atlantic, moving north along the coast of Iberia and south along the coast of West Africa—which, as noted in Chapter 5, the commander Hanno explored and colonized. Pushing their influence even farther, they established a trading post at the island of Mogador more than 600 miles down the Atlantic coast of Africa.

Carthaginian culture (or Punic culture, to use the Romans' name for the people with whom they would soon be at war; see Chapter 7) took on important elements of Hellenistic culture. For example, some Carthaginians went to Athens to become philosophers. Also, the design of their sanctuaries, temples, and other public buildings reveals a marriage of styles: Greek-style pediments and columns mixed with Punic designs and measurements, and local North African motifs and structures added to the mix. The splendid jewelry that Phoenician women adorned themselves with reflected styles from Egypt, such as ornate necklaces of gold and earrings of lapis-lazuli. The finest tableware and pottery were imports from Etruscans in Italy, and coinage and innovative ideas on political theory and warfare came from the Greek city-states.

ECONOMIC CHANGES: PLANTATION SLAVERY AND MONEY-BASED ECONOMIES

The main economic innovation that accompanied unification of the Mediterranean world was the use of large numbers of slaves in agricultural production—especially in Italy, Sicily, and North African regions close to Carthage. After all, Alexander's conquests and Rome's political rise produced unprecedented wealth for a small elite. These men and women used their riches to acquire huge tracts of land and to purchase slaves (either kidnapped individuals or conquered peoples) on a scale and with a degree of managerial organization never seen before.

The slave plantations, wholly devoted to producing surplus crops for profit, became one of the engines driving a new Mediterranean economy. The estates created vast wealth for their owners—though at a heavy price to others, as reliance on slave labor now left the free peasants who used to work the fields with no option but to move into overcrowded cities, where employment was hard to find. However, the sudden importation of so many slaves to work in harsh conditions had an unanticipated outcome. Between 135 and 70 BCE, authorities on Sicily and in southern Italy faced several massive slave uprisings, led by the religious seer Eunus in 130 and the slave gladiator Spartacus in the late 70s. These were among the greatest slave wars in world history. The superior

Early Roman Coin. Coins like this one were the standard means by which the state paid its expenditures; they later were widely used in ordinary commercial dealings. This coin features the prow of a ship with an "evil eye" decoration and armed beak for ramming other ships. The legend ROMA at the bottom signals that Rome is a state with the power and autonomy to have its own money.

military force of the Roman state prevailed in all three wars, and the rebels were finally defeated. But the political repercussions of the wars had a fundamental impact in the subsequent political crises that transformed the Roman state.

The circulation of money reinforced the effects of forced labor. With more cash in the economy, wealthy landowners, urban elites, and merchants could more easily do business. The increasing use of Greek-style coins to pay for goods and services (in place of barter) promoted the importation of commodities such as wine from elsewhere in the Mediterranean. As coined money became even more available, it led to even more commercial exchanges. The forced transfer of precious metals to the Mediterranean from Southwest Asia by Alexander's conquests actually caused the price of gold to fall. In the west, Carthage now began to mint its own coins—at first mainly in gold, but later in other metals. Rome moved to a money economy at the same time. By the 270s and 260s BCE, the Romans were issuing coins on a large scale under the pressures of their first war with Carthage (264–241 BCE). By the end of the third century, even borderland peoples such as the Gauls had begun to mint coins, imitating the galloping-horse images found on Macedonia's gold coins. So, too, did kingdoms in North Africa, where the coins of kings Massinissa and Syphax bore the same Macedonian royal imagery. By the end of this period, inhabitants of the entire Mediterranean basin and surrounding lands were using coins to buy and sell all manner of commodities.

To pay for the goods that satisfied their newly acquired tastes, Celtic chieftains in the regions encompassing modern-day France began selling their own people in the expanding slave markets of the Mediterranean. Slavery and slave trading also became central to the economies of the Iberian Peninsula—especially in the hinterlands of large river valleys like the Ebro, where local elites founded urban centers imitating Greek styles. If Alexander's triumphs broadcast political and military influences from the Hellenistic world, the more influential aftershocks were economic and cultural. From North Africa to South Asia and beyond, Hellenistic influences and the very idea of a universal culture incorporating all urban, settled peoples reverberated.

Roman Slaves. One of the most profitable occupations for peoples living beyond the northwestern frontiers of the Roman Empire, in what was called Germania, was providing bodies for sale to Roman merchants. In this relief, we see chained German prisoners whose fate was to become slaves in the empire. This stone picture supported columns in front of the headquarters of the Roman fortress at Mainz-Kästrich.

CONVERGING INFLUENCES IN CENTRAL AND SOUTH ASIA

> → *How did Hellenistic and pastoral nomadic cultures influence central and South Asia?*

The mountains of what we know today as Afghanistan are formidable but not impenetrable. Their passes, between the high plateau of Iran to the west and the towering ranges of Tibet to the east, are pinched like the narrow neck of an hourglass—but they offer the shortest route through the mountains.

The Bolan Pass. The formidable Bolan Pass separated India from the highland of Baluchistan. It was both an artery for transportation and a strategic military spot.

By crossing those passes, Alexander's armies expanded the routes between the eastern and western portions of Afro-Eurasia, fashioned a land bridge that has remained open to this day, and brought about massive political and cultural changes in central and South Asia. Their routes created avenues for unprecedented cross-cultural exchange that eventually remapped entire regions. Conquerors moving from west to east (like Alexander) and from east to west (like the later nomads from central Asia) pressed southward, through the mountains, into the rich plains of the Indus and Ganges river valleys. At the same time, trade and religious influences from South Asia moved northward toward routes running west to east along what became known as the Silk Road. The incorporation of central Asia and South Asia into this east-west axis set the stage for exchanges that would penetrate North Africa and then work their way into East Africa and parts of sub-Saharan Africa.

INFLUENCES FROM THE MAURYAN EMPIRE

Alexander's brief occupation of the Indus Valley (327–325 BCE) helped pave the way for South Asia's most powerful and durable polity before the Common Era. Before the arrival of Alexander's forces, South Asia had been a conglomerate of small warring states. Its political instability came to an abrupt halt when, in 321 BCE, an ambitious young man named Chandragupta Mori ascended the throne of the Magadha kingdom and launched a series of successful military expeditions in what is now northern India.

THE REGIME OF CHANDRAGUPTA Magadha, located on the lower Ganges plain, held great advantages over other states. For one thing, it contained rich iron ores and fertile rice paddies. Moreover, on the northeast Deccan plateau ample woods supported herds of elephants, the mainstay of the potent Magadha cavalries. The Mori family, or Mauryans, did not start out as a distinguished ruling family, but economic strength and military skill elevated them over their rivals. Alexander's retreat created a momentary political vacuum that gave the Mauryans an opportunity to extend the dynasty's claims to the northwest areas of South Asia, the region previously controlled by the Persian Empire.

Chandragupta's regime, which historians call the Mauryan Empire, constituted the first empire in South Asia and served as a model for later Indian empire-builders. The contemporary Greek world knew this empire as "India," stretching from the Indus River eastward. Indeed, the Mauryan regime began to etch out the territorial contours of what would become, many centuries later, modern India.

Chandragupta (r. 321–297 BCE) used his military resources to reach beyond the Ganges plain to the northwest into the Punjab ("Five Rivers," the area around the upper stream of the Indus where four tributaries join it). Here he pushed up to the border with the Seleucid kingdom, the largest successor kingdom of Alexander's empire. Its king, Seleucus Nicator, fretted about his neighbor's challenge and invaded Mauryan territory—only to face Chandragupta's impregnable defenses. Soon thereafter, a treaty between the two powers gave a large portion of Afghanistan to the Mauryan Empire. This territory remained Greek-speaking for centuries, and some **garrison towns** developed into genuine Greek-style city-states. The treaty yielded a round of gift exchanges and diplomacy. One of the daughters of Seleucus went to the Mauryan court at Pataliputra, accompanied by a group of Greek women. Seleucus also sent an ambassador, Megasthenes, to Chandragupta's court. Megasthenes lived in South Asia for years, gathering his observations of life there in a book titled *Indica*. In return the Mauryans sent Seleucus many South Asian valuables, including hundreds of elephants, which the Greeks soon learned to use in battles.

Megasthenes's *Indica* depicted a well-ordered and highly stratified society divided into seven groups: philosophers, farmers, soldiers, herdsmen, artisans, magistrates, and councilors. People respected the boundaries between groups and honored rituals that reinforced their identities; members of different groups did not intermarry or even eat together. Meanwhile, Megasthenes noted some ways in which rulers integrated the region—for example, with extensive roads connecting major cities. These arteries were lined with trees and mileage stones to beautify the realm. If these roads helped traders, they also enabled the ruler's troops to march around his dominions. According to Megasthenes, soldiers were a profession separate from the rest of the population. This surprised the Greek observer, who was more accustomed to the idea of the military closely integrated into civil society. Mauryan troops did not pretend to work when there was no war. They constituted a standing force of immense proportions, ready to obey their commander. This military force was huge, boasting cavalry divisions of mounted horses, war elephants, and scores of infantry. Most of the fighters evolved into a warrior caste of their own.

THE REGIME OF AŚOKA   The Mauryan Empire reached its height during the reign of the third king, Aśoka (r. 268–231 BCE), Chandragupta's grandson. Aśoka's lands comprised almost the entirety of South Asia, including the Deccan plateau; only the southern tip of the peninsula remained

outside his control. In 261 BCE, Aśoka waged the dynasty's last campaign: the conquest of Kalinga, a kingdom on the east coast of the South Asian peninsula. It was a gruesome and despicable operation. The Mauryan army triumphed, but at a high price: about 100,000 soldiers died in battle, many more perished in its aftermath, and some 150,000 people endured forcible relocation. Aśoka himself, when he learned of the devastation, was shocked and appalled at his own handiwork, and in a fit of guilt he issued a famous edict renouncing his brutal ways.

Aśoka was a faithful follower and patron of Buddhism. In fact, the Kalinga campaign redoubled his devotion to Buddhism, which informed his peaceable edict. (See Primary Source: Aśoka's Kalinga Edict.) All over his domain he built **stupas**, or dome monuments, marking the burial sites of relics of the Buddha. In the Kalinga edict, he claimed to rule over his subjects according to **dhamma** (a vernacular form of the Sanskrit word *dharma*), a set of moral regulations that applied to all—including the priestly Brahmans, Buddhists, members of other religious sects, and even the Greeks. Dhamma or dharma became a concept that all religious schools in South Asia used, irrespective of faith; it was an encompassing moral code for all sects. Using dhamma as a unifying symbol, Aśoka wanted all people, whatever their religious practices and cultural customs, to consider themselves his subjects, to respect him as their father, and to conform to his moral code—starting with the precept that people of different religions or sects should get

Aśoka. Buddhist legend claims that Aśoka placed relics of the Buddha into the many stupas he had built. The stupa at Sarnath (*left*) is the best-preserved one from the time of Aśoka. Aśoka had his edicts carved on pillars like the one on the right all over India. The majestic lion at the top of the pillar shows the influence of Persian art, in which the lion was the symbol of royalty.

Primary Source

AŚOKA'S KALINGA EDICT

After the Kalinga war, Aśoka issued an edict to express his regret at the miseries it had caused his people. From this edict, we can tell that Aśoka ruled a country of many different cultures and religions.

Beloved of the Gods, is that those who dwell there, whether brahmans, *śramanas*, or those of other sects, or householders who show obedience to their superiors, obedience to mother and father, obedience to their teachers and behave well and devotedly towards their friends, acquaintances, colleagues, relatives, slaves, and servants suffer violence, murder, and separation from their loved ones. Even those who are fortunate to have escaped, and whose love is undiminished [by the brutalizing effect of war], suffer from the misfortunes of their friends, acquaintances, colleagues, and relatives. This participation of all men in suffering weighs heavily on the mind of the Beloved of the Gods. Except among the Greeks, there is no land where the religious orders of brahmans and *śramanas* are not to be found, and there is no land anywhere where men do not support one sect or another. Today if a hundredth or a thousandth part of those people who were killed or died or were deported when Kaliṅga was annexed were to suffer similarly, it would weigh heavily on the mind of the Beloved of the Gods.

The Beloved of the Gods believes that one who does wrong should be forgiven as far as it is possible to forgive him. And the Beloved of the Gods conciliates the forest tribes of his empire, but he warns them that he has power even in his remorse, and he asks them to repent, lest they be killed. For the Beloved of the Gods wishes that all beings should be unharmed, self-controlled, calm in mind, and gentle.

The Beloved of the Gods considers victory by *Dhamma* to be the foremost victory. And moreover the Beloved of the Gods has gained this victory on all his frontiers to a distance of six hundred *yojanas* [i.e., about 1,500 miles], where reigns the Greek king named Antiochus, and beyond the realm of that Antiochus in the lands of the four kings named Ptolemy, Antigonus, Magas, and Alexander; and in the south over the Colas and Pāndyas as far as Ceylon. Likewise here in the imperial territories among the Greeks and the Kambojas, Nābhakas and Nābhapanktis, Bhojas and Pitinikas, Andhras and Pārindas, everywhere the people follow the Beloved of the Gods' instructions in *Dhamma*. Even where the envoys of the Beloved of the Gods have not gone, people hear of his conduct according to *Dhamma*, his precepts and his instruction in *Dhamma*, and they follow *Dhamma* and will continue to follow it.

What is obtained by this is victory everywhere, and everywhere victory is pleasant. This pleasure has been obtained through victory by *Dhamma*—yet it is but a slight pleasure, for the Beloved of the Gods only looks upon that as important in its results which pertains to the next world.

This inscription of *Dhamma* has been engraved so that any sons or great grandsons that I may have should not think of gaining new conquests, and in whatever victories they may gain should be satisfied with patience and light punishment. They should only consider conquest by *Dhamma* to be a true conquest, and delight in *Dhamma* should be their whole delight, for this is of value in both this world and the next.

→ *Why would Aśoka refer to himself as "the Beloved of the Gods"? Whose gods might he be referring to?*

→ *Aśoka was a follower of Buddhism, which held that mortals passed through cycles of life, death, and rebirth. What parts of this passage reflect that belief?*

→ *Aśoka promises to rule his people with* Dhamma *(Dharma in Sanskrit). Whereas Buddhist doctrine considers* Dharma *to encompass religious teachings that guided the Buddha's followers, Aśoka's* Dhamma *refers to a general moral standard that applied to all religious and ethnic communities—Buddhists or not. Why do you suppose he emphasizes this broader meaning?*

SOURCE: Romila Thapar, *Aśoka and the Decline of the Maurya*, 2nd ed. (Delhi: Oxford University Press, 1973), 255–57.

along. He also lauded the benefits of agrarian progress and banned large-scale cattle sacrifice as detrimental to agriculture. Meanwhile, he warned the "forest people," the hunters and gatherers living beyond the reach of government, to avoid making trouble and be wary of his punitive wrath.

To explain and implement this dhamma Aśoka regularly issued decrees, which he displayed on stone pillars and boulders in every corner of his domain; occasionally he also issued edicts to explain his own Buddhist faith. All were inscribed in local languages. While most of his decrees were in dialects of Sanskrit, those published in northwestern regions were in Greek or Aramaic, the administrative script of old Persia. Aśoka's legal pronouncements helped legitimize the Greek-speaking population that had arrived with Alexander and now resided in Greek-style towns.

The works of art created under Aśoka's patronage celebrated the copious cultural and economic exchanges among Greeks, Persians, and Indians. The most famous monument was the edict pillar that Aśoka erected in Sarnath at the Deer Garden, where the Buddha gave his first sermon. Atop the pillar, four lions sat facing four directions. Beneath the four lions were four wheels representing universal rule; they were separated by a bull, a horse, elephants, and another lion. The majestic images of lions, animals not found in the Ganges plain, represented an Indian version of the Persian royal symbol. Its artistic technique displayed Greek influence as well, in vivid, animated style.

Elephant Cavalry. As shown by this terra-cotta statuette from 200 BCE, elephant cavalry was an important component of the Greek military. In their exchanges with India, Hellenist states demanded numerous elephants for their army.

THE SELEUCID EMPIRE AND GREEK INFLUENCES

Alexander's military thrust into Asia reached as far as the Punjab. There he defeated several rulers of Gandhara in 326 BCE. In the course of this campaign he planted many garrison towns—especially in eastern Iran, northern Afghanistan, and the Punjab, where he needed to protect his easternmost territorial acquisition. These towns were originally stations for soldiers, but they soon became centers of Hellenistic culture. Many of these outposts, such as those at Ghazni, Kandahar, Kapisi, and Bactra (modern Balkh), displayed the characteristic features of a Greek polis: a colonnaded main street lined by temples to patron gods or goddesses, a theater, a gymnasium for education, a palace administration center, a marketplace.

After Alexander's death, Seleucus Nikator (358–281 BCE), ruler of the Hellenistic successor state in this area, built more Greek garrison towns. Seleucus, who also controlled Mesopotamia, Syria, and Persia, named sixteen cities "Antioch" after his father, five "Laodiceas" after his mother, nine "Seleucia" after himself, three "Apamea" after his wife Apama, and "Stratonicea" after another wife. These towns, too, became major Hellenistic centers.

Most of the Greek invaders integrated themselves into the local societies. Once the soldiers realized they would be spending their lives far from their homeland, they married local women and started families. Bringing their native customs to the local populations, they established institutions familiar to them from the polis. Greek was the official language; but because local women used their native tongues in daily life, subsequent generations were bilingual. For centuries the traditional Greek institutions—especially Greek language and writing—survived many political changes and much cultural assimilation, providing a common basis of engagement in a long strip of land stretching from the Mediterranean to South Asia.

THE KINGDOM OF BACTRIA AND THE YAVANA KINGS

Hellenistic influences were even more pronounced in the Seleucid successor regimes of central Asia of the late third century BCE. The Seleucid state took over the entire Persian realm, including its central Asian and South Asian territory.

The Hellenistic kingdom of Bactria broke away from the Seleucids to establish a strong state, which included the Gandhara region in modern Pakistan, around 200 BCE. As Mauryan power receded from the northwestern part of India, the Bactrian rulers extended their conquests into this area. Because the cities that the Bactrian Greeks founded included many Indian residents, and thus were a mix of cultural influences, they have been called "Indo-Greek." Those in Gandhara incorporated familiar features of the Greek polis, but inhabitants still revered Indian patron gods and goddesses.

Hellenistic Bactria served as a bridge between South Asia and the Greek world of the Mediterranean. Among the goods that the Bactrians sent west were elephants, which were vital to the Greek armies. In fact, the Greeks' fascination with Indian war elephants found frequent expression in Greek art. The Greek king Demetrius, who invaded India around 200 BCE, had coins minted portraying himself wearing an elephant cap (a headdress with an elephant's trunk). In subsequent decades, Bactrian Greek invaders not only revived the cities in India left by Alexander but also founded new Hellenistic cities in the Gandhara region. Demetrius entrusted the extension of his empire in the northern region of India to his generals, many of whom became independent rulers after his death. Sanskrit literature refers to these Greek rulers as the Yavana kings—a word derived from "Ionia," a region whose name applied to all those who spoke Greek or came from the Mediterranean.

Remains of a Greek garrison town, unearthed under the site of the ancient city of Samarkand in Uzbekistan, attest to the strength of Hellenistic influences. In the 1960s, archaeologists at Aï Khanoum on the Oxus River (now the Amu) in present-day Afghanistan were stunned to find the ruins of nearly an entire Greek city. Miraculously, Aï Khanoum was able to avoid the reconstructions and devastations that befell so many other Hellenistic cities in this region. It was clearly an administrative center, if not the capital city, of the Bactrian state. The Greek-style architecture and inscriptions indicate that the original residents were soldiers from Greece. Following the typical pattern, they married local women and stayed; but they also established fundamental institutions of a Greek polis.

Aï Khanoum's characteristic Greek structures included a palace complex, a gymnasium, a theater, an arsenal, several temples, and elite residences. Featuring marble columns with Corinthian capitals, the palace contained an administrative section, storage rooms, and a library. A main road divided the city into lower and higher parts, with the palace and main religious buildings located in the lower city. Though far from Greece, the elite Greek residents read poetry and philosophy and staged Greek dramas in the theater. The palace baths had a mosaic floor of colored pebbles obtained from the nearby riverbank. Grape cultivation supported a festival of

Three Coins. *Top*: Wearing an elephant cap, Demetrius of Bactria titled himself the king of Indians as well as Greeks. On the other side of the coin is Hercules. *Middle*: The king Menander is remembered by Buddhists for his curiosity about their theology. His image appears on one side of the coin with a Greek legend of his name and title. On the other side, Athena is surrounded by Kharoshthi script, an Indian writing. *Bottom*: The Scythian king Maues used Greek to claim "King of Kings" on one side of his coin. On the other side, the goddess Nike is surrounded by Kharoshthi letters.

wine drinking, associated with the god Dionysus. The main temple housed a gigantic marble statue of an unknown deity; only its huge marble foot has survived the ravages of time. The remains of various statues indicate that the residents not only revered the Greek deity Athena and the demigod Heracles but also paid homage to the Zoroastrian religion and worshipped Mesopotamian gods.

The Hellenistic cities in the area of modern Uzbekistan, Afghanistan, and northern India maintained Greek culture, also educating young people in gymnasia and performing

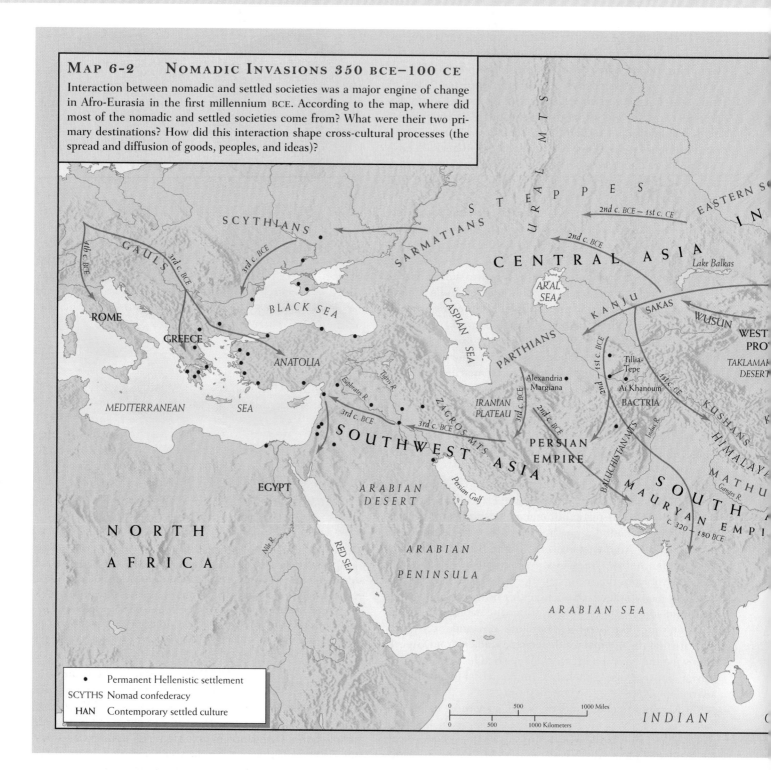

MAP 6-2   NOMADIC INVASIONS 350 BCE–100 CE

Interaction between nomadic and settled societies was a major engine of change in Afro-Eurasia in the first millennium BCE. According to the map, where did most of the nomadic and settled societies come from? What were their two primary destinations? How did this interaction shape cross-cultural processes (the spread and diffusion of goods, peoples, and ideas)?

• Permanent Hellenistic settlement
SCYTHS Nomad confederacy
HAN Contemporary settled culture

Greek dramas in their theaters. Because Greek religious practices were highly inclusive, temples were suitable places for cultural assimilation; there, local deities donned Greek garb to protect the city. As the Greeks planted familiar crops from their homeland, vineyards and olive orchards flourished. A material culture, such as tableware associated with wine drinking, also thrived. Cities and kings issued coins with Greek inscriptions, or legends, in the standard weights of the Greek world. Most men and women spoke and wrote some Greek, often as a second language.

Perhaps the most adept ruler at mingling Greek and Indian influences was Menander, the best-known Yavana city-state king of the mid-second century BCE. Using images and legends on coins to promote both traditions among his subjects,

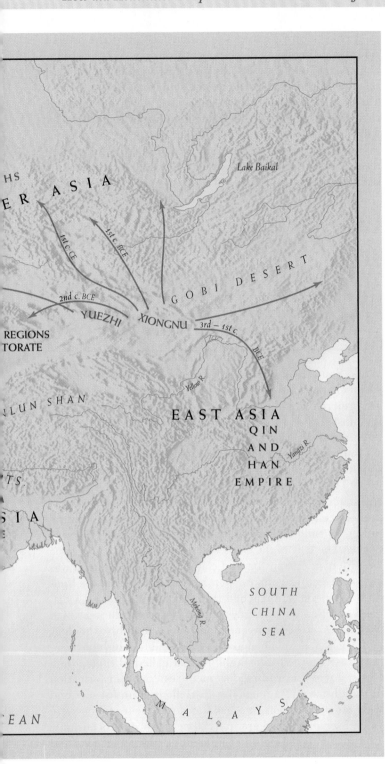

essential to communication and trade around the Indian Ocean rim.

NOMADIC INFLUENCES OF PARTHIANS AND KUSHANS

Although much of central and Southwest Asia came under the control of Alexander's successor kingdoms (and some smaller independent kingdoms), nomadic populations continued to be influential in this period. (See Map 6-2.) First to feel the impact of nomads was the Seleucid state in Iran. Having lost control of Bactria, it now came under relentless pressure from nomadic peoples living on the steppes to the north. The first to prey on them were the horse-riding Parthians, who wiped out the Greek kingdoms in Iran. The Parthians then extended their power all the way to the Mediterranean, where they would ultimately encounter the Roman Empire in Anatolia and Mesopotamia.

THE PARTHIANS The Parthian people had moved south from present-day Turkmenistan and settled in the region comprising the modern states of Iraq and Iran. Unlike the Persians before them, the Parthians had a social order founded on nomadic pastoralism and a war capability based on technical advances in mounted horseback warfare. Reliance on horses made their style of fighting highly mobile and ideal for warfare on arid plains and deserts. They perfected the so-called Parthian shot: the arrow shot from a bow with great accuracy at long distance and from horseback at a gallop. On the flat, open plains of Iran and Iraq, the Parthians had a decisive advantage over slow-moving, cumbersome mass infantry formations that had developed for war in the Mediterranean. Eventually the expansionist states of Parthia and Rome became archenemies: they confronted each other in Mesopotamia for nearly four centuries. Because the Parthians probably did not have their own writing system, their empire left no historical record. We know it only through the descriptions of Greek observers who remained in central Asia after the Greek powers retreated. According to these sources, the Hellenistic caravan cities on the Roman Empire's eastern frontier continued to trade with the east in spite of the conflicts between Romans and Parthians. From the eastern shore of the Mediterranean all the way to Afghanistan, Greek was still the essential language for commercial activities.

During a second wave of invasions, other nomadic peoples swept out of Mongolia and central Asia around 130 BCE. They filled some of the vacuum left by the disintegration of Alexander's and Aśoka's empires, infusing South Asian societies with the nomadic and equestrian values of the steppe. In the process, they blended Hellenism and Buddhist religious thought with a culture that glorified nomadic and pastoral ways and institutions. A modified Hellenistic culture

Menander claimed legitimacy as an Indian ruler but also cultivated Greek cultural forms. The face of his coins bore his regal image surrounded by the Greek words *Basileus Sōtēr Menandros* ("King, Savior, Menander"). The reverse side featured the Greek goddess Athena and the king's title in the local Pakrit language. These legacies persisted long after the Hellenistic regimes collapsed, because they remained

and the Greek language now became more vital than before. Even as its connections to Greece weakened, Hellenism's influence over Buddhism and other South Asian cultures grew stronger.

The new rulers galloping down from the steppe in waves forced their predecessors to seek new tribal domains. In the second century BCE, a vast tribal confederacy called the Xiongnu became dominant in the East Asian steppe lands. While consolidating their power, the Xiongnu drove many other pastoral groups out of their homelands. Meanwhile, the Parthians (who had supplanted the Greek Seleucids in Iran) also entered the Indus Valley—from the northwest, through the mountain passes of Baluchistan.

THE KUSHANS The most dynamic and powerful of the nomadic groups were the Yuezhi-Kushans, who appeared as a political force around 50 CE. Led by their chief, the Yuezhi unified the region's tribes and established the Kushan dynasty in Afghanistan and the Indus River basin. The Kushans' empire embraced a large and diverse territory and was critical in the formation of the Silk Road.

Like the Parthians, the Kushans had been an illiterate people, but they adopted Greek as their official language. The face of a gold coin of Wima Kadphises (the second Kushan king to rule South Asia) features the king's bust surrounded by Greek legends. The reverse side shows the Hindu god Shiva with his cow. Until the end of the Kushan Empire in the early third century CE, Greek letters continued to appear on Kushan coins. Their rulers kept alive the influence of Hellenism in an area strategically located on the Silk Road, even though by this time few Greek speakers were left in the population. Mediterranean traders arriving in the Kushan markets to purchase silks from China, as well as Indian gemstones and spices, conducted their transactions in Greek. The coins they used—struck to Roman weight standards (themselves derived from Greek coinage) and inscribed in Greek—served their needs perfectly.

These diverse nomadic groups did not undermine local cultural traditions or the Hellenistic heritage, but they introduced a powerful new cultural ingredient: equestrianism. The proud Kushans carried their horse-riding skills into India and, in spite of the hot climate, continued to wear their trademark cone-shaped leather hats, knee-length robes, trousers, and boots. Since the time of the Vedic invaders (see Chapter 3), horses had been valued imports into the region—and under the Kushans they became the most prestigious status symbol of the ruling elite. At the same time, the Kushans began consuming exotic goods that arrived from as far east as China and as far west as the Mediterranean. Their rule also stabilized the trading routes through central Asia that stretched from the steppes in the east to the Parthian Empire in the west. This would become a major segment of the Silk Road.

The Kushans also courted the local population by patronizing local religious cults. In Bactria, where they encountered the shrines of many different gods, the Kushan kings had their coins cast with images of various deities on the reverse side. They also donated generously to shrines of Zoroastrian, Vedic, and Buddhist cults. Around Kushan political centers, religious shrines mushroomed and sculptural works reached a high artistic level. Kushan kings also built royal dynastic shrines, beside which they placed statues of themselves as patrons of the local deities. Governors and generals followed their example of patronizing local religions, as did traders, artisans, and other urbanites. Wealth flowed into religious institutions, especially Buddhist monasteries later on.

THE TRANSFORMATION OF BUDDHISM

> → *In what ways did the transformation of Buddhism represent cultural integration in South Asia?*

While South Asia was undergoing noteworthy political and social change caused by encroaching nomadic tribes, it was also experiencing upheavals in the religious sphere. Perhaps the most surprising repercussion of the spread of Hellenism after Alexander was the transformation of Buddhism.

Impressed by Hellenistic thought, South Asian peoples sought to blend it with their own ethical and religious traditions. This merging began among the Yavana (that is, Greek) city-states in the northwest, where Buddhism's sway was most pronounced—and readily absorbed into the mix of cultural pulses swirling throughout the area. (See Primary Source: Sâgala: The City of the Gods.) Here, for example, the Yavana king Menander went beyond claiming that the Buddha was an inspired ethical philosopher; he held instead that the Buddha was a god. He reached this conclusion through a discussion with a Buddhist sage named Nagasena, during which Menander asked many questions about Buddhist theology and Nagasena explained away all his doubts. This conversation was recorded in a Buddhist text called *Milindapunha* (*Questions of King Milinda*). Nonetheless, the transformation of Buddhism into a religion with Hellenistic influences and wide-ranging support in other states was far from complete when Menander died around 130 BCE. It would occur only after accommodating other influences, and other gods and beliefs (see Chapter 8).

INDIA AS A SPIRITUAL CROSSROADS

Hellenism was not the sole cultural movement to affect other cultures. The nomads in India added another layer of cultural change, as did Arab and other seafarers. The latter's mastery of the monsoon trade winds opened the Indian Ocean to commerce (see below) and made India the hub for

Primary Source

SÂGALA: THE CITY OF THE GODS

The Indo-Greek king Menander was a famous patron of Buddhism, as described in the Questions of King Milinda. *The book, written in Pāli, a northwestern dialect of Sanskrit, begins with a description of the kingdom of Milinda (Menander) located in the country of Yonakas, the Pāli name for Greeks. This kingdom, according to the following passage, is a center of prosperous trade and people of many creeds, with a city called Sâgala whose glory rivals that of "the city of the gods."*

Thus hath it been handed down by tradition—There is in the country of the Yonakas a great centre of trade, a city that is called Sâgala, situated in a delightful country well watered and hilly, abounding in parks and gardens and groves and lakes and tanks, a paradise of rivers and mountains and woods. Wise architects have laid it out, and its people know of no oppression, since all their enemies and adversaries have been put down. Brave is its defence, with many and various strong towers and ramparts, with superb gates and entrance archways; and with the royal citadel in its midst, white walled and deeply moated. Well laid out are its streets, squares, cross roads, and market places. Well displayed are the innumerable sorts of costly merchandise with which its shops are filled. It is richly adorned with hundreds of almshalls of various kinds; and splendid with hundreds of thousands of magnificent mansions, which rise aloft like the mountain peaks of the Himâlayas. Its streets are filled with elephants, horses, carriages, and foot-passengers, frequented by groups of handsome men and beautiful women, and crowded by men of all sorts and conditions, Brahmans, nobles, artificers, and servants. They resound with cries of welcome to the teachers of every creed, and the city is the resort of the leading men of each of the differing sects. Shops are there for the sale of Benares muslin, of Kotumbara stuffs and of other cloths of various kinds; and sweet odours are exhaled from the bazaars, where all sorts of flowers and perfumes are tastefully set out. Jewels are there in plenty, such as men's hearts desire, and guilds of traders in all sorts of finery display their goods in the bazaars that face all quarters of the sky. So full is the city of money, and of gold and silver ware, of copper and stone ware, that it is a very mine of dazzling treasures. And there is laid up there much store of property and corn and things of value in warehouses—foods and drinks of every sort, syrups and sweetmeats of every kind. In wealth it rivals Uttara-kuru, and in glory it is as Âlakamandâ, the city of the gods.

→ *The city Sâgala is in the country of the Yonakas, that of the Greeks. Judging from the references to elephants, horses, and the Himalayas, where approximately would it have been located?*

→ *What kinds of people lived there?*

→ *Why do you suppose Buddhist ideas found easy acceptance there?*

SOURCE: *The Questions of King Milinda,* translated by T. W. Rhys Davis (1890; reprint, Delhi: Motilal Banarsidass, 1975), 2–3.

long-distance ocean traders and travelers. In fact, all land and sea roads seemed to lead to India. During this era the region became a melting pot of ideas and institutions, from which a powerful spiritual synthesis emerged. Indeed, the combined influences of Hellenism, nomadism, and Arab seafaring culture profoundly transformed Buddhism.

As a result, Buddhism changed dramatically from the early days when the Buddha walked from city to city preaching to his community of followers (*sangha*) and general audiences. Under the Kushans, whom we noted earlier as energetic patrons of many religions, the Buddhist *sangha* grew so rich through India's commercial prosperity that monks began to live in elegant monastic complexes. The center of each was a stupa decorated with sculptures depicting the Buddha's life and teachings. Such monasteries provided generously for the monks, with halls where they gathered and worshipped and rooms where they meditated and slept. During this age, Buddhist monasteries also opened to the public as places for worship.

THE NEW BUDDHISM: THE MAHAYANA SCHOOL

The mixing of new ways—nomadic, Hellenistic, Persian, and Mesopotamian—with traditional Buddhism produced a spectacular spiritual and religious synthesis. A new school of

Stupa Staircase. These risers from the staircase of a large stupa in the Gandhara region display scenes from Buddhist stories. The upper one shows men in nomads' clothing playing music, including the Greek-style lira. On the middle one, men and women in Greek clothing drink and make merry. The people on the lower riser wear little clothing but are as happy as those on the other two panels.

theology, **Mahayana Buddhism**, appeared at this time. For at least a hundred years, Buddhist scholars had debated whether the Buddha was a god or a wise human being. The Mahayana Buddhists resolved this dispute in the first two centuries of the Common Era with a ringing affirmation: the Buddha was, indeed, a deity. Mahayana Buddhism was worldly and accommodating, a spiritual pluralism that positioned Indian believers as a cosmopolitan people—welcoming contacts with peoples from other parts of Afro-Eurasia and laying the spiritual foundations for a region that had become a crossroads of world cultures.

As Buddhism adapted to external impulses, Mahayana Buddhism appealed especially to foreigners and immigrants who traded or settled in India. It made the Buddha as a god

easier to understand. Hitherto, the Buddha's preaching had stressed life's suffering and the renunciation of desire to end suffering and achieve nirvana. This was a tough road to a better life. As we saw in Chapter 5, those who did not believe in reincarnation found it difficult to understand the appeal of nirvana. Newcomers such as migrants or traders were unlikely to embrace the nonexistence it offered; they saw no need to escape painful cycles of birth, growth, death, and rebirth that were so ingrained in the mental worlds of local populations. This sharp dichotomy between a real world of hardship and the Buddha's abstract one of nirvana gave way to a greater variety of conditions in the Mahayana cosmos; the latter appealed to diverse peoples as a way of conceiving, and practicing, the way to a better life. In the Mahayana Buddhists'

→ *In what ways did the transformation of Buddhism represent cultural integration in South Asia?*

Buddhist Cave Temple at Ajanta. Buddhists excavated cave temples along the trade routes between ports on the west coast of India and places inland. Paintings and sculptures from Ajanta became the models of Buddhist art in central Asia and China.

vision, **bodhisattvas** (enlightened demigods who were ready to reach nirvana but delayed doing so in order to help others attain it) prepared "Buddha-lands" and heavens—spiritual halfway points—to welcome deceased devotees not yet ready to release desires and enter nirvana. In this fashion the universe of the afterlife in Mahayana Buddhism was colorful and pleasant, presenting an array of alternatives to the tough real existence of worldly living.

Mahayana ("Great Vehicle") Buddhism would enable all individuals—the poor and powerless as well as the rich and powerful—to move from a life of suffering into a happy existence. Early Buddhism had left suffering devotees with little relief because of the uncertainty of achieving nirvana and the lack of a guide to lead them there, since the Buddha had already moved on to nirvana. The new Buddhist brokers—the bodhisattvas—were effective instruments for helping all classes find their way to heaven. They were the way stations, the escorts. One of these bodhisattvas, Avalokiteshvara, proclaimed his willingness to stay in this world to guide people out of trouble—especially those who traveled in caravans and had the misfortune of running into murderous robbers, or those who had to navigate unwieldy ships through violent storms. As Avalokiteshvara guided and protected the living rather than appease the deceased, lay followers, especially traveling merchants, invoked him constantly and spread the cult along the trade routes.

Just as Buddhism absorbed outside influences, became more appealing, and developed a cadre of spiritual brokers, it also inspired a new genre of literature to portray the Buddha and the bodhisattvas to audiences. This was the advent of Sanskrit Buddhist texts. Many were devoted to conveying the life of the Buddha and his message far and wide, reaching far corners of Asia. Aśvaghosa (80?–150? CE), a great Buddhist thinker and the first known Sanskrit writer, wrote a biography of the Buddha. This work, known as the Buddhacarita, set the Buddha's life story within the commercial urban environment of the Kushan Empire (instead of in the rural Shakya republic in the Himalaya foothills, where he had actually lived). Aśvaghosa said that the Buddha was born as a prince into a life of extreme luxury, becoming aware of human suffering only after experiencing heavenly revelations. To escape his mundane life, the young prince left home in the middle of the night, riding on a white horse. This largely fictive version of the Buddha's life story spread rapidly throughout India and beyond, introducing Buddha and his teachings to many new potential converts.

CULTURAL INTEGRATION

The colorful images of Sanskrit Buddhist texts of the first centuries CE gave rise to a large repertoire of Buddhist sculptural art and drama. On Buddhist stupas and shrines, artisans carved scenes of the Buddha's life, figures of bodhisattvas, and statues of patrons and donors. Buddhist sculptures from the northern Kushan territory, fashioned from gray schist rock, are called Gandharan art; those from the central region of India, created mainly from local red sandstone, are called Mathuran art. Gandharan Buddhist art shows strong Greek and Roman influences, whereas the Mathuran style evolved from the carved idols of folk gods and goddesses.

Despite their stylistic differences, the schools shared themes and cultural elements. Inspired by Hellenistic art and religious tradition, both took the bold step of sculpting the Buddha and bodhisattvas in realistic human, rather than symbolic, form (such as a bodhi tree, which symbolizes Buddha's enlightenment). Though the Buddha wore no decorations because he had cut off all links to the world, bodhisattvas were dressed as princes because they were still in this world, generously helping others. What was important was bringing the symbolic world of Buddhism closer to the people.

Buddhist art depicted a society of diverse populations, reflecting a spiritual system that appealed to people of diverse

Buddhas. The bronze Buddha on the left often strikes viewers as a Jesus Christ. Greco-Roman influence on the iconography of Buddha was probably responsible for the Gandharan-style attire and facial expression of Buddhas and bodhisattvas. The Mathuran Buddha of Gupta times (*right*) is more refined than the Buddhas of the Kushan era. The robe is so transparent that the artist must have had very fine silk in mind when sculpturing.

cultural backgrounds. Consider the clothes of the patron figures. For male and female figures alike, the garments were simple and well adapted to tropical climates. Those indigenous to the semitropical land had nude upper bodies and, covering their lower bodies, a wrapping akin to the modern *dhoti*, or loincloth. Jewelry adorned their headdresses and bodies. By contrast, the nomadic patron figures wore traditional cone-shaped leather hats, knee-length robes, trousers, and boots. Figures with Greek clothing demonstrate continuing Hellenistic influence, and those wearing Roman togas reveal imperial Rome's influence. The jumble of clothing styles illustrates that Buddhist devotees could share a faith while retaining their ethnic or regional differences.

The many peoples who lived under Kushan rule had important cultural traits in common. They preferred Hellenistic or pseudo-Hellenistic architecture, particularly favoring columns, and they reveled in Greek music and dance. We can recognize many of their musical instruments: the lira (a small version of the harp), the flute, the cymbal, the drum, the xylophone. In their carvings, grape and grape-leaf motifs celebrated wine's intoxicating pleasures; in fact, those found near Buddhist shrines often highlighted festive drinking scenes. The story of the Buddha also celebrated the horse, an important

nomadic cultural symbol. Under the Kushans, Buddhist monasteries were cosmopolitan organizations where Greco-Roman, Indic, and steppe nomadic cultural themes blended together. These organizations also welcomed traders converging on India over mountain passes or from the Indian Ocean, bringing incense and jewels to decorate bodhisattvas and stupas.

THE FORMATION OF THE SILK ROAD

> → *How did long-distance exchanges affect the cultural geography of Afro-Eurasia?*

In the first century BCE, trade routes stretching from China to central Asia and westward had merged into one route. It became famously known as the Silk Road. Though caravans transported many commodities, it was silk that exemplified the commercial integration of the Afro-Eurasian world. Traders traveled segments of the route, passing their goods on to others who took them farther along the road and, in turn, passed them on. The Silk Road owed much to earlier overland routes through which merchants had exchanged frankincense and myrrh from the Arabian Peninsula for copper, tin, iron, gemstones, and textiles. (See Map 6-3.)

The expansion of commerce between the Mediterranean and South Asia reinforced a frenetic rise in commercial activity within each region. Over land and across the seas, traders loaded textiles, spices, and precious metals onto the backs of camels and into the holds of oceangoing vessels destined for distant markets. Trade thereby strengthened the political, intellectual, and spiritual shift: other areas that had once been on the fringes of the Southwest Asian heartlands were becoming heartlands in their own right.

A NEW MIDDLE GROUND

The effects of long-distance exchanges altered the political geography of Afro-Eurasia. Egypt and Mesopotamia faded as sources of innovation and knowledge, becoming instead a crossroads for peoples on either side. The former borderlanders emerged as new imperial centers. What we now call the Middle East literally became a commercial middle ground between centers of culture and political expansion of the Mediterranean in the west and India in the east.

East Asia, principally China, finally connected with the Mediterranean via central Asia and South Asia. Through China, a connection then developed with Japan, Korea, and Southeast Asia, whose traders penetrated Bali and other Indonesian islands. However, China remained politically and culturally a mysterious land to those from the Mediterranean. Although Alexander had marched as far as the Indus Valley, the Himalayas and Pamir Mountains kept the Chinese insulated. Products made of silk (a word derived from *Sēres,* the Greek and Roman name for the people of northwestern China) revealed to the Greeks and Romans that an advanced society lay far to the east, though the Greeks and Romans knew little more about it.

NOMADS, FRONTIERS, AND TRADE ROUTES

Without the activities of the horse-riding nomads from Inner Afro-Eurasia, long-distance trade would never have reached the heights that it attained. Accustomed in the course of their migrations to carry their own vital supplies, nomads gradually learned to trade goods from one region for goods produced elsewhere. They were the pioneers of a slow but powerful commercial transformation of Afro-Eurasia. In the second millennium BCE their arid homelands became deserts, so they sent out conquering armies that eventually traversed entire regions and facilitated trade and interactions between distant communities (see Chapter 3).

One other advantage proved crucial to the nomads' interactions with other populations: because of their movements from place to place, they were exposed to—and acquired resistance to—a greater variety of microbes than settled peoples did. Their relative immunity to disease aided the launch of early overland trade routes in the middle of the second millennium BCE. This was the time when chariots appeared in central Asia and pastoral groups began to link the North China plain to Turkestan (Xinjiang), Mongolia, and Manchuria. Around 600 BCE, horse-riding nomads on the steppe became skillful archers on horseback, whose advantages in fighting emboldened them to range farther from their homelands. These long-distance marauders eventually learned the skills of mediating between cultures, blending terror and traffic to bring diverse Afro-Eurasian worlds together.

Even more important were the ways in which nomads raced into political vacuums and installed new regimes that would link northwest China and the Iranian plateau. At first, the most important of these nomadic peoples were the Xiongnu (Hsiung-nu) pastoralists, originally from the eastern part of the Asian steppe in modern Mongolia. By the third century BCE their mastery of bronze technology made them the most powerful nomadic community in the area.

In time as the power of the Xiongnu waned, a new, more powerful empire, that of the now familiar Kushans, arose in their place. Though they too were fearsome warriors, the Kushans were key players in keeping the Silk Road open to merchants. Indeed, the nomadic groups of central Asia were vital to creating, maintaining, and enhancing the land bridge that joined parts of Afro-Eurasia. Both the land routes linking the Roman trading depot of Palmyra to central Asia and the sea routes carrying ships from the Red Sea to ports on the western coast of India had to pass through the territory of the Kushan Empire. At the eastern end of this chain of political and commercial contacts, the Chinese state was also beginning to protect outposts and frontiers, enabling caravans to move more easily. Chinese silk textiles were reaching the Roman market, and glassware from the Mediterranean, incense from the Arabian Peninsula, and gemstones from India were reaching China. The Silk Road now connected the Mediterranean and Pacific coasts.

EARLY OVERLAND TRADE AND CARAVAN CITIES

As nomads moved southward, here too they created new trade routes, in this case a new set of networks, parallel to and south and west of the original systems that penetrated the valleys and crossed the mountain passes into South Asia.

This enormous surge in trade produced a new kind of commercial hub: the **caravan city**. Established at strategic locations (often at the edges of deserts or in oases) these cities became locations where vast trading groups assembled

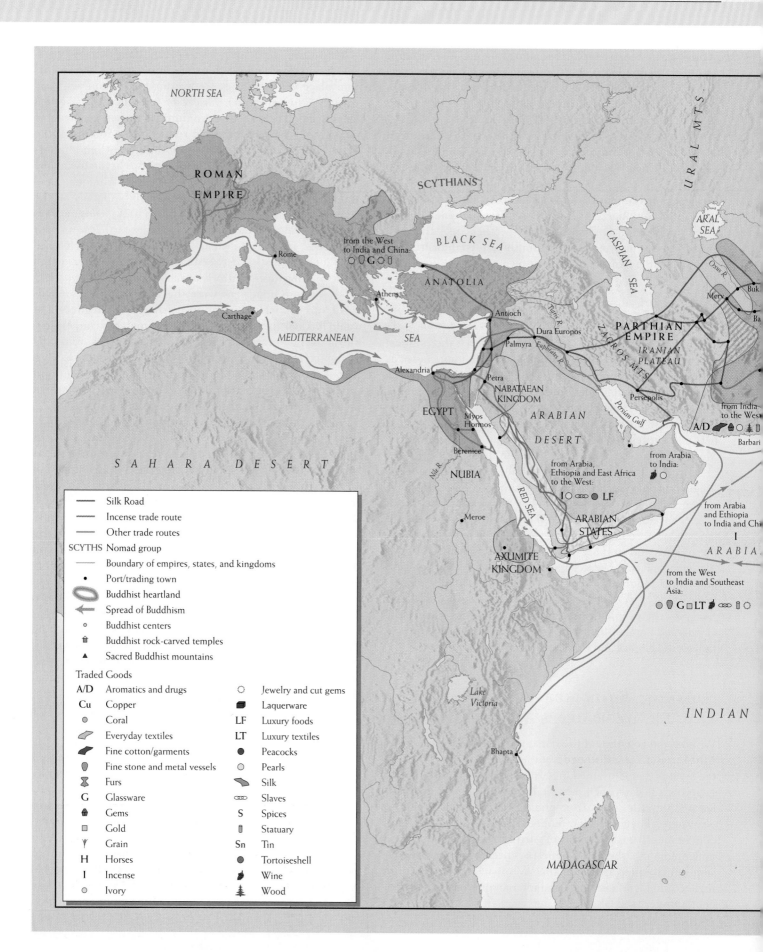

NORTH SEA

ROMAN
EMPIRE

SCYTHIANS

BLACK SEA

URAL MTS.

ARAL
SEA

CASPIAN
SEA

Oxus R.

from the West
to India and China:

ANATOLIA

Merv

Bük

Ba

Rome

Athens

Antioch

Dura Europos

PARTHIAN
EMPIRE

ZAGROS MTS.

IRANIAN
PLATEAU

Tigris R.

Palmyra

Euphrates R.

Carthage

MEDITERRANEAN   SEA

Alexandria

Petra

NABATAEAN
KINGDOM

Persepolis

Persian Gulf

from India
to the West:

A/D

Barbari

EGYPT

Myos
Hormos

ARABIAN

DESERT

from Arabia
to India:

SAHARA   DESERT

Berenice

Nile R.

NUBIA

RED SEA

from Arabia,
Ethiopia and East Africa
to the West:

I ⊙ ⊂⊃ ● LF

from Arabia
and Ethiopia
to India and Ch

A R A B I A

Meroe

ARABIAN
STATES

AXUMITE
KINGDOM

from the West
to India and Southeast
Asia:

⬤ ⬤ G □ LT 🍷 ⊂⊃ 🏺 ⬤

I

Lake
Victoria

INDIAN

Bhapta

MADAGASCAR

Legend

—— Silk Road
—— Incense trade route
—— Other trade routes
SCYTHS Nomad group
—— Boundary of empires, states, and kingdoms
• Port/trading town
⬭ Buddhist heartland
⬅ Spread of Buddhism
∘ Buddhist centers
🛕 Buddhist rock-carved temples
▲ Sacred Buddhist mountains

Traded Goods

A/D	Aromatics and drugs	⊙	Jewelry and cut gems
Cu	Copper	▰	Laquerware
●	Coral	LF	Luxury foods
⬎	Everyday textiles	LT	Luxury textiles
⬏	Fine cotton/garments	●	Peacocks
⬙	Fine stone and metal vessels	∘	Pearls
⧓	Furs	⬎	Silk
G	Glassware	⊂⊃	Slaves
✿	Gems	S	Spices
□	Gold	🏺	Statuary
Y	Grain	Sn	Tin
H	Horses	●	Tortoiseshell
I	Incense	🍷	Wine
∘	Ivory	🌲	Wood

→ *How did long-distance exchanges affect the cultural geography of Afro-Eurasia?*

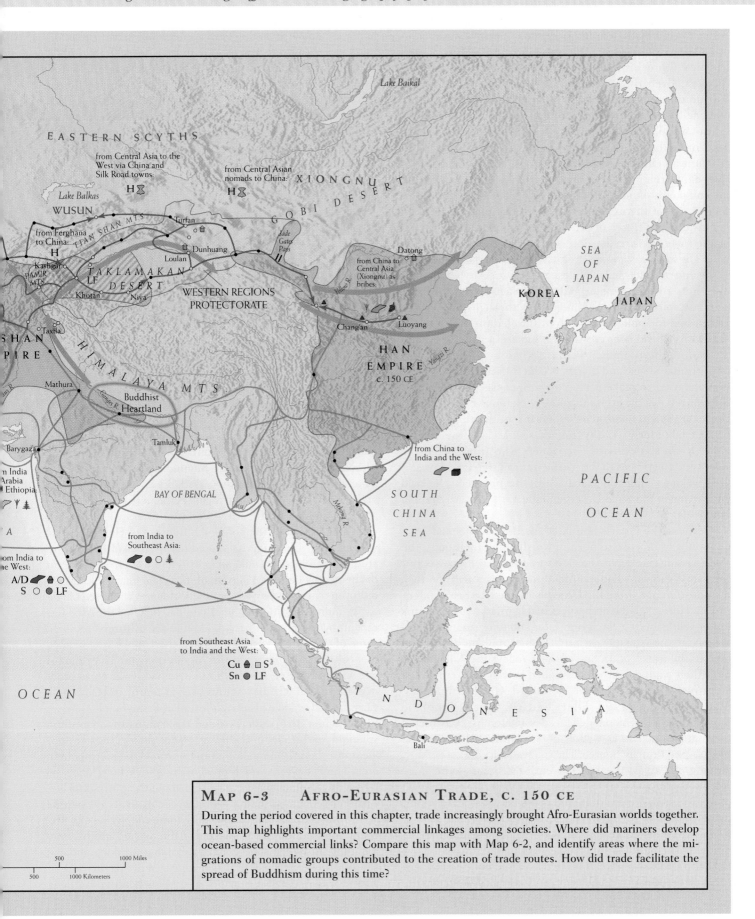

MAP 6-3   AFRO-EURASIAN TRADE, C. 150 CE

During the period covered in this chapter, trade increasingly brought Afro-Eurasian worlds together. This map highlights important commercial linkages among societies. Where did mariners develop ocean-based commercial links? Compare this map with Map 6-2, and identify areas where the migrations of nomadic groups contributed to the creation of trade routes. How did trade facilitate the spread of Buddhism during this time?

before beginning their arduous journeys. Some caravan cities originating as Greek garrison towns became centers of Hellenistic culture, displaying such staples of the polis as public theaters. Even those founded by Arab traders had a Hellenistic tinge, as local traders often admired Greek culture and had frequent commercial interactions with the Mediterranean world. They wrote in Greek, sometimes speaking it in addition to their native tongues.

Caravan cities were among the most spectacular and resplendent urban centers of this era. They often emerged at the end points of major trade arteries. One such end point for traders was at the extreme southwestern tip of the Arabian Peninsula, in the area of present-day Yemen, a land watered by the same rains responsible for the annual flooding of the Nile. The area was a wonder of its own, a vivid patch of green at the end of 1,200 miles of desert. Its prosperity was in part due to its role as a major gathering place—both for long-distance spice traders heading north through the Arabian Desert and for sailors whose ships traveled the Red and the Arabian seas and later crossed the Indian Ocean.

The southern Arabian Peninsula had long been famous for its frankincense and myrrh, products that the Greeks and Romans used to make perfume and incense. They reached their buyers via an overland route sometimes called the Incense or Spice Road. The Sabaeans of southern Arabia became fabulously wealthy from these sales and from the Indian Ocean spice trade. The traders who transported the spices and fragrances to the Mediterranean were another Arabic-speaking people: the Nabataeans, sheepherders who eked out a living in the Sinai Desert and the northwestern Arabian Peninsula.

Because the Greeks and later the Romans needed large quantities of incense to burn in worshipping their gods, the trade passing through this region was extremely lucrative. But the camel caravans had a difficult journey through the rock ravines stretching from the Dead Sea to the Red Sea's Gulf of Aqaba. Here, Nabataean herders had learned to cut cisterns out of solid stone to catch rainwater and to create cave shelters. Now the Nabataeans profited by supplying water and food to the travelers. In one of these valleys the Nabataeans built their capital—a rock city called Petra ("rock" in Greek is *petros*)—which displayed abundant Greek influences. Many of the houses and shrines were cut directly out of the mountains. Their colonnaded facades and tombs, constructed for common people as well as nobles, projected Hellenistic motifs. (See Primary Source: The Caravan City of Petra.) Most striking was a vast theater. The entire structure—the stage platform, orchestra, and forty-five rows of seats—was carved out of the sandstone terrain and could accommodate an audience of 6,000 to 10,000 people. Actors performed plays at first in Greek and later in Latin, for being cosmopolitan required participating in the language of high culture.

Petra's power and wealth lasted from the mid-second century BCE to the early second century CE. Greek persisted as the common language among Petran merchants seeking to maintain their trading ties. The caravan traders, the ruling elite of the rock city, controlled the supply of spices and fragrances from Arabia, North Africa, and India to the ever-expanding Roman Empire. During these years, Nabataean traders based in Petra traveled throughout the eastern Mediterranean, erecting temples wherever they established trading communities. Yet the glory of this commercial people dimmed with the coming of the Romans, who took over the province of Arabia—and with it, the profitable Spice Road trade.

THE WESTERN END OF THE SILK ROAD: PALMYRA

As trading hubs proliferated in central Asia, similar commercial cities thrived in Southwest Asia as well. They soon overshadowed the older political or religious capitals. With Petra's decline during the Roman period, another settlement became the most important caravan city at the western end of the Silk Road: Palmyra. Rich citizens of Rome relied on the Palmyran traders to procure luxury goods for them, importing Chinese silks for women's clothing and incense for religious rituals, as well as gemstones, pearls, and many other precious items.

Administered by the chiefs of local tribes, Palmyra had considerable autonomy even under formal Roman control. Although the Palmyrans used a Semitic dialect in daily life, for state affairs and business they used Greek. Their merchants had learned Greek when the region came under Seleucid rule, and it remained useful when doing business with caravans from afar, long after the political influences of Hellenism had waned. Palmyran traders handled many kinds of textiles, including cotton from India and cashmere wool from Kashmir or the nearby central Asian highlands. The many silk textiles discovered at this site were products of Han China (see Chapter 7), indicating that the Silk Road had reached the Mediterranean by the first century CE. While the oligarchs retained some of the exquisite silks for themselves, most were headed to wealthier consumers in the Mediterranean. The Romans not only purchased silk cloth but also had it woven to order in eastern Mediterranean cities such as Beirut and Gaza. Silk yarns and dyes have also been found at Palmyra.

This lucrative trade enabled the Palmyrans to build a splendid marble city in the desert. A colonnade, theater, senate house, agora, and major temples formed the metropolitan area. The Palmyrans worshipped many deities, both local and Greek, but seemed most concerned about their own afterlife. Like Petra, Palmyra had a cemetery as big as its residential area, with marble sculptures on the tombs depicting city life. Many tombs showed the master or the master and his wife reclining on Greek-style couches, holding drinking goblets. The clothes on those statues appear more Iranian than Greek: robes with wide stripes and hems bearing exquisite

Primary Source

THE CARAVAN CITY OF PETRA

Petra was a city cut out of the pink rock cliffs in the valley between the Dead Sea and the Red Sea. The Nabataeans built the city to host traders from west and east; from here, caravans headed out to trading centers in the Mediterranean and on the Iranian plateau. Petra's good fortune ran out under the Roman Empire when the silk trade favored another caravan city, Palmyra. Yet even today the rock structure of the city shining in the sun is an imposing sight, as this account by a modern traveler makes vividly clear.

When one descends into the valley from the surrounding heights towards the place where the river has cut for itself a passage between the dark-red rocks, one seems to be gazing at some large and fantastic excrescence—a piece of reddish-mauve raw flesh set between the gold of the desert and the green of the hills. It is a most extraordinary sight, which becomes even more extraordinary when the cavalcade slowly descends into the river valley, and the rocky walls of the ever-narrowing gorge tower up to the right and left, speckled with red, orange, mauve, grey, and green layers. Wild and beautiful they are, with their contrasts of light and shade; the light blinding, the shadows black. And there is seldom even anything to remind the visitor that this gorge served for centuries as a main road, trodden by camels, mules, and horses, and that along it rode Bedouin merchants who must have felt like ourselves its horror and its mystic fascination. Yet suddenly one may be confronted with the façade of a tomb-tower with dog-tooth design, or with an altar set high up on one of the vertical walls, bearing a greeting or prayer to some god, inscribed in the Nabataean tongue. Our caravan advanced slowly along the gorge, until an unexpected bend disclosed to us an apparition sparkling pinky-orange in the sun, which must once have been the front of a temple or tomb. Elegant columns joined by fascinating pediments and arches form the frames of the niches in which its statues stand. All this rose up before us dressed in a garb of classicism yet in a style new and unexpected even by those well acquainted with antiquity. It was as though the magnificent scenery of some Hellenistic theatre had appeared, . . . chiselled in the rock.

Petra. This beautiful building is known as El-Khaznah, or The Treasury, at Petra. The wealth created by the region's long-distance trade is manifest in the magnificent buildings at the center of the city. Both the face of the building and its interior are cut out of the sandstone rock that forms the cliffs surrounding Petra.

→ *What features in the description of Petra and the monuments in and around the city suggest that it hosted a variety of cultures with different art forms?*

→ *Imagine being part of a caravan arriving in bustling Petra via the route described here. What feelings would the atmosphere evoke in you?*

SOURCE: M. Rostovtzeff, *Caravan Cities* (Oxford: Clarendon Press, 1932), 42–43.

Palmyran Tomb Sculpture. This tombstone relief sculpture shows a wealthy young Palmyran, attended by a servant—probably a household slave. Palmyra was at the crossroads of the major cultural influences traversing Southwest Asia at the time. The style of the clothing—the flowing pants and top—and the couch and pillows reflect the trading contacts of the Palmyran elite, in this case with India to the east. The hairstyle and mode of self-presentation signal influences from the Mediterranean to the west.

designs. Sculptures of camel caravans and horses tell us that the deceased were caravan traders in this world who anticipated continuing their rewarding occupation in the afterlife.

Palmyra rapidly became a commercial powerhouse. The city not only provided supplies and financial services to passing caravans but also hosted self-contained trading communities—complexes of hostels, storage houses, offices, and temples. Palmyra achieved its golden age at the same time that the Silk Road was the major route for silk and other luxuries traveling from China to the eastern rim of the Indian Ocean. Some of the goods went across the Iranian plateau, reaching the Mediterranean via Syria's desert routes. Another artery went through Afghanistan, the Indus, and the west coast of India, then across the Indian Ocean to the Red Sea. Aiding the success of the Silk Road was the shared Hellenistic culture, which lingered for centuries after Greek political power had vanished from this region.

REACHING CHINA ALONG THE SILK ROAD

China was the ultimate end point and beginning point of the Silk Road. Its flourishing economy owed much to the fact that Chinese silks were the most sought-after commodity in long-distance trade. As thousands of precious bales made their way to Indian, central Asian, and Mediterranean markets, silk became the ultimate prestige commodity of the re-

gions' ruling classes. But the exchange between eastern and western portions of the Silk Road was increasingly mediated by Persian, Xiongnu, and other middlemen at the great oases and trading centers that grew up in central Asia. Local communities took profitable advantage of the silk trade from China based on their increased knowledge and contacts.

THE SILK ECONOMY Not only was silk China's most valuable export, but it also served as a tool in diplomacy with the nomadic kingdoms on China's western frontiers and in underwriting the Chinese armies. The country's rulers used silk to pay off neighboring nomads and borderlanders, buying both horses and peaceful borders with the fabric. During the Zhou dynasty, it served as a precious medium of exchange and trade.

Silk has always been prized as a material for clothing; as a filament made by spinning the protein fibers extracted from the cocoons of silkworms, it is smooth yet strong. Whereas cloth spun from hemp, flax, and other fibers tends to be rough, silk looks and feels rich. Moreover, it is cool against the skin in hot summers and warm in the winter. Silk also has immense tensile strength, being useful for bows, lute strings, and fishing lines. Artisans even spun it into a tight fabric to make light body armor or light bags for transporting liquids (particularly useful for traders crossing arid expanses). Before the Chinese invented paper, silk was a popular writing material that was more durable than bamboo or wood. Brush writing on silk was the medium of choice for correspondence, maps, and illustrations and important texts written on silk often joined other funerary objects in the tombs of aristocratic lords and wealthy individuals.

Whereas economic life in ancient China had centered on the agricultural manors of powerful landowners, after 300 BCE independent farmers increasingly produced commercial crops for the marketplaces along land routes as well as rivers, canals, and lakes. As the market economy grew, merchants organized themselves into influential family lineages and occupational guilds. Now power shifted away from agrarian elites and into the hands of urban financiers and traders. The latter benefited from the improvement in roads and waterways, which eased the transportation of grain, hides, horses, and silk from the villages to the new towns and cities. By the second century BCE, wealthy merchants such as the Fan family were ennobled as local magnates and wore the clothing that marked their official status. Bronze coins of various sizes and shapes (such as the spade-shaped money of several semi-autonomous Warring States; see photo in Chapter 5), as well as cloth and silk used in barter, also spurred long-distance trade. As commerce expanded, regional lords opened local customs offices along land routes and waterways to extract a share of the money and products for themselves.

THE ROLE OF THE STATE Facilitating trade was also a key concern of the state. For example, merchant ships now enjoyed the protection of military boats, able to cover seventy-five miles in a day and carry fifty soldiers and supplies for a three-month voyage. Though China still had little intellectual interaction with the rest of Afro-Eurasia, its commercial exchanges skyrocketed. Southern silk was only the first of many Chinese commodities that reached the world beyond the Taklamakan Desert. China also became an export center for lacquer, hemp, and linen. From Sichuan came iron, steel, flint, hard stone, silver, and animals, while jade came from the northwest. At the same time, China was importing Mediterranean, Indian, and central Asian commodities.

Despite its early development of commerce, China still had no major ports that could compare to the oasis hub of Palmyra. Internal, interregional trade predominated, and it fed into the Silk Road through decentralized networks. Most cities in the landlocked north were administrative centers where farmers and traders gathered under the regional states' political and military protection. The larger cities had gates that closed between sunset and sunrise; during the night, mounted soldiers patrolled the streets. Newer towns along the southeastern seacoast still looked upriver to trade with inland agrarian communities, which also produced silk for export. Later, during the sixth and seventh centuries, China would become the site of massive trading centers.

The Chinese people and the Chinese state remained little affected by Hellenism and Mahayana Buddhism, which were so important elsewhere during this period. China went about dealing with its own crises, laying the foundations for the magnificent Han Empire (see Chapter 7).

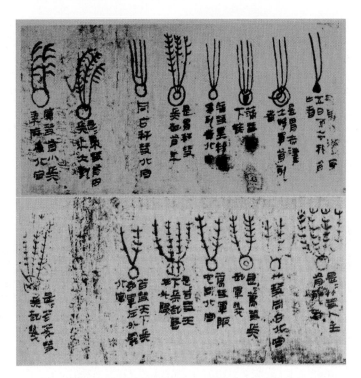

Silk Texts. Before the invention of paper, silk was widely used as writing material because it was more mobile and durable than bamboo or wood for correspondence, maps, illustrations, and important texts included as funerary objects in the tombs of aristocrats. The Mawangdui silk texts shown here are from a Hunan tomb that was closed in 168 BCE and opened in 1973.

THE SPREAD OF BUDDHISM ALONG THE TRADE ROUTES

Silk traders were not the only individuals who traversed Afro-Eurasian trade arteries. Monks also plied these roads to spread the word of new religions. The chief expansionist faith in this period came out of India, inspired in part by the successful spread of Hellenism. The Buddha was no longer just a sage departed to the state of nirvana; he was also a god whom people could worship like any Greek deity.

Under Kushan patronage during the first centuries CE, Buddhism reached out from India to China and central Asia, following the Silk Road. Monks from the Kushan Empire accompanied traders to Luoyang, the eastern capital of the Han Empire. There they translated Buddhist texts into Chinese, aided by Chinese converts who were also traders. Buddhist ideas were slow to gain acceptance, however. It took several centuries, and a new wave of nomadic migrations, for Buddhism to take root in China.

Buddhism fared less well when it followed the commercial arteries westward. Although Buddhists did gain some followers in the Parthian Empire, the religion never became established on the Iranian plateau and made no further headway toward the Mediterranean. The main barrier was

Zoroastrianism, which had been a state religion in the Persian Empire during the fifth and fourth centuries BCE (see Chapter 4); by the time Buddhism began to spread, Zoroastrianism had long been established in Iran. Iranian Hellenism had done little to weaken the power of Zoroastrianism, whose adherents formed city-based religious communities affiliated primarily with traders. Following the Silk Road, Zoroastrian traders traveled both eastward to China and westward to the coast of the Mediterranean, impeding the westward spread of Buddhism.

TAKING TO THE SEAS: COMMERCE ON THE RED SEA AND INDIAN OCEAN

> ⇥ *What factors promoted sea trade on the Indian Ocean?*

Although land routes were the tried-and-true avenues for migrants, traders, and wayfarers, they carried only what could be borne on the backs of humans and animals. Travel on them was slow, and they were vulnerable to marauders. With time, some risk takers found ways of traversing waterways—eventually on an unprecedented scale and with an ease unimaginable to earlier merchants. These risk takers were Arabs, from the commercial middle ground of the Afro-Eurasian trading system.

Arab traders had long carried such spices as frankincense and myrrh to the Egyptians, who used them in religious and funerary rites, and later to the Greeks and Romans. Metals such as bronze, tin, and iron passed along overland routes from Anatolia, as did gold, silver, and chlorite from the Iranian plateau. Gold, ivory, and other goods from the northern part of India passed through Taxila (the capital of Gandhara) and the Hindu Kush Mountains into Persia as early as the sixth century BCE. Following the expansion of the Hellenistic world, however, ships increasingly conducted long-distance trade. They sailed down the Red Sea and across the Indian Ocean as they carried goods between the tip of the Arabian Peninsula and the ports of the Indian landmass.

Arab seafarers led the way into the Indian Ocean, forging links that joined East Africa, the eastern Mediterranean, and the Arabian Peninsula with India, Southeast Asia, and East Asia. Such voyages involved longer stays at sea and were far more dangerous than sailing in the Mediterranean. Yet by the first century CE, Arab and Indian sailors were transporting Chinese silks, central Asian furs, and fragrances from Himalayan trees across the Indian Ocean. The city of Alexandria in Egypt soon emerged as a key transit point between the Mediterranean Sea and the Indian Ocean. Boats carried Mediterranean exports of olives and olive oil, wine, drinking vessels, glassware, linen and wool textiles, and red coral up

the Nile, stopping at Koptos and other port cities from which camel caravans took the goods to the Red Sea ports of Myos Hormos and Berenice. For centuries, Mediterranean merchants had considered the Arabian Peninsula to be the end of the Spice Road. But after Alexander's expedition and the establishment of colonies between Egypt and Afghanistan, they began to value the wealth and opportunities that lay along the shores of the Indian Ocean.

Arab sailors who ventured into the Indian Ocean benefited from new navigational techniques, especially celestial bearings (using the position of the stars to determine the position of the ship and the direction to sail). They used large ships called *dhows,* whose sails were rigged to easily capture the wind; these forerunners of modern cargo vessels were capable of long hauls in rough waters. Beginning about 120 BCE, mariners came to understand the seasonal rain-filled monsoon winds, which blow from the southwest between October and April and then from the northeast between April and October—knowledge that propelled the maritime trade connecting the Mediterranean with the Indian Ocean.

Mariners accumulated the new sailing knowledge in books—each called a **periplus** ("sailing around")—in which sea captains recorded the landing spots and ports between their destinations, as well as their precious cargoes. (See Global Connections & Disconnections: The Worlds of *Periplus.*) From such books, for example, we learn that trading ships left the southern Arabian coast with the monsoon winds behind them, heading for the entrepôts (trading centers) of India. Barbaricum, at the mouth of the Indus, was the first Indian port reached from the west. On their arrival, traders unloaded linen textiles, red coral, glassware, wine, and money from the Mediterranean and Egypt, as well as frankincense and storax, aromatic gum resins from Southwest Asia. These cargoes were headed to the upper Indus region of the Punjab and Gandhara. While at harbor in India, traders loaded their ships with treasures from the east: fragrances or spices from the Himalayas and India, such as costus root and bdellium, turquoise from Khorasan in Iran, lapis lazuli from Badakhshan in Afghanistan, indigo dye and cotton textiles from India, furs from central Asia, and silk textiles and yarn from China.

By now, the revolution in navigational techniques and knowledge had dramatically reduced the cost of long-distance shipping and multiplied the ports of call around large bodies of water. Some historians have argued that there were now two Silk Roads: one by land and one by sea.

 **CONCLUSION**

Alexander's conquests were awesome in their scale and brilliant in their execution. But his empire was as transitory as it was huge. Though it crumbled upon his death, this empire

THE WORLDS OF *PERIPLUS*

Periplus Maris Erythraei, or *Periplus of the Red Sea*, was written in Greek by an Egyptian sailor and trader late in the first century CE. Its author, a shrewd businessman, keen observer, and experienced navigator, described the whole world of commerce of the Red Sea, the Mediterranean, and the Indian Ocean. He catalogued the navigable routes and listed the goods that were marketed in the ports; starting from the Red Sea, he moved southward along East Africa's coast and then eastward all the way to India. The result is the first historical record of the city-states existing along the coast of East Africa and one of the earliest accounts of Africa south of the Sahara. Throughout, he supplied data on currencies, customs, and the political regimes that controlled the ports and radiated into their hinterlands.

The author's voyage began from Berenice. After leaving this Red Sea port, he encountered tribal countries on the coastal lands of today's Sudan and Eritrea. The *Periplus* named the region Barbaria, the land of barbarians, and identified its inhabitants with such labels as "eaters of fish" and "eaters of wild animals." Farther south, the author noted the coastal area of a former Ptolemaic Egyptian colony that had fallen into decline and now exported only tortoise shells and ivory. On the other side of the Red Sea lay the coast of Arabia, where the waters were so calm that ships did not need to be anchored but where pirates from the Nabataean tribes preyed on them.

Once it sailed out of the narrow strait, the ship entered the Gulf of Aden, famed as the land of frankincense and myrrh. Beyond the territory from which incense was exported, traders brought ivory, tortoise shells, and slaves to the markets. The Somali ports received goods from India such as rice and ghee (clarified butter), sesame oil, cotton textiles, and sugar. The southernmost port along the east coast of Africa known to the author was Bhapta, nearly 3,000 miles from Berenice. This region had fallen under the influence of Arabs through intermarriage and trade.

Next the ship headed back up along the East African coast and proceeded across the Arabian Sea toward India. The most important Indian port at the time was Barygaza on the Gulf of Khambhat (Cambay), near the modern city of Broach in Gujarat, but its harbor was very difficult to navigate. The coast was rugged, the sea bottom was uneven, and the tidal waves were high and variable. Local fishermen under the king's service came out to guide foreign ships to the harbor. In fact, the entire northwestern and western parts of India were connected to the Mediterranean through Barygaza. Here the author focused on the abundance of Greek influences. For example, he noted that in the market of Barygaza old drachmas (coins) of the Indo-Greek kings Apollodotus and Menander, inscribed with Greek letters, were still circulating. Although he often garbled the names of places and people, his general point was clear: Greek culture played a critical role in the long-distance trade of India.

Map from a *Periplus*

had effects more profound than those of any military or political regime that preceded it. Alexander's armies ushered in an age of thinking and practices that transformed Greek achievements into a common culture—Hellenism—whose influences, both direct and indirect, touched far-flung societies for centuries thereafter.

This Hellenistic movement was most strongly represented by a common, simpler Greek language, which linked culture, institutions, and trade. However, many Greek-speaking peoples and their descendants in parts of Southwest and central Asia integrated local cultural practices with their own ways, creating diverse and rich cultures. Thus the influences of culture flowed both ways. The economic story is equally complex. In many respects, Alexander and his successors followed pathways established by previous kingdoms and empires. If anything, Alexander's successors helped strengthen and expand the existing trade routes and centers of commercial activity, which ultimately led to the creation of the Silk Road.

Although the effects of this Hellenistic age lasted longer than most cultural systems and had a wider appeal than previous philosophical and spiritual ideas, they did not sweep away everything before it. Indigenous cultures accommodated to this movement or fought against it with all their might, fearing the loss of their own cultural identities. Others took from it what they liked and discarded the rest. The citizens of Rome admired its achievements and steeped themselves in it while fashioning their own Latin-based culture. Eventually, they created an imperial polity that outdistanced Alexander's. In North Africa, the commercially talented Carthaginians saw some of these Greek means of expression as useful for new elites like themselves.

Of all those exposed to Hellenistic thinking, the South Asian peoples produced the most varied responses because they represented a multitude of cultures. Once opened to the influences of Macedonian invaders, steppe nomads, and Arab seafarers, South Asia became the confluence of the currents moving swiftly across Afro-Eurasia. The most telling responses were in the realm of spiritual and ethical norms, where Buddhist doctrines evolved toward a full-fledged world religious system.

Greater political integration helped fashion highways for commerce and enabled the spread of Buddhism. Nomads left their steppe lands and exchanged wares across great distances. As they found greater opportunities for business, their trade routes shifted farther south, radiating out of the oases of central Asia. Eventually merchants, rather than the trading nomads, seized the opportunities provided by new technologies, especially in sailing and navigation. These commercial transformations connected distant parts of Afro-Eurasia. Accompanying the spread of Greek ways was the opening of trade. Alexander's campaigns had followed some of the trade routes east, and his conquests opened up permanent channels of exchange. In the wake of conquests, the Silk Road and proliferating sea-lanes connected ports and caravan cities from North Africa to South China, creating new social classes, producing new urban settings, supported powerful new polities, and transported Buddhism to China, where it would ultimately proliferate on an even grander, more lasting scale than it did in South Asia.

Chronology

	400 BCE	300 BCE	200 BCE
SOUTHWEST ASIA AND NORTHERN AFRICA		◆–––◆ 334–323 BCE Conquests of Alexander the Great ◆ 323 BCE Emergence of Hellenistic "successor kingdoms" begins	◆––––◆ 240 BCE–224 CE Parthian kingdom
THE MEDITERRANEAN		◆ 330s and 320s BCE Roman expansion in the Italian Peninsula begins 264–241 BCE Roman-Carthage war ◆–––––––◆	
CENTRAL ASIA		◆––◆ 334–323 BCE Conquests of Alexander the Great 250–130 BCE Bactrian kingdom ◆-------	
SOUTH ASIA		321–184 BCE Mauryan Empire ◆-------------------------------◆ c. 200 BCE Yavana kings emerge ◆ c. 200 BCE Saka invasions from central Asia ◆	
EAST ASIA	403–221 BCE Warring States period ◆------------------------------◆ 2nd or 3rd century BCE Xiongnu Confederacy in the Mongolian steppes ◆ 221 BCE Unification of China under the Qin dynasty ◆ 206 BCE Emergence of Han Empire ◆		Han expands into the Silk Road

Review and research materials are available at StudySpace: ⊚ WWNORTON.COM/STUDYSPACE

KEY TERMS

Alexander the Great (p. 208)
bodhisattva (p. 227)
caravan city (p. 229)
dhamma (p. 218)
garrison towns (p. 217)

Hellenism (p. 204)
Mahayana Buddhism (p. 226)
periplus (p. 236)
Silk Road (p. 205)
stupa (p. 218)

STUDY QUESTIONS

1. Analyze the impact of Alexander's conquest on the Afro-Eurasian world. How did his military pursuits, and those of his successors, bring together various worlds?
2. Describe the influence of Hellenism on societies outside the Greek homeland. What aspects of Hellenistic culture held broad appeal for diverse groups?
3. Compare and contrast Judean, Roman, and Carthaginian responses to Hellenistic influences. How receptive was each society to Greek cultural influences?
4. Explain how South Asia (or India) became a melting pot for the intellectual, political, and economic currents sweeping across Afro-Eurasia between 350 BCE and 250 CE. How did this development affect Buddhist doctrine?
5. Analyze the extent to which long-distance trade routes connected societies during this period. Which societies were involved? How did commercial linkages affect them?
6. Analyze the influence of nomadic pastoral groups in Afro-Eurasia during this period. What role did they play in integrating cultures and economies?
7. Explain how interregional contacts transformed Buddhism. How did it expand across a variety of cultures?
8. Explain how art, architecture, and other forms of material culture in Afro-Eurasian societies reflected broader patterns of cultural, political, and economic integration during this period. In particular, how did caravan cities reflect new cultural configurations?

---

100 BCE   **1** CE   **100** CE   **200** CE

1st–3rd centuries CE *(established 60* CE*) Kushan kingdom*

◆ *1st century* CE *Transformation of Buddhism begins*

Chapter

7

HAN DYNASTY CHINA AND IMPERIAL ROME, 300 BCE–300 CE

In the third century BCE, the Eastern Zhou state of Qin absorbed the remaining Warring States (see Chapter 5) and set the stage for the epic Han dynasty. The chief minister of the Qin state, Li Si, urged his king to dispense with niceties and to seize opportunities: a man who aimed at great achievements must exploit the advantages offered to him. By combining his fearsome armies and his own personal virtues, the king could sweep away his rivals as if dusting ashes from a kitchen hearth—he could eliminate them all. In this way he could establish a truly imperial rule and unify the entire world. "This is the one moment in ten thousand ages," Li Si whispered. The king listened carefully. He followed the advice. He laid the foundations for a mighty empire.

We saw in Chapter 5 how the Qin state emerged as the dominant "warring state" in Zhou China. The Qin king relied on his massive army to make himself China's First Emperor and to begin a cycle that spun out the first great land-based empire in East Asia. But the Qin Empire collapsed in 207 BCE, and soon the Han

Empire took its place. Following the Qin model, the Han defeated other regional groups and established the first long-lasting Chinese empire. Subjects of Han basked in a society whose landholding elites, free farmers, trained artisans, itinerant traders, and urban merchants were building an era that emulated the statecraft ideals of antiquity—unlike those of the cruel Qin.

At the other end of Afro-Eurasia another great state, imperial Rome, also met its rivals in war, emerged victorious, and consolidated its power into a vast empire. The Romans achieved this feat by using violent force on a scale hitherto unseen in their part of the globe. The result was a state of huge size, astonishingly unified and stable. Living in the Roman Empire in the mid-70s CE, a man of middle rank, Pliny the Elder, could write glowingly about the unity of the imperial state. In his eyes, all the benefits that flowed from its extensive reach derived from the boundless greatness of a peace that joined diverse peoples under one benevolent emperor.

The Han and the Roman states were not just new ways of organizing resources to plow them into large-scale military and administrative functions. They were not just new in the reasons rulers gave for their rulership. They were novel in laying out the political boundaries of regions we now recognize as "China" and "Christendom." Nowadays, the boundaries of both bear remarkable resemblance to those defined by these two empires at their peak. This chapter addresses how these regimes transcended the limits of previous territorial kingdoms by deploying resources and reasons of state in new ways. They concentrated military power in professionalized military elites that owed allegiance above all to the state, not to its ruler. They modernized tax collecting to support large-scale killing machines—that is, armies. They wrote laws and codes for their subjects. And they promoted the idea that the state should support schooling, the arts, architecture, and a learned society as ways to bring peace and prosperity to the realm. In this basic sense, ever since, we have come to associate the ideal of empire with these two founders at either end of Afro-Eurasia.

Just as we see these empires as models for world history, we must understand how they were built—for they did not emerge as the inevitable consequences of destiny. They were crafted of a delicate mixture of coercion, coaxing, and convincing—and not just to prove that empires were exalted and enjoyed benefits that faraway neighbors did not. They actually had to deliver on these promises in order to endure. These were no short lasting conquerings, like Alexander the Great's. They enjoyed the institutional muscle to outlive any particular ruler.

CHINA AND ROME: HOW EMPIRES ARE BUILT

> → *How did the Roman and Han empires differ from earlier large states?*

Afro-Eurasia had seen empires come and go, emerging out of territorial kingdoms to exercise their power over neighboring states as clients, often demanding tribute in return for protection. The Romans and the Han took expansion to the next level: not content to exercise influence over neighbors, they wanted to incorporate them fully into their realm. What distinguished these two from their predecessors was their commitment to integrating conquered neighbors and rivals into the system—by extending laws, offering systems of representation, exporting belief systems, colonizing lands, and promoting trade within and beyond the empires. In effect, subject peoples became members of empires, not just the vanquished. Those who resisted not only waved away the ben-

Focus Questions

Ⓢ WWNORTON.COM/STUDYSPACE

→ *How did the Roman and Han empires differ from earlier large states?*

→ *What policies did the Qin leaders use to integrate their empire?*

→ *How did Han leaders promote peace and stability?*

→ *Were the policies and institutions that integrated the Roman Empire similar to those of Han dynasty China?*

MAIN THEMES

→ *At both ends of Afro-Eurasia two great empires rise, flourish, and fall at roughly the same time.*
→ *Han China and imperial Rome exercise greater power over more people and larger expanses of territory than any previous state.*
→ *The two empires create long-lasting foundations for China and Christendom.*

FOCUS ON *Comparing the Two Empires*

+ Han China and imperial Rome assimilate diverse peoples to their ways and regard outsiders as uncivilized.
+ Both empires develop professional military elites, codify laws, and value the role of the state (not just the ruler) in supporting their societies.

+ Both empires serve as models for successor states in their regions.
+ The empires differ in their ideals and the officials they value: Han China values civilian bureaucrats and magistrates; Rome values soldiers and military governors.

efits of living under an imperial mantle but also became the targets for awesome and relentless armies.

EMPIRE AND CULTURAL IDENTITY

The mere existence of these two vast imperial states meant that at least one out of every two human beings in Afro-Eurasia now fell directly under the control of China or Rome. What did it mean to live under the imperial umbrella of these giants?

To be "Han Chinese" meant that elites shared a common written language based on the Confucian classics, which qualified them for public office. It also meant that commoners from all walks of life shared the elites' belief system based on ancestor worship, ritual practices stressing appropriate decorum and dress for each social level, and a view that the Han as an agrarian-based empire was a small-scale model of the entire cosmos. Those who lived beyond the realm of the Han were considered uncivilized.

In the fifth century BCE, being Roman meant being a citizen of the city of Rome, speaking Latin (the regional language of central Italy), and eating and dressing like Latin-speaking people. By the late second century BCE, however, the concept of citizenship expanded to include anyone who had formal membership in the larger territorial state that the Romans were building.

By the beginning of the third century CE, even this bigger view was no longer true. Now being Roman meant simply being a subject of the Roman emperors. This identity became so deeply rooted that when the western parts of the empire disintegrated two centuries later, the inhabitants of the surviving eastern parts—who had no connection with Rome, did not speak Latin, and did not dress or eat like the original Romans—still considered themselves "Romans" in this broader sense.

PATTERNS OF IMPERIAL EXPANSION

Despite their similarities, the empires reflected different patterns of development, types of public servants, and ideals for the best kind of government. For example, whereas the civilian magistrate and the bureaucrat were typical of the Han Empire, the citizen, the soldier, and the military governor stood for the Roman Empire. In China, dynastic empires fashioned themselves according to the models of past empires. The Chinese treated imperial culture as an ideal descended from the past that had to be emulated in the present. By contrast, Rome began as a collectively ruled city-state and pursued a pragmatic road to domination of its world as if creating something anew. Only by a long, sometimes violent process of trial and error did the Romans achieve a political system of one-man rule by emperors. Nonetheless, they, like the Chinese, were strongly traditional. They also idealized their ancestors. But they were less fascinated with the earlier major powers. What characterized Roman expansion and empire building was a process of continual experimentation, innovation, and adaptation.

The new empires united huge landmasses and extraordinarily diverse populations. For example, the scale of the Han dynasty was unprecedented. A land survey by the imperial government in 2 CE revealed a registered population of 12,233,062 households, or around 58 million people. These households paid taxes, provided military recruits, and supplied laborers for public works. At its height, the Han Empire covered some 3 million square miles in China proper and, for a while, another 1 million square miles in central Asia. The extent of the Yellow and Yangzi river systems that the Han dominated was also unprecedented, as each river was almost as long as the Nile. The Yellow River, nearly 3,500 miles long, drained an area of a third of a million square miles in the north, while the Yangzi River drained a basin of three-quarters of a million square miles in the south as it flowed almost 4,000 miles from central Asia to the East China Sea. The Roman Empire governed an area and a population that were as great as those of Han China.

Both empires left indelible legacies; following their collapses, both survived as models. Successor states in the Mediterranean sought to become the Second Rome, and after the Han dynasty fell, the Chinese people always identified themselves and their language simply as "Han." Both empires raised life to a new level throughout Afro-Eurasia—now people could share a common identity on a grander scale than ever before. It was a vision that would never be lost.

THE QIN DYNASTY

> → *What policies did the Qin leaders use to integrate their empire?*

The Qin dynasty's contributions to political unity and economic growth were essential to its far more powerful Han successor state. (See Map 7-1.) Together, the Qin and Han created the political, social, economic, and cultural foundations that would characterize imperial China thereafter. Through conquest and a strong bureaucracy, the Qin forged a central state whose administrative organizations, laws, and standardized measures that the Qin rulers put in place would last well beyond their own rule.

King Zheng of Qin defeated the remaining Warring States between 230 and 221 BCE, ending one of the most violent periods in Chinese history. With the help of able ministers and generals and a large conscripted army, as well as a system of taxation that financed all-out war, he assumed the mandate of heaven from the Zhou and unified the states into a centralized empire. Having accomplished this feat, he declared himself Shi Huangdi, or "First August Emperor" (much as Rome's first emperor also called himself Augustus).

He took the title of emperor (*di*) to distinguish himself from both the Zhou ruler and the rulers of the Warring States, all of whom had called themselves kings (*wang*). To further consolidate his power he forced the defeated rulers and their families to move to Xianyang, the Qin capital—where, under his watchful eye, they would be unable to gather rebel armies.

ADMINISTRATION AND CONTROL

After securing loyalty from the defeated states, the First August Emperor divided up China so that the new dynasty could rule the massive state effectively. He parceled the territory into thirty-six provinces, or **commanderies** (*jun*), which he subdivided into counties (*xian*). Each commandery had a civilian and a military governor answering to an imperial inspector. Crucial to this administrative strategy were requirements that regional and local officials answer directly to the emperor and that he could dismiss them at will. Moreover, he made sure that civilian governors did not serve in their home areas and often got reassigned to new posts—calculated moves that prevented them from building up power for themselves.

Clerks registered the common people in order to observe, control, and punish them. Registration, required of all males when they reached maturity (age sixteen or seventeen, and five feet in height), provided the basis for taxation and conscription. All able-bodied males had to serve in the army and work on public projects: building border walls, imperial roads, canals, and huge palaces in the capital. Imperial rule was harsh, and censorship was rife. These practices imposed a social order that had been lacking during nearly two and a half centuries of warfare and chaos.

To further unify varied systems surviving from the Warring States period, the Qin emperor established standard weights and measures, as well as a standard currency. Circular copper coins with square holes in the center (to string them together) replaced the coins shaped like miniature spades or knives that had characterized the different states' economies. To rule out currency forging and ensure that these coins kept their value (thus being more than mere symbols), the new Qin and later the Han "Pan Liang" copper coins bore simple

Qin Coin. After centuries of distinctive regional currencies, the Qin unified the currency as part of its general unification policy. Thereafter bronze or copper cash was the standard imperial currency in China.

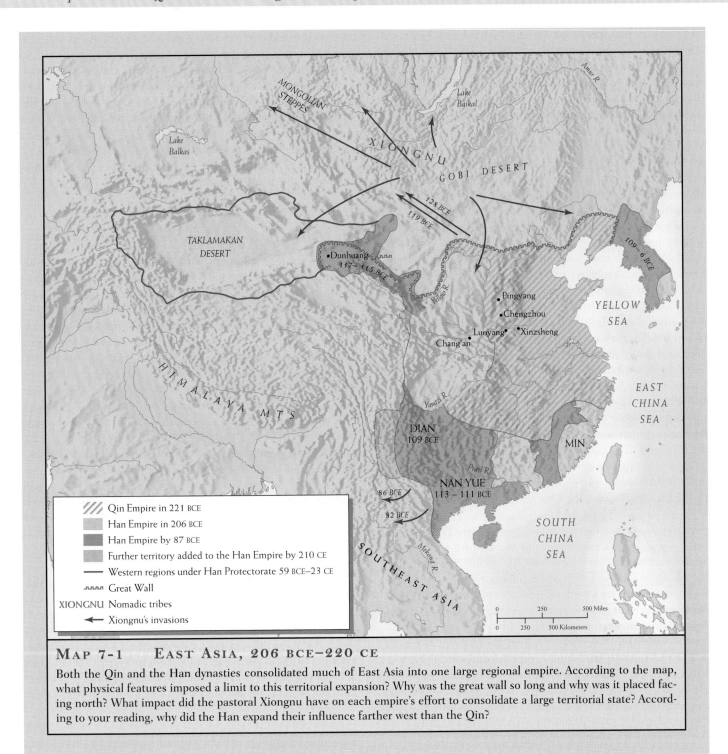

MAP 7-1   EAST ASIA, 206 BCE–220 CE

Both the Qin and the Han dynasties consolidated much of East Asia into one large regional empire. According to the map, what physical features imposed a limit to this territorial expansion? Why was the great wall so long and why was it placed facing north? What impact did the pastoral Xiongnu have on each empire's effort to consolidate a large territorial state? According to your reading, why did the Han expand their influence farther west than the Qin?

etchings that identified their value. While coins were nothing new, the Qin pioneered effective minting techniques.

The Qin extended China's boundaries in the northeast to the Korean Peninsula, in the south to present-day Vietnam, and in the west into central Asia. Han Fei, a minor official from the state of Han, introduced the notion of a "grand

unity" that appealed to the Qin rulers and ministers as a guiding political idea. The chief minister of the Qin Empire, Li Si, used it to justify the harsh measures that the state enacted to unify the Central Plain states.

Both Han Fei and Li Si subscribed to the principles of Legalism developed during the Warring States period (see

Chapter 5). This philosophy valued written law codes, administrative regulations, and inflexible punishments more highly than rituals and ethics (which the Confucians emphasized) or spontaneity and the natural order (which the Daoists stressed). Determined to bring order to a turbulent society, they enacted unambiguous laws and regulations, as well as harsh punishments that applied to everyone regardless of rank or wealth. (Such punishments included beheading, mutilation by cutting off a person's nose or foot, tattooing, shaving off a person's beard or hair, hard labor, and loss of office and rank.) After registering people in groups of five and ten, officials made them all responsible for one another—and subject to punishment for any crime that any one of them might commit.

The Qin also improved communication systems. For example, they constructed roads radiating out from their capital to all parts of the empire. These immense thoroughfares were 115 feet wide, with three lanes to accommodate vehicles, pedestrians, animals, and soldiers. Their thick embankments of soil bristled with reinforcing metal poles and pine trees to check erosion. Officials required vehicles to have a standard axle length so that all wheels would fit in the same dirt ruts. Dusty in the dry seasons, the roads were often muddy and rutted when the spring rains came. Elite men and women who traveled in elegant carts with enclosed interiors would find the dust and stench almost unbearable as they journeyed along the hundreds of miles from local towns and villages to the capital and back. After several days of travel, merchants would be lucky if their wares and goods survived undamaged.

Just as crucial was the Qin effort to standardize writing. Banning regional variants in written characters, which had characterized the Warring States period, the Qin required scribes and ministers throughout the empire to adopt the "small seal script," a revised form of writing that resembled the pictographic forms carved on ancient Shang oracle bones (see Chapter 3). Its simpler characters evolved into the less complicated style of bureaucratic writing, known as "clerical script," prominent during the Han dynasty.

The standardized script helped the Qin disseminate their vision of the state and weed out competing ideas from the Warring States era. It also eased the work of regional elites and clerks, who now served as bureaucratic intermediaries between the imperial capital and local government. Standardization

also eliminated troublesome ideas that might disturb the new imperial unity. In 213 BCE, a Qin decree ordered officials to confiscate and burn all books in residents' private possession (except for technical works on medicine, divination, and agriculture). In addition, the court prosecuted teachers who used outlawed classical books, including some Confucian works that troublemakers could cite to criticize the Qin regime. Education and learning were now under the exclusive control of state officials. (See Primary Source: A Qin Legal Document: Memorial on the Burning of Books.)

ECONOMIC AND SOCIAL CHANGES

The Qin rulers expanded their agrarian empire through conquest. During the Warring States period, landownership had shifted from aristocratic clans to the peasantry, who no longer shouldered the burden of paying tribute to regional lords. An agrarian bonanza had yielded wealth that the state could tax, and increased tax revenues meant more resources for imposing order. Now, under the Qin Empire, the government issued rules on working the fields (with severe penalties for failure to follow regulations), taxed farming households, and conscripted laborers to build irrigation systems and canals so that even more land could come under cultivation. Whereas the Greek city-states and the Roman Empire relied on slave labor, the Qin and (later) the Han dynasties championed free farmers and conscripted able-bodied sons into their huge armies. Free to work their own land, and paying only a small portion of their crops in taxes, peasant families were the economic bedrock of the Chinese empire.

Consolidation of power led to major economic changes, as self-sufficient royal manors gave way to farms that produced goods for the marketplace. As production rose, landowners—some of them peasants—could enjoy profiting from their surpluses. Increasingly, public royal domains and private employers used contracts and money to strike bargains with laborers and with one another. A similar shift toward contracts occurred throughout Chinese society and government. Previously, blood ties had been all-important, but as trade and commerce boomed, farmers and traders began to dominate public and private business.

Agricultural surpluses fueled long-distance commerce—the source of even more wealth and revenues. The burgeoning money economy produced a class of merchants in China's cities, which became market centers (rather than fortresses) in the dynamic world of region-based networks. Merchants peddled foodstuffs as well as weapons, metals, horses, dogs, hides, furs, silk, and salt—all produced in different regions. Moreover, the new roads and canals not only aided soldiers' movements but also promoted commerce, carrying both goods and tax revenues from commanderies far and wide. Nonetheless, the central government continued to value the production of crops and goods over trade, and it imposed ever-higher taxes on goods in transit and in the markets.

Small Seal Script. Under the Qin, the "large seal" script of the Zhou Dynasty was unified and simplified into a smaller version "small seal" writing.

A QIN LEGAL DOCUMENT: MEMORIAL ON THE BURNING OF BOOKS

When the first Qin emperor came to power, his minister, Li Si, devised a policy to enhance state power through a unified political ideology. Any traditions of learning that differed from the Qin orthodoxy were targets for elimination. The most serious threat to Qin power came from the Five Classics (said to have been compiled by Confucius), which stressed moral rectitude, personal character, and political responsibility while holding office. Such texts were an affront to imperial power, Li thought, so he called for their destruction and the execution of scholars who defended them in public.

In earlier times the empire disintegrated and fell into disorder, and no one was capable of unifying it. Thereupon the various feudal lords rose to power. In their discourses they all praised the past in order to disparage the present and embellished empty words to confuse the truth. Everyone cherished his own favorite school of learning and criticized what had been instituted by the authorities. But at present Your Majesty possesses a unified empire, has regulated the distinctions of black and white, and has firmly established for yourself a position of sole supremacy. And yet these independent schools, joining with each other, criticize the codes of laws and instructions. Hearing of the promulgation of a decree, they criticize it, each from the standpoint of his own school. At home they disapprove of it in their hearts; going out they criticize it in the thoroughfare. They seek a reputation by discrediting their sovereign; they appear superior by expressing contrary views, and they lead the lowly multitude in the spreading of slander. If such license is not prohibited, the sovereign power will decline above and partisan factions will form below. It would be well to prohibit this.

Your servant suggests that all books in the imperial archives, save the memoirs of Qin, be burned. All persons in the empire, except members of the Academy of Learned Scholars, in possession of the *Classic of Odes, the Classic of Documents,* and discourses of the hundred philosophers should take them to the local governors and have them indiscriminately burned. Those who dare to talk to each other about the *Odes* and *Documents* should be executed and their bodies exposed in the marketplace. Anyone referring to the past to criticize the present should, together with all members of his family, be put to death. Officials who fail to report cases that have come under their attention are equally guilty. After thirty days from the time of issuing the decree, those who have not destroyed their books are to be branded and sent to build the Great Wall. Books not to be destroyed will be those on medicine and pharmacy, divination by the turtle and milfoil, and agriculture and arboriculture. People wishing to pursue learning should take the officials as their teachers.

→ *According to Li Si, how would the burning of classic texts help the Qin emperor keep "a unified empire" and "sole supremacy"?*

→ *What types of books were still acceptable? Why would the first Qin emperor want to keep these practical works alive?*

SOURCE: "A Qin Legal Document: Memorial on the Burning of the Books" from *Sources of Chinese Tradition,* Volume 1, eds. William Theodore de Bary and Irene Bloom, © 1999 Columbia University Press. Reprinted with the permission of the publisher.

NOMADS AND THE QIN ALONG THE NORTHERN FRONTIER

Both the Qin dynasty and, later, the Han dynasty grappled with the need to expand and defend their borders. During the last centuries of the Warring States period, states along the northern border had expanded by conquering nomadic frontier peoples (see Chapter 5). When the Qin united those states into an empire and then started looking beyond to the north and west, it encountered nomadic warrior peoples—especially the proud Xiongnu, who dominated the steppes. Like the Qin, the Han faced the same limits.

Relations between these nomadic peoples and the settled Chinese teetered in a precarious balance until 215 BCE, when the Qin Empire pushed north into the middle of the Yellow River basin. At that time, the First Emperor sent troops against the Xiongnu to seize their pasturelands. To secure those lands for settlement, Qin officials built roads between the frontier and the nearest cities, such as Liye in Longshan County, in Hunan. They also directed conscripts and criminals in building

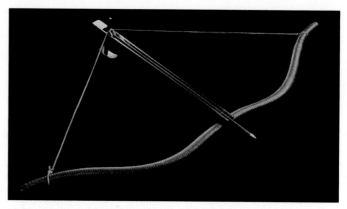

Qin Archer and Crossbow. This kneeling archer (*left*) was discovered in the tomb of the First Emperor. Notice his breastplate. The wooden bow he was holding has disintegrated, but a replica appears to the right. The bronze arrowhead and trigger mechanism in this reproduction were found with the terra-cotta army.

a massive defensive wall along the northern border (the beginnings of the Great Wall of China—though north of the current wall, which was constructed more than a millennium later). As a result of these imperial efforts, in 211 BCE the Qin settled 30,000 colonists in the steppe lands of Inner Eurasia.

THE QIN DEBACLE

Despite its military power, the Qin dynasty collapsed quickly. Its rule weighed heavily on taxpayers because of constant warfare, which consumed not just massive tax revenues but also huge numbers of laborers. Dissension at court became apparent when Chief Minister Li Si was implicated in a conspiracy and executed. When desperate conscripted workers mutinied in 211 BCE, they found allies in descendants of Warring States nobles, local military leaders, and influential merchants. The rebels swept up thousands of supporters

with their call to arms against the "tyrannical" Qin. Shortly before the First Emperor died in 210, even the educated elite joined former lords and regional vassals in revolt. The second Qin emperor committed suicide early in 207, and his weak successor surrendered to the leader of the Han forces later that year. The resurgent Xiongnu confederacy also reconquered their old pasturelands as the Qin dynasty fell.

In the aftermath of the Qin's fall, the insurgents' leader, Xiang Yu, tried to restore the Zhou system of powerful regional states—so he established nineteen feudal states. In the ensuing civil war among them, an unheralded commoner and former policeman named Liu Bang (r. 206–195 BCE) declared himself prince of his home area of Han. In 202 BCE, after Xiang Yu committed suicide, Liu proclaimed himself the first Han emperor.

Emphasizing his peasant origins, Liu demonstrated his initial disdain for intellectuals by urinating into the hat of a court scholar. But he quickly learned that power would be better served through good manners. Confucian scholars loyal to the Han soon were busy justifying Liu Bang's victory by depicting his Qin predecessors as cruel dynasts and ruthless despots. For their part, the Han court and its officials denied any link to the Qin, affirming instead Confucian ideas about the moral and cultural foundations of state power. For example, the scholar Jia Yi (c. 200–168 BCE) argued that the Qin had fallen "because the ruler lacked moral values." (See Primary Source: Jia Yi on the Faults of the Qin.) Under the cover of receiving the mandate of heaven, the Han portrayed the Qin as evil, even as they adopted the Qin's bureaucratic system.

In reality—as we can see from a cache of Qin penal codes and administrative ordinances, written on some 1,000 bamboo slips—Qin laws were no crueler than those of the later Han. Punishments suited the crimes, and the laws themselves resembled the later Han penal code.

Primary Source

JIA YI ON THE FAULTS OF THE QIN

After the Qin dynasty disintegrated, Confucians sought to explain the fall of so strong a military power that had unified China just fourteen years before. Jia Yi tied the dynasty's collapse to its autocratic rule and mean-spirited policies. Rather than blame the imperial system itself, Jia blamed the immorality of the Qin penal code and the first Qin emperor's totalitarian policies for his loss of the mandate of heaven. If the Qin had ruled according to Confucian teachings and ritual guidelines, Jia contended, the dynasty would have endured.

[Later] when the First Emperor ascended [the throne] he flourished and furthered the accomplishments of the six generations before him. Brandishing his long whip, he drove the world before him; destroying the feudal lords, he swallowed up the domains of the two Zhou dynasties. He reached the pinnacle of power and ordered all in the Six Directions, whipping the rest of the world into submission and thus spreading his might through the Four Seas. . . . He then abolished the ways of ancient sage kings and put to the torch the writings of the Hundred Schools in an attempt to keep the people in ignorance. He demolished the walls of major cities and put to death men of fame and talent, collected all the arms of the realm at Xianyang and had the spears and arrowheads melted down to form twelve huge statues in human form—all with the aim of weakening his people. Then he . . . posted capable generals and expert bowmen at important passes and placed trusted officials and well-trained soldiers in strategic array to challenge all who passed. With the empire thus pacified, the First Emperor believed that, with the capital secure within the pass and prosperous cities stretching for ten thousand *li*, he had indeed created an imperial structure to be enjoyed by his royal descendants for ten thousand generations to come.

Even after the death of the First Emperor, his reputation continued to sway the people. Chen She was a man who grew up in humble circumstances in a hut with broken pots for windows and ropes as door hinges and was a mere hired field hand and roving conscript of mediocre talent. He could neither equal the worth of Confucius and Mozi nor match the wealth of Tao Zhu or Yi Dun, yet, even stumbling as he did amidst the ranks of common soldiers and shuffling through the fields, he called forth a tired motley crowd and a mob of several hundred to turn upon the Qin. Cutting down trees to make weapons, and hoisting their flags on garden poles, they had the whole world come to them like gathering clouds, with people bringing their own food and following them like shadows. These men of courage from the East rose together, and in the end they defeated and extinguished the House of Qin.

. . . Qin, from a tiny base, had become a great power, ruling the land and receiving homage from all quarters for a hundred-odd years. Yet after they had unified the land and secured themselves within the pass, a single common rustic could nevertheless challenge this empire and cause its ancestral temples to topple and its ruler to die at the hand of others, a laughingstock in the eyes of all. Why? Because the ruler lacked humaneness and rightness; because preserving power differs fundamentally from seizing power.

✦ *According to the reading, what specific steps did the Qin emperor take that were mean-spirited and autocratic?*

✦ *What details in this reading help you to imagine the peasant rebellion? What did the peasants use for weapons? What was their typical dwelling like?*

✦ *Why would Jia Yi want to preserve imperial government after the Qin had been so cruel?*

SOURCE: "Faults of the Qin" from *Sources of Chinese Tradition*, Volume 1, eds. William Theodore de Bary and Irene Bloom, © 1999 Columbia University Press. Reprinted with the permission of the publisher.

THE HAN DYNASTY

> → *How did Han leaders promote peace and stability?*

The Han dynasty, which lasted 400 years (206 BCE–220 CE), became China's formative empire and ultimately oversaw a blossoming of peace and prosperity. (See Map 7-2.) Its armies swelled with some 50,000 crossbowmen who brandished mass-produced weapons made from bronze and iron. Armed with the crossbow, foot soldiers and mounted archers extended Han imperial lands in all directions. Following the Qin practice, the Han also relied on a huge conscripted labor force for special projects such as building canals, roads, and defensive walls.

The first part of the dynastic cycle, known as the Western (or Former) Han dynasty (206 BCE–9 CE), brought economic prosperity and the expansion of empire. This was especially the case under Emperor Wu or Wudi, known as the "Martial Emperor" because of his many military campaigns (r. 140–87 BCE). Emperor Wu's more stringent penal code eliminated the powerful officials who got in his way. In a single year, his

Emperor Wu. This idealized representation of Emperor Wu (156–87 BCE, r. 141–87 BCE) welcoming a man of letters was one of a series of seventeenth-century silk paintings of Chinese emperors.

court system prosecuted over a thousand such cases. (See Primary Source: Han Legal Philosophy from Dong Zhongshu.) After Wu's reign, a burden of poor harvests, heavy taxes, and increased debt forced many peasants to sell their land to the wealthy, causing social tensions to simmer. A usurper who tried to introduce land reforms took power from 9 to 23 CE, but he lost control to a coalition of landowners and peasants who restored the Han dynasty to power. Thereafter Liu Xiu reconsolidated the Han Empire as the Eastern (or Later) Han dynasty (25—220 CE) and moved the capital to Luoyang on the North China plain.

Out of the experience of the Han, the Chinese produced a political narrative known as the **dynastic cycle**. In this scheme, influential families would vie for supremacy. Upon gaining power, they legitimated their authority by claiming to be the heirs of previous grand dynasts and by preserving or revitalizing the ancestors' virtuous governing ways. This continuity conferred divine support, and with it the rulers more easily united China. Dynasties rose and fell, and heaven could potentially grant its mandate to anyone who unified the empire. Indeed, the imperial continuity established by the Han was extraordinarily long-lasting, enduring more than 2,000 years until 1911.

FOUNDATIONS OF HAN POWER

The Han and Roman empires relied on political institutions, ideological supports, and control of economic assets to maintain power. Yet they differed in their use of civil bureaucracy, the military, and ideologies to ensure their subjects' consent. Undergirding the Han Empire was the tight-knit alliance between the imperial family and the new elite—the scholar-gentry class—who shared a determination to impose order on the Chinese population.

POWER AND ADMINISTRATION The first Han emperors had no choice but to compromise with the aristocratic groups who had helped overthrow the Qin. To win their favor, Liu Bang showered land grants on military supporters as well as on his relatives. Still, all power emanated from the ruling family. Members of the Qin imperial family ruled those lands that were under their direct power, while governors appointed by the emperor administered the commanderies. A "grand counselor," chosen by the emperor, headed a civil bureaucracy of educated men who represented powerful local communities. Early in the Han dynasty, the central government was careful not to interfere with regional communities. The court followed the same flexible policy toward border peoples, using marriage alliances to gain control over their territories.

The Han had the most highly centralized bureaucracy in the world at this time, even more centralized than Rome's. That structure became the source of its enduring power. As

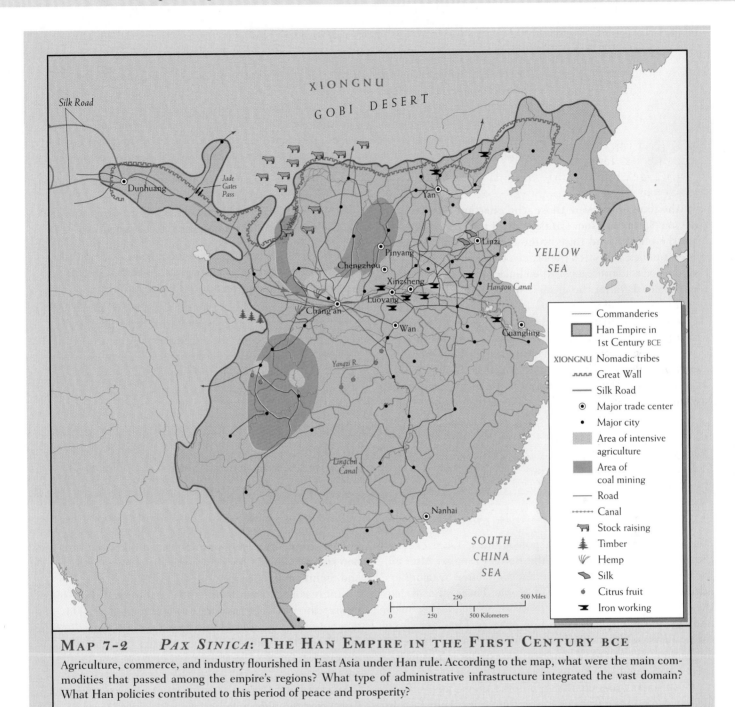

MAP 7-2 *PAX SINICA*: THE HAN EMPIRE IN THE FIRST CENTURY BCE

Agriculture, commerce, and industry flourished in East Asia under Han rule. According to the map, what were the main commodities that passed among the empire's regions? What type of administrative infrastructure integrated the vast domain? What Han policies contributed to this period of peace and prosperity?

under the Qin, the bureaucracy touched everyone because all males had to register, pay taxes, and serve in the military. At first, regional officials seldom intervened at the local level, simply making sure that local officials came up with the usual tax revenues and army conscripts. But the Han court was quick to tighten its grip on regional administration. First it removed powerful princes, crushed rebellions, and took over the areas controlled by regional lords. As princes lost power,

regional officials managed these aristocratic enclaves as imperial commanderies. According to arrangements instituted in 106 BCE by Emperor Wu, the empire consisted of thirteen provinces under imperial inspectors. Like the Romans' *dictator*, who was appointed in emergencies, Wu also appointed governors-general during floods or famine.

A civilian official and a commandant for military affairs shared the work of administering each commandery. These

HAN LEGAL PHILOSOPHY FROM DONG ZHONGSHU

The Qin legal system was considered brutal in its application of uniform punishments against criminals. Scholars claimed that the Qin punished all equally, regardless of the accused's motive or social status. Under the Han emperor Wu, Dong Zhongshu devised an ingenious way to humanize the Han penal code by using Confucian philosophy, so that jurists could consider the litigant's social status and personal motives behind allegedly criminal behavior. In essence, Dong as a Confucian argued that the spirit of the law took precedence over its letter when true justice was the goal.

At the time, there were those who questioned the verdict saying: "A had no son. On the side of the road, he picked up the child B and raised him as his own son. When B grew up, he committed the crime of murder. The contents of the accusation [against B] included [the fact that] A had concealed B [after the crime]. What should be the judgment regarding A?"

Tung Chung-shu passed judgment saying: "A had no son. He restored [B] to life and raised him [as his own son]. Although B was not A's natural son, who would think of seeing [B] as anyone but [A's] son? The *Poetry [Classic]* says: 'The mulberry-tree caterpillar has little ones, but the wasp raises them.' According to the intent of the *Annals*, a father must cover up for his son. A accordingly concealed B. The verdict: A does not deserve to be punished."

→ *Mulberry-tree caterpillars are silkworms. What does the use of this example in a classic text indicate about the importance of that creature to Chinese culture?*
→ *Why would the Han penal code exonerate a stepfather for harboring his son even though the son had committed a serious crime?*

SOURCE: Pan Ku, *Han-shu* 3:1714 (*chüan* 30); quoted in Benjamin A. Elman, *Classicism, Politics, and Kinship: The Ch'ang-chou School of New Text Confucianism in Late Imperial China* (Berkeley: University of California Press, 1990), p. 262.

---

men shouldered immense responsibilities, far exceeding those of their counterparts in the Roman Empire. After all, the commanderies covered vast lands inhabited by countless ethnic groups totaling millions of people. These officials, like their Roman equivalents, had to maintain political stability and ensure the efficient collection of taxes. However, given the immense numbers under their jurisdiction and the heavy duties they bore, the local administrative staff was in many respects inadequate.

Government schools that promoted the scholar-official ideal became fertile sources for recruiting local officials. In fact, the Han established formal institutions of learning to ensure adequate numbers of well-trained bureaucrats. Emperor Wu founded a college for classical scholars in 136 BCE and soon expanded it into the Imperial University. By the second century CE it boasted 30,000 members, dwarfing the number of students in the largest Roman schools. Not only did they study the classics, but Han scholars also were naturalists and inventors. They made important medical discoveries, dealing with rational diagnoses of the body's functions and the role of wind and temperature in transmitting diseases. They also invented the magnetic compass and developed high-quality paper, which replaced silk, wood, and bamboo strips as media for communicating laws, ideas, rituals, and technical knowledge.

Increasingly, even local elites encouraged their sons to master the classical teachings of Confucianism. This practice not only guaranteed a future entrée into the ruling class but also planted the Confucian classics at the heart of the imperial state.

CONFUCIAN IDEOLOGY AND LEGITIMATE RULE

Confucian thought stood as the ideological buttress of the Han empire. According to Han political philosophy, the people's welfare was the foundation of legitimate rule. (See Primary Source: Dong Zhongshu on Responsibilities of Han Rulership.) When the Confucian scholar and official Jia Yi wrote that "the state, the ruler, and the officials all depend on the people for their mandate," he was underscoring "the primacy of the people" in affirming the mandate of heaven. Claims like these promoted classical political principles of civilizing the people and supporting local elites. However, such principles did *not* imply that the people actually chose their own leaders (as in the Greek-city states; see Chapter 5).

The Wuliang Shrine. This rubbing of a Wuliang Shrine stele depicts Han scholars sitting on mats on the floor. Chairs were not used until late medieval times.

The people's only power was the ability to reject rulers who did not promote general well-being.

By 50 BCE, three Confucian ideals reigned as the official doctrine of the Han Empire: honoring tradition, respecting the lessons of history, and emphasizing the emperor's responsibility to heaven. Confucian scholars now tutored the princes. To mark the lessons of the past, the grand historian Sima Qian provided a historical vision of good and evil Shang and Zhou rulers. By embracing Confucian political ideals, the Han rulers established a polity based on the people's mandate and crafted a careful balance between two arms of government in which the officials provided a counterweight to the emperor's autocratic strength. Of course, when the interests of the court and the bureaucracy clashed, the emperor's will was paramount.

THE NEW SOCIAL ORDER AND THE ECONOMY

Part of the Han's genius was their ability to win the support of diverse social groups that had been squabbling for centuries. They did so by forming alliances with key leaders—for example, by letting aristocratic Qin survivors reacquire some of their former power and status. They also urged enterprising peasants who had worked the nobles' lands to become local leaders in the countryside. Successful merchants won permission to extend their influence in cities, and in local areas scholars found themselves in the role of masters when their lords were removed.

Out of a massive agrarian base flowed a steady stream of tax revenues and labor for military forces and public works. The Han court also drew revenues from state-owned imperial preserves, mining, and mints; tribute from outlying domains; household taxes on the nobility; and surplus grains from wealthy merchants who were hungry for noble ranks, official appointments, or smaller tax burdens. Emperor Wu established state monopolies in salt, iron, and wine to fund his expensive military campaigns. His policies fueled silk production and iron production—especially iron weapons and everyday tools—and controlled profiteering through price controls. He also minted standardized copper coins and imposed stiff penalties for counterfeiting. All these efforts aimed at expanding the imperial economy and supporting the emperor's ambitions.

Laid out in an orderly grid, Han cities—particularly capitals—reflected their political functions. Bustling markets south of the palace complex served as public areas. Carriages transported rich families up and down the wide avenues (and they paid dearly for the privilege, for keeping a horse required as much grain as a family of six could consume). Court palaces became forbidden inner cities, off-limits to all but those in the imperial lineage or the government. Monumental architecture in China announced the palaces and tombs of rulers rather than the sites of mass entertainment (like the Colosseum in Rome).

DAILY LIFE Wealthy families took pride in their several-story homes displaying richly carved crossbeams and rafters. They cushioned their floors with embroidered pillows, wool rugs, and mats. Fine embroideries hung as drapes, and screens in the rooms secured privacy. Families also sharply distinguished gender roles to redouble the authority of the father figure. Women and children stayed cloistered in inner quarters, preserving the sense that the family patriarch's role

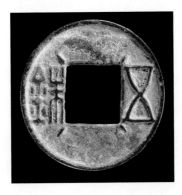

Wuzhu Coin. This copper coin was issued by Emperor Xuandi during the Western Han Dynasty, 73–49 BCE. *Wuzhu*, which means "five grains," refers to the weight of the coin (1 wuzhu = 5 grains = 4 grams). The wuzhu was in circulation until 621 CE.

Primary Source

DONG ZHONGSHU ON RESPONSIBILITIES OF HAN RULERSHIP

Early Han dynasty officials sought to enhance the government's legitimacy by replacing the Legalist defense of an autocratic state with a Confucian view of the ruler as the moral and cosmological foundation of government. Thus the philosopher Dong Zhongshu offered a new theory to legitimize the Han dynasty, while criticizing the Qin's mismanagement of government. Under the guidance of Confucian officials, Dong argued, the imperial system would nourish the people and promote upright officials who would maintain the Han dynasty's mandate to govern, rather than ruling through fear and intimidation.

He who rules the people is the foundation of the state. Now in administering the state, nothing is more important for transforming [the people] than reverence for the foundation. . . . What do I mean by the foundation? Heaven, Earth, and humankind are the foundation of all living things. Heaven engenders all living things, Earth nourishes them, and humankind completes them. With filial and brotherly love, Heaven engenders them; with food and clothing, Earth nourishes them; and with rites and music, humankind completes them. These three assist one another just as the hands and feet join to complete the body. None can be dispensed with because without filial and brotherly love, people lack the means to live; without food and clothing, people lack the means to be nourished; and without rites and music, people lack the means to become complete. If all three are lost, people become like deer, each person following his own desires and each family practicing its own customs. Fathers will not be able to order their sons, and rulers will not be able to order their ministers. Although possessing inner and outer walls, [the ruler's city] will become known as "an empty settlement." Under such circumstances, the ruler will lie down with a clod of earth for his pillow. Although no one endangers him, he will naturally be endangered; although no one destroys him, he will naturally be destroyed. This is called "spontaneous punishment." When it arrives, even if he is hidden in a stone vault or barricaded in a narrow pass, the ruler will not be able to avoid "spontaneous punishment."

One who is an enlightened master and worthy ruler believes such things. For this reason he respectfully and carefully attends to the three foundations. He reverently enacts the suburban sacrifice, dutifully serves his ancestors, manifests filial and brotherly love, encourages filial conduct, and serves the foundation of Heaven in this way. He takes up the plough handle to till the soil, plucks the mulberry leaves and nourishes the silkworms, reclaims the wilds, plants grain, opens new lands to provide sufficient food and clothing, and serves the foundation of Earth in this way. He establishes academies and schools in towns and villages to teach filial piety, brotherly love, reverence, and humility, enlightens [the people] with education, moves [them] with rites and music, and serves the foundation of humanity in this way.

If these three foundations are all served, the people will resemble sons and brothers who do not dare usurp authority, while the ruler will resemble fathers and mothers. He will not rely on favors to demonstrate his love for his people nor severe measures to prompt them to act. . . . [W]hen the ruler relies on virtue to administer the state, it is sweeter than honey or sugar and firmer than glue or lacquer. This is why sages and worthies exert themselves to revere the foundation and do not dare depart from it.

→ *Count the number of times the following words appear in this reading:* fathers, sons, brothers, filial conduct. *What do these words tell us about Han officials' view of the proper relationship between rulers and subjects?*

→ *How does this reading reflect the gender ideology of Han China?*

→ *Why was the emperor so important in Dong Zhongshu's vision of Han political culture after the fall of the Qin?*

SOURCE: "Responsibilities of Han Rulership" from *Sources of Chinese Tradition*, Volume 1, eds. William Theodore de Bary and Irene Bloom, © 1999 Columbia University Press. Reprinted with the permission of the publisher.

was to protect mothers, wives, and children from the harsh society. But this did not deprive women from following careers of their own. Elite women, often literate, enjoyed respect as teachers and managers within the family while their husbands served as officials away from home. Women who were commoners led less protected lives; many worked in the fields, and some joined troupes of entertainers to sing and dance for food at the open markets.

Silk was abundant and available to all classes, though in winter only the rich wrapped themselves in furs while everyone else stayed warm in woolens and ferret skins. The rich also wore distinctive slippers inlaid with leather or lined with silk. No longer were wine and meat reserved only for festivals, leading critics to decry the debauches of the well-to-do. In the cooked-meat stalls of the markets, those who could afford them pushed and shoved to buy their piglets, dog cutlets, or chopped liver. These tasty victuals came to the dinner tables of the wealthy on vessels fashioned with silver inlay or golden handles.

Entertainment for those who could afford it included performing animals, tiger fights, and foreign dancing girls. Some gambled, betting for high stakes at *liubo*, a board game that involved shaking bamboo sticks out of a cup. Live music was popular at private homes, and rich families kept their own orchestras, complete with bells and drums. Although events like these had occurred during the Zhou dynasty, they had marked only public ritual occasions. Now, Han elites called on the gods for their own spiritual and private benefits. They still took funerary rites very seriously, however: the rich ordered the finest wood for their coffins, and even the poor had at least their coffin lids painted.

SOCIAL HIERARCHY At the base of Han society was a free peasantry—farmers who owned and tilled their own land. The Han court upheld an agrarian ideal by honoring the peasants' productive labors, while subjecting merchants to a range of controls (including regulations on luxury consumption) and belittling them for not doing physical labor. Confucians and Daoists supported this hierarchy, but we will see below that the Daoists later challenged the status quo. The Confucians, for instance, envisioned scholar-officials as working hard for the ruler to enhance a moral economy in which profiteering by greedy merchants would be minimal. In reality, however, the first century of Han rule perpetuated powerful elites. At the apex were the imperial clan and nobles, followed, in order, by high-ranking officials and scholars, great merchants and manufacturers, and a regionally based class of local magnates. Below these elites, lesser clerks, medium and small landowners, free farmers, artisans, small merchants, poor tenant farmers, and hired laborers eked out a living. The more destitute became government slaves and relied on the state for food and clothing. At the bottom was a thin layer of convicts and private slaves.

Between 100 BCE and 200 CE, scholar-officials stood as the bulwark of imperial authority and legitimacy. In their official capacity, they linked the imperial center with local society. At first, their political clout and prestige complemented the power of landlords and large clans, but over time their autonomy grew as they gained wealth by acquiring private property. Following the fall of the Han, they emerged as the dominant aristocratic clans.

In the long run, the imperial court's struggle to limit the power of local lords and magnates failed. Indeed, dynasts had to rely on local officials to enforce their rule, but those officials could rarely stand up to the powerful men they were supposed to be governing. And when central rule proved too onerous for local elites, they always had the option of rebelling. Local uprisings against the Han that began in 99 BCE forced the court to relax its measures and left landlords and local magnates as dominant powers in the provinces. Below these privileged groups, powerless agrarian groups turned to Daoist religious organizations to provide the framework that crystallized into potent cells of dissent.

Model of a Han House. Elite families in Chang'an and other Han cities typically lived in two-story houses with carved crossbeams and rafters and enclosed courtyards. The floors were covered with embroidered cushions, wool rugs, and mats for sitting. Screens were used for privacy. Women and children were cloistered in the inner quarters.

Han Entertainment. Han entertainment included dancing, particularly by foreign girls (*top left*), and acrobatics, for which the Chinese remain famous today (*bottom left*). Music was often played at the homes of rich families, who kept their own orchestras complete with bells and drums. Musical events became so popular, for both the entertainers (note the face in the Han statue on the right) and the entertained, that performances ceased being only somber ritual occasions.

RELIGION AND OMENS Under Emperor Wu, Confucianism took on religious overtones. Dong Zhongshu, Wu's chief minister, advocated a more powerful view of Confucius, promoting texts that cast Confucius as a man who possessed aspects of divinity. One treatise portrayed him not as a humble teacher but as an uncrowned monarch, and even as a demigod and a giver of laws.

Classical learning was not just state orthodoxy; it also informed popular religion. In the early Han world dominated by social elites, religion linked scholars and officials to the peasantry. Although classical learning remained the preserve of the Confucians at court, many local communities practiced forms of a remarkably dynamic popular Chinese religion.

Imperial cults, magic, and sorcery reinforced the court's interest in astronomical omens—such as the appearance of a nova (a suddenly bright star), solar halos, meteors, and lunar and solar eclipses. Unpredictable celestial events, as well as earthquakes and famines, were taken as signs of the emperor's lack of virtue, and powerful ministers exploited them to intimidate their ruler. A cluster of calamities, prodigies, and heavenly omens usually meant that the emperor had lost the mandate of heaven. At the same time, people of high and low social position alike took witchcraft very seriously, believing that its practitioners could manipulate natural events and interfere with the will of heaven. Though the Chinese were not a deeply religious or otherwordly people like the Romans, thought about the supernatural did affect imperial power, usually buttressing it but then at times of disorder promoting dissident leaders and movements.

EXPANSION OF THE EMPIRE AND THE SILK ROAD

Empires seldom stand on shared political and cultural beliefs alone. More often, they survive by force. The Han Chinese were no exception to the general rule. Like their Roman counterparts, they created a ruthless military machine that was effective at expanding their borders and enforcing stability around the borderlands. Peace was good for business, specifically for creating stable conditions that allowed the safe transit of goods over the Silk Road.

Emperor Wu did much to transform the military forces. Following the Qin precedent, he again made military service compulsory. The number of men under arms was stunning: some 100,000 crack troops in the Imperial Guard were stationed in the capital, and more than a million in the standing army. In contrast, the armies of Athens, the largest Greek city-state, rarely exceeded 20,000 men; even the Roman field armies rarely exceeded 30,000. The Han simply created armies on an entirely different scale.

EXPANDING BORDERS During the reign of Emperor Wu, Han control extended from southeastern China to northern Vietnam. Because of similar strife in the northeast, pro-Han Koreans could appeal for Han help against rulers in their internal squabbles. After Emperor Wu's expeditionary force defeated the Korean king, four Han commanderies sprang up in northern Korea. Incursions into Sichuan and the southwestern border areas were less successful, as both mountainous terrain and malaria hampered the Han armies. Nevertheless, a commandery took root in southern Sichuan in 135 BCE, and soon it opened trading routes to Southeast Asia.

THE XIONGNU, THE YUEZHI, AND THE HAN DYNASTY Mighty as this empire was, expansion invariably renewed conflicts along more extended borders. The Han's most serious military threat came from nomadic peoples in the north, especially the Xiongnu. The Han inherited from the Qin a symbiotic relationship with these proud, horse-riding nomads from outside the frontier's defensive wall. Merchants of the Han Empire brought silk cloth and thread, bronze mirrors, and lacquerware to the nomadic chiefs, exchanging them for furs, horses, and cattle.

At first, the Han suffered humiliating defeats at the hands of the Xiongnu. But as the regime grew more powerful, the tables turned. Under Emperor Wu, the Han launched offensive campaigns across the Mongolian steppe to drive back the raiders. Between 129 and 124 BCE, they repelled several Xiongnu invasions. In subsequent campaigns Han forces penetrated deep into Xiongnu territory, reaching as far as the northern Mongolian steppe. Eventually the Han armies split the Xiongnu tribes. The southern tribes surrendered, but the northern ones moved westward—toward the Mediterranean,

Bronze Horsemen. Two bronze horsemen holding *Chi*-halberds from the Later Han dynasty, circa second century CE. These statues were excavated in 1969 in Gansu along the Silk Road. Note the size and strength of these Ferghana horses from central Asia.

where they eventually threatened the eastern flank of the Roman Empire.

THE CHINESE PEACE: TRADE, OASES, AND THE SILK ROAD The retreat of the Xiongnu (and other nomadic peoples) introduced a glorious period of peace and prosperity. Now China achieved a *Pax Sinica* (149–87 BCE) that was much like the *Pax Romana* (25 BCE–235 CE) in the west. Long-distance trade flourished, cities ballooned, standards of living rose, and the population surged. As a result of their military campaigns, Emperor Wu and his successors became monarchs enjoying tribute from distant vassal states. Normally the Han did not intervene in the domestic policy of such states unless they rebelled. Instead, the Han relied on trade and markets to induce their vassals to work within the tribute system and become prosperous satellite states.

Although clashes occurred between the nomadic Xiongnu and the sedentary Chinese farmers, more often relations in the borderlands produced benefits for both sides. After all, Han expansion coincided with the flourishing of the Silk

The Jade Gate. From the Jade Gate, the most significant pass on the Silk Road, foods, fruits, and religions of the "Western Regions" were introduced into central China during the Han dynasty. Chinese inventions, such as paper during the Later Han and then the compass and gunpowder, traveled in the opposite direction.

Road, where Xiongnu nomads were key middlemen. When the Xiongnu were no longer a threat to the north, Emperor Wu expanded westward. By 100 BCE, he had extended the northern defensive wall from the Tianshan Mountains to the Gobi Desert. Along the wall stood signal beacons for sending emergency messages, and its gates opened periodically for trading fairs. The westernmost gate was called the Jade Gate, since jade from the Taklamakan Desert passed through it. Wu also built garrison cities at oases to protect the trade routes; farthest west was Dunhuang, which later become a culturally diverse center of Buddhist thought and activity.

It was expensive to maintain a strong military force in such a remote and barren country, so Wu established military and farming settlements in the semidesert region. The state even encouraged soldiers to bring their families to settle on the frontier. As warfare in these territories was relatively infrequent, soldiers could spend time digging wells, building canals, and reclaiming wastelands. The government gave them seeds, tools, and technical support.

Soon after its military power expanded beyond the Jade Gate, the Han government set up a similar system of oases on the rim of the Taklamakan Desert. With irrigation, oasis agriculture attracted many more settlers. Traders now could find food for themselves and fodder for their animals as the Xiongnu fled westward. Trade routes passing through deserts and oases now were safer and more reliable than the steppe routes, which they gradually replaced. These new desert routes would flourish for another century, until fierce Tibetan tribes challenged the distant Han frontiers.

SOCIAL CONVULSIONS AND THE USURPER

Emperor Wu's dramatic military expansions required the stationing of soldiers in garrisons from central Asia to the Pacific and from Korea to Vietnam. However, further conquests failed to bolster the state's coffers, and the huge expenses of maintaining a gigantic army exhausted the imperial treasury. Wu raised taxes, which put a strain on small landholders and peasants—the bedrock of the empire. The strain continued after his death, and by the end of the first century BCE the Chinese empire was drained financially.

During this epoch large segments of the population suffered a dramatic economic blow, as natural disasters led to crop failures. These worsened the plight of poor farmers, for their taxes were based not on their crop yield but on the size of their holdings. Unable to pay their taxes, many free peasants had to sell their land to large landholders; they then became tenant farmers and sometimes slaves. As local landlords rebuilt their power and their landholdings, they accumulated even more wealth, which enabled them to obtain classical educations and pursue careers as government officials. As a burgeoning population faced land shortages in the countryside, the social fabric of Han society finally tore apart. In desperation, the dispossessed peasants rebelled.

This crisis led Wang Mang (r. 9–23 CE), a former Han minister and regent to a child emperor, to take over the throne and establish a new dynasty, as he believed that the Han had lost the mandate of heaven. After usurping power, he enacted reforms to help the poor. He fostered economic activity by confiscating gold from wealthy landowners and merchants and by depreciating the value of state coinage so that peasants could pay their taxes and their debts. He broke up large estates by limiting the amount of land each family could own, and he even prohibited the purchase and sale of land. His goal was to redistribute excess land equitably on the basis of an ancient ideal of a "well-field" land system: all families would work their own parcels and share in cultivating a communal plot whose crops would become tax surplus for the state. Wang Mang imposed higher taxes on artisans, hunters, fishermen, and silk weavers to pay for a storehouse system that would alleviate grain shortages, and he forbade slavery. Unfortunately, his reforms did not succeed.

NATURAL DISASTER AND REBELLION

Wang Mang succumbed to a violent upheaval by peasants and large landholders against central authority. Bad luck also played a part. Up to 5 million Chinese lived along the great northern plain south of the Yellow River, whose course—unluckily for Wang—changed soon after he assumed power. In 11 CE, the river broke through its dikes. Rather than bending northward on the Central Plain, it flowed due southward toward the Yellow Sea.

This demographic catastrophe plunged the north part of China into famine and banditry; it would repeat itself several more times in Chinese history. Each time it changed course from north to south and then back again, "China's Sorrow," as the river was called, unleashed tremendous flooding that caused mass death and vast migrations. Peasant impoverishment and revolt followed with chilling regularity. Researchers estimate that the floods of 11 CE affected some 28 million Chinese, or half the population.

Wang Mang's reforming regime was utterly unable to cope with a cataclysm of such magnitude. Rebellious peasants, led by Daoist clerics, used the disaster as a pretext to march on Wang's capital at Chang'an. The peasants painted their foreheads red and called themselves Red Eyebrows in imitation of demon warriors, and their leaders spoke to them through inspired religious mediums. By 23 CE they had overthrown Wang Mang.

Wang's enemies attributed the natural disaster to the emperor's unbridled misuse of power. They created a history of legitimate Han dynastic power that Wang Mang had illegitimately overturned, and soon Wang became the model of the evil usurper. His fall also brought an end to his reformist policies, as the statecraft tradition of the first half of the Han dynasty died out. Instead, a conservative ethos emerged during the Later Han dynasty that favored the hereditary privileged elite, who used Wang Mang's sudden fall to justify their own social and political power.

THE LATER HAN DYNASTY

After Wang Mang's fall, problems of social, political, and economic inequalities fatally diluted the central power of the emperor and the court. As a result, the Later Han dynasty (25–220 CE) followed a hands-off economic policy under which large landowners and merchants amassed more wealth and more property. Decentralizing the regime was also good for local business and long-distance trade, as the Silk Road continued to flourish. Chinese silk became popular as far away as the Roman Empire. In return, China received glass, jade, horses, precious stones, tortoiseshells, and fabrics.

By the second century CE, landed elites were enjoying the fruits of their success in manipulating the Later Han tax system. (In fact, it granted them so many land and labor ex-emptions that the government never again firmly controlled its human and agricultural resources as Emperor Wu had.) As the court refocused on the new capital in Luoyang, local power fell into the hands of great aristocratic families, who acquired even more privately owned land and forced free peasants to become their tenants.

Such prosperity bred greater social inequity and a new source of turmoil. Pressure grew on tenants to pay high rents, on the remaining free peasants to pay most of the taxes, and on poor migrant workers to serve as laborers. As the Later Han state's political arm weakened, its ritual tasks became more formalized. The simmering tensions between landholders and peasants boiled over in a full-scale rebellion in 184 CE. Popular religious groups, such as the Red Eyebrows, championed new ideas among commoners and elites during the Later Han dynasty. Confucius was no longer an exemplary figure: the new models were a mythical Yellow Emperor, extolled as the inventor of traditional Chinese writing and medicine; and the Daoist sage Master Laozi, the voice of naturalness and spontaneity. Laozi was now treated as a god. Although scholars scorned folk cults and magical practices, both commoners and local magnates in rural communities kept these beliefs alive.

At this propitious moment, Buddhist clerics from central Asia arrived in northern China preaching personal enlightenment for the elite and millenarian salvation for the masses. (A **millenarian movement** is a broad, popular upheaval calling for the restoration of a bygone moral age, often led by charismatic spiritual prophets.) Their message received a warm welcome from an increasingly disaffected population. Yet the most powerful challenge to the Later Han came not from the Buddhists but from the Daoists. As idiosyncratic Daoist masters challenged Confucian ritual conformity, they advanced their ideas in the name of a theocracy that would redeem all people. This motivated officials who were unhappy with Wang Mang's usurpation, and other political outcasts, to

Jade Burial Shroud. Shown here is the jade burial suit of Princess Tou Wan, late second century BCE.

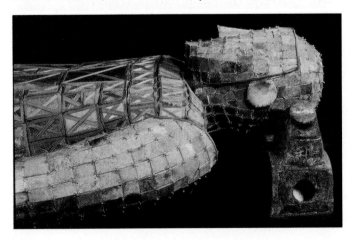

EMPIRES, ALLIES, AND FRONTIERS

Both the Han and the Roman empires faced threats on their frontiers and used allies as well as their own military prowess to counter such threats. Keeping good relations with frontier allies was essential to the statecraft of empires. It could also yield important intelligence for rulers in capitals.

THE HAN Consider how the Han dealt with their enemies, the Xiongnu. Emperor Wu sent a special envoy to the Yuezhi, whom he thought would be willing to ally with him against the Xiongnu. His emissary was Zhang Qian, who had volunteered to undertake the journey into the dangerous steppe. In 139 BCE, Zhang set out with a group of 100 people; one was a former slave from the steppe, Ganfu, who guided the travelers and used his bow to kill wild animals when they ran out of food. Aware of the envoy's purpose, the Xiongnu chief detained the group when they tried to pass through his territory. The Xiongnu kept Zhang Qian for ten years, during which time he married a Xiongnu woman and had children. Zhang learned much of steppe life and geography, but he did not forget his mission; together with Ganfu, he eventually managed to escape. At last, they reached the Yuezhi camp on the northern bank of the Oxus River.

Zhang Qian. This painting shows Zhang Qian crossing the Yellow River during his journey to the Yuezhi. Although he failed to forge an alliance for Emperor Wu, he returned home with valuable information about frontier areas of central Asia.

Unfortunately, Zhang Qian did not succeed in enlisting the support of the Yuezhi. Their surviving leaders had little inclination to return to the steppe to again battle the fierce Xiongnu, especially as they could see before them the fertile Bactrian plain dotted with Hellenistic cities (see Chapter 6). Zhang Qian accompanied the Yuezhi court in touring the land of Bactria. After consuming a year in futile negotiations with the Yuezhi leaders, Zhang set out for home, bearing much information about the cultures and products of Bactria and regions beyond, including India and Persia. He finally reached Chang'an, the Han capital, thirteen years after beginning his expedition. Although he had failed in his diplomatic mission, Zhang had collected invaluable information for Wudi about the frontier areas in central Asia.

THE ROMANS The Romans also had to deal with their frontiers. To the north they contended with "barbarians," and to the east they ran up against the powerful kingdoms of the Parthians and the Sasanians. But the Romans did have occasional contacts with kingdoms far to the east. For example, in the reign of Augustus (r. 27 BCE–14 CE) an embassy came from Poros, a king in India. In a letter that his ambassadors carried, Poros described himself as the king over 600 other kings, and he offered any help that the emperor Augustus might want of him. With the letter came gifts carried by eight slaves, naked except for their scented loincloths: a "freak," a number of large snakes, a huge turtle, and a partridge larger than a vulture.

Although embassies of this sort did bring information from far afield, Rome knew little of communities outside the empire to the east except for the peoples and provinces of the Parthian and Sasanian empires, which were closest to its frontiers. Most of this knowledge was very local in nature, gained not through formal channels but in contacts between the two states over military or territorial problems or from merchants and other travelers. Diplomacy did exist, but the Roman Empire had no centralized office to manage intelligence reports.

More important than statecraft were exchanges along the Silk Road that brought news, rumors, and impressions of distant empires. The Chinese were the source of the most expensive item in the Roman Empire: the highly valued commodity silk. But in Roman eyes, the Chinese were still very remote and unknown. As Pliny the Elder wrote, "Though mild in character, the Chinese still resemble wild animals in that they shun the company of the rest of humankind, and wait for trade to come to them." Although connected, the two empires that so dominated their own worlds were still worlds apart.

head up strong dissident groups and eventually form local movements. Under their leadership, religious groups such as the Yellow Turbans—so called because of the yellow scarves that they wrapped around their heads—championed Daoist millenarian movements across the empire.

Proclaiming the Daoist millenarian belief in a future "Great Peace," the Yellow Turbans demanded fairer treatment by the Han state and equal distribution of all farm lands. When agrarian conditions got worse, widespread famine ensued—a catastrophe that, in the rebels' view, demonstrated the emperor's loss of the mandate of heaven. The economy disintegrated when people refused to pay taxes and provide forced labor, and internal wars engulfed the dynasty. After the 180s CE, three competing states replaced the Han: the Wei in the northwest, the Shu in the southwest, and the Wu in the south. A unified empire did not return until three centuries later.

THE ROMAN EMPIRE

> → *Were the policies and institutions that integrated the Roman Empire similar to those of Han dynasty China?*

The other large empire of the time flexed its muscle at the other end of Afro-Eurasia. There, Rome was a great power ruling 60 to 70 million subjects. The Roman Empire at its height encompassed lands from the highlands of what is now Scotland to the lower reaches of the Nile River in modern-day Egypt and part of Sudan, and from the borders of the Inner Eurasian steppe in Ukraine and the Caucasus to the Atlantic shores of North Africa. (See Map 7-3.) It was comparable in size to Han dynasty China.

Whereas China dominated an enormous and unbroken landmass, the Roman Empire dominated lands around the Mediterranean Sea. Like Han China, though, the Romans acquired command over their world through an unprecedented exercise of violence. By the first century CE, almost unceasing wars against their neighbors had enabled the Romans to forge an unparalleled number of ethnic groups and minor states into a single, large political state. (See Global Connections & Disconnections: Empires, Allies, and Frontiers.) This achievement was so striking that the Jewish historian and general Josephus, writing in the 90s CE, saw the empire as the unchallengeable work of God on earth. We can easily see how the Latin word that the Romans used to designate command over their subjects—*imperium*—became the source for the English words *empire* and *imperialism*.

FOUNDATIONS OF THE ROMAN EMPIRE

The emergence of Rome as a world-dominating power was a surprise. Although the Romans might have looked to the Persians or to Alexander the Great for imperial models, they did not. And unlike the Han, they had no great imperial

War Elephants. There are no contemporary illustrations of the elephants that Hannibal brought when he invaded Italy in 217 BCE. Hannibal was influenced by the Hellenistic armies in the east who had borrowed the idea of war elephants, and the elephants themselves, from Indian rulers. This painting, by an artist from the school of the Renaissance painter Raphael, highlights the terrifying aspect of the elephants and reduces the human warriors to bit players. In fact, the elephants were not decisive in the winning of any major battle in Italy in the Second Roman-Carthaginian War. Hannibal won them all by superior generalship.

ancestors. Down to the 350s BCE, the Romans were just one of a number of Latin-speaking communities in Latium, a region in the center of the Italian peninsula. Although Rome was one of the largest urban centers there, it was still only a city-state that had to ally with other towns for self-defense. However, Rome soon began an extraordinary phase of military and territorial expansion, and by 265 BCE it had taken control of most of the peninsula. At least two factors contributed to this achievement: a migration of foreign peoples, and the Romans' own military and political innovations.

POPULATION MOVEMENTS   Between 450 and 250 BCE, migrations from northern and central Europe brought large numbers of Celts to settle in lands around the Mediterranean Sea. They convulsed the northern rim of the Mediterranean, staging armed forays into lands from what is now Spain in the west to present-day Turkey in the east.

One of these migrations involved dozens of Gallic peoples in a series of violent incursions into northern Italy that ultimately—around 390 BCE—led to the seizure of Rome. The important result for the Romans was not their city's capture, which was temporary (they paid the Gauls to go away), but the permanent dislocation that the invaders inflicted on the city-states of the Etruscans, who until then had dominated the Italian peninsula. The Etruscans survived and, with great effort, drove the invading Gauls back northward. However, Etruscan cities never recovered their ability to dominate other peoples in Italy, including the Romans. Thus the Gallic migrations removed one of the most formidable roadblocks to Roman expansion in Italy.

MILITARY INSTITUTIONS AND THE WAR ETHOS
Rome's unparalleled expansion could not have occurred without the unique military and political institutions that it developed. Basically, the Romans were more successful and more efficient in killing other humans than any other people in their part of the world. They achieved unassailable military power by organizing the communities that they conquered in Italy into a system that generated huge reservoirs of manpower for their army. This development began between 340 and 335 BCE, when the Romans faced a concerted attack by their fellow Latin city-states. By then, the Latins were viewing Rome not as an ally in a system of mutual defense but as a growing threat to their own independence. After overcoming the nearby Latins, the Romans charged on to defeat one community after another in Italy. Their main demand of all defeated enemies was to provide men for the Roman army every year. The result was a snowball-like accumulation of military manpower.

By 265 BCE, Rome controlled the Italian peninsula. It next entered into three wars with the Carthaginians, the major power located in the northern parts of present-day Tunisia. The First Punic War (264–241 BCE) was a prolonged naval battle over the island of Sicily. With their victory, the Romans acquired a dominant position in the western Mediterranean.

The Second Punic War (218–201 BCE), however, revealed the real strength and might of Roman arms. The Carthaginian general Hannibal realized that if his troops were to have any hope of victory, they would have to attack the Italian peninsula

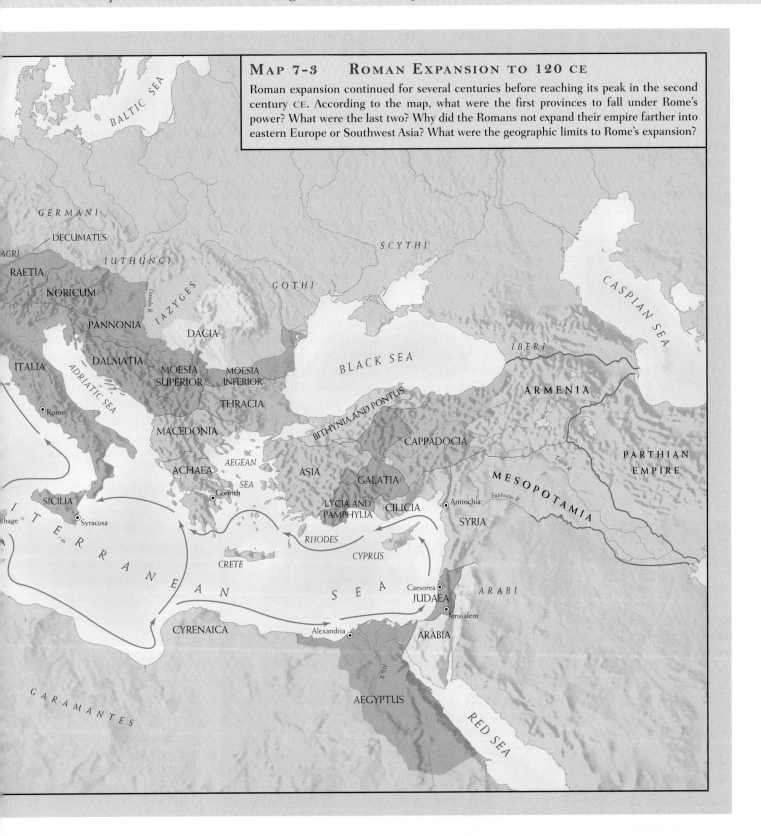

MAP 7-3 ROMAN EXPANSION TO 120 CE

Roman expansion continued for several centuries before reaching its peak in the second century CE. According to the map, what were the first provinces to fall under Rome's power? What were the last two? Why did the Romans not expand their empire farther into eastern Europe or Southwest Asia? What were the geographic limits to Rome's expansion?

itself. The new Roman military system, however, made a Roman victory almost certain. Whereas the Carthaginians' resources were those of a large city-state, Rome was more like a modern nation-state drafting manpower from a huge population. Nonetheless Hannibal moved his foot soldiers and cavalry from southern Spain toward the Italian peninsula. After the heroic feat of crossing the Pyrenees and the Alps with his war elephants, he entered Italy with a force of only about 20,000 men. In contrast, Rome could draw on reserves of more than 750,000 men. With those numbers, Roman commanders could afford to lose battles—which they proceeded to do, suffering casualties of about 60,000 to 80,000 dead in three great encounters with the Carthaginian general—and still win the war. They finally did so in 201 BCE. In the end, not even a strategic and tactical genius like Hannibal could prevail against the Roman military system. In a final war of extermination, waged between 150 and 146 BCE, the Romans used their overwhelming advantage in manpower, ships, and other resources to bring the four-centuries-long hegemony of Carthage in the western Mediterranean to an end.

In addition to their overwhelming advantage in manpower, the Romans cultivated an unusual **war ethos**. A heightened sense of honor drove Roman men to push themselves into battle again and again, and never to accept defeat. They were educated to imitate the example of such soldiers as Marcus Sergius. Wounded twenty-three times in battle, Sergius was crippled in both hands and both feet. In the war with Hannibal he lost one hand but continued to serve, using a false right hand made out of iron. He was twice taken prisoner by Hannibal, each time escaping despite being kept in chains. Going into action four times with his artificial hand tied to the stump of his arm, Sergius helped to rescue major Roman cities from Carthaginian sieges—and twice the horse that he was riding was cut out from under him. Such men set a high standard of commitment to war. What also propelled Roman soldiers was an unusual regime of training and

discipline, in which minor infractions of duty were punishable by death (in Greek armies, by contrast, misconduct merely drew fines). Disobedience by a whole unit led to a savage mass punishment, called "decimation," in which every tenth man was arbitrarily selected and executed. For men like Sergius, going out on the annual spring campaigns in the month dedicated to Mars (still called March today), the Roman god of war, had an almost biological rhythm.

Displaying an unrelenting compulsion to war, the Romans continued to draft, train, and field extraordinary numbers of men. Soldiers, conscripted at age seventeen or eighteen, could expect to serve for up to ten years at a time. With so many young men devoted to war for such long spans, the war ethos became deeply embedded in the ideals of every generation. After 200 BCE the Romans unleashed this successful war machine on the kingdoms of the eastern Mediterranean—with devastating results. In one year, 146 BCE, the Romans achieved the final extermination of what was left of Carthage in the west—killing all its adult males and selling all its women and children into slavery—and the parallel obliteration of the great Greek city-state of Corinth in the east. Their monopoly of power over the entire Mediterranean basin was now unchallenged.

Roman military forces served under men who knew they could win not just glory and territory for the state, but also enormous rewards for themselves. They were talented men driven by burning ambition, from Scipio Africanus in the 200s BCE, the conqueror of Carthage (a man who claimed that he personally communicated with the gods), to

Roman Farmers and Soldiers. In the late Republic most Roman soldiers came from rural Italy, where small farms were being absorbed into the landholdings of the wealthy and powerful. In the empire, soldiers were recruited from rural provincial regions. They sometimes worked small fields of their own and sometimes worked the lands of the wealthy—like the domain in the Roman province of Africa (in modern-day Tunisia) that is depicted in this mosaic.

Julius Caesar, the great general of the 50s BCE. A man of prodigious abilities, the greatest orator of his age, and a writer of boundless persuasion, Julius Caesar (100–44 BCE) allegedly could dictate seven letters simultaneously while attending to other duties. He was also a mass killer who kept an exact body count: he knew that he had killed precisely 1,192,000 of the enemy in his wars. And that number did not include his fellow citizens, whose murders during civil wars he refused to acknowledge or add to the total. The eight-year-long cycle of his wars in Gaul (modern-day France and the Rhine valley) was one of the most murderous of his expeditions. By Caesar's own estimation, his army killed more than 1 million Gauls and enslaved another million. The Western world had never witnessed war on this scale; it had no equal anywhere, except in China.

POLITICAL INSTITUTIONS AND INTERNAL CONFLICT

The conquest of the Mediterranean placed unprecedented power and wealth into the hands of a few men in the Roman social elite. The rush of battlefield successes had kept Romans and their Italian allies preoccupied with the demands of army service overseas. Once this process of territorial expansion slowed, social and political problems that had been lying dormant back home began to resurface.

Following the traditional date of its foundation in 509 BCE, the Romans had lived in a state that they called the "public thing," or *Res publica* (hence, "republic"). Here, policy and rules of behavior issued from the Senate—a body of permanent members, 300 to 600 of Rome's most powerful and wealthy citizens—and from popular assemblies of the citizens. The Republic would remain the only form of Roman government for the next five centuries. Every year the citizens elected the officials of state, principally two consuls who held power for a year and commanded the armies. In addition, the people annually elected ten men who, as tribunes of the plebs ("the common people"), had the special task of protecting their interests against those of the rich and the powerful. In severe political crises, the Romans sometimes chose one man to hold absolute power over the state; his words, or *dicta,* were law—so he was called a *dictator.* (Under a similar device in China, centrally designated overlords were charged with stabilizing unruly provinces.) Ordinarily the dictator could hold those powers for no longer than six months. The problems with using these institutions, originally devised for a city-state, to rule a Mediterranean-sized empire became glaringly apparent by the second century BCE.

Rome's power elite exploited the wealth from its Mediterranean conquests to acquire huge tracts of land in Italy and Sicily, and then they imported enormous numbers of slaves from all around the Mediterranean to work them. This process drove the free citizen farmers, the backbone of the army, off their lands and into the cities. The result was a severe agrarian and recruiting crisis. In 133 and 123–121 BCE

Julius Caesar. This full-size statue represents Caesar as a high-ranking Roman army commander and conveys some of the power and influence that a charismatic military and political leader like Caesar had over both soldiers and citizen voters. Caesar belonged to a generation of Roman politicians who were immensely attentive to their public images.

two tribunes, the brothers Tiberius and Gaius Gracchus, tried to institute land reforms guaranteeing to all of Rome's poor citizens a basic amount of land that would qualify them for army service. But political enemies assassinated both men. Thereafter, poor Roman citizens looked not to state institutions but to army commanders, to whom they gave their loyalty and support, to provide them with land and a decent income. These generals thus became increasingly powerful and started to compete with one another, ignoring the Senate and the traditional rules of politics. As they sought control of the state and their supporters took sides, a long series of civil wars began in 90 BCE. The tremendous resources built up during the conquest of the Mediterranean were now turned inward by the Romans on themselves. These civil wars threatened to tear the empire to pieces from the inside.

EMPERORS, AUTHORITARIAN RULE, AND ADMINISTRATION

It is ironic that the most warlike of all ancient Mediterranean states was responsible for creating the most pervasive and long-lasting peace of its time—the *Pax Romana* ("Roman Peace"; 25 BCE–235 CE). Worn out by half a century of savage civil wars, by the 30s BCE the Romans, including their warlike governing elite, were ready to change their values. They were now prepared to embrace the virtues of peace.

However, political stability came at a price: authoritarian one-man rule. Peace depended on the power of one man who possessed enough authority to enforce an orderly competition among Roman aristocrats. Ultimately, Julius Caesar's adopted son, Octavian (63 BCE–14 CE), would reunite the fractured empire and emerge as undisputed master of the Roman world. Octavian concentrated most of the state's surplus wealth, the most important official titles, and the positions of power in his own hands. To signal the transition to a new political order in which he alone would control the army, the provinces, and the political processes in Rome, he assumed a new name, Augustus ("the Revered One"). He also assumed a series of titles: *imperator,* or "commander in chief" (compare the English word *emperor*); *princeps,* or "first man" (whence the English *prince*); and *caesar* (pronounced "kaisar" in Latin and the source of the words *tsar* in Russian and *kaiser* in German). Augustus became the first of dozens of men who, over the next five centuries, were to rule over Rome's vast dominions as emperors.

Rome's subjects tended to see these emperors as heroic or semidivine beings in life, and to think of the good ones as becoming gods on their death. This propensity to deify good emperors prompted the Emperor Vespasian's famous deathbed joke: "Dear me, I think I'm turning into a god!" Yet emperors were always careful to present themselves as civil rulers whose power ultimately depended on the consent of Roman citizens and the might of the army. They contrasted themselves with the image of "king," or absolute tyrannical ruler, whom the Romans for centuries had learned to detest. The emperors' powers were nevertheless immense. Moreover, many of them deployed their powers arbitrarily and whimsically, exciting a profound fear of emperors in general. One such emperor was Caligula (r. 37–41 CE), who presented himself as a living god on earth, engaged in casual incest with his sister, and kept books filled with the names of persons he wanted to kill. His violent behavior was so erratic that people thought he suffered from serious mental disorders; those who feared him called him a living monster.

Being a Roman emperor was a high-wire act that required finesse and talent, and few succeeded at it. Of the twenty-two emperors who held power in the most stable period of Roman history (between the first Roman emperor, Augustus, and the early third century), fifteen met their end by murder or suicide. As powerful as he might be, no individual emperor alone could govern an empire of such great size and population, encompassing a multitude of languages and cultures. He needed institutions and competent people to help him. In terms of sheer power, the most important institution was the army. So the emperors systematically transformed the army into a full-time professional force. Men now entered the imperial army not as citizen volunteers but as paid experts who signed up for life and swore loyalty to the emperor and his family. And it was part of the emperor's image to present himself as a victorious battlefield commander, inflicting

Symbols of Roman Power. Roman power was conveyed to people as much by symbols as by actual words. In this piece of sculpture from Santo Omobono in Rome dating to the third century BCE, we see symbols of imperial power. The winged figures to the left and right of the military shield represent the idea of Victory; the eagle on the shield, holding lightning bolts in its claws, represents brute power; and the garland at the top of the shield represents the wealth and rewards of empire. These powerful images have been copied by many modern states in the West.

defeat on the "barbarians" who threatened the empire's frontiers. Such a warrior emperor, like Trajan, was a "good" emperor.

For most emperors, however, governance was largely a daily chore of listening to complaints, answering petitions, deciding court cases, and hearing reports from civil administrators and military commanders. By the second century CE, the empire encompassed more than forty provinces or administrative units; as in Han China, each had a governor appointed or approved by the emperor. In turn, these governors depended on lower-ranking officials. Compared with the Chinese imperial state, however, which had its ranks of senior and junior officials, the Roman empire of this period was relatively understaffed in terms of central government officials. The emperor and his provincial governors had to depend very much on local help, sometimes aided by elite slaves and freedmen (former slaves) serving as government bureaucrats. With these few full-time assistants and an entourage of friends and acquaintances, the governor was expected to guarantee peace and collect taxes for his province. For many essential tasks, though, especially the collection of imperial taxes, even these helpers were insufficient. Thus the state had to rely on private companies, a measure that set up a tension between the profit motives of the publicans (the men in the companies that took up government contracts) and expectations of fair government among the empire's subjects.

TOWN AND CITY LIFE

Above all, the emperor counted on local elites to see him as a presence that guaranteed the stability of their world and their personal well-being. Because of the unusual concentration of wealth that imperial unity generated, core areas of the empire—central Italy, southern Spain, northern Africa, and the western parts of present-day Turkey—had surprising densities of urban settlements. Perhaps up to one in every twenty persons in these regions lived in a town.

MUNICIPALITIES Inasmuch as these towns imitated Roman forms of government, they provided the backbone of local administration for the empire. (See Primary Source: Municipal Charter of a Roman Town.) This system of municipalities would become a permanent legacy of Roman government to the Western world. Some of our best records of how these towns operated come from Spain, which later flourished as a colonial power that exported Roman forms of municipal life to the Americas.

Remarkable physical records of such towns come from Pompeii and Herculaneum in southern Italy. Both towns were almost perfectly preserved by the ash and debris that buried them following the explosion of a nearby volcano, Mount Vesuvius, in 79 CE. Their excavation has provided

A Roman Town. Roman towns featured many of the standard elements of modern towns and cities. Streets and avenues crossed at right angles; streets were paved; sidewalks ran between streets and houses. The houses were often several stories high and had wide windows and open balconies. All these elements can be seen in this street from Herculaneum, nicely preserved by the pyroclastic flow that ran down the slopes of nearby Mount Vesuvius when its volcano erupted in August of 79 CE, burying the town and its inhabitants.

astounding information. Towns often were walled, and inside those walls the streets and avenues ran at right angles. A large, open-air, rectangular area called the *forum* dominated the town center. Around it clustered the main public buildings: the markets, the main temples of principal gods and goddesses, and the building that housed city administrators. Residential areas featured regular blocks of houses, usually tiled with bright red roof tiles, close together and fronting on the streets. Larger towns like Ostia, the port city of Rome, contained large apartment blocks that were not much different from the four- and five-story buildings in any modern city. In the smaller towns, sanitary and alimentary conditions were reasonably good. Human skeletons discovered at Herculaneum in the 1970s revealed people in good health, with much better teeth than many people have today—a difference we can explain largely by the lack of sugar in their diet.

ROME The imperial metropolis of Rome was another matter. With well over a million inhabitants, it was an almost grotesque exaggeration of everything good and bad in Roman city life. (The only other urban centers of comparable size at the time were Xianyang and Chang'an—the Qin and Han capitals, respectively—each with a population of between 300,000 and 500,000.) Rome's inhabitants were privileged, because there the emperor's power and state's wealth guaranteed them a basic food supply. Thirteen huge and vastly

Primary Source

MUNICIPAL CHARTER OF A ROMAN TOWN

Town governments in the Roman Empire followed standard rules and regulations that developed during the Roman conquest of Italy. In 1981, detailed copies of some of these regulations came to light in southern Spain at Molino del Postero (called Irni in Roman times). The Roman governor of Spain in 81 CE had the rules incised on ten plates of bronze for public display in the town's forum. By following these and other rules, the residents of a Spanish community learned how to govern themselves as the Romans did (see a Roman municipal charter on the facing page).

XIX ON AEDILES: The aediles [the two town business managers] . . . are to have the right and power of managing the grain supply, the sacred buildings, the sacred and holy places, the town and its roads and neighborhoods, the drains and sewers, the baths, the marketplace, and of checking weights and measures; and also of setting a night watch if the need arises.

XX CONCERNING THE RIGHT AND POWER OF QUAESTORS: The quaestors [the two town financial officers] . . . are to have the right and power of collecting, spending, storing, administering, and managing the common funds of the municipality at the discretion of the *duumviri* [the two town mayors]. And they are allowed to have the public slaves belonging to the municipality to help them.

XXI HOW ROMAN CITIZENSHIP IS ACQUIRED IN THE MUNICIPALITY: When those who are senators, decurions [town councillors], or conscripted town councillors who have been or are chosen as town magistrates according to the terms of this law, have completed their term of office, they are to become Roman citizens, along with their parents and wives and any children who have been born out of legal marriages and who are in the power of their parents, and likewise grandsons and granddaughters born to a son. . . .

XXVIII CONCERNING THE FREEING OF SLAVES BEFORE THE MAYORS: If any citizen of the municipality of Flavian Irni . . . in the presence of a *duumvir* [mayor] of that municipality in charge of the administration of justice sets free his male or female slave from slavery into freedom or orders him or her to be free . . . then any male slave who has been manumitted or ordered to be free in this way is to be free, any female slave who has been manumitted or ordered to be free in this way is also to be free. . . . Someone who is under twenty years of age may manumit his or her slave only if the number of town councillors necessary for decrees passed under this law to be valid decides that the grounds for said manumission are proper.

➤ *What were some of the titles of civil servants in a typical Roman town or municipality?*

➤ *According to this charter, what different types of people were part of the normal social structure?*

➤ *In what ways could certain inhabitants of towns such as Irni become Roman citizens?*

➤ *Why would making small towns uniform in design and function be important to the Roman Empire?*

SOURCE: J. González, "The *Lex Irnitana*: A New Copy of the Flavian Municipal Law," from *Journal of Roman Studies*, Vol. 76 (1986). Reprinted with permission of the Society for the Promotion of Roman Studies. Translated by Brent Shaw.

A Roman Municipal Charter. This bronze tablet inscribed in Latin is part of a group of six bronze tablets discovered in 1981 at the Roman town of Irni, near modern Molino del Postero, in southern Spain. Charters like this one, set up for public display in the forum or central open area of the town, displayed regulations for the conduct of public life in a Roman town, from rules governing family inheritance and property transfers to the election of town officials and definitions of their powers and duties. For some of these rules, see the Primary Source box on the facing page.

expensive aqueducts provided a dependable supply of water, sometimes flowing in from great distances. Most adult citizens regularly received a free, basic amount of wheat (and, later, olive oil and pork). But living conditions were often appalling, with people jammed into ramshackle high-rise apartments that threatened to collapse on their renters or go up in flames. And Romans constantly complained of crime and violence. Even worse was the lack of sanitary conditions—despite the sewage and drainage works that were wonders of their time. Rome was disease-ridden; its inhabitants died from infection at a fearsome rate—malarial infections were particularly bad—so the city required a substantial input of immigrants every year just to maintain its population.

MASS ENTERTAINMENT Every self-respecting Roman town had at least two major entertainment venues. One was an adoption from Hellenistic culture: a theater devoted to plays, dances, and other popular events. The other was a Roman innovation that combined two horseshoe-shaped theaters into a single, more elaborate structure called an amphitheater. A much larger seating capacity than in a regular theater surrounded the oval performance area at its center. The emperors Vespasian and Titus completed the Flavian

Amphitheater in Rome and dedicated it in 80 CE. It is the vast structure that we know today as the Colosseum, after the colossal statue of the emperor Nero that used to stand beside it. It was a state-of-the-art facility whose floor area, the arena, could handle elaborate hunts of exotic wild animals such as giraffes and elephants. The arena could also be flooded to stage naval battles between hostile fleets, much to the delight of the audience, or it could provide a venue for a Roman invention, gladiatorial games. In these expensive public entertainments, heavily armed and well-trained men—most of them slaves and prisoners of war, but sometimes free men who volunteered—fought each other, wounding or

Aqueduct. The Romans built aqueducts to transport to Rome the huge amounts of water needed for the city's population of over a million. The idea soon spread to the provinces, where these structures were built to bring water to Roman-style cities developing in the peripheral regions of Roman rule. This aqueduct at Segovia in modern Spain is one of the best preserved.

North African Amphitheater. This huge amphitheater is in the remains of the Roman city of Thysdrus in North Africa (the town of el-Jem in modern-day Tunisia). The wealth of the Africans under the empire enabled them to build colossal entertainment venues that competed with the one at Rome in scale and grandeur.

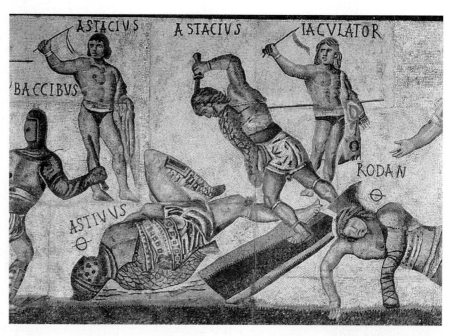

Roman Gladiators. In this brilliant mosaic from Rome, we see two gladiators at the end of a full combat in which Astacius has killed Astivus. The Greek letter theta, or "th" (the circle with crossbar through it), beside the names of Astivus and Rodan indicates that these men are dead—*thanatos* being the Greek word for "death."

killing for the enjoyment of the huge crowds of appreciative spectators.

Westerners tend to think of these structures for public entertainment as ordinary and normal. Seen from a contemporary Chinese perspective, however, they were strange and unusual. Among the Han, local elites and the imperial family created gigantic palace complexes complete with hunting parks to impress and amuse themselves, not the general public. In contrast, the public entertainment facilities of a Roman town reflected attitudes that stressed the importance of citizens in town life.

SOCIAL AND GENDER RELATIONS

Even more significant than political forums and game venues were the personal relations that linked the rich and powerful with the mass of average citizens. Men and women of wealth and high social status acted as **patrons**, protecting and supporting dependents or "clients" of a lower class. From the emperor at the top to the local municipal man at the bottom, these relationships were reinforced by generous distributions of food and entertainments from wealthy men to their people. The bonds between these groups in each city found formal expression in legal definitions of patrons' responsibilities to clients; at the same time, the informal social code raised expectations that the wealthy would be public benefactors. For example, a senator, Pliny the Younger, constructed for his hometown a public library and a bathhouse; supported a teacher of Latin; and established a fund to support the sons and daughters of former slaves. The emperors at the very top were no different. Augustus documented the scale of his gifts to the Roman people in his autobiography, gifts that exceeded hundreds of millions of sesterces (a small silver or bronze coin) in expenditures from his own pocket. A later emperor, Trajan, established a social scheme for feeding the children of poor Roman citizens in Italy—a benefaction that he advertised on coins and in pictures on arches in Beneventum and other towns in Italy.

The essence of Roman civil society, though, involved the formal relationships governed by Rome's laws and courts. Public courts heard all disputes, and decisions issued from judges and, sometimes, large juries. By the last century BCE, the Roman state's complex legal system featured not only a rich body of written law but also institutions for settling legal disputes and a growing number of highly educated men who specialized in interpreting the law. The apparatus of Roman law eventually appeared in every town and city of the empire, creating a deeply entrenched civil culture. It is no surprise that this legal infrastructure persisted long after the empire's political and military institutions had disappeared.

Municipal charters and civil laws—as well as secular philosophers and, later, Christian writers—placed the family at the very foundation of the Roman social order. The authoritarian *paterfamilias* ("father of the family") headed the family. Legally speaking, he had nearly total power over his

Primary Source

BIRTHDAY INVITATION OF CLAUDIA SEVERA

The ability to write in Latin became so widespread under the Roman Empire that even its frontier areas could boast basic literacy. Excavations of a Roman army base at Vindolanda, in northern England, have unearthed a cache of documents written on thin sheets of wood. These reveal the normal use of Latin writing for everyday activities late in the first century CE. Officers' wives were just as skilled in writing as the men. One of these elite women, Claudia Severa, sent a letter inviting a good friend (whom she addresses affectionately as "sister") to her birthday party. The elegant handwriting on several documents is almost certainly that of Claudia herself. The second letter is her friend's reply.

[Address on the outside:] To Sulpicia Lepidina, wife of Cerialis, from Severa.
[Claudia Severa to her Lepidina, Greetings!]

My sister, I am sending an invitation to you to attend my birthday festivities on the third day before the Ides of September [September 11 in our calendar]—just to make sure that you come to visit us. Your presence will make the day all the more enjoyable for me. Please convey my greetings to your Cerialis [i.e., Lepidina's husband]. My Aelius and our little son send him their warmest greetings.

I await your arrival, my sister.

I bid you goodbye, my sister, my dearest soul. Be well.

[Sulpicia Lepidina to Claudia Severa] Greeting.

Just as I had told you, my sister, and had promised that I would ask your Brocchus [i.e., Claudia Severa's husband, Aelius Brocchus] for permission to come to visit you, he replied to me that I was, of course, always most welcome to come. . . . [I shall try] to come to you by whatever way I can, for there are certain things that we must do . . . on which matter you will receive a letter from me so that you will know what I am going to do. . . .

Farewell, my sister, my dearest and most-desired soul . . .

→ *What does the writing of letters in Latin at this far edge of the empire tell us about Roman culture?*

→ *Sulpicia mentions asking Claudia's husband for permission to visit Claudia. Why would she do this? Do you think it indicates that the women's husbands were of different military rank, or that Sulpicia was merely following Roman social customs for women—or both? Or something else?*

→ *What does the very existence of these letters tell us about Roman women?*

SOURCE: Alan K. Bowman and J. David Thomas, with contributions by J. N. Adams, *The Vindolanda Writing-Tablets (Tabulae Vindolandenses II)* (London: British Museum Press, 1994), nos. 291 and 292, pp. 256–62. Translated by Brent Shaw.

dependents, including his wife, children, grandchildren, and the slaves whom he owned. Imperial society heightened the importance of the basic family unit of mother, father, and children in the urban centers. As in Han dynasty China, the Roman state regularly undertook a census, rigorously counting the empire's inhabitants and assessing their property for tax purposes—a process that underscored the family as the core unit of society.

This system might seem to place women under the domineering rule of fathers and husbands. That is certainly the picture presented in the repressive laws that Roman men drafted and in the histories that Roman men wrote. But com-pared with women in most Greek city-states, Roman women, even those of only modest wealth and status, had much greater freedom of action and much greater control of their own wealth and property. (See Primary Source: Birthday Invitation of Claudia Severa.) Thus Terentia, the wife of the Republican senator Cicero, bought and sold properties on her own, made decisions regarding her family and wealth without consulting her husband (much to his chagrin—he later divorced her), and apparently fared well following her separation from Cicero. Her behavior was normal for a woman of her status: she was well educated, literate, well connected, and in control of her own life—despite what the laws and ideas of Roman males might suggest. The daily lives of ordinary women that we know of from papyrus documents found in the Roman province of Egypt, for example, show them buying, selling, renting, and leasing with no sign that the legal constraints subjecting them to male control had any significant effect on their dealings.

Terentia reminds us of Ban Zhao, the younger sister of the historian Ban Gu (32–92 CE). She became the first female Chinese historian and lived relatively unconstrained. After marrying the local resident, Cao Shishu, at the age of fourteen, she was called Madame Cao at court. Subsequently she completed her elder brother's *History of the Former Han Dynasty* when he was imprisoned and executed. In addition to completing the first full dynastic history in China, Ban Zhao wrote *Lessons for Women*, in which she described the status of elite women and presented the ideal woman in light of her virtue, her type of work, and the words she spoke and wrote. Ban represented a conservative version of the perennial "talented woman" in China, whose virtue was never eclipsed by her literary production or lifestyle.

ECONOMY AND NEW SCALES OF PRODUCTION

Rome achieved staggering transformations in the production of agricultural, manufactured, and mined goods. Public and private demand for metals, for example, led the Romans to mine lead, silver, and copper in Spain in operations so

Coin Hoard. The use of coins for a wide spectrum of economic exchanges became common in the Roman Empire. Looking at the batches buried for safekeeping gives us an idea of the range of coins in circulation at any one time. This coin hoard was found near Didcot in Oxfordshire, England. Buried about 165 CE, it contained about 125 gold coins minted between the 50s and 160s CE and represents the equivalent of about eleven years' pay for a Roman soldier. Gold coins were used for expensive transactions or to store wealth. Most ordinary purchases or payments were made with silver or brass coins.

Roman Roads. Like Qin and Han China, the Roman Empire was characterized by large-scale road building, which began as early as the late fourth century BCE. Roads eventually connected most land areas and larger urban centers in the empire, considerably easing ordinary travel, as well as trade and commerce. Here we see part of the Via Appia, the great highway that connected Rome with the southern parts of Italy.

massive that traces of the air pollution they generated remain in ice core samples taken from Greenland today. Evidence from Mediterranean shipwrecks similarly indicates a seaborne trade on an unprecedented scale. The area of land surveyed and cultivated rose steadily throughout this period, as Romans reached into arid lands on the periphery of the Sahara Desert to the south and opened up heavily forested regions in present-day France and Germany to the north. (See Map 7-4.)

The Romans also built an unprecedented number of roads to connect far-flung parts of their empire. Although many roads did not have the high-quality flagstone paving and excellent drainage exhibited by highways in Italy, such as the Via Appia, most were systematically marked by milestones (for the first time in this part of the world) so that travelers would know their precise location and the distance to the next town. Also for the first time, complex land maps and itineraries specified all major roads and distances between towns. Adding to the roads' significance was their deliberate coordination with Mediterranean sea routes to support the smooth and safe flow of traffic, commerce, and ideas on land and at sea.

The mines produced copper, tin, silver, and gold—out of which the Roman state produced the most massive coinage known in the Western world before early modern times.

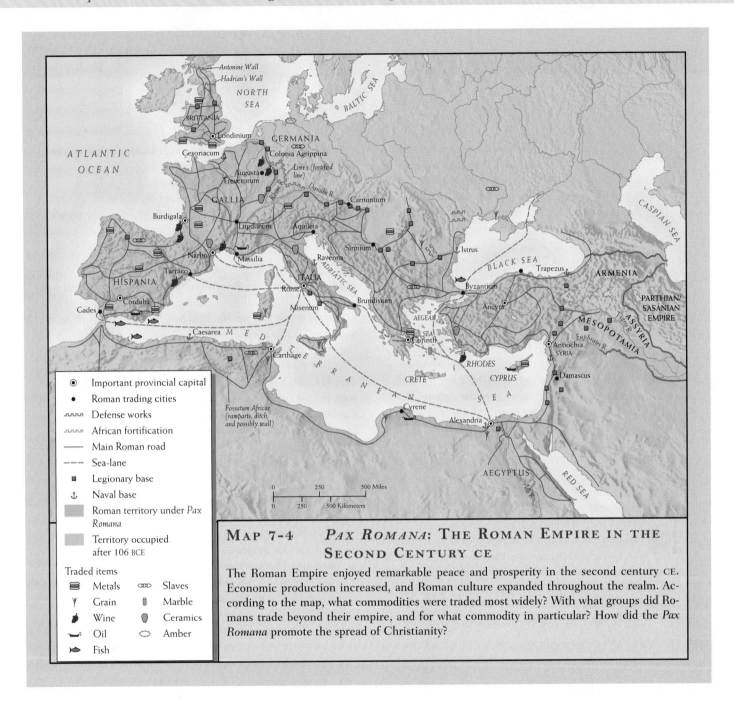

MAP 7-4 — *PAX ROMANA*: THE ROMAN EMPIRE IN THE SECOND CENTURY CE

The Roman Empire enjoyed remarkable peace and prosperity in the second century CE. Economic production increased, and Roman culture expanded throughout the realm. According to the map, what commodities were traded most widely? With what groups did Romans trade beyond their empire, and for what commodity in particular? How did the *Pax Romana* promote the spread of Christianity?

Coinage facilitated the exchange of commodities and services, which now carried standard values. Throughout the Roman Empire, from small towns on the edge of the Sahara Desert to army towns along the northern frontiers, people appraised, purchased, and sold goods in coin denominations. Taxes were assessed and hired laborers were paid in coin. The economy in its leading sectors functioned more efficiently because of the production of coins on an immense scale (paralleled only by the coinage output of Han dynasty China and its successors).

Roman mining, as well as other sizable operations, relied on chattel slaves—human beings purchased as private property. The massive concentration of wealth and slaves at the center of the Roman world led to the first large-scale commercial plantation agriculture, along with the first technical handbooks on how to run such operations for profit. These estates specialized in products destined for the big urban markets: wheat, grapes, and olives, as well as cattle and sheep. Such developments rested on a bedrock belief that private property and its ownership were sacrosanct. In fact, the Roman senator Cicero

Primary Source

CICERO ON THE ROLE OF THE ROMAN STATE

Whereas Greek thinkers debated ethics and morals, the role of the good life, and the nature of the universe, Romans deliberated more about the nature of government and the role of the state. This focus reflects their pragmatic attitudes and their possession of a huge empire. In the following passage, Marcus Tullius Cicero, one of the leading Roman politicians from the 60s to the 40s BCE, discusses how any man who holds public office in the Roman state has a duty to defend the state's main function.

That man who undertakes responsibility for public office in the state must make it his first priority to see that every person can continue to hold what is his and that no inroads are made into the goods or property of private persons by the state. It was a bad policy when Philippus, when he was tribune of the plebs [about 104 BCE], proposed an agrarian reform law. When his law was defeated, he took the defeat well and was moderate in his response. In the debates themselves, however, he tried to curry popular favor and acted in a bad way when he said, "In our community there are not more than two thousand men who have real property."

That speech ought to be condemned outright for attempting to advocate equality of property holdings. What policy could be more dangerous? It was for this very reason—that each person should be able to keep his own property—that states and local governments were founded. Although it was by the leadership of nature herself that men gathered together in communities, it was for the hope of keeping their own property that they sought the protection of states. . . .

Some men want to become known as popular politicians and for this reason they engage in making revolutionary proposals about land, with the result that owners are driven from their homes and money lent out by creditors is simply given free to the borrowers with no need for repayment. Such men are shaking the very foundations of the state. First of all, they are destroying that goodwill and sense of trust which can no longer exist when money is simply taken from some people and given to others [by the state]. And then they take away fairness, which is totally destroyed if each person is not permitted to keep what is his own. For, as I have already said, it is the peculiar function of the state and of local government to make sure that each person should be able to keep his own things freely and without any worry.

→ *According to Cicero, what is the main function of the Roman state and the main reason men "sought the protection of states"?*

→ *How does the protection of private property rights affect the claims that citizens had on their rulers?*

→ *And how does this differ from the role of the state in contemporary Han dynasty China?*

SOURCE: *De Officiis (On Duties)*, 2.21.73, 22.78; translated by Brent Shaw.

argued that the defense and enjoyment of private property constituted basic reasons for the existence of the state. (See Primary Source: Cicero on the Role of the Roman State.) Roman law more clearly defined and more strictly enforced the rights of the private owner than any previous legal system had done. The extension of private ownership of land and other property to regions having little or no prior knowledge of it—Egypt in the east, Spain in the west, the lands of western Europe—was one of the most enduring effects of the Roman Empire.

RELIGIOUS CULTS AND THE RISE OF CHRISTIANITY

The political unification of the Mediterranean also suggested the possibility of uniting the beliefs of its diverse peoples. The world of gods, spirits, and demons remained hugely important, even as the region had seen the spread of new religions as part of the Hellenistic movement. Indeed, the municipal charters of Roman towns required local councilors to institute and maintain the support of official and semiofficial cults of a wide variety of gods and goddesses.

If there was any religion of empire, it was **Christianity**, although it did not achieve official recognition as the state religion until the fourth century CE. Its foundations lay in a direct confrontation with Roman imperial authority: the trial of Yeshua ben Yosef (Joshua son of Joseph). He preached the new doctrines of what was originally a sect of Judaism, and we know him today by the Greek form of his name, Jesus. A Roman governor, Pontius Pilatus, tried Jesus in a typical Roman provincial trial; he was found guilty of sedition and executed, along with two bandits, by a standard Roman penalty—crucifixion.

We know of Jesus only after his death. No reference to him survives from his own lifetime. Two years after the crucifixion, Paul of Tarsus, a Jew and a Roman citizen from southeastern Anatolia, claimed to have seen Jesus in full glory outside the city of Damascus. Paul and the communities to whom he preached between 40 and 60 CE were the first to call Yeshua "Jesus." They also referred to him as "the Christ"—*ho Christos*—or the Anointed One (i.e., the Messiah), and thought of him as a god.

Paul had not been one of Jesus's original disciples. Only much later did four of those men—Matthew, Mark, Luke, and John—write about his life and record his sayings in accounts that came to be called the Gospels. (That early English word translates their name in the original Greek, *Evangeliai*, or "Good News.") The Gospels all sought to tell the world not what Jesus had said, but who he had been. They served as answers to the question that Jesus reportedly asked his disciples a few months before he died: "Who do people say that I am?" (Mark 8:27).

Jesus's preachings could not have been more Jewish. He taught that God is the father of his people—sinners who are always liable to fall away. But God is like a good shepherd to them. Scrambling down dangerous ravines, the good shepherd seeks those who have gone astray, joyfully carrying home on his shoulders even a single lost lamb (see John 10:1–18). We have already met the image of the great king as shepherd of his people in both Egypt and Mesopotamia (see Chapter 3). With Jesus, this ancient image took on a new intimacy. Not a distant monarch but a preacher, Jesus had set out on God's behalf to gather a new, small flock. Jesus's teachings (like those of the Buddha) comforted people who lived at a distance from power, such as scholars, merchants, and farmers.

To his followers, Jesus was a man who had slowly revealed an awesome, hidden identity. He was crucified not for what he had preached but for what he (or others) claimed that he was. Through the preaching of Paul in Greek and the textual portraits painted in the Gospels, also in Greek, this image of Jesus rapidly spread beyond Palestine (where Jesus had preached only to Jews and only in the local language, Aramaic) and entered the religious bloodstream of the Mediterranean. Core elements of Jesus's message, such as the special responsibilities of the well-off for the poor and the promised eventual empowerment of "the meek," appealed to huge numbers of ordinary persons in the wider Mediterranean world. But it was the apostle Paul who was especially responsible for recasting this message for a wider audience. While Jesus directed his teachings to villagers and peasants and cast his metaphors in that light, Paul's writing and preaching dealt with a world heavily populated by slaves. For him, God was a father figure who set converts free and embraced them as His children. His message was immediately accessible to the dwellers of the towns and cities of the Roman Empire.

Just half a century after Jesus's crucifixion, the followers of Jesus saw in his life not the wanderings of an amiable Jewish charismatic but a moment of head-on conflict between "God" and "the world." (A **charismatic** is a person who uses his personal strengths or virtues, often laced with a divine aura, to command followers.) Jesus had "overcome" the "world" and had even broken the boundaries of the human condition: God had raised him from the dead. Thus, the preaching that his followers brought to confront this world was no longer the preaching of a man. It was the message of a god—who, for thirty years half a century before, had moved (largely unrecognized) among human beings. The followers formed a church: a permanent gathering committed to the charge of leaders chosen by God and by their fellow believers. For these leaders and their followers, death—death for Jesus—was the hallmark of their faith. In dying they witnessed for the faith. Indeed, the defining experience for Christians was that of the Roman trial and the idea of "witnessing" to God. The Greek word *martus* means a witness in a trial. From this came the English term *martyr* and the concept of martyrdom.

The persecutions of Christians were sporadic and intensely local. Like imperial power itself, persecutions were responses to local concerns. Not until the emperor Decius, in the mid-third century ce, did the state direct an empire-wide attack on Christians. And that attempt failed. Decius died within the year, and Christians interpreted their persecutor's death as evidence of the hand of God in human affairs. By the last decades of the third century, Christian communities of various kinds, reflecting the different strands of their movement through the Mediterranean as well as the local cultures in which they settled, were present in every society in the empire.

THE LIMITS OF EMPIRE

The empire labeled outsiders as those whom it excluded. A crucial part of that process was the exercise of force in extending its borders. (See Map 7-5.) The limitations of that force determined who belonged in the empire and was subject to it, and who was outside it and therefore excluded. To the west the Romans pushed their authority to the shores of

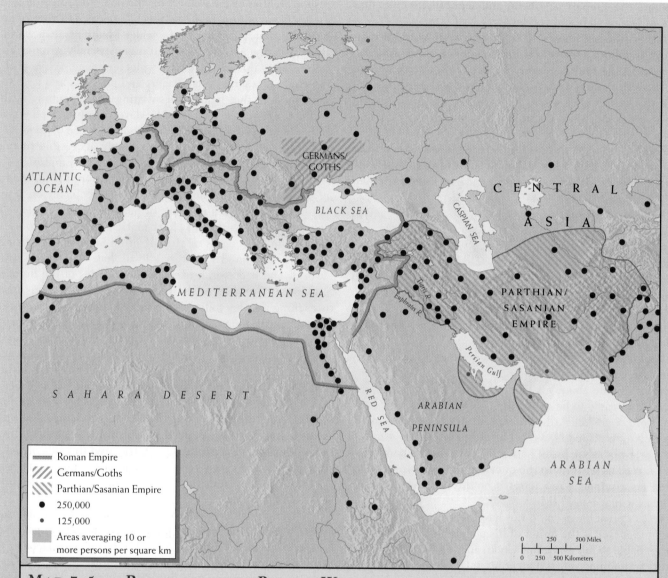

MAP 7-5 POPULATION OF ROMAN WORLD IN 362 CE

Roman frontiers at the northern and eastern limits of the empire were persistent sources of anxiety and concern for imperial leaders. While not as densely populated as the Roman Empire, these regions contained large population centers as well. Name some of the major groups of peoples that lived just beyond Roman rule in the areas of eastern Europe and Southwest Asia. What were the geographical limits of the Roman Empire? According to your reading, why were Roman armies never able to subdue these neighboring peoples?

the Atlantic Ocean, and to the south they drove it to the edges of the Sahara Desert. In both cases, little farther land was available to dominate for profit. To the east and north, however, things were different.

On Rome's eastern frontiers, powerful Romans such as Marcus Licinius Crassus in the mid-50s BCE and Mark Antony in the early 30s BCE wished to imitate the achievements of

Alexander the Great and conquer the arid lands beyond Judea and Syria. But they failed miserably, stopped by the Parthian Empire and their successors the Sasanian Empire (see Chapter 6 for a full discussion of the Parthians and Chapter 8 for more on the Sasanians). The Sasanians expanded the technical advances in mounted horseback warfare that the Parthians had used so successfully in open

Soldier versus Barbarian. On the frontiers of the Roman Empire, the legionary soldiers faced the non-Roman "barbarians" from the lands beyond. In this piece of a stone-carved picture from the northwestern frontier, we see a civilized and disciplined Roman soldier, to the left, facing a German "barbarian"—hair uncut and unkempt, without formal armor, his house a thatched hut. Frontier realities were never so clear-cut, of course. Roman soldiers, often recruited from the "barbarian" peoples, were a lot more like them than was convenient to admit, and the "barbarians" were influenced by and closer to Roman cultural models than this picture indicates.

desert warfare against the slow-moving Roman mass infantry formations. King Shapur I (Shabuhr), their greatest monarch, exploited the weaknesses of the Roman Empire in the mid-third century, even capturing the Roman emperor Valerian. As successful as Parthians and Sasanians were in fighting the Romans, however, they could never equal the Romans' sway, and were not a threat to expand. Their highly decentralized political structure limited their coordination and resources, and their equestrian-style warfare was ill-suited to fight around the more rocky and hilly environment of the Mediterranean world. In the lands across the Rhine and Danube, to the north, environmental conditions largely determined the limits of empire. The long and harsh winters, but excellent soil and growing conditions, produced hardy populations clustered densely across vast distances. These illiterate, kin-based agricultural societies had changed little since the first millennium BCE. And because their warrior elites still engaged in armed competitions, war and violence characterized their connections with the Roman Empire. As the empire fixed its northern frontiers along the

Rhine and Danube rivers, two factors determined its relationship with the Germans and Goths on the rivers' other side. First, these small societies had only one commodity for which the empire was willing to pay: human bodies. So the slave trade out of the land across the Rhine and Danube became immense: gold, silver, coins, wine, arms, and other luxury items flowed across the rivers in one direction in exchange for slaves in the other. Second, their wars were unremitting, as every emperor faced the expectation of dealing harshly with the "barbarians." These connections, involving arms and violence, were to enmesh the Romans ever more tightly with the tribal societies. They even overlapped, as internal conflicts within the Roman Empire ultimately prompted increasing use of "barbarians" as soldiers and officers who served the empire.

CONCLUSION

China and Rome both constructed empires of unprecedented scale and duration, yet they differed in fundamental ways. Starting out with a less numerous and less dense population than China, Rome relied on slaves and "barbarian" immigrants to expand and diversify its workforce. While about 1 percent of the Chinese population was enslaved, more than 10 percent were slaves in the Roman Empire. Also, the lifeblood of the Chinese rural economy was a huge population of free peasant farmers; this enormous labor pool, together with a remarkable bureaucracy, enabled the Han to achieve great political stability. In contrast, the millions of peasant farmers who formed the backbone of rural society in the Roman Empire were much more loosely integrated into the state structure. They never unified to revolt against their government and overthrow it, as did the raging millenarian peasant movements of Later Han China. By comparison with their counterparts in China, the peasants in the Roman Empire were not as well connected in their proximity or density, or as united by similar modes of production. Here, too, the Mediterranean environment accented separation and difference.

By Chinese standards, the Roman Empire was relatively fragmented and underadministered. Moreover, philosophy and religion never underpinned the Roman state in the way that Confucianism buttressed the dynasties of China. Both empires, however, benefited from the spread of a uniform language and imperial culture. The process was more comprehensive in China (which possessed a single language that the elites used, a literary language based on classical Chinese) than in Rome (whose empire spanned a two-language world: Latin in the western Mediterranean, Greek in the east). Both states fostered a common imperial culture across all levels of society. Once entrenched, these cultures and languages lasted well after the end of empire.

Differences in human resources, languages, and ideas led the Roman and Han states to evolve in unique ways. In both places, however, the faiths of outsiders—Christians and Buddhists—eclipsed the classical ideals that grounded their states' ideological foundations of a distinctly secular sort. Transmission of these new faiths benefited from expanded communications networks. The new religions added to the cultural mix that succeeded the Roman Empire and the Han dynasty.

At their height, both states surpassed their forebears by translating unprecedented military power into the fullest form of state-based organization. Each state's complex organization involved the systematic control, counting, and taxing of its population. In both cases, the general increase of the population, the growth of huge cities, and the success of long-distance trade contributed to the new scales of magnitude. The Han would not be superseded in East Asia as the model empire until the Tang dynasty in the seventh century. In western Afro-Eurasia, the Roman Empire would not be surpassed in scale or intensity of development until the rise of powerful European nation-states more than a millennium later.

Review and research materials are available at StudySpace: Ⓢ WWNORTON.COM/STUDYSPACE

KEY TERMS

charismatic (p. 275)
Christianity (p. 275)
commanderies (p. 244)
dynastic cycle (p. 250)
millenarian movement (p. 259)

patrons (p. 270)
Pax Romana (p. 257)
Pax Sinica (p. 257)
war ethos (p. 264)

Chronology

	400 BCE	300 BCE	200 BCE	100 BCE
THE MEDITERRANEAN		◆-----------◆ 350–265 BCE *Roman city-state expansion in Italian peninsula*		90–30 BCE *Civil wars divide Romans*
		265–146 BCE *Rome defeats Carthage in three Punic wars* ◆-------------		
SOUTHWEST ASIA			129 BCE *Parthian Empire established in Southwest Asia* ◆	
EAST ASIA		221–207 BCE *Qin Empire* ◆---◆		
		206 BCE–220 CE *Han dynasty* ◆-------------		
		206 BCE–9 CE *Western (Former) Han* ◆-------------		
		140–87 BCE *Expansion of Han Empire under Emperor Wu* ◆-------------		

STUDY QUESTIONS

1. Analyze the impact of Xiongnu pastoralists on imperial policies of the Qin and Han dynasties. How did each dynasty counter the threat of nomadic incursions into its territorial heartlands?

2. Explain the influence of Confucian ideas during the Han dynasty. How did these ideas shape political and social hierarchies during this period?

3. Describe the process through which the Roman city-state created a vast empire in the Mediterranean world. How did Roman attitudes toward military service influence the empire's growth?

4. Explain the social and legal hierarchies that governed Roman urban life. To what extent did residents enjoy personal autonomy?

5. Explain the concepts of *Pax Sinica* and *Pax Romana*. How did Han and Roman leaders promote long periods of peace and prosperity in eastern and western Afro-Eurasia, respectively?

6. Compare and contrast the concept of emperor in the Han dynasty with that in the Roman Empire. What role did emperors play in the governing structure of their respective empires?

7. Compare and contrast the methods through which Han and Roman leaders enlisted their subjects' support. What emphasis did each state place on ideology, civil bureaucracy, and military organization?

8. Compare and contrast the labor systems in the Qin and Han dynasties with that of the Roman Empire. To what extent did each rely on forced labor?

9. Compare and contrast Roman strategies for promoting stability along its borders with those of the Han dynasty. How different were the threats that each empire faced from borderland peoples?

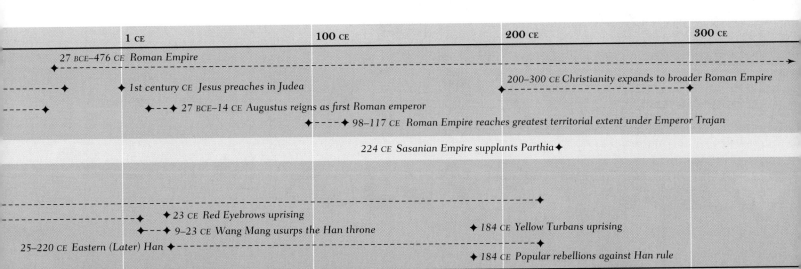

1 CE   **100** CE   **200** CE   **300** CE

27 BCE–476 CE Roman Empire

200–300 CE Christianity expands to broader Roman Empire

1st century CE Jesus preaches in Judea

27 BCE–14 CE Augustus reigns as first Roman emperor

98–117 CE Roman Empire reaches greatest territorial extent under Emperor Trajan

224 CE Sasanian Empire supplants Parthia

23 CE Red Eyebrows uprising

9–23 CE Wang Mang usurps the Han throne

184 CE Yellow Turbans uprising

25–220 CE Eastern (Later) Han

184 CE Popular rebellions against Han rule

THE RISE OF UNIVERSAL RELIGIONS, 300–600 CE

Around 180 CE, a humble group of three men and three women stood trial before the provincial governor at Carthage. They claimed to be Christians, and their crime was refusal to worship the gods of the Roman Empire. The governor was unimpressed; his god was "the protecting spirit of our lord the emperor." One Christian retorted that his god was also an emperor, but that he could not be seen, for he stood "above all kings and . . . all nations." There was an unbridgeable gap between the governor and the Christians. So the governor read out a death sentence, ordering their immediate execution. "Thanks be to God!" cried the Christians, and straightaway they were beheaded.

As the centuries unfolded, the tables would turn dramatically. Old ideas of the supremacy of an emperor-lord gave way to those of the Lord God as emperor. Previously, the impulse toward universalism had come from ambitious empire builders, like Alexander the Great and the Roman emperors. Now, for the first time, religious leaders became the agents of universalist messages and worked to convert humanity to their belief systems. This period, which witnessed the bonding of religions to universal aspirations, spread religious tenets across the Afro-Eurasian landmass. What gave these religions, notably Christianity and Buddhism, their universalistic message and their widespread appeal to diverse peoples and cultures? In effect, in this era spiritual and religious fervor became an even more powerful force of integration than political ambitions, while also triggering new world divides. This advent of religion as a global influence was anything but simple. It also built on the expansive reach of the Roman and Han empires while shaping the institutions of these states. It profited from the closer commercial and intellectual connections between east and west. This chapter tells the story of how Christianity and Buddhism became universal religions forever changing world history.

UNIVERSAL RELIGIONS AND COMMON CULTURES

> → *How did religion bring worlds together and drive them apart?*

From 300 to 600 CE, the entire Afro-Eurasian landmass experienced a surge of religious ferment. In the West, Christianity became the state faith of the Roman Empire. In India, Vedic religion (Brahmanism) evolved into a more formal spiritual system called Hinduism. In northern India, central Asia, and even China, Buddhism—originally a code of ethics—became a religion. Across much of the world, spiritual concerns affected everyday life and integrated scattered communities into shared faiths.

Two faiths in particular aspired to universality in this era—Christianity and Buddhism. They were to be joined by Islam several centuries later. What made them universalistic in comparison with, say, Judaism, Hinduism, and traditional African religious beliefs was that they were not tied to a locality. Hinduism was the belief system of Hindi speakers of South Asia. Judaism was tied to a specific ethnicity, while traditional African religious beliefs varied from people to people. In contrast, Christianity and Buddhism appealed to diverse populations (men and women, freeborn and slaves, rich and poor), proved adaptable as they moved from one cultural and geographical area to another, were promoted by energetic and charismatic missionizing agents, and despite their many and insistent demands provided a deep sense of community to their converts. In the case of Christianity, though to a lesser extent Buddhism, these religions also benefited from the support of powerful empires.

The new spirituality blossomed inside and also outside empires (see Map 8-1). In western Europe, Christianity arose alongside a decaying Roman state. In the eastern Mediterranean, it inspired a revived Roman *imperium* at Byzantium. In India, Hinduism and Buddhism vied for cultural preeminence; in central Asia and China, Buddhism flourished as the old polities foundered.

The peoples living in sub-Saharan Africa and the Americas, too, reached beyond local communities and wove common spiritual worlds. In Africa, the Bantu-speaking peoples, residing in the southeastern corner of present-day Nigeria, began to spread their way of life throughout the entire southern half of the landmass. Similarly, across the Atlantic Ocean, the Mayans established political and cultural institutions over a large portion of Mesoamerica.

A wide variety of societies experienced spiritual ferment. This does not mean that people became more excitable or more otherworldly; it means that religion touched more areas of society and in more demanding ways. People felt deeply about religion because it was through religious filters that

Focus Questions

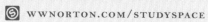

ⓢ WWNORTON.COM/STUDYSPACE

→ *How did religion bring worlds together and drive them apart?*

→ *How did empires such as the Roman and Sasanian help religions such as Christianity become universalizing?*

→ *How did central Asians influence the spread of universal religions and other cross-cultural developments during this time?*

→ *To what extent did South Asia develop a common culture despite political, religious, and social diversity?*

→ *To what extent did influences from other parts of Afro-Eurasia transform Chinese culture and politics?*

→ *How similar and different were spiritual and cultural developments in worlds apart from Afro-Eurasia during this time?*

MAIN THEMES

→ *Afro-Eurasia and the Americas witness the rise of universalizing religions and unifying cultural beliefs.*

→ *Two religions—Christianity and Buddhism—aspire to world missions and challenge the power of secular rulers and thinkers.*

→ *While undermining Roman emperors, Indian satraps, and Chinese dynasts, these new religions also win important statesmen to their cause and use the authority of the state to gain converts and spread their faiths.*

FOCUS ON *Religions and Regions*

Western and Eastern Europe and Southwest Asia

✦ **Christianity** moves from a minority, persecuted faith to a state religion in the Roman Empire.

✦ Both Christianity and South Asian religious tenets buttress the powerful Sasanian state based in Iran.

Sub-Saharan Africa and Mesoamerica

✦ Large parts of Africa and the Americas develop common cultures based on religious beliefs shared by large, widely dispersed groups.

South Asia and East Asia

✦ Brahmanism, or **Hinduism**, becomes the dominant religion among the Vedic peoples of South Asia.

✦ **Buddhism** spreads out of South Asia along the Silk Road through central Asia and into East Asia.

---

they processed the meaning of what was important to them. They discussed issues of truth, loyalty, and solidarity in terms framed by spiritual leaders who claimed to know the truth about an invisible other world.

Consider how many questions in our own world are assumed to be answerable by science. In many respects, religion functioned in that age as science does in ours. It claimed to give clear answers about the nature of human beings, why they lived in society, why they married and had children, whom they should obey, and the degree of allegiance they owed to something unseen (God, the gods, or a supernaturally guaranteed code of conduct) rather than to any ruler. Even more, as the case of the Christian martyrs showed, religion told them what they should die for.

Because religion claimed to help its followers distinguish between right and wrong, it freed people from the past. The fact that local religious practices might have existed for ages did not make the old beliefs true. As cultures shrugged off their older heritages, shared faith brought people together and enabled them to identify with people and places beyond their own local worlds. Some religious systems, such as Buddhism and Christianity, spread far and wide because they professed universal rules and principles to guide behavior that transcended place, time, and specific cultural practices; later, Islam would follow the same pattern (see Chapter 9).

Sharp distinctions between right and wrong also drew new lines between peoples. Religion became a wedge that drove worlds apart, as absolute conviction left little room for tolerance. Centuries of harmonious interaction offered few protections to neighbors now perceived to be "wrong" in their beliefs—and their errors could get them ostracized, exiled, or killed. For wrong beliefs were considered as dangerous as today's counterfeit medicines. Like noxious drugs, they had to be removed from circulation as quickly as possible. Conflict, even violence and religious persecution, accompanied this new sense of certainty.

Moreover, religious beliefs came to apply equally from one end of Afro-Eurasia to the other. Religious leaders carrying written texts (books, scrolls, or tablets of wood or palm leaf) often traveled widely. Everywhere, universal religions were on the move. Christians from Persia went to China. Buddhists journeyed from South Asia to Afghanistan and used the caravan routes of central Asia to reach China. In 643 CE, the Chinese Buddhist Xuanzang brought back to Chang'an

FOREST NOMADIC HUNTERS

NORTH AMERICA

PLAINS NOMADIC HUNTERS

Great Lakes

Mississippi R.

St. Lawrence R.

ATLANTIC OCEAN

Gulf of Mexico

Teotihuacán

MAYAN CITY STATES

WEST INDIES

ROCKY MOUNTAINS

CELTIC PEOPLES

GERMAN

GOTHS

Carthage

KINGDOM OF THE VANDALS

SAHARA

SAHAR PEOPL

Niger R.

ANDES MOUNTAINS

Amazon R.

CHAVIN

SOUTH AMERICA

PACIFIC OCEAN

ANDES MOUNTAINS

	Qi
	Tuoba
	Hephthalites
	Sasanian
	Gupta
	Eastern Roman
	Mayan
VANDALS	Kingdom
BANTU	People
•	City

0   1000   2000 Miles

0   1000   2000 Kilometers

→ *How did religion bring worlds together and drive them apart?*

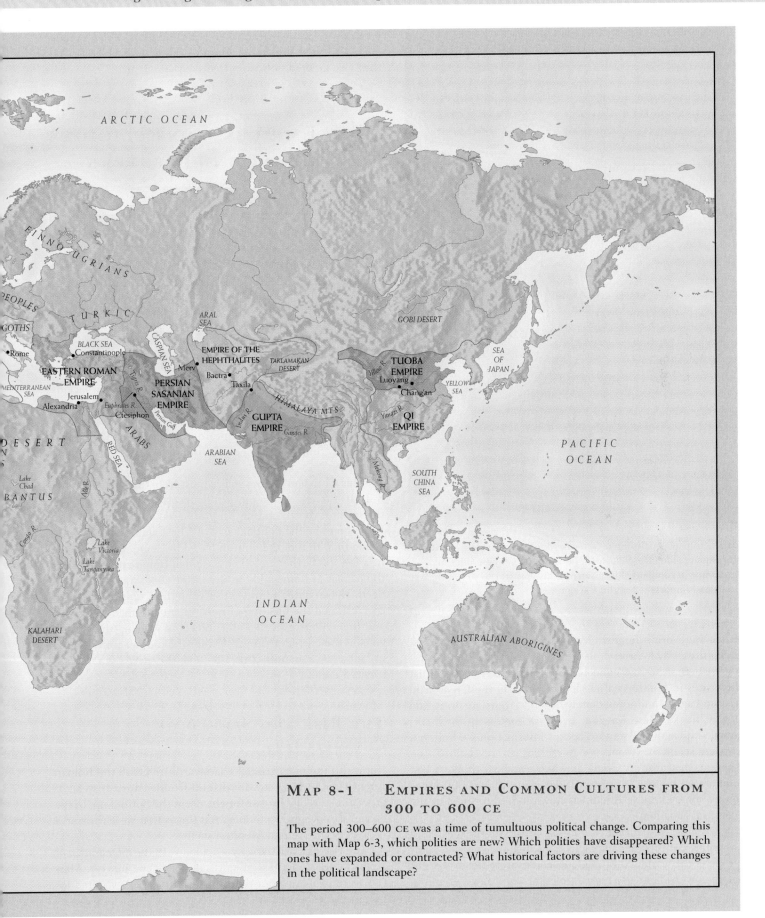

MAP 8-1 EMPIRES AND COMMON CULTURES FROM 300 TO 600 CE

The period 300–600 CE was a time of tumultuous political change. Comparing this map with Map 6-3, which polities are new? Which polities have disappeared? Which ones have expanded or contracted? What historical factors are driving these changes in the political landscape?

Xuanzang. This painting c. 900 CE, which survives in the caves of Dunhuang along the Silk Road, portrays the Chinese pilgrim Xuanzang accompanied by a tiger on his epic travels to South Asia to collect important Buddhist scriptures.

(then the world's largest city) an entire library of Buddhist scriptures—527 boxes of writings and 192 birch-bark tablets—that he had collected on a pilgrimage to Buddhist holy sites in South Asia. He lodged them in the Great Wild Goose Pagoda and immediately began to translate every line into Chinese. Here was the "truth" of Buddhism for Xuanzang, similar to the way we accept information we find in a modern science textbook, and as exciting as a revelation when they reached distant China as when Buddhist thinkers had elaborated them in northern India, more than 5,000 miles away. Some Chinese Buddhists now referred to India as the "Central Kingdom."

Voyages, translations, long-distance pilgrimages, and sweeping conversion campaigns remapped the spiritual landscape of the world. New religious leaders were the brokers of more universal but also more intolerant worldviews, premised on a new relationship between gods and their subjects. Religions and their brokers profoundly integrated societies. But they also created new ways to drive them apart.

EMPIRES AND RELIGIOUS CHANGE IN WESTERN AFRO-EURASIA

> → *How did empires such as the Roman and Sasanian help religions such as Christianity become universalizing?*

In western Afro-Eurasia, the Roman Empire was hardly the political and military juggernaut it had been 300 years earlier. Surrounded by peoples who coveted its wealth while resisting its power, Rome was fragmenting. Yet its endurance was a boon to the new religious ferment, which took hold in its decaying political institutions. Although so-called barbarians eventually overran the western parts of the empire, in many ways those areas still felt "Roman." They looked to the new faith of Christianity to maintain continuity with the past, eventually founding a papacy in Rome to rule the remnants of empire.

This Christian empire split almost from the start (see Map 8-2). In Rome's east, a powerful successor state appeared in the form of the Byzantine Empire based at Constantinople. Its claim to be the political arm of Christianity seemed more viable than that of the church based in Rome. But it faced a new foe still farther east. The Sasanian Empire of Persia, like the papacy at Rome and the Byzantine state, was unique. Indeed, these states represented something unprecedented: they claimed the blessing of new (or transformed) religions, and their rulers expected all subjects to worship the correct gods in the correct manner. Those who did not were treated as outsiders, in both this life and the next—where hell awaited them.

THE RISE AND SPREAD OF CHRISTIANITY

Ironically, the most crucial change ever to befall the Roman Empire had little to do with distant frontier wars. Instead, it grew from a religious war fought, from the bottom up, in the peaceful and tightly administered towns that were the nerve centers of the Roman Mediterranean.

The rise of Christianity coincided with the appearance of a new figure in matters of spiritual belief: the **martyr**. Martyrs were people whom the Roman authorities executed for

→ *How did empires such as the Roman and Sasanian help religions such as Christianity become universalizing?*

persisting in their Christian beliefs instead of submitting to pagan (polytheistic) ritual or belief. Many of them were remarkable witnesses to their faith. In 203 CE, a well-to-do mother in her early twenties, Vibia Perpetua, faced a horrible punishment for refusing to sacrifice to the Roman gods. Denied the benefit of a human executioner, she and her companions were condemned to face wild beasts in the amphitheater of Carthage. The amphitheater is still there, south of modern Tunis. It is a mean, small place—not a gigantic stadium. The condemned and the spectators would have had eye contact with one another throughout the fatal encounter.

Before her death, Perpetua dictated a prison diary that is unique in Roman literature. Here a woman speaks with a full

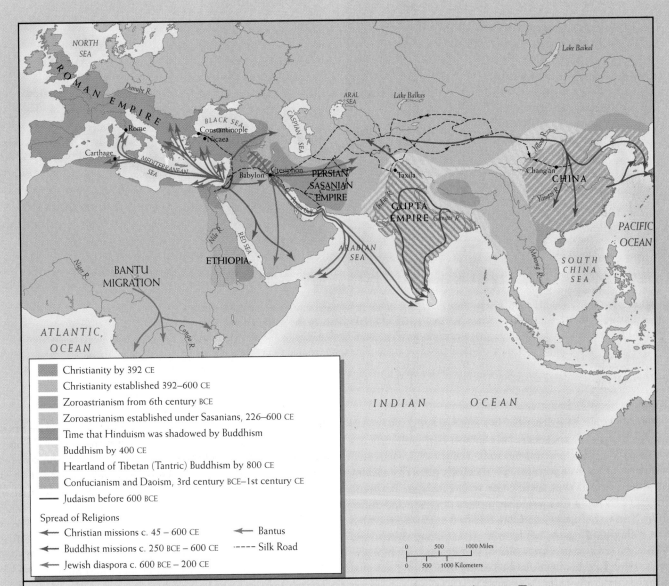

MAP 8-2 THE SPREAD OF UNIVERSAL RELIGIONS IN AFRO-EURASIA, 300–600 CE

The spread of universal religions and the shifting political landscape were intimately connected. Using Map 8-1, identify the major polities in Afro-Eurasia during this era. How did these political configurations differ from those in the era covered in Chapter 7? Compare and contrast Map 8-1 with Map 8-2. Where did Hinduism, Buddhism, and Christianity emerge, and where did they spread? How did the rise and fall of empires affect the expansion of universal religions?

Christian Martyrs. The Christian martyr Perpetua (*left*) came to be represented as an upper-class Roman matron with carefully covered hair. Set in a circle of bright blue, in the golden dome of a church, she looks out from a distant, peaceful Heaven. The detail from a mosaic found in a Roman circus in North Africa (*right*) shows a criminal tied to a stake and being pushed on a little cart toward a lunging leopard. Christian martyrs were treated much the same as criminals: they were executed—exposed to animals without even the "privilege" of suffering at the hands of a human executioner.

religious message. She describes her relief at being allowed to have her baby stay with her: "My prison had suddenly become a palace, so that I wanted to be there rather than anywhere else." More important, she recounts powerful visions of the next world that fortify her with courage. Perpetua stepped every night into paradise, a place of peace and abundance: "I saw an immense garden, and in it a gray-haired man sat in a shepherd's garb; tall he was, and milking sheep. And around him were many thousands of people clad in white garments. He raised his head, looked at me and said: 'I am glad you have come, my child.'"

Other religions, including Judaism and later Islam, honored martyrs who died for their faith. But because Christianity claimed to be based directly on "the blood of martyrs," in the words of Tertullian (197 CE), martyrdom gained unusual significance in the early church. Moreover, the remembered heroism of women martyrs balanced the increasingly all-male leadership—bishops and clergy—of the institutionalized Christian church.

RELIGIOUS DEBATE AND CHRISTIAN UNIVERSALISM
The spread of religious ideas in the Roman Empire changed the way people viewed their existence. Believing implied that an important "other" world loomed beyond the world of physical matter. Feeling contact with it gave worshippers a sense of worth; it guided them in this life, and they anticipated someday meeting their guides and spiritual friends there. The fervor for paradise was so potent that scarcely a century after Perpetua's execution, the Roman emperor Constantine believed that a vision sent by Christ had brought him military victory. Thereafter Constantine and his successors placed the awesome authority of the Roman state behind a Christian church that until then had been marginal and often persecuted.

No longer were the gods local powers to be placated by archaic rituals in sacred places. Many became omnipresent figures whom mortals could touch through loving attachment. As ordinary mortals now could hope to meet these divine beings in another, happier world, the sense of an afterlife glowed brighter.

Above all, the gods now expected to be obeyed, as one would obey a human lord. And it was on the issue of obedience to God, rather than to a human ruler, that the Christians sparked a Mediterranean-wide debate on the nature of religion. Like the Jews, the Christians possessed divinely inspired scriptures that told them what to believe and do, even when those actions went against the empire's laws.

In their emphasis on texts, the Christians were moving with the times. After 200 CE, published writings circulated widely in the Roman world. By 300 CE, a revolution in book production had taken place. The scroll that all ancient readers had used (and that survives in the Torah scrolls of Jewish synagogues) gave way to the codex: separate pages bound together as a book. Christians spoke of their scriptures as "a divine codex." Bound in a compact volume or set of volumes, this was the definitive Code of God's law.

THE CONVERSION OF CONSTANTINE Crucial in spurring Christianity's eastward expansion was the transformative experience of a man named Constantine (c. 280–337 CE). Born near the Danubian frontier, he belonged to a class of professional soldiers whose careers took them far from the Mediterranean. His troops proclaimed him emperor after the death of his father, the emperor Constantius. It was a time of political confusion when several claimants fought for power. In 312 CE, Constantine's armies closed in on Rome in his first bid to rule the Mediterranean heartlands.

Like earlier Roman emperors, Constantine looked for signs from the gods. Before the decisive battle for Rome, which took place for control of a strategic bridge, he supposedly had a dream in which he saw an emblem bearing the words "In this sign conquer." He was told to place this mysterious sign on his soldiers' shields. It took the form of an X (the Greek letter chi, representing a "ch" sound) placed over P (the Greek letter rho, or "r")—the opening letters of the name of Christ. In the ensuing battle, the rival troops were routed and the rival emperor was pushed off the bridge and drowned. Thereafter, Constantine's visionary sign became known all over the Roman world.

The persecuted Christian church was the beneficiary of Constantine's vision, as he soon issued a proclamation exalting the work of Christian bishops and giving them significant

Scroll and Codex. (*Left*) The Torah scroll still used in Jewish synagogues is the same as that used in the ancient world. Sheets of papyrus were carefully glued together to produce a continuous roll. (*Right*) The codex of the Christian Scriptures is written in simple letters. Each column of text is put on a separate page, and the pages are then bound together to form a book.

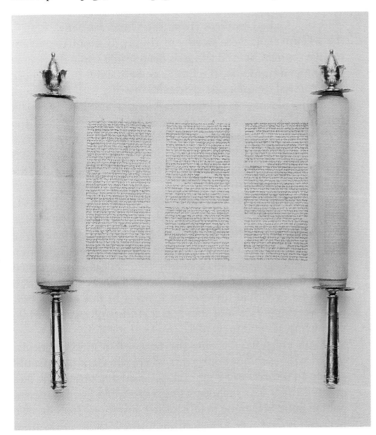

The Conversion of Constantine. In this painting, the seventeenth-century artist Rubens uses "period" details for historical accuracy: the XP (the first letters of the name of Christ in Greek) in the sky; beneath them, the "dragon" standard of the Roman cavalry of the year 312 (the standard came from China and passed to Rome via the cavalry-nomads of central Asia); beside the dragon, the eagle of the traditional Roman standard.

tax exemptions. But the edict's significance was much broader. Being evidence for the so-called **conversion of Constantine**, it took a typically Roman approach to a powerful new god: it gave privileges to a favored religious group who were responsible for that god's worship. The edict's effects were long-lasting, for it would be through the institutions and across the byways of the Roman Empire that Christianity would spread.

By the time that Constantine embraced Christianity, it had already made considerable progress within the Roman Empire. At the outset, it was only one of many different new sects competing for attention within the empire. It prevailed in the face of stiff competition and intense persecution from the imperial authorities largely because of the universalistic aspects of its message, the charisma of its holy men and women, the sacred aura surrounding its scriptural canon, and the fit that existed between its doctrines and popular preexisting religious beliefs and practices. The new religion made few distinctions. It appealed alike to rich and poor, city dwellers and peasants, slave and free, young and old, and men and women.

CHRISTIANITY IN THE CITIES   After 312 CE, the large churches built in every major city, many with imperial funding, signaled Christianity's growing strength. These gigantic meeting halls often accommodated over a thousand wor-

shippers. Called *basilicas* (from the Greek *basileus*, "king"), the solemn halls were worthy of royalty. But unlike ancient temples, which housed the gods deep inside while the people worshipped outdoors, the basilicas were open to all. Those who entered found a vast space shimmering with the light of oil lamps playing on shining marble and mosaics. Rich silk hangings, swaying between rows of columns, increased the sense of mystery and directed the eye to the far end of the building—a semicircular apse furnished with particular splendor. Worshippers had come into a different world. This was heaven on earth.

And it was a very orderly heaven. The bishop and priests sat under the dome of the apse, which represented the dome of heaven. The bishop had a special throne, or *cathedra* (the Latin word for both a teacher's seat and a governor's throne). Low marble screens and especially vivid floor mosaics marked off the holy space around the bishop and clergy. (The church at Verona even had under-floor heating in this area!) Ordinary worshippers would stand, as a gesture of respect, while the bishop sat and preached.

Such churches became the new urban public forums, ringed with spacious courtyards where the city's poor would gather. In return for the tax exemptions that Constantine had granted them, the bishops were responsible for the metropolitan poor, becoming in effect their governors. Bishops also became judges, as Constantine turned their arbitration process for disputes between Christians into a kind of small claims court.

It was by such means—offering the poor shelter, quick justice, and moments of unearthly splendor in grand basilicas—that bishops throughout the Roman world secured a position that would last until modern times. And in their basilicas, "Rome" lived on for centuries after the empire had disappeared.

THE CHRISTIAN EMPIRE

Constantine and his successors were impressed by the Christian church's emphasis on expansion. Indeed, Christianity was spreading into the hinterlands of Africa and Southwest Asia, and these efforts required the breaking of language barriers. After around 300 CE, the Christian clergy in Egypt replaced hieroglyphs—which only a few temple priests could read—with a more accessible script based on Greek letters: it is known today as Coptic (from the Greek *Aigyptios,* "Egyptian"). With this innovation the Christian clergy brought the countryside and its local languages closer to the towns, and the towns closer to the countryside.

A similar pattern unfolded in Nubia and Ethiopia, as each developed its own scripts and language under Christian influence. And in the crucial corridor that joined Antioch to

Basilica Interior. The interior of a basilica was dominated by rows of ancient marble columns and was filled with light from upper windows, so that the eye was led directly to the apse of the church, where the bishop and clergy would sit under a dome, close to the altar.

Mesopotamia, Syriac, an offshoot of the Semitic language Aramaic, became a major Christian language. Christianity also spread farther east, to Georgia in the Caucasus and to Armenia. Christian clergy created the written languages that are still used in those regions.

In 325 CE, Constantine celebrated his final conquest of the eastern provinces by summoning all the bishops to Nicaea (modern Iznik in western Turkey). Though their religion has since produced many denominations, all Christians still regard the Council of Nicaea as the foundational moment when their faith was summed up in a **creed** (from the Latin *credo,* "I believe"). It was a statement of religious belief formulated in technical, philosophical terms. It asked believers to balance three separate Gods in one supreme being—God "the father," "the son," and "the holy spirit." Also at Nicaea the bishops agreed to hold Easter, the day on which Christians celebrate Christ's resurrection from the tomb, on the same day in every church of the Christian world.

Constantine died in 337 CE, and his legacy was monumental. He had converted to Christianity, but in such a way that Christianity itself became the religion of the Roman Empire. Writing near the end of Constantine's reign, an elderly bishop in Palestine named Eusebius presented a vision of the "reconciled" Roman Empire that would have surprised the martyrs of Carthage, who had willingly died rather than recognize any "empire of this world." (See Primary Source: Eusebius: In Praise of "One Unity and Concord.") From the time of Constantine onward, many Christians around the eastern Mediterranean believed that Christianity, empire, and culture had flowed together.

THE FALL OF ROME: A TAKEOVER FROM THE MARGINS

Soon, however, the Roman world began to fall apart (see Map 8-3). After 400 CE the western European provinces went their own way, as the presence of Roman armies and cities along the Rhine and Danube had blurred the boundary between Roman and non-Roman worlds.

WHO WERE THE BARBARIANS? The so-called barbarian invasions of the late fourth and fifth centuries CE were simply a more violent and chaotic form of a steady immigration of young fighting men from the frontiers of the empire. Today the term *barbarian* implies uncultivated or savage, but its core meaning is "foreigner" (with overtones of inferiority). Inhabitants of the western provinces had become used to non-Roman soldiers from across the frontiers, and for them *barbarian* was synonymous with "soldier." Soldiers could be destructive, but nobody feared that the presence of barbarians fighting in armies on Roman territory would bring the end of Roman culture.

Primary Source

EUSEBIUS: IN PRAISE OF "ONE UNITY AND CONCORD"

Eusebius (c. 263–339?) believed that the Roman Empire owed its success to divine providence. He viewed the birth of Christ during the rule of the emperor Augustus as no coincidence: it showed God's choice to come to earth at a time when the preaching of his message could coincide with a blessed era of peace and unity in the Roman world. Christianity had ridden to its favored position on the providential tide of a unified world empire. The excerpt below is from a speech commemorating thirty years of Constantine's rule.

Now formerly all the peoples of the earth were divided, and the whole human race cut up into provinces and tribal and local governments, states ruled by despots or by mobs. Because of this continuous battles and wars, with their attendant devastations and enslavements, gave them no respite in countryside or city. . . .

But now two great powers—the Roman Empire, which became a monarchy at that time, and the teaching of Christ—proceeding as if from a single starting point, at once tamed and reconciled all to friendship. Thus each blossomed at the same time and place as the other. For while the power of our Savior destroyed the multiple rule and polytheism of the demons [the old gods] and heralded the one kingdom of God to Greeks and barbarians and all men to the furthest end of the earth, the Roman Empire, now that the causes of manifold governments had been abolished, subdued the visible governments of, in order to merge the entire race into one unity and concord. . . .

Moreover, as One God and one knowledge of this God is heralded to all, one empire has waxed strong among men, and the entire race of mankind has been re-directed into peace and friendship as all acknowledged each other as brothers. . . . All at once, as if sons and daughters of one father, the One God, and children of one mother, true religion, they greeted and received each other peaceably, so

that from that time the whole inhabited world differed in no way from a single well-ordered and related household. It became possible for anyone who pleased to make a journey and to leave home for wherever he might wish with all ease. Thus some from the East moved freely to the West, while others went from here [the East] back there, as easily as if traveling to their native lands.

→ *The elderly Eusebius was a bishop in Palestine, and as a younger man he had witnessed the persecution of Christians. Can you find evidence of this background in his praise of Constantine as the first Christian emperor, who fostered "one unity and concord" among "the whole human race"?*

→ *Being patriarchal, Roman society highly valued the family unit. What lines in the excerpt reflect this outlook?*

→ *What elements in the history of Christianity would have led Eusebius to emphasize its role as a unifying force in the Roman world?*

SOURCE: Eusebius, *Tricennial Oration* 16.2–7 [Jubilee Oration on the Thirtieth Year of the Reign of Constantine, delivered on July 25, 336], translated by H. L. Drake in *In Praise of Constantine: A Historical Study and New Translation of Eusebius' Tricennial Orations* (Berkeley: University of California Press, 1976), pp. 119–21.

THE GOTHS The popular image of bloodthirsty barbarian hordes streaming into the empire bears little resemblance to reality. In fact, it was the Romans' need for soldiers that drew the barbarians in. The process reached a crisis point when Gothic tribes petitioned the emperor Valens (r. 365–378 CE) to let them immigrate into the empire. Desperate for manpower, Valens encouraged their entrance. But the Roman authorities failed to feed their guests. Thus it was a lethal combination of famine and anger at the breakdown of supplies—not innate bloodlust—that turned the Goths against

Valens. When he marched against them at the flat plains outside Adrianople in the hot August of 378 CE, he was not seeking to halt a barbarian invasion. Rather, he was planning to teach a lesson in obedience to his new recruits. But the Goths had brought cavalry from the steppes, and its thunderous charge proved decisive. Valens and a large part of the Roman army of the East vanished in a cloud of red dust, trampled to death by the men and horses they had hoped to hire.

Even the most notorious invasions followed a similar pattern, drawn into the crumbling empire by its civil wars.

Intermittent civil wars had long been a feature of Roman society, but the state could not survive this bout, constantly fed by non-Roman recruits. Thus the "fall" of the empire in western Europe was the result of a long process of overextension. Rome could never be as strong along its frontiers as it was around the Mediterranean, because those frontiers were too far away. Despite the famous Roman roads, travel time between the Rhine border and Rome was more than thirty days. Lacking the vast network of canals that enabled Chinese emperors to move goods and soldiers by water, Roman power could survive in the north only at the cost of constant effort and high taxes.

But after 400 CE the western emperors could no longer raise enough taxes to maintain control of the provinces. While some loss of revenue was attributable to military defeat and civil wars, the primary cause may have been the rise of an aristocracy of Roman landowners throughout the western provinces. These big estate owners welcomed the Goths as a

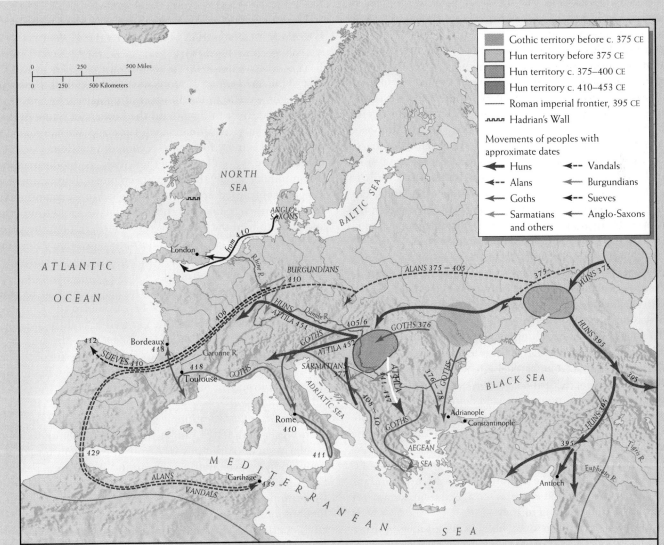

MAP 8-3 WESTERN AFRO-EURASIA: WAR, IMMIGRATION, AND SETTLEMENT IN THE ROMAN WORLD, 375–450 CE

Invasions and migrations brought about the reconstitution of the Roman Empire at this time. Using the map, identify the people who migrated to or invaded the Roman Empire. Where were they from, and where did they go? How did they reshape the political landscape of western Afro-Eurasia? Considering these effects, was the Roman depiction of these groups as "barbarians" a fair assessment?

kind of local militia who would maintain law and order in what had become increasingly lawless regions.

In 418 CE, the Goths settled in southwest Gaul. Ruled by their own king, who kept his military in order, they suppressed the peasants' revolts that were occurring with alarming frequency. Though never as savage or widespread as the uprisings that had undermined the Han dynasty in China, they created a mood of emergency. Now the Roman landowners of Gaul and elsewhere anxiously allied themselves with the new military leaders rather than face social revolution and the raids of even more dangerous armies. The Goths came as allies of the aristocracy, not as enemies of Rome.

CONTINUITY IN CHANGE Romans and non-Romans also drew together because both suddenly confronted a common enemy. As happened many times in the history of Afro-Eurasia, a nomad confederation—in this case, that of the Huns—threatened the edge of western Europe. For twenty chilling years a single king, Attila (406–453 CE), imposed himself as sole ruler of all the Hunnish tribes. He was a harsh overlord who frightened the Germanic peoples even more than he frightened the Romans. The Romans had walls to hide behind—Hadrian's Wall, town walls, villa walls, city walls. In the open plains north of the Danube, however, the Hunnish cavalry found only scattered villages and open fields, whose harvests they plundered on a regular basis.

Attila intended to be a "real" emperor. Having seized (perhaps from the Chinese empire) the notion of a "mandate of heaven"—in his case, a divine right to rule the tribes of the north—he fashioned the first opposing empire that Rome ever had to face in northern Europe. Its traces remain in the archaeology of Ukraine, Hungary, and central Europe. Spectacular jewelry of a Hunnish style, often bearing dragon motifs originating in China, reveals a true warrior-aristocracy. Rather than selling his people's services to Rome, Attila extracted thousands of pounds of gold coins from the Roman emperors in tribute. With Roman gold, he could dominate the barbarian world. The result: the Roman Empire in the west vanished only twenty years after his death. In 476, the last Roman emperor of the west, a young boy named Romulus Augustulus (namesake of both Rome's founder and, as "Mini-Augustus," its first emperor) resigned to make way for a so-called barbarian king in Italy.

Rule from Rome was over, but not its legacies. Future rulers had to ally with the surviving Roman landowners of southern Europe, and among them the Goths felt fully at home. Their king called himself Alaric II, underscoring his connection to the man who had sacked Rome in 410 CE. At the same time, he enjoyed the warm support of the Roman landowners, some of whom claimed to be descendants of ancient Roman senators. Alaric II issued for them a simplified code of imperial law that owed nothing to the non-Roman world. It provided his Roman subjects with all that was necessary to maintain a Roman way of life in a world without empire.

Now the sense of unity of the Roman Empire ceded to a sense of the continued unity of the church. The Catholic Church (*Catholic* meaning "universal") became the one institution to which all Christians in western Europe, Romans and non-Romans alike, felt that they belonged. As a result, the bishops of Rome emerged as popes—the symbolic head of the western churches. Rome became a spiritual capital instead of an imperial one. By 700 CE, the great Roman landowning families had vanished (unlike the more tenacious elites of China). Replacing them in the power structure were religious leaders with vast moral authority.

BYZANTIUM, ROME IN THE EAST: THE RISE OF CONSTANTINOPLE

Elsewhere the Roman Empire was alive and well. From the borders of Greece to the borders of modern Iraq, and from the Danube River to Egypt and the borders of Saudi Arabia, the empire survived undamaged. Rich and self-confident, it saw itself as a more fortunate version of Old Rome.

However we call it (whether with its modern name, Byzantium, or simply the surviving empire of Rome), this was a highly centralized empire. All roads led to Constantinople. All decisions were made in the great palace. Gold from taxes and grain to feed the city arrived regularly. In fact, the speed of sea travel in the eastern Mediterranean facilitated this centralization. As long as emperors of Constantinople controlled the sea lanes, they controlled the heart of their empire.

The new Roman empire of the East now had its own Rome. In 324 CE, a year before he assembled the Christian bishops at Nicaea, Constantine decided to build a grandiose city on the European side of the Bosporus—the waterway that separates Europe from Asia. He chose the site of the ancient Greek city of Byzantium and called it New Rome, but it soon took on the name "Constantine's City" (in Greek, *Kōnstantinou polis*).

Thereafter Constantinople grew explosively, becoming an even bigger and better Rome. It was one of the most spectacularly successful cities in Afro-Eurasia, soon boasting a population of over half a million and 4,000 new palaces. Every year, more than 20,000 tons of grain arrived from Egypt, unloaded on a dockside over a mile long. A gigantic hippodrome echoing Rome's Circus Maximus straddled the city's central ridge, flanking an imperial palace whose opulent, enclosed spaces stretched down to the busy shore. As in Rome, the emperor would sit in his imperial box, witnessing chariot races as rival teams careened around the stadium. The Hippodrome also featured displays of eastern imperial might, as ambassadors came from as far away as central Asia, northern India, and Nubia.

Constantinople had the resources of a world capital. Long after their western colleagues had been declared bankrupt, its emperors had a yearly budget of 8,500,000 gold pieces. No other state west of China had tax revenues so gigantic. It was a

Justinian and Theodora. These portraits face each other on either side of the altar in the apse of the church of San Vitale at Ravenna. Both Justinian and Theodora are shown presenting lavish gifts. As emperor, Justinian heads the procession. On his left are the clergy; on his right are guards with Constantine's XP symbol on their shields and his lay advisers. Thus, both church and state line up behind their leader, the emperor. Theodora is more secluded. She is surrounded by ladies with veiled heads and by beardless eunuchs. The curtain is pulled back to enable Theodora to place her gift on the altar.

predominantly Greek city whose residents were proud to live under Roman law, a circumstance that made them "Romans." This was the Constantinople to which the future emperor Justinian came, as a young man from an obscure Balkan village, to seek his fortune. When he became emperor in 527 CE, he considered himself the successor of a long line of forceful Roman emperors—and he was determined to outdo them.

First, Justinian reformed the Roman laws. Within six years a commission of lawyers had created the *Digest*: a volume of 800,000 words that condensed the contents of 1,528 Latin law books. Its companion volume was the *Institutes*, a teacher's manual for schools of Roman law. These works were the foundation of what later ages came to know as "Roman law," followed in both eastern and western Europe.

The Hagia Sophia. After the conquest of Constantinople by the Muslim Ottomans in 1453, the Hagia Sophia was made into a mosque by having minarets (slender, high towers) added to each corner. Otherwise, it looks exactly as it did in the days of Justinian. In modern times, it became the model for the domed mosques that appear all over the Islamic world.

Justinian was equally determined to reassert Roman imperial authority in the western Mediterranean. Relying on naval superiority and regiments of crack troops (which included Hunnish horse archers wielding the most advanced bows), he crushed the once-formidable Vandals in Africa and made Carthage part of the "true" Roman Empire once again. He then turned to the heart of the old empire, wresting Rome itself from the Goths and reclaiming the former imperial capital of Ravenna in northern Italy.

Reflecting the marriage of Christianity with empire was the church of the Hagia Sophia at one end of the Hippodrome. Constructed on the spot where the city's old basilica church was destroyed during a riot, Hagia Sophia ("Holy Wisdom") must have astounded those who first entered it. The nave was twice the span of the former basilica—230 feet wide—and the new church was more than twice as high. The largest church built by Constantine, the basilica of Saint Peter in Rome, would have reached only as high as its lower galleries. Above all, the solemn straight lines of the traditional

Christian basilica were transformed. Great cliffs of stone, sheathed in multicolored marble and supported on gigantic columns of green and purple granite, rose to a dreamlike height. Audaciously curved semicircular niches placed at every corner made the entire building seem to dance. And a spectacular dome lined with gleaming gold mosaics floated almost 200 feet above it all.

In later centuries Greek and non-Greek Christians of the east called Hagia Sophia "the eye of the civilized world." It represented the flowing together of Christianity and imperial culture that, for another thousand years, would mark the eastern Roman empire of Constantinople.

SASANIAN PERSIA

Justinian had the misfortune of ruling an empire at the edge of Asia when Asia itself was changing dramatically (see Map 8-4). To begin with, the contacts between east and west were

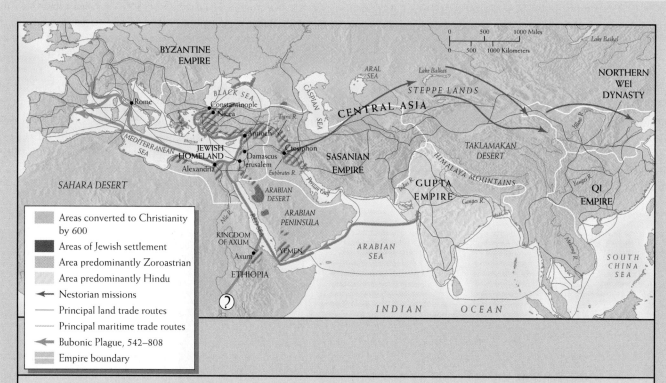

Areas converted to Christianity by 600
Areas of Jewish settlement
Area predominantly Zoroastrian
Area predominantly Hindu
Nestorian missions
Principal land trade routes
Principal maritime trade routes
Bubonic Plague, 542–808
Empire boundary

MAP 8-4 SOUTHWEST ASIA, 300–600 CE

Southwest Asia remained the crossroads of Afro-Eurasia in a variety of ways. Trade goods flowing between west and east passed through this region, as did universal religions. Using your finger, trace the principal trade routes and maritime routes. What were the areas of major religious influence? What was the relationship between trade routes and the areas of major religious influence? Then point out each area of religious influence. How did religious geography correspond to political geography? How was Southwest Asia affected by other regions, such as sub-Saharan Africa and central Asia, and how did it shape developments in these regions? The question mark in eastern Africa indicates scholars' uncertainty about the origination of the plague.

intensifying. The most unexpected reminder of this was a sudden onslaught of the bubonic plague—the grim gift of the Indian Ocean. In 542 CE, the plague first appeared in an Egyptian port that linked the Mediterranean to commercial routes in the Red Sea and the Indian Ocean. Scholars are unsure where the plague originated—South Asia or Africa—but it quickly emptied the cities of the Mediterranean. One third of the population of Constantinople died within weeks. Justinian himself survived, but thereafter he ruled an empire whose heartland was decimated.

Another reminder of growing interconnectedness was an escalating rivalry for territorial control. Justinian's empire struggled with a formidable eastern rival for the control of Southwest Asia. Beginning at the Euphrates River and stretching for eighty days of slow travel across the modern territories of Iraq, Iran, Afghanistan, and much of central Asia, the Sasanian Empire of Persia encompassed all the land routes of western Asia.

KING OF KINGS OF ERAN AND AN-ERAN   As we saw in Chapter 7, the Sasanians had replaced the Parthians as rulers of the Iranian plateau and Mesopotamia. Westerners (Romans included) called this domain the empire of Persia, but its precise title is more revealing of the Sasanians' universalistic aspirations: the Sasanian ruler was the King of Kings of Eran and An-Eran—"of the Iranian and non-Iranian lands." The ancient, irrigated fields of what is modern Iraq became the economic heart of this empire. Its capital, Ctesiphon, arose where the Tigris and the Euphrates rivers come close, only twenty miles south of modern Baghdad. Symbolizing the king's presence was a 110-foot-high vaulted arch decorated with rows of smaller, window-like arches. The structure, the Great Arch of Khusro, took its name from that

of Justinian's rival, Khusro I Anoshirwan (Khusro of the Righteous Soul).

As his name implied, Khusro Anoshirwan exemplified the model ruler: strong and just. His image in the east (as an ideal monarch) was as glorious as that of Justinian in the west (as an ideal Christian Roman emperor). For both Persians and Arab Muslims of later ages, the Arch of Khusro was as awe-inspiring as Justinian's Hagia Sophia was to Christians.

As Khusro's reign unfolded, it became obvious that the **Sasanian Empire** was more than the equal of the Mediterranean empire of Rome, for it controlled the trade crossroads of Afro-Eurasia. (See Global Connections & Disconnections: Religious Conflict in Imperial Borderlands.) But control of trade was only part of the story. Christian forces also met their match in the form of Iranian armored cavalry, a fighting machine adapted from years of competition with the nomads of central Asia. These fearless Persian horsemen fought covered from head to foot in flexible armor (small plates of iron sewn onto leather) and chain mail, riding "blood-sweating horses" draped in thickly padded cloth. Their lethal swords were light and flexible owing to steel-making techniques imported from northern India. With such cavalry, Khusro sacked Antioch in 540 CE. The campaign was a warning, at the height of Justinian's glory, that Mesopotamia could reach out once again to conquer the eastern Mediterranean shoreline.

Under Khusro II the confrontation between Persia and Rome escalated into the greatest war of centuries. Between 604 and 628 CE, Persian forces conquered Egypt and Syria and even reached Constantinople. Khusro II finally fell to the emperor Heraclius in a series of brilliant campaigns in northern Mesopotamia. Never had either empire reached so far into the heart of the other, and the effort exhausted both. For

The Great Arch. For a Persian king-of-kings, the prime symbol of royal majesty was the great arch marking the entrance gate of his palace. Here, in a Middle Eastern tradition that reached back for millennia, the king would appear to his subjects to deliver judgment. This building was associated with Khusro I, who came to be remembered as an ideal ruler.

Through the Persian Gulf, the Sasanian Empire reached out to control the trade on the Indian Ocean. This effort brought Persians into conflict with Roman merchants, who strove to reach India from the Red Sea. The entire region bounded by present-day Ethiopia (at the western end of the Red Sea), Yemen (in southern Arabia), and the Persian Gulf became a field of conflict between the Roman and Sasanian empires.

Their clash took religious as well as commercial and political form. Both Axum (modern-day Ethiopia) and Himyar (modern-day Yemen) had embraced monotheism, expressed in the worship of a Most High God known as

Granite Obelisks from Axum. The giant obelisks shown above, built around 100 BCE, reflect the warrior culture of ancient Axum.

al-Rahmānān (the Merciful One). In Axum, this monotheism was Christian: Christ was the protector of its kings, and the Cross of Christ was their talisman in battle. In contrast, the leaders of Himyar and the southern coast of Arabia were Jewish, and they dismissed Jesus as a crucified sorcerer.

The kings of Axum occupied the African side of the southern end of the Red Sea, looking down from the foothills of the well-watered and populous mountains of Ethiopia. Their formidable warrior-kingdom stretched as far as the Nile to the northwest, south into equatorial Africa, and eastward across the Red Sea to southern Arabia and Yemen. Axum's rulers, who became Christian around 340 CE, celebrated their victories on gigantic granite obelisks; they were monuments to a God that was very much a god of battles.

Faced by the aggressive Christian kingdom of Axum, the Sasanians reached out to support the kings of Himyar, who since 380 CE had been Jewish. Thus two monotheisms faced each other across the narrow southern opening of the Red Sea. Each was associated with a rich and aggressive kingdom. Each was backed by a Great Power—Axum by Christian Rome and Himyar by the Persians.

Between 522 and 530 CE, a Jewish king of Himyar popularly known as Dhu-Nuwas (the Man with the Forelock) drove the Ethiopian Christian garrisons out of southern Arabia. He turned churches into synagogues (just as, in the Christian empire far to the north, many synagogues had been turned into churches). In 523 CE, the Christians of the oasis city of Najran were ordered to become Jewish. Those who refused to do so, Dhu-Nuwas burned on pyres of brushwood piled into a deep trench.

Swept by these rivalries, the Arabian Peninsula was no longer a world apart, shut off from "civilization" by its cruel deserts and by its inhabitants' nomadic lifestyle. Far from it. Arabia had become a giant soundboard that amplified claims about the pros and cons of Judaism and Christianity, argued over with unusual intensity for an entire century. The "nonaligned" Arabs of the intermediate regions (between southern Arabia and Mesopotamia) still worshipped their ancestral tribal gods. But they had heard much, of late, about Jews and Christians, Romans and Persians. Arab tribes around Yathrib (modern Medina) adopted Judaism and remained in touch with the rabbis of Galilee along the caravan routes of northern Arabia. Here was a new kind of borderland between empires and between religions. In fact, it would be from this borderland that a new religion and a new prophet would emerge. His name was Muhammad.

THE SILK ROAD | **299**

→ *How did central Asians influence the spread of universal religions and other cross-cultural developments during this time?*

that reason, both fell easily to an Arab invasion only a few years later (see Chapter 9).

AN EMPIRE AT THE CROSSROADS   In their confrontations with Rome, Khusro I and Khusro II had the benefit of several factors. Culturally, Southwest Asia was already more united than its political boundaries implied. The political frontier cut across an exuberant common zone where Syriac was the main language and Christianity was making inroads. The Sasanians themselves were devout Zoroastrians, but they were forbearing rulers. Indeed, Jews and Christians enjoyed a tolerance in Mesopotamia that no Christian emperor had extended to non-Christians within the Roman Empire. Protected by the King of Kings, the rabbis of Mesopotamia compiled the monumental Babylonian Talmud at a time when their western peers, in Roman Palestine, were feeling cramped under the Christian state.

But the Sasanian court not only was interested in western religions such as Christianity and Judaism. It also embraced offerings from northern India, including the *Pancantantra* stories (moral tales played out in a legendary kingdom of the animals), polo, and the game of chess. In this regard Khusro's was truly an empire of crossroads, where the cultures of central Asia and India met that of the eastern Mediterranean.

Christians flourished in the Sasanian Empire, establishing dynamic communities in northern Mesopotamia, at the head of the Persian Gulf, and along the trade routes of central Asia. Named by their enemies "Nestorian" Christians (from Nestorius, a former bishop of Constantinople), these members of the "Church of the East" exploited Sasanian trade and diplomacy to spread their faith more widely. As Nestorian merchants passed along the Silk Road, they settled numerous communities and even established monasteries and a church in Chang'an, China. Others operating out of the Persian Gulf founded colonies on the west coast of southern India. Although they were Nestorian Christians, these colonists asserted a special claim for themselves as having been converted by Thomas the Apostle, the companion of Jesus. The Christians of this part of India are still called "Saint Thomas Christians."

THE SILK ROAD

> → *How did central Asians influence the spread of universal religions and other cross-cultural developments during this time?*

Crucial to growing interconnectedness was central Asia. Wending their way across its difficult terrains, a steady parade of merchants, scholars, and travelers transmitted commodities, technologies, and ideas between the Mediterranean worlds and China, and across the Himalayas into northern India, exploiting a series of commercial routes that have come to be known as the Silk Road.

The sharing of knowledge between the Mediterranean world and China began in earnest during the period when Christianity and Buddhism were spreading and when Vedic religion (Brahmanism) was developing a scholarly written tradition. Byzantium dispatched ambassadors from Constantinople to the nomads of eastern central Asia. In 568 CE these emissaries brought back glowing firsthand reports of the great empire of China.

Chinese observers likewise admired aspects of the eastern and western Roman empires. According to the historian Fan Ye, writing in the fifth century CE, "They have no permanent rulers, but when an extraordinary calamity visits the country, they elect a new king."

The great oasis cities of central Asia played a crucial role in the effective functioning of the Silk Road. While the Sasanians controlled Merv in the west, nomadic rulers became the overlords of Sogdiana and Tukharistan and extracted tribute from the cities of Samarkand and Panjikent in the east. The tribal confederacies in this region maintained the links between west and east by patrolling the Silk Road between Iran and China. Like the Kushans, they also joined north to south as they passed through the mountains of Afghanistan into the plains of northern India. As a result, central Asia between 400 and 600 CE was the hub of a vibrant system of religious and cultural contacts covering the whole of Afro-Eurasia. (See Map 8-5.)

THE SOGDIANS AS LORDS OF THE SILK ROAD

Sogdians in the oasis cities of Samarkand and Panjikent served as human links between the two ends of Afro-Eurasia. Their religion was a blend of Zoroastrian and Mesopotamian beliefs, touched with Brahmanic influences. Their language was the common tongue of the early Silk Road, and their shaggy camels bore the commodities that passed through their entrepôts. Moreover, their splendid mansions (excavated at Panjikent) show strong influences from the warrior-aristocracy culture of Iran. The palace walls display gripping frescoes of armored riders, reflecting the revolutionary change to cavalry warfare from Rome to China. The **Sogdians** were known as far away as China as merchants. To the Chinese, they were persons "with honey on their tongues and gum on their fingers"—to sweet-talk money out of others' pockets and to catch every stray coin. (See Primary Source: A Letter from a Sogdian Merchant Chief.)

Through the Sogdians, products from western Asia and North Africa found their way to the eastern end of the landmass. Carefully packed for the long trek on

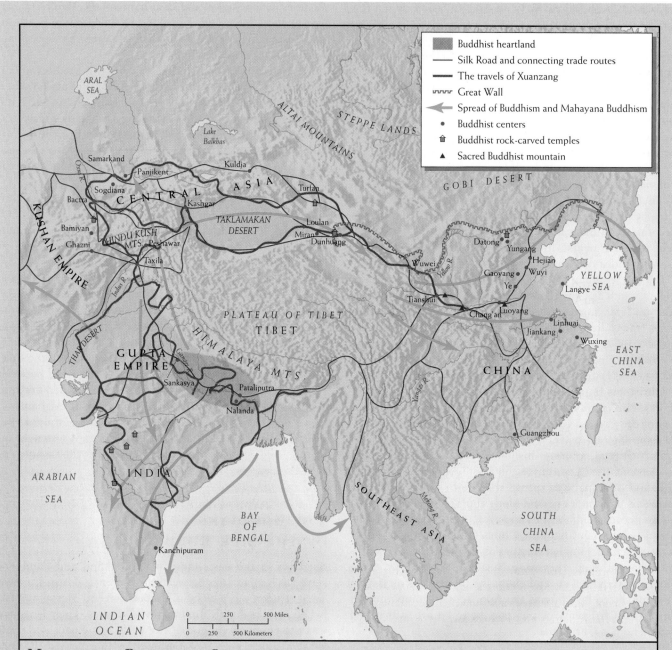

MAP 8-5   BUDDHIST LANDSCAPES, 300–600 CE

Buddhism spread from its heartland in northern India to central and East Asia at this time. Using your finger, trace the red lines of trade routes and then the green arrows showing the spread of Buddhism. According to the map, what role did increasingly extensive trade routes play in pushing this movement? What was the relationship among Buddhist centers and rock-carved temples, trade routes, and the spread of this universal faith? How did the travels of Xuanzang symbolize growing connections between East and South Asia?

Primary Source

A LETTER FROM A SOGDIAN MERCHANT CHIEF

Perhaps the clearest demonstration of how the Sogdians linked the ends of Afro-Eurasia is a document discovered in western China. In 313 CE (during a period of upheaval following the fall of the Han dynasty), a Sogdian merchant chief wrote a letter from China to his partner in Samarkand, his homeland some 2,000 miles to the west. He describes a state of civil war made more violent by invading barbarian armies. He also describes the "business as usual" attitude of traders. The letter never reached Samarkand, however. It was among several Sogdian letters in a mailbag found in one of the guard posts of the Great Wall of China.

And sirs, it is three years since a Sogdian came from "inside" [i.e., from China]. And now no one comes from there so that I might write to you about the Sogdians who went inside, how they fared and which countries they reached. And, sirs, the last emperor, so they say, fled from Luoyang because of the famine and fire was set to his palace and to the city, and the palace was burnt and the city [destroyed]. Luoyang is no more, Ye is no more! And sirs, we do not know whether the remaining Chinese were able to expel the Huns [from] Chany'an, from China, or whether they took the country beyond . . .

And from Dunhuang up to Jincheng . . . to sell, linen cloth is going [selling well?], and whoever has made cloth or woolen cloth . . .

And, sirs, as for us, whoever dwells in the region from Ji[ncheng] up to Dunhuang, we only survive so long as the . . . lives, and we are without family, old and on the point of death. . . .

. . . Moreover, four years ago, I sent another man named Artikhu-vandak. When the caravan left Guzang, Wakhushakk . . . was there, and when they reached Luoyang . . . the Indians and the Sogdians there had all died of starvation.

→ *What does the letter reveal about the difficulties and dangers of trade along the Silk Road?*

→ *What does it reveal about the fall of Luoyang—and about the way news traveled over long distances at this time?*

→ *The letter seems to imply that cloth is in high demand in northern areas of China. How might this indicate the effects of civil war and invasions disrupting local agriculture and trade?*

SOURCE: Annette L. Juliano and Judith A. Lerner (eds.), *Monks and Merchants: Silk Road Treasures from Northwest China Gansu and Ningxia, 4th–7th Century* (New York: Harry N. Abrams with the Asia Society, 2001), p. 49.

Simurgh, the legendary dog-headed bird of Persian mythology, as shown on this seventh-century silver plate from Sasanian Persia, was a favored motif on textiles, sculptures, paintings, and architecture from the Byzantine Empire to Tang China.

jostling camel caravans, goods displaying Persian motifs (such as the legendary simurgh bird and prancing rams with fluttering ribbons that, in Iran, were the symbol of good fortune and royalty) rode side by side with Roman glass from Mediterranean cities. Along with Sasanian silver coins and gold pieces minted in Constantinople, these exotic products found eager buyers as far east as China and Japan.

BUDDHISM ON THE SILK ROAD

Unstable political systems did not hinder the flow of ideas or commodities. Instead, the civil wars marking the end of the Han Empire rendered China more open to the cultures of its far western regions. South of the Hindu Kush Mountains, in northern India, nomadic groups made the roads into central Asia safe to travel, enabling Buddhism to spread northward

and eastward via the mountainous corridor of Afghanistan into China. Here, Buddhist monks were the primary missionizing agents, the purveyors of a universal message as they traveled across the roads of central Asia, bearing holy books, offering salvation to commoners, and establishing themselves more securely in host communities than did armies, diplomats, or merchants.

Starting at Bamiyan, a valley of the Hindu Kush—where two gigantic statues of the Buddha, 121 and 180 feet in height, were hewn from the stone face of the cliff during the fourth and fifth centuries CE—travelers found welcoming cave monasteries at oases all along the way from the Taklamakan Desert to northern China. They also encountered five huge Buddhas carved from cliffs in Yungang. While those at Bamiyan stood tall with royal majesty, the Buddhas of Yungang sat in postures of meditation. Surrounding the Buddhas, over fifty caves sheltered more than 50,000 statues representing Buddhist deities and patrons. The Yungang Buddhas, seated just inside the Great Wall, welcomed travelers to the market in China and marked the eastern end of the central Asian Silk Road.

The Bamiyan and Yungang Buddhas, placed more than 2,500 miles apart, are a reminder that by now religious ideas were creating world empires of the mind. Religions such as early Christianity and Buddhism saw themselves as transcending kingdoms of this world: they were bringing a universal message contained in holy scriptures. And they enjoyed greater reach than the ponderous empires that *were* of this world—whether Roman or Chinese. Religion traveled light and traveled faster than did armies.

Yungang Buddha. This is one of the five giant statues of the Buddha in Yungang, created under the emperors of the Northern Wei, a dynasty built by nomads who invaded and occupied north China. Sitting at the foothills of the Great Wall, the Buddhas marked the eastern destination of the central Asian Silk Road.

POLITICAL AND RELIGIOUS CHANGE IN SOUTH ASIA

> → *To what extent did South Asia develop a common culture despite political, religious, and social diversity?*

A Gold Coin of Chandra Gupta II. The Gupta dynasty, based in the middle and lower Ganges plain, was known for its promotion of indigenous Indian culture. Here, Chandra Gupta II, the most famous king of the dynasty, is shown riding a horse in the style of the invaders from the central Asian steppes.

South Asia, especially the area of modern India, also enjoyed religious enthusiasm (see again Map 8-5). Its major cultural system, Brahmanism (Vedic religion), did not claim to be a universal faith with aspirations to reach outside India. But it did strive to meet all needs and to explain all theological problems, much as its rival, Buddhism, had done. Like Christianity in the Mediterranean and Southwest Asia and Buddhism in China, religion in India unified diverse peoples. And again, political opportunities aided its spread.

Religious change took a dramatic turn during the Gupta dynasty. The largest political entity in South Asia from the early fourth to the mid-sixth century CE, it provided stability that facilitated commercial and cultural exchange (much as the Roman Empire had done in its united territories). Chandragupta (r. c. 320–335 CE) called himself "King of Kings, Great King." His son expanded the Gupta territory to the entire northern Indian plain and made a long expedition to southern India. Even more military achievements occurred under later Gupta dynasts.

The poetry during the reign of Chandragupta, a generous patron of the arts, expressed the widespread religious yearnings and popular sentiments of the age. Kalidasa, a prolific poet and playwright, and other poets, for instance, worked with the motifs and episodes from two early epics, *Mahabharata* and *Ramayana* (see Chapter 4), to address new problems and to extol new virtues. In their hands what had once been lyric dramas and narrative poems, written to provide entertainment, now served as collective memories of the past and underscored religious commands for ideal behavior. The heroes and deeds that the poets praised served as models for kings and their subjects. Because these epics were intended to become part of the religious canon, they were rendered in classical Sanskrit and embodied religious teachings.

Nonetheless, these works preserve stories from ancient times and offer insights into those eras. Consider the original *Mahabharata* epic, which told of a king who left his court for an assertive woman of a forest society. In Kalidasa's accounting, what had been a saga of love and suffering becomes a morality play about holding to strict religious precepts. The main character, Sakuntala, now portrayed as a shy girl who had been adopted by a forest ascetic but who had neglected her religious duties, was made to suffer punishments and to live out her life in great misery. The moral of Kalidasa's story was that misfortune comes from failing to follow Brahmanical religious rules.

THE TRANSFORMATION OF THE BUDDHA

During the Gupta period, the two main schools of Buddhism acquired universalistic features. Initially regarded as a contemplative ascetic (someone who chooses a simple, hard life of self-denial), the Buddha now came to be worshipped as a god.

The doctrines of both schools—Mahayana (Greater Vehicle); and the school of elders, Hinayana (Lesser Vehicle), also referred to as Theraveda—had become quite different from what the Buddha preached centuries earlier. As we saw in Chapter 5, the historical Buddha was a sage who was believed to enter *nirvana*, ending the pain of consciousness. In the earliest Buddhist doctrine, god and supernatural powers did not exist. But by 200 CE a crucial transformation had occurred: his followers started to view the Buddha as a god (see Chapter 6). **Mahayana Buddhism** also extended worship to the many bodhisattvas who bridged the gulf between the Buddha's perfection and the world's sadly imperfect peoples.

Some Buddhists fully accepted the Buddha as god but could not accept the divinity of bodhisattvas; these adherents belonged to the more monkish school of old-fashioned **Hinayana Buddhism**, later called Theraveda in Ceylon and Southeast Asia. They rejected the Sanskrit canon on the supernatural power of bodhisattvas and cleaved to the early Buddhist texts, which were probably based on the words of Buddha himself. Hinayana temples barred all colorful idols of bodhisattvas and other heavenly beings and contained only the image of the Buddha.

It was especially in the Mahayana school that Buddhism became a universal religion, whose adherents worshipped divinities rather than simply acknowledging the worth of great men. Spreading along the Silk Road, this new religion (with claims to universality that rivaled Christianity's) eventually appealed to peoples all over East Asia.

The religion's universalizing transformation also involved rituals that recognized powerful local spirits. Consider the observations of Faxian, a Chinese pilgrim to India around 400 CE. He described the city of Sankasya, where both Mayahana and Hinayana took hold, as being home to a Buddhist *sangha* whose patron was "a white-eared dragon." Believing that it brought rain at propitious times to guarantee a good harvest, the Buddhists constructed a shrine in its honor and offered it food daily. At the end of the summer rainy period, "the dragon appears in the form of a white-eared snake. Monks recognize him and offer some cheese in a copper bowl. . . . The snake then moves from the high seats to the low seats of the sangha, as if sending his regards to everyone. Then he disappears. This happens every year." This Buddhist ritual likely reflects the local agrarian lifestyle and traditions of propitiating spirits from the natural world.

THE HINDU TRANSFORMATION

During this period, the ancient Brahmanic Vedic religion also spread widely and became the dominant religion of South Asia. Because Buddhism and Jainism (see Chapter 5) had many devotees in cities and commercial communities, conservative Brahmans turned their attention to rural India and refashioned their religion, bringing it in accord with rural life and agrarian values. As a result of these changes, the Brahmanic religion emerged as the dominant faith in Indian society as what we know today as **Hinduism**.

Hinduism is a modern word coined from *Hindu*, the people who live in Hind, the Arabic word for India. In the religion's new form, believers became vegetarians, forsaking the animal sacrifices that had been important to their earlier rituals.

Hindu Statue. This huge statue of a three-headed god in a cave on a small island near Mumbai (Bombay) represents the monotheistic theology of Hinduism. Brahma, the creator, Vishnu, the keeper, and Siva, the destroyer, are all from one *atma,* or the single soul of the universe.

They abandoned long-held customs associated with pastoralists and nomads and even absorbed Buddhist and Jain practices, as they identified themselves with agrarian culture. Their new rituals were linked to self-sacrifice—denying themselves meat rather than offering up slaughtered animals to the gods, as they had done previously. Three major deities—Brahma, Vishnu, and Siva—formed a trinity representing the three phases of the universe (birth, existence, and destruction, respectively) and the three expressions of the eternal self, or *atma*. As the universe was already born and its destruction was yet to come, the god in charge of the current world, Vishnu, was the most prominent. Next in importance was Siva, who was especially meaningful for those fearing the end of the world.

Vishnu, who embodied the present, was the most popular of the three deities. Believers thought he revealed himself to the world in various avatars (incarnations). One of these was Krishna, the dark-skinned cattle herder and charioteer of the ancient hero Arjuna in the epic poem *Mahabharata*, who also became a religious teacher to Arjuna. A vital part of this poem revolves around the final battle between two warring confederations of Vedic tribes. Arjuna, the best warrior of one of these confederations, holds back from the fray, afraid to fight against his enemies because many of them are his cousins. At a crucial moment his spiritual guide, Krishna, intervenes, commanding him to slay his foes—even those related to him. Krishna reminds Arjuna that the warrior caste, the Kshatriyas, to whom Arjuna belongs, have been put on earth to govern and to fight against the community's enemies. In the early rendition of this tale the episode takes up little space; but by the Gupta period the story had become a lengthy poem, *The Bhagavad Gita* (Song of the God). In this form it prescribed religious and ethical precepts (*dharma*) for people in all walks of life and served as a major canon of Hindu spirituality.

Hindus also absorbed other religions' deities into their pantheon, even regarding the Buddha as an avatar of Vishnu. Thus the Hindu pantheon became larger and more accessible than the Vedic one, enabling more believers to share a single faith. Hindus did not wish to approach the gods only through sacrificial rituals at which Brahmans alone could officiate. They preferred to devote their passion and faith to an individual form of each of the great gods. For example, one could be a devotee exclusively of Rama or his wife, Sita. Women, especially widows, tended to worship Krishna and kept a small idol of him in the home. Evidence from later times shows that worshippers of Krishna, Rama, Siva, or any other deity often gathered to sing, dance, and parade. This practice of personal devotion to gods was called **bhakti**. It attracted Hindus of all social strata, while the body of mythological literature wove the deities into an intriguing heavenly order presided over by the trinity of Brahma, Vishnu, and Siva. The Hindu trinity enabled believers to claim to be monotheists, since the three gods embodied a single god, Atma. The trinity also represented a divine hierarchy. In this sense the Hindu trinity may

THE LAWS OF MANU: CASTES AND OCCUPATIONS   Hinduism

Brahmans compiled the Laws of Manu during the first or the second century CE, when the Kushans from the northern steppes ruled over much of South Asia. It was a time of constant social upheaval. Among the many law codes that appeared throughout Indian history, that of Manu (father of the human race) holds the most authority among Hindus because it is the most comprehensive. It describes the origins of the four castes and clearly designates the occupations that provide members of each with their livelihood.

87. But in order to protect this universe He, the most resplendent one, assigned separate (duties and) occupations to those who sprang from his mouth, arms, thighs, and feet.

88. To Brâhmanas he assigned teaching and studying (the Veda), sacrificing for their own benefit and for others, giving and accepting (of alms).

89. The Kschatriya he commanded to protect the people, to bestow gifts, to offer sacrifices, to study (the Veda), and to abstain from attaching himself to sensual pleasures;

90. The Vaisya to tend cattle, to bestow gifts, to offer sacrifices, to study (the Veda), to trade, to lend money, and to cultivate land.

91. One occupation only the lord prescribed to the Sûdra, to serve meekly even these (other) three castes.

→ *According to Hindu belief, the four castes sprang from "the mouth, arms, thighs, and feet" of "the most resplendent one." In what ways is it significant that the Brahman caste sprang from the mouth?*

→ *What caste do soldiers belong to? What caste do farmers and merchants belong to? Which caste do you suppose represents the majority of the population?*

→ *How are the different caste statuses reflected in the jobs that their members can take?*

SOURCE: *The Laws of Manu*, I.87–91; translated by G. Bühler, vol. 25 of *The Sacred Books of the East* (Oxford: Clarendon Press, 1886), p. 24.

---

have taken inspiration from Christianity, as Christians had been living in India for centuries.

During this period Buddhism and Hinduism lived side by side, competing for followers by building ornate temples and sculptures of gods and by holding elaborate rituals and festivities. Hindu temples and Buddhist monasteries also developed into centers of education, as both communities learned from each other in all lines of knowledge.

A CODE OF CONDUCT
INSTEAD OF AN EMPIRE

Besides setting heaven in order, Hinduism sought to establish a "correct" social order on earth. What emerged were new ways of thinking about the bonds between rulers and subjects. Although these ideas could not transcend the region's political differences, they introduced an alternative ethic of governing—steeped in religious faith—that would eventually integrate the society.

THE LAWS OF MANU   Unlike China and Rome, India did not have a centralized empire that the new governing ethic could revitalize. After the fall of the Mauryan Empire in the second century BCE (see Chapter 6), northern India came under the rule of distant rulers who had no contact with the people from whom they collected taxes and tariffs. Local populations relied on religious and social institutions such as castes and guilds to maintain order during periods of frequent warfare. But now, to maintain order, the Brahmans compiled law codes drawing on Hindu moral rules and customary law. Among them, the Laws of Manu were the most comprehensive. In Hindu mythology, Manu ("human") was the father of the human race, and the Laws of Manu applied to all persons no matter where they lived. Kingdoms might come and go, but the "true" order of society, summed up in the Laws of Manu, remained the same.

Above all, the **Laws of Manu** offered guidance for living within the caste system, whose origins lay centuries earlier. (See Primary Source: The Laws of Manu: Castes and Occupations.) Every person had to marry within his or her caste and follow its profession and dietary rules in order to perpetuate its status. Thus social and religious pressure, not government coercion, kept all individuals within orderly categories.

Though seemingly rigid, the Laws of Manu offered a way to cope with a constantly changing Indian society, for the code's purview extended far beyond the major states of northern India. In providing mechanisms for absorbing new groups into the caste system, it propelled Hinduism into areas beyond the reach of the state.

The code also reinforced what it meant to belong to a community of believers, especially as the faithful no longer lived close to one another. In this sense, the Laws of Manu functioned like the Jewish Torah, the Confucian Analects, Christianity's New Testament, and eventually the Islamic Quran. These texts were easy to transport. Powerful weapons in the arsenal of religious conversion, and carried in the earnest hands of the faithful, such holy scriptures could travel into distant regions within India for sharing among those who were not yet members of the community of believers.

INTERNAL COLONIZATION Behind these developments was a remarkable movement of internal colonization, as settlers from northern India pushed southward into lands formerly outside the Brahmans' domain. In these territories Brahmans encountered Buddhists and competed with them to win followers. The mixing of these two groups and the intertwining of their ideas and institutions ultimately created a common "Indic" culture organized around a shared vocabulary addressing concepts such as the nature of the universe and the cyclical pattern of life and death. The arenas in which much of this mixing of ideas took place were schools, universities, and monasteries. On their side, the Buddhists already possessed large monasteries, such as Nolanda in northeast India, where 10,000 residential faculty and students assembled, and more than 100 smaller establishments in southeast India housing at least 10,000 monks. In these settings Buddhists teachers debated such topics as theology, theories of the structure of the universe, mathematics, logic, and botany, and did so always in Sanscrit. In response, the Brahmans established schools, called *mathu*, where similar high intellectual topics were discussed and where Buddhist and Brahmanic Hindu ideas were fused.

The resulting widespread Indic cultural unity covered around one million square miles (the greatest extent of the Roman Empire) and affected a highly diverse population. Although India was not one polity (as was China) and did not adhere to one religious system (as would happen in the Christian Roman Empire and in medieval western Europe), it was developing a distinctive culture based on the intertwining of two shared major religious traditions. Even outsiders recognized it. Xuanzang, a Chinese Buddhist pilgrim, began his account of a visit to India in the 630s–640s CE by discussing the name *Indu*. For him and others, Indu (what we today call

India) began after a traveler crossed the valley of the Hindu Kush from the northwest. Its other boundaries were oceans on three sides and the snowy Himalayas to the north. Although the region comprised more than seventy states, he found it to be culturally cohesive. Throughout this large land, Xuanzang observed, the Brahmans were the highest caste, so he suggested calling the territory "the land of the Brahmans." In short, he described an area of greatly diverse regimes, climates, and customs. But it was a unity nonetheless—possibly even a country.

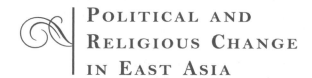

POLITICAL AND RELIGIOUS CHANGE IN EAST ASIA

> → *To what extent did influences from other parts of Afro-Eurasia transform Chinese culture and politics?*

In the first century CE, Han China had been the largest state in the world, with as great a population as the Roman Empire had at its height. Its emperor ruled an area more than twice the size of the Roman Empire, extracted an annual income of millions of pounds of rice and bolts of cloth, and conscripted millions of workers whose families paid tribute through their labor. Later Chinese regarded the end of the Han Empire as a disaster just as great as western Europeans regarded the end of the Roman Empire. Successive generations recalled the centuries after the fall of the Han as a period marked by barbarization.

In reality (as with the Roman Empire), "barbarization" meant the opening up of a proud society to cultures along its margins. In post-Han China, new influences emanated from the Silk Road, the nomads' military talents, and the proselytizing of Buddhist monks from the so-called Western Regions (see again Map 8-5). In this process Buddhism took much the same role as Christianity played in Rome, adapting to the Chinese empire and gaining popularity through imperial and elite patronage. Here Buddhism evolved into a Chinese religion with universal appeal, even extending into Korea and Japan (see Chapter 9).

NORTHERN AND SOUTHERN CHINA

After the fall of the Han in 220 CE, several kingdoms—initially three, though at times as many as sixteen—competed for total power. Civil wars raged for roughly three centuries, a time called the Six Dynasties period, when no single state was able to conquer more than half of China's territory.

Ultimately, the most successful regime was that of the Tuoba, a people originally from Inner Mongolia. Nearly seventy-five years after their first contact with the northern Chinese rulers, the Tuoba founded the **Northern Wei dynasty** in 386 CE; it lasted one and a half centuries. As a result of such northern invasions, China spent roughly three centuries divided by polity, culture, and ethnicity.

Undeterred by the Han's contempt for them, the "barbarian" rulers in northern China maintained many of their preconquest forms of state and society. Because they had lived for generations within the Chinese orbit as tributary states, they were "civilized" by imperial standards. They even maintained many Chinese traditions of statecraft and court life: they taxed land and labor on the basis of a census, conferred official ranks and titles, practiced court rituals, preserved historical archives, and promoted classical learning and the use of classical Chinese for record keeping and political discourse. Though they were nomadic warriors, they adapted their large standing armies to city-based military technology, which required dikes, fortifications, canals, and walls. Following the Qin and Han precedent, they drafted huge numbers of workers to complete such enormous projects as rebuilding a capital city at Luoyang.

Among the challenges facing the Northern Wei was the need to consolidate authority over their own highly competitive nomadic people. One strategy, which they pursued with little success for nearly a century, was to make their own government more "Chinese." Under Emperor Xiaomen (r. 471–499), for example, the Tuoba royal family adopted the Chinese family name of Yuan and required all court officials to speak Chinese and wear Chinese clothing. However, the Tuoba warrior families resisted these policies. They blatantly spoke their native tongues, shaved most of their heads and tied their remaining hair in pigtails, and continued wearing loose-fitting pants and shirts more typical of the warrior on horseback than the flowing gowns of urbane Han Chinese civilians riding in carts or walking the streets.

At the same time, the Wei rulers sought stronger relationships with the Han families of Luoyang that had not fled south. The Wei offered them more political power (as officials in the Wei bureaucracy) and more land. A key figure in this effort was the Dowager Empress Fang (regent 476–490), grandmother of Emperor Xiaomen. (As widows, such dowagers often held power over their young emperor sons and controlled their own property, or dower, which was derived from their deceased husbands, the former emperors.) Her most substantial initiative involved progressive land reforms: all young men—whether Han or Wei—who agreed to cultivate the land would receive two allotments, one at age eleven and one at fifteen, which they could pass on to their heirs. After age seventy, they would no longer have to pay taxes on it. But even this plan failed to bridge the cultural divides between the "civilized" Han of Luoyang and the "barbarian" Tuoba Wei because the latter showed no interest in farming.

The boldest attempt to unify northern China came under Emperor Xiaomen, who rebuilt the old Han capital of Luoyang based on classical architectural models dating from the Han dynasty (see Chapter 7) and made it the seat of his government. To gain political legitimacy, members of the Wei court supported Buddhist temples and monumental cave sites in an appeal to their Tuoba roots while also honoring Confucian traditions dating to the ancient Zhou period. Emperor Xiaomen's untimely death cut short his efforts to unify the north, however. Several decades of intense fighting among military rulers followed, leading ultimately to the downfall of the Northern Wei dynasty.

BUDDHISM IN CHINA

By the third and fourth centuries CE, Buddhist travelers from central Asia had become frequent visitors in the streets and temples of the competing capitals: Chang'an, Luoyang, and Nanjing. (See Primary Source: The Art of Religious Fervor in China.)

MADHYAMIKA BUDDHISM AND CULTURAL CHANGE
Spreading the increasingly universalizing faith required brokers, endowed with texts or codes, to convey its message. Kumarajiva (344–413 CE), a renowned Buddhist scholar and missionary, was the right man, in the right place, at the right time to spread Buddhism in China—where it already coexisted with other faiths. He was, above all, a bearer of exotic holy books (not unlike the Christians of the Roman Empire), and his influence on Chinese Buddhist thought was critical. Not only did he translate previously unknown Buddhist texts into Chinese, but he also clarified Buddhist terminology and philosophical concepts. He and his disciples established a Mahayana branch known as **Madhyamika (Middle Way) Buddhism**, which used irony and paradox to show that reason was limited. For example, they contended that all reality was transient because nothing abided over time unchanged. They sought enlightenment through transcendental visions and spurned experiences in the material world of sights and sounds.

Kumarajiva represented the beginning of a profound cultural shift. After 300 CE Buddhism began to expand in northwestern China, taking advantage of imperial disintegration and the decline of state-sponsored classical learning. The Buddhists stressed devotional acts (such as daily prayers and mantras, which included seated meditations in solitude requiring mind and breath control), as well as the saving power of the Buddha and the saintly bodhisattvas who postponed their own salvation for the sake of others. They even encouraged the Chinese to join the clergy. The idea that persons could be defined by faith rather than kinship was not new in Chinese society (as the Han dynasty Daoist rebels had showed; see Chapter 7), but it had special appeal in a time of

THE ART OF RELIGIOUS FERVOR IN CHINA: THE PAGODA

Religious fervor changed the visual environment of China. For example, the decorations on pottery and metal objects from this time show strong central Asian and Sasanian influences, transmitted primarily through Buddhism. The impact on architecture was even more striking. In India, Buddhists had adapted a form of dome-shaped tombs (called stupas) into shrines for housing relics of the Buddha. Now, in China, huge pagodas represented an attempt—mostly in wood—to imitate the stone and brick stupas of India. Regarded by Koreans and Japanese (and later by Westerners) as quintessentially Chinese, the pagoda was in fact a distant echo, on Chinese soil, of northern Indian Buddhism. Similarly, the complexes of cave temples at Longmen and Yungang reflect Indian and central Asian influences. In these ways, a universal religion created common artistic themes that stretched from central to East Asia.

One site that featured the work of central Asian artisans was the oasis city of Dunhuang. Located along the Silk Road, it contained a number of cave temples. Starting in 400 CE they were adorned with paintings and statues, and between the fifth and eighth centuries hundreds of them were decorated with wall paintings. Some illustrated Buddhist legends, and others depicted scenes of paradise. The caves were sealed in 1035 to save them from raids by Tibetans, and they have survived to this day. In 1900, the cave housing the great Buddhist library at Dunhuang was found unopened. The dry climate had preserved thousands of manuscripts, including Buddhist texts and works of popular literature.

→ *What do the architectural links from India to China, Japan, and Korea tell us about Buddhism?*
→ *Why do you suppose the Dunhuang caves are essential to our understanding of Chinese Buddhism at this time?*

Pagoda on Mount Song. This is probably the earliest pagoda in China. The solid stone structure shows the influence of pagodas in the contemporary eastern part of India, such as the one in Mahabodhi Monastery in Bodhgaya.

The Western Pure Land. This mural painting of the Western Pure Land (a place where enlightenment is achieved) is from Dunhuang, close to the eastern end of the Silk Road. The facial features of the celestial beings and the art style are more Chinese than Indian. Lazulite blue, a pigment made from lapis lazuli from Badakshan, Afghanistan, is the dominant color here, as it is on all the cave art along the central Asian Silk Road.

Amitabha. This exquisite tapestry is an illustration for the *Amitabha Sutra,* the "Sutra of the Western Pureland." Since the text was translated into Chinese by Kumarajiva in the fourth century CE, Amitabha has been one of the most popular bodhisattvas in China. A devotee who invokes the name of Amitabha ten times before death would be saved to this Western Pure Land, where the Seven Treasures decorated the quiet landscape.

unprecedented crisis. In the south, the immigrants from the north found that membership in the Buddhist clergy and monastic orders offered a way to restore their lost prestige.

Even more important, in the northern states—now part-Chinese, part-barbarian—Buddhism provided legitimacy. With Buddhists holding prominent positions in government, medicine, and astronomy, the Wei's ruling houses could espouse a philosophy that was just as legitimate as that of the Han Chinese. As a Tuoba who ruled at the height of the Northern Wei, Emperor Xuanwu, for instance, was an avid Buddhist. During his reign he made Mahayana Buddhism the state religion.

Despite its appeals to universalism, Buddhism, which did not have a central ecclesiastical authority like the pope in Christianity, acquired different forms throughout South and East Asia. It did not have the hard edges that defined Christianity in the Roman Empire as a religion that sought to be the same in all places and at all times. On the contrary, as the expression of a cosmic truth as timeless and varied as the world itself, Buddhism showed a high level of adaptability, easily absorbing as its own the gods and the wisdom of every country it touched. A particularly interesting variant emerged in southern China, where Buddhism and Daoism borrowed extensively from each other. In fact, the two faiths became so amalgamated that only scholars could identify fine distinctions between them. In effect, Buddhism in southern China gained a Chinese tinge through its borrowing from Daoist practices.

DAOISM, ALCHEMY, AND THE TRANSMUTATION OF THE SELF Daoism, a popular Chinese religion under the Han and a challenge to the Confucian state and its scholar-officials (see Chapter 7), lost its political edge and adapted to the new realities in this period of disunity. Two new traditions of Daoist thought flourished in this era of self-doubt. The first, which was community oriented, involved heavenly masters who as mortals guided local religious groups or parishes. Followers sought salvation through virtue, confession, and liturgical ceremonies. Through ecstatic initiation rites, often achieved via an "external alchemy"—the use of hallucinatory drugs—the Daoist clergy also brought believers into contact with the divine.

A second Daoist tradition was more individualistic. In the Yangzi delta, personal expressions of religious faith emerged. For example, Ge Hong (283–343) sought to reconcile Confucian classical learning with Daoist religious beliefs in the occult and magical. He focused on "internal alchemy"—the use of trance and meditation to control human physiology. Through such mental and physical exertions, an adept, both as believer and practitioner, believed that the soul could accumulate enough religious merit to prolong his life. A recommended set of nine body postures involved full chest breathing combined with extensive stretching to facilitate the healthy flow of Qi, the life force circulating throughout the body. Adepts complemented this extension of life via trance and physiological control by taking elixirs, boiling exquisite teas as medical beverages, and knowing the specific effects of herbs and minerals.

The concept of merit and demerit in Daoist circles echoed the Buddhist notion of karmic retribution (the cosmic assessment of one's acts in this life that determines one's rebirth into a better or worse next life; see Chapter 5). For the Daoists, however, eternal life was the ultimate goal—not the Buddhists' ideal of release from the cycle of life, death, and rebirth.

By 400 CE China had more than 1,700 Buddhist monasteries and about 80,000 monks and nuns. By contrast, in 600 CE (after two centuries of monastic growth), Gaul and Italy—the two richest regions of western Europe—had, altogether, only 320 monasteries, many with fewer than 30 monks. Yet, in the two ends of Afro-Eurasia the principal bearers of the new religions were monks. Set apart from "worldly" affairs in their refuges, they enjoyed the pious support of royal courts and warriors whose lifestyles differed sharply from their own. It would be through their devoted faith in the divine and the support of secular rulers that these two universalizing religions would continue to grow, flourish, and revitalize themselves.

FAITH AND CULTURES IN THE WORLDS APART

> → *How similar and different were spiritual and cultural developments in worlds apart from Afro-Eurasia during this time?*

In most areas of sub-Saharan Africa and the Americas, it was not easy for ideas, institutions, peoples, and commodities to circulate broadly. Thus we do not see the development of universalizing faiths. Rather, belief systems and their deities were localized.

This is not to say that sub-Saharan Africa and the Americas lacked the elements for creating communities of faith. Indeed, Africans and Americans alike had prophetic figures who, they believed, communicated with deities and brought to humankind divinely prescribed rules of behavior. Moreover, peoples in both regions honored beliefs and rules that were passed down orally from generation to generation. These spiritual traditions guided behavior, established social customs, and determined people's fates. In fact, relationships with deities and spirits governed the calendar of rituals across these regions.

BANTUS OF SUB-SAHARAN AFRICA

Today, most of Africa south of the equator is home to peoples who speak some variant of more than 400 Bantu languages. Early Bantu history is shrouded in mystery. At present, scholars using oral traditions and linguistic evidence can trace the narrative of these peoples no further back than 1000 CE (see Map 8-6).

The first Bantu speakers apparently lived in the southeastern part of modern Nigeria, where about 4,000 or 5,000 years ago they shifted from hunting, gathering, and fishing to practicing settled agriculture. The areas they spread into, being tropical rain forest, demanded an immense amount of work. To ready a new acre for cultivation required removing some 600 tons of moist vegetation, and the migrants brought to the task only simple tools (mainly machetes and billhooks). In fact, their most effective technique was controlled burning. Moreover, the African equatorial forests were almost totally devoid of food plants. So these peoples made do with woodland plants such as yams and mushrooms, as well as palm oils and kernels.

BANTU MIGRATIONS   Following riverbeds and elephant trails, Bantu migrants traveled out of West Africa in two great waves. One group moved across the Congo forest region to East Africa, aided by their knowledge of iron smelting, which enabled them to use iron tools for agriculture. Because their new habitats supported a mixed economy of animal husbandry and sedentary agriculture, this group became relatively prosperous. The second wave of migrants moved southward through the rain forests in present-day Congo, eventually reaching the Kalahari Desert. They were not so fortunate. The tsetse fly–infested environment did not permit them to rear livestock, so they were limited to subsistence farming. These Bantus learned to use iron later than those who had moved to the east.

Precisely when the **Bantu migrations** began is unclear, but once under way the travelers moved with extraordinary rapidity. Genetic and linguistic evidence reveals that they swept all else before them, absorbing most of the hunting-and-gathering populations who originally inhabited these areas.

What enabled the Bantus to prevail and then to prosper was their skill as settled agriculturalists. They knew how to cultivate the soil, and they adapted their farming techniques to widely different environments. They thrived equally well in the tropical rain forests of the Congo River basin, the high grasslands around Lake Nyanza (Lake Victoria), and the highlands of Kenya, even though they had to grow different crops in each location.

For the Bantu of the rain forests of central Africa (the Western Bantu), the introduction of the banana plant was decisive. Linguistic evidence suggests that it first arrived in the Upper Nile region and then traveled into the rest of Africa with small groups migrating from one favorable location to another; the earliest proof of its presence is a record from the East African coast dating to 525 CE. When it reached the equatorial rain forests, its adaptability to local conditions was unmatched. Not only did it provide more nutrients than the yam crop, but it better withstood heavy rainfalls. In addition, banana plantings required the clearing of fewer trees than yam cultivation and created an environment free of the anopheles mosquito, which carried malaria. Exploiting the benefits of banana cultivation, the Western Bantu filled up the equatorial rain forests of central Africa—perhaps as early as 500 CE, certainly by 1000 CE.

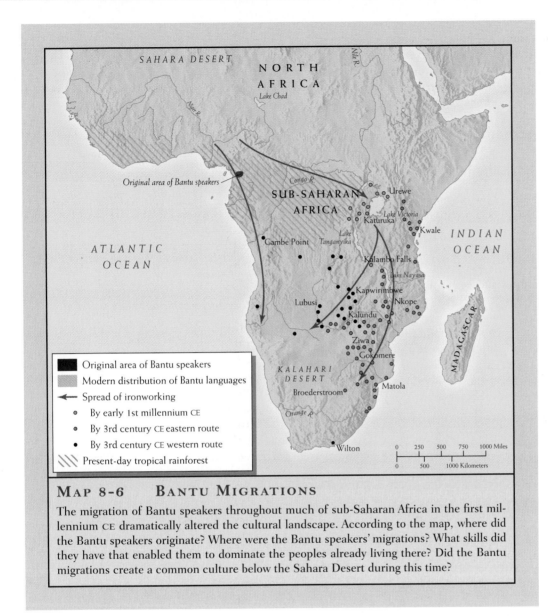

MAP 8-6   BANTU MIGRATIONS

The migration of Bantu speakers throughout much of sub-Saharan Africa in the first millennium CE dramatically altered the cultural landscape. According to the map, where did the Bantu speakers originate? Where were the Bantu speakers' migrations? What skills did they have that enabled them to dominate the peoples already living there? Did the Bantu migrations create a common culture below the Sahara Desert during this time?

socially and politically into age groups, the most important of which were the ruling elders. Within these age-based networks, individuals who demonstrated talent in warfare, commerce, and politics provided leadership.

Age-grading tended to impose certain rights and duties on different social groups based mainly on their physical age. Many such societies established three age grades for males and two for females. Males moved from (1) being children and learning male roles from older men, to (2) acquiring warrior status, when they defended the community, raided for livestock, and acquired new lands for the community, and then (3) becoming the politically ruling age grade—the elders. Females' age grades consisted of childhood and marriage. Bonds among age grades were powerful, and movement from one to the next was marked by meaningful and well-remembered rituals.

Lacking chiefs and kings, the loosely organized Bantu societies rallied around individuals of talent—so-called **big men**—whose abilities attracted followers and thereby promoted territorial expansion. Their courage, military valor, and wisdom won them many supporters, but rarely did their high positions pass along to offspring or relatives. Invariably, other dynamic individuals arose to compete for power. In the rain forest, land was abundant but labor was in short supply. Thus, individuals who could attract a large community of followers, marry many women, and sire many children could lead their bands into new locations and establish dominant communities.

Although dispersed, these rain forest communities embraced a common worldview. They believed that the natural world was inhabited by spirits, many of whom were their own heroic ancestors. These spiritual beings intervened in mortals' lives and required constant appeasement. Diviners helped men and women understand the spirits' ways, and charms warded off the misfortune that aggrieved spirits might

BANTU CULTURES, EAST AND WEST   Did these peoples create a common Bantu culture? Clearly, they could not establish the same political, social, and cultural institutions in widely different ecological zones. In the Great Lakes area of the East African savanna lands, where communication was relatively easy, the Bantu speakers developed centralized polities whose kings ruled by divine right. Mostly, however, they moved into heavily forested areas similar to those they had left in southeastern Nigeria. These locations supported a way of life that remained fundamentally unaltered for perhaps a millennium and a half, withstanding the later impact of the Atlantic slave trade and withering only under European colonialism in the twentieth century.

The western Bantu-speaking communities of the lower Congo River rain forests formed small-scale societies based on family and clan connections. They organized themselves

INSTRUCTIONS TO A YOUNG MAN IN WEST AFRICA

The words that were traditionally spoken to young men coming of age in the Cameroons in West Africa (an area where the Bantus likely originated) reflect the importance that families attached to being a strong and enterprising individual.

The grandfather gave an ivory bracelet and said:
"This elephant which I put on your arm, become a man of crowds,
a hero in war, a man with women
rich in children, and in many objects of wealth
prosper within the family, and be famous throughout the villages."

The grandmother gave a charm of success as a belt and said:
"Father, you who are becoming a man
Let toughness and fame be with you as this sap of the [*Baillonella toxisperma*] tree is glued to this thread.
Become dominant, *a great man,*
a hero in war, who surpasses strangers and visitors;
prosper, Have us named!"

→ *Think about the Bantu speakers' environment. Why would a bracelet made from elephant tusk carry special meaning?*

→ *How do the words and gifts (typically charms) offered above reflect a belief that spirits inhabited the natural world?*

→ *According to the chapter text, why did the sub-Saharan peoples organize themselves around "big men" rather than kings or other sorts of rulers?*

→ *Have you ever had or attended a coming-of-age ceremony? Were certain words or gifts significant? Have you ever owned any good-luck charms? What were (or are) they?*

SOURCE: Jan Vansina, *Paths in the Rainforests: Toward a History of Political Tradition in Equatorial Africa* (Madison: University of Wisconsin Press, 1990), pp. 73–74.

wish to inflict. Diviners and charms also protected against the injuries that living beings—witches and sorcerers—could inflict. In fact, much of the misfortune that occurred in the Bantu world was attributed to these malevolent forces. The Bantus believed their big men could control such forces and use them to punish opponents and reward friends. These beliefs survived unchallenged for well over a millennium. (See Primary Source: Instructions to a Young Man in West Africa.)

The Bantu migrations ultimately filled up more than half the African landmass and introduced settled agriculture throughout its southern part. They spread a political and social order based on family and clan structures that allowed considerable leeway for individual achievement—and maintained an intense relationship to the world of nature that they believed, for good or ill, was shot through with supernatural forces.

MESOAMERICANS

As in sub-Saharan Africa, the process of settlement and expansion in Mesoamerica differed from that in the large empires of Afro-Eurasia. Mesoamerica had no integrating artery of a giant river and its floodplain, and thus it lacked the extensive resources that the state could harness for its monumental ambitions. What Mesoamericans achieved was therefore remarkable if we bear this in mind.

In the case of Teotihuacán, the first major community to emerge since the Olmecs (see Chapter 5), we see the growth of a city-state that ruled over a large, mountainous valley in the area of present-day Mexico (see Map 8-7). While it did not evolve into a territorial state, it traded and warred with neighboring peoples and created a smaller-scale common culture. In the case of the Mayans, we witness the emergence of a common culture that ruled over large stretches of Mesoamerica under a series of kingdoms built around ritual centers rather than cities. The Mayans aggressively engaged in warfare and trade, expanding their borders through tributary relationships. The extraordinary feature of Mayan society was that its people were defined not by a great ruler or a great capital city, but by their shared religious beliefs, worldview, and sense of purpose.

However, there is a mystery at the heart of Mesoamerican societies. For as great as the Olmec, Teotihuacán, and Mayan societies were, there was little carryover from one society to the next. Cultural development was much less cumulative here than in Afro-Eurasia, where new regimes built on the old—often by absorbing their predecessors. In the Americas, decline usually set in before newcomers could apply all of their predecessors' learning and breakthroughs.

TEOTIHUACÁN Around 300 BCE, people in the central plateau and the southeastern districts of Mesoamerica (where the dispersed villages of Olmec culture had risen and fallen; see Chapter 5) began to gather in larger settlements and to create state systems. Soon, political and social integration led to city-states. The largest was **Teotihuacán,** in the heart of the fertile valley of central Mexico; it became the largest center of the Americas before the Aztecs almost a half-millennium later.

Fertile land and ample water from the valley's marshes and lakes fostered high agricultural productivity despite the inhabitants' technologically rustic methods of cultivation. The local food supply sustained a metropolis of between 100,000 and 200,000 residents, living in more than 2,000 apartment compounds lining the city's streets. At one corner rose the massive pyramids of the sun and the moon— the focus of spiritual life for the city dwellers. Marking the city's center was the huge royal compound, or Ciudadela; the grandeur and refinement of its stepped stone pyramid, the Temple of the Feathered Serpent, were famous throughout Mesoamerica and probably influenced Mayan pyramid builders. The feathered serpent was the anchor for their spiritual lives. It was a symbol of fertility, a deity that governed reproduction and life, often bearing powerful maternal

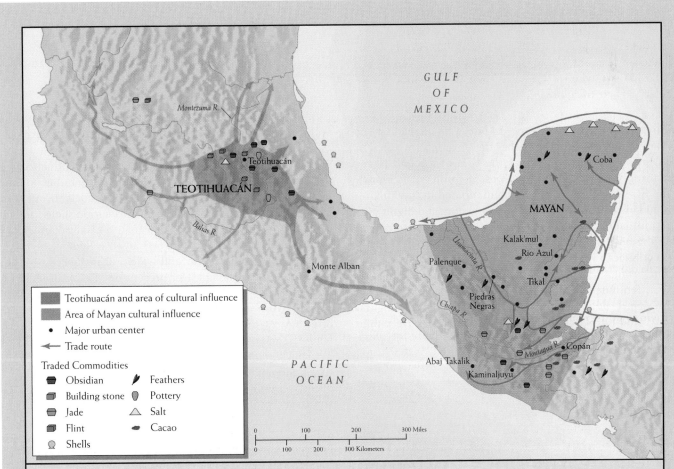

MAP 8-7 MESOAMERICAN WORLDS, 200–700 CE

At this time, two groups dominated Mesoamerica: one was located at the city of Teotihuacán in the center, and the other, the Mayans, was in the south. What commodities did these cultures trade? Look at the symbols for Traded Commodities in the map key, and find them all on the map. Judging by what you see, how did each group create a common culture in surrounding regions? To what extent do you believe the people of the Teotihuacán and Mayan worlds influenced each other?

Teotihuacán. The ruins of Teotihuacán convey the importance of monumental architecture to Aztec culture. In the foreground is the Plaza of the Moon, leading to the Street of the Dead, with the Pyramid of the Sun to the left. These massive structures were meant to confirm the importance of spiritual affairs in urban life.

features—despite the fearsome (to our eyes) appearance of the fangs and jaws, and the snakes that invariably writhed in the deity's grip. Its temple was the core of a much larger structure. From it radiated the awesome promenade known as the Street of the Dead, which culminated in the hulking Pyramid of the Moon. Here foreign warriors and dignitaries were mutilated, sacrificed, and often buried alive to consecrate the holy structure.

Teotihuacán was a powerful city-state. Its military muscle was imposing. After overwhelming or annexing its rivals, by 300 CE Teotihuacán controlled the entire basin of the Valley of Mexico. It dominated its neighbors and demanded gifts, tribute, and humans for ritual sacrifice. Its massive public architecture displayed art that commemorated decisive battles, defeated neighbors, and captured fighters.

Beyond the basin, though, the city's political influence was limited. Far more important was its cultural and economic diffusion, for Teotihuacán's merchants traded throughout Mesoamerica. Ceramics, ornaments of marine shells, and all sorts of decorative and valued objects (especially of green obsidian) made by Teotihuacáno artisans traveled on the backs of porters for exchange far and wide. For instance, a Mayan community near the coast of present-day Belize used Teotihuacáno green obsidian objects, such as elegant figurines resembling the Temple of the Feathered Serpent, in burial offerings. At the same time, Teotihuacán imported pottery, feathers, and other goods from distant lowlands.

This kind of expansion left much of the political and cultural independence of neighbors intact, with only the threat of force keeping them in check. But for some unknown reason that threat apparently waned, for late in the fifth century CE the city fell at the hands of invaders. They burned it and smashed the carved figurines of the central temples and palaces, targeting Teotihuacán's institutional and spiritual core.

Quetzalcoatl. The artisans of Teotihuacán decorated the sides of their monumental buildings with sculptures. Here, feathered serpents, denoting the god Quetzalcoatl, burst from the sides of a wall to stare menacingly at passers-by.

FAITH AND CULTURES IN THE WORLDS APART | **315**

→ *How similar and different were spiritual and cultural developments in worlds apart from Afro-Eurasia during this time?*

THE MAYANS   Teotihuacán's power eventually spread as far as the Caribbean region of the Yucatán and its interior. Here the Mayan people arose and flourished from about 250 CE to their zenith in the eighth century. The **Mayans** have been a never-ending mystery to historians and archaeologists. They lived in an inhospitable region—hot, infertile, lacking navigable river systems, and vulnerable to hurricanes. Still, their communities, grouped into large settlements, conducted long-distance trade and produced stunning scientific and mathematical innovations. The Mayans were also great artists and builders, and it is largely from the remains of their prodigious constructions that scholars know much about them. Like the earlier Olmecs, the Mayans accomplished magnificent feats only to collapse, leaving their centers deserted for centuries and entire provinces utterly depopulated.

In contrast to the inhabitants of Teotihuacán (or Baghdad or Constantinople), the Mayans achieved greatness without founding a single metropolis. Instead, they established hundreds, possibly thousands, of agrarian villages scattered across present-day southern Mexico to western El Salvador. In this region of diverse ecological zones, people shared the same Mayan language and the benefits of trade. Villages were also linked through tribute payments, chiefly from lesser settlements to sacred towns. At their peak the Mayans may have numbered as many as 10 million—a figure that qualifies them as a "big" culture. Bigness in a cultural system without big cities made them unique.

MAYAN POLITICAL AND SOCIAL STRUCTURE   The Mayans established a variety of kingdoms around major hubs and their hinterlands. Palenque, Copán, and Piedras Negras, for instance, embodied the model of a city-state with hinterlands (similar in some respects to Mesopotamian city-states surrounded by transhumant societies; see Chapter 3). Such hubs were politically independent but culturally and economically interconnected. Some larger polities, such as Tikal and Kalak'mul, became sprawling cities with dependent provinces. Ambitious rulers in these larger states frequently engaged in hostilities with one another.

Thus a single culture encompassed about a dozen kingdoms that shared many features. Each was highly stratified, displaying an elaborate class structure. At the center was a shamanistic king who legitimated his position by extolling his lineage, which reached back to a founding father and, ultimately, the gods. While there was a vast pantheon of gods and each subregion had its own patron, there were some common features. There was a creator (indeed, there were tiers, or generations, of creator gods), and there were deities for rain, maize, war, and the sun—as well as of bees and midwifery. The importance of reproduction is evident in this lineup. The creation of humans was only one act in an eternal cycle of births, deaths, and renewals that constituted the

Palenque. Deep in the Lacandon jungle lies the ruin of the Mayan city of Palenque. Its pyramid, on the left, overlooks the site; on the right, the Tower of the Palace shadows a magnificent courtyard where religious figures and nobles gathered. There is no mistaking how a city like Palenque could command its hinterland with religious authority.

entire population of the cosmos. Gods were neither especially cruel nor benevolent; they were just very busy with the work, or dance, that sustained the axis connecting the underworld and the skies. What humans had to worry about was making sure that the gods got the attention and reverence they needed.

This was the job of Mayan rulers. Kings sponsored elaborate public rituals to reinforce their divine heritages, including ornate processions down their cities' main boulevards to pay homage to gods and their descendants, the rulers. Lords and their wives performed ritual blood sacrifice to feed their ancestors. Though there may have been a powerful priestly elite, the pillars of these societies were their scribes, legal experts, military advisers, and skilled artisans. Indeed, many artists and scribes rose to high political positions because they bestowed an aura of greatness on their rulers.

Most of the Mayan people remained tied to the land, which could sustain a high population only through dispersed settlements. In much of the region, the soil was poor and quickly exhausted. Limited water also prevented large-scale agriculture, as major rivers or irrigation systems were lacking. Mayans therefore employed a combination of agrarian systems adapted to the ecology. Where possible they created terraces and drained fields for intensive cultivation. But in much of the region they relied on slash-and-burn agriculture, which pushed the arable frontier farther into the dense jungle. The result: a subsistence economy of diversified agrarian production. Villagers cultivated maize, beans, and squash, rotating them to prevent the depletion of soil nutrients. Where possible, farmers supplemented these staples with root crops such as sweet potato and cassava. Cotton was the basic fiber used for robes, dresses, and blouses; it frequently grew amid rows of other crops as part of a diversified mix.

MAYAN WRITING, MATHEMATICS, AND ARCHITECTURE Commerce connected the dispersed Mayan worlds, as did a common set of beliefs, codes, and values that rulers supported. Villagers spoke dialects of roughly the same language. Writing developed very early, though only recently have epigraphers deciphered the Mayan script. The advent of writing created an important caste of scribes who were vital to the society's integration. Rulers rewarded them with great titles and honors, as well as material comforts, for writing grand epics about dynasties and their founders, major battles, marriages, deaths, and sacrifices. Such writings taught generations of Mayan subjects that they shared common histories, beliefs, and gods—always associated with the narratives of ruling families. The inscriptions reflected elaborate narratives that were ritually performed for commoners and rulers alike. These took the form of dances that rehearsed epic triumphs before warriors went off to battle, or acts of illusion intended to trick and humor the audiences to remind them of some devious antecedent. And there were magnificent costumes made of shells, feathers, and hides to masquerade dancers and actors as gods, enemies, or royal neighbors.

The combination of writings and performances created a historic memory to serve rulers' power and to venerate the gods whose patronage they required. The best-known surviving text is the Popol Vuh, a "Book of Community." It narrates one community's creation myth, extolling its founders (twin heroes) and trials and tribulations—wars, natural disasters, human ingenuity—that enabled a royal genealogy to rule the Quiché Kingdom. It begins, as many creation myths do, with the gods' creation of the earth, in this case the work of three water-dwelling plumed serpents. And it ends with the elaboration of rituals to which the kingdom's tribes must subscribe if they are to avoid losing their way, which had occurred several times throughout their history. After all, to be a "community" required sharing and honoring a historic memory of the gods' work. One must note, however, in the use of Mayan "written" texts like the Popol Vuh, that they comprise narratives recited to later Spanish sources. They are not texts inscribed in the Classical Mayan era.

The Mayans also were skilled mathematicians, devising a calendar and studying astronomy. They charted regular celestial movements with amazing accuracy and marked the passage of time by precise lunar and solar cycles. Keen read-

Wood Tablet. This detail of a wood-carved tablet from a temple in the city of Tikal (c. 741 CE) is a fine example of the ornate form of scribal activity, which combined images and portraits with glyphs that tell a narrative.

ers of the stars, the Mayans could map heavenly motions onto their sacred calendars and rigorously observe their rituals at the proper times. Indeed, the movement of the stars and the chronology of the calendar governed annual ritual cycles. Each change in the cycle had particular rituals, dances, performances, and offerings, including the offering of human blood to honor the gods with life's sustenance. The most sacred blood was drawn from ears, tongues, and the foreskins of penises, to open pathways to the gods through which "donors" could hear, speak, and participate in heavenly reproduction. This was one reason why the rituals took place like clockwork according to the precise angles and movements of the heavenly bodies.

Here, then, was a world characterized by political divisions and often crippling warfare, but with common religious and cultural features. A common faith provided a powerful human resource that rulers could exploit. Indeed, cities reflected a ruler's ability to summon his subjects to contribute to the kingdom's greatness. Plazas, ball courts,

POP	UO	ZIP	ZOTZ	TZEC
XUL	YAXKIN	MOL	CHEN	YAX
ZAC	CEH	MAC	KANKIN	MUAN
PAX	KAYAB	CUMHU	uayeb	

Mayan Pictograms. The Mayans were famous for keeping records of time with an elaborate calendar. Pictograms, each with a separate image, represented the months of the year. All literate Mayans would have recognized this index.

terraces, and palaces sprouted out from neighborhoods in an early form of urban sprawl. Activity revolved around grand royal palaces and massive ball courts, where competing teams treated enthusiastic audiences to contests that were more religious ritual than game (see discussion of Olmec ball courts in Chapter 5). Moreover, rulers exhorted their people to build not just outward but upward. The Mayans excelled at building skyscrapers—especially as tombs. In Tikal, for instance, surviving buildings include six steep and massive funerary pyramids featuring thick masonry walls and vaulted ceilings and chambers; the tallest temple soars above the treetops, more than 220 feet high. Embellishing the outsides are giant carvings and paintings, and deep within lie the crypts of royal family members. For example, the famous Bonampak site (in current-day southern Mexico) has a magnificent Temple of the Murals with the finest examples of Classical Mayan painting. These depict a series of events in precise detail—from an orchestra performing, to nobles discussing current affairs, to captured warriors being prepared for human sacrifice. The artwork dates from 790 CE. This kind of artwork likely adorned other Mayan centers as well.

MAYAN BLOODLETTING AND WARFARE The elites were obsessed with blood, for spilling it was a way to honor dynastic lineages as well as gods. This rite led to chronic warfare, especially among rival dynasties, the goal of which was to capture victims for the bloody rituals. Rulers also would shed their own blood at intervals set by the calendar. Royal wives drew blood from their tongues; men had their penises perforated by a stingray spine or sharpened bone. Such bloodletting was

reserved for those of noble descent, with the aid of elaborately adorned and sanctified instruments; carvings and paintings portray blood cascading from rulers' mutilated bodies.

The spiral of warfare doomed the Mayans, especially after devastating confrontations between Tikal and Kalak'mul during the fourth through seventh centuries CE. With each outbreak, rulers drafted larger armies and sacrificed greater numbers of captives, and their resolve fueled the carnage. Crops perished. People fled. Food supplies dwindled. After centuries of misery, it must have seemed as if the gods themselves were abandoning the Mayan people.

As warfare engulfed the fractured Mayan communities and ruling households collapsed, entire states fell. The cycle of violence destroyed the cultural underpinnings of elite rule that had held the Mayan world together. There was no single catastrophic event, no great defeat by a rival power. The Mayan people simply abandoned their spiritual centers, and cities became ghost towns. As populations declined, jungles overtook temples. Eventually, the hallmark of Mayan unity— the ability to read a shared script—vanished.

CONCLUSION

The breakdown of two imperial systems—Rome around the Mediterranean, and Han China in East Asia—introduced an era in which religion and shared culture (rather than military conquest and political institutions) linked large areas of Afro-Eurasia.

The Roman Empire gave way to a religious unity, first represented by Christian dissenters and then co-opted by the emperor Constantine. In western Europe, the sense of unity unlimited by imperial frontiers gave rise to a universal, or "Catholic," church—the "true" Christian religion that believers felt all peoples should share. In the eastern Mediterranean, where the Roman Empire survived, Christianity and empire coalesced to reinforce the feeling that true religion, high culture, and empire went hand in hand. Christians here held that beliefs about God and Jesus found their most correct expression within the eastern Roman Empire and in its capital, Constantinople.

Similarly, in East Asia, the weakening of the Han dynasty enabled Buddhism to dominate Chinese culture. Without a unified state in China, Confucian officials languished in obscurity, while Buddhist priests and monks enjoyed patronage from regional rulers, local warriors, and commoners. In India, too, a political vacuum allowed the unfolding of a new culture: the Brahman elites exploited population movements beyond the reach of traditional rulers as they established ritual forms for daily life on every level of society.

Not all regions felt the spread of universalizing religions, however. In most of sub-Saharan Africa (though not Sudan and Ethiopia, where Christianity set down deep roots) belief systems were much more localized. The same pattern emerged in the Americas, where long-distance transportation was harder and language systems had not yielded texts to share with nonbelievers. But spiritual life was no less profound. Here, it was the strong sense of a shared worldview, a shared sense of purpose, and a shared sense of faith that enabled common cultures to develop. Indeed, the Bantus and Mayans became large-scale common cultures—but ruled at the local level.

Thus, the period 300–600 CE saw the emergence of three great cultural units in Afro-Eurasia, each defined in religious terms: Christianity in the Mediterranean and Southwest Asia, Brahmanism in South Asia, and Buddhism in East Asia. They illustrated the ways in which peoples were converging under larger religious tents, while also becoming more distinct. Universal religions, whether Christian or Buddhist, and universal codes of behavior, such as the Brahmanic Laws of Manu, gave people a new way to define themselves and their loyalties.

But the pattern would soon change. As we will see, empire would return to East Asia in the form of the mighty Tang dynasty. And the zone stretching from Morocco to central Asia would find itself united in a gigantic imperial system fashioned by followers of the Prophet Muhammad.

Review and research materials are available at StudySpace: Ⓢ WWNORTON.COM/STUDYSPACE

KEY TERMS

Bantu migrations (p. 310)
bhakti (p. 304)
big men (p. 311)
conversion of Constantine (p. 290)
creed (p. 291)
Hinayana (Lesser Vehicle) Buddhism (p. 303)
Hinduism (p. 304)
Laws of Manu (p. 305)

Madhyamika (Middle Way) Buddhism (p. 307)
Mahayana (Greater Vehicle) Buddhism (p. 303)
martyr (p. 286)
Mayans (p. 315)
Northern Wei dynasty (p. 307)
Sasanian Empire (p. 297)
Sogdians (p. 299)
Teotihuacán (p. 313)

Chronology

	1 CE	100 CE	200 CE	300 CE	400 CE
THE MEDITERRANEAN AND NORTH AFRICA		313 CE Emperor Constantine legalizes Christianity in Roman Empire ✦		✦ 325 CE Nicene Creed developed	
			late 4th and 5th centuries "Barbarian" invasions of Roman Empire ✦ - - - - - - - -		
SOUTHWEST ASIA	220s Sasanians create empire in Iran, Mesopotamia ✦				
		324 CE Constantine establishes new Roman capital at Constantinople ✦			
			400 CE Jewish Talmud produced in the Levant ✦		
		✦ Buddhism spreads through central Asia			
CENTRAL ASIA	Sogdian merchant communities dominant trade routes through central Asia ✦				
		✦ Buddhism spreads through central Asia			
SOUTH ASIA	✦ 1st or 2nd centuries CE Transformation of Brahmanism to Hinduism begins				
		320–550 CE Gupta dynasty rules much of northern India ✦ - - - - - - - - - - - - - -			
EAST ASIA			c. 220 CE Han Empire collapses		
		220–589 CE Six Dynasties Period ✦ -			
			Daoism reforms and revives in popularity ✦	✦ - - - - -	
		300–600 CE Buddhism spreads among Chinese society ✦ - - - - - - - - - -			
SUB-SAHARAN AFRICA	◄ 3000 BCE–1000 CE Bantu migrations from West Africa into central and southern Africa				
MESOAMERICA	250 CE Early Classic Mayan Period begins in Yucatan Peninsula ✦				
	300 CE to late 5th century City of Teotihuacán dominates valley of Mexico ✦ - - - - - - -				

STUDY QUESTIONS

1. Describe the connections between the growing power of Christianity and the political reconfiguration of the Roman Empire. What was the appeal of Christianity in the Roman Empire?

2. Analyze the Sasanian Empire's role in facilitating the spread of universal religions and the development of common cultures in Afro-Eurasia. How did the empire's geographic location support this cross-cultural dissemination?

3. Explain the role of Sogdians and other central Asian peoples in the dispersion of universal religions. How did they influence East Asian societies in particular?

4. Describe how Brahmanism (Vedic religion) evolved into Hinduism during this era. What factors contributed to this development?

5. Identify key changes in Buddhist thought and practice in South Asia at this time. How did these refinements aid the spread of this religious outlook beyond its homeland?

6. Explain the role of written texts (such as the Laws of Manu, the Talmud, the Analects, and the New Testament) in universalizing religion. How did these texts reshape social attitudes toward spiritual behavior and identity?

7. Analyze the ways in which political decentralization affected the growing popularity of Buddhist and other religious ideas in East Asia. To what extent did they challenge Confucian ideas on social and political organization?

8. Analyze the impact of Bantu migrations on the social and cultural geography of sub-Saharan Africa. What set of beliefs helped unite societies in this region?

9. Compare and contrast Mayan society with that of Teotihuacán. To what extent did each represent a common religious and cultural outlook in Mesoamerica at different times?

10. Analyze the extent to which universal religions brought worlds together and pushed them apart. How did religion create new cultural boundaries and rivalries in Afro-Eurasia at this time?

| 500 CE | 600 CE | 700 CE | 800 CE | 900 CE | 1000 CE |

◆ 5th century CE Collapse of Roman authority in western empire

◆ 500 CE Byzantine Empire flourishes in the eastern part of former Roman Empire

◆◆ 533–540 CE Emperor Justinian attempts to revive Roman Empire

◆ 542 CE Bubonic plague begins to ravish southwest Asia

◆ Sasanian/Byzantine Wars

◆ 560 CE Turkish Confederacy begins to rule much of central Asia

◆ 5th–7th centuries CE Nestorian Christianity spreads along the Silk Road

◆ ◆ 630s, 640s Xuanzang, Chinese Buddhist pilgrim, visits South Asia

◆ 386–534 CE Tuoba Wei dynasty rule in northern China

◆ 8th century Mayan culture reaches its zenith

Chapter 9

NEW EMPIRES AND COMMON CULTURES, 600–1000 CE

*I*n 754 CE, the Muslim caliph (ruler) al-Mansur decided to relocate his capital city. Islam was barely a century old, yet flourishing under its second dynasty, the Abbasids. Al-Mansur wanted to relocate power away from Damascus (the capital of Islam's first dynasty) to the Abbasids' home region on the Iranian plateau to signal its new dawn. After traveling the length of the Tigris and Euphrates rivers in search of a perfect site, the caliph decided to build his capital near an unimposing village called Baghdad.

He had good reasons for this selection. The site lay between Mesopotamia's two great rivers at the juncture of the canals that linked them. It was also a powerful symbolic location: close to the ancient capital of the Sasanian Empire, Ctesiphon, where the Arch of Khusro was still standing. It was also the site of earlier Sumerian and Babylonian power. By building at Baghdad, al-Mansur could reaffirm Mesopotamia's centrality in the world and exalt the universalizing ambitions of Islam. Within five years of laying the first brick, towering walls surrounded what soon became known as the "round city," so named because of the way in which the different segments radiated out from the administrative and religious center."

Al-Mansur's choice had enduring effects. As the new capital of Islam, Baghdad also became a vital crossroads for commerce. Overnight, the city exploded into a bustling world entrepôt. Chinese goods arrived by land and sea; commodities from Inner Eurasia flowed in over the Silk Road; and cargo-laden camel caravans wound across Baghdad's western desert, linking the capital with Syria, Egypt, North Africa, and southern Spain. In effect, the unity that the Abbasids imposed from Baghdad intensified the movement of peoples, ideas, innovations, and commodities.

Baghdad's eminence and prosperity reflected its role as the center of the Islamic world. Yet, while Islam was gaining ground in central Afro-Eurasia, Chinese might was surging in East Asia—powerfully under the Tang—and Christianity was striving to extend its domains and add to its converts. Unquestionably, however, the two imperial powerhouses of this period were Islam and Tang China, and they are the focus of this chapter.

Islam and Tang China were manifestly different worlds. The Islamic state had a universalizing religious mission: to bring humankind under the authority of the religion espoused by the Prophet Muhammad. In contrast, the Tang had no such grandiose religious aspirations, and while the ruling elite supported religious pluralism within China, they did not use Buddhism to expand their control into areas outside China. Instead, the Tang rulers expected that their neighbors would emulate Chinese institutions and pay tribute as symbols of respect to the greatness of the Tang Empire. As Islam's warriors and scholars crossed into Europe and as Chinese influences took deeper root in East Asia, religion and empire once again intertwined to serve as the social foundation across much of Afro-Eurasia.

RELIGIONS AND EMPIRES

> → *Why did the new religion of Islam arise in the Arabian Peninsula, and what outside factors influenced Muhammad's religious messages?*

How religion and empire connect can vary in important ways. In the cases of Christianity and Buddhism, empire was the main vehicle for their growth. In the case of Islam, though, it was religion that created empire. Having swept aside their predecessors in Southwest Asia, Muslim leaders had to form their own institutional system; and as their spiritual aspirations spread, the political imagination evolved into an imperial one. Although they borrowed from the Byzantines and Persians, their reason for establishing an empire was new: to secure, defend, and spread their religion. Whereas Christianity, Buddhism, and Zoroastrianism converted already-existing empires to their own views, Islam created its empire from scratch.

Given the recent surge of religious energy across Afro-Eurasia, it was perhaps only a matter of time before a prophetic figure would arise among the Arabs. Christianity and Buddhism were laying claim to universal truths, spreading their faiths across wide geographic areas outside their places of origin, and competing groups now had to speak the language of universal religion. Only the Tang dynasty resisted the universalizing faiths, as Confucianism and Daoism withstood the upsurge of Chinese Buddhism—revealing that China would follow a different path by maintaining past traditions. In the seventh century, Arab peoples would become

Focus Questions

Ⓢ WWNORTON.COM/STUDYSPACE

→ *Why did the new religion of Islam arise in the Arabian Peninsula, and what outside factors influenced Muhammad's religious messages?*

→ *What factors created a common cultural outlook among Muslim communities in Afro-Eurasia during this era?*

→ *How did the Tang state balance its restoration of Confucian principles with the growth of new universal religions?*

→ *To what extent did Japanese and Korean polities imitate Tang China?*

→ *How did two Christianities come to exist in western Afro-Eurasia?*

MAIN THEMES

→ *The universalizing religion of Islam, based on the message of the prophet Muhammad, originates on the Arabian Peninsula and spreads rapidly across Afro-Eurasia.*

→ *Two distinctly different imperial powerhouses—Islam and Tang China—dominate much of Afro-Eurasia.*

→ *Christianity splits over doctrinal and political differences, leading to a western church based on the papacy in Rome and Eastern Orthodoxy based in Constantinople.*

FOCUS ON *Faith and Empire*

The Islamic Empire

✦ Warriors from the Arabian Peninsula defeat Byzantine and Sasanian armies and establish an Islamic empire stretching from Morocco to South Asia.

✦ The Abbasid state takes over from the Umayyads, crystallizes the main Islamic institutions of the caliphate and Islamic law, and promotes cultural achievements in religion, philosophy, and science.

✦ Disputes over Muhammad's succession lead to a deep and enduring split between Sunnis and Shiites.

Tang China

✦ The Tang dynasty dominates East Asia, including Japan and Korea.

✦ Tang dynasts balance Confucian ideals with Buddhist thought and practice.

✦ A common written language and shared philosophy, rather than a universalizing religion, integrate the Chinese state.

Christian Europe

✦ Monks, nuns, and Rome-based popes spread Christianity throughout western Europe.

✦ Constantinople-based Eastern Orthodoxy survives the spread of Islam.

---

the makers of their own universal faith, which would join and jostle with predecessors in Afro-Eurasia.

THE ORIGINS AND SPREAD OF ISLAM

> → *What factors created a common cultural outlook among Muslim communities in Afro-Eurasia during this era?*

Islam began inside Arabia. Despite its remoteness and sparse population, by the sixth century CE Arabia was brushing up against exciting outside currents: long-distance trade, religious debate, and imperial politics. Byzantine and Sasanian imperial pressures already had intruded deeply into Arabia (see Chapter 8); commodities from Egypt, Syria, and Iraq cir-

culated in local markets; and learned men debated the doctrines of Christianity and Judaism. The Hijaz—the western region bordering the Red Sea—knew the outside world through trading routes reaching up the coast to the Mediterranean. While one of the world's major universalizing faiths would be born in a remote region of Southwest Asia, Islam would quickly take advantage of the dynamic trade routes stretching across Southwest Asia and North Africa to spread its faith and political empire.

Mecca, in the Hijaz, was not an imposing place. A pre-Islamic poet wrote that its "winter and summer are equally intolerable. No waters flow . . . [and there is] not a blade of grass on which to rest the eye; no, nor hunting. [Here there are] only merchants, the most despicable of professions" (Peters, p. 23). Hardly more than a village of simple mud huts, Mecca's inhabitants sustained themselves less as traders than as caretakers of a revered sanctuary called the kaaba. They regarded this collection of unmortared rocks piled on top of one another as the dwelling place of deities, whom the polytheistic Meccans worshiped. Here a great prophet was born.

Mecca. At the great mosque at Mecca, which many consider the most sacred site in Islam, hundreds of thousands of worshippers gather for Friday prayers. Many are performing their religious duty to go on a pilgrimage to the holy places in the Arabian Peninsula.

A VISION, A TEXT

Born in Mecca around 570 CE into a well-respected tribal family, **Muhammad** enjoyed only moderate success as a trader. Little in his early life suggested that momentous events would soon occur. Then came a revelation, which would convert this broker of commodities into a proselytizer of a new faith. In 610 CE, while Muhammad was on a month-long spiritual retreat in a cave near Mecca, he believed that God came to him in a vision and commanded him to recite these words:

> Recite in the Name of the Lord who createth,
> Createth man from a clot
> Recite: And thy Lord is the most Bounteous who
>   teacheth by the pen
> Teacheth man that which he knew not.

Further revelations followed. The early ones were like the first: short, powerful, emphasizing a single, all-powerful God (Allah), and full of instructions for Muhammad's fellow Meccans to carry this message to nonbelievers. The words were eminently memorable, an important feature in an oral culture where poetry recitation was the highest art form. Muhammad's early preaching had a clear message. He urged his small band of followers to act righteously, to set aside false deities, to submit themselves to the one and only true God, and to care for the less fortunate—for the Day of Judgment was imminent. Muhammad's most insistent message was the oneness of God, a belief that has remained central to the Islamic faith ever since.

These teachings, compiled into an authoritative version after the Prophet's death, constituted the foundational text of Islam: the **Quran.** Its 114 chapters, known as suras, occur in descending order of length; the longest has three hundred verses and the shortest, a mere three. Accepted as the very word of God, they flowed without flaw through God's perfect instrument, the Prophet Muhammad. (See Primary Source: The Quran: Two Suras in Praise of God.) Like the Jewish Torah, the Christian Bible, and other foundational texts, this one proclaimed the tenets of a new faith to unite a people and to expand its spiritual frontiers. Its message already had universalist elements, though how far it was to be extended, whether to the tribesmen living in the Arabian Peninsula or well beyond, was not at all clear at first.

Muhammad believed that he was a prophet in the tradition of Moses, other Hebrew prophets, and Jesus, and that he communicated with the same God that they did. As we have seen, Christian and Jewish communities existed in the Arabian Peninsula at this time. The city of Yathrib (later called Medina) held a substantial Jewish community. Just how deeply Muhammad understood the tenets of Judaism and Christianity is difficult to determine, but his professed indebtedness to their tradition is a part of Islamic belief.

THE MOVE TO MEDINA

Muslims date the beginning of the Muslim era from the year 622 CE. At this time Muhammad and a small group of followers, opposed by Mecca's leaders because of their radical

Primary Source

THE QURAN: TWO SURAS IN PRAISE OF GOD

These two suras from the Quran are relatively short, but they convey some of the essence of Muhammad's message. The Quran opens with a sura known as the fatiha ("of the opening"), which in its powerfully prayerlike quality lends itself to frequent recitation. Sura 87, "The Most High," provides a deeper insight into the nature of humanity's relationship with God.

The Fatiha

In the Name of God the Compassionate the merciful
Praise be to God, Lord of the Universe,
The Compassionate, the Merciful,
Sovereign of the Day of Judgement!
You alone we worship, and to You alone we turn for help.
Guide us to the straight path,
The path of those whom You have favoured,
Not of those who have incurred Your wrath,
Nor of those who have gone astray.   (1.1–1.7)

The Most High

In the Name of God, the Compassionate, the merciful
Praise the name of your Lord, the Most High, who has
    created all things and proportioned
them; who has ordained their destinies and guided them;
    who brings forth the green pasture, then turns it to
    withered grass.
We shall make you recite our revelations, so that you
    shall forget none of them except as God pleases. He

has knowledge of all that is manifest, and all that is hidden.

We shall guide you to the smoothest path. Therefore give warning, if warning will avail. He that fears God will heed it, but the wicked sinner will flout it. He shall burn in the gigantic Fire, where he shall neither die nor live. Happy shall be the man who purifies himself, who remembers the name of his Lord and prays.

Yet you prefer this life, although the life to come is better and more lasting.

All this is written in earlier scriptures; the scriptures of Abraham and Moses.   (87.1–87.19)

→ *What themes do these passages reveal about Islam's view of the relationship between God and mortals?*
→ *Do you find any similarities to the tenets of Judaism and Christianity as you have encountered them in this volume?*

SOURCE: From *The Koran*, translated and with notes by N. J. Dawood (Penguin Classics 1956, Fifth revised edition 1990). Copyright © N. J. Dawood, 1956, 1959, 1966, 1968, 1974, 1990, 1993, 1997, 1999, 2003. Reproduced by permission of Penguin Books Ltd.

---

religious tenets and their challenge to the ruling elite's authority, escaped to Medina. Known as *the hijra* ("breaking off of relations" or "departure"), the perilous 200-mile journey yielded a new form of communal unity: the *umma* ("band of the faithful").

The city of Medina had been facing tribal and religious tensions, and by inviting Muhammad and his followers to take up residence there, its elders hoped that his leadership and charisma would bring peace and unity to their city. Early in his stay Muhammad promulgated a document, the Constitution of Medina, requiring the community's people to refer all disputes to God and him. Medina thus became the birthplace of a new faith called **Islam** ("submission"—in this case, to the will of God) and a new community called Muslims ("those who submit"). Now the residents were expected to replace traditional family, clan, and tribal affiliations with loyalty to Muhammad as the one and true Prophet of God. From Medina the faithful broadcast their faith and their mission, at first mainly by military means, to the recalcitrants of Mecca and then to all of Arabia and then later to the entire world. In this way, Islam joined Christianity in seeking to bring the whole known world under its authority.

CONQUESTS

In 632, in his early sixties, the Prophet passed away. Islam might have withered without its leader, but the movement remained vibrant thanks to the energy of the early followers—especially Muhammad's first four successors, the "rightly

The Battle of Badr. This image depicts the battle of Badr, which took place in 624 and marked the beginning of Muhammad's reconquest of Mecca from his new base in the city of Medina.

guided caliphs." The Arabic word *khalīfa* means "successor," and in this context it referred to Muhammad's successors as political rulers over Muslim peoples and the expanding state. Their breakthrough was to institutionalize the new faith. They set the new religion on the pathway to imperial greatness and linked religious uprightness with territorial expansion, empire-building, and an appeal to all peoples.

Now Islam's expansive spiritual force galvanized its political authority. But what kind of polity would this be? Driven by religious fervor and a desire to acquire the wealth of conquered territories, Muslim soldiers embarked on military conquests and sought to found a far-reaching territorial empire. This expansion of the Islamic state was one aspect of the struggle that they called *jihad*. From the outset Muslim religious and political leaders divided the world into two units: the *dar al-Islam* (or the world of Islam) and the *dar al-harb*

(the world of warfare), seeking nothing less than world domination. Within fifteen years Muslim soldiers had grasped Syria, Egypt, and Iraq—centerpieces of the former Byzantine and Sasanian empires that now became pillars undergirding an even larger Islamic empire. Mastery of desert warfare and inspired military leadership yielded these astonishing exploits, as did the exhaustion of the Byzantine and Sasanian empires after generations of warfare.

The Byzantines saved the core of their empire by pulling back to the highlands of Anatolia, where they had readily defensible frontiers. In contrast, the Sasanians gambled all on a final effort: they hurled their remaining military resources against the Muslim armies, only to be crushed. Having lost Iraq and unable to defend the Iranian plateau, the Sasanian Empire passed out of existence, its remnants absorbed into a new imperial regime. The result: Islam acquired political foundations within a generation of its birth.

AN EMPIRE OF ARABS

Creating an empire and stabilizing it were two different things. We have seen some come and go, like Alexander's. Others had more stamina. How would Islam fare? For a while, it was unclear. After the assassination of the last of the "rightly guided caliphs," Ali, a political vacuum opened. At this point a branch of one of the Meccan clans, the Umayyads, laid claim to Ali's legacy. Having been governors of the province of Syria under Ali, this first dynasty moved the core of Islam out of Arabia to the Syrian city of Damascus. They also introduced a hereditary monarchy to resolve leadership disputes. These adaptable, cosmopolitan traders ruled from Damascus until the Abbasids overthrew them in 750 CE.

By then, the core practices and beliefs of every Muslim had crystallized as the five "pillars" of Islam, which found clear expression in the Quran. Building on long-standing Arabian customs and certain familiar Jewish practices, these pillars undergirded Islamic practice early in Muhammad's career as a prophet and gave the imperial system a doctrinal and legal structure and a broad appeal to diverse populations.

The five pillars of Islam established clear-cut demands on believers. Converts were expected to adhere to and repeat the phrase that there is no God but God and that Muhammad was His Prophet. They were required to pray five times daily facing Mecca, to fast from sunup until sundown during the month of Ramadan, to make a pilgrimage to Mecca at least once in a lifetime if their personal resources permitted, and to pay alms in the form of taxation that would alleviate the hardships of the poor. These core doctrines, especially the crucial pillar affirming belief in one God and the prophecy of Muhammad, likely attracted early converts.

There was, however, a political limit to Islam's welcoming embrace. Although tolerant of conquered populations, Umayyad dynasts did not permit non-Arabic-speaking converts to hold high political offices. Not until the overthrow of Umayyad rule did the "Arabs only" empire come to an end and non-Arab populations become incorporated into the Islamic core. This changed the nature of the emerging empire. For as the political center of Islam moved out of Arabia to Syria (at Damascus), and then with the Abbasids to Mesopotamia, ethnic and geographical diversity replaced what had been ethnic purity. Thus even as the universalizing religion strove to create a common spiritual world, it became more diverse within its political dimensions.

THE ABBASID REVOLUTION

As the Umayyad dynasts spread Islam beyond Arabia, some peoples resented the rulers' high-handed ways. For example, the central Asian province of Khurasan was home to many converts who chafed at their subordination to Arab peoples. Here, religious reformers and political dissidents stressed doctrines of religious purity and depicted the Umayyads as irreligious and politically repressive.

A coalition emerged under the Abbasi family, which claimed descent from the Prophet. Soon disgruntled provincial authorities and their military allies, as well as non-Arab converts, joined the movement. These individuals had embraced Islam and learned Arabic, only to discover that they were still second-class citizens. After amassing a sizable military force, the Abbasid coalition trounced the Umayyad ruler in 750 CE. Thereafter the center of the caliphate shifted to Iraq (at Baghdad; recall the opening anecdote about al-Mansur), signifying the eastward sprawl of the faith and its empire. It also represented a success for non-Arab groups within Islam without eliminating Arab influence at the dynasty's center—the capital, Baghdad, in Arabic-speaking Iraq.

Ultimately, conversion to Islam rested on the zeal of evangelizers and the faith's appeal to converts. Some turned to it for practical reasons, seeking reduced taxes or enhanced power. Others, particularly those living in ethnically and religiously diverse regions, welcomed the message of a single all-powerful God and a single community united by a clear code of laws; they saw it as offering superior answers to thorny secular and spiritual questions. Not only did the Abbasids open Islam to Persian peoples, but they also embraced Greek and Hellenistic learning, Indian science, and Chinese innovations. In this fashion, Islam, drawing its original impetus from the teachings and actions of a prophetic figure, followed the trajectory of Christianity and Buddhism and became a faith with a universalist message and appeal. It owed much of its success to its ability to merge the contributions of vastly different geographic and intellectual territories into a rich yet unified culture (see Map 9-1).

THE CALIPHATE An early challenge for the Abbasid rulers was to determine how traditional, or "Arab," they could be and still rule so vast an empire. They chose to keep the bedrock political institution of the early Islamic state—the **caliphate**. Signifying both the political and spiritual head of the Islamic community, this institution had arisen as the successor to Muhammad's shining leadership. Although the caliphs exercised political and spiritual authority over the Muslim community, they did not inherit his prophetic powers. Nor were they authorities in religious doctrine. That power was reserved for religious scholars, called **ulama**; some of these men were schooled in Islamic law, others were experts in Quranic interpretation, and still others were religious thinkers.

Imperial rule reflected borrowed practices from successful predecessors. The caliphates' leadership style was a mixture of Persian absolute authority and the royal seclusion of the Byzantine emperors who lived in palaces far removed from their subjects. Imperial Islam mingled absolute authority with decentralized power through its envoys in the provinces. This involved a delicate and ultimately unsustainable balancing act. As the empire expanded it became increasingly decentralized, enabling wily regional governors and competing caliphates in Spain and Egypt to grab power. The political result was an Islamic world shot through with multiple centers of power, nominally led by a weakened Abbasid caliphate. Even as Islam's political center diffused, though, its spiritual center remained fixed in Mecca, where many of the faithful gathered to circle the kaaba and to reaffirm their devotion to Islam as part of their pilgrimage obligation.

THE ARMY The Abbasids, like all rulers, relied on force to integrate their empire. For imperial Islam (as for the Romans), exercising military power required marshalling warriors and soldiers from across Afro-Eurasia.

How "Arab" should the Muslim armies be? In the early stages, leaders had conscripted military forces from local Arab populations, creating citizen armies. But as Arab populations settled down in garrison cities, the Abbasid rulers turned to professional soldiers from the empire's peripheries. Now they recruited from Turkish-speaking communities in central Asia, and from the non-Arab, Berber-speaking peoples of North Africa and West Africans. Their reliance on foreign—that is, non-Arab—military personnel represented a major shift in the Islamic world. Not only did the change infuse the empire with dynamic new populations, but soon these groups gained political authority (just as the "barbarians" had done in the last centuries of the Roman Empire; see Chapters 6 and 8). Having begun as an Arab state and then incorporated strong Persian influence, the Islamic empire now especially embraced Turkish elements from the pastoral belts of central Asia.

ISLAMIC LAW (THE *SHARIA*) AND THEOLOGY In the Abbasid period, not just the caliphate but also Islamic law took shape. The **sharia** stands as the crucial foundation of

Islam. It covers all aspects of practical and spiritual life, providing legal principles for marriage contracts, trade regulations, and religious prescriptions such as prayer, pilgrimage rites, and ritual fasting. It reflects the work of generations of religious scholars, rather than soldiers, courtiers, and bureaucrats. And it has remained vital throughout the Muslim world, independent of empires, to the present day.

Early Muslim communities prepared the ground for the *sharia*, endeavoring (guided by the Quran) to handle legal matters in ways that they thought Muhammad would have wanted. However, because the Quran mainly addressed family concerns, religious beliefs, and social relations (such as marriage, divorce, inheritance, dietary restrictions, and treatment of women) but not other legal questions, local judges exercised their own judgment where the Quran was silent. The most influential early legal scholar was an eighth-century Palestinian-born Arab, al-Shafi'i, who wanted to make the empire's laws entirely Islamic. He insisted that Muhammad's laws as laid out in the Quran, in addition to his sayings and actions as written in later reports (*hadith*), provided all the legal guidance that Islamic judges needed.

The triumph of scholars such as Shafi'i was deeply significant: it placed the *ulama*, the Muslim scholars, at the heart of Islam. *Ulama*, not princes and kings, became the lawmakers, insisting that the caliphs could not define religious law. Only the scholarly class could interpret the Quran and determine which *hadith* were authentic. The *ulama*'s ascendance opened a sharp division within Islam: between the secular realm, where caliphs and their representatives exercised power, and the religious sphere, where religious officials and scholars (judges, experts on Islamic jurisprudence, teachers, and holy men) exercised their authority.

GENDER IN EARLY ISLAM Pre-Islamic Arabia was one of the last regions in Southwest Asia where patriarchy had not triumphed. Instead, men still married into women's families and moved to those families' locations, as was common in tribal communities. Some women engaged in a variety of occupations and even, if they became wealthy, married more than one husband. But contact with the rest of Southwest Asia, where men's power over women prevailed, was already altering women's status in the Arabian Peninsula before the birth of Muhammad.

Muhammad's relations with women reflected these changes. As a young man, he married a woman fifteen years his senior—Khadija, an independent trader—and took no other wives before she died. It was Khadija to whom he went in fear following his first revelations. She wrapped him in a blanket and assured him of his sanity. She was also his first convert. Later in life, however, he took younger wives and insisted on their veiling. He

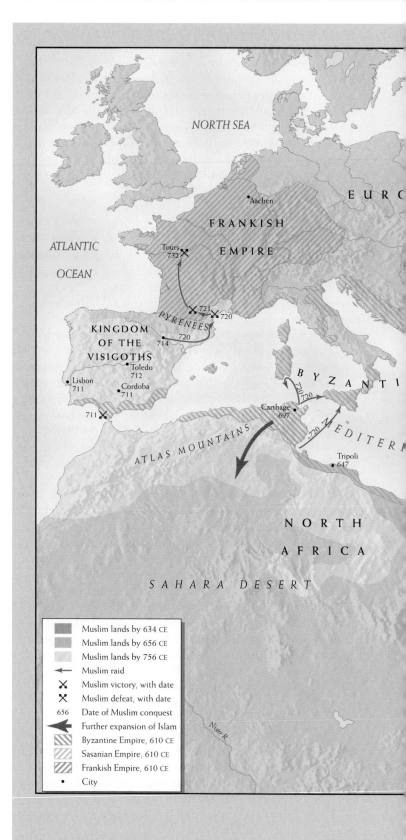

> ➔ *What factors created a common cultural outlook among Muslim communities in Afro-Eurasia during this era?*

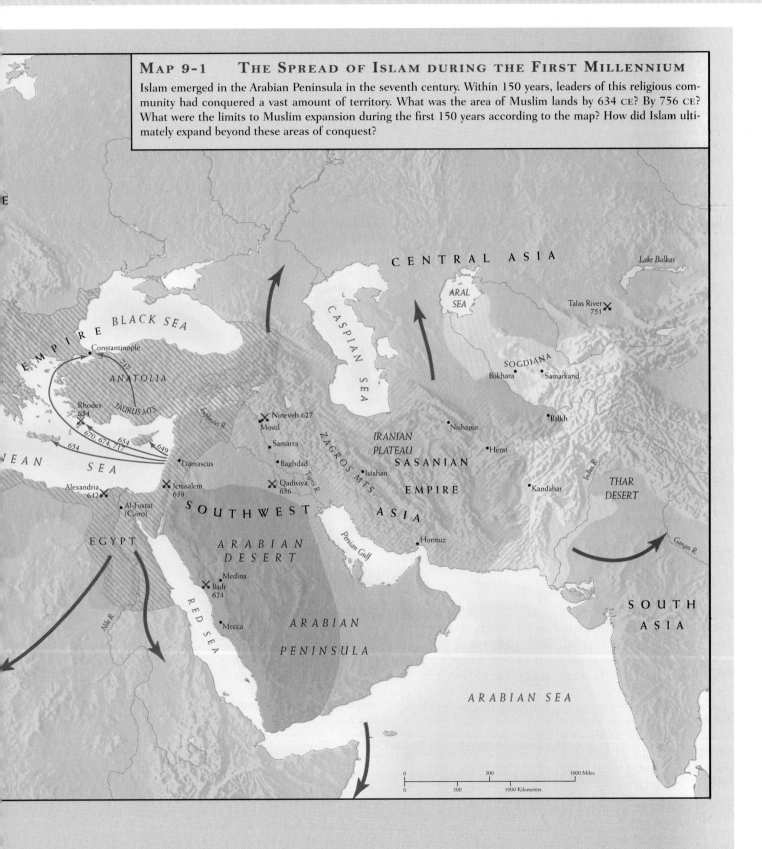

MAP 9-1   THE SPREAD OF ISLAM DURING THE FIRST MILLENNIUM

Islam emerged in the Arabian Peninsula in the seventh century. Within 150 years, leaders of this religious community had conquered a vast amount of territory. What was the area of Muslim lands by 634 CE? By 756 CE? What were the limits to Muslim expansion during the first 150 years according to the map? How did Islam ultimately expand beyond these areas of conquest?

PREMODERN LIBRARIES: FROM ROYAL ARCHIVES TO REPOSITORIES OF UNIVERSAL KNOWLEDGE

Libraries invariably accompanied urbanization, centralized governments, and writing. In the ninth and tenth centuries the biggest, most carefully organized, and most actively used libraries were in the Islamic and Chinese empires. These were great centers of learning and government; their cultures extolled the written word.

The Islamic world had special respect for books and libraries, for in the Quran Muhammad had brought the very words of God to his followers. Later generations added to Islam's traditions by collecting sayings attributed to the Prophet, his companions, and the early caliphs (*hadith*); writing treatises on religious law (*sharia*); and assimilating the knowledge of Greeks, Persians, Indians, and Chinese. Moreover, since Egypt and Southwest Asia had seen the world's earliest writing, these areas—the heartland of Islam—already had strong literary and library traditions.

The world's first libraries arose in Mesopotamia, where writing itself originated. These facilities were quite different from modern repositories of learning. They did house literary masterpieces (such as the Sumerian *Epic of Gilgamesh*), but they mainly served as government archives, holding important records that future rulers and bureaucrats might need to consult. Most likely the first storehouse of written materials was that of King Ashurbanipal of Assyria in the seventh century BCE. Like other monarchs aspiring to universal sway, he collected all significant literary works. His library at Nineveh contained as many as 25,000 tablets preserving omens, incantations, and hymns;

it also held the literatures of the many Mesopotamian languages, including Assyrian, Sumerian, Ugaritic, and Aramaic.

Because the "books" of Ashurbanipal II's library were clay tablets etched in cuneiform, hardened through baking in kilns, they were safe from fire—the destroyer of many later libraries. Those in its famous successor in Alexandria were not so fortunate. Housed in several buildings, that magnificent library was the pride of Ptolemy I and Ptolemy II (r. 323–285, 285–246 BCE), two enlightened kings who believed that Greek arts, sciences, and literature were an unmatched legacy for future generations. They set their administrators the task of collecting anything written in Greek. Though the size of Alexandria's holdings is unknown (as few as 40,000 scrolls or as many as half a million works), it was almost unimaginably large for the period. But beginning in the first century BCE, these collections were repeatedly subject to burning and looting. By the fourth century CE the immense body of literature was almost entirely lost.

The Muslims led the way, as impressive libraries arose in the heartland of Islam. They appeared first in the early mosques, including those in Cairo, Damascus, and Baghdad. But book and manuscript collecting spread rapidly to the outskirts of the Islamic world, where libraries in Timbuktu in West Africa, Samarkand in central Asia, and Jakarta in Southeast Asia earned high reputations for their extraordinary collections of religious and scientific treatises.

---

married his favorite wife, Aisha, when she was only nine or ten years old.

Hence, by the time Islam reached Southwest Asia and North Africa, where strict gender rules and women's subordinate status were entrenched, the new faith was adopting a patriarchal outlook. Muslim men could divorce freely; women could not. A man could take four wives and numerous concubines; a woman could have only one husband. Well-to-do women, always veiled, lived secluded from male society. Still, the Quran did offer women some protections. Men had to treat each wife with respect if they took more than one. Women could inherit property (although only half of what a man inherited). Infanticide was taboo. Marriage dowries went

directly to the bride rather than to her guardian, indicating women's independent legal standing; and while a woman's adultery drew harsh punishment, its proof required eyewitness testimony. The result was a legal system that reinforced men's dominance over women but empowered magistrates to oversee the definition of male honor and proper behavior.

THE BLOSSOMING OF ABBASID CULTURE

The arts flourished during the Abbasid period, a blossoming that left its imprint throughout society. Within a century, Ara-

Compared with those in Christian Europe, the Muslim libraries were immense. The library at Cordova (in Muslim Spain) reportedly held 600,000 books, or more than two books for every household in the city. Ibn Sina, the great Muslim scholar of the eleventh century, marveled at the library holdings of the Saminid court in Persia. There he found Greek books that he had not seen anywhere else and that were barely known to even the best Muslim scholars. Probably the largest collection was Cairo's vast House of Learning, assembled by the Fatimid caliphs. At its height it may have held 1.5 million books. By contrast, Germany's Reichenau, one of the largest monastic libraries in Christian Europe, had only 450 volumes in parchment—almost one-third of them prayer books. It did, however, have a catalog and a system of interlibrary loans that served monasteries across Germany, northern Italy, and France.

China was very much the equal of the Islamic world in its wealth of libraries. The Chinese had invented paper during the Western Han dynasty and printing during the Tang era. As a result, scholarship, book production, and libraries became vital to the region's cultural fabric. Accompanying the classical works printed for literati were works of popular literature and primers that circulated among a common audience.

The Chinese infatuation with the printed word bred an elite class of bibliophiles (book collectors). These individuals located source materials and created the reference works necessary to found coherent scholarly disciplines. Although Chinese libraries housed printed books, unpublished manuscripts formed a more substantial portion of many collections.

Under the Han, private libraries did not exceed 10,000 "rolls" (each holding about a chapter) of books or manuscripts. But under the Tang, many Buddhist monasteries accumulated thousands of books and religious sutras. Some 30,000 rolls, for example, survived in the precious Buddhist grottoes of Dunhuang along the Silk Road. The largest collection graced the imperial library in the capital. Here in this library scholars toiled as collators and editors to recompile the Confucian classics and dynastic histories for the civil service examination system—and for posterity. The Tang imperial catalog indicates that by the early eighth century this library contained some 54,000 unique titles and, including duplicates, about 200,000 rolls. Then as now, libraries were crucial repositories of knowledge and culture.

Dunhuang Cave Temple. Buddhist temples such as this one served as repositories for tens of thousands of manuscript rolls.

bic had superseded Greek as the Muslim world's preferred language for poetry, literature, medicine, science, and philosophy. Like Greek, it spread beyond native speakers to become the language of the educated classes.

Arabic scholarship now made significant contributions, including the preservation and extension of Greek and Roman thought and the transmission of Greek and Latin treatises to Europe. Scholars at Baghdad translated the principal works of Aristotle; essays by Plato's followers; works by Hippocrates, Ptolemy, and Archimedes; and the medical treatises of Galen. To house such manuscripts, patrons of the arts and sciences—including the caliphs—opened magnificent libraries. (See Global Connections & Disconnections: Premodern Libraries: From Royal Archives to Repositories of Universal Knowledge.)

The intense borrowing, translating, storing, and diffusing of written works brought worlds together. The Muslim world absorbed scientific breakthroughs from China and other areas, incorporated the use of paper from China, adopted siege warfare from China and Byzantium, and applied knowledge of plants from the ancient Greeks. From Indian sources, scholars borrowed a numbering system based on the concept of zero and units of ten—what we today call Arabic numerals. Arab mathematicians were pioneers in arithmetic, geometry, and algebra, and they expanded the frontiers of plane and spherical trigonometry.

ISLAM IN A WIDER WORLD

As Islam spread and became decentralized, it generated dazzling and often competitive dynasties in Spain, North Africa, and points farther east. Each dynastic state revealed the Muslim talent for achieving high levels of artistry far from its heartland. As more peoples came under the roof provided by the Quran, they invigorated a broad world of Islamic learning and science. But growing diversity led to a problem: Islam's political structures could not hold its widely dispersed believers under a single regime. Although its polities shared many legal elements (especially those controlled by Islamic texts and its enforcers), in terms of secular power Islam was deeply divided—and remains so to this day (see Map 9-2).

DAZZLING CITIES IN SPAIN One extraordinary Muslim state arose in Spain under Abd al-Rahman III, al-

Nasir (the Victorious; r. 912–961 CE), the successor ruler of a Muslim kingdom founded there over a century earlier. Abd al-Rahman brought peace and stability to a violent frontier region where civil conflict had disrupted commerce and intellectual exchange. His evenhanded governance promoted amicable relations among Muslims, Christians, and Jews, and his diplomatic relations with Christian potentates as far away as France, Germany, and Scandinavia generated prosperity across western Europe and North Africa. He expanded and beautified the capital city of Cordoba, and his successor made the Great Mosque of Cordoba one of Spain's most stunning sites.

The Great Mosque of Cordoba, known in Spanish as la Mezquita, is the oldest standing Muslim building on the Iberian Peninsula. It is a stirring tribute to the architectural brilliance and religious zeal of Iberia's Muslims. Conceived of in 785 CE by the Umayyad ruler Abd al-Rahman I, it was

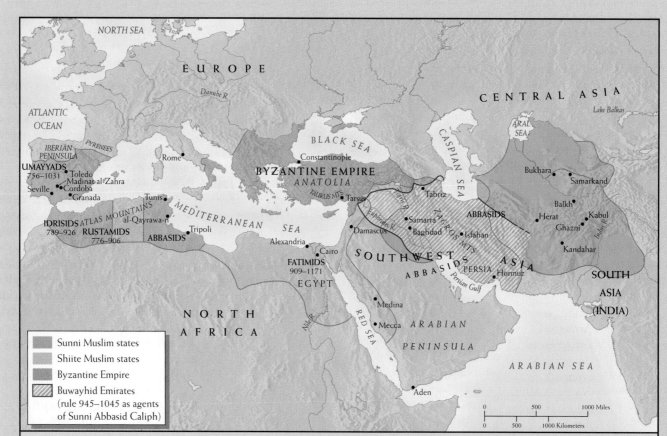

MAP 9-2   POLITICAL FRAGMENTATION IN THE ISLAMIC WORLD, 750–1000

By 1000, the Islamic world was politically fractured and decentralized. The Abbasid caliphs still reigned in Baghdad, but they wielded very limited political authority. Looking at the map, first point to Baghdad and then point out all the areas under Abbasid control. What are the regions where major Islamic powers emerged? What areas were Sunni versus Shiite? Why were the Abbasids unable to sustain political unity in the Islamic world?

The Great Mosque of Cordoba. The great mosque of Cordoba was built in the eighth century by the Umayyad ruler Abd al-Rahman I and added to by other Muslim rulers, including al-Hakim II, who succeeded Abd al-Rahman III, considered by many historians to have been the most powerful and effective of the Spanish Umayyad caliphs.

finished within a year of the laying of the foundations. It arose on a site with a rich cultural and political history. Here had existed a Roman temple and later a Gothic church, which after the Arab Muslim conquest housed both Muslim and Christian believers (the latter permitted by the Muslim conquerors to worship under the same roof). Convinced that this building could no longer accommodate the area's increasing Muslim population, Abd al-Rahman I sketched out the plan of the mosque. He commanded that it be built in the form of a perfect square. Its most striking features were alternating red and white arches, made of jasper, onyx, marble, and granite and fashioned from materials from the Roman temple and other buildings in the vicinity. These huge double arches hoisted the ceiling to forty feet and filled the interior with light and cooling breezes. Around the doors and across the walls Arabic calligraphy proclaimed Muhammad's message and asserted the superiority of Arabic as God's chosen language.

At this time, competition among rival rulers spurred artistic creativity. Soon the Islamic world resembled a series of dazzling lanterns, each vying to outdo the others in brilliance. When Abd al-Rahman III built an extravagant city, Madinat al-Zahra, next to Cordoba, his goal was to overshadow the splendor of Islam's most fabled cities, including Baghdad and al-Qayrawān (in northeast Tunisia). He surrounded the city's administrative offices and mosque with verdant gardens of lush tropical and semitropical plants, tranquil pools, fountains that spouted cooling waters, and sturdy aqueducts that carried potable water to the city's inhabitants. Madinat al-Zahra was meant to be paradise on earth.

A CENTRAL ASIAN GALAXY OF TALENT The other end of the Islamic empire, 8,000 miles east of Spain, enjoyed an equally spectacular cultural flowering. In a territory where Greek culture had once sparkled and where Sogdians had become leading intellectuals, Islam was now the dominant faith and the source of intellectual ferment.

The Abbasid rulers in Baghdad delighted in surrounding themselves with learned men from this region. The Barmaki family, who for several generations held high administrative offices under the Abbasids, came from the central Asian city of Balkh. They had been Buddhists living under the serene gaze of the great carved Buddhas of Bamiyan (see Chapter 8). This family prospered under Islam and enjoyed remarkable influence in Baghdad. Loyal servants of the caliph, they made sure that all wealth and talent from the crossroads of Asia found their way to Baghdad, as they themselves had done.

In turn, the Barmakis were devoted patrons of the arts. They promoted and collected Arabic translations of Persian, Greek, and Sanskrit manuscripts, and they encouraged central Asian scholars to enhance their learning by moving to Baghdad. One of their protégés, the Islamic cleric al-Bukhari (d. 870 CE), was Islam's most dedicated collector of *hadith*, which provided vital knowledge about the Prophet's life.

Others made notable contributions to science and mathematics. Al-Khwarizmi (c. 780–850 CE) modified Indian digits into Arabic numerals and wrote the first book on algebra. The renowned Abbasid philosopher al-Farabi (d. 950 CE), from a Turkish military family, also made his way to Baghdad, where he studied Hellenistic Christian teachings. Although he considered himself a Muslim, he thought good societies

Ibn Sina. Ibn Sina was a versatile scholar, most famous for his *Canon of Medicine*.

would succeed only if their rulers implemented political tenets espoused in Plato's *Republic*. He championed a virtuous "first chief" to rule over an Islamic commonwealth in the same way that Plato had favored a philosopher-king.

In the eleventh century the Abbasid caliphate began to decline, weakening under overextension and the influx of outsider groups (the same problems the Roman Empire had faced). Scholars no longer trekked to the court at Baghdad.

Yet the region's intellectual vitality remained strong, for young men of learning found patrons among local rulers. Consider Ibn Sina, known in the west as Avicenna (980–1037 CE). He grew to adulthood in Bukhara, practiced medicine in the courts of various Islamic rulers, and spent his later life in central Persia. Schooled in the Quran, Arabic secular literature, philosophy, geometry, and Indian and Euclidean mathematics, Ibn Sina was a master of many disciplines. His *Canon of Medicine* stood as the standard medical text in both Southwest Asia and Europe for centuries.

ISLAM IN SUB-SAHARAN AFRICA Islam also crossed the Sahara Desert and penetrated well into Africa, carried by traders and scholars (see Map 9-3). By the seventh and eighth centuries, Islamic adventurers were pouring into sub-Saharan West Africa, where they exchanged weapons and textiles for gold, salt, and slaves. Trade did more than join West Africa to North Africa. It also generated prodigious wealth, which allowed centralized political kingdoms to develop. The most celebrated was Ghana, which lay at the terminus of North Africa's major trading routes.

Of Ghana, scholars know little. The first to mention it was a Baghdadi scholar, who in the eighth century described it as "the land of gold." A century later, an Arab geographer wrote of "the kingdom of Ghana, the king of which is very powerful. In his country there are gold mines. Under his authority are other kingdoms . . . and gold is found in all of these regions" (Fage, p. 15). Although Muslim traders frequented the state, its rulers were not Muslims. Still, Ghana's pomp and power impressed visitors; in 1067–1068, a geographer from the Muslim province of Andalusia in Spain, wrote of a resplendent king who heard "grievances against officials in a domed pavilion around which stand ten horses covered with gold-embroidered materials. Behind the king stand ten pages holding shields and swords decorated with gold and on his right are the sons of the (vassal) kings of his country wearing splendid garments and their hair plaited with gold" (Levtzion and Spaulding, p. 16). (See also Primary Source: Ghana as Seen by a Muslim Observer in the Eleventh Century.)

Seafaring Muslim traders carried Islam into East Africa via the Indian Ocean. There is evidence of a small eighth-century Islamic trading community at Lamu, along the northern coast of present-day Kenya; and by the mid-ninth century other coastal trading communities had sprung up. They all exported ivory and, possibly, slaves. On the island of Pate, off the coast of Kenya, the inhabitants of Shanga constructed the region's first mosque. This simple structure was replaced 200 years later by a mosque capable of holding all adult members of the community when they gathered for their Friday prayers. By the tenth century, the East African coast featured a mixed African-Arab culture. The region's evolving Bantu language absorbed Arabic words and before long gained a new name, Swahili (derived from the Arabic plural of the word meaning "coast").

→ *What factors created a common cultural outlook among Muslim communities in Afro-Eurasia during this era?*

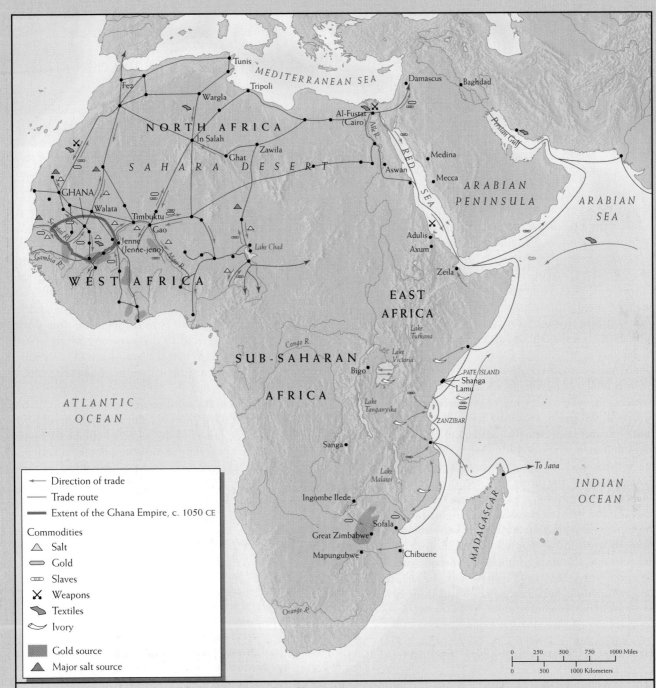

MAP 9-3   ISLAM AND TRADE IN SUB-SAHARAN AFRICA, 700–1000

Islamic merchants and scholars, not Islamic armies, carried Islam into sub-Saharan Africa. Trace the trade routes in Africa, being sure to follow the correct direction of trade. According to the map key and icons, what commodities were Islamic merchants seeking below the Sahara? What were the major trade routes and the direction of trade in Africa? How did trade and commerce lead to the geographic expansion of the Islamic faith?

Primary Source

GHANA AS SEEN BY A MUSLIM OBSERVER IN THE ELEVENTH CENTURY

The following excerpt is from an eleventh-century manuscript written by a Muslim serving under the Umayyads in Spain. Its author, Abdullah Abu Ubayd al-Bakri, produced a massive general geography and history of the known world, as did many Muslim scholars of the period. This manuscript has special value because it provides information about West Africa, a region in which the Spanish rulers had great interest and into which Islam had been spreading for several centuries.

Ghana is the title of the king of the people. The name of the country is Aoukar. The ruler who governs the people at the present time—the year 460 AH (after the Hijra and 1067–68 CE)—is called Tenkamein. He came to the throne in 455 AH. His predecessor, who was named Beci, began his reign at the age of 85. He was a prince worthy of great praise as much for his personal conduct as for his zeal in the pursuit of justice and his friendship to Muslims. . . .

Ghana is composed of two towns situated in a plain. The one inhabited by Muslims is large and contains twelve mosques, in which the congregants celebrate the Friday prayer. All of these mosques have their imams, their muezzins, and their salaried readers. The city possesses judges and men of great erudition. . . . The city where the king resides is six miles away and carries the name el-Ghaba, meaning "the forest." The territory separating these two locations is covered with dwellings, constructed out of rocks and the wood of the acacia tree. The dwelling of the king consists of a chateau and several surrounding huts, all of which are enclosed by a wall-like structure. In the ruler's town, close to the royal tribunal, is a mosque where Muslims come when they have business with the ruler in order to carry out their prayers. . . . The royal interpreters are chosen from the Muslim population, as was the state treasurer and the majority of the state ministers. . . .

The opening of a royal meeting is announced by the noise of a drum, which they call a *deba*, and which is formed from a long piece of dug-out wood. Upon hearing the drumming, the inhabitants assemble. When the king's coreligionists [people of the same religion] appear before him, they genuflect and throw dust on their heads. Such is the way in which they salute their sovereign. The Muslims show their respect for the king by clapping their hands. The religion of the Negroes is paganism and fetishism. . . . The land of Ghana is not healthy and has few people. Travelers who pass through the area during the height of the agricultural season are rarely able to avoid becoming sick. When the grains are at their fullest and are ready for harvesting is the time when mortality affects visitors.

The best gold in the land comes from Ghiarou, a town located eighteen days journey from the capital. All of the gold found in the mines of the empire belongs to the sovereign, but the sovereign allows the people to take gold dust. Without this precaution, the gold would become so abundant that it would lose much of its value. . . . It is claimed that the king owns a piece of gold as large as an enormous rock.

➤ *From this excerpt, how much can you learn about the kingdom of Ghana? Try drawing a sketch of the region based on the description in the second paragraph.*

➤ *What influence did Islam have in the empire? What aspects of the excerpt reveal the extent of Islam's acceptance?*

➤ *What elements of Ghana most interested the author?*

SOURCE: Abou-Obeïd-el-Bekri, *Description de l'Afrique septentrionale*, revised and corrected edition, translated by [William] Mac Guckin de Slane (Paris: A. Maisonneuve, 1965), pp. 327–31; translated from the French by Robert Tignor.

Jenne Mosque. This fabulous mosque arose in the kingdom of Mali when that kingdom was at the height of its power. The mosque speaks to the depth and importance of Islam's roots in the Malian kingdom.

OPPOSITION WITHIN ISLAM, SHIISM, AND THE RISE OF THE FATIMIDS

Islam's whirlwind rise generated internal tensions from the start. It is hardly surprising that a religion that extolled territorial conquests and created a large empire in its first decades would also spawn dissident religious movements that challenged the existing imperial structures. Muslims shared a reverence for a basic text and a single God, but little else. Religious and political divisions grew deeper as Islam spread into new corners of Afro-Eurasia. Once the charismatic prophet died, believers disagreed over who should take his place and how to preserve authority. Strains associated with selecting the first four caliphs after Muhammad's death left a legacy of protest; to this day, they represent the greatest challenge facing Islam's efforts to create a unified culture.

SUNNIS AND SHIITES   The most powerful opposition movement arose in North Africa, lower Iraq, and the Iranian plateau. The questions that fueled disagreements were who should succeed the Prophet, how the succession should take place, and who should lead Islam's expansion into the wider world. The vast majority of Muslims today are **Sunnis** (from the Arabic word meaning "tradition"). They accept the political succession to the Prophet through the four rightly guided caliphs and then to the Umayyad and Abbasid dynasties was the correct one. Dissidents, like the Shiites,

contest this version. Over time the Sunnis and Shiites diverged even more than these political disputes would have indicated. Both groups had their own versions of the *sharia*, their own collections of *hadith*, and their own theological tenets.

Shiites ("members of the party of Ali"), among the earliest dissidents, felt that the proper successors should have been Ali, who had married the Prophet's daughter Fatima, and his descendants. Ali was one of the early converts to Islam and one of the band of Meccans who had migrated with the Prophet to Medina. The fourth of the rightly guided caliphs, he ruled over the Muslim community from 656 to 661 CE, dying at the hands of an assassin who struck him down as he was praying in a mosque in Kufa, Iraq. Shiites believe that Ali's descendants, whom they call *imams*, have religious and prophetic power as well as political authority—and thus should enjoy spiritual primacy. Shiism appealed to groups whom the Umayyads and Abbasids had excluded from power; it became Islam's most potent dissident force and created a permanent divide within Islam. Shiism was well established in the first century of Islam's existence.

FATIMIDS   After 300 years of struggling, the Shiites finally seized power. Repressed in Iraq and Iran, Shiite activists made their way to North Africa, where they joined with dissident Berber groups to topple several rulers. In 909 CE, a Shiite religious and military leader, Abu Abdallah, overthrew the Sunni ruler there. Thus began the Fatimid regime.

After conquering Egypt in 969 CE, the Fatimids set themselves against the Abbasid caliphs of Baghdad, refusing to acknowledge their legitimacy and claiming to speak for the whole Islamic world. The Fatimid rulers established their capital in a new city that arose alongside al-Fustat, the old Umayyad capital. They called this place al-Qahira (or Cairo), "the Victorious," and promoted its beauty. Early on they founded a place of worship and learning, the al-Azhar mosque, which attracted scholars from all over Afro-Eurasia and spread Islamic learning outward; they also built other elegant mosques and centers of learning. The Fatimid regime lasted until the late twelfth century, though its rulers made little headway in persuading the Egyptian population to embrace their Shiite beliefs. Most of the population remained Sunnis.

AGRICULTURE IN THE MUSLIM WORLD

At the time Islam was spreading, the Muslim world was also experiencing significant developments in agriculture; indeed, rural bounty gave the new belief system resources to plow into its expansion.

By now, India had replaced Mesopotamia as the source of a dazzling array of new crops. Most of them originated in Southeast Asia, made their way to India, and dispersed from there throughout the Muslim world. These crops included rice, taro, sour oranges, lemons, limes, and most likely coconut palm trees, sugarcane, bananas, plantains, and mangoes. Sorghum and possibly cotton and watermelons arrived from Africa. Only the eggplant was indigenous to India. Although these staple crops spread quickly to East Asia, their westward movement was slower. Not until the Muslim conquest of Sindh in northern India in 711 CE did territories to the west fully discover the crop innovations pioneered in Southeast Asia.

India fascinated the Arabs, and they exploited its agricultural offerings to the hilt. Soon a revolution in crops and diet swept through the Muslim world. Sorghum supplanted millet and the other grains of antiquity because it was hardier, had higher yields, and required a shorter growing season. Citrus trees added flavor to the diet and provided refreshing drinks during the summer heat. Increased cotton cultivation led to a greater demand for textiles.

For over three hundred years, farmers from northwest India to Spain, Morocco, and West Africa made impressive use of the new crops. They increased agricultural output, slashed fallow periods, and grew as many as three crops on lands that formerly yielded one. (See Map 9-4.) As a result, farmers could feed larger urban communities; as cities grew, the countryside became more densely populated and even more productive.

Al-Azhar Mosque. The mosque of al-Azhar is Cairo's most important ancient mosque. Built in the tenth century by the Fatimid conquerors and rulers of Egypt, it quickly became a leading center for worship and learning, frequented by Muslim clerics and admired in Europe.

→ *What factors created a common cultural outlook among Muslim communities in Afro-Eurasia during this era?*

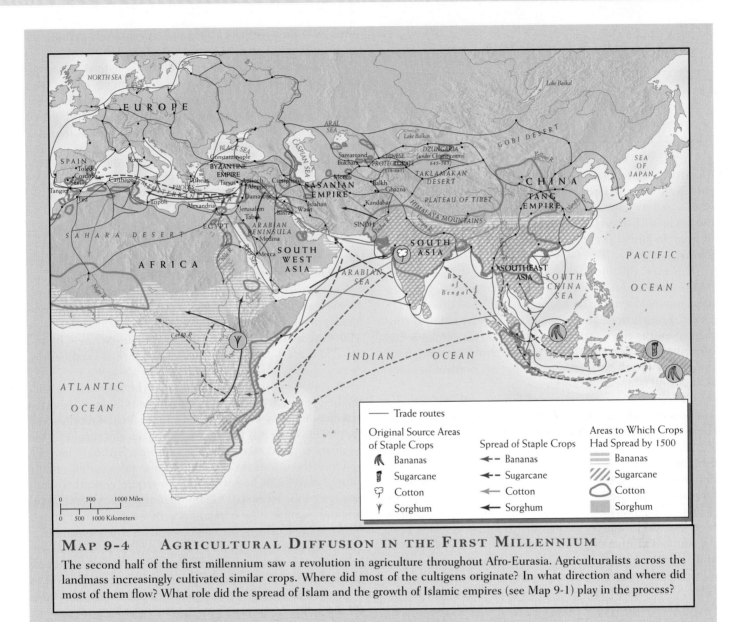

MAP 9-4   AGRICULTURAL DIFFUSION IN THE FIRST MILLENNIUM

The second half of the first millennium saw a revolution in agriculture throughout Afro-Eurasia. Agriculturalists across the landmass increasingly cultivated similar crops. Where did most of the cultigens originate? In what direction and where did most of them flow? What role did the spread of Islam and the growth of Islamic empires (see Map 9-1) play in the process?

By 1000 CE Islam, which had originated as a radical religious revolt in a small corner of the Arabian Peninsula, had grown into a vast political and religious empire. It had become the dominant political and cultural force in the middle regions of Afro-Eurasia. Like its rival in this part of the world, Christianity, it aspired to universality. But unlike Christianity, it was linked from its outset to political power. Muhammad and his early followers created an empire to facilitate the expansion of their faith while their Christian counterparts inherited an empire when Constantine embraced the new faith. A vision of a world under the jurisdiction of Muslim caliphs, adhering to the dictates of the *sharia,* drove Muslim armies, merchants, and scholars to territories thousands of miles away from Mecca and Medina. Yet the impulse to expand ran out of energy at the fringes of Islam's reach, creating political fragmentation within the Muslim world and leaving much of western Europe and China untouched. But it also had important internal consequences: Muslims were no longer the minority within their own lands, owing to the conversion of Christians, Jews, and other populations under Muslim emperors.

 # THE TANG STATE

> → *How did the Tang state balance its restoration of Confucian principles with the growth of new universal religions?*

The rise of the Sui and Tang empires in China, and their impact on Korea and Japan, paralleled Islam's explosion out of Arabia and its impact throughout Afro-Eurasia. Once again the landmass had two centers of power, as Islam replaced the Roman Empire in counterbalancing the power and wealth of China.

However, this bipolar world differed significantly from that of the Roman and Han empires: in the centuries since their waning, Eurasian and African worlds had drawn much closer through trade, conversion, and regular political contacts. Now the two powerhouses competed for dominance in central Asia, sharing influences and even mobile populations that weaved back and forth across porous borders between Islamic and Chinese territories.

China was both a recipient of foreign influences and a source of influences on its neighbors. Indeed, it was becoming the hub of East Asian integration. Like the Umayyads and the Abbasids, the **Tang dynasty** (608–907 CE) promoted a cosmopolitan culture. Under its rule Buddhism, medicine, and mathematics from India gave China's chief cities an international flavor. Buddhist monks from Bactria; Greeks, Armenians, and Jews from Constantinople; Muslim envoys from Samarkand and Persia; Vietnamese tributary missions from Annam; nomadic chieftains from the Siberian plains; officials and students from Korea; and monkish visitors from Japan all rubbed elbows in the streets of Chang'an and Luoyang. Ideas traveled east as well—notably to Korea and Japan, where Daoism and Buddhism made inroads. Similarly, Chinese statecraft, as expressed through the Confucian classics, struck the early Koreans and Japanese as the best model for their own state building.

AGRICULTURE IN CHINA

The agrarian transformation that swept through South Asia and the Muslim world also took East Asia by storm (see above). Indeed, China received the same crops that Islamic cultivators were carrying westward. Rice was critical. New varieties entered from the south, and groups migrating from the north (after the collapse of the Han Empire) eagerly took them up. Soon Chinese farmers became the world's most intensive wet-field rice cultivators. Early- and late-ripening seeds supported two or three plantings a year. Champa rice,

introduced from central Vietnam, was especially popular for its drought resistance and rapid ripening.

Because rice needs ample water, Chinese hydraulic engineers went into the field to design water-lifting devices, which peasant farmers used to construct hillside rice paddies. They also dug more canals linking rivers and lakes (see Map 9-5) and even drained swamps, alleviating the malaria that had long troubled the region. Their efforts yielded a booming and constantly moving rice frontier.

TERRITORIAL EXPANSION UNDER THE TANG DYNASTY

After the fall of the Han, China had faced a long period of political instability (see Chapter 8). Ultimately, though, Tang rulers restored Han models of empire building. Their claims that an imperial system could outperform small states found a receptive audience in a populace fatigued by internal chaos. The Tang dynasty expanded the boundaries of the Chinese state and reestablished its dominance in East and central Asia.

A sudden change in the course of the Yellow River (not the first such environmental calamity; see Chapter 7) caused extensive flooding on the North China plain and set the stage for the emergence of the Tang dynasty. Revolts ensued as the population faced starvation. Li Yuan marched on Chang'an and took the throne for himself. He promptly established the Tang dynasty and began building a strong central government. First he increased the number of provinces and counties and expanded the bureaucracy. By doubling the number of government offices, the emperor tightened his control over individual governors. By 624 CE the initial steps of establishing the Tang dynasty were complete. But the fruits of these gains slipped into the hands of Li Yuan's ambitious son Li Shimin, who forced his father to abdicate and took the throne for himself in 627 CE.

THE ARMY AND IMPERIAL CAMPAIGNING

The Chinese empire created armies, and big armies reinforced the empire on a massive scale. An expanding Tang state required a large and professionally trained army, capable of defending far-flung frontiers and squelching rebellious populations. Toward these efforts the Tang built a military organization of aristocratic cavalry and peasant soldiers. The cavalry regularly clashed on the northern steppes with encroaching nomadic peoples, who also fought on horseback; at its height the Tang military had some 700,000 horses. At the same time, between 1 and 2 million peasant soldiers garrisoned the south and toiled on public works projects.

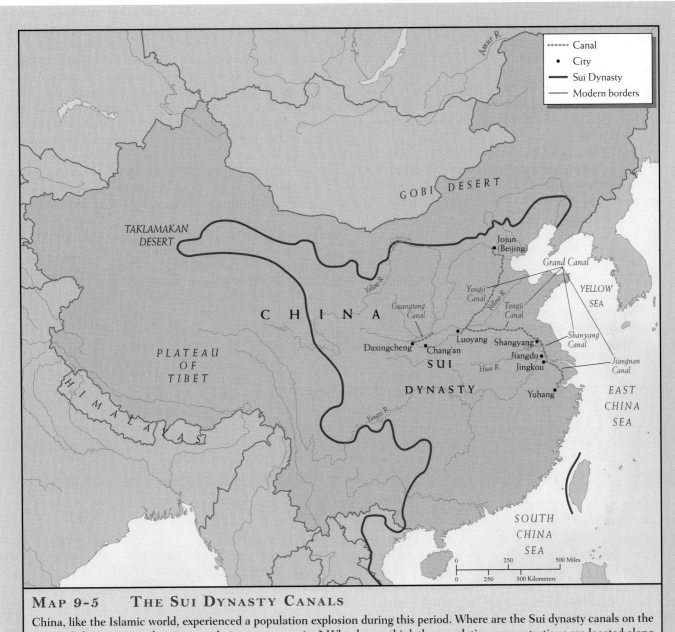

MAP 9-5   THE SUI DYNASTY CANALS

China, like the Islamic world, experienced a population explosion during this period. Where are the Sui dynasty canals on the map and the two areas showing population concentration? Why do you think the population concentrations are located along the canals? What other roles might the canals have played in addition to fostering population growth in this period within China?

Much like the Islamic forces, the Tang's frontier armies increasingly relied on pastoral nomadic soldiers from the Inner Eurasian steppe. Notable were the Uighurs, Turkish-speaking peoples who had moved into western China and by 750 CE constituted the empire's most potent military force. These hard-riding and hard-drinking warriors galvanized fearsome cavalries, fired longbows at distant range, and wielded steel swords and knives in hand-to-hand combat. The Tang military also pushed the state into Tibet, the Red River valley in northern Vietnam, Manchuria, and Bohai (near Korea).

By 650 CE, as Islamic armies were moving toward central Asia, the Tang were already the region's new colossus. At the empire's height, Tang armies controlled more than 4 million square miles of territory—an area as large as the entire

Islamic world in the ninth and tenth centuries. Once the Tang administrators brought South China's rich farmlands under cultivation (by draining swamps, building an intricate network of canals and channels, and connecting lakes and rivers to the rice lands), the state was able to collect taxes from roughly 10 million families, representing 57 million individuals. Most of these taxes took the form of agricultural labor, which propelled the expansion of cultivated frontiers throughout the south.

In spite of the Abbasid Empire's precocious spread, China in 750 CE was the most powerful, most advanced, and best administered empire in the world (see Map 9-6). Korea and Japan recognized its superiority in every material aspect of life. Mus-

lims were among the people who arrived at Chang'an to pay homage. Persians, Armenians, and Turks brought tribute and merchandise via the busy Silk Road or by sea, and other travelers and traders came from Southeast Asia, Korea, and Japan.

The peak of Chinese power occurred just as the Abbasids were expanding into Tang portions of central Asia. Rivalry brought these worlds together, but not peaceably. Muslim forces drove the Tang from Turkistan in 751 CE at the battle of Talas River, and their success emboldened groups such as the Sogdians and Tibetans to challenge the Tang in the west. As a result, the Tang retreated into the old heartlands along the Yellow and Yangzi rivers. They even saw their capital fall to invading Tibetans and Sogdians. Thereafter misrule, court

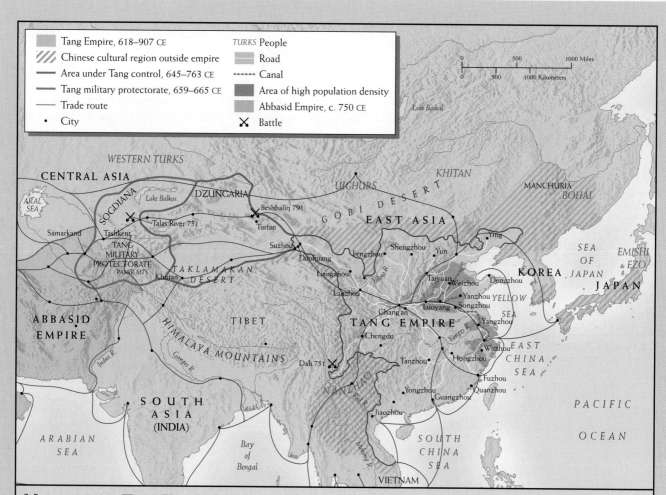

MAP 9-6   THE TANG STATE IN EAST ASIA, 750 CE

The Tang dynasty, at its territorial peak in 750, controlled a state that extended from central Asia to the East China Sea. What foreign areas are under Tang control? What areas were heavily influenced by Tang government and culture? How can we tell from the map that China was undergoing an economic revolution during the Tang period? How did the Tang maintain order and stability in such a large, dynamic realm?

China Trade. In this seventh-century silk painting, we see envoys from the busy Silk Road bearing tribute to gain access to the lucrative China trade.

intrigues, economic exploitation, and popular rebellions weakened the empire, but the dynasty held on for over a century more until northern invaders toppled it in 907 CE.

ORGANIZING AN EMPIRE

The Tang Empire, a worthy successor to the Han, ranks as one of China's great dynastic polities. Although its rulers emulated the Han in many ways (for example, by compiling a legal code based on the Han's), they also introduced new institutions.

CONFUCIAN ADMINISTRATORS Despite the Tang's reliance on military force, the day-to-day control of the empire required an efficient and loyal civil service. Whereas a shared spiritual commitment to Islam held together the multilingual, multiethnic, and even multireligious Islamic empire, the Tang found other ways to integrate remote territories and diverse groups. Their ingenious efforts produced an empire-wide political culture based on Confucian teachings composed in the written language of Mandarin-speaking officials and classically educated elites.

Chinese integration began at the top. Entry into the ruling group required knowledge of Confucian ideas and all of the commentaries on the Confucian classics. It also required skill in the intricate classical Chinese language, in which this literature was written. These skills were as crucial in forging a Chinese cultural and political solidarity as Islam was for the Abbasid state or Christianity was for Europe and the Byzantine Empire.

Most important in reinforcing the Tang state were the world's first fully written **civil service examinations.** These examinations, which tested sophisticated literary skills and the Confucian classics, were the only route to the top echelons of power and the ultimate means of uniting the Chinese state. Candidates for office, whom local elites recommended, gathered in the capital triennially to take qualifying exams. They had been trained since the age of three in the Classics and Histories, either by their families or in Buddhist temple schools. Most failed the grueling competition, however. Those who were successful underwent further trials to evaluate their character and determine the level of their appointments. New officials were selected from the pool of graduates on the basis of social conduct, eloquence, skill in calligraphy and mathematics, and legal knowledge. (See Primary Source: The Pressures of Maintaining Empire by Examination.) When Emperor Li Shimin observed the new officials obediently parading out of the

Tang Official. Tang officials were selected through competitive civil examinations in order to limit the power of Buddhist and Daoist clerics. This painted clay figure of a Tang official c. 717 was excavated in 1972.

THE PRESSURES OF MAINTAINING EMPIRE BY EXAMINATION

Young and old competed equally in the Tang examination halls. The rituals of success were alluring to youths, while the tortures of failure weighed heavily on older competitors still seeking an elusive degree. For all, the tensions of seeing the posted list of successful candidates—following years of preparation for young boys, and even more years of defeat for old men—were intensely personal responses to success or failure. The few who passed would look back on that day with relief and pride.

In the Southern Court they posted the list. (The Southern Court was where the Board of Rites ran the administration and accepted documents. All prescribed forms together with the stipulations for each [degree] category were usually publicized here.) The wall for hanging the list was by the eastern wall of the Southern Court. In a separate building a screen was erected which stood over ten feet tall, and it was surrounded with a fence. Before dawn they took the list from the Northern Court to the Southern Court where it was hung for display.

In the sixth year of Yuanhe [AD 811] a student at the University, Guo Dongli, broke through the thorn hedge. (The thorn hedge was below the fence. There was another outside the main gate of the Southern Court.) He then ripped up the ornamental list [*wenbang*]. It was because of this that afterwards they often came out of the gateway of the Department [of State Affairs] with a mock list. The real list was displayed a little later.

→ *Why were the stakes so high in the civil examinations? What happened to those who failed?*

→ *Was the Tang civil examination system an open system that tested talent—that is, a meritocracy?*

→ *Can you relate to the candidates' anxiety in terms of your own experiences—for example, waiting for college acceptance letters or your year-end grade point average?*

SOURCE: Wang Dingbao (870–940), quoted in Oliver J. Moore, *Rituals of Recruitment in Tang China* (Leiden: Brill, 2004), p. 175.

examination hall, he slyly noted, "The heroes of the empire are all in my pocket!" (Miyazaki, *China's Examination Hell*, 13). Overall, the civil service system gave rise in China to the perennial belief in the value of a classically trained **meritocracy** (rule by persons of talent), which lasted into modern times.

Having assumed the mandate of heaven (see Chapter 4), the Tang rulers and their supporters sought to establish a code of moral values for the whole empire. Building on Han models, they expanded the state school in the capital into an empire-wide series of select schools that accepted only fully literate candidates for the civil examinations. They also allowed the use of Daoist classics as texts for the exams, believing that the early Daoists represented an important stream of ancient wisdom. Ultimately the Tang amalgamated this range of texts, codes, and tests into a common intellectual and moral credo for the governing classes.

Although official careers were in theory open to anyone of proven talent, in practice they were closed to certain groups. Despite Empress Wu's prominence (see below), women were not permitted to serve, nor were sons of merchants, nor those who could not afford a classical education. Over time, Tang civil examinations forced aristocrats to compete with commoner southern families, whose growing wealth (from trade) and access to educational resources made them the equals of the old elites. Through examinations, this new elite eventually outdistanced the sons of the northern aristocracy in the Tang government by out-studying them.

The system also brought a few benefits to the poor by underscoring education as the primary avenue for success. Even impoverished families sought the best classical education they could afford for their sons. Although few succeeded in the civil examinations, many boys and even some girls learned the fundamentals of reading and writing. In fact, the Buddhists played a crucial role in extending education across society: as part of their charitable mission, their temple schools introduced many children to primers based on classical texts. Buddhist monks would never admit that many in their own ranks had initially hoped to become Confucian officials, but in reality quite a few entered the clergy only after not qualifying for or failing the civil examinations.

CHINA'S FEMALE EMPEROR   Not all Tang power brokers were men. Women also wielded influence in the court—usually behind the scenes, but sometimes publicly. Consider Empress Wu, who dominated the court in the late seventh and early eighth centuries. She deftly exploited the examination system to check the power of aristocratic families and consolidated courtly authority by creating groups of loyal bureaucrats, who in turn preserved loyalty to the dynasty at the local level.

Born into a noble family, Wu Zhao played music and mastered the Chinese classics as a young girl. By age thirteen, because she was witty, intelligent, and beautiful, Wu was recruited to Li Shimin's court, where she became his favorite concubine. She also fell in love with his son. When Li Shimin died, his son assumed power and became the Emperor Gaozong. Wu became the new emperor's favorite concubine and gave birth to the sons he required to succeed him. As the mother of the future emperor, Wu enjoyed heightened political power. Subsequently, she took the place of Gaozong's Empress Wang by accusing her (falsely) of killing Wu's newborn daughter. Gaozong believed Wu and married her.

After Gaozong suffered a stroke, Wu became administrator of the court, a position equal to the emperor's. She created a secret police force to spy on her opposition, and she jailed or killed those who stood in her way, including Empress Wang. Upon the emperor's death Wu outmaneuvered her eldest sons, placed her youngest son in power, and named herself as his regent. Shortly thereafter she seized power in her own right as Empress Wu (r. 684–705 CE), becoming the only female ruler in Chinese history. She expanded the military and recruited her administrators from the civil examination candidates to oppose her enemies at court.

Challenging Confucian beliefs that subordinated women, Wu elevated their position. She ordered scholars to write biographies of famous women, and she empowered her mother's clan by assigning high political posts to her relatives. Later, she moved her court from Chang'an to Luoyang, where she tried to establish a new "Zhou dynasty" in imitation of the Confucian period.

Empress Wu. When she seized power in her own right as Empress Wu, Wu Zhao became the first and only female ruler in Chinese history.

Despite Wu's ruthless climb to power, her rule was relatively benign and competent. She elevated Buddhism over Daoism as the favored state religion, invited the most gifted Buddhist scholars to her capital at Luoyang, built Buddhist temples, and subsidized spectacular cave sculptures. In fact, Chinese Buddhism achieved its highest officially sponsored development in this period.

EUNUCHS   Tang rulers protected themselves and their possessions, including their women, with loyal and well-compensated men. So did the Abbasids. The caliphs in Baghdad chose young male slaves as their personal guards, although males known as **eunuchs** (who were surgically castrated as youths and thus sexually impotent) also protected the harem. Similarly, Tang emperors relied on castrated males from the lower classes to protect the royal family. By the late eighth century, more than 4,500 eunuchs were fully entrenched in the Tang Empire's institutions, wielding significantly more court power than the male slaves in Baghdad.

The Chief Eunuch controlled the military. Through him, the military power of court eunuchs extended to every province and garrison station in the empire, forming an all-encompassing network. In effect, the eunuch bureaucracy mediated between the emperor and the provincial governments.

Under Emperor Xianzong (r. 806–820 CE), eunuchs acted as a third pillar of the government, working alongside the official bureaucracy and the imperial court. By establishing clear career patterns for eunuchs that paralleled those in the civil service, Xianzong sparked a striking rise in their levels of literacy and their cultural attainments. Yet by 838 CE, the delicate balance of power among throne, eunuchs, and civil officials had evaporated. Eunuchs became an unruly political force in late Tang politics, and their scheming plots equaled those of the slaves guarding the Abbasid caliph and his harem.

AN ECONOMIC REVOLUTION

In both the Abbasid caliphate and Tang China, political stability fueled remarkable economic achievements. Highlighting China's success were rising agricultural production based on an egalitarian land allotment system, an increasingly fine handicrafts industry, a diverse commodity market, and a dynamic urban life.

An earlier dynasty, the Sui, had started this economic progress by reunifying China and building canals, especially the Grand Canal linking the north and south (see again Map 9-5). The Tang continued by centering their efforts on the Grand Canal and the Yangzi River, which flows from west to east. These waterways aided communication and transport

The Tang Court. This tenth-century painting of elegant ladies of the Tang imperial court enjoying a feast and music (*left*) tells us a great deal about the aesthetic tastes of elite women in this era. It also shows the secluded "inner quarters," where court ladies passed their daily lives far from the hurly-burly of imperial politics. Castrated males, known as eunuchs (*right*), guarded the harem and protected the royal family of Tang emperors. By the late eighth century, eunuchs were fully integrated into the government and wielded a great deal of military and political power.

throughout the empire and helped raise living standards. The south grew richer, largely through the backbreaking labor of immigrants from the north. Fertile land along the Yangzi became China's new granary, and areas south of the Yangzi became its demographic center.

Chinese merchants took full advantage of the Silk Road to trade with India and the Islamic world; but when rebellions in northwest China and the rise of Islam in central Asia jeopardized the land route, the "silk road by sea" became the avenue of choice. From all over Asia and Africa, merchant ships arrived in South China ports bearing intoxicating cargoes of spices, medicines, and jewelry in exchange for Chinese silks and porcelain (see again Map 9-6). Chang'an became the richest city in the world, with its million or so residents including foreigners of every description.

In the large cities of the Yangzi delta—in some ways a nascent industrial heartland—workshops proliferated. Their reputations spread far and wide for the elegance of their wares, which included rich brocades (silk fabrics), fine paper, intricately printed woodblocks, unique iron casts, and exquisite porcelains. Art collectors especially valued Tang "tricolor pottery," fired up to 900 degrees Celsius in the Sui (1200–1300°C in Song) and decorated with brilliant hues of yellow, green, white, brown, and blue. Meanwhile, Chi-

nese artisans transformed locally grown cotton into highest-quality clothing. The textile industry prospered as painting and dyeing technology improved and superb silk products generated significant tax revenue. Such Chinese luxuries dominated the trading networks that reached Southwest Asia, Europe, and Africa via the Silk Road and the Indian Ocean.

ACCOMMODATING WORLD RELIGIONS

The early Tang emperors tolerated remarkable religious diversity, for the Confucian ideology at heart was secular. Although it posited a heaven from which the ruling dynasty claimed the authority to govern, it did not promise an afterlife or threaten nonbelievers with eternal damnation. Thus Nestorian Christianity, Zoroastrianism, and Manichaeanism (a radical Christian sect) had entered China from Persia during the time of the Sasanian Empire. Islam came later. These spiritual impulses—together with Buddhism and the indigenous teachings of Daoism and Confucianism—spread throughout the Tang Empire and at first did not conflict with state power.

THE GROWTH OF BUDDHISM Buddhism, in particular, thrived under Tang rule. In fact, many students from Korea and Japan journeyed to China in the Tang's early years to study it. Initially, Emperor Li Shimin distrusted Buddhist monks because they avoided serving the government and paying taxes. Yet after Buddhism gained acceptance as one of the "three ways" of learning—joining Daoism and Confucianism—Li endowed huge monasteries, sent emissaries to India to collect texts and relics, and commissioned Buddhist paintings and statuary. Caves along the Silk Road, such as those at Dunhuang, provided ideal venues for monks to paint the inside walls of caves where religious rites and meditation took place. Soon the caves boasted "bright" color paintings and massive statues of the Buddha and the bodhisattvas. Before long, giant carvings of the Buddha in northwestern temple sanctuaries dotted the trading routes to central Asia, and temples filled with ornate statuary offered religious refuge throughout South China.

ANTI-BUDDHIST CAMPAIGNS By the mid-ninth century, the Tang Empire contained nearly 50,000 monasteries and hundreds of thousands of Buddhist monks and nuns. (In contrast, Charlemagne's empire in France had only 700 major monasteries.) Such success by a foreign religion, in conjunction with the initial decline of the Tang dynasty, threatened China's Confucian and Daoist leaders. So they attacked Buddhism, arguing that its values conflicted with Confucian and Daoist traditions.

One of the first to attack was the scholar-official Han Yu, who represented the rising literati from the south. His Memorial of 819 protested the emperor's plan to bring a relic of the Buddha to the capital for exhibition. Striking a note that would have been inconceivable under the early Tang's cosmopolitanism, Han Yu attacked Buddhism as a foreign doctrine of barbarian peoples who were different in language, culture, and knowledge. These objections earned him exile to the southern province of Guangdong.

Yet, two decades later the state began suppressing Buddhist monasteries and confiscating their wealth, fearing that religious loyalties would undermine political ones. Increasingly intolerant Confucian scholar-administrators argued that the Buddhist monastic establishment threatened the imperial order. They accused Buddhists of undermining kinship values and traditional family relations. They claimed that members of the clergy were conspiring to destroy the state, the family, and the body.

Gradually the Tang government began challenging the power of monastic communities. Piecemeal measures against the monastic orders gave way in the 840s CE to open persecution. Emperor Wuzong, for instance, closed more than 4,600 monasteries and destroyed 40,000 temples and shrines. More than 260,000 Buddhist monks and nuns endured a forced return to secular life, after which the state parceled out monastery lands to taxpaying landlords and peasant farmers. To expunge the cultural impact of Buddhism, classically trained literati revived ancient prose styles and the teachings of Confucius and his followers. Linking classical scholarship, ancient literature, and Confucian morality, they constructed a cultural fortress that reversed the early Buddhist successes in China.

The persecution of Buddhism in this period raises two important points. First, in China, it was government (the Tang) that brought religion (the Buddhist monastic communities) under its control; in Latin Europe, in contrast, it was religion (the Christian church) that dominated government (the

One of the Four Sacred Mountains. This monastery on Mount Song is famous because in 527 an Indian priest, Bodhidharma, arrived there to initiate the Zen school of Buddhism in China.

feudal states). Second, because the Chinese bureaucracy was steeped in the traditions of Confucianism and Daoism, it had a power base that Buddhism lacked. China's most prominent universalizing religion was thus vulnerable once Emperor Wuzong began to persecute it.

Ultimately, the Tang era represented the triumph of homegrown ideologies (Confucianism and Daoism) over universalizing religion (Buddhism). The result was persistent religious pluralism within China.

THE FALL OF TANG CHINA

China's deteriorating economic conditions in the ninth century led to peasant uprisings, some led by unsuccessful examination candidates. These revolts eventually brought down the dynasty. In the tenth century, China fragmented into regional states and entered a new era of decentralization. Even the Song dynasty that emerged in 960 CE could not overcome the disunity. Only the Mongols, invading steppe peoples, were later able to restore the glory of the Han and Tang empires.

EARLY KOREA AND JAPAN

> → *To what extent did Japanese and Korean polities imitate Tang China?*

While China was opening up to the cultures of its western regions, its own culture was reaching out to the east—to Korea and, eventually, to Japan (see Map 9-7). Being colored by Buddhism, these influences were somewhat flexible and less distinctly Chinese, although Confucianism in Japan, Korea, and Vietnam was tailored to each country's scale and needs. To comprehend Korean and Japanese history of this era, we need to explore developments that predated the Koryo kingdom of Korea and the Japanese experience of the ninth and tenth centuries.

EARLY KOREA

Scholars have documented Chinese cultural influences in Korea as early as the third century BCE. By the fourth century CE, three independent states had emerged on the peninsula. This division into the "Three Kingdoms" of Korea lasted until 668 CE, when one of these states, Silla, gained control over the entire peninsula and unified it.

UNIFICATION UNDER THE SILLA Unification enabled the Koreans to establish a government modeled on the Tang

imperial state. Now Silla dispatched annual embassies to the Chinese capital and regularly sent students and monks. As a result, literary Chinese became the written language of Korean elites—not their vernacular (as Latin did among diverse populations in medieval Europe). Koreans much later in the fifteenth century devised a phonetic system for writing their own language based on simplified Chinese characters, but most official writing continued in the literary Chinese form.

In spite of Chinese influences the loyalty of most non-Chinese Koreans was to their kinship groups. These early Koreans believed that birth, not displays of learned achievement, should be the source of influence in religious and political life. Korean holy men and women (known today as shamans), who interceded with gods, demons, and ancestral spirits, remained prominent in local village life. The culture stressed small-scale agriculture for harvesting grains, fishing along the coasts, and hunting in the vast northern forests.

Silla's fortunes became entwined with the Tang's to such an extent that once the Tang declined, Silla also began to fragment. Moreover, it had never established a full-blown Tang-style government.

THE KORYO DYNASTY In 936 CE, Wang Kon, a rebel leader, absorbed Silla into the northern-based Koryo kingdom, an act that tenuously reunified the country. The Koryo dynasty (from which the country's modern name derives) began to construct a new cultural identity by enacting a bureaucratic system, which replaced the archaic tribal system that the Silla had maintained. The Koryo went beyond earlier Silla reforms and fully established Tang-style civil service examinations to select officials who would govern at court and in the provinces. Wang Kon's heirs consolidated control over the peninsula and strengthened its political and economic foundations by following the Tang's bureaucratic and land allotment systems.

During this period Korea, like Tang China itself, suffered continual harassment from northern tribes such as the Khitan. This particular group exploited the fall of the Tang dynasty to control northern Chinese lands after 907 CE, establishing themselves in what is modern-day Manchuria. Reflecting the repercussions of this troubled period, Korean artisans anxiously carved wooden printing blocks for 81,258 scriptures from the Buddhist canon as an offering to the Buddha to protect them from invading enemies—but in vain. The Korean royal family at the time was under siege, and they hoped that the woodblocks would elicit a change in fortune. The scriptures were hidden away in a single temple, and when rediscovered they represented the most comprehensive and intact version of the Buddhist canon written in the Chinese script. After being overwhelmed by the Khitan in 1010, the Koryo dynasty revived, only to be invaded by the Mongols in 1231 (see Chapter 10). Nevertheless, the dynasty managed to last until 1392.

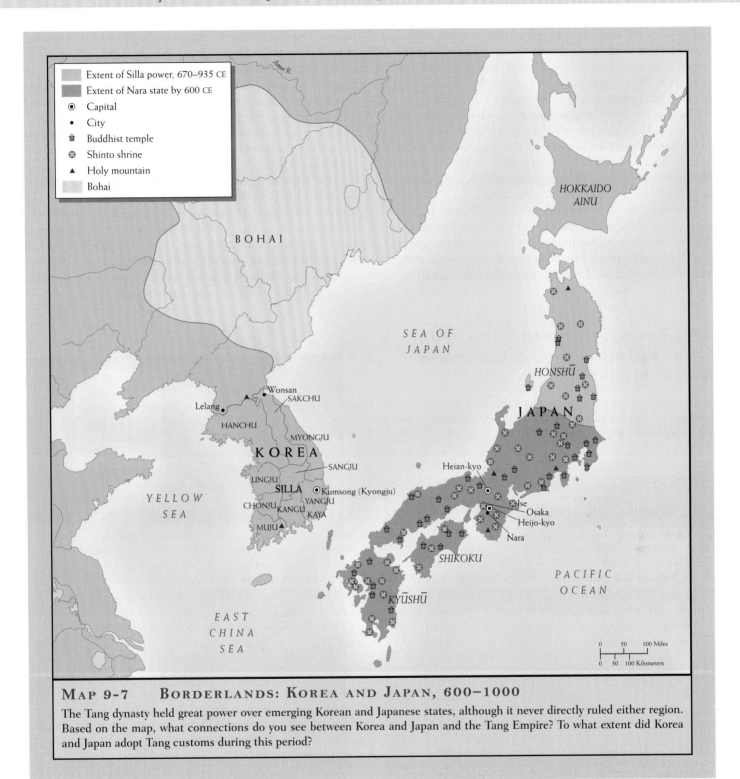

Legend:
- Extent of Silla power, 670–935 CE
- Extent of Nara state by 600 CE
- ⊙ Capital
- • City
- Buddhist temple
- ⊛ Shinto shrine
- ▲ Holy mountain
- Bohai

MAP 9-7   BORDERLANDS: KOREA AND JAPAN, 600–1000

The Tang dynasty held great power over emerging Korean and Japanese states, although it never directly ruled either region. Based on the map, what connections do you see between Korea and Japan and the Tang Empire? To what extent did Korea and Japan adopt Tang customs during this period?

EARLY JAPAN

Like Korea, Japan also felt influences emanating from China, and it responded by thwarting and accommodating them at the same time. But Japan enjoyed added autonomy: it was an archipelago of islands, more easily separated from the main-land although also internally more fragmented. Beginning in the Ice Age, tribal groups known as the Jomon (from 10,000 years ago to 400 BCE) and the Yayoi (400 BCE–250 CE) dominated prehistoric Japan. The early Jomon wandered into "Japan" when it was still part of the Asian mainland (see Chapter 1). Thereafter, several nomadic groups from Asia migrated to Japan via Korea. Subsequently, in the mid-third century, a warlike group also originating in Asia arrived by sea from Korea and imposed military and social power on southern Japan. These conquerors—known as the "Tomb Culture" because of their elevated burial sites—unified Japan by extolling their imperial ancestors and maintaining their social hierarchy. They also introduced a belief in the power of female shamans, who married into the imperial clans. These women became rulers of early Japanese kinship groups, combining religious and political power much like the early Korean holy men and women described above.

Chinese dynastic records describe the early Japanese, with whom imperial China had contact in this period, as a "dwarf" people who maintained a rice and fishing economy. The Japanese farmers also mastered Chinese-style sericulture: the production of raw silk by raising silkworms.

THE YAMATO EMPEROR AND THE SHINTO ORIGINS OF THE JAPANESE SACRED IDENTITY

In time, the complex aristocratic society that had developed within the Tomb Culture gave rise to a Yamato-dominated Japanese state that incorporated native Japanese as well as

Korean migrants. In becoming the ruling faction, the Yamato clan elevated themselves along with their belief system, based on ancestor worship, into a national religion known as **Shinto.** (Shinto means "the way of the deities.") Shinto beliefs derived from the early Japanese groups who believed that after death a person's soul (or spirit) became a Shinto *kami*, or local deity, provided that it was nourished and purified through proper rituals and festivals. (This burial tradition continues in Japan today.) Before the imperial Yamato clan became dominant, each clan had its own ancestral deities; but after 500 CE all Japanese increasingly worshipped the Yamato ancestors. Their origins went back to the fourth-century Tomb Culture of the Yamato plain (the region now known as Nara, south of Osaka). Other regional ancestral deities later became subordinate to the Yamato deities, who claimed direct lineage from the primary Shinto deity Amaterasu, the Sun Goddess and creator of the sacred islands of Japan.

Creation Myth. Tsukioka Yoshitoshi (1839–1892) depicted Japan's creation myth in "Amaterasu Appearing from the Cave." To lure Amaterasu, the goddess of the sun, out so that light would return to the world, the other gods performed a ribald dance.

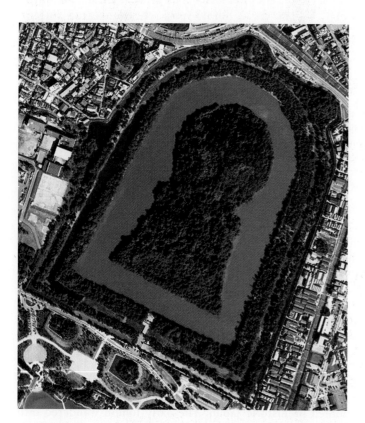

Tomb Culture. Daisenryo Kofun, in Osaka, is allegedly the tomb of Emperor Nintoku, dating from the fifth century.

→ *To what extent did Japanese and Korean polities imitate Tang China?*

PRINCE SHOTOKU AND THE TAIKA POLITICAL RE-FORMS After 587 CE the Soga kinship group—originally from Korea but by 500 CE a minor branch of the Yamato imperial family—became Japan's leading family and controlled the Japanese court through intermarriage. Soon, they were attributing everything that was innovative in their culture to their own Prince Shotoku (574–622 CE), a direct descendant of the Soga and thus of the Yamato imperial family as well.

Contemporary Japanese scribes claimed that Prince Shotoku, rather than Korean immigrants, introduced Buddhism to Japan and that his illustrious reign sparked Japan's rise as an exceptional island kingdom. Shotoku promoted both Buddhism and Confucianism, thus enabling Japan, like its neighbor China, to be accommodating to numerous religions. Although earlier Korean immigrants had laid the groundwork for the growth of these views, Shotoku was credited with introducing these faiths into the native religious culture, Shinto. The prince also had ties with several Buddhist temples modeled on Tang pagodas and halls; one of these, in Nara (Japan's first imperial capital), is Horyuji Temple, the oldest surviving wooden structure in the world. Its frescoes include figures derived from the art of Iran and central Asia. They are a reminder that within two centuries Buddhism had dispersed its visual culture along the full length of the Silk Road—from Afghanistan to China, and then on to Korea and the island kingdom of Japan.

Political integration under Prince Shotoku did not mean political stability, however. In 645 CE, the Nakatomi kinship group seized the throne and eliminated the Soga and their allies. Via intermarriage with the imperial clan, the Nakatomi became the new spokesmen for the Yamato tradition. Thereafter Nakatomi no Kamatari (614–669 CE) enacted a series of reforms, known as the Taika Reform, which reflected Confucian principles of government allegedly enunciated by Shotoku. These reforms enhanced the power of the ruler, no longer portrayed simply as an ancestral kinship group leader but now depicted as an exalted "emperor" (*tenno*) who ruled by the mandate of heaven, as in China, and exercised absolute authority.

MAHAYANA BUDDHISM AND THE SANCTITY OF THE JAPANESE STATE Religious influences continued to flow into Japan, contributing to spiritual pluralism while bolstering the Yamato rulers. Although Prince Shotoku and later Japanese emperors turned to Confucian models for government, they also dabbled in occult arts and Daoist purification rituals. In addition, the Taika edicts promoted Buddhism as the state religion of Japan. Although the imperial family continued to support native Shinto traditions, association with Buddhism gave the Japanese state extra status by lending it the prestige of a universal religion whose appeal stretched to Korea, China, and India.

State-sponsored spiritual diversity led native Shinto cults to formalize a creed of their own. Indeed, the introduction of Confucianism and Buddhism motivated Shinto adherents to assemble their diverse religious practices into a well-organized belief system. Shinto priests now collected ancient liturgies, and Shinto rituals (such as purification rites to ward off demons and impurities) gained recognition in the official Department of Religion.

Prince Shotoku Taishi. Shotoku was instrumental in the establishment of Buddhism in Japan, although his actual historical role was overstated. In this hanging scroll painting from the early fourteenth century (*left*), he is idealized as a sixteen-year-old son, holding an incense censer and praying for the recovery of his sick father, the Emperor Yomei (r. 585–587 CE). The main hall of the Horyuji Temple in Nara, Japan (*right*).

Although the Japanese welcomed elements of the Buddhist faith, they did not fully accept the traditional Buddhist view that the state was merely a vehicle to propagate moral and social justice for the ruler and his subjects. Instead, the Japanese saw their emperor (the embodiment of the state) as an object of worship, a sacred ruler, one in a line of luminous Shinto gods, a supreme *kami*—a divine force in his own right. Thus, Buddhism as imported from China and Korea changed in Japan to serve the interests of the state (much as Christianity served the interests of European monarchs, and Islam served the Islamic dynasties).

THE CHRISTIAN WEST

> → *How did two Christianities come to exist in western Afro-Eurasia?*

Seen from the Mediterranean and the Islamic worlds, Europe by now seemed little more than a warrior-dominated realm. In the fifth century, the mighty Roman military machine gave way to a multitude of warrior leaders whose principal allegiances were local affiliations. Yet major innovations were under way. The leading force was Christianity, and its universalizing agents were missionaries and monks. The political ideal of the Roman Empire cast a vast shadow over the western Europeans, but the inheritor of the mantle of Rome was a spiritual institution—the Roman Catholic Church—whose powerful head, the pope, was based in Rome (see Map 9-8.)

CHARLEMAGNE'S FLEDGLING EMPIRE

In 802 CE, Harun al-Rashid, the ruler of Baghdad, sent the gift of an elephant to Charlemagne, the king of the Franks, in northern Europe. The elephant caused a sensation among the Franks, who saw the gift as an acknowledgment of Charlemagne's power. In fact, Harun often sent rare beasts to distant rulers as a gracious reminder of his own formidable power. In his eyes, Charlemagne's "empire" was a minor principality.

This was an empire that Charlemagne ruled for over forty years, often traveling 2,000 miles a year on campaigns of plunder and conquest. He ultimately controlled much of western Europe, which was a significant accomplishment; yet compared with the Islamic world's rulers, he was a political lightweight. His empire had a population of less than 15 million; he rarely commanded armies larger than 5,000; and he had a rudimentary tax system. At a time when the palace quarters of the caliph at Baghdad covered nearly 250 acres,

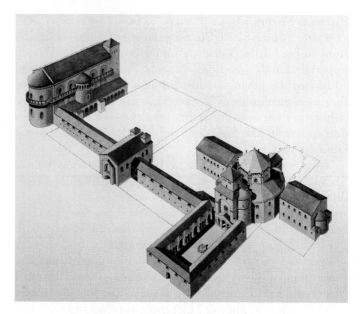

Charlemagne's Palace and Chapel. Though not large by Byzantine or Islamic standards, Charlemagne's palace and chapel were heavy with symbolic meaning. A royal hall for banqueting in Frankish, "barbarian" style was linked by a covered walkway to the imperial domed chapel, which was meant to look like a miniature version of the Hagia Sophia of Constantinople. Outside the chapel was a courtyard, like that outside the shrine of Saint Peter at Rome.

Charlemagne's palace at Aachen was merely 330 by 655 feet. Baghdad itself was almost 40 square miles in area, whereas there was no "town" outside the palace at Aachen. It was little more than a large country house set in open countryside, close to the Ardennes woods where Charlemagne and his Franks loved to hunt wild boar on horseback.

He and his men were representatives of the warrior class that dominated post-Roman western Europe. For a time, Roman rule had imposed an alien way of life in this rough world. After that empire faded, however, war became once again the duty and joy of the aristocrat. Buoyed up by their chieftains' mead—a heavy beer made with honey, "yellow, sweet and ensnaring"—young men eagerly followed their lords into battle "among the war horses and the blood-stained armor" (Aneirin, *Y Gododdin*, ll. 102, 840).

And although the Franks vigorously engaged in trade, that trade was based on war. In fact, Europe's principal export at this time was Europeans, and the massive sale of prisoners of war financed the Frankish empire. From Venice, which grew rich from its role as middleman, captives were sent as slaves across the sea to Alexandria, Tunis, and southern Spain. The main victims of this trade were Slavic-speaking peoples, tribal hunters and cultivators from eastern Europe. Their long oppression is preserved in the English language, for the medieval Latin *sclavus* ("Slavic") replaced the classical Latin *servus* to denote "slave"; *servus,* by contrast, applied to those

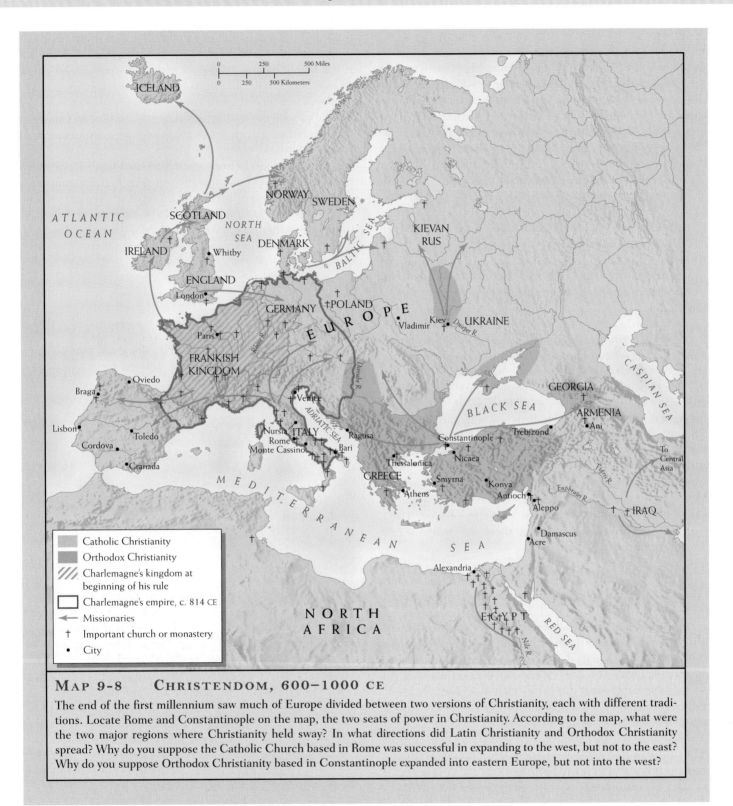

MAP 9-8   CHRISTENDOM, 600–1000 CE

The end of the first millennium saw much of Europe divided between two versions of Christianity, each with different traditions. Locate Rome and Constantinople on the map, the two seats of power in Christianity. According to the map, what were the two major regions where Christianity held sway? In what directions did Latin Christianity and Orthodox Christianity spread? Why do you suppose the Catholic Church based in Rome was successful in expanding to the west, but not to the east? Why do you suppose Orthodox Christianity based in Constantinople expanded into eastern Europe, but not into the west?

who stayed at home and became "serfs"—peasants tied for life to the estates of the aristocracy.

Yet this seemingly uncivilized and inhospitable zone offered fertile ground for Christianity to sink down roots. Although its worldwide expansion did not occur for centuries, its spiritual conquest of European peoples established institutions and fired enthusiasms that would later drive believers to carry its message to faraway lands.

A CHRISTIANITY FOR THE NORTH

Charlemagne's empire was unquestionably primitive when compared with the Islamic empire or the Tang Empire of China. What made it significant was its location. Far removed from the old centers of high culture, it was a polity of the borderlands. It also featured an expansionist Christianity that drew energy from its rough frontier mentality. Indeed, Christianity now entered a world profoundly different from the Mediterranean cities in which it had taken form.

AUGUSTINE AND THE UNIVERSAL CATHOLIC CHURCH
Christians of the west felt that theirs was the one truly universal religion. (See Primary Source: Christendom on the Edge: A View of Empire in Ireland.) Their goal was to bring rival groups into a single "catholic" church that was replacing a political unity lost in western Europe when the Roman Empire fell.

As far back as 410 CE, reacting to the Goths' sack of Rome, the Christian bishop Augustine of Hippo (a seaport in modern Algeria) had laid down the outlines of this belief. His book *The City of God* assured contemporary Christians that the barbarian takeover happening around them was not the end of the world. The "city of God" would take earthly shape in the form of the Catholic Church, and the Catholic Church was not just for Romans—it was for all times and for all peoples, "in a wide world which has always been inhabited by many differing peoples, that have so many different customs and languages, so many different forms of organization and so many languages, and who have had so many different religions" (Augustine, *City of God,* 14.1). Only one organization would bring them all to paradise: the Catholic Church.

Several developments gave rise to this attitude. First, the arrival of Christianity in northern Europe had provoked a cultural revolution. Preliterate societies now encountered a sacred text—the Bible—in a language that seemed utterly strange. Latin had become a sacred language, and books themselves were vehicles of the holy. The bound codex (see Chapter 8), which had replaced the clumsy scroll, was still a messy object. It had no divisions between words, no punctuation, no paragraphs, no chapter headings. Readers who knew Latin as a spoken language could understand the script. But Irishmen, Saxons, and Franks could not, for they had never spoken Latin. Hence the care lavished in the newly Christian north on the Latin scriptures. The few parchment texts that circulated there were carefully prepared with words separated, sentences correctly punctuated and introduced by uppercase letters, and chapter headings provided. They were far more like this textbook than anything available to Romans at the height of the empire.

Second, those who produced the Bibles were starkly different from ordinary men and women. They were monks and nuns. **Monasticism** had originated in Egypt, but it suited the missionary tendencies of Christianity in northern Europe particularly well. (The root of "monastic" and "monk" is the Greek *monos,* "alone": a man or a woman who chose to live alone, without the support of marriage or family.) Monasticism placed small groups of men and women in the middle of societies with which they had nothing in common. It appealed to a deep sense that the very men and women who had little in common with "normal" people were best suited to mediate between believers and God. Laypersons (common believers, not clergy) gave gifts to the monasteries and offered them protection. In return, they gained the prayers of monks and nuns and the reassurance that although they themselves were warriors and men of blood, the monks' and nuns' intercessions would keep them from going to hell.

Celtic Bible. Unlike the simple codex of early Christian times, the Bible came to be presented in Ireland and elsewhere in the northern world as a magical book. Its pages were filled with mysterious, intricate patterns, which imitated on parchment the jewelry and treasure for which early medieval warlords yearned.

Primary Source

CHRISTENDOM ON THE EDGE: A VIEW OF EMPIRE IN IRELAND

A young Christian Briton of Roman citizenship who lived near Hadrian's Wall experienced the pull of Christianity around 400. Captured by Irish slave raiders as a teenager, Patricius spent six years herding pigs on the Atlantic coast of Mayo. He escaped but years later returned in order to convert his former captors to Christianity. He believed that in making the fierce Irish Christians, he also made them "Romans." He thus brought Christianity to the Atlantic edge of the known world. Patricius is remembered today as Saint Patrick.

16 But after I reached Ireland, well, I pastured the flocks every day. . . . I would even stay in the forests and on the mountain and would wake to pray before dawn in all weathers, snow, frost, rain. . . .

17 And it was in fact there that one night while asleep I heard a voice saying to me: 'You do well to fast, since you will soon be going to your home country;' and again, very shortly after, I heard this prophecy: 'See, your ship is ready.' And it was not near at hand but was perhaps two hundred miles away, and I had never been there and did not know a living soul there. And then I soon ran away and abandoned the man with whom I had been for six years . . . till I reached the ship.

23 And again a few years later I was in Britain with my kinsfolk. . . . And it was there that I saw one night in a vision a man coming as it were from Ireland . . . with countless letters, and he gave me one of them, and I read the heading of the letter, 'The Voice of the Irish,' and as I read these opening words aloud, I imagined at that very instant that I heard the voice of those who were beside the forest of Foclut which is near the western sea; and thus they cried, as though with one voice: 'We beg you, holy boy, to come and walk again among us.'

→ *What does this passage reveal about life in the Celtic worlds?*

→ *How many voices or visions does Patricius experience in this passage? What other religious figure have you read about in this chapter who had a vision or a revelation?*

→ *Based on your reading, how do St. Patrick's spiritual experiences compare to those of rulers and priests in the older Christian communities of Rome and Constantinople?*

SOURCE: *St. Patrick: His Writings and Muirchu's Life,* edited and translated by A. B. E. Hood (London: Phillimore, 1978), pp. 41, 44–46, 50.

MONKS, NUNS, AND POPES With the spread of monasticism, the Christianity of the north took a decisive turn. In Muslim (as in Jewish) societies, religious leaders emphasized what they had in common with those around them: many Islamic scholars, theologians, and mystics were married men just like the public, even merchants and courtiers. In the Christian West, the opposite was true: warrior societies honored small groups of men and women (the monks and nuns) who were utterly unlike themselves: unmarried, unfit for warfare, and intensely literate in an incomprehensible tongue. Even their hair looked different. Unlike warriors, these men were close-shaven; by contrast, the Orthodox clergy of the eastern Roman empire grew long, silvery beards (signifying wisdom and maturity; not, as in the west, the warrior's masculine strength). Catholic monks and priests shaved their heads as well.

The Catholic Church of northern Europe owed its missionary zeal to the same principles that explained the spread of Buddhism: it was a religion of monks, whose communities represented an otherworldly alternative to the warrior societies of the time. By 800 CE, most regions of northern Europe held great monasteries, many of which were far larger than the local villages. Supported by thousands of serfs donated by kings and local warlords, the monasteries became powerhouses of prayer that kept the regions safe.

Northern Christianity also gained new ties to an old center: the city of Rome. The Christian bishop of Rome had always enjoyed much prestige. But being only one bishop among many, he often took second place to his peers in Carthage, Alexandria, Antioch, and Constantinople. Though people spoke of him with respect as *papa* ("the grand old man"), many others shared that title.

Monasticism. The great monasteries of the age of Charlemagne, such as the St. Gallen Monastery (*left*), were like Roman legionary settlements. Placed on the frontiers of Germany, they were vast, stone buildings, around which entire towns would gather. Their libraries, the largest in Europe, were filled with parchment volumes, carefully written out and often lavishly decorated in a "northern," Celtic style. Monasticism was also about the lonely search for God at the very end of the world, which took place in these Irish monasteries (*right*) on the Atlantic coast. The cells, made of loose stones piled in round domes, are called "beehives."

By 800 CE, this picture had changed. As believers looked down from the distant north, they saw only one *papa* left in western Europe: Rome's pope. The papacy as we know it arose because of the fervor with which the Catholic Church of western Europe united behind one symbolic center, represented by the popes at Rome and the desire of new Christians in northern borderlands to find a religious leader for their hopes.

Charlemagne recognized this desire very well. In 800 CE, he went out of his way to celebrate Christmas Day by visiting the shrine of Saint Peter at Rome. There, Pope Leo III acclaimed him as the new "emperor" of the west. The ceremony ratified the aspirations of an age. A "modern" Rome—inhabited by popes, famous for shrines of the martyrs, and protected by a "modern" Christian monarch from the north—was what his subjects wanted.

THE AGE OF THE VIKINGS

Harun's elephant died in 813 CE, one year before Charlemagne himself. The elephant's death was noteworthy because the Franks viewed it as an omen of coming disasters. The great beast keeled over when his handlers marched him out to confront a Viking army from Denmark. In the next half-century, the Vikings from Scandinavia exposed the weakness of Charlemagne's self-confident regime. His empire of bor-

derland peoples met its match on the widest border of all: that between the European landmass and the mighty Atlantic (see Map 9-9).

The Vikings' motives were announced in their name, which derives from the Old Norse *vik*, "to be on the warpath." The **Vikings** sought to loot the now-wealthy Franks and replace them as the dominant warrior class of northern Europe. It was their turn to extract plunder and to sell droves of slaves across the water. They succeeded because of a deadly technological advantage: ships of unparalleled sophistication, developed by Scandinavian sailors in the Baltic Sea and the long fjords of Norway. Light and agile, with a shallow draft, they could penetrate far up the rivers of northern Europe and even be carried overland from one river system to another. Under sail, the same boats could tackle open water and cross the unexplored wastes of the North Atlantic.

In the ninth century, the Vikings set their ships on both courses. They emptied northern Europe of its treasure, sacking the great monasteries along the coasts of Ireland and Britain and overlooking the Rhine and the Seine—rivers that led into the heart of Charlemagne's empire. At the same time, Norwegian adventurers colonized the uninhabited island of Iceland, and then Greenland. By 982 CE, they had even reached the New World and established a settlement at L'Anse aux Meadows on the Labrador coast. Viking goods have been found as far west as the Inuit settlements of Baffin Island to

The Coronation of Charlemagne. This is how the coronation of Charlemagne at Rome in 800 CE was remembered in medieval western Europe. This painting stresses the fact that it was the pope who placed the crown on Charlemagne's head, thereby claiming him as a ruler set up by the Catholic Church for the Catholic Church. But in 800 contemporaries saw the pope as recognizing the fact that Charlemagne had already deserved to be emperor. The rise of the papacy to greater prominence and power in later medieval Europe caused this significant "re-remembering" of the event.

the north of Hudson Bay, carried there along trading routes by Native Americans.

The consequences of this spectacular reach across the ocean to America were short-lived, but the penetration of eastern Europe had lasting effects. Supremely well equipped to traverse long river systems, the Vikings sailed east along the Baltic and then turned south, edging up the rivers that

Oseberg Ship. The Viking ship was a triumph of design. It could be rowed up the great rivers of Europe, and, at the same time, its sail could take it across the Atlantic.

crossed the watershed of central Russia. Here the Dnieper, the Don, and the Volga begin to flow south into the Black Sea and the Caspian. By opening this link between the Baltic and what is now Kiev in modern Ukraine, the Vikings created an avenue of commerce that linked Scandinavia and the Baltic directly to Constantinople and Baghdad. And they added yet more slaves: Muslim geographers bluntly called this route "The Highway of the Slaves."

THE SURVIVAL OF THE CHRISTIAN EMPIRE OF THE EAST

On reaching the Black Sea, the Vikings made straight for Constantinople. In 860 CE, more than 200 Viking long ships gathered ominously in the straits of the Bosporus, beneath the walls of Constantinople. What they found was not Charlemagne's rustic Aachen, but a proud city with a population exceeding 100,000 surrounded by well-engineered late Roman walls.

The Vikings had come up against a state hardened by battle. For two centuries the empire of "East Rome," centered on Constantinople, had held Islamic armies at bay. From 640 to 840 CE they faced almost yearly campaigns launched by the Islamic empire of Damascus and Baghdad, powerhouses that grew to be ten times greater than their own. For years on end, Muslim armies and navies came within striking distance of Constantinople. Each time they failed, outmaneuvered by highly professional generals and blocked by a skillfully

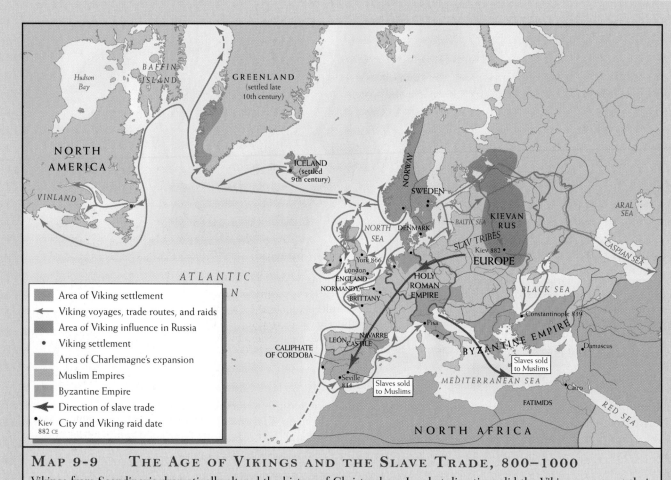

MAP 9-9   **THE AGE OF VIKINGS AND THE SLAVE TRADE, 800–1000**

Vikings from Scandinavia dramatically altered the history of Christendom. In what directions did the Vikings carry out their voyages, trade routes, and raids? What were the geographic limits of the Viking explorations in each direction? In what direction did the slave trade move, and what role did the Vikings and the Holy Roman emperors play in expanding the slave trade?

constructed line of fortresses that controlled the roads across Anatolia. The Christian empire of East Rome fought the caliphs of Baghdad to a draw. The Viking fleet was even less well suited to assault Constantinople, as the empire of "East Rome" had a deadly technological advantage in naval warfare: Greek fire, a combination of petroleum and potassium that, when sprayed from siphons, would explode in a great sheet of flame on the water. A previous emperor had used it to destroy the Muslim fleet as it lay at anchor within sight of Constantinople. Now, a century and a half later, the experience and weaponry of East Rome were too much for the Vikings, and their raid was a spectacular failure.

GREEK ORTHODOX CHRISTIANITY   In the long run, the sense of having outlasted so many military emergencies bolstered the morale of East Roman Christianity and led to its unexpected flowering. Not just Constantinople but Justinian's glorious church, the Hagia Sophia—its heart—had survived. That great building and the solemn Greek liturgy that reverberated within its domed spaces might not impress Catholic Franks, but upon seeing it the Scandinavian adventurers were awestruck. Here was the central church of a Christian empire that for half a millennium had represented all that was most venerable in the Christian tradition. In the tenth century, as Charlemagne's empire collapsed in western Europe, large areas of eastern Europe became Greek Orthodox, not Catholic. As a result, Greek Christianity gained a spiritual empire in Southwest Asia.

The conversion of Russian peoples and Balkan Slavs to Greek Orthodox Christianity was a complex process. It reflected a deep admiration for Constantinople on the part of Russians, Bulgarians, and other Slav princes. It was an admiration as intense as that of any Western Catholic for the Roman popes. This admiration amounted to awe, as shown by the famous story of the conversion to Greek Christianity of the rulers of Kiev (descendants of Vikings):

> The envoys reported[,] . . . "We went among the Germans [the Catholic Franks] and we saw them performing many ceremonies in their churches; but we beheld no glory there. Then we went to Greece [in fact, to Constantinople and Hagia Sophia], and the Greeks led us to the edifices where they worship their God, and we knew not whether we were in heaven or on earth. For on earth there is no such splendor or such beauty, and we are at a loss to describe it. . . . [W]e can not forget that beauty. (Cross and Sherbowitz-Westor, *The Russian Primary Chronicle*, 111)

By the year 1000, there were two Christianities: the new and confident "borderland" **Roman Catholicism** of western Europe, and an ancient **Greek Orthodoxy**, protected against extinction by the iron framework of a "Roman" state inherited from Constantine and Justinian. Together both strands of the faith constituted the realm of **Christendom:** the entire portion of the world in which Christianity prevailed. Western Catholics believed that their church was destined to expand everywhere. East Romans were less euphoric but more tenacious. They believed that their church would forever survive the regular ravages of invasion. It was a significant difference in attitude and neither side liked the other. East Romans considered the Franks barbarous and grasping; Western Catholics contemptuously called the East Romans "Greeks" and condemned them for their "Byzantine" cunning.

Thus, like Islam, the Christian world was divided. But its differences were not about the basic tenets of the faith, like those of Shiite and Sunni Islam. They were differences in heritage, customs, and levels of civilization. At that time, the orthodox world was considerably more ancient and more cultured than the world of the Catholic west. And it dealt with Islam differently. At Constantinople, eastern Christianity held off Muslim forces that constantly threatened the integrity of the great city and its Christian hinterlands. In the west, by contrast, Muslim expansionism reached all the way to the Iberian Peninsula. Western Christendom, led by the Roman papacy, did not feel the same intimidation from Islam. It set about spreading Christianity to pagan tribes in the north, and it began to contemplate retaking lands from the Muslims.

The period 600–1000 CE saw heightened movement across cultural boundaries as well as an insistence on the distinctiveness of individual societies. Commodities, technological innovations, ideas, merchants, adventurers, and scholars traveled from one end of Afro-Eurasia to the other, and up and down coastal Africa. Spreading religion into new frontiers accompanied this mercantile activity. The proximity of the period's two powerhouses—Abbasid Islam and Tang China—facilitated the dynamic movement.

Jelling Stone. Carved on the side of this great stone, Christ appears to be almost swallowed up in an intricate pattern of lines. For the Vikings, complicated interweaving like serpents or twisted gold jewelry was a sign of majesty: hence, in this, the first Christian monument in Denmark, Christ is part of an ancient pattern of carving, which brought good luck and victory to the king.

 CONCLUSION

Despite the intermixing, new political and cultural boundaries were developing that would split this landmass in ways it could never have imagined. The most important dividing force was Islam, which challenged and slowed the spread of Christianity. As a consequence, Afro-Eurasia's major cultural zones began to compete in terms of religious and cultural doctrines. The Islamic Abbasid Empire pushed back the borders of the Tang Empire. But the conflict grew particularly intense between the Islamic and Christian worlds, where the clash involved faith as well as frontiers.

The Tang Empire revived Confucianism, insisting on its political and moral primacy as the foundation of a new imperial order, and it embraced the classical written language as another unifying element. By doing so the Tang counteracted universalizing foreign religions—notably Buddhism but also Islam—spreading into the Chinese state. The same adaptive strategies influenced new systems on the Korean peninsula and in Japan.

In some circumstances, faith followed empire and relied on rulers' support or tolerance to spread the word. This was the case especially in East Asia. At the opposite extreme, empire followed faith—as in the case of Islam, whose believers endeavored to spread their empire in every conceivable direction. The Islamic empire and its successors represented a new force: expanding political power backed by one God whose instructions were to spread his message. In the worlds of Christianity, a common faith absorbed elements of a common culture (shared books, a language for learned classes). But in the west, political rulers never overcame inhabitants' intense allegiance to local authority.

While universalizing religions expanded and common cultures grew, debate raged within each religion over foundational principles. In spite of the diffusion of basic texts in "official" languages, variations of Christianity, Islam, and Buddhism proliferated as each belief system spread. The period demonstrated that religion, reinforced by prosperity and imperial resources, could bring peoples together in unprecedented ways. But it could also, as the next chapter will illustrate, drive them apart in bloodcurdling confrontations.

Review and research materials are available at StudySpace: Ⓢ WWNORTON.COM/STUDYSPACE

KEY TERMS

caliphate (p. 327)
Christendom (p. 359)
civil service examinations
    (p. 343)
eunuchs (p. 345)
Greek Orthodoxy
    (p. 359)
Islam (p. 325)
jihad (p. 326)
meritocracy (p. 344)
monasticism (p. 354)

Muhammad (p. 324)
Quran (p. 324)
Roman Catholicism
    (p. 359)
sharia (p. 327)
Shiites (p. 337)
Shinto (p. 350)
Sunnis (p. 337)
Tang dynasty (p. 340)
ulama (p. 327)
Vikings (p. 356)

Chronology

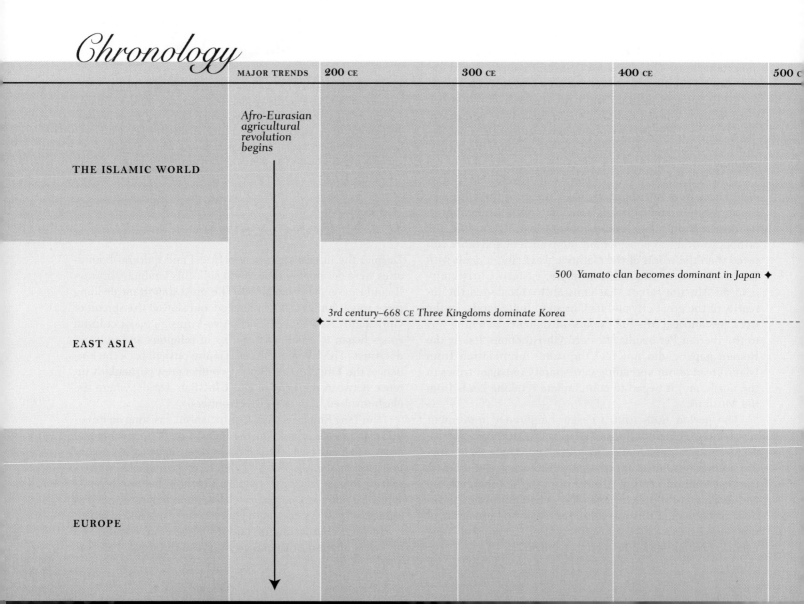

	MAJOR TRENDS	200 CE	300 CE	400 CE	500 C
THE ISLAMIC WORLD	*Afro-Eurasian agricultural revolution begins*				
EAST ASIA		◆ 3rd century–668 CE *Three Kingdoms dominate Korea*		500 *Yamato clan becomes dominant in Japan* ◆	
EUROPE					

STUDY QUESTIONS

1. Analyze the impact of the spread of Islam on Afro-Asian societies. How did the large Islamic empire shape the movement of peoples, ideas, innovations, and commodities across the vast landmass?

2. Describe the process through which an expanding Islam fostered an agricultural revolution. What crops and cultivation techniques were involved?

3. Compare and contrast the spread of Islam, Christianity, and Buddhism between 600 and 1000. What was the geographic range of each religious community? Through which methods did each religion gain new converts?

4. Explain the origins and basic concepts of Islam. How similar to and different from other religions that began in Southwest Asia—such as Judaism, Christianity, and Zoroastrianism—was this new religious outlook?

5. Analyze the successes and failures of Islamic leaders in creating one large empire to govern Islamic communities. What opponents challenged this goal?

6. Describe the Tang dynasty's attempts to restore political unity to East Asia. How did Tang leaders react to the growth of universal religions within their realm?

7. Describe the state structure that emerged in Korea and Japan during this era. How did other developments in Afro-Eurasia, such as the spread of universal religions, shape these new states?

8. Compare and contrast Christian communities in western Europe to those in eastern Europe and the Byzantine Empire. What factors contributed to each region's distinctiveness?

9. Analyze the Vikings' impact on world history during this era. How did they shape developments in the Christian world especially?

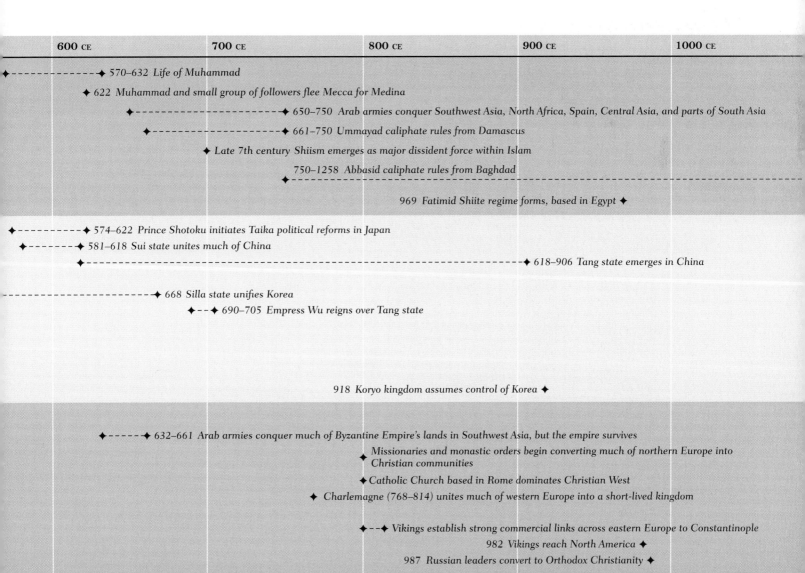

| 600 CE | 700 CE | 800 CE | 900 CE | 1000 CE |

◆-------------→ 570–632 Life of Muhammad

◆ 622 Muhammad and small group of followers flee Mecca for Medina

◆----------------→ 650–750 Arab armies conquer Southwest Asia, North Africa, Spain, Central Asia, and parts of South Asia

◆----------------→ 661–750 Ummayad caliphate rules from Damascus

◆ Late 7th century Shiism emerges as major dissident force within Islam

750–1258 Abbasid caliphate rules from Baghdad

969 Fatimid Shiite regime forms, based in Egypt ◆

◆--------→ 574–622 Prince Shotoku initiates Taika political reforms in Japan

◆------→ 581–618 Sui state unites much of China

◆-------------------→ 618–906 Tang state emerges in China

◆------------→ 668 Silla state unifies Korea

◆--◆ 690–705 Empress Wu reigns over Tang state

918 Koryo kingdom assumes control of Korea ◆

◆-----◆ 632–661 Arab armies conquer much of Byzantine Empire's lands in Southwest Asia, but the empire survives

Missionaries and monastic orders begin converting much of northern Europe into Christian communities

Catholic Church based in Rome dominates Christian West

◆ Charlemagne (768–814) unites much of western Europe into a short-lived kingdom

◆--◆ Vikings establish strong commercial links across eastern Europe to Constantinople

982 Vikings reach North America ◆

987 Russian leaders convert to Orthodox Christianity ◆

Becoming "The World,"
1000–1300 CE

In the late 1270s two Christian monks, Bar Sāwmā and Markōs, voyaged into the heart of Islam. They were not Europeans. They were Uighurs, a Turkish people of central Asia, many of whom had converted to Christianity centuries earlier. Sent by the mighty Mongol ruler Kubilai Khan as he prepared to become the first emperor of China's Yuan dynasty, the monks were supposed to worship at the temple in Jerusalem. But the Great Khan also had political ambitions. He was eager to conquer Jerusalem, held by the Muslims. Accordingly, he dispatched the monks as agents to make alliances with Christian kings in the area and to gather intelligence about his potential enemy in Palestine.

By 1280, conflict and conquest had transformed many parts of the world. But friction was simply one manifestation of cultures brushing up against one another. More important was trade. Indeed, Bar Sāwmā and Markōs lingered at the magnificent trading hub of Kashgar in far western China, where caravan routes converged in a market for jade, exotic spices, and precious silks. Later, at Baghdad, the monks parted ways. Bar Sāwmā visited

Constantinople (where the king gave him gold and silver), Rome (where he met with the pope at the shrine of Saint Peter), and Paris (where he saw that city's vibrant university) before deciding to return to China, where the Christians of the east awaited his reports. In the end, neither monk ever returned. Yet their voyages exemplified the crisscrossing of people, money, and goods along the trade routes and sea-lanes that connected the world's regions. For just as religious conflict was a hallmark of this age, so was a surge in trade, migration, and global exchange.

The period brought to a climax many centuries of human development, and it ushered in a new, very long cycle of cultural interaction from which emerge three interrelated themes. First, trade was shifting from land-based routes to sea-based routes. Coastal trading cities began to dramatically expand. Second, intensified trade and linguistic and religious integration generated the world's four major cultural "spheres," whose inhabitants were linked by shared institutions and beliefs: China, India, Islam, and Europe. Not all cultures turned into "spheres," though. In the Americas and sub-Saharan Africa there was not the same impulse to integrate regions, which remained more fragmented but thrived nonetheless. Third, the rise of the Mongol Empire represented the peak in the long history of ties and tensions between settled and mobile peoples. From China to Persia and as far as eastern Europe, the Mongols ruled over much land in the world's major cultural spheres.

COMMERCIAL CONNECTIONS

> → *What factors led to the explosion of global trading between 1000 and 1300?*

REVOLUTIONS AT SEA

By the tenth century, sea routes were eclipsing land networks for long-distance trade. Improved navigational aids, refinements in shipbuilding, better mapmaking, and new legal arrangements and accounting practices made shipping easier and slashed the costs of seaborne trade. The numbers testify to the power of the maritime revolution: while a porter could carry about 10 pounds over long distances, and animal-drawn wagons could move 100 pounds of goods, the Arab dhows plying the Indian Ocean were capable of transporting up to 5 tons of cargo. (**Dhows** are ships with triangle-shaped sails, called lateens, that maximize the monsoon trade winds on the Arabian Sea and the Indian Ocean.) As a result some coastal ports, like Mogadishu in eastern Africa, became vast transshipment centers for a thriving trade across the Indian Ocean.

A new navigational instrument spurred this boom: the needle compass. This Chinese invention initially identified prom-

Focus Questions

WWNORTON.COM/STUDYSPACE

→ *What factors led to the explosion of global trading between 1000 and 1300?*

→ *How did trade and migration affect sub-Saharan Africa between 1000 and 1300?*

→ *How did trade, conversion, and migration affect the Islamic world between 1000 and 1300?*

→ *In what ways did India remain a cultural mosaic?*

→ *What transformations in communication, education, and commerce promoted a distinct Chinese identity during this era?*

→ *How were Southeast Asia, Japan, and Korea influenced by sustained contact with other regions?*

→ *How did Christianity produce a distinct identity among the diverse peoples of Europe?*

→ *Where did societies in the Americas demonstrate strong commercial expansionist impulses?*

→ *How did Mongol conquests affect cross-cultural contacts and regional development in Afro-Eurasia?*

ising locations for houses and tombs, but eleventh-century sailors from Canton used it to find their way on the high seas. The device spread rapidly. Not only did it allow sailing under cloudy skies, but it also improved mapmaking. And it made all the oceans, including the Atlantic, easier to navigate.

Now shipping became less dangerous. Navigators relied on lateen-rigged dhows between the Indian Ocean and the Red Sea, heavy junks in the South China seas, and Atlantic "cogs," which linked Genoa to locations as distant as the Azores and Iceland. They also enjoyed the protection of political authorities, such as the Song dynasts in China, in guiding the trading fleets in and out of harbors. The Fatimid caliphate in Egypt, for instance, profited from maritime trade and defended merchant fleets from pirates. Armed convoys of ships escorted commercial fleets in a system called **karim** (a loose confederation of shippers banding together to protect convoys) that regularized the ocean traffic. The system soon spread to North Africa and southern Spain. Most *karimi* firms were family-based, and they sent young men of the family, sometimes servants or slaves, to work in India. Housewives in Cairo could expect gifts from their husbands to arrive with the *karimi* fleet.

Changes in navigation ushered in the demise of overland routes. Silk Road merchants eventually gave up using camel trains, caravansaries (inns for travelers), and oasis hubs as they switched to the sea-lanes. The shift took centuries, but overland routes and camels were no match for multiple-masted cargo ships.

Dhow. This modern dhow in the harbor of Zanzibar displays the characteristic triangle sail. The triangle sail can make good use of the trade monsoon and thus has guided dhows on the Arabian Sea since ancient times.

COMMERCIAL CONTACTS

The opening of the sea-lanes also tapped into changes occurring in world agriculture (see Map 10-1). By 1000 CE, major innovations in irrigation techniques, carried out over many centuries and in numerous locations, had yielded enormous returns. New strains of cereals—and in the Americas, the refinement of maize—led to grain cultivation in vast areas that had been too cold and arid to sustain them previously. Clover, alfalfa, and other newly domesticated grasses became fodder for healthier, stronger, and fatter animals. Agriculture pushed into new regions, buoying population growth and surpluses that now could be shipped over great distances.

GLOBAL COMMERCIAL HUBS

Long-distance trade spawned the growth of commercial cities. These entrepôts became cosmopolitan nerve centers of an increasingly integrated world. (**Entrepôts** are transshipment centers, located between borders or in ports, where traders exchange commodities and replenish supplies.) Beginning in the late tenth century, four places became major anchorages of the maritime trade: in the west, the Egyptian port cities of Alexandria and Cairo; in the east, the Chinese city of Quanzhou; in the Malaysian Archipelago, the city of Melaka; and near the tip of the Indian peninsula, the port of Quilon. These hubs thrived under the political stability of powerful dynasts who recognized that the free-for-all of trade and market life would generate wealth for their regimes. Yemeni rulers, for instance, offered shelter to *karimi* fleets in return for taxes collected on cargoes; so did Egyptian governments for fleets moving through the Red Sea.

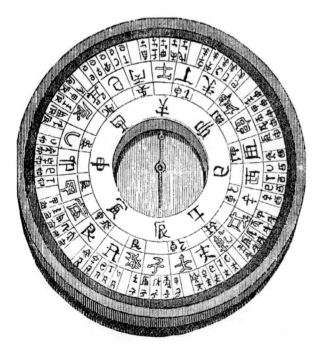

Antique Chinese Compass. Chinese sailors from Canton started to use needle compasses in the eleventh century. By the thirteenth century, needle compasses were widely used on ships in the Indian Ocean and were starting to appear in the Mediterranean.

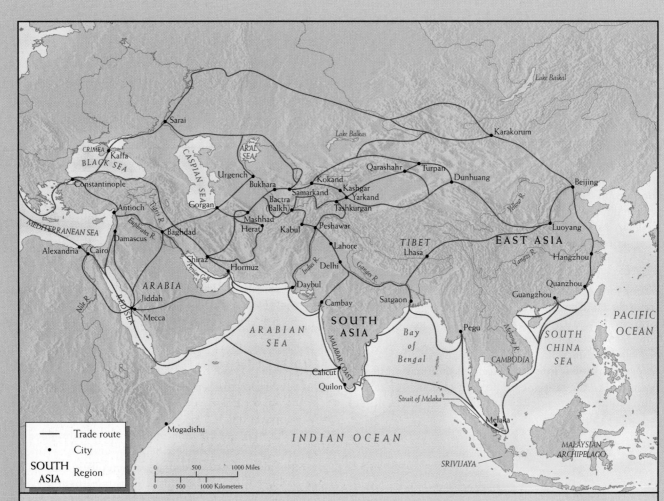

MAP 10-1 AFRO-EURASIAN TRADE, 1000–1300

During the early second millennium, Afro-Eurasian merchants increasingly turned to the Indian Ocean to transport their goods. Locate the global hubs of Quilon, Alexandria, Cairo, and Guangzhou on this map. What regions do each of these global hubs represent? Based on the map, why would sea travel have been preferable to overland travel? According to the text, what revolutions in maritime travel facilitated this development?

THE EGYPTIAN ANCHORAGE Cairo and Alexandria were the Mediterranean's main maritime commercial centers. Cairo was home to numerous Muslim and Jewish trading firms, and Alexandria was their lookout post on the Mediterranean.

Silk yarn and textiles were the most popular commodities in the global trade involving Egypt. It was through Alexandria that Europeans acquired silks from China, especially the coveted *zaytuni* (satin) fabric from Quanzhou. Spanish silks also passed through Alexandria, heading to eastern Mediterranean markets. But the entrepôts handled much more. Goods from the Mediterranean included olive oil, glassware, flax, corals, and metals. Gemstones and aromatic perfumes poured in from India. Also changing hands were minerals and

chemicals for dyeing or tanning, and raw materials such as timber and bamboo. The real novelties were paper and books. Hand-copied Bibles, Talmuds, legal and moral works, grammars in various languages, and Arabic books became the first best sellers of the Mediterranean.

Cairo and Alexandria prospered under Islamic leaders' commercial institutions. Success required states to protect merchants from predators. Armed convoys sent by Fatimid caliphs to escort commercial fleets in the Mediterranean and the Red Sea were so effective that fleets arrived on schedule and were relied on for postal service. Thus, when an Egyptian trader in Quilon (India) around 1100 was delayed on his journey home, he could send a consoling message to his wife in Cairo. He apologized for his absence but promised gifts

Mazu. Many Quanzhou sailors sought protection at the shrine of the goddess Mazu. According to legend, before assuming godhood Mazu had performed many miracles. Her temple became prominent after 1123, when Quanzhou's governor survived a storm at sea while returning from Korea. After that, sailors and their families burned incense for the goddess and prayed for her aid in keeping them safe at sea.

including pearl bracelets, red silk garments, a bronze basin, a ewer, and a slave girl: "I shall send them, if God wills it, with somebody who is traveling home in the *Karim*" (Goitein, "New Light," 179).

The Islamic legal system also promoted a favorable business environment. Consider how legal specialists got around the rule that might have brought commerce to a halt—the *sharia*'s (see Chapter 9) prohibition against earning interest on loans. With the clerics' blessing, Muslim traders formed partnerships between those who had capital to lend and those who needed money to expand their businesses. These partnerships enabled owners of capital to entrust their money or commodities to agents who, after completing their work, returned the investment and a share of the profits to the owners—and kept the rest as their reward. The English word "risk" derives from the Arabic *rizq*, the extra allowance paid to merchants in lieu of interest.

THE ANCHORAGE OF QUANZHOU In China, Quanzhou was as busy as Cairo and Alexandria. The Song government set up offices of Seafaring Affairs in its three major ports: Canton, Quanzhou, and an area near present-day Shanghai in the Yangzi delta. In return for a portion of the taxes, these offices registered cargoes, sailors, and traders, while guards kept a keen eye on the traffic.

All foreign traders were guests of the governor, who doubled as the Chief of Seafaring Affairs. Part of his mandate was to summon favorable winds for shipping. Every year, the governor took his place on a high perch facing the harbor, in front of a rock cliff filled with inscriptions that recorded the wind-calling rituals. Traders of every origin witnessed the rite, then joined the dignitaries for a sumptuous banquet.

Ships departing from Quanzhou and other Chinese ports were junks—large, flat-bottomed ships with internal sealed bulkheads and stern-mounted rudders. Their multiple watertight compartments increased stability; the largest ones boasted four decks, six masts, and a dozen sails and could carry 500 men. Those departing Quanzhou headed for Srivijaya (Java) in the Malay Archipelago, navigating through the Strait of Melaka, a choke point between the South China Sea and the Indian Ocean. The final destination was Quilon on the coast of southwest India. Traders heading farther west in Arab-dominated seas unloaded their cargo and boarded small Arabian dhows.

Arabs, Persians, Jews, and Indians (as well as Chinese) traded at Quanzhou, and some stayed on to manage their businesses. Perhaps as many as 100,000 Muslims lived there during the Song dynasty. And traders could become power brokers in their own right. Consider the Pu family, which owned several hundred ships ferrying goods between India and Islamic countries. For generations the family made donations for public projects such as bridges, and the contributions garnered them official positions.

Although most foreign merchants did not reside apart from the rest of the city, they had their own buildings for

MAIN THEMES

↬ *Trade routes shift from land to sea, transforming coastal cities into global trading hubs and elevating Afro-Eurasian trade to unprecedented levels.*

↬ *Intensified trade, linguistic, and religious integration generate the foundational cultural spheres that we recognize today: China, India, Islam, and Europe.*

↬ *The rise of the Mongol Empire integrates the world's foundational cultural spheres.*

FOCUS ON *Foundational Cultural Spheres*

The Islamic World

+ Islam undergoes a burst of expansion, prosperity, and cultural diversification but remains politically fractured.

+ Arab merchants and sufi mystics spread Islam over great distances and make it more appealing to other cultures, helping to transform Islam into a foundational world.

+ Islam travels across the Sahara Desert; the powerful gold- and slave-supplying empire of Mali arises in West Africa.

China

+ The Song dynasty reunites China after three centuries of fragmented rulership, reaching into the past to re-establish a sense of a "true" Chinese identity as the Han, through a widespread print culture and denigration of outsiders.

+ Breakthroughs in iron metallurgy allow agricultural expansion to support 120 million people and undergird Han commercial success.

+ China undergoes the world's first manufacturing revolution: gunpowder, porcelain, and handicrafts are produced on a large scale for widespread consumption.

India

+ India remains a mosaic under the canopy of Hinduism despite cultural interconnections and increasing prosperity.

+ The invasion of Turkish Muslims leads to the Dehli Sultanate, which rules over India for three centuries, strengthening cultural diversity and tolerance.

Christian Europe

+ Catholicism becomes a "mass" faith and helps to create a common European cultural identity.

+ An emphasis on religious education spawns numerous universities and a new intellectual elite.

+ Feudalism causes a fundamental reordering of the elite–peasant relationship, leading to agricultural and commercial expansion.

+ Europe's growing confidence is manifest in the Crusades and Reconquista, an effort to drive Islam out of Christian lands.

---

religious worship. A mosque from this period is still standing on a busy street. Hindu traders living in Quanzhou worshipped in a Buddhist shrine where statues of Hindu deities stood alongside those of Buddhist gods.

THE CROSSROADS OF AFRO-EURASIA: MELAKA Because of its strategic location and proximity to Malayan tropical produce, Melaka became a key cosmopolitan city. Indian, Javanese, and Chinese merchants and sailors spent months at a time in such ports selling their goods, purchasing return cargo, and waiting for the winds to change so they could reach their next destination. During peak season, Southeast Asian ports teemed with colorfully dressed foreign sailors,

local Javanese artisans who produced finely textured batik handicrafts (using melted wax applied to cloth before dipping it into blue and brown dyes), and money-grubbing traders. The latter converged from all over Asia to flood the markets with their merchandise and to search for pungent herbs, aromatic spices, and agrarian staples such as quick-ripening strains of rice to ship out. In a sense, each bustling port represented the cosmopolitan mosaic that Southeast Asia had become.

THE TIP OF INDIA In the tenth century, the Chola dynasty in south India supported a nerve center of maritime trade between China and the Red Sea and the Mediterranean. Although the Chola golden age lasted only about two generations, trade continued to flourish. Many Muslim traders settled in Malabar, on the southwest coast of the Indian peninsula, and Quilon became a major cosmopolitan hub. Dhows arrived, laden not only with goods from the Red Sea and Africa but also with traders, sojourners, and fugitives. Chinese junks unloaded silks and porcelain, and picked up passengers and commodities for East Asian markets. Sailors and traders strictly observed the customs of this entrepôt, for it was good business to respect others' norms and values while doing business with them.

Muslims, the largest foreign community, lived in their own neighborhoods. They shipped horses from Arab countries to India and the southeast islands, where kings viewed them as symbols of royalty. Because the animals could not survive in those climates, the demand was constant. There was even trade in elephants and cattle from tropical countries, though most goods were spices, perfumes, and textiles. Traders knew each other well, and personal relationships were key. When striking a deal with a local merchant, a Chinese trader would mention his Indian neighbor in Quanzhou and that family's residence in Quilon. Global commercial hubs relied on friendship and family to keep their businesses thriving across religious and regional divides.

SUB-SAHARAN AFRICA COMES TOGETHER

> → *How did trade and migration affect sub-Saharan Africa between 1000 and 1300?*

During this period sub-Saharan Africa's relationship to the rest of the world changed dramatically. Before 1000 CE sub-Saharan Africa had never been a world entirely apart, but now its integration became firmer. Africans and outsiders were determined to overcome the sea, river, and desert barriers that had blocked sub-Saharan peoples from participating in long-distance trade and intellectual exchanges (see Map 10-2). Increasingly, interior hinterlands found themselves touched by the commercial and migratory impulses emanating from the Indian Ocean and Arabian Sea transformations.

WEST AFRICA AND THE MANDE-SPEAKING PEOPLES

Once the camel bridged the Sahara Desert (see Chapter 9), the flow of commodities and ideas linked sub-Saharan Africa to the Muslim world of North Africa and Southwest Asia. As the savanna region became increasingly connected to developments in Afro-Eurasia, Mande-speaking peoples emerged as the primary agents for integration within and beyond West

Africa. Exploiting their expertise in commerce and political organization, the Mande edged out rivals.

The Mande, or Mandinka, homeland was a vast area between the bend in the Senegal River to the west and the bend of the Niger River to the east (1,000 miles wide), stretching from the Senegal River in the north to the Bandama River in the south (more than 2,000 miles). This was where the kingdom of Ghana had arisen (see Chapter 9) and where Ghana's successor state—the Mandinka state of Mali, discussed below—emerged around 1100.

The Mande-speaking peoples were constantly on the go and marvelously adaptable. By the eleventh century they were spreading their cultural, commercial, and political hegemony from the high savanna grasslands southward into the woodlands and tropical rainforests stretching to the Atlantic Ocean. Those dwelling in the rainforests organized small-scale societies led by local councils, while those in the savanna lands developed centralized forms of government under sacred kingships. These peoples believed that their kings had descended from the gods and that they enjoyed the gods' blessing.

As the Mande broadened their territory to the Atlantic coast, they gained access to tradable items that residents of the interior were eager to have—notably kola nuts and malaguetta peppers, for which the Mande exchanged iron products and textile manufactures. By 1300 the Mandinka merchants had followed the Senegal River to its outlet on the coast and then pushed their commercial frontiers farther inland and down the coast. Thus, even before European explorers and traders arrived in the mid-fifteenth century, West African peoples had created dynamic networks linking the hinterlands with coastal trading hubs.

From the eleventh century to the late fifteenth century, the most vigorous businesses were those that spanned the Sahara Desert. The Mande-speaking peoples, with their far-flung commercial networks and highly dispersed populations, dominated this trade as well. Here one of the most prized commodities was salt, mined in the northern Sahel around the city of Taghaza; it was in demand on both sides of the Sahara. Another valuable commodity was gold, mined within the Mande homeland and borne by camel caravans to the far northern side of the Sahara, where traders exchanged it for various manufactures. Equally important in West African commerce were slaves, who were shipped to the settled Muslim communities of North Africa and Egypt.

THE EMPIRE OF MALI

As booming trade spawned new political organizations, the empire of Mali became the Mande successor state to the kingdom of Ghana. Founded in the twelfth century, it exercised political sway over a vast area for three centuries.

The Mali Empire represented the triumph of horse warriors, and its origins are enshrined in an epic involving the dynasty's founder, the legendary Sundiata, *The Epic of Sundiata*. Many

MAP 10-2 SUB-SAHARAN AFRICA, 1300

Increased commercial contacts influenced the religious and political dimensions of sub-Saharan Africa at this time. Compare this map to Map 9-3 (p. 335). Where had strong Islamic communities emerged by 1300? According to this map, what types of activity were affecting the Mande homeland? To what extent had sub-Saharan Africa "come together"?

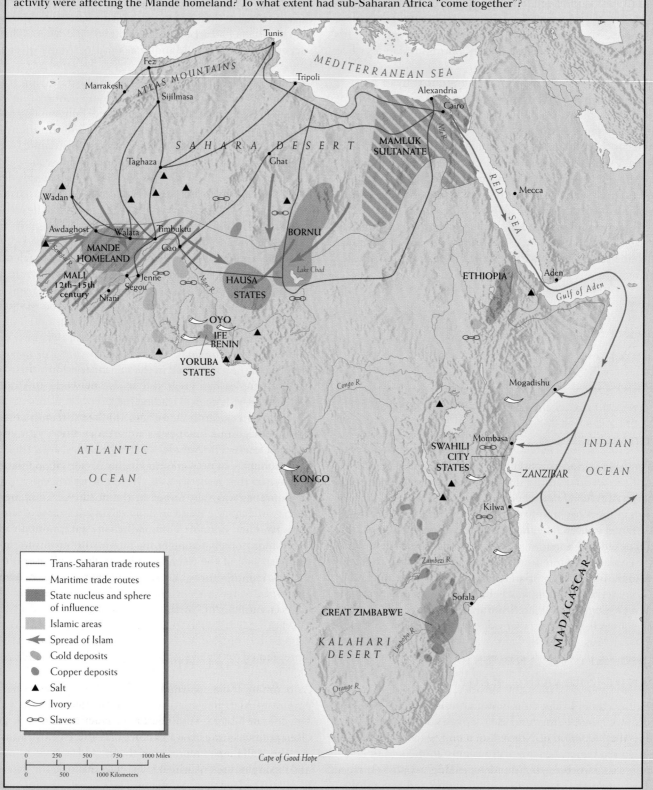

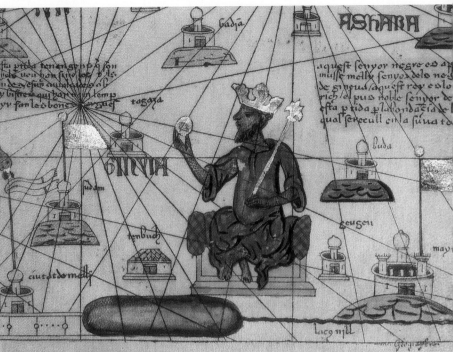

West African Asante Gold. Although this gold head from the kingdom of Asante (*left*) was made in the eighteenth century, it shows the artistic abilities of the West African peoples. The head probably belonged to the Asante ruler, known as the Asantehene, and symbolized his power and wealth. This 1375 picture (*right*) shows the king of Mali on his throne, surrounded by images of gold.

historians believe that Sundiata actually existed, noting that the Arab historian Ibn Khaldun referred to him by name and reported that he was "their [Mali's] greatest king" (Levtzion and Pouwels, p. 64). His triumph, which occurred in the fourteenth century, marked the victory of new cavalry forces over traditional footsoldiers. Henceforth, horses—which had always existed in some parts of Africa—became prestige objects of the savanna peoples, symbols of state power. (See Primary Source: An African Epic.)

Under the Mali Empire, commerce was in full swing. With Mande trade routes extending to the Atlantic Ocean and spanning the Sahara Desert, West Africa was no longer an isolated periphery of the central Muslim lands. Mali's most famous sovereign, Mansa Musa (r. 1312–1332), made a celebrated hajj, or pilgrimage to Mecca, in 1325–1326, traveling through Cairo and impressing crowds with the size of his retinue and his displays of wealth, especially many dazzling items made of gold.

Mansa Musa's visit to Cairo was a sensation in its time. The stopover in one of Islam's primary cities astonished the Egyptian elite and awakened much of the world to the fact that Islam had spread far below the Sahara and that a sub-Saharan state could mount such an ostentatious display. Mansa Musa spared no expense to impress his hosts. He sent ahead an enormous gift of 50,000 dinars (a unit of money widely used in the Islamic world at this time), and his entourage included soldiers, wives, consorts, and as many as 12,000 slaves, many

wearing rich brocades woven of Persian silks. And there was gold—a lot of it. He brought immense quantities and distributed it lavishly during his three-month stay. Preceding his retinue as it crossed the desert were 500 slaves, each carrying a golden staff. The caravan also included around 100 camels, each bearing two 300-pound sacks of gold.

The Mali Empire boasted two of West Africa's largest cities. Jenne, an ancient entrepôt, was a vital assembly point for caravans laden with salt, gold, and slaves preparing for journeys west to the Atlantic coast and north over the Sahara. The city had originated as an urban settlement around 200 BCE; by 1000 CE most substantial structures were made of brick. Around the city ran an impressive wall over eleven feet thick at its base and extending over a mile in length. More spectacular was the city of Timbuktu; founded around 1100 as a seasonal camp for nomads, it grew in size and importance under the patronage of various Malian kings. By the fourteenth century it was a thriving commercial and religious center famed for its two large mosques, which are still standing. Timbuktu was also renowned for its intellectual vitality. Here, West African Muslim scholars congregated to debate the tenets of Islam and to ensure that the faithful, even when distant from the Muslim heartland, practiced their religion with no taint of pagan observances. These clerics acquired treatises on Islam from all over the world for their personal libraries, remnants of which remain to this day.

AN AFRICAN EPIC

The traditional story of the founding of the kingdom of Mali was passed down orally from generation to generation by griots, counselors and other official historians to the royal family. Only in 1960 was it finally written down in French. The narrative recounts the life of Sundiata, the heroic founder of the Mali state. The following passage provides insight into the role of the narrator (the griot) in the Malian kingdom, as well as some of the qualities of good and bad rulers.

Griots know the history of kings and kingdoms and that is why they are the best counsellors of kings. Every king wants to have a singer to perpetuate his memory, for it is the griot who rescues the memories of kings from oblivion, as men have short memories.

Kings have prescribed destinies just like men, and seers who probe the future know it. They have knowledge of the future, whereas we griots are depositories of the knowledge of the past. But whoever knows the history of a country can read its future.

Other peoples use writing to record the past, but this invention has killed the faculty of memory among them. They do not feel the past any more, for writing lacks the warmth of the human voice. . . .

I, Djeli Mamoudou Kouyaté, am the result of a long tradition. For generations we have passed on the history of kings from father to son. The narrative was passed on to me without alteration and I deliver it without alteration, for I received it free from all untruth.

Listen now to the story of Sundiata, the Na'Kamma, the man who had a mission to accomplish.

At the time when Sundiata was preparing to assert his claim over the kingdom of his fathers, Soumaoro was the king of kings, the most powerful king in all the lands of the setting sun. The fortified town of Sosso was the bulwark of fetishism against the word of Allah. For a long time Soumaoro defied the whole world. Since his accession to the throne of Sosso he had defeated nine kings whose heads served him as fetishes in his macabre chamber. Their skins served as seats and he cut his footwear from human skin. Soumaoro was not like other men, for the jinn had revealed themselves to him and his power was beyond measure. So his countless sofas [soldiers] were very brave since they believed their king to be invincible. But Soumaoro was an evil demon and his reign had produced nothing but bloodshed. Nothing was taboo for him. His greatest pleasure was publicly to flog venerable old men. He had defiled every family and everywhere in his vast empire there were villages populated by girls whom he had forcibly abducted from their families without marrying them.

→ *Are you able to understand the function of the griot after reading this passage?*

→ *How reliable do you think this kind of oral history is?*

→ *Soumaoro, the adversary of Sundiata, exemplified the characteristics of a bad ruler. What were they? Can you tell, indirectly, what the characteristics of a good ruler (like Sundiata) were?*

SOURCE: *Sundiata: An Epic of Old Mali,* translated by D. T. Niane (Harlow: Longman Group, 1965), pp. 40–41.

EAST AFRICA AND THE INDIAN OCEAN

Africa's eastern and southern regions were also integrated into long-distance trading systems. Because of monsoon winds, East Africa was a logical end point for much of the Indian Ocean trade. Thus Swahili peoples living along that coast became brokers for the trade coming and going from the Arabian Peninsula, the Persian Gulf territories, and the western coast of India. Merchants in the city of Kilwa along the coast of present-day Tanzania brought ivory, slaves, gold, and other items from the interior and shipped them to destinations around the Indian Ocean.

The most valued commodity in the trade was gold. Shona-speaking peoples grew rich by mining the ore in the highlands between the Limpopo and Zambezi rivers. By the year 1000, the Shona had founded up to fifty small religious and political centers, each one erected from stone to display

Great Zimbabwe. These walls surrounded the city of Great Zimbabwe, which was a center of the gold trade between the East African coastal peoples and traders sailing on the Indian Ocean. Great Zimbabwe flourished during the thirteenth, fourteenth, and fifteenth centuries.

THE TRANS-SAHARAN AND INDIAN OCEAN SLAVE TRADE

African slaves were as valuable as African gold in shipments to the Mediterranean and Indian Ocean markets. There had been a lively trade in African slaves (mainly from Nubia) into pharaonic Egypt well before the Common Era. After Islam spread into Africa and sailing techniques improved, the slave trade across the Sahara Desert and Indian Ocean boomed.

Although the Quran attempted to mitigate the severity of slavery, requiring Muslim slave owners to treat their slaves kindly and praising manumission as an act of **piety** (a strong sense of religious duty and devoutness, often inspiring extraordinary actions), nonetheless the African slave trade flourished under Islam.

Slave Market. Slaves were a common commodity in the marketplaces of the Islamic world. Turkish conquests during the years from 1000 to 1300 put many prisoners into the slave market.

its power over the peasant villages surrounding it. Around 1100 one of these centers, Great Zimbabwe, stood supreme among the Shona. Built on the fortunes made from gold, its most impressive landmark was a massive elliptical building— 32 feet high, 17 feet thick in parts, and extending more than 800 feet—made of stone so expertly that its fittings needed no grouting. The buildings of Great Zimbabwe probably housed the king and may also have contained smelters for melting down gold.

One of the key meeting grounds of the Indian Ocean trading system was the island of Madagascar. So intense was the interchange of peoples, plants, and animals from mainland Africa and around the rest of the Indian Ocean that Madagascar became one of the most multicultural places in the world at this time. Among the early inhabitants of the island were seafarers from Indonesia who plied the oceans with seaworthy outrigger canoes, likely picking up Bantu-speaking mainlanders from East Africa. The first evidence of human settlement there dates to the eighth century CE. Subsequently the island became a regular stopover point, as well as an import-export market, for traders crossing the Indian Ocean.

Africans became slaves during this period much as they had before: some were prisoners of war; others were considered criminals and sold into slavery as punishment. Their duties were varied. Some slaves were pressed into military service, rising in a few instances to positions of high authority. Others with seafaring skills worked as crewmen on dhows or as dockworkers. Still others, mainly women, were domestic servants, and many became concubines of Muslim political figures and businessmen. Slaves also did forced labor on plantations, the most oppressive being the agricultural estates of lower Iraq. There, slaves endured fearsome discipline and revolted in the ninth century. Yet in this era plantation-slave labor like that which later became prominent in the Americas was the exception, not the rule. Slaves were more prized as additions to family labor or as status symbols for their owners.

Dervishes. Today, the whirling dance of dervishes is almost a tourist attraction, as shown in this picture from the Jerash Cultural Festival in Jordan. Though Sufis in the early second millennium CE were not this neatly dressed, the whirling dance was an important means of reaching union with God.

ISLAM IN A TIME OF POLITICAL FRAGMENTATION

> → *How did trade, conversion, and migration affect the Islamic world between 1000 and 1300?*

Islam underwent the same burst of expansion, prosperity, and cultural diversification that swept through the rest of Afro-Eurasia (see Map 10-3 and Map 10-4). However, whereas prosperity fostered greater integration in other regions, the peoples of Islam remained politically fractured. As in China, efforts to unite under a common rulership failed, giving way to defeats by marauding outsiders. The attempt to uphold centralized rule ended cataclysmically in 1258 with the Mongol sacking of Baghdad. But unlike China, Muslim leaders were unable to reunite after their collapse.

BECOMING THE "MIDDLE EAST"

Islam responded to political fragmentation by undergoing major changes, many prompted by contacts (and conflicts) with neighbors. Commercial networks, sustained by Muslim merchants, carried the word of the Quran far and wide. As Islam spread, it attracted more converts.

Decisive in the spread of Islam was a popular form of the religion, highly mystical and communal, called **Sufism.** The term *Sufi* comes from the Arabic word for wool (*suf*), which many of the early mystics wrapped themselves in to mark their penitence. Seeking closer union with God, they also performed ecstatic rituals such as repeating over and over again the name of God. In time, groups of devotees gathered to read aloud the Quran and other religious tracts. Although

many clerics despised the Sufis and loathed their seeming lack of theological rigor, the movement spread with astonishing speed. Sufism's emotional content and strong social bonds, sustained in Sufi brotherhoods or lodges, made its appeal to common folk irresistible. Sufi missionaries carried the universalizing faith to India, across the Sahara Desert, and to many other distant locations. It was from within these brotherhoods that Islam became truly a religion for the people.

Sufism had an intellectual and artistic dynamism that complemented its missionizing zeal. This was especially true of poetry, where the mystics' desire to experience God's love found ready expression. Most admired of Islam's mystical love poets was Jalal al-Din Rumi, spiritual founder of the Medlevi Sufi order that became famous for the ceremonial dancing of its whirling devotees, known as dervishes. Rumi, who wrote in Persian, celebrated all forms of love, spiritual and sexual, and preached a universalistic religious message:

> What is to be done of Muslims? For I do not recognize myself.
> I am neither Christian, nor Jew, nor Gabr (Zoroastrian), nor Muslim.

Another Sufi mystic and advocate of the universality of religions, the Spanish Muslim poet Ibn Arabi, wrote in Arabic:

> My heart has been of every form; it is a pasture for gazelles and a convent for Christian monks.
> And a temple for idols and the pilgrim's kaaba, and the tables of the Torah and the book of the Quran.

As trade increased and more converts appeared in the Islamic lands, urban and peasant populations came to understand the faith practiced by the political, commercial, and scholarly upper classes even while they remained attached to their

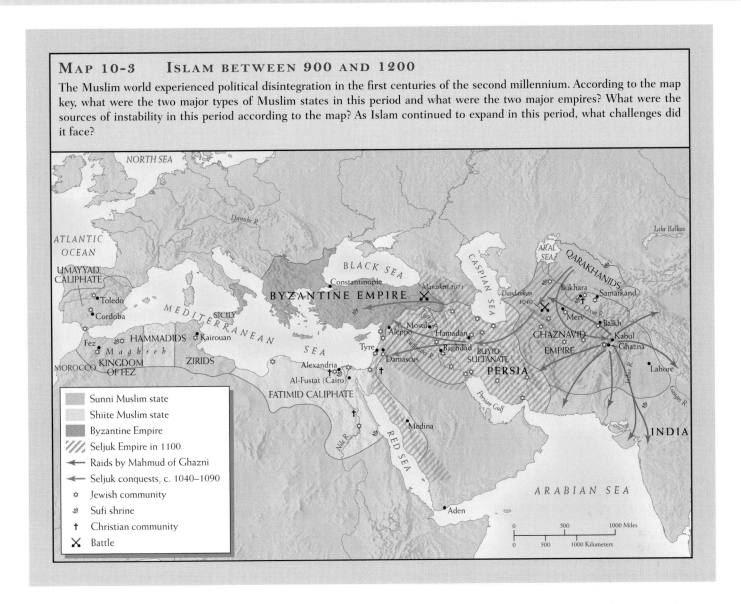

MAP 10-3   ISLAM BETWEEN 900 AND 1200

The Muslim world experienced political disintegration in the first centuries of the second millennium. According to the map key, what were the two major types of Muslim states in this period and what were the two major empires? What were the sources of instability in this period according to the map? As Islam continued to expand in this period, what challenges did it face?

Sunni Muslim state
Shiite Muslim state
Byzantine Empire
Seljuk Empire in 1100
Raids by Mahmud of Ghazni
Seljuk conquests, c. 1040–1090
Jewish community
Sufi shrine
Christian community
Battle

Sufi brotherhood ways. Islam became even more accommodating, embracing Persian literature, Turkish ruling skills, and Arabic-language contributions in law, religion, literature, and science. In this way the world acquired a "core" region centered in what we now call the Middle East (the lands west of the "Far East" of China and Japan, and including the "Near East" of the eastern Mediterranean), united by a shared faith and pulsating with religious and commercial energies.

AFRO-EURASIAN MERCHANTS

By the thirteenth century, as the old Islamic heartland became the crossroads for commercial networks, Muslim merchants were the world's premier traders. As diverse as their businesses, these merchants were proof that a universal religion, an imagined political unity (projected by the Abbasid caliphate), the spread of the Arabic language, and Islamic law

allowed entrepreneurs of varied backgrounds to flourish. The traders were not only Muslims but also Armenians, Indians, and Jews; working out of Islam's major cities; and they all had connections with families in North Africa and central Asia. (See Primary Source: The Merchants of Egypt.)

Long-distance trade surged under the protection of a sophisticated legal framework. The traders drew up elaborate contracts knowing that if breaches of contract occurred, they could take their cases to the courts. Many Jewish, Armenian, and Christian merchants went before Islamic judges, whose expertise in commercial matters they admired. Yet legal recourse was rarely necessary because the merchant community was self-policing—its members severely punished those who violated trust, sometimes ending their careers. Relying on partnerships, letters of credit, and a thorough knowledge of local trading customs and currencies, traders and their customers were confident that agreements made in India would be honored in Southeast Asia, Egypt, and North Africa.

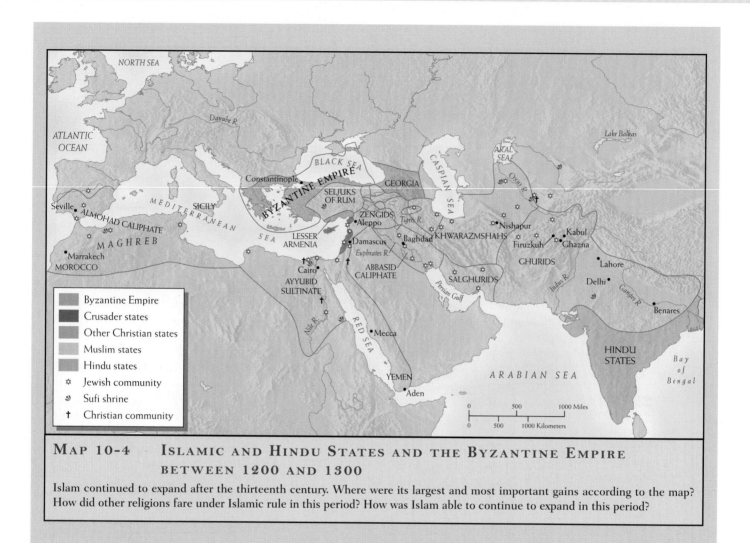

MAP 10-4   ISLAMIC AND HINDU STATES AND THE BYZANTINE EMPIRE BETWEEN 1200 AND 1300

Islam continued to expand after the thirteenth century. Where were its largest and most important gains according to the map? How did other religions fare under Islamic rule in this period? How was Islam able to continue to expand in this period?

DIVERSITY AND UNIFORMITY IN ISLAM

Not until the ninth and tenth centuries did Muslims become a majority within their own Abbasid Empire (see Chapter 9). From the outset, Muslim rulers and clerics had to deal with large non-Muslim populations, even as these groups were converting to Islam. Rulers through the dhimma system accorded non-Muslims religious toleration as long as the non-Muslims accepted Islam's political dominion. Thus Jewish, Christian, and Zoroastrian communities were free to choose their own religious leaders and to settle internal disputes in their own religious courts. They did, however, have to pay a special tax, the *jizya,* and be deferential to their rulers. The dhimma system spared the Islamic world some of the religious conflict that afflicted other areas, and it made Islamic cities hospitable environments for traders from around the world.

While tolerant, Islam was an expansionist, universalizing faith. Intense proselytizing carried the sacred word to new frontiers and, in the process, reinforced the spread of Islamic institutions that supported commercial exchange. There were also moments of intense religious passion within Islam's frontiers, especially when Muslim rulers feared that Christian minorities would align with the Europeans pressing on their borders. Ugly incidents left some Christian churches in flames. Pressures to convert to Islam were unremitting at this time. After a surge of conversions to Islam from the ninth century onward, for example, the Christian Copts of Egypt shrank to a small community and never recovered their numbers.

POLITICAL INTEGRATION AND DISINTEGRATION

Just as the Islamic faith was increasing its reach from Africa to India and ultimately to Southeast Asia, its political institutions began to fragment. From 950 to 1050, it appeared that Shiism would be the vehicle for uniting the Islamic

THE MERCHANTS OF EGYPT

The most comprehensive collection of eleventh- and twelfth-century commercial materials from the Islamic world comes from a repository connected to the Jewish synagogue in Cairo. (It was the custom of the Jewish community to preserve, in a special storeroom, all texts that mention God.) These papers, a rich source of information about the Jewish community in Egypt at that time, touch on all manner of activities: cultural, religious, judicial, political, and commercial. The following letter is addressed to Joseph ibn 'Awkal, one of Egypt's leading merchants in the eleventh century.

Dear and beloved elder and leader, may God prolong your life, never take away your rank, and increase his favors and benefactions to you.

I inform you, my elder, that I have arrived safely. I have written you a letter before, but have seen no answer. Happy preoccupations—I hope. In that letter I provided you with all the necessary information.

I loaded nine pieces of antimony (kohl), five in baskets and four in complete pieces, on the boat of Ibn Jubār—may God keep it; these are for you personally, sent by Mūsā Ibn al-Majjānī. On this boat, I have in partnership with you—may God keep you—a load of cast copper, a basket with (copper) fragments, and two pieces of antimony. I hope God will grant their safe arrival. Kindly take delivery of everything, my lord.

I have also sent with Banāna a camel load for you from Ibn al-Majjānī and a camel load for me in partnership with you—may God keep you. He also carries another partnership of mine, namely, with 'Ammā r Ibn Yijū, four small jugs (of oil).

With Abū Zayd I have a shipload of tin in partnership with Salāma al-Mahdawī. Your share in this partnership with him is fifty pounds. I also have seventeen small jugs of s[oap]. I hope they arrive safely. They belong to a man [called . . .]r b. Salmūn, who entrusted them to me at his own risk. Also a bundle of hammered copper, belonging to [a Muslim] man from the Maghreb, called Abū Bakr Ibn Rizq Allah. Two other bundles, on one is written Abraham, on the other M[. . .]. I agreed with the shipowner that he would transport the goods to their destination. I wish my brother Abū Nasr—may God preserve him—to take care of all the goods and carry them to his place until I shall arrive, if God wills.

Please sell the tin for me at whatever price God may grant and leave its "purse" (the money received for it) until my arrival. I am ready to travel, but must stay until I can unload the tar and oil from the ships.

Please take care of this matter and take from him the price of five skins (filled with oil). The account is with Salāma.

Al-Sabbāgh of Tripoli has bribed Bu 'l-'Alā the agent, and I shall unload my goods soon.

Kindest regards to your noble self and to my master [. . . and] Abu 'l-Fadl, may God keep them.

→ *List all the different kinds of commodities that the letter talks about.*
→ *How many different people are named as owners, partners, dealers, and agents?*
→ *What does the letter reveal about the ties among merchants and about how they conducted their business?*

SOURCE: *Letters of Medieval Jewish Traders,* translated with introductions and notes by S. D. Goitein (Princeton, NJ: Princeton University Press, 1973), pp. 85–87.

world. While the Fatimid Shiites established their authority over Egypt and much of North Africa (see Chapter 9), the Abbasid state in Baghdad fell under the sway of a Shiite family. Each group created universities (in Cairo and Baghdad, respectively), ensuring that leading centers of higher learning were Shiite. But divisions also sapped Shiism, as Sunni Muslims began to challenge Shiite power and establish their own strongholds. The last of the Shiite Fatimid rulers gave way to a new Sunni regime in Egypt. In Baghdad, the Shiite Buyid family surrendered to a group of unrelated Sunni strongmen.

The new strongmen were mainly Turks. Their people had been migrating into the Islamic heartland from the Asian steppes since the eighth century, bringing superior military skills and an intense devotion to Sunni Islam. Once established in Baghdad, they founded outposts in Syria and Palestine, and then moved into Anatolia after defeating

Byzantine forces in 1071. But this Turkish state also crumbled, as tribesmen quarreled for preeminence. Thus by the thirteenth century the Islamic heartland had fractured into three regions. In the east (central Asia, Iran, and eastern Iraq), the remnants of the old Abbasid state persevered. Caliphs succeeded one another, still claiming to speak for all of Islam yet deferring to their Turkish military commanders. Even in the core of the Islamic world (Egypt, Syria, and the Arabian Peninsula), where Arabic was the primary tongue, military men of non-Arab origin held the reins of power. Farther west (in the Maghreb), Arab rulers prevailed—but there the influence of Berbers, some from the northern Sahara, was extensive. Islam was a vibrant faith, but its polities were splintered.

WHAT WAS ISLAM?

Buoyed by Arab dhows on the high seas and carried on the backs of camels, following commercial networks, Islam had been transformed from Muhammad's original goal of creating a religion for Arab peoples. By 1300, its influence spanned Afro-Eurasia. It attracted urbanites and rural peasants alike, as well as its original audience of desert nomads. Its extraordinary universal appeal generated an intense Islamic cultural flowering in 1000 CE.

Some people worried about the preservation of Islam's true nature as, for example, Arabic ceased to be the language of many Islamic believers when it spread beyond the Arab peoples. True, the devout read and recited the Quran in its original tongue, as the religion mandated. But Persian was now the language of Muslim philosophy and art, and Turkish was the language of law and administration. Moreover, Jerusalem and Baghdad no longer stood alone as Islamic cultural capitals. Other cities, housing universities and other centers of learning, promoted alternative, vernacular versions of Islam. In fact, some of the most dynamic thought came from Islam's fringes.

At the same time, heterogeneity fostered cultural blossoming in all fields of high learning. Arabic remained a preeminent language of science, literature, and religion in 1300. Indicative of Islam's and Arabic's prominence in thought was the legendary Ibn Rushd (1126–1198). Known as Averroës in the western world, where scholars pored over his writings, he wrestled with the same theological issues that troubled western scholars. Steeped in the writings of Aristotle, Ibn Rushd became Islam's most thoroughgoing advocate for the use of reason in understanding the universe. His knowledge of Aristotle was so great that it influenced the thinking of the Christian world's leading philosopher and theologian, Thomas of Aquino (Thomas Aquinas, 1225–1274). Above all, Ibn Rushd believed that faith and reason could be compatible. He also argued for a social hierarchy in which learned men would command influence akin to Confucian scholars in China or Greek philosophers in Athens. Ibn Rushd believed that the proper forms of reasoning had to be entrusted to the educated class—in the case of Islam, the *ulama*—which would serve the common folk.

Equally powerful works appeared in Persian, which by now was expressing the most sophisticated ideas of culture and religion. Best representing the new Persian ethnic pride was Abu al-Qasim Firdawsi (920–1020), a devout Muslim who also believed in the importance of pre-Islamic Sasanian traditions. In the epic poem *Shah Namah*, or *Book of Kings*, he celebrated the origins of Persian culture and narrated the history of the Iranian highland peoples from the dawn of time to the Muslim conquest. As part of his effort to extol a pure Persian culture, Firdawsi attempted to compose his entire poem in Persian unblemished by other languages, even avoiding Arabic words.

By the fourteenth century, Islam had achieved what early converts would have considered unthinkable. No longer a religion of a minority of peoples living amid Christian, Zoroastrian, and Jewish communities, it had become the people's faith. The agents of conversion were mainly Sufi saints and Sufi brotherhoods—not the *ulama*, whose exhortations had little impact on common people. The Sufis had carried their faith far and wide to North African Berbers, to Anatolian villagers, and to West African animists (who believed that things in nature have souls). Indeed, Ibn Rushd worried about the growing appeal of what he considered an "irrational" piety. But his message failed, because he did not appreciate that Islam's expansionist powers rested on its appeal to common folk. While the *sharia* was the core of Islam for the educated and scholarly classes, Sufism spoke to ordinary men and women.

INDIA AS A CULTURAL MOSAIC

> → *In what ways did India remain a cultural mosaic?*

Trade and migration affected India, just as it did the rest of Asia and Africa. As in the case of Islam, India's growing cultural interconnections and increasing prosperity produced little political integration. Under the canopy of Hinduism it remained a cultural mosaic; in fact, the Islamic faith now joined others to make the region even more diverse (see Map 10-5). India, in this sense, illustrates how cross-cultural integration can just as easily preserve diversity as promote internal unity.

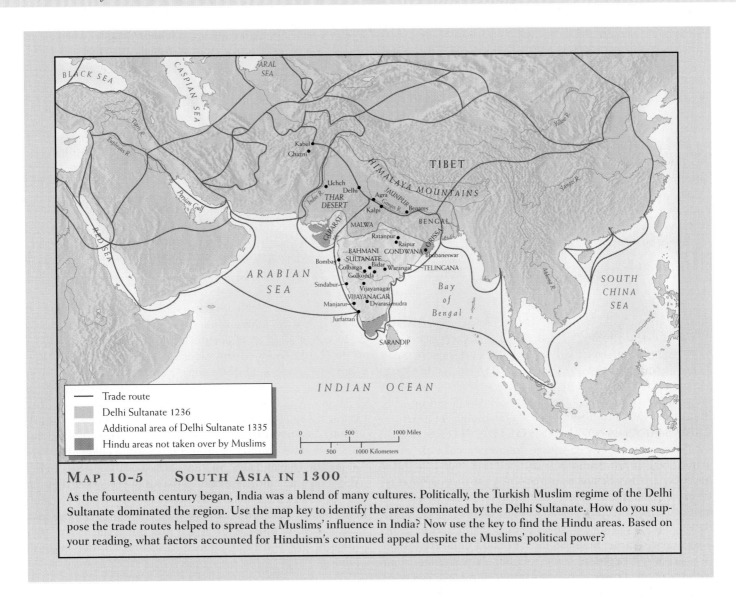

MAP 10-5   SOUTH ASIA IN 1300

As the fourteenth century began, India was a blend of many cultures. Politically, the Turkish Muslim regime of the Delhi Sultanate dominated the region. Use the map key to identify the areas dominated by the Delhi Sultanate. How do you suppose the trade routes helped to spread the Muslims' influence in India? Now use the key to find the Hindu areas. Based on your reading, what factors accounted for Hinduism's continued appeal despite the Muslims' political power?

RAJAS AND SULTANS

Turks spilled into India as they had the Islamic heartlands, bringing their newfound Islamic beliefs. But the newcomers encountered an ethnic and religious mix that they would add to without upsetting the balance. India became an intersection for the trade, migration, and culture of Afro-Eurasian peoples. Moreover, with 80 million inhabitants in 1000 CE, it had the second-largest population in the region, not far behind China's 120 million.

Before the Turks arrived, India was splintered among rival chiefs called *rajas*. (**Rajas** considered themselves kings; the term also denotes the head of a family or the person who controlled land and resources.) These leaders solicited support from high-caste Brahmans by giving them land. Much of it was uncultivated, so the Brahmans set out to make it

arable: they built temples, converted the indigenous hunter-gatherer peoples to the Hindu faith, and then taught the converts how to cultivate the land. In this way the Brahmans simultaneously spread their faith and expanded the agrarian tax base for themselves and the rajas. The Brahmans reciprocated the rajas' support by compiling elaborate genealogies for them and endowing them with a lengthy (and legitimizing) ancestry. For their part, the rajas demonstrated that they were well versed in Sanskrit culture, including equestrian skills and courtly etiquette, and became the patrons of artists and poets. Ultimately, many of the warriors and their heirs became Indian rajas. However, the Turkish invaders were armed with Islam, so the conquerors remained sultans instead of becoming rajas. (Unlike rajas, **sultans** were political leaders who combined a warrior ethos with a devotion to Islam.)

Hindu Temple. When Buddhism started to decline in India, Hinduism was on the rise. Numerous Hindu temples were built, many of them adorned with ornate carvings like this small tenth-century temple in Bhubaneshwar, east India.

INVASIONS AND CONSOLIDATIONS

When the Turkish warlords began entering India, the rajas had neither the will nor resources to resist them after centuries of fighting off invaders. The Turks introduced their own customs while accepting local social structures, such as the caste system. Concerned to promote Islamic culture, the Turks constructed grandiose mosques and built impressive libraries where scholars could toil and share their wisdom with the court. Previous invaders from central Asia had reinforced the rajas' power base through intermarriage. But the Turks upset the balance of the raja kingdoms. For example, Mahmud of Ghazna (971–1030) launched many expeditions from the Afghan heartland into northern India and wanted to make his capital, Ghazni, a center of Islamic learning in order to win status within Islam. Subsequently, Muhammad Ghuri in the 1180s led another wave of Islamic Turkish invasions from Afghanistan and dispersed across the Delhi region in northern India. Wars raged between the Indus and Ganges rivers until one by one, all the way to the lower Ganges valley, the fractured kingdoms of the rajas toppled.

The most powerful and enduring of the Turkish Muslim regimes of northern India was the **Delhi Sultanate** (1206–1526), whose rulers strengthened the cultural diversity and tolerance that were already a hallmark of the Indian social order. Sultans recruited local artisans for numerous building projects, and palaces and mosques became displays of Indian architectural tastes adopted by Turkish newcomers. But the sultans did not force their subjects to convert, so that South Asia never became an Islamic-dominant country. Nor did they have an interest in the flourishing commercial life along the Indian coast. So they permitted these areas to develop on their own. Persian Zoroastrian traders settled on the coast around modern-day Mumbai (Bombay). The Malabar coast to the south became the preserve of Arab traders. The Delhi Sultanate was a rich and powerful regime that brought political integration but did not enforce cultural homogeneity.

WHAT WAS INDIA?

During the eleventh, twelfth, and thirteenth centuries India became the most diverse and, in some respects, most tolerant region in Afro-Eurasia. It is from this era that India as an impressive but fragile mosaic of cultures, religions, and ethnicities truly arises. Not even Islam's entry into the region undermined this intense cultural mixing.

When the Turks arrived, the local Hindu population, having had much experience with foreign invaders and immigrants, assimilated these intruders as they had done earlier peoples. And the Turks cooperated. Before long, they thought of themselves as Indians who, however, retained their Islamic beliefs and steppe ways. They continued to wear their distinctive trousers and robes and flaunted their horse-riding skills. At the same time, the local population embraced some of their conquerors' ways, donning the tunics and trousers that characterized Central Asian peoples.

Lodi Gardens. The Lodi Dynasty was the last Delhi sultan dynasty. Lodi Gardens, the cemetery of Lodi sultans, places central Asian Islamic architecture in the Indian landscape, thereby creating a scene of "heaven on the earth."

Diversity and cultural mixing became most visible in the multiple languages that flourished in India. Although the sultans spoke Turkish languages, they regarded Persian literature as a high cultural achievement and made Persian their courtly and administrative language. Meanwhile, most of their Hindu subjects spoke local languages (which had evolved out of Sanskrit) and followed their caste regulations. Despite living under Muslim rulers, the subject populations adhered to their local adaptations of the Hindu faith. Here the rulers did what Muslim rulers did with Christian and Jewish communities living in their midst: they collected the *jizya* tax and permitted communities to worship as they saw fit and to administer their own communal law. Ultimately, Islam proved in India that it did not have to be a conquering religion to prosper. As rulers, sultans granted lands to ulama (Islamic scholars) and Sufi saints, much as Hindu rajas had earlier granted lands to Brahmans (see Chapter 8). These scholars and saints in turn attracted followers to their large estates and forests to enjoy the benefits of membership in a community of believers.

Although newcomers and locals cleaved to separate religious traditions, nonetheless their customs began to merge.

Vishnu. With Buddhism disappearing from India, Buddha was absorbed by the cult of Vishnu and became one of the incarnations of the Hindu god. This late-twelfth-century Angkor Wat–style sculpture from Cambodia shows Vishnu asleep; from his nostril sprouts the lotus that will give birth to Buddha.

Sultans maintained their steppe lifestyle and equestrian culture and took delight in the fact that their subjects adopted Central Asian–style clothing. Within only a few decades, once the subject peoples realized that sultans and Islam were there to stay, they embraced the fashions of the court. In turn, their Muslim rulers understood that ruling effectively meant mastering the local language. Before long, court scholars and Sufi holy men were writing and teaching proficiently in local dialects. Hindustani was the result, an Indian language incorporating Persian and Arabic words; in time, it became the root language of Hindi and Urdu.

This exchange of skills among diverse communities was not confined to governance and religion. It spilled over into the economic arena as well. The foreign artisans who had arrived with their rulers brought silk textiles, rugs, and appliances to irrigate gardens that the leading families of Delhi cherished. Soon the artisans' talents were influencing local manufacturing techniques. Native-born Indians learned from Muslims how to extract long filaments from silk cocoons and were themselves weaving fine silk textiles.

Although Buddhism had been in decline in India for centuries, it, too, became part of the cultural intermixing of these centuries. As Vedic Brahmanism evolved into Hinduism (see Chapter 8), it absorbed many Buddhist doctrines and practices, such as *ahimsa* (non-killing) and vegetarianism. The two religions became so similar that Hindus simply considered the Buddha to be one of their deities—an incarnation of the great god Vishnu. Many Buddhist moral teachings mixed with and became Hindu stories. Artistic motifs reflect a similar process of adoption and adaptation. Goddesses, some beautiful and others fierce, appeared alongside Buddhas, Vishnus, and Sivas as their consorts. The Turkish invaders' destruction of major monasteries in the thirteenth century deprived Buddhism of local spiritual leaders. Lacking dynastic support, Buddhists in India were thus more easily assimilated into the Hindu population or converted to Islam.

SONG CHINA: INSIDERS VERSUS OUTSIDERS

> → *What transformations in communication, education, and commerce promoted a distinct Chinese identity during this era?*

The preeminent world power in 1000 CE was still China, despite its recent turmoil. Once dampened, that turbulence yielded to a long era of stability and splendor—a combination that made China a regional engine of Afro-Eurasian prosperity.

After the end of the Tang dynasty (907 CE), North and South China splintered into regional kingdoms, mostly led by military generals. In 960 CE one of those generals, Zhao Kuangyin, ended the fragmentation. Overthrowing the boy emperor of his own kingdom, Zhao reunified China by conquering regional kingdoms. After his death, his younger brother annexed the remaining kingdoms. Thus, the Song dynasty took over the mandate of heaven.

The following three centuries witnessed many economic and political successes, but northern nomadic tribes kept the Song from completely securing their reign (see Map 10-6 and Map 10-7). Their efforts to deter these warriors were ulti-

mately unsuccessful, and in 1127 the Song lost control of northern China to the Jurchen (ancestors of the Manchu, who would rule China from the seventeenth until the twentieth century). After reconstituting their dynasty in southern China, their empire's most economically robust region, the Song enjoyed another century and a half of rule before falling to the Mongols.

CHINA'S ECONOMIC PROGRESS

China, like India and the Islamic world, participated in Afro-Eurasia's powerful long-distance trade. Indeed, Chinese merchants were as energetic as their Muslim and Indian counterparts. Yet China's commercial successes could not have occurred without the country's strong agrarian base—especially its vast rice fields, which sustained a population that reached 120 million. Agriculture benefited from breakthroughs in metalworking that yielded stronger iron plows, which the Song harnessed to sturdy water buffalo to extend the farming frontier. In 1078, for example, total Song iron production reached between 75,000 and 150,000 tons, roughly the equivalent of European iron production in the early eighteenth century. The Chinese piston bellows were a marvel, and of a size unsurpassed until the nineteenth century.

Manufacturing also flourished. In the early tenth century, Chinese alchemists mixed saltpeter with sulfur and charcoal to produce a product that would burn and could be deployed on the battlefield: gunpowder. Soon, Song entrepreneurs were inventing a remarkable array of incendiary devices that flowed from their mastery of techniques for controlling explosions. Moreover, artisans produced increasingly light, durable, and exquisitely beautiful porcelains. Before long, their porcelain (now called "china") was the envy of all Afro-Eurasia. Also flowing from the artisans' skillful hands were vast amounts of clothing and handicrafts, made from the fibers grown by Song farmers. In effect, the Song Chinese oversaw the world's first manufacturing revolution, producing finished goods on a large scale for consumption far and wide.

MONEY AND INFLATION

Expanding commerce transformed the role of money and its wide circulation. By now the Song government was annually minting nearly two million strings of currency, each containing 1,000 copper coins. In fact, the supply of metal currency could not match the demand. (The result: East Asia's thirst for gold from East Africa.) At the same time, merchant guilds in northwestern Shanxi developed the first letters of exchange, called "flying cash." These letters linked northern traders with their colleagues in the south. Before long,

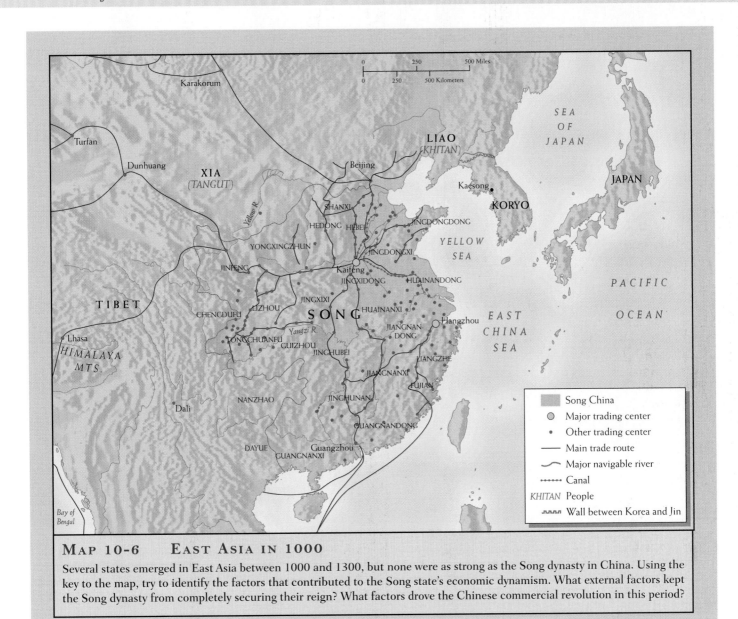

MAP 10-6   EAST ASIA IN 1000

Several states emerged in East Asia between 1000 and 1300, but none were as strong as the Song dynasty in China. Using the key to the map, try to identify the factors that contributed to the Song state's economic dynamism. What external factors kept the Song dynasty from completely securing their reign? What factors drove the Chinese commercial revolution in this period?

printed money had eclipsed coins. Even the government collected more than half its tax revenues in cash rather than grain and cloth. The government also issued more notes to pay its bills—a practice that ultimately contributed to the world's first case of runaway inflation.

NEW ELITES

Song emperors ushered in a period of social and cultural vitality. They established a central bureaucracy of scholar-officials chosen through competitive civil service examinations. Zhao Kuangyin, or Emperor Taizu (r. 960–976 CE), himself

administered the final test for all who had passed the highest-level palace examination. In subsequent dynasties, the emperor was the nation's premier examiner, symbolically demanding oaths of allegiance from successful candidates. By 1100 these ranks of learned men had accumulated sufficient power to become China's new ruling elite.

The introduction of the civil service examination system was crucial to a dramatic shift in power from a hereditary aristocracy to a less wealthy but more highly schooled class of scholar officials. Consider the career of the infamous Northern Song reformer Wang Anshi (1021–1086), who ascended to power from a commoner family outside of Hangzhou in the south. He owed his rise to power to success

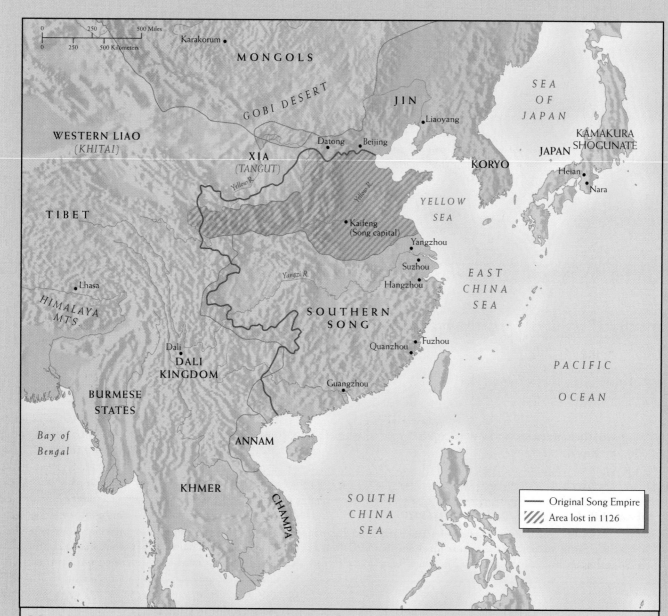

MAP 10-7   EAST ASIA IN 1200

The Song dynasty regularly dealt with "barbarian" neighbors. What were the major "barbarian" tribes during this period? Approximately what percentage of Song China was lost to the Jin in 1126? How did the "barbarian" tribes affect the Han Chinese identity in this period?

in Song state examinations—a not insignificant achievement, for in nearby Fujian province alone, of the roughly 18,000 candidates who gathered triennially to take the provincial examination, over 90 percent failed! After gaining the emperor's ear, Wang eventually challenged the political and cultural influence of the old Tang dynasty elites from the northwest.

NEGOTIATING WITH NEIGHBORS

As the Song flourished, nomads on the outskirts eyed the Chinese successes closely. To the north, Khitan, Tungusic, Tangut, and Jurchen nomadic societies formed their own dynasties and adopted Chinese techniques. Located within the "greater China" established by the Han and Tang dynasties,

Wang Anshi. He owed his rise from a commoner family to a powerful position as a reformer to the Song state examinations.

these non-Chinese nomads saw China proper as an object of conquest.

In military power the Song dynasts were relatively weak: despite their sophisticated weapons, they could not match their steppe foes when the latter united against them. Yes, steel tips improved the arrows that their soldiers shot from their crossbows, and flame throwers and "crouching tiger catapults" sent incendiary bombs streaking into their enemies' ranks; none of these breakthroughs was secret. Warrior neighbors on the steppe mastered the new arts of war more fully than did the Song dynasts themselves.

China's strength as a manufacturing powerhouse made economic diplomacy an option, so the Song relied on "gifts" and generous trade agreements with the borderlanders. For example, after losing militarily to the Khitan Liao dynasty, the Song agreed to make annual payments of 100,000 ounces of silver and 200,000 bolts of silk. The treaty allowed them to live in relative peace for more than a century. Securing peace meant emptying the state coffers and then printing more paper money. The resulting inflation added economic instability to military weakness, making the Song an easy target when Jurchen invaders made their final assault.

WHAT WAS CHINA?

Paradoxically, the increasing exchange between outsiders and insiders within China hardened the lines that divided them and gave residents of China's interior a highly developed sense of themselves as a distinctive people possessing a superior culture. Exchanges with outsiders nurtured a "Chinese" identity among those who considered themselves true insiders and referred to themselves as Han. Improvements in communications and education further intensified this Han sense that they were the authentic Chinese, and that outsiders were radically different. Driven from their ancient homeland in the eleventh century, they grew increasingly suspicious and resentful toward the outsiders living in their midst. They called these outsiders "barbarians" and treated them accordingly.

Chinese and Barbarian. After losing the north, the Han Chinese grew resentful of outsiders. They drew a dividing line between their own agrarian society and the nomadic warriors, calling them "barbarians." Such identities were not fixed, however. Chinese and so-called barbarians were mutually dependent.

Vital in crystallizing this sense of a distinct Chinese identity was print culture. In fact, of all Afro-Eurasian societies in 1300, the Chinese were the most advanced in their use of printing and book publishing and circulation. The Song government used its plentiful supply of paper to print books, especially medical texts, and to distribute calendars. The private publishing industry also expanded. Printing houses throughout the country produced Confucian classics, works on history, philosophical treatises, and literature—all of which figured in the civil examinations. Buddhist publications, too, were available everywhere. The dramatic expansion of the print culture was further emblematic of this great period of stability and splendor in China.

CHINA'S NEIGHBORS ADAPT TO CHANGE

> → *How were Southeast Asia, Japan, and Korea influenced by sustained contact with other regions?*

Feeling the pull of Chinese economic and political gravity, cultures around China's rim consolidated internal political authority to resist being swallowed up, while increasing their commercial transactions.

THE RISE OF WARRIORS IN JAPAN

In Japan, rulers sought to create a stable regime out of feuding warrior factions, so they combined the Heian court's imperial authority with the military power of provincial warriors. At first, entrenched court nobles in the new capital of Heian (today's Kyoto) dominated Japan (see Map 10-7); later, rough-and-ready warriors won possession of the throne to "protect" its sanctity as an object of popular veneration.

The most influential of these ruling groups was the Fujiwara family, ancestors of the Nakatomi kinship group (see Chapter 9). During the tenth and eleventh centuries the Fujiwara presided over Japanese society in what is known as the Heian period (794–1185). They exchanged poetry written in classical Chinese and their native language, and dressed in the elegant costumes that have influenced Japanese taste up to this day.

In time, however, power shifted to elites in the provinces. In a new hierarchy of land tenures, peasant cultivators were at the bottom, managers and estate officials in the middle, and absentee patrons at the top. Soon these large estates controlled more than half of Japan's rice land, and the state's revenue and power plummeted. In the midst of such privatization, Heian aristocrats became politically weak but culturally influential—while the hinterlands provided their economic wealth.

Heian aristocrats disdained the military and even abolished the conscription system used to raise imperial armies. In the provinces, however, trained warriors affiliated with kinship groups gathered strength. Protected by lightweight leather armor, these expert horsemen defended their private estates with remarkable long-range bowmanship and superbly crafted, single-edged long steel swords for close combat. Formidable in warfare, they formed local warrior organizations in the outlying regions and prepared the way for the rise of a warrior or samurai society.

Japan now smoldered with multiple sources of political and cultural power: an endangered aristocracy, an imperial family, and local samurai warriors. It was a combustible mix of refined high culture in the capital versus uncouth warriors in the provinces. Such a mix generated social intrigue in marriage politics and political double-dealing in the capital. Lady Murasaki Shikibu (c. 976–c. 1031), writing in native Japanese script, captured this world of elegant lives and sordid affairs of courtiers and their women in *The Tale of Genji*, Japan's—and possibly the world's—first novel. (See Primary Source: *The Tale of Genji*.)

SOUTHEAST ASIA: A MARITIME MOSAIC

Southeast Asia, like India, now became a crossroads of Afro-Eurasian influences. Its sparse population (probably around 10 million in 1000 CE—tiny compared with that of China and India) was not immune, however, to the foreign influences riding the sea-lanes into the archipelago. Indeed, the Malay Peninsula became home to many trading ports and stopovers for traders shuttling between India and China, because it connected the Bay of Bengal and the Indian Ocean with the South China Sea (see Map 10-8).

"INDO-CHINESE" INFLUENCES   Indian influence had been prominent both on the Asian mainland and in island portions of Southeast Asia since 800 CE, but Islamic expansion into the islands after 1200 gradually superseded these influences. Only Bali and a few other islands far to the east of Malaya preserved their Vedic religious origins. Elsewhere in Java and Sumatra, Islam became the dominant religion. In Vietnam and northern portions of mainland Southeast Asia, Chinese cultural influences and northern schools of Mahayana Buddhism were especially prominent.

Heiji Rebellion. This illustration from the Kamakura period depicts a battle during the Heiji Rebellion, which was fought between rival subjects of the cloistered emperor Go-Shirakawa in 1159. Riding in full armor on horseback, the fighters on both sides are armed with devastating long bows.

Primary Source

THE TALE OF GENJI

Lacking a written language of their own, Heian aristocrats adopted classical Chinese as the official written language while continuing to speak Japanese. Men at the court took great pains to master the Chinese literary forms, but Japanese court ladies were not expected to do so. Lady Murasaki Shikibu, the author of The Tale of Genji, *hid her knowledge of Chinese, fearing that she would be criticized. In the meantime, the Japanese developed a native syllabary (a table of syllables) based on Chinese written graphs. Using this syllabary, Murasaki kept a diary in Japanese that gave vivid accounts of Heian court life. Her story—possibly the world's first novel—relates the adventures of a dashing young courtier named Genji. In the passage below, Genji evidently speaks for Murasaki in explaining why fiction can be as truthful as a work of history in capturing human life and its historical significance.*

Genji . . . smiled, and went on: "But I have a theory of my own about what this art of the novel is, and how it came into being. To begin with, it does not simply consist in the author's telling a story about the adventures of some other person. On the contrary, it happens because the storyteller's own experience of men and things, whether for good or ill— not only what he has passed through himself, but even events which he has only witnessed or been told of—has moved him to an emotion so passionate that he can no longer keep it shut up in his heart. Again and again something in his own life or in that around him will seem to the writer so important that he cannot bear to let it pass into oblivion. There must never come a time, he feels, when men do not know about it. That is my view of how this art arose.

"Clearly then, it is no part of the storyteller's craft to describe only what is good or beautiful. Sometimes, of course, virtue will be his theme, and he may then make such play with it as he will. But he is just as likely to have been struck by numerous examples of vice and folly in the world around him, and about them he has exactly the same feelings as about the pre-eminently good deeds which he encounters: they are more important and must all be garnered in. Thus anything whatsoever may become the subject of a novel, provided only that it happens in this mundane life and not in some fairyland beyond our human ken.

"The outward forms of this art will not of course be everywhere the same. At the court of China and in other foreign lands both the genius of the writers and their actual methods of composition are necessarily very different from ours; and even here in Japan the art of storytelling has in course of time undergone great changes. There will, too, always be a distinction between the lighter and the more serious forms of fiction. . . . So too, I think, may it be said that the art of fiction must not lose our allegiance because, in the pursuit of the main purpose to which I have alluded above, it sets virtue by the side of vice, or mingles wisdom with folly. Viewed in this light the novel is seen to be not, as is usually supposed, a mixture of useful truth with idle invention, but something which at every stage and in every part has a definite and serious purpose."

→ *According to this passage, what motivates an author to write a story (i.e., fiction)?*

→ *Genji feels it is appropriate for a writer to address not only "what is good or beautiful" but also "vice and folly." What explanation does he give? Do you agree?*

SOURCE: *Sources of Japanese Tradition*, compiled by Ryūsaku Tsunoda, Wm. Theodore de Bary, and Donald Keene (New York: Columbia University Press, 1964), vol. 1, pp. 177–79.

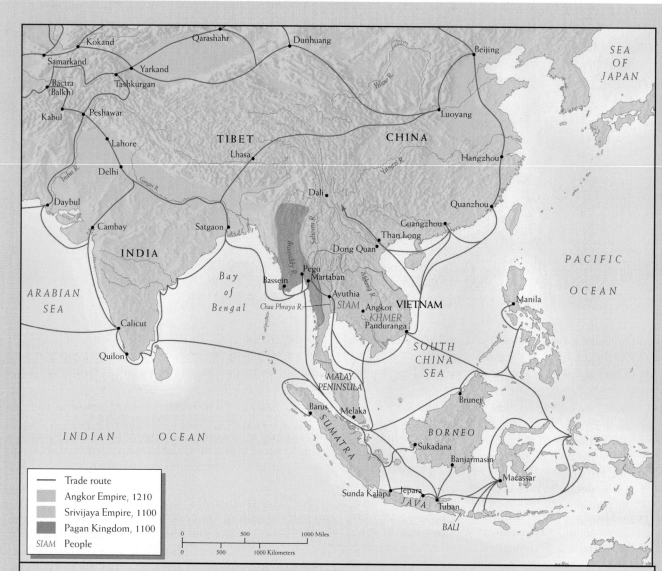

MAP 10-8 SOUTHEAST ASIA, 1000–1300

Cross-cultural influences affected Southeast Asian societies during this period. What makes Southeast Asia unique geographically compared to other regions of the world? Based on the map, why were the kingdoms of Southeast Asia exposed to so many cross-cultural influences? In this chapter, the term "mosaic" describes both South and Southeast Asia. Compare Map 10-5 with this map, and explain how the mosaic of Southeast Asia differed from the mosaic of India.

MAINLAND BUFFER KINGDOMS During this period Cambodian, Burmese, and Thai peoples founded powerful mixed polities along the Mekong, Salween, Chao Phraya, and Irriwaddy river basins of the Asian mainland. Important Vedic and Buddhist kingdoms emerged here as political buffers between the strong states in China and India and brought stability and further commercial prosperity to the region.

Consider the kingdom that ruled Angkor in present-day Cambodia. With their capital in Angkor, the Khmers (889–

1431) created the most powerful and wealthy empire in Southeast Asia. Countless water reservoirs enabled them to flourish on the great plain to the west of the Mekong River after the loss of eastern territories. Public works and magnificent temples dedicated to the revived Vedic gods from India went hand in hand with the earlier influence of Indian Buddhism. Eventually the Khmer kings united adjacent kingdoms and extended Khmer influence to the Thai and Burmese states along the Chaophraya and Irriwaddy rivers.

Angkor Wat. Mistaken by later European explorers as a remnant of Alexander the Great's conquests, the enormous temple complexes built by the Khmer people in Angkor borrowed their intricate layout and stupa (a moundlike structure containing religious relics) architecture from the Brahmanist Indian temples of the time. As the capital, Angkor was a microcosm of the world for the Khmer, who aspired to represent the macrocosm of the universe in the magnificence of Angkor's buildings and their geometric layout.

One of the greatest temple complexes in Angkor exemplified the Khmers' heavy borrowing from Vedic Indian architecture. Angkor aspired to represent the universe in the magnificence of its buildings. As signs of the ruler's power, the pagodas, pyramids, and terra-cotta friezes (ornamented walls) presented the life of the gods on earth. The crowning structure of the royal palace was the magnificent temple of **Angkor Wat,** possibly the largest religious structure ever built. In ornate detail and with great artistry, its buildings and statues represented the revival of the Hindu pantheon within the Khmer royal state. Far less Buddhist influence is visible.

 CHRISTIAN EUROPE

> → *How did Christianity produce a distinct identity among the diverse peoples of Europe?*

In the far western corner of Afro-Eurasia, people were building a culture revealingly different. Although their numbers were small compared with the rest of Afro-Eurasia in 1000 CE (36 million in Europe, compared to 80 million in India and 120 million in China), their population would soar to 80 million before the arrival of the Black Death in the fourteenth century.

This was a region of contrasts. On the one hand, the period 1000–1300 witnessed an intense localization of politics because there was no successor to the Roman Empire or Charlemagne's (see Chapter 9). On the other hand, the territory united under a shared sense of its place in the world. Indeed, some inhabitants even began to believe in the existence of something called "Europe" and increasingly referred to themselves as "Europeans" (see Map 10-9).

WESTERN AND NORTHERN EUROPE

The collapse of Charlemagne's empire had exposed much of northern Europe to invasion, principally from the Vikings, and left the peasantry with no central authority to protect them from local warlords. Armed with deadly weapons, these strongmen collected taxes, imposed forced labor, and became the unchallenged rulers of society. Within this growing warrior aristocracy, northern France led the way. The Franks (later called Frenchmen) were the trendsetters of eleventh- and twelfth-century western Europe.

The most important change was the peasantry's subjugation to the knightly class. Previously, well-to-do peasants had carried arms as "free" men. The moment the farmers lost the right to carry arms, they were no longer free. They slipped back to being mere agricultural laborers. Each peasant toiled under the authority of a lord, who controlled every detail of his or her life. This was the basis of a system known as **feudalism.**

Assured of control of the peasantry, feudal lords watched over an agrarian breakthrough—which fueled a commercial transformation that drew Europe into the rest of the global trading networks. Lordly protection and more advanced metal tools like axes and plows, combined with heavier livestock to pull plows through the root-infested sods of northern

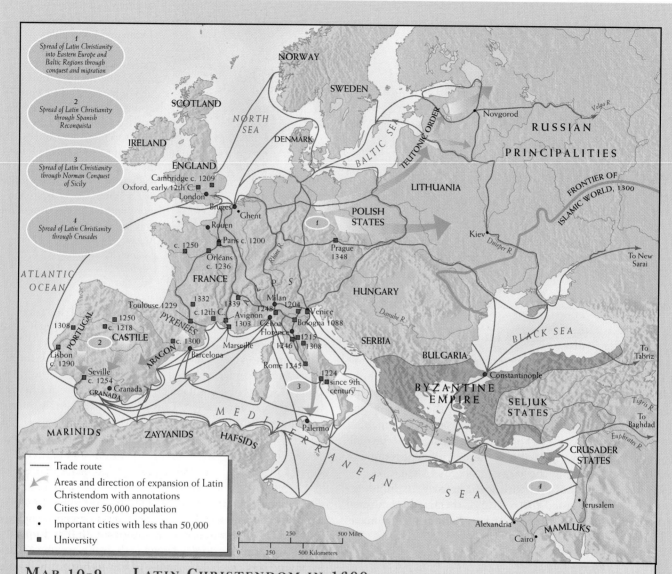

Trade route

Areas and direction of expansion of Latin Christendom with annotations

• **Cities over 50,000 population**

· **Important cities with less than 50,000**

■ **University**

1 — Spread of Latin Christianity into Eastern Europe and Baltic Regions through conquest and migration

2 — Spread of Latin Christianity through Spanish Reconquista

3 — Spread of Latin Christianity through Norman Conquest of Sicily

4 — Spread of Latin Christianity through Crusades

MAP 10-9   LATIN CHRISTENDOM IN 1300

Catholic Europe expanded geographically and integrated culturally during this era. According to this map, into what areas did western Christendom successfully expand? What factors contributed to the growth of a widespread common culture and shared ideas? How did long-distance trade shape the history of the region during this time?

Europe, led to massive deforestation. Above this clearing activity stood the castle. Its threatening presence ensured that the peasantry stayed within range of the collector of rents for the lords and of tithes (shares of crops, earmarked as "donations") for the church. In this blunt way, "feudalism" harnessed agrarian energy to its own needs. The population of western Europe as a whole leaped forward, most spectacularly in the north. As a result, northern Europe (from England to Poland) ceased to be an underdeveloped "barbarian" appendage of the Mediterranean.

EASTERN EUROPE

Nowhere did pioneering peasants develop more land than in the wide-open spaces of eastern Europe, the region's land of opportunity. Between 1100 and 1200, some 200,000 farmers emigrated from Flanders (modern Belgium), Holland, and northern Germany into eastern frontiers. Well-watered landscapes, covered with vast forests, filled up what are now Poland, the Czech Republic, Hungary, and the Baltic states. "Little Europes," whose castles, churches, and towns echoed

The Bayeux Tapestry. This tapestry was prepared by a queen and her ladies to celebrate the victories of William, known as the Conqueror because of his successful invasion of England in 1066. It shows the fascination of the entire "feudal" class, even women, with war on which they depended—great horses, tightly meshed chain mail, long shields, and the stirrups that made such cavalry warfare possible.

the landscape of France, now replaced economies that had been based on gathering honey, hunting, and the slave trade. For a thousand miles along the Baltic Sea, forest clearings dotted with new farmsteads and small towns edged inward from the coast up the river valleys.

The social structure here was a marriage of convenience between migrating peasants and local elites. The area offered the promise of freedom from the feudal lords' arbitrary justice and imposition of forced labor. Even the harsh landscape of the eastern Baltic (where the sea froze every year and impenetrable forests blocked settlers from the coast) was preferable to life in the feudal west. For their part, the elites of eastern Europe—the nobility of Poland, Bohemia, and Hungary and the princes of the Baltic—wished to live well, in the "French"

Olavinlinna Castle. This castle in Finland was the easternmost extension of a "western," feudal style of rule through great castles. It was built at the very end of the Baltic, to keep away the Russians of Novgorod.

style. But they could do so only if they attracted manpower to their lands by offering newcomers a liberty that they had no hope of enjoying in the west.

THE RUSSIAN LANDS

In Russian lands, western settlers and knights met an eastern brand of Christian devotion. This world looked toward Byzantium, not Rome. Russia was a giant borderland between the steppes of Eurasia and the booming feudalisms of Europe. Its cities lay at the crossroads of overland trade and migration, and Kiev became one of the region's greatest cities. Standing on a bluff above the Dnieper River, it straddled newly opened trade routes. With a population exceeding 20,000, including merchants from eastern and western Europe and the Middle East, Kiev was larger than Paris—larger even than the much-diminished city of Rome.

Kiev looked south to the Black Sea and to Constantinople. Under Iaroslav the Wise (1016–1054), it became a small-scale Constantinople on the Dnieper. A stone church called St. Sophia stood (as in Constantinople) beside the imperial palace. Indeed, with its distinctive "Byzantine" domes, it was a miniature Hagia Sophia (see Chapter 8). Its highest dome towered a hundred feet above the floor, and its splendid mosaics depicting Byzantine saints echoed the religious art of Constantinople. But the message was political as well, for the ruler of Kiev was cast in the mold of the emperor of Constantinople. He now took the title *tsar* from the ancient Roman name given to the emperor, Caesar. From this time onward, *tsar* was the title of rulers in Russia.

The Russian form of Christianity replicated the Byzantine style of churches all along the great rivers leading to the trading cities of the north and northeast. These were not agrarian centers, but hubs of expanding long-distance trade.

Hagia Sophia, Novgorod.
The cathedral of Novgorod (as that of Kiev) was called Hagia Sophia. It was a deliberate imitation of the Hagia Sophia of Constantinople, showing Russia's roots in a glorious Roman/Byzantine past that had nothing to do with western Europe.

(See Primary Source: The Birch Bark Letters of Novgorod.) Each city became a small-scale Kiev, and thus a smaller-scale echo of Constantinople. The Orthodox religion looked to Byzantium's Hagia Sophia rather than the Catholic faith associated with the popes in Rome. Russian Christianity remained the Christianity of a borderland—vivid oases of high culture set against the backdrop of vast forests and widely scattered settlements.

WHAT WAS CHRISTIAN EUROPE?

In this era Catholicism became a universalizing faith that transformed the region becoming known as "Europe." The Christianity of post-Roman Europe had been a religion of monks, and its most dynamic centers were great monasteries. Members of the laity were expected to revere and support their monks, nuns, and clergy, but not to imitate them. By 1200, all this had changed. The internal colonization of western Europe—the clearing of woods and founding of villages—ensured that parish churches arose in all but the wildest landscapes. Their spires were visible and their bells were audible from one valley to the next. Church graveyards were the only places where good Christians could be buried; criminals' and outlaws' bodies piled up in "heathen" graves outside the cemetery walls. Even the bones of the believers helped make Europe Christian.

Now the clergy reached more deeply into the private lives of the laity. Marriage and divorce, previously considered family matters, became a full-time preoccupation of the church. And sin was no longer an offense that just "happened"; it was

a matter that every person could do something about. Soon, regular confession to a priest became obligatory for all Catholic, western Christians. The followers of Francis of Assisi (1182–1226) emerged as an order of preachers who brought a message of repentance. They did not tell their audiences to enter the monastery (as would have been the case in the early Middle Ages). Instead, their listeners were to weep, confess their sins to local priests, and strive to be better Christians. Franciscans instilled in the hearts of all believers a Europe-wide Catholicism based on daily remorse and daily contemplation of the sufferings of Christ and his mother, Mary. From Ireland to Riga and Budapest, Catholic Christians came to share a common piety.

UNIVERSITIES AND INTELLECTUALS Vital to the creation of Europe's Christian identity was the emergence of universities, for it was during this era that Europe acquired its first class of intellectuals. Since the late twelfth century, scholars had gathered in Paris, where they formed a *universitas*—a term borrowed from merchant communities, where it denoted a type of union. Those who belonged to the *universitas* enjoyed protection by their fellows and freedom to continue their trade. Similarly protected by their own "union," the scholars of Paris began wrestling with the new learning from Arab lands. When the bishop of Paris forbade this undertaking, they simply moved to the Left Bank of the Seine, so as to place the river between themselves and the bishop's officials, who lived around the cathedral of Notre Dame.

The scholars' ability to organize themselves gave them an advantage that their Arab contemporaries lacked. For all his

THE BIRCH BARK LETTERS OF NOVGOROD

The city of Novgorod was a vibrant trading center with a diverse population. From 1951 onward, Russian archaeologists in Novgorod have excavated almost a thousand letters and accounts scratched on birch bark and preserved in the sodden, frequently frozen ground. Reading them, we realize how timeless people's basic concerns can be.

First, we meet the merchants. Many letters are notes by creditors of the debts owed to them by trading partners. The sums are often expressed in precious animal furs. They contain advice to relatives or to partners in other cities:

> Giorgii sends his respects to his father and mother: Sell the house and come here to Smolensk or to Kiev: for the bread is cheap there.

Then we meet neighborhood disputes:

> From Anna to Klemiata: Help me, my lord brother, in my matter with Konstantin. . . . [For I asked him,] "Why have you been so angry with my sister and her daughter. You called her a cow and her daughter a whore. And now Fedor has thrown them both out of the house."

There are even glimpses of real love. A secret marriage is planned:

> Mikiti to Ulianitza: Come to me. I love you, and you me. Ignato will act as witness.

And a poignant note from a woman was discovered in 1993:

> I have written to you three times. What is it that you hold against me, that you did not come to see me this Sunday? I regarded you as I would my own brother. Did I really offend you by that which I sent to you? If you had been pleased you would have torn yourself away from company and come to me. Write to me. If in my clumsiness I have offended you and you should spurn me, then let God be my judge. I love you.

→ *What does the range of people writing on birch bark tell us about these people?*
→ *Think of the messages you send to friends and relatives today. Even if texting and e-mailing seem centuries distant from writing on birch bark, can you relate in any way to these ancient letter-writers?*

SOURCE: A. V. Artsikhovskii and V. I. Borkovski, *Novgorodskie Gramoty na Bereste*, 11 vols. (Moscow: Izd-vo Akademii nauk SSSR, 1951–2004), document nos. 424, 531, 377, and 752.

---

genius, Ibn Rushd had to spend his life courting the favor of individual monarchs to protect him from conservative fellow Muslims, who frequently burned his books. Ironically, European scholars congregating in Paris could quietly absorb the most persuasive elements of Arabic thought, like Ibn Rushd's. Yet they endeavored to prove that Christianity was the only religion that fully met the aspirations of all rational human beings. Such was the message of the great intellectual Thomas Aquinas, who wrote *Summa contra Gentiles* (Summary of Christian Belief against Non-Christians) in 1264.

The Europe of 1300 was more culturally unified than in previous centuries. It was permeated by Catholicism, and its leading intellectuals extolled the virtues of Christian learning. Such a confident region was not, however, a tolerant place for heretics, Jews, or Muslims.

CHRISTIAN EUROPE ON THE MOVE: THE CRUSADES AND IBERIA

By the tenth and eleventh centuries, western Christianity was on the move, spreading into Scandinavia, southern Italy, the Baltic, and eastern Europe. Its ambitions to reconquer Spain and Portugal (which had been under Islamic control since the eighth century CE) demonstrated one of the effects of feudal power: the lords' self-confidence, their belief in their military capability, and their pious sense of destiny were all inflated. Besides, the wealth of the east was irresistible to those whose piety entwined with an appetite for plunder. Yet the two Christendoms formed an uneasy alliance to roll back the expanding frontiers of Islam. The result: Europeans zealously took war outside their own borders.

Global Connections & Disconnections

THE CRUSADES FROM DUAL PERSPECTIVES

In 1095, Pope Urban II called for the First Crusade in the following words:

> Oh, race of Franks, race from across the mountains, race chosen and beloved by God, as shines forth in very many of your works, set apart from all nations by the situation of your country, as well as by your Catholic faith and the honor of the Holy Church! To you our discourse is addressed, and for you our exhortation is intended. We wish you to know what a grievous cause has led us to your country, what peril, threatening you and all the faithful, has brought us.

The "grievous cause" was the occupation of the Holy City of Jerusalem by the Islamic empire. Formed within the complex relationship between the Byzantine Empire and the western Christian papacy and kingdoms of Europe, the religious motivation behind the Crusades became the subject of many literary renditions of the tumultuous events. It also generated emotionally stirring and polemical (argumentative) writing, depicting either a Muslim or Christian enemy (depending on the work's author).

Polemics are often passionate, harsh, and emotional. They also inspire and reinforce the conviction of fellow believers, with little concern for accuracy. Thus authors of polemic in the time of the Crusades were usually too biased or too misinformed to present accurate portraits of their enemies. But occasionally, firsthand accounts in the form of chronicles and histories offer us unique glimpses into Christian-Muslim relations in the age of the Crusades.

Consider Usāmah ibn Munqidh (1095–1188), the learned ruler of the city of Shaizar in western Syria. Skirmishes, truces, and the ransoming of prisoners were part of his daily life, and Usāmah socialized with his Frankish neighbors as much as he fought with them. He offers a dismissive opinion of his enemies. Basically, they struck him as "animals possessing the virtues of courage and fighting, but nothing else." In particular, their medical practice appalled him. More strange, the Franks allowed their wives to walk about freely and to talk to strangers unaccompanied by male guardians. How could men be at once so brave and yet so lacking in a proper, Arab sense of honor, which would lead a man to protect his women? Unlike other Muslim authors of his time, however, Usāmah does not refer to the Franks in derogatory terms such as "infidels" or "devils." In fact, he occasionally refers to some of them as his companions and writes of a Frank who called him "my brother" (*An Arab-Syrian Gentleman and Warrior in the Time of the Crusades*, 16).

CRUSADES In the late eleventh century, western Europeans launched a wave of attacks known as the **Crusades.** The First Crusade began in 1095, when Pope Urban II appealed to the warrior nobility of France to put their violence to good use: they should combine their role as pilgrims to Jerusalem with that of soldiers, and free Jerusalem from Muslim rule. What the clergy proposed was a novel kind of war. Whereas previously war had been a dirty business and a source of sin, now the clergy told the knights that good and just wars were possible. Such wars could cancel out the sins of those who waged them.

Starting in 1097, an armed host of around 60,000, men moved all the way from northwestern Europe to Jerusalem. This was a huge crowd. But it was divided. Knights in heavy armor led, as they did in Europe. But in the eastern Mediterranean they depended on poor masses who joined the movement to help besiege cities and construct a network of castles as the Christian knights drove their frontier forward. Later Crusaders brought their wives, especially those from the upper class. As in many colonial societies away from the homeland, these women felt freer. Eleanor of Aquitaine, for example, led her own army. Also, queens were crucial in opening up to the local populations. Consider the Armenian queen, Melisende (r. 1131–1152): regarded as wise and experienced in affairs of the state, she was popular with local Christians. As a result, the society of the Crusader states remained more open to women and the lower classes than in Europe. Above all, the Crusades could not have happened without the sailors and merchants of Italy. It was the fleets of Venice, Genoa, and Pisa that transported the later Crusaders and supplied their kingdom.

Christian authors had similar interests in documenting the customs of their enemies in battle. Jean de Joinville (1224/1225–1317) was a chronicler of medieval France. During one crusade, while in the service of the king, Joinville had occasion to note the Muslims' social behavior:

> Whenever the Sultan was in the camp, the men of the personal Guard were quartered all round his lodging, and appointed to guard his person. At the door of the Sultan's lodging there was a little tent for the Sultan's door-keepers, and for his musicians, who had Arabian horns and drums and kettledrums; and they used to make such a din at daybreak and at nightfall that people near them could not hear one another speak, and that they could be heard plainly all through the camp. The musicians never dared sound their instruments in the daytime unless by the order of the Chief of the Guard. Thus it was, that whenever the Sultan had a proclamation to make he used to send for the Chief of the Guard, and give him the order; and then the Chief would cause all the Sultan's instruments to be sounded; and thereupon all the host would come to hear the Sultan's commands.

Although scholars regard such literary renditions with caution, they are useful for gleaning personal details that other types of works omit. The colorful accounts by authors such as Usāmah ibn Munqidh and Joinville are invaluable resources for the social history of the Crusaders.

Jeane de Joinville. Joinville dictating his Memoir of St. Louis, in which he described the Seventh Crusade.

There were five Crusades in all, spread out over two centuries. None of the coalitions, in the end, created permanent Christian kingdoms in the lands they "reconquered." Only a small proportion of Crusaders remained in southwest Asia, and those who did met their match in Muslim armies. (See Global Connections & Disconnections: The Crusades from Dual Perspectives.) Part of the problem was that few Crusaders had any intention of becoming colonists. Only a small proportion remained to defend the Kingdom of Jerusalem after the First Crusade. Most knights returned home, their epic pilgrimage completed. The remaining fragile network of Crusader lordships could barely threaten the Islamic heartlands.

Muslim leaders, however, did not see the Frankish knights as a threat. For them, the Crusades were irrelevant. And as far as the average Muslim of the region was concerned, the Crusaders hardly mattered at all. Jerusalem and Palestine had always been fringe areas in the Middle East. Real prosperity and the capital cities of Muslim kingdoms lay inland, away from the coast—at Cairo, Damascus, and Baghdad. The assaults' long-term effect was to harden Muslim feelings against the Franks and the millions of non-Western Christians who had previously lived peacefully in Egypt and Syria. Muslims viewed the Crusaders as brave but uncivilized warriors. A neighboring Muslim wrote: "The Franks possess none of the virtues of men except courage. . . . Nobody counts for them except knights." Their lack of medical knowledge shocked this observer. He noted that they would rather chop off a man's leg than administer ointments, as Muslim doctors would have advised.

Other campaigns of Christian expansion were more successful. Consider the Spanish driving the Muslims out of the

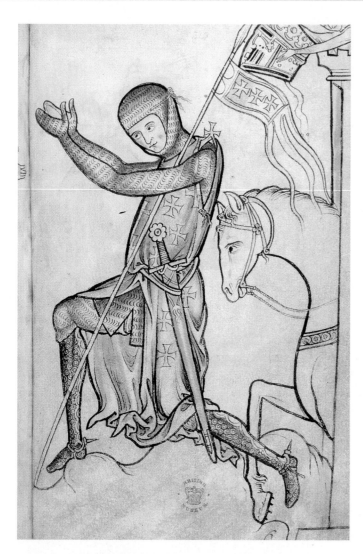

Crusader. Kneeling, this Crusader promises to serve God (as he would serve a feudal lord) by going to fight on a Crusade (as he would fight for any lord to whom he had sworn loyalty). The two kinds of loyalty—to God and to one's lord—were deliberately confused in Crusader ideology. Both were about war. But fighting for God was unambiguously good, while fighting for a lord was not always so clear-cut.

Iberian Peninsula. Beginning with the capture of Toledo in 1061, the Christian kings of northern Spain (who could count on support from Christian neighbors across the Pyrenees) slowly pushed back the Muslims. Eventually they reached the heart of Andalusia and conquered Seville, adding more than 100,000 square miles of territory to Christian Europe. Another force from northern France crossed Italy to conquer Muslim-held Sicily, ensuring Christian rule in the strategically located mid-Mediterranean island. These two conquests—not the Crusaders' fragile foothold at the edge of the Middle East—turned the tide in relations between Christian and Muslim power.

 THE AMERICAS

> → *Where did societies in the Americas demonstrate strong commercial expansionist impulses?*

During this period, the Americas were untouched by the connections reverberating across Afro-Eurasia. After all, navigators still could not cross the large oceans that separated the Americas from other lands. Yet, here, too, commercial and expansionist impulses fostered closer contact among peoples who lived there.

ANDEAN STATES

Growth and prosperity in the Andean region gave rise to South America's first empire. Known as the Chimú Empire, it developed early in the second millennium in the fertile Moche Valley bordering the Pacific Ocean (see Map 10-10). Ultimately the Moche people expanded their influence across numerous valleys and ecological zones, from pastoral highlands to rich valley floodplains to the fecund fishing grounds of the Pacific Coast. As their geographical reach grew, so did their wealth. The Chimú regime lasted until Incan armies invaded in the 1460s and incorporated the Pacific state into their own immense empire.

A THRIVING LOWLAND ECONOMY   The Chimú economy was successful because it was highly commercialized. Agriculture was its base, and complex irrigation systems turned the arid coast into a string of fertile oases capable of feeding an increasingly dispersed population. Cotton became a lucrative export to distant markets along the Andes. Parades of llamas and porters lugged these commodities up and down the steep mountain chains that are the spine of South America. As in China, a well-trained bureaucracy oversaw the construction and maintenance of canals, with a hierarchy of provincial administrators watching over commercial hinterlands.

Between 850 and 900 CE, the Moche peoples founded their biggest city, Chan Chan, with a core population of 30,000 inhabitants. A sprawling walled metropolis, covering nearly ten square miles with extensive roads circulating through neighborhoods, it boasted ten huge palaces at its center. Protected by thick walls thirty feet high, these opulent residence halls bespoke the rulers' power. Within the compound, emperors erected mortuary monuments for storing their accumulated riches: fine cloth, gold and silver objects, splendid *Spondylus* shells, and other luxury goods. Around the compound spread neighborhoods for nobles and artisans; farther out stood rows of commoners' houses.

AN INVENTIVE HIGH-LAND STATE The Andes also saw its first highland empires during this period. On the shores of the plateau lake Titicaca, the people of Tiahuanaco forged a high-altitude state. Though neither as large nor as wealthy as the Chimú Empire, its residents converted the inhospitable highlands into an environment where farmers and herders thrived. There is evidence of long-distance trade with neighbors in semitropical valleys, and even signs of highlanders migrating to the lowlands to produce agrarian staples for their kin in the mountains. Dried fish and cotton came from the coast; fruits and vegetables came from lowland valleys. Trade sustained an enormous urban population of up to 115,000 people. Looming over the skyline of Tiahuanaco was an imposing pyramid of massive sandstone blocks. Its advanced engineering system conveyed water to the summit, from which an imitation rainfall coursed down the carefully carved sides—an awesome spectacle of engineering prowess in such an arid region.

CONNECTIONS TO THE NORTH

Additional hubs of regional trade developed farther north, showing once again that even in areas of relative geographic isolation, cultures could flourish and interact within expanding regional spheres. The Toltecs and the Cahokians are superb examples.

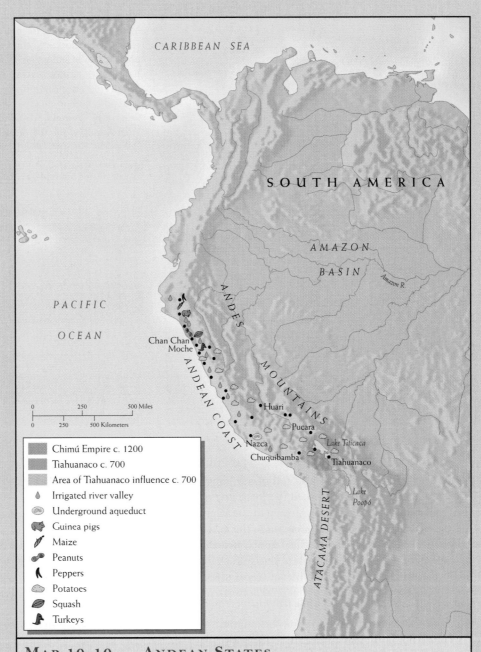

MAP 10-10   ANDEAN STATES

Although the Andes region of South America was isolated from Afro-Eurasian developments before 1500, it was not stagnant. Indeed, political and cultural integration brought the peoples of this region closer together. Where are the areas of the Chimú Empire and Tiahuanaco influence on the map? What kinds of ecological niches did they govern? According to your reading, how did each polity encourage greater cultural and economic integration?

Andean States. The image to the left shows what remains of Chan Chan. The city covered fifteen square miles and was divided into neighborhoods for nobles, artisans, and commoners, with the elites living closest to the hub of governmental and spiritual power. The buildings of Tiahuanaco (below) were made of giant, hand-hewn stones assembled without mortar. Engineers had not discovered the principle of curved arches and keystones and instead relied on massive slabs atop gateways. Gateways were important symbolic features, for they were places where people acknowledged the importance of sun and moon gods.

THE TOLTECS IN MESOAMERICA By 1000 CE, Mesoamerica had seen the rise and fall of several complex societies. Caravans of porters worked the intricate roads that connected the coast of the Gulf of Mexico to the Pacific, and the southern lowlands of Central America to the arid regions of modern Texas (see Map 10-11). The region's heartland was the rich valley of central Mexico. Here the Toltecs filled the political vacuum left by the decline of Teotihuacán (see Chapter 8) and tapped into the commercial network radiating from the valley.

The Toltecs were a combination of migrant groups, refugees from the south, and farmers from the north. They settled northwest of Teotihuacán as the city waned, making their capital at Tula. They relied on a maize-based economy supplemented by beans, squash, and dog, deer, and rabbit meat. Their rulers, however, made sure that enterprising merchants provided them with status goods such as ornamental pottery, rare shells and stones, and precious skins and feathers.

Tula was a commercial hub, a political capital, and a ceremonial center. While its layout differed from Teotihuacán's, many features revealed borrowings from other Mesoamerican peoples. Temples consisted of giant pyramids topped by colossal stone soldiers, and ball courts where subjects and conquered peoples alike played their ritual sport were ubiquitous. The architecture and monumental art bespoke the mixed and migratory origins of the Toltecs: a combination of Mayan and Teotihuacáno influences. At its height, the Toltec capital teemed with 60,000 people—a huge metropolis by contemporary European standards.

THE CAHOKIANS IN NORTH AMERICA Cities took shape at the hubs of trading networks all across North America. The largest was **Cahokia,** along the Mississippi River near modern-day East St. Louis. A city of about 15,000, it approximated the size of London at the time. Farmers and hunters settled in the region around 600 CE, attracted by its rich soil, its woodlands for fuel and game, and its access to the trading artery of the Mississippi. Eventually, fields of maize and other crops fanned out toward the horizon. The hoe replaced the trusty digging stick, and satellite towns erected granaries to hold the increased yields.

Now Cahokia became a commercial center for regional and long-distance trade. The hinterlands produced staples for Cahokia's urban consumers, and in return its crafts rode inland on the backs of porters and to distant markets in canoes. The city's woven fabrics and ceramics were especially desirable. In exchange, traders brought mica from the Appalachian Mountains, seashells and sharks' teeth from the Gulf of Mexico, and copper from the upper Great Lakes. Indeed, Cahokia became more than an importer and exporter:

→ *Where did societies in the Americas demonstrate strong commercial expansionist impulses?*

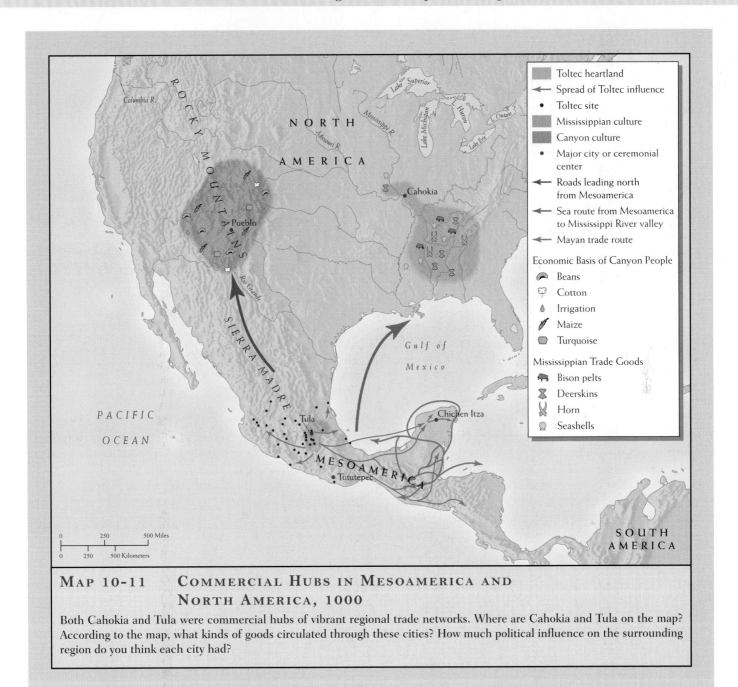

MAP 10-11   COMMERCIAL HUBS IN MESOAMERICA AND NORTH AMERICA, 1000

Both Cahokia and Tula were commercial hubs of vibrant regional trade networks. Where are Cahokia and Tula on the map? According to the map, what kinds of goods circulated through these cities? How much political influence on the surrounding region do you think each city had?

it was the entrepôt for an entire regional network trafficking in salt, tools, pottery, woven stuffs, jewelry, and ceremonial goods.

Dominating Cahokia's urban landscape were enormous mounds (thus the nickname "mound people"). These earthen monuments reveal a sophisticated design and careful maintenance: for example, their builders applied layers of sand and clay to prevent the foundations from drying and cracking. It was from these artificial hills that the people paid homage to spiritual forces. Of course, building this kind of infra-

structure without draft animals, hydraulic tools, or even wheels was labor-intensive, so the Cahokians recruited neighboring people to help. A palisade around the city protected the metropolis from marauders.

Ultimately the city outgrew its environment, and its success bred its downfall. As woodlands fell to the axe and arable soil lost nutrients, timber and food became scarce. Because the city lacked a means of transportation to ship bulky items over long distances (in contrast to the sturdy dhows of the Arabian Sea and the bulky junks of the China Sea), its river

Toltec Temple. Tula, the capital of the Toltec Empire, carried on the Mesoamerican tradition of locating ceremonial architecture at the center of the city. The Pyramid of the Morning Star cast its shadow over all other buildings. And above them stood columns of the Atlantes, carved Toltec god-warriors, the figurative pillars of the empire itself. The walls of this pyramid were likely embellished with images of snakes and skulls. The north face of the pyramid has the image of a snake devouring a human.

canoes could carry only limited cargoes. Thus Cahokia's commercial networks met their limits. When the creeks that fed its water system could not keep up with demand, engineers changed their course, but to no avail. By 1350 the city was practically empty. Nevertheless, Cahokia was a remarkable entrepôt while it lasted. It represented the growing networks of trade and migration, and the ability of North Americans to organize vibrant commercial societies.

Cahokia Mounds. This is all that is left of what was once a large city organized around temple mounds in what today is Illinois. The largest of the temples, known as Monks' Mound, was likely a burial site, with four separate terraces for crowds to gather. Centuries of neglect and erosion have taken their toll on what was once the largest human-made earthen mound in North America.

THE MONGOL TRANSFORMATION OF AFRO-EURASIA

> → *How did Mongol conquests affect cross-cultural contacts and regional development in Afro-Eurasia?*

The world's sea-lanes grew crowded with ships; ports buzzed with activity. Commercial networks were clearly one way to integrate the world. But just as long-distance trade connected people, so could conquerors—as we have seen throughout the history of the world. Now, transformative conquerors came from the Inner Eurasian steppes, the same place that centuries earlier had unleashed horse-riding warriors such as the Xiongnu (see Chapters 6 and 7).

Like the Xiongnu and the Kushans before them, the Mongols not only conquered but intensified trade and cultural exchange. By consolidating a latticework of states across northern and central Asia, they created an empire that straddled east and west (see Map 10-12). It was unstable and not as durable as other dynasties. It did not even have a shared faith; the mother of the conquering emperors, Hulagu and Kubilai Khan, was a devout Christian, reflecting Nestorian missionaries' centuries-long efforts to convert the animistic nomads. Many Europeans prayed that the entire empire would convert. But it did not; the Mongols were a religious patchwork of Afro-Eurasian belief systems. Yet they brought far-flung parts of the world together as they conquered territories much larger than their own.

WHO WERE THE MONGOLS?

The **Mongols** were a combination of forest and prairie peoples. Residing in circular, felt-covered tents, which they shared with some of their animals, they lived by hunting and livestock herding. They changed campgrounds with the seasons. Life on the steppes was such a constant struggle that only the strong survived. Their food, primarily animal products, provided high levels of protein, which built up their muscle mass and their strength. Always on the march, their society resembled a perpetual standing army with bands of well-disciplined military units led by commanders chosen for their skill.

MILITARY SKILLS   Mongol archers were uniquely skilled. Wielding heavy compound bows made of sinew, wood, and horns, they were deadly accurate at over 200 yards—even at full gallop. Their small but sturdy horses, capable of withstanding extreme cold, bore saddles with high supports in front and back, enabling the warriors to maneuver at high speeds. With their feet secure in iron stirrups, the archers could rise in their saddles to aim their arrows without stopping. These expert horsemen often remained in the saddle all day and night, even sleeping while their horses continued on. Each warrior kept many horses, replacing tired mounts with fresh ones so that the armies could cover up to seventy miles per day.

Mongol Warriors. This miniature painting is one of the illustrations for *History* by Rashid al Din, the most outstanding scholar under the Mongol regimes. Note the relatively small horses and strong bows used by the Mongol soldiers.

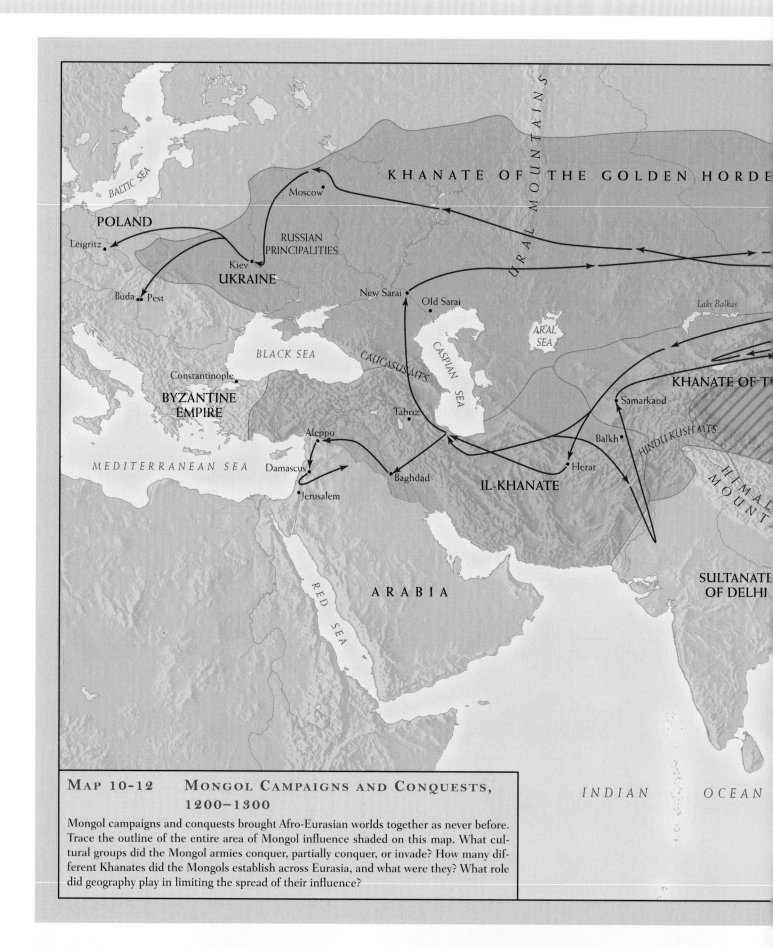

BALTIC SEA
POLAND
Leigritz
Moscow
RUSSIAN
PRINCIPALITIES
Kiev
UKRAINE
Buda • Pest
BLACK SEA
Constantinople
BYZANTINE
EMPIRE
Aleppo
MEDITERRANEAN SEA
Damascus
Jerusalem
Baghdad
RED SEA
ARABIA
KHANATE OF THE GOLDEN HORDE
URAL MOUNTAINS
New Sarai
Old Sarai
ARAL SEA
Lake Balkas
CAUCASUS MTS.
CASPIAN SEA
Tabriz
IL-KHANATE
Samarkand
Balkh
Herat
HINDU KUSH MTS.
KHANATE OF T
HIMAL
MOUNTA
SULTANATE
OF DELHI
INDIAN OCEAN

MAP 10-12   MONGOL CAMPAIGNS AND CONQUESTS, 1200–1300

Mongol campaigns and conquests brought Afro-Eurasian worlds together as never before. Trace the outline of the entire area of Mongol influence shaded on this map. What cultural groups did the Mongol armies conquer, partially conquer, or invade? How many different Khanates did the Mongols establish across Eurasia, and what were they? What role did geography play in limiting the spread of their influence?

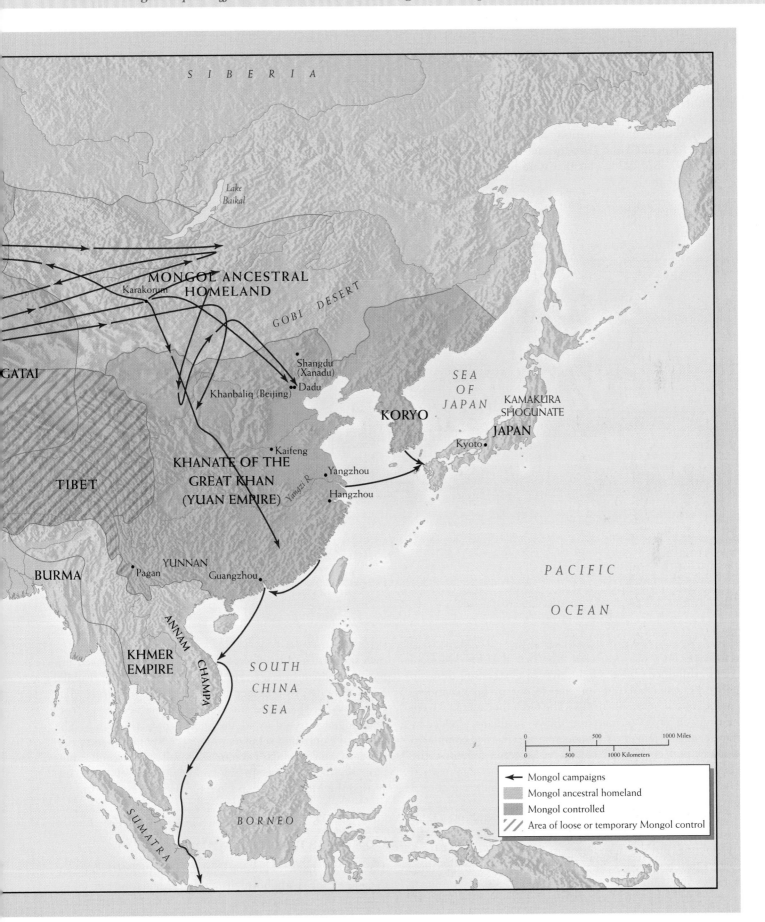

Global Connections & Disconnections

THE TRAVELS OF MARCO POLO AND IBN BATTUTA

The most famous of the thirteenth- and fourteenth-century travelers were Marco Polo and Ibn Battuta. They encountered a world linked by trade routes that often had as their ultimate destination the imperial court of the Great Khan in China. These two men, and less celebrated travelers, observed worlds that were highly localized and yet culturally unified.

In 1271, Marco Polo (1254–1324), the son of an enterprising Venetian merchant, set out with his father and uncle on a journey to East Asia. Making their way along the fabled Silk Road across central Asia, the Polos arrived in Xanadu, the summer capital of the Mongol Empire, after a three-and-a-half-year journey. There they remained for more than two decades. When they returned

Marco Polo. This medieval painting shows the caravan of Marco Polo's father and uncle crossing Asia.

KINSHIP NETWORKS AND SOCIAL ROLES Mongol tribes solidified their conquests by extending kinship networks, thus building an empire out of an expanding confederation of familial tribes. The tents (households) were interrelated mostly by marriage: they were alliances sealed by the exchange of daughters. Conquering men married conquered women, and conquered men were selected to marry the conquerors' women. Chinggis Khan may have had more than 500 wives, most of them daughters of tribes that he conquered or that allied with him.

Women in Mongol society were responsible for child-rearing, shearing and milking livestock, and processing pelts for clothing. But they also took part in battles. Kubilai Khan's niece Khutulun became famous for besting men in wrestling matches and claiming their horses as spoils. Although women were often bought and sold, Mongol wives had the right to

own property and to divorce. Elite women even played important political roles. Consider Sorghaghtani Beki, Kubilai Khan's mother, who helped to engineer her sons' rule. Illiterate herself, she made sure that each son acquired a second language to aid in administering conquered lands. She gathered Confucian scholars to prepare Kubilai Khan to rule China. Chabi, Kubilai's senior wife, followed a similar pattern, offering patronage to Tibetan monks who set about converting the Mongol elite in China to Tibetan Buddhism.

CONQUEST AND EMPIRE

The nomads' need for grazing lands contributed to their desire to conquer the splendors of distant fertile belts and rich cities. Then, as they acquired new lands, they increasingly craved

Ibn Battuta. During his journey, Ibn Battuta traveled throughout Africa. In this woodcut, he is depicted in Morocco.

A half-century after Polo began his travels, the Moroccan-born scholar Muhammad ibn Abdullah ibn Battuta (1304–1369) embarked on a journey of his own. Then just twenty-one, he vowed to visit the whole of the Islamic world without traveling the same road twice. It was an ambitious goal, for Islam's domain extended from one end of the Eurasian landmass to the other and far into Africa as well. On his journey, Ibn Battuta eventually covered some 75,000 miles. Along his way, he claimed to have met at least sixty rulers, and in his book he recorded the names of more than 2,000 persons whom he knew personally.

The writings of Marco Polo and Ibn Battuta provide a wealth of information on the well-traversed lands of Africa, Europe, and Asia. What they and other travelers observed was the extreme diversity of Afro-Eurasian peoples, reflecting numerous ethnicities, political formations, and religious faiths. In addition, they observed that the vast majority of people lived deeply localized lives, primarily seeking to obtain the basic necessities of everyday life. Yet, they were also aware the same societies welcomed trade and cultural exchange. In fact, they wrote most eloquently about how each of the four major cultural systems of the landmass—Christian, Muslim, Indian, and Chinese—struggled to define itself. Interestingly, if Ibn Battuta and Marco Polo had been able to travel in the "unknown" worlds—the African hinterlands, the Americas, and Oceania—they would have witnessed to varying degrees similar phenomena and challenges.

to Venice in 1295, fellow townsmen greeted them with astonishment, believing that the Polos had perished years before. So, too, Marco Polo's published account of his travels generated an incredulous reaction. Some of his European readers considered his tales of eastern wonders to be mere fantasy, yet others found their appetites for Asian splendor whetted by his descriptions.

control of richer agricultural and urban areas nearby to increase their wealth and power through tribute. Trade disputes also likely spurred their expeditions. The Mongols depended on settled peoples for grain and manufactured goods (including iron for tools, wagons, weapons, bridles, and stirrups), and their first expansionist forays followed caravan routes.

The expansionist thrust began in 1206 under a united cluster of tribes. A gathering of clan heads acclaimed one of those present as Chinggis (Genghis) Khan, or Supreme Ruler. Chinggis (c. 1155–1227) subsequently launched a series of conquests southward across the Great Wall of China, and westward to Afghanistan and Persia. The Mongols also invaded Korea in 1231. The armies of Chinggis's son reached both the Pacific Ocean and the Adriatic Sea. His grandsons founded dynasties in China, in Persia, and on the southern Eurasian steppes. One of them, Kubilai Khan, enlisted thou-

sands of Koryo men and ships for (ill-fated) invasions of Japan. Thus, a realm took shape that touched all four of Afro-Eurasia's main worlds.

Mongol raiders ultimately built a permanent empire by incorporating conquered peoples and some of their ways. Their feat of unification was far more surprising and sudden than the ties developed incrementally by traders and travelers on ships. Now, Afro-Eurasian regions were connected by land and by sea, in historically unparalleled ways.

MONGOLS IN CHINA

Mongol forces under Chinggis Khan entered northern China at the beginning of the thirteenth century, defeating the Jin army that was no match for the Mongols' superior cavalry on the North China plain. But below the Yangzi River, where the climate and weather changed, the Mongol horsemen fell ill from diseases such as malaria, and their horses perished from the heat. To conquer the semitropical south, the Mongols took to boats and fought along rivers and canals. **Kubilai Khan** (1215–1294) seized the grandest prize of all—southern China—after 1260. His cavalries penetrated the higher plateaus of southwest China and then attacked South China's economic heartland from the west. The Southern Song army fell before his warriors brandishing the latest gunpowder-based weapons (which the Mongols had borrowed from Chinese inventors only to be used against them).

THE FALL OF HANGZHOU Hangzhou, the last Song capital, succumbed in 1276. Rather than see the invaders pillage the city and their emperors' tombs, the Southern Song bowed to the inevitable. Kubilai Khan's most able commander, Bayan, led his crack Mongol forces in seizing town after town, ever closer to the capital. The Empress Dowager tried to buy them off, proposing substantial tribute payments, but Bayan had his eye on the prize: Hangzhou, which fell under Mongol control but survived reasonably intact. Bayan escorted the emperor and the Empress Dowager to Beijing, where Kubilai treated them with honor. Within three years, Song China's defeat was complete. With all of South China in their grip, the Mongols established the Yuan dynasty with a new capital at Dadu ("Great Capital," present-day Beijing).

Although it fell to Mongol control, Hangzhou survived reasonably intact. It was still one of the greatest cities in the world when the Venetian traveler Marco Polo visited in the 1280s and the Muslim traveler Ibn Battuta in the 1340s. Both men agreed that neither Europe nor the Islamic world had anything like it. (See Global Connections & Disconnections: The Travels of Marco Polo and Ibn Battuta.)

OUTSIDERS TAKE CONTROL The Mongol conquest both north and south changed the political and social landscape. However, Mongol rule did not impose rough steppeland ways on the "civilized" urbanite Chinese. Outsiders, non-Chinese, took political control. They themselves were a heterogeneous group of Mongols, Tanguts, Khitan, Jurchen, Muslims, Tibetans, Persians, Turks, Nestorians, Jews, Armenians—a conquering elite that ruled over a vast Han majority. The result was a segmented ruling system in which incumbent Chinese elites governed locally, while newcomers managed the central dynastic polity and collected taxes for the Mongols.

MONGOL REVERBERATIONS IN SOUTHEAST ASIA

Southeast Asia also felt the whiplash of conquest. Circling Song defenses in southern China, the Mongols galloped southwest and conquered states in Yunnan and in Burma. From there, in the 1270s, the armies headed directly back east into

Mongols on Horseback. Even after the Mongols became the rulers of China, the emperors remembered their steppe origin and maintained the skills of horse-riding nomads. This detail from a thirteenth/fourteenth-century silk painting shows Kubilai Khan hunting.

the soft underbelly of the Song state. In this sweep, portions of mainland Southeast Asia became annexed to China for the first time. Even the distant Khmer regime felt repercussions when the Mongol fleet (which grew out of the conquered Song navy) passed by on its way to attack Java—unsuccessfully—in 1293. Kubilai Khan used the conquered Chinese fleets to push his expansionism onto the high seas—with little success during the unsuccessful 1274 and 1281 invasions of Japan from Korea. The ill-fated Javanese expedition was his last.

THE FALL OF BAGHDAD

In the thirteenth century, Mongol tribesmen streamed out of the steppes, crossing the whole of Asia and entering the eastern parts of Europe. Mongke Khan, a grandson of Chinggis, made clear the Mongol aspiration for world domination: he appointed his brother Kubilai to rule over China, Tibet, and the northern parts of India; and he commanded another brother, Hulagu, to conquer Iran, Syria, Egypt, Byzantium, and Armenia.

When Hulagu reached Baghdad in 1258, he encountered a feeble foe and a city that was a shadow of its former glorious self. Merely 10,000 horsemen faced his army of 200,000 soldiers, who were eager to acquire the booty of a wealthy city. Even before the battle had taken place, Baghdadi poets were composing elegies for their dead and mourning the defeat of Islam.

The slaughter was vast. Hulagu himself boasted of taking the lives of at least 200,000 people. The Mongols pursued their adversaries everywhere. They hunted them in wells, latrines, and sewers and followed them into the upper floors of buildings, killing them on rooftops until, as an Iraqi Arab historian observed, "blood poured from the gutters into the streets. . . . The same happened in the mosques" (Lewis, pp. 82–83). In a few weeks of sheer terror, the venerable Abbasid caliphate was demolished. Hulagu's forces showed no mercy to the caliph himself, who was rolled up in a carpet and trampled to death by horses, his blood soaked up by the rug so it would leave no mark on the ground. With Baghdad crushed, the Mongol armies pushed on to Syria, slaughtering Muslims along the way.

In the end, the Egyptian Mamluks stemmed the advancing Mongol armies and prevented Egypt from falling into their hands. The Mongol Empire had reached its outer limits. Better at conquering than governing, the Mongols struggled to rule their vast possessions in makeshift states. Bit by bit, they ceded control to local administrators and dynasts who governed as their surrogates. There was also chronic feuding among the Mongol dynasts themselves. In China and in Persia, Mongol rule collapsed in the fourteenth century.

Mongol conquest reshaped Afro-Eurasia's social landscape. Islam would never again have a unifying authority like the caliphate or a powerful center like Baghdad. China, too, was divided and changed, but in other ways. The Mongols introduced Persian, Islamic, and Byzantine influences on China's architecture, art, science, and medicine. The Yuan policy of benign tolerance also brought elements from Christianity, Judaism, Zoroastrianism, and Islam into the Chinese mix. The Mongol thrust thus led to a great opening, as fine goods, traders, and technology flowed from China to the rest of the world in ensuing centuries. Finally, the Mongol state promoted an Afro-Eurasian interconnectedness that this huge landmass had not known before and would not experience again for hundreds of years. Out of conquest and warfare would come centuries of trade, migration, and increasing contacts among Africa, Europe, and Asia.

 ## CONCLUSION

Between 1000 and 1300, Afro-Eurasia was forming large cultural spheres. As trade and migration spanned longer distances, these spheres prospered and became more inte-grated. In central Afro-Eurasia, Islam was firmly established, its merchants, scholars, and travelers acting as commercial and cultural intermediaries joining the landmass together, as they spread their universalizing faith. As seaborne trade expanded, India, too, became a commercial crossroads. Merchants in its port cities welcomed traders arriving from Arab lands to the west, from China, and from Southeast Asia. China also boomed, pouring its manufactures into trading networks that reached throughout Afro-Eurasia and even into Africa. Christian Europe had two centers, both of which were at war with Islam. In the east, Byzantium was a formidable empire with a resplendent and unconquerable capital city, Constantinople, in many ways the pride of Christianity. In the west, the Catholic papacy had risen from the ashes of the Roman Empire and sought to extend its ecclesiastical authority over Rome's territories in western Europe.

Trade helped outline the parts of the world. The prosperity it brought also supported new classes of people—thinkers, writers, and naturalists—who clarified what it meant to belong to the regions of Afro-Eurasia. By 1300, learned priests and writers had begun to reimagine these regions as more than just territories: they were maturing into cultures with definable—and defensible—geographic boundaries. Increasingly these intellectuals delivered their messages to commoners as well as to rulers.

Neither the Americas nor sub-Saharan Africa saw the same degree of integration, but trade and migration in these areas did have profound effects. Certain African cultures flourished as they encountered the commercial energy of trade on the Indian Ocean. Indeed, Africans' trade with one another linked coastal and interior regions in an ever more integrated world. American peoples also built cities that dominated cultural areas and thrived through trade. American cultures shared significant features: reliance on trade, maize, and the exchange of goods such as shells and precious feathers. And larger areas honored the same spiritual centers.

By 1300, trade, migration, and conflict were connecting Afro-Eurasian worlds in unprecedented ways. When Mongol armies swept into China, into Southeast Asia, and into the heart of Islam, they applied a thin, surface-like coating of political integration to these widespread regions and built on existing trade links. At the same time, most people's lives remained quite local, driven by the need for subsistence and governed by spiritual and governmental representatives acting at the behest of distant authorities. Still, locals noticed the evidence of cross-cultural exchanges everywhere—in the clothing styles of provincial elites, such as Chinese silks in Paris or Quetzal plumes in northern Mexico; in enticements to move (and forced removals) to new frontiers; in the news of faraway conquests or advancing armies. Worlds were coming together within themselves and across territorial boundaries, while remaining apart as they sought to maintain their own identity and traditions. In Afro-Eurasia especially, as the movement of goods and peoples shifted from ancient land routes to sea-lanes, these contacts were more frequent and far-reaching. Never before had the world seen so much activity connecting its parts. Nor within them had there been so much shared cultural similarity—linguistic, religious, legal, and military. Indeed, by the time the Mongol Empire arose, the regions composing the globe were those that we now recognize as the cultural spheres of today's world. These were truly worlds together and worlds apart.

Review and research materials are available at StudySpace: Ⓢ WWNORTON.COM/STUDYSPACE

KEY TERMS

Angkor Wat (p. 389)

Cahokia (p. 398)

Crusades (p. 394)

Delhi Sultanate (p. 380)

dhows (p. 364)

entrepôts (p. 365)

feudalism (p. 389)

karim (p. 365)

Kubilai Khan (p. 405)

Mongols (p. 401)

piety (p. 373)

rajas (p. 379)

Sufism (p. 374)

sultans (p. 379)

Chronology

	700 CE	800 CE	900 CE	1000 CE
SUB-SAHARAN AFRICA		Mandinka merchants establish vast commercial networks linking West Africa ◆		
THE AMERICAS			c. 1000 Cahokia flourishes as a commercial hub in Mississippi River valley ◆	
		c. 900 Moche people found Chan Chan ◆		
		c. 900–1100 Toltec Empire in Mexico Valley ◆ - - - - - - - - - - - - - - - - -		
			1000–1460 Chimú Empire ◆ - - -	
THE ISLAMIC WORLD				
SOUTH ASIA			Turkish invasions from Central Asia begin ◆	
EAST ASIA	794–1185 Heian period in Japan ◆ -			
			Song dynasty founded 960 ◆	
		918–1392 Koryo dynasty rules ◆ - - - - - - - - - - - - - - - - -		
				Gunpowder invented ◆
SOUTHEAST ASIA		899–1431 Khmer kingdom ◆ - - - - - - - - - - - - - - - - -		
CHRISTIAN EUROPE				

STUDY QUESTIONS

1. List the four major cultural regions in Afro-Eurasia, and briefly explain the defining characteristics of each. What did the various people and groups in these geographic areas all have in common that distinguished them from others?

2. Explain the role of global commercial hubs in India, China, and Egypt in fostering commercial contacts across Afro-Eurasia. How did they reflect revolutions in maritime transportation?

3. Which areas of sub-Saharan Africa were parts of the larger Afro-Eurasian world by 1300? How did contact with other regions shape political and cultural developments in sub-Saharan Africa?

4. Describe the cultural diversity within the Islamic world during this era. How did diverse Islamic communities achieve a uniform regional identity?

5. Analyze the impact of Muslim Turkish invaders on India. To what extent did India remain distinct from the Islamic world in this era?

6. Describe how the Song dynasty reacted to the military strength of its nomadic pastoral neighbors. How did these relationships foster a distinct Chinese identity?

7. Compare and contrast cultural and political developments in Korea, Japan, and Southeast Asia during this era. How did other regional cultures influence these societies?

8. Describe how Christianity expanded its geographic reach during this era. How did this expansion affect Latin Christianity in western Europe and Orthodox Christianity in eastern Europe?

9. Analyze the extent to which peoples in the Americas established closer contact with each other. How extensive were these contacts compared with those in the Afro-Eurasian world?

10. Describe the empire that the Mongols created in the thirteenth century. How did their policies promote greater contact among the various regions of Afro-Eurasia?

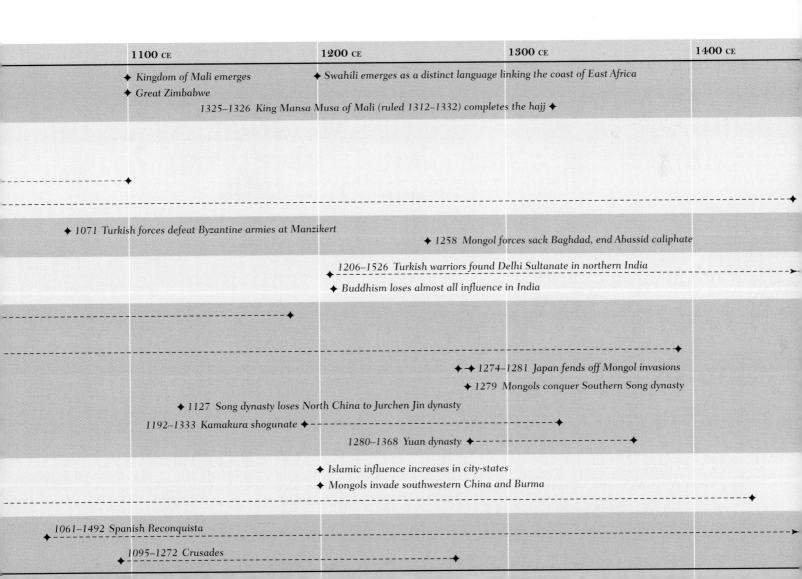

1100 CE	1200 CE	1300 CE	1400 CE

◆ Kingdom of Mali emerges

◆ Great Zimbabwe

◆ Swahili emerges as a distinct language linking the coast of East Africa

1325–1326 King Mansa Musa of Mali (ruled 1312–1332) completes the hajj ◆

◆ 1071 Turkish forces defeat Byzantine armies at Manzikert

◆ 1258 Mongol forces sack Baghdad, end Abassid caliphate

1206–1526 Turkish warriors found Delhi Sultanate in northern India

◆ Buddhism loses almost all influence in India

◆ 1274–1281 Japan fends off Mongol invasions

◆ 1279 Mongols conquer Southern Song dynasty

◆ 1127 Song dynasty loses North China to Jurchen Jin dynasty

1192–1333 Kamakura shogunate ◆

1280–1368 Yuan dynasty ◆

◆ Islamic influence increases in city-states

◆ Mongols invade southwestern China and Burma

1061–1492 Spanish Reconquista

1095–1272 Crusades

Further Readings

Chapter 1 Becoming Human

Arsuaga, Juan Luis, *The Neanderthal's Necklace: In Search of the First Thinkers*, translated by Anthony Klatt (2002). A stimulating overview of prehistory that focuses on the Neanderthals and compares them with *Homo sapiens*.

Barker, Graeme, *Agricultural Revolution in Prehistory: Why Did Foragers Become Farmers* (2006). The most recent, truly global, and up-to-date study of this momentous event in world history.

Bellwood, Peter, *First Farmers: The Origins of Agricultural Societies* (2005). A state-of-the-art global history of the origins of agriculture including recent archaeological, linguistic, and microbiological data.

Bogucki, Peter, *The Origins of Human Society* (1999). An authoritative overview of prehistory.

Cauvin, Jacques, *The Birth of the Gods and the Origins of Agriculture*, translated by Trevor Watkins from the original 1994 French publication (2000). An important work on the agricultural revolution of Southwest Asia and the evolution of symbolic thinking at this time.

Cavalli-Sforza, Luigi Luca, *Genes, Peoples, and Languages*, translated by Mark Selestad from the original 1996 French publication (2000). An expert's introduction to the use of gene research for revealing new information about the evolution of human beings in the distant past.

Childe, V. Gordon, *What Happened in History* (1964). A classic work by one of the pioneers in studying the early history and evolution of human beings. Though superseded in many respects, it is still an important place to start one's reading and a work of great power and emotion.

Clark, J. Desmond, and Steven A. Brandt (eds.), *From Hunters to Farmers: The Causes and Consequences of Food Production in Africa* (1984). Excellent essays on the agricultural revolution.

Coon, Carleton Stevens, *The Story of Man; from the First Human to Primitive Culture and Beyond*, 2nd ed. (1962). An important early work on the evolution of humans, emphasizing the distinctiveness of "races" around the world.

Cunliffe, Barry (ed.), *The Oxford Illustrated Prehistory of Europe* (1994). The definitive work on early European history.

Ehrenberg, Margaret, *Women in Prehistory* (1989). What was the role of women in hunting and gathering societies, and how greatly were women affected by the agricultural revolution? The author offers a number of stimulating generalizations.

Ehret, Christopher, *The Civilizations of Africa: A History to 1800* (2002). Although this is a general history of Africa, the author, a linguist and an expert on early African history, offers new information and new overviews of African peoples in very ancient times.

Fagan, Brian, *People of the Earth: An Introduction to World Prehistory* (1989). An authoritative overview of early history, widely used in classrooms.

Fage, J. D., and Roland Oliver (eds.), *The Cambridge History of Africa*, 8 vols. (1975–1984). A pioneering work of synthesis by two of the first and foremost scholars of the history of Africa. Volume 1 deals with African prehistory.

Frison, George C., *Survival by Hunting: Prehistoric Human Predators and Animal Prey* (2004). An archaeologist applies his knowledge of animal habitats, behavior, and hunting strategies to an examination of prehistoric hunting practices in the North American Great Plains and Rocky Mountains.

Gebauer, Anne Birgitte, and T. Douglas Price (eds.), *Transition to Agriculture in Prehistory* (1992). Excellent essays on the agricultural revolution, especially those written by the two editors.

Johnson, Donald, Lenora Johnson, and Blake Edgar, *Ancestors: In Search of Human Origins* (1999). A good overview of human evolution, with insightful essays on *Homo erectus* and *Homo sapiens*.

Jones, Steve, Robert Martin, and David Pilbeam (eds.), *The Cambridge Encyclopedia of Human Evolution* (1992). A superb guide to a wide range of subjects, crammed with up-to-date information on the most controversial and obscure topics of human evolution and early history.

Ki-Zerbo, J. (ed.), *Methodology and African Prehistory*, vol. 1 of the UNESCO General History of Africa (1981). A general history of Africa, written for the most part by scholars of African descent.

Klein, Richard G., and Blake Edger, *The Dawn of Human Culture* (2002). A fine and reliable guide to the tangled history of human evolution.

Leakey, Richard, *The Origin of Humankind* (1994). A readable and exciting account of human evolution, written by the son of the pioneering archaeologists Louis and Mary Leakey, a scholar of equal stature to his parents.

Lewin, Roger, *The Origin of Modern Humans* (1993). Yet another good overview of human evolution, with useful chapters on early art and the use of symbols.

Loewe, Michael, and Edward Shaughnessy (eds.), *The Cambridge History of Ancient China: From the Origins of Civilization to 221 B.C.* (1999). A good review of the archaeology of ancient China.

Mellaart, James, *Çatal Höyük: A Neolithic Town in Anatolia* (1967). A detailed description of one of the first towns associated with the agricultural revolution in Southwest Asia.

Mithen, Steven, *The Prehistory of the Mind: The Cognitive Origins of Art and Science* (1996). A stimulating discussion of the impact of biological and cultural evolution on the cognitive structure of the human mind.

Olson, Steve, *Mapping Human History: Genes, Race, and Our Common Origins* (2003). Using the findings of genetics and attacking the racial thinking of an earlier generation of archaeologists, the author writes powerfully about the unity of all human beings.

Price, T. Douglas (ed.), *Europe's First Farmers* (2000). A discussion of the agricultural revolution in Europe.

Price, T. Douglas, and Anne Birgitte Gebauer (eds.), *Last Hunters– First Farmers: New Perspectives on the Prehistoric Transition to Agriculture* (1996). An exciting collection of essays by some of the leading scholars in the field studying the transition from hunting and gathering to settled agriculture.

Scarre, Chris (ed.), *The Human Past: World Prehistory and the Development of Human Societies* (2005). An encyclopedia and an overview rolled up into one mammoth volume, written by leading figures in the field of early human history.

Shaw, Thurstan, Paul Sinclair, Bassey Andah, and Alex Okpoko (eds.), *The Archaeology of Africa: Food, Metals, and Towns* (1993). Up-to-date research on the earliest history of human beings in Africa.

Smith, Bruce D., *The Emergence of Agriculture* (1995). How early humans domesticated wild animals and plants.

Stringer, Christopher, and Robin McKie, *African Exodus: The Origins of Modern Humanity* (1996). Detailed data on why Africa was the source of human origins and why *Homo sapiens* is a recent wanderer out of Africa.

Tattersall, Ian, *The Fossil Trail: How We Know What We Think We Know about Human Evolution* (1995). A passionately written book about early archaeological discoveries and the centrality of Africa in human evolution.

Tattersall, Ian, *The World from Beginnings to 4000 BCE* (2008). A brief up-to-date overview of humanity's early history by a leading authority.

Van Oosterzee, Penny, *Dragon Bones: The Story of Peking Man* (2000). Describes how the late-nineteenth-century unearthing of sites in China containing fossils of animals used for medicinal purposes led to the discovery of the fossils of the Peking Man.

Weiss, Mark L., and Alan E. Mann, *Human Biology and Behavior: An Anthropological Perspective* (1996). The authors stress the contribution that biological research has made and continues to make to unravel the mystery of human evolution.

Chapter 2 Rivers, Cities, and First States, 4000–2000 BCE

Adams, Robert McCormick, *The Evolution of Urban Society* (1966). A classic study of the social, political, and economic processes that led to the development of the first urban civilizations.

Algaze, Guillermo, *The Uruk World System: The Dynamics of Expansion of Early Mesopotamian Civilization* (1993). A compelling argument for the colonization of the Tigris and Euphrates valley by the proto-Sumerians at the end of the fourth millennium BCE.

Andrews, Carol, *Egyptian Mummies* (1998). An illustrated summary of Egyptian mummification and burial practices.

Bagley, Robert, *Ancient Sichuan: Treasures from a Lost Civilization* (2001). Describes the remarkable findings in Southwest China, particularly at Sanxingdui, which have challenged earlier accounts of the Shang dynasty's central role in the rise of early Chinese civilization.

Bar-Yosef, Ofar, and Anatoly Khazanov (eds.), *Pastoralism in the Levant: Archaeological Materials in Anthropological Perspectives* (1992). Classic study of the role of nomads in the development of societies in the Levant during the Neolithic period.

Bruhns, Karen Olsen, *Ancient South America* (1994). The best basic text on pre-Columbian South American cultures.

Butzer, Karl W., *Early Hydraulic Civilization in Egypt: A Study of Cultural Ecology* (1976). The best work on how the Egyptians dealt with the Nile floods and the influence that these arrangements had on the overall organization of society.

Cunliffe, Barry, *Europe Between the Oceans, 9000 BC–AD 1000* (2008), a very up-to-date and spectacularly illustrated account of early Europe.

Habu, Junko, *Ancient Jomon of Japan* (2004). Study of prehistoric Jomon hunter-gatherers on the Japanese archipelago that incorporates several different aspects of anthropological studies, including hunter-gatherer archaeology, settlement archaeology, and pottery analysis.

Jacobsen, Thorkild, *The Treasures of Darkness: A History of Mesopotamian Religion* (1976). Best introduction to the religious and philosophical thought of ancient Mesopotamia.

Kemp, Barry J., *Ancient Egypt: Anatomy of a Civilization* (1989). A synthetic overview of the culture of the pharaohs.

Kramer, Samuel Noah, *The Sumerians: Their History, Culture and Character* (1963). Classic study of the Sumerians and their culture by a pioneer in Sumerian studies.

Pollock, Susan, *Ancient Mesopotamia: The Eden That Never Was* (1999). An analysis of the social and economic development of Mesopotamia from the beginnings of settlement until the reign of Hammurapi.

Possehl, Gregory L., *Indus Age: The Beginnings* (1999). The second of four volumes analyzing the history of the Indus Valley civilization.

Postgate, J. N., *Early Mesopotamia: Society and Economy at the Dawn of History* (1992). A study of the economic and political development of the Sumerian civilization.

Preziosi, Donald, and L. A. Hitchcock, *Aegean Art and Architecture* (1999). One of the best general guides to the figurative and decorative art produced both by the Minoans and Mycenaeans and by related early societies in the region of the Aegean.

Ratnagar, Shereen, *Trading Encounters: From the Euphrates to the Indus in the Bronze Age*, 2nd ed. (2004). A comprehensive presentation of the evidence for the relationship between the Indus Valley and its western neighbors.

———, *Understanding Harappa: Civilization in the Greater Indus Valley* (2001). Harappan site archaeological data of the last century organized into a historical narrative comprehensible to the general audience.

Rice, Michael, *Egypt's Legacy: The Archetypes of Western Civilization, 3000–300 BC* (1997). The author argues for the decisive influence of Egyptian culture on the whole of the Mediterranean and its later historical development.

Roaf, Michael, *Cultural Atlas of Mesopotamia and the Ancient Near East* (1990). A comprehensive compendium of the historical and cultural development of the Mesopotamian civilization from the Neolithic background through the Persian Empire.

Shaw, Ian (ed.), *The Oxford History of Ancient Egypt* (2000). The most up-to-date and comprehensive account of the history of Egypt down to the Greek invasion.

Thorp, Robert, *The Chinese Neolithic: Trajectories to Early States* (2005). Uses the latest archaeological evidence to describe the development of early Bronze Age cultures in North and Northwestern China from about 2000 BCE.

Chapter 3 Nomads, Territorial States, and Microsocieties, 2000–1200 BCE

Allan, Sarah, *The Shape of the Turtle: Myth, Art and Cosmos in Early China* (1991). Explains the roles of divination and sacrifice in artistic representations of the Shang cosmology.

Allen, James P., *Middle Egyptian: An Introduction to the Language and Culture of Hieroglyphs* (2000). An introduction to the system of writing and its use in Ancient Egypt.

Anthony, David W., *The Horse, the Wheel, and Language: How Bronze-Age Riders from the Eurasian Steppes Shaped the Modern World* (2007). A superb analysis of the origins and spread of the Indo-European peoples.

Arnold, Dieter, *Building in Ancient Egypt: Pharaonic Stone Masonry* (1996). Details the complex construction of monumental stone architecture in ancient Egypt.

Baines, John, and Jaromir Málek, *Atlas of Ancient Egypt* (1980). Useful compilation of information on ancient Egyptian society, religion, history, and geography.

Beal, Richard H., *The Organization of the Hittite Military* (1992). A detailed study based on textual sources of the world's first chariot-based army.

Bogucki, Peter, and Pam J. Crabtree (eds.), *Ancient Europe 8000 BC–AD 1000: Encyclopedia of the Barbarian World*, 2 vols. (2004). An indispensable handbook on the economic, social, artistic, and religious life in Europe during this period.

Bruhns, Karen Olsen, *Ancient South America* (1994). The best basic text on pre-Columbian South American cultures.

Bryant, Edwin, *The Quest for the Origins of Vedic Culture: The Indo-Aryan Migration Debate* (2001). Insight into the highly charged debate on who the Indo-European speakers were, where they originated, and where they migrated to.

Castleden, Rodney, *The Mycenaeans* (2005). One of the best current surveys of all aspects of the Mycenaean Greeks.

Chadwick, John, *The Decipherment of Linear B*, 2nd ed. (1968). Not only a retelling of the story of the decipherment of the Linear B script but also an introduction to the actual content and function of the tablets themselves.

Cline, E. H., *Sailing the Wine-Dark Sea: International Trade and the Late Bronze Age Aegean* (1994). An excellent account of the trade and contacts between the Aegean and other areas of the Mediterranean, Europe, and the Near East during the late Bronze Age.

Cunliffe, Barry, *Facing the Ocean: The Atlantic and Its Peoples, 8000 BC–AD 1500* (2001). An in-depth, highly useful treatment of western Europe during this period.

Cunliffe, Barry (ed.), *Prehistoric Europe: An Illustrated History* (1997). A state-of-the-art treatment of first farmers, agricultural developments, and material culture in prehistoric Europe.

Davis, W. V., and L. Schofield, *Egypt, the Aegean and the Levant: Interconnections in the Second Millennium BC* (1995). A discussion of the complex interactions in the eastern Mediterranean during the "international age."

Doumas, Christos, *Thera: Pompeii of the Ancient Aegean* (1983). A study of the tremendous volcanic eruption and explosion that destroyed the Minoan settlement on the island of Thera.

Drews, Robert, *Coming of the Greeks: Indo-European Conquests in the Aegean and the Near East* (1988). A good survey of the evidence for the "invasions" or "movements of peoples" that reconfigured the world of the eastern Mediterranean and Near East.

Finley, M. I., *The World of Odysseus*, 2nd rev. ed. (1977; reprint, 2002). The classic work that describes what might be recovered about the social values and behaviors of men and women in the period of the so-called Dark Ages of early Greek history.

Frankfort, Henri, *Ancient Egyptian Religion: An Interpretation* (1948; reprint, 2000). A classic study of Egyptian religion and culture during the pharaonic period.

Keightley, David N., *The Ancestral Landscape: Time, Space, and Community in Late Shang China, ca. 1200–1045 B.C.* (2000). Provides insights into the nature of royal kinship that undergirded the Shang court and its regional domains.

Kemp, Barry J., *Ancient Egypt: Anatomy of a Civilization* (2006). A definitive presentation of the history, culture, and religion of ancient Egypt.

Klein, Jacob, "The Marriage of Martu: The Urbanization of 'Barbaric' Nomads," in *Mutual Influences of Peoples and Cultures in the Ancient Near East*, ed. Meir Malul (1996).

Kristiansen, Kristian, *Europe before History* (1998). The finest recent survey of all the major developmental phases of European prehistory.

McIntosh, Jane, *Handbook to Life in Prehistoric Europe* (2006). Highlights the archaeological evidence that enables us to re-create the day-to-day life of different prehistoric communities in Europe.

Preziosi, Donald, and L. A. Hitchcock, *Aegean Art and Architecture* (1999). One of the best general guides to the figurative and decorative art produced both by the Minoans and Mycenaeans and by related early societies in the region of the Aegean.

Quirke, Stephen, *Ancient Egyptian Religion* (1992). A highly readable presentation of ancient Egyptian religion that summarizes the roles and attributions of the many Egyptian gods.

Robins, Gay, *The Art of Ancient Egypt* (1997). The most comprehensive survey to date of the art of pharaonic Egypt.

———, *Women in Ancient Egypt* (1993). An interesting survey of the place of women in Ancient Egyptian society.

Romer, John, *Ancient Lives: Daily Life in Egypt of the Pharaohs* (1990). A discussion of the economic and social lives of everyday ancient Egyptians.

Sandars, N. K., *The Sea Peoples: Warriors of the Ancient Mediterranean* (1985). A readable discussion of a very complex period of Levantine history.

Simpson, William Kelly (ed.), *The Literature of Ancient Egypt: An Anthology of Stories, Instructions, and Poetry* (1972). A compilation of the most important works of literature from Ancient Egypt.

Thorp, Robert L., *China in the Early Bronze Age: Shang Civilization* (2005). Reviews the archaeological discoveries near Anyang, site of two capitals of the Shang kings.

Warren, Peter, *The Aegean Civilizations: From Ancient Crete to Mycenae*, 2nd ed. (1989). An excellent textual and pictorial guide to all the basic aspects of the Minoan and Mycenaean societies.

Wilson, John A., *The Culture of Ancient Egypt* (1951). A classic study of the history and culture of pharaonic Egypt.

Yadin, Yigael, *The Art of Warfare in Biblical Lands in the Light of Archaeological Discovery* (1963). A well-illustrated presentation of the machinery of war in the second and first millennia BCE.

Chapter 4   First Empires and Common Cultures in Afro-Eurasia, 1250–325 BCE

Ahlström, Gosta W., *The History of Ancient Palestine from the Paleolithic Period to Alexander's Conquests* (1993). An excellent survey of the history of the region by a renowned expert, with good attention to the recent archaeological evidence.

Aubet, Maria Eugenia, *The Phoenicians and the West*, 2nd ed. (2001). The basic survey of the Phoenician colonization of the western Mediterranean and Atlantic, with special attention to recent archaeological discoveries.

Briant, Pierre, *From Cyrus to Alexander: A History of the Persian Empire*, trans. Peter T. Daniels (2002). A complex and comprehensive history of the Persian Empire by its finest modern scholar.

Bright, John, *A History of Israel*, 4th ed. (2000). An updated version of a classic and still very useful overview of the whole history of the Israelite people down to the end of the period covered in this chapter.

Cook, J. M., *The Persian Empire* (1983). An older but still useful, and highly readable, standard history of the Persian Empire.

Falkenhausen, Lothar von, *Chinese Society in the Age of Confucius (1000–250 BC): The Archaeological Evidence* (2006). A timely reassessment of early Chinese history that compares the literary texts on which it has traditionally been based to the new archaeological evidence.

Frye, Richard N., *The Heritage of Persia* (1963). This classic study of ancient Iran gives the political and literary history of the Persians and their successors.

Grayson, A. K., "Assyrian Civilization," in *Cambridge Ancient History*, vol. 3, pt. 2, pp. 194–228. The Assyrian and Babylonian empires and other states of the Near East, from the eighth to the sixth century BCE.

Hornung, Erik, *Akhenaten and the Religion of Light*, translated from the German by David Lorton (1999). An important, brief biography of Egypt's most controversial pharaoh.

———, *History of Ancient Egypt: An Introduction*, translated from the German by David Lorton (1999). An accessible overview of the history of ancient Egypt by a leading Egyptologist.

Isserlin, Benedikt J., *The Israelites* (1998). A very well-written and heavily illustrated history of all aspects of life in the regions of the Levant inhabited by the Israelites, equally good on the latest scholarship and the archaeological data.

Lancel, Serge, *Carthage: A History*, trans. Antonia Nevill (1997). By far the best single-volume history of the most important Phoenician colony in the Mediterranean (the first three chapters are especially relevant to materials covered in this chapter).

Lemche, Niels Peter, *Ancient Israel: A New History of Israelite Society* (1988). A quick, readable, and still up-to-date summary of the main phases and themes.

Lewis, Mark Edward, *Writing and Authority in Early China* (1999). A work that traces the changing uses of writing to command assent and obedience in early China.

Markoe, Glenn E., *Phoenicians* (2000). A thorough survey of the Phoenicians and their society as it first developed in the Levant and then expanded over the Mediterranean, with excellent illustrations of the diverse archaeological sites.

Matthews, Victor H., and Don C. Benjamin, *Social World of Ancient Israel, 1350–587* BCE (1993). A thematic overview of the main occupational groups and social roles that characterized ancient Israelite society.

Oates, Joan, and David Oates, *Nimrud: An Assyrian Imperial City Revealed* (2001). A fine and highly readable summary of the state of our knowledge of the Assyrian Empire from the perspective of the early capital of Assurnasirpal II.

Oded, Bustenay, *Mass Deportations and Deportees in the Neo-Assyrian Empire* (1979). A detailed textual examination of the deportation strategy of the Assyrian kings. Good for in-depth research of the question.

Potts, D. T., *The Archaeology of Elam: Formation and Transformation of an Ancient Iranian State* (1999). The definitive study of the archaeology of western Iran from the Neolithic period through the Persian Empire.

Shaughnessy, Edward L., *Sources of Western Zhou History: Inscribed Bronze Vessels* (1992). Detailed work on the historiography and interpretation of the thousands of ritual bronze vessels discovered by China's archaeologists.

Thapar, Romila, *From Lineage to State* (1984). The only book on early India that uses religious literature historically and analyzes major lineages to reveal the transition from tribal society to state institutions.

Tignor, Robert L., *Egypt: A Short History* (2010). A succinct treatment of the entire history of Egypt from the pharaohs to the present, with three chapters on the ancient period.

Tubb, Jonathan N., *Canaanites* (1998). The best recent survey, well illustrated, of one of the main ethnic groups dominating the culture of the Levant.

Chapter 5 Worlds Turned Inside Out, 1000–350 BCE

Adams, William Y., *Nubia: Corridor to Africa* (1977). The authoritative historical overview of Nubia, the area of present-day Sudan just south of Egypt and a geographical connecting point between the Mediterranean and sub-Saharan Africa.

Aubet, Maria Eugenia, *The Phoenicians and the West*, 2nd ed. (2001). The basic survey of the Phoenician colonization of the western Mediterranean and Atlantic, with special attention to recent archaeological discoveries.

Barker, Graeme, and Tom Rasmussen, *The Etruscans* (1998). The most up-to-date introduction to this important pre-Roman society in the Italian peninsula, with strong emphasis on broad social and material patterns of development as indicated by the archaeological evidence.

Burkert, Walter, *Greek Religion*, trans. John Raffan (1985). The best one-volume introduction to early Greek religion, placing the Greeks in their larger Mediterranean and Near Eastern contexts.

Burns, Karen Olsen, *Ancient South America* (1994). A very useful overview of recent debates and conclusions about pre-Columbian archaeology in South America, including both the Andes and the lowland and coastal regions.

Cartledge, Paul (ed.), *The Cambridge Illustrated History of Ancient Greece* (2002). An excellent history of the Greek city-states down to the time of Alexander the Great.

Chakravarti, Uma, *The Social Dimensions of Early Buddhism* (1987). A description of the life of Buddha drawn from early Buddhist texts.

Cho-yun, Hsu, *Ancient China in Transition* (1965). An account of the political, economic, social, and intellectual changes that occurred during the Warring States period.

Coarelli, Filippo (ed.), *Etruscan Cities* (1975). A brilliantly and lavishly illustrated guide to the material remains of the Etruscans: their cities, their magnificent tombs, and their architecture, painting, sculpture, and other art.

Coe, Michael, et al. (eds.), *The Olmec World: Ritual and Rulership* (1996). A collection of field-synthesizing articles with important illustrations, based on one of the most comprehensive exhibitions of Olmec art in the world.

Confucius, *The Analects (Lun Yü)*, trans. D. C. Lau (1979). An outstanding translation of the words of Confucius as recorded by his major disciples. Includes valuable historical material needed to provide the context for Confucius's teachings.

Finley, M. I., and H. W. Pleket, *The Olympic Games: The First Thousand Years* (2005). A fine description of the most famous of the Greek games; it explains how they exemplify the competitive spirit that marked many aspects of the Greek city-states.

Garlan, Yvon, *Slavery in Ancient Greece*, trans. Janet Lloyd (1988). A treatment of the emergence, development, and institutionalization of chattel slavery in the Greek city-states.

———, *War in the Ancient World: A Social History*, trans. Janet Lloyd (1976). A discussion of the emergence of the forms of warfare, including male citizens fighting in hoplite phalanxes and the development of siege warfare, that were typical of the Greek city-states.

Iliffe, John, *Africans: The History of a Continent*, 2nd ed. (2007). A first-rate scholarly survey of Africa from its beginnings, with a strong emphasis on demography.

Kagan, Donald, *The Peloponnesian War* (2004). A vivid description of the war that pitted the major Greek city-states, including Athens and Sparta, against each other over the latter half of the fifth century BCE.

Lancel, Serge, *Carthage: A History*, trans. Antonia Nevill (1997). By far the best single-volume history of the most important Phoenician colony in the Mediterranean.

Lewis, Mark Edward, *Sanctioned Violence in Early China* (1990). An analysis of the use of sanctioned violence as an element of statecraft from the Warring States period to the formation of the Qin and Han empires in the second half of the first millennium BCE.

———, *Writing and Authority in Early China* (1999). A revisionist account of the central role of writing and persuasion in models for the invention of a Chinese world empire.

Lloyd, G. E. R., *Early Greek Science: Thales to Aristotle* (1970). An especially clear and concise introduction to the main developments and intellectuals that marked the emergence of critical secular thinking in the early Greek world.

Lloyd, G. E. R., and Nathan Sivin, *The Way and the Word: Science and Medicine in Early China and Greece* (2002). A comprehensive rethinking of the social and political settings in ancient China and city-state Greece that contributed to the different views of science and medicine that emerged in each place.

Murray, Oswyn, *Early Greece*, 2nd ed. (1993). One of the best introductions to the emergence of the Greek city-states down to the end of the archaic age.

Osborne, Robin, *Archaic and Classical Greek Art* (1998). An outstanding book that clearly explains the main innovations in Greek art, setting them in their historical context.

———, *Greece in the Making, 1200–479 BC* (1999). The standard history of the whole early period of the Greek city-states characterized by an especially fine and judicious mix of archaeological data and literary sources.

Pallottino, Massimo, *The Etruscans*, rev. ed., trans. J. Cremona (1975). A fairly traditional but still classic survey of all aspects of Etruscan history, political and social institutions.

Redford, Donald B., *From Slave to Pharaoh: The Black Experience of Ancient Egypt* (2004). A description of Egypt's twenty-fifth dynasty, which was made up of Sudanese conquerors.

Schaberg, David, *A Patterned Past: Form and Thought in Early Chinese Historiography* (2002). A comprehensive study of the intellectual content of historical anecdotes by the followers of Confucius collected around the fourth century BCE.

Schaps, David, *The Invention of Coinage and the Monetization of Ancient Greece* (2004). A new analysis that offers a broad overview of the emergence of coined money in the Near East and the eastern Mediterranean and its effects on the spread of money-based markets.

Sharma, J. P., *Republics in Ancient India, c. 1500 B.C.–500 B.C.* (1968). Relying on information from early Buddhist texts, this book first revealed that South Asia had not only monarchies but also alternative polities.

Shaw, Thurston, *Nigeria: Its Archaeology and Early History* (1978). An important introduction to the early history of Nigeria by one of that country's leading archaeologists.

Shinnie, P. L., *Ancient Nubia* (1996). An excellent account of the history of the ancient Nubians, who, we are discovering, had great influence on Egypt and on the rest of tropical Africa.

Snodgrass, Anthony, *Archaic Greece: The Age of Experiment* (1981). A good introduction to the archaeological evidence of archaic Greece.

Taylor, Christopher, Richard Hare, and Jonathan Barnes, *Greek Philosophers* (1999). A fine, succinct, one-volume introduction to the major aspects of the three big thinkers who dominated the high period of classical Greek philosophy: Socrates, Plato, and Aristotle.

Torok, Laszlo, *Meroe: Six Studies on the Cultural Identity of an Ancient African State* (1995). A good collection of essays on the most recent work on Meroe.

Welsby, Derek A., *The Kingdom of Kush: The Napatan and Meroitic Empires* (1996). A fine book on these two important Nubian kingdoms.

Chapter 6 Shrinking the Afro-Eurasian World, 350 BCE–250 CE

Bradley, Keith, *Slavery and Rebellion in the Roman World, 140 B.C.–70 B.C.* (1989). A description of the rise of large-scale plantation slavery in Sicily and Italy, and a detailed account of the three great slave wars.

Browning, Iain, *Palmyra* (1979). A narrative of the history of the important desert city that linked eastern and western trade routes.

Casson, Lionel, *The Periplus Maris Erythraei* (1989). An introduction to a typical ancient sailing manual, this one of the Red Sea and Indian Ocean.

———, *Ships and Seamanship in the Ancient World* (1995). The classic account of the ships and sailors that powered commerce and war on the high seas.

Colledge, Malcolm, *The Art of Palmyra* (1976). A well-illustrated introduction to the unusual art of Palmyra with its mixture of eastern and western elements.

Fowler, Barbara H., *The Hellenistic Aesthetic* (1989). How the artists in this new age saw and portrayed their world in new and different ways.

Green, Peter, *Alexander to Actium: The Historical Evolution of the Hellenistic Age* (1990). The best general guide to the whole period in all of its various aspects, and well illustrated.

Habicht, Christian, *Athens from Alexander to Antony,* trans. Deborah L. Schneider (1997). The authoritative account of what happened to the great city-state of Athens in this period.

Holt, Frank L., *Thundering Zeus: The Making of Hellenistic Bactria* (1999). A basic history of the most eastern of the kingdoms spawned by the conquests of Alexander the Great.

Hopkirk, Peter, *Foreign Devils on the Silk Road* (1984). A historiography of the explorations and researches on the central Asian Silk Road of the nineteenth and early twentieth centuries.

Juliano, Annette L., and Judith A. Lerner (eds.), *Nomads, Traders and Holy Men Along China's Silk Road* (2003). A description of the travelers along the Silk Road in human terms, focusing on warfare, markets, and religion.

Lane Fox, Robin, *Alexander the Great* (1973). Still the most readable and in many ways the sanest biography of the world conqueror.

Lewis, Naphtali, *Greeks in Ptolemaic Egypt* (1986). An account of the relationships between Greeks and Egyptians as seen through the lives of individual Greek settlers and colonists.

Liu, Xinru, *Ancient India and Ancient China* (1988). The first work to connect political and economic developments in India and China with the evolution and spread of Buddhism in the first half of the first millennium.

Long, Antony A., *Hellenistic Philosophy: Stoics, Epicureans, Sceptics*, 2nd ed. (1986). One of the clearest guides to the main new trends in Greek philosophical thinking in the period.

Martin, Luther H., *Hellenistic Religions: An Introduction* (1987). An introduction to the principal new Hellenistic religions and cults that emerged in this period.

Mendels, Doron, *The Rise and Fall of Jewish Nationalism* (1992). A sophisticated account of the various phases of Jewish resistance in Judah to foreign domination.

Miller, James Innes, *The Spice Trade of the Roman Empire, 29 B.C. to A.D. 641* (1969). A first-rate study of the spice trade in the Roman Empire.

Pomeroy, Sarah B., *Women in Hellenistic Egypt: From Alexander to Cleopatra* (1990). A highly readable investigation of women and family in the best-documented region of the Hellenistic world.

Ray, Himanshu P., *The Wind of Change, Buddhism and the Maritime Links of Early South Asia* (1994). Ray's study of Buddhism and maritime trade stretches from the Arabian Sea to the navigations between South Asia and Southeast Asia.

Rosenfield, John, *The Dynastic Art of the Kushans* (1967). Instead of focusing on the Gandharan Buddhist art itself, Rosenfield selects sculptures of Kushan royals and those representing nomadic populations in religious shrines to display the central Asian aspect of artworks of the period.

Rostovtzeff, Michael Ivanovich, *Caravan Cities*, trans. D. and T. Talbot Rice (1932). Though published more than seven decades ago, this small volume contains accurate descriptions of the ruins of many caravan cities in modern Jordan and Syria.

———, *The Social and Economic History of the Hellenistic World* (1941). A monumental achievement. One of the great works of history written in the twentieth century. An unsurpassed overview of all aspects of the politics and social and economic movements of the period. Despite its age, there is still nothing like it.

Schoff, Wilfred H. (ed. and trans.), *The Periplus of the Erythraean Sea* (1912). An invaluable tool for mapping the names and places from the Red Sea to Indian coastal areas during this period.

Shipley, Graham, *The Greek World after Alexander, 323–30 B.C.* (2000). A more up-to-date survey than Peter Green's work (above), with more emphasis on the historical detail in each period.

Tarn, W. W., *Greeks in Bactria and India* (1984). The most comprehensive coverage of Greek sources on Hellenistic states in Afghanistan and northwest India.

Thapar, Romila, *Ashoka and the Decline of the Mauryas* (1973). Using all available primary sources, including the edicts of Ashoka and Greek authors' accounts, Thapar gives the most authoritative analysis of the first and the most important empire in Indian history.

Vainker, Shelagh, *Chinese Silk: A Cultural History* (2004). A work that traces the cultural history of silk in China from its early origins to the twentieth century and considers its relationship to the other decorative arts. The author draws on the most recent archaeological evidence to emphasize the role of silk in Chinese history, trade, religion, and literature.

Wood, Francis, *The Silk Road: Two Thousand Years in the Heart of Asia* (2004). Illustrated with drawings, manuscripts, paintings, and artifacts to trace the Silk Road to its origins as far back as Alexander the Great, with an emphasis on its importance to cultural and religious movements.

Young, Gary K., *Rome's Eastern Trade: International Commerce and Imperial Policy, 31 BC–AD 305* (2001). This study examines the taxation and profits of eastern trade from the perspective of the Roman government.

Chapter 7 Han Dynasty China and Imperial Rome, 300 BCE–300 CE

Bodde, Derk, *China's First Unifier: A Study of the Ch'in Dynasty as Seen in the Life of Li Ssu (280?–208 B.C.)* (1938). A classic account of the key Legalist adviser, Li Si, who formulated the Qin policy to enhance its autocratic power.

Bowman, Alan K., *Life and Letters on the Roman Frontier: Vindolanda and Its Peoples* (1994). An introduction to the exciting discovery of writing tablets at a Roman army base in northern Britain.

Bradley, Keith, *Slavery and Society at Rome* (1994). The best single overview of the major aspects of the slave system in the Roman Empire.

Chevallier, Raymond, *Roman Roads*, trans. N. H. Field (1976). A guide to the fundamentals of the construction, maintenance, administration, and mapping of Roman roads.

Coarelli, Fillipo (ed.), *Pompeii*, trans. Patricia Cockram (2006). A lavishly illustrated large volume that allows the reader to sense some of the wondrous wealth of the buried city of Pompeii.

Colledge, Malcolm A. R., *The Parthians* (1967). A bit dated but still a fundamental introduction to the Parthians, the major power on the eastern frontier of the Roman Empire.

Cornell, Tim, *The Beginnings of Rome: Italy and Rome from the Bronze Age to the Punic Wars, c. 2000 to 264 B.C.* (1995). The single best one-volume history of Rome through its early history to the first war with Carthage.

Cornell, Tim, and John Matthews, *Atlas of the Roman World* (1982). A history of the Roman world; much more than simply an atlas. It is provided not only with good maps and a gazetteer but also with marvelous color illustrations and a text that guides the reader through the basics of Roman history.

Csikszentmihalyi, Mark, *Readings in Han Chinese Thought* (2006). A volume presenting a representative selection of primary sources to illustrate the growth of ideas in early imperial times; a useful introduction to the key strains of thought during this crucial period.

Dixon, Suzanne, *The Roman Family* (1992). The best one-volume guide to the nature of the Roman family and family relations.

Garnsey, Peter, and Richard Saller, *The Roman Empire: Economy, Society, and Culture* (1987). A perceptive and critical introduction to three basic aspects of social life in the empire.

Giardina, Andrea (ed.), *The Romans*, trans. Lydia Cochrane (1993). Individual studies of important typical figures in Roman society, from the peasant and the bandit to the merchant and the soldier.

Goldsworthy, Adrian, *The Roman Army at War: 100 B.C.–A.D. 200* (1996). A summary history and analysis of the Roman army in action during the late Republic and early Empire.

Goodman, Martin, *The Roman World: 44 B.C.–A.D. 180* (1997). A newer basic history text covering the high Roman Empire.

Harris, William, *Ancient Literacy* (1989). A basic survey of what is known about communication in the form of writing and books in the Roman Empire.

Hopkins, Keith, *Death and Renewal: Sociological Studies in Roman History*, vol. 2 (1983). Innovative studies in Roman history, including one of the best on gladiators and another on death and funerals.

———, *A World Full of Gods: Pagans, Jews and Christians in the Roman Empire* (1999). A somewhat unusual but interesting and provocative look at the world of religions in the Roman Empire.

Juliano, Annette L., and Judith A. Lerner (eds.), *Nomads, Traders and Holy Men along China's Silk Road* (2003). A description of the travelers along the Silk Road in human terms, focusing on warfare, markets, and religion.

Kraus, Theodore, and Leonard von Matt, *Pompeii and Herculaneum: The Living Cities of the Dead*, trans. Robert E. Wolf (1975). A huge, lavishly illustrated compendium of all aspects of life in the buried cities of Pompeii and Herculaneum as preserved in the archaeological record.

Loewe, Michael, *The Government of the Qin and Han Empires: 221 BCE–220 CE* (2006). A useful overview of the government of the early empires of China. Topics include the structure of central government, provincial and local government, the armed forces, officials, government communications, the laws of the empire, and control of the people and the land.

Millar, Fergus, *The Crowd in the Late Republic* (1998). An innovative study of the democratic power of the citizens in the city of Rome itself.

———, *The Emperor in the Roman World, 31 B.C.–A.D. 337* (1992). Everything you might want to know about the Roman emperor, with special emphasis on his civil role as the administrator of an empire.

Potter, David, *Roman Empire at Bay: A.D. 180–395* (2004). A new basic text covering the later Roman Empire, including the critical transition to a Christian state.

Potter, David S., and David J. Mattingly (eds.), *Life, Death, and Entertainment in the Roman Empire* (1999). A good introduction to basic aspects of Roman life in the empire, including the family, feeding the cities, religion, and popular entertainment.

Qian, Sima, *Records of the Grand Historian: Qin Dynasty,* trans. Burton Watson, 3rd ed. (1995). The classic work of Chinese history in a readable translation. The Han dynasty's Grand Historian describes the slow rise and meteoric fall of the Qin dynasty from the point of view of the succeeding dynasty, which Sima Qian witnessed or heard of during his lifetime.

Southern, Pat, *The Roman Army: A Social and Institutional History* (2006). A fundamental guide to all aspects of the Roman army.

Todd, Malcolm, *The Early Germans*, rev. ed. (2004). A basic survey of the peoples in central and western Europe at the time of the Roman Empire.

Vainker, Shelagh, *Chinese Silk: A Cultural History* (2004). A work that traces the cultural history of silk in China from its early origins to the twentieth century and considers its relationship to the other decorative arts. The author draws on the most recent archaeological evidence to emphasize the role of silk in Chinese history, trade, religion, and literature.

Wells, Peter S., *The Barbarians Speak: How the Conquered Peoples Shaped Roman Europe* (1999). The cultures of the peoples of central and northern Europe at the time of the Roman Empire and their impact on Roman culture.

Wood, Francis, *The Silk Road: Two Thousand Years in the Heart of Asia* (2004). A work illustrated with drawings, manuscripts, paintings, and artifacts to trace the Silk Road to its origins as far back as Alexander the Great. The author stresses the importance of the Silk Road to cultural and religious movements.

Woolf, Greg (ed.), *The Cambridge Illustrated History of the Roman World* (2005). A good guide to various aspects of Roman history, culture, and provincial life.

Chapter 8 The Rise of Universal Religions, 300–600 CE

Bowersock, Glen W., Peter Brown, and Oleg Grabar, *Late Antiquity: A Guide to the Postclassical World* (1999). Essays and items for the entire period 150–750 CE. The volume covers the Roman, East Roman, Sasanian, and early Islamic worlds.

Brown, Peter, *The Rise of Western Christendom: Triumph and Diversity, A.D. 200–1000*, 2nd ed. (2003). The rise and spread of Christianity in Europe and Asia, with up-to-date bibliographies on all topics, maps, and time charts.

———, *The World of Late Antiquity: From Marcus Aurelius to Muhammad, AD 150–750* (1989). A social, religious, and cultural history of the late Roman and Sasanian empires, with illustrations and a time chart.

Bühler, G. (trans.), *The Laws of Manu* (1886). The classic translation of one of India's most important historical, legal, and religious texts.

Coe, Michael D., *The Maya*, 6th ed. (1999). A work by the world's most famous Mayanologist, with recent evidence, analyses, and illustrations.

Cowgill, George L., "The Central Mexican Highlands and the Rise of Teotihuacan to the Decline of Tula," in Richard Adams and Murdo Macleod (eds.), *The Cambridge History of the Native Peoples of the Americas*, vol. 2, *Mesoamerica, Part 1* (2000). A thorough review of findings about urban states in central Mexico.

Fash, William L., *Scribes, Warriors and Kings: The City of Copan and the Ancient Maya* (2001). A fascinating and comprehensive study of one of the most elaborate of the Mayan city-kingdoms.

Fowden, Elizabeth Key, *The Barbarian Plain: Saint Sergius between Rome and Iran* (1999). The study of a major Christian shrine and its relations to Romans, Persians, and Arabs.

Fowden, Garth, *Empire to Commonwealth: The Consequences of Monotheism in Late Antiquity* (1993). A study of the relation between empire and world religions in western Asia.

Gombrich, Richard F., and Sheldon Pollack (eds.), *Clay Sanskrit Library* (2005–2006). All major works from the Gupta and post-Gupta periods, in both Sanskrit and English versions. During the Gupta period, classical Sanskrit literature reached its apex, with abundant drama, poetry, and folk stories.

Gordon, Charles, *The Age of Attila* (1960). The last century of the Roman Empire in western Europe, vividly illustrated from contemporary sources.

Harper, Prudence, *The Royal Hunter: The Art of the Sasanian Empire* (1978). The ideology of the Sasanian Empire as shown through excavated hoards of precious silverware.

Heather, Peter, *The Fall of the Roman Empire: A New History of Rome and the Barbarians* (2006). A military and political narrative based on up-to-date archaeological material.

Herrmann, Georgina, *Iranian Revival* (1977). The structure and horizons of the Sasanian Empire as revealed in its monuments.

Hillgarth, Jocelyn (ed.), *Christianity and Paganism, 350–750: The Conversion of Western Europe*, rev. ed. (1986). A collection of contemporary sources.

Holcombe, Charles, *In the Shadow of the Han: Literati Thought and Society at the Beginning of the Southern Dynasties* (1994). A clear and concise account of the evolution of thought in China after the fall of the Han dynasty in 220 CE. The book presents the rise of Buddhism and Daoism as popular religions as well as elite interests in classical learning in a time of political division and barbarian conquest in North and South China.

La Vaissière, Étienne de, *Sogdian Traders: A History*, trans. James Ward (2005). A summary of historical facts about the most important trading community and its commercial networks on the Silk Road, from the early centuries CE to its demise in the ninth century CE.

Liu, Xinru, and Lynda Norene Shaffer, *Connections across Eurasia: Transportation, Communication, and Cultural Exchanges on the Silk Roads* (2007). A survey of trade and religious activities on the Silk Road.

Maas, Michael, *Readings in Late Antiquity: A Source Book* (1999). Well-chosen extracts that illustrate the interrelation of Romans and non-Romans, and of Christians, Jews, and pagans.

Maas, Michael (ed.), *The Cambridge Companion to the Age of Justinian* (2005). A survey of all aspects of the eastern Roman Empire in the sixth century CE.

Moffett, Samuel, *A History of Christianity in Asia*, vol. 1 (1993). Particularly valuable on Christians in China and India.

Munro-Hay, Stuart, *Aksum: An African Civilization of Late Antiquity* (1991). The origins of the Christian kingdom of Ethiopia.

Murdock, George P., *Africa: Its Peoples and Their History* (1959). A vital introduction to the peoples of Africa and their history.

Oliver, Roland, *The African Experience: From Olduvai Gorge to the Twenty-First Century* (1999). An important overview, written by one of the pioneering scholars of African history and one of the leading authorities on the Bantu migrations.

Pregadio, Fabrizio, *Great Clarity: Daoism and Alchemy in Early Medieval China* (2006). An examination of the religious aspects of Daoism. The book focuses on the relation of alchemy to the Daoist traditions of the third to sixth centuries CE and shows how alchemy was integrated into the elaborate body of doctrines and practices of Daoists at that time.

Tempels, Placide, *Bantu Philosophy* (1959). A highly influential effort to argue for the underlying cultural unity of all the Bantu peoples.

Vansina, Jan, *Paths in the Rainforests: Toward a History of Political Tradition in Equatorial Africa* (1990). The best work on Bantu history.

Walker, Joel, *The Legend of Mar Kardagh: Narrative and Christian Heroism in Late Antique Iraq* (2006). Christians and Zoroastrians in northern Iraq and in Iran.

Wells, Peter, *The Barbarians Speak: How the Conquered Peoples Shaped the Roman Empire* (1999). A view, based on archaeology, of the Roman Empire from the non-Roman side of the frontier.

Yarshater, Ehsan, *Encyclopedia Iranica* (1982–). A guide to all aspects of the Sasanian Empire and to religion and culture in the regions between Mesopotamia and central Asia.

Xuanzang, *Faxianzhuan Jiaoxhu*. Text excerpt translated by Xinru Liu.

Zürcher, E., *The Buddhist Conquest of China: The Spread and Adaptation of Buddhism in Early Medieval China*, 3rd ed. (2007). A reissue of the classic account of the assimilation of Buddhism in China during the medieval period, with particular focus on the religious and philosophical success of Buddhism among Chinese elites in South China.

Chapter 9 New Empires and Common Cultures, 600–1000 CE

Ahmed, Leila, *Women and Gender in Islam* (1992). A superb overview of the relations between men and women throughout the history of Islam.

Aneirin, *Y Gododdin: Britain's Oldest Heroic Poem*, ed. and trans. A. O. H. Jarman (1988). A sixth-century Welsh text that describes the battle of the last Britons against the invading Anglo-Saxons.

Arberry, Arthur J., introduction to *The Koran Interpreted: A Translation*, trans. Arthur J. Arberry (1986). One of the most eloquent appreciations of this classical work of religion.

Augustine, *The City of God*, trans. H. Bettenson (1976). An excellent translation of Augustine's monumental work of history, philosophy, and religion.

Berkey, Jonathan P., *The Formation of Islam: Religion and Society in the Near East, 600–1800* (2005). A recent overview of the history of Islam before the modern era. It is particularly sensitive to the influence of external elements on the history of the Muslim peoples.

Bol, Peter, *This Culture of Ours: Intellectual Transitions in T'ang and Sung China* (1994). A study tracing the transformation of the shared culture of the Chinese learned elite from the seventh to the twelfth centuries.

Brown, Peter, *The Rise of Western Christendom: Triumph and Diversity,* AD 200–1000, 2nd ed. (2003). A description of the changes in Christianity in northern Europe and the emergence of the new cultures and political structures that coincided with this development.

Bulliet, Richard W., *Conversion to Islam in the Medieval Period: An Essay in Quantitative History* (1979). A study of the rate at which the populations overrun by Arab conquerors in the seventh century CE embraced the religion of their rulers.

Cook, Michael, *The Koran: A Very Short Introduction* (2000). A useful overview of Islam's holy book.

———, *Muhammad* (1983). A brief but careful life of the Prophet that takes full account of the prolific and often controversial preexisting scholarship.

Creswell, K. A. C., *A Short Account of Early Muslim Architecture, Revised and supplemented by James W. Allan* (1992). The definitive treatment of the subject, brought up to date.

Cross, S. H., and O. P. Sherbowitz-Westor, trans., *The Russian Primary Chronicle* (1953). A vivid record of the Viking settlement of Kiev, of the conversion of Kiev, and of the princes of Kiev in the tenth and eleventh centuries.

Donner, Fred M., *The Early Islamic Conquests* (1981). The best account of the Arab conquests in the Persian and Byzantine empires in the seventh century.

Duncan, John, *The Origins of the Chosŏn Dynasty* (2000). A historical account of the early Korean dynasties from 900 to 1400.

Fage, J. D., *Ghana: A Historical Introduction* (1966). A brief but authoritative history of Ghana from earliest times to the present.

Fisher, Humphrey J., *Slavery in the History of Muslim Black Africa* (2001). A general history of the relations between North Africa and black Africa, focusing on one of the most important aspects of contact—the slave trade.

Graham-Campbell, James, *Cultural Atlas of the Viking World* (1994). A positioning of the Vikings against their wider background in both western and eastern Europe.

Hawting, G. R., *The First Dynasty of Islam: The Umayyad Caliphate,* A.D. 661–750 (2000). The essential scholarly treatment of Islam's first dynasty.

Herrmann, Georgina, *Iranian Revival* (1977). The structure and horizons of the Sasanian Empire as revealed in its monuments.

Hillgarth, J. N. (ed.), *Christianity and Paganism, 350–750: The Conversion of Western Europe,* rev. ed. (1986). A collection of contemporary sources.

Hodges, Richard, and David Whitehouse, *Mohammed, Charlemagne, and the Origins of Europe* (1983). A spirited comparison of Islam and the rise of Europe.

Hodgson, Marshall G. S., *The Venture of Islam: Conscience and History in a World Civilization* (1977), 3 vols. A magnificent history of the Islamic peoples. Its first volume, *The Classical Age of Islam,* is basic reading for anyone interested in the history of the Muslim world.

Holdsworth, May, *Women of the Tang Dynasty* (1999). An account of women's lives during the Tang dynasty.

Hourani, Albert, *History of the Arab Peoples* (2002). The best overview of Arab history.

Jones, Gwynn, *The Norse Atlantic Saga* (1986). The Viking discovery of America.

Kennedy, Hugh, *The Prophet and the Age of the Caliphate: The Islamic Near East from the Sixth to the Eleventh Century* (2004). A very good recent synthesis of the rise and spread of Islam.

Lee, Peter, et al. (eds.), *Sources of Korean Tradition,* vol. 1 (1996). A unique view of Korean history through the eyes and words of the participants or witnesses themselves, as provided in translations of official documents, letters, and policies.

Levtzion, Nehemia, *Ancient Ghana and Mali* (1980). The best introduction to the kingdoms of West Africa.

Levtzion, Nehemia, and Jay Spaulding, *Medieval West Africa: Views from Arab Scholars and Merchants* (2003). An indispensable source book on early West African history.

Lewis, Bernard, *The Middle East: Two Thousand Years of History from the Rise of Christianity to the Present Day* (1995). A stimulating introduction to an area that has seen the emergence of three of the great world religions.

——— (trans.), *Islam from the Prophet Muhammad to the Capture of Constantinople* (1974). Vol. 2: Religion and Society. A fine collection of original sources that portray various aspects of classical Islamic society.

Lewis, David Levering, *God's Crucible: Islam and the Making of Europe, 570–1215* (2008). An exciting and well-written overview of the high period of Islamic power and cultural attainments.

Middleton, John, *The Swahili: The Social Landscape of a Mercantile Community* (2000). An exciting synthesis of the Swahili culture of East Africa.

Miyazaki, Ichisada, *China's Examination Hell* (1981). A study of China's examination system.

Nurse, Derek, and Thomas Spear, *The Swahili: Reconstructing the History and Language of an African Society, 800–1500* (1984). A work that explores the history of the Muslim peoples who lived along the coast of East Africa.

Peters, F. E., *Muhammad and the Origins of Islam* (1994). A work that explores the early history of Islam and highlights the critical role that Muhammad played in promoting a new religion and a powerful Arab identity.

Schirokauer, Conrad, et al., *A Brief History of Japanese Civilization,* 2nd ed. (2005). A balanced account; chapters focus on developments in art, religion, literature, and thought as well as on Japan's economic, political, and social history in medieval times.

Smith, Julia, *Europe after Rome: A New Cultural History, 500–1000* (2005). A vivid analysis of society and culture in so-called Dark Age Europe.

Totman, Conrad, *History of Japan* (2004). A recent and readable summary of Japanese history from ancient to modern times.

Twitchett, Denis, *The Birth of the Chinese Meritocracy: Bureaucrats and Examinations in T'ang China* (1976). A description of the role of the written civil examinations that began during the Tang dynasty.

———, *Financial Administration under the T'ang Dynasty* (1970). A pioneering account—based on rare Dunhuang documents that survived from medieval times in Buddhist grottoes in central Asia—of the political and economic system undergirding the Chinese imperial state.

Whittow, Mark, *The Making of Byzantium, 600–1025* (1996). A study on the survival and revival of the eastern Roman empire as a major power in eastern Europe and Southwest Asia.

Wood, Ian, *The Missionary Life: Saints and the Evangelization of Europe, 400–1050* (2001). The horizons of Christians on the frontiers of Europe.

Chapter 10 Becoming "The World," 1000–1300 CE

Allsen, Thomas, *Commodity and Exchange in the Mongol Empire: A Cultural History of Islamic Textiles* (1997). A study that uses golden brocade, the textile most treasured by Mongol rulers, as a lens through which to analyze the vast commercial networks facilitated by the Mongol conquests and control.

———, *Culture and Conquest in Mongol Eurasia* (2001). A work that emphasizes the cultural and scientific exchanges that took place across Afro-Eurasia as a result of the Mongol conquest.

Bartlett, Robert, *The Making of Europe: Conquest, Colonization and Cultural Change, 950–1350* (1993). The modes of cultural, political, and demographic expansion of feudal Europe along its frontiers, especially in eastern Europe.

Bay, Edna G., *Wives of the Leopards: Gender, Politics, and Culture in the Kingdom of Dahomey* (1998). A work that stresses the role of women in an important West African society and dips into the early history of this area.

Beach, D. N., *Shona and Zimbabwe, 900–1850: An Outline of Shona History* (1980). A good place to start for exploring the history of Great Zimbabwe.

Brooks, George E., *Landlords and Strangers: Ecology, Society, and Trade in Western Africa, 1000–1630* (1993). A survey assembled from primary sources of early West African history that stresses transregional connections.

Buzurg ibn Shahriyar of Ramhormuz, *The Book of the Wonders of India: Mainland, Sea and Islands,* ed. and trans. G. S. P. Freeman-Greenville (1981). A collection of stories told by sailors, both true and fantastic; they help us imagine the lives of sailors of the era.

Chappell, Sally A. Kitt, *Cahokia: Mirror of the Cosmos* (2002). A thorough and vivid account of the "mound people"; it explores not just what we know of Cahokia but how we know it.

Christian, David, *A Short History of Russia, Central Asia, and Mongolia,* vol. 1, *Inner Eurasia from Prehistory to the Mongol Empire* (1998). Essential reading for students interested in interconnections across the Afro-Eurasian landmass.

Curtin, Philip, *Cross-Cultural Trade in World History* (1984). A groundbreaking book on intercultural trade with a primary focus on Africa, especially the cross-Saharan trade and Swahili coastal trade.

Dawson, Christopher, *Mission to Asia* (1980). Accounts of China and the Mongol Empire brought back by Catholic missionaries and diplomats after 1240 CE.

Foltz, Richard C., *Religions of the Silk Road: Overland Trade and Cultural Exchange from Antiquity to the Fifteenth Century* (1999). A study of the populations and the cities of the Silk Road as transmitters of culture across long distances.

Franklin, Simon, and Jonathan Shepherd, *The Emergence of Rus: 750–1200* (1996). The formation of medieval Russia between the Baltic and Black seas.

Gibb, Hamilton A. R., *Saladin: Studies in Islamic History,* ed. Yusuf Ibish (1974). A sympathetic portrait of one of Islam's leading political and military figures.

Goitein, S. D., *Letters of Medieval Jewish Traders* (1973). The classic study of medieval Jewish trading communities based on the commercial papers deposited in the Cairo Geniza (a synagogue storeroom) during the tenth and eleventh centuries; it explores not only commercial activities but also the personal lives of the traders around the Indian Ocean basin.

———, *A Mediterranean Society: An Abridgment in One Volume,* rev. and ed. Jacob Lassner (1999). A portrait of the Jewish merchant community with ties across the Afro-Eurasian landmass, based largely on the documents from the Cairo Geniza (of which Goitein was the primary researcher and interpreter).

———, "New Light on the Beginnings of the Karim Merchant," *Journal of Social and Economic History of the Orient* 1 (1958). Goitein's description of Egyptian trade.

Harris, Joseph E., *The African Presence in Asia: Consequences of the East African Slave Trade* (1971). One of the few books that looks broadly at the impact of Africans and African slavery on the societies of Asia.

Hartwell, Robert, "Demographic, Political, and Social Transformations of China, 750–1550," *Harvard Journal of Asiatic Studies* 42 (1982): 365–442. A pioneering study of the demographic changes that overtook China during the Tang and Song dynasties, which are described in light of political reform movements and social changes in this crucial era.

Historical Relations across the Indian Ocean: Report and Papers of the Meeting of Experts Organized by UNESCO at Port Louis, Mauritius, from 15 to 19 July, 1974 (1980). Excellent essays on the connections of Africa with Asia across the Indian Ocean.

Hitti, Philip, *An Arab-Syrian Gentleman and Warrior in the Period of the Crusades: Memoirs of Usāmah ibn-Munqidh* (1929). The Crusaders seen through Muslim eyes.

Hodgson, Natasha, *Women, Crusading, and the Holy Land in Historical Narrative* (2007). A book dealing with the Crusades and focusing on the place of women in them.

Holt, P. M., *The Age of the Crusades: The Near East from the Eleventh Century to 1517* (1984). The Crusades period as seen from the eastern Mediterranean and through the lens of a leading British scholar of the area.

Hymes, Robert, and Conrad Schirokauer (eds.), *Ordering the World: Approaches to State and Society in Sung Dynasty China* (1993). A collection of essays that traces the intellectual, social, and political movements that shaped the Song state and its elites.

Ibn Battuta, *The Travels of Ibn Battuta,* trans. H. A. R. Gibb (2002). A readable translation of the classic book, originally published in 1929.

Ibn Fadlan, Ahmad, *Ibn Fadlan's Journey to Russia: A Tenth Century Traveler from Baghdad to the Volga River,* trans. with commentary by Richard Frye (2005). A coherent summary of the observations of an envoy who traveled from Baghdad to Russia.

Irwin, Robert, *The Middle East in the Middle Ages: The Early Mamluk Sultanate, 1250–1582* (1986). Egypt under Mamluk rule.

Jeppie, Shamil, and Diagne, Souleymane Bachir, editors, *The Meanings of Timbuktu* (2008). New materials on the ancient Muslim city of Timbuktu by scholars who have been preserving its manuscripts and writing about its historical importance.

Lancaster, Lewis, Kikun Suh, and Chai-shin Yu (eds.), *Buddhism in Koryo: A Royal Religion* (1996). A description of Buddhism at its height in the Koryo period, when the religion made significant contributions to the development of Korean culture.

Levtzion, Nehemia, and Randall L. Pouwels (eds.), *The History of Islam in Africa* (2000). A useful general survey of the place of Islam in African history.

Lewis, Bernard (trans.), *Islam: From the Prophet Muhammad to the Capture of Constantinople* (1974). Vol. 2: *Religion and Society*. A fine collection of original sources that portray various aspects of classical Islamic society.

Lopez, Robert S., *The Commercial Revolution of the Middle Ages, 950–1350* (1976). An account focusing on the development around the Mediterranean of commercial practices such as the use of currency, accounting, and credit.

Maalouf, Amin, *The Crusades through Muslim Eyes,* trans. Jon Rothschild (1984). The European Crusaders as seen by the Muslim world.

Marcus, Harold G., *A History of Ethiopia* (2002). An authoritative overview of the history of this great culture.

Mass, Jeffrey, *Yoritomo and the Founding of the First Bakufu: The Origins of Dual Government in Japan* (1999). A revisionist account of how the Kamakura military leader Minamoto Yoritomo established the "dual polity" of court and warrior government in Japan.

McDermott, Joseph, *A Social History of the Chinese Book: Books and Literati Culture in Late Imperial China* (2006). The history of the book in China since the Song dynasty, with comparisons to the book's role in other civilizations, particularly the European.

McIntosh, Roderik, *The Peoples of the Middle Niger: The Island of Gold* (1988). A historical survey of an area often omitted from other textbooks.

Moore, Jerry D., *Cultural Landscapes in the Ancient Andes: Archaeologies of Place* (2005). The most recent and up-to-date analysis of findings based on recent archaeological evidence, emphasizing the importance of local cultures and diversity in the Andes.

Niane, D. T. (ed.), *Africa from the Twelfth to the Sixteenth Century,* vol. 4 of *General History of Africa* (1984). The general UNESCO history of Africa's volume on four centuries of African history. This work features the scholarship of Africans.

Oliver, Roland (ed.), *From c. 1050 to c. 1600,* vol. 3 of *The Cambridge History of Africa,* ed. J. D. Fage and Roland Oliver (1977). Another general survey of African history. This volume draws heavily on the work of British scholars.

Peters, Edward, *The First Crusade* (1971). The Crusaders as seen through their own eyes.

Petry, Carl F. (ed.), *Islamic Egypt, 640–1517,* vol. 1 of *The Cambridge History of Egypt,* ed. M. W. Daly (1998). A solid overview of the history of Islamic Egypt up to the Ottoman conquest.

Polo, Marco, *The Travels of Marco Polo,* ed. Manuel Komroff (1926). A solid translation of Marco Polo's famous account.

Popovic, Alexandre, *The Revolt of African Slaves in Iraq in the 3rd/9th Century,* trans. Leon King (1999). The account of a massive revolt against their slave masters by African slaves taken to labor in Iraq's mines and fields.

Scott, Robert, *Gothic Enterprise: A Guide to Understanding the Medieval Cathedral* (2003). The meaning and social function of religious building in medieval cities in northern Europe.

Shaffer, Lynda Norene, *Maritime Southeast Asia to 1500* (1996). A history of the peoples of the southeast fringe of the Eastern Hemisphere, up to the time that they became connected to the global commercial networks of the world.

Shimada, Izumi, "Evolution of Andean Diversity: Regional Formations (500 BCE–CE 600)," in Frank Salomon and Stuart Schwartz (eds.), *South America,* vol. 3 of *The Cambridge History of the Native Peoples of the Americas* (1999), part 1, pp. 350–517. A splendid overview that contrasts the varieties of lowland and highland cultures.

Steinberg, David Joel, et al., *In Search of Southeast Asia: A Modern History* (1987). An account of the emergence of the modern Southeast Asian polities of Cambodia, Burma, Thailand, and Indonesia.

Tyerman, Christopher, *God's War: A New History of the Crusades* (2006). The balance of religious and nonreligious motivations in the Crusades.

Waley, Daniel, *The Italian City-Republics,* 3rd ed. (1988). The structures and culture of the new cities of medieval Italy.

Watson, Andrew, *Agricultural Innovation in the Early Islamic World: The Diffusion of Crops and Farming Techniques, 700–1100* (1983). An impressive study of the spread of new crops throughout the Muslim world.

Abd al-Rahman III Islamic ruler in Spain who held a countercaliphate and reigned from 912 to 961 CE.

aborigines Original, native inhabitants of a region, as opposed to invaders, colonizers, or later peoples of mixed ancestry.

absolute monarchy Form of government where one body, usually the monarch, controls the right to tax, judge, make war, and coin money. The term *enlightened absolutists* was often used to refer to state monarchies in seventeenth- and eighteenth-century Europe.

acid rain Precipitation containing large amounts of sulfur, mainly from coal-fired plants.

adaptation Ability to alter behavior and to innovate, finding new ways of doing things.

African National Congress (ANC) Multiracial organization founded in 1912 in an effort to end racial discrimination in South Africa.

Afrikaners Descendants of the original Dutch settlers of South Africa; formerly referred to as Boers.

Agones Athletic contests in ancient Greece.

Ahmosis Egyptian ruler in the southern part of the country who ruled from 1550 to 1525 BCE; Ahmosis used Hyksos weaponry—horse chariots in particular—to defeat the Hyksos themselves.

Ahura Mazda Supreme God of the Persians believed to have created the world and all that is good and to have appointed earthly kings.

AIDS (Acquired Immunodeficiency Syndrome) Virus that compromises the ability of the infected person's immune system to ward off disease. First detected in 1981, AIDS was initially stigmatized as a "gay cancer," but as it spread to heterosexuals, public awareness about it increased. In its first two decades, AIDS killed 12 million people.

Akbarnamah Mughal intellectual Abulfazl's *Book of Akbar*, which attempted to reconcile the traditional Sufi interest in the inner life within the worldly context of a great empire.

Alaric II Visigothic king who issued a simplified code of innovative imperial law.

Alexander the Great (356–323 BCE) Leader who used novel tactics and new kinds of armed forces to conquer the Persian Empire, which extended from Egypt and the Mediterranean Sea to the interior of what is now Afghanistan and as far as the Indus River valley. Alexander's conquests broke down barriers between the Mediterranean world and Southwest Asia and transferred massive amounts of wealth and power to the Mediterranean, transforming it into a more unified world of economic and cultural exchange.

Alexandria Port city in Egypt named after Alexander the Great. Alexandria was a model city in the Hellenistic world. It was built up by a multiethnic population from around the Mediterranean world.

Al-Khwarizmi Scientist and mathematician who lived from 780 to 850 CE and is known for having modified Indian digits into Arabic numerals.

Allied powers Name given to the alliance between Britain, France, Russia, and Italy, who fought against Germany and Austria-Hungary (the Central powers) in World War I. In World War II the name was used for the alliance between Britain, France, and America, who fought against the Axis powers (Germany, Italy, and Japan).

allomothering System by which mothers relied on other women, including their own mothers, daughters, sisters, and friends, to help in the nurturing and protecting of children.

alluvium Area of land created by river deposits.

American Railway Union Workers' union that initiated the Pullman Strike of 1894, which led to violence and ended in the leaders' arrest.

Amnesty International Non-governmental organization formed to defend "prisoners of conscience"—those detained for their beliefs, race, sex, ethnic origin, language, or religion.

Amorites Name that Mesopotamian urbanites called the transhumant herders from the Arabian desert. Around 2300 BCE, the Amorites, along with the Elamites, were at the center of newly formed dynasties in southern Mesopotamia.

Amun Once insignificant Egyptian god elevated to higher status by Amenemhet (1991–1962 BCE). *Amun* means "hidden" in Ancient Egyptian; the name was meant to convey the god's omnipresence.

Analects Texts that included the teachings and cultural ideals of Confucius.

anarchism Belief that society should be a free association of its members, not subject to government, laws, or police.

Anatolia Now mainly the area known as modern Turkey; in the sixth millennium BCE, people from Anatolia, Greece, and the Levant took to boats and populated the Aegean. Their small villages endured almost unchanged for two millennia.

Angkor Wat Magnificent Khmer Vaishnavite temple that crowned the royal palace in Angkor. It had statues representing the Hindu pantheon of gods.

Anglo-Boer War (1899–1902) Anticolonial struggle in South Africa between the British and the Afrikaners over the gold-rich Transvaal. In response to the Afrikaners' guerrilla tactics and in order to contain the local population, the British instituted the first concentration camps. Ultimately, Britain won the conflict.

animal domestication Gradual process that occurred simultaneously with or just before the domestication of plants, depending on the region.

annals Historical records. Notable annals are the cuneiform inscriptions that record successful Assyrian military campaigns.

Anti-Federalists Critics of the U.S. Constitution who sought to defend the people against the power of the federal government and insisted on a bill of rights to protect individual liberties from government intrusion.

Apartheid Racial segregation policy of the Afrikaner-dominated South African government. Legislated in 1948 by the Afrikaner National Party, it had existed in South Africa for many years.

Arab-Israeli War of 1948–1949 Conflict between Israeli and Arab armies that arose in the wake of a U.N. vote to partition Palestine into Arab and Jewish territories. The war shattered the legitimacy of Arab ruling elites.

Aramaic Dialect of a Semitic language spoken in Southwest Asia; it became the lingua franca of the Persian Empire.

Aristotle (384–322 BCE) Philosopher who studied under Plato but came to different conclusions about nature and politics. Aristotle believed in collecting observations about nature and discerning patterns to ascertain how things worked.

Aryans Nomadic charioteers who spoke Indo-European languages and entered South Asia in 1500 BCE. The early Aryan settlers were herders.

Asante state State located in present-day Ghana, founded by the Asantes at the end of the seventeenth century. It grew in power in the next century because of its access to gold and its involvement in the slave trade.

ascetic One who rejects material possessions and physical pleasures.

Asiatic Society Cultural organization founded by British Orientalists who supported native culture but still believed in colonial rule.

Aśoka Emperor of the Mauryan dynasty from 268 to 231 BCE; he was a great conqueror and unifier of India. He is said to have embraced Buddhism toward the end of his life.

Assur One of two cities on the upper reaches of the Tigris River that were the heart of Assyria proper (the other was Nineveh).

Aśvaghosa First known Sanskrit writer. He may have lived from 80 to 150 CE and may have composed a biography of the Buddha.

Ataturk, Mustafa Kemal (1881–1938) Ottoman army officer and military hero who helped forge the modern Turkish nation-state. He and his followers deposed the sultan, declared Turkey a republic, and constructed a European-like secular state, eliminating Islam's hold over civil and political affairs.

Atlantic system New system of trade and expansion that linked Europe, Africa, and the Americas. It emerged in the wake of European voyages across the Atlantic Ocean.

Atma Vedic term signifying the eternal self, represented by the trinity of deities.

Atman In the Upanishads, an eternal being who exists everywhere. The atman never perishes but is reborn or transmigrates into another life.

Attila Sole ruler of all Hunnish tribes from 433 to 453 CE. Harsh and much feared, he formed the first empire to oppose Rome in northern Europe.

Augustus Title meaning "Revered One," assumed in 27 BCE by the Roman ruler Octavian (63–14 BCE). This was one of many titles he assumed; others included *imperator*, *princeps*, and *Caesar*.

Australopithecines Hominid species that appeared 3 million years ago and, unlike other animals, walked on two legs. Their brain capacity was a little less than one-third of a modern human's or about the size of the brain capacity of today's African apes. Although not humans, they carried the genetic and biological material out of which modern humans would later emerge.

Austro-Hungarian Empire Dual monarchy established by the Habsburg family in 1867; it collapsed at the end of World War I.

authoritarianism Centralized and dictatorial form of government, proclaimed by its adherents to be superior to parliamentary democracy and especially effective at mobilizing the masses. This idea was widely accepted in parts of the world during the 1930s.

Avesta Compilation of holy works transmitted orally by priests for millennia and eventually recorded in the sixth century BCE.

Axis powers The three aggressor states in World War II: Germany, Japan, and Italy.

Aztec Empire Mesoamerican empire that originated with a league of three Mexica cities in 1430 and gradually expanded through the Central Valley of Mexico, uniting numerous small, independent states under a single monarch who ruled with the help of counselors, military leaders, and priests. By the late fifteenth century, the Aztec realm may have embraced 25 million people. In 1521, they were defeated by the conquistador Hernán Cortés.

baby boom Post–World War II upswing in U.S. birth rates; it reversed a century of decline.

bactrian camel Two-humped animal domesticated in central Asia around 2500 BCE. The bactrian camel was heartier than the one-humped dromedary and became the animal of choice for the harsh and varied climates typical of Silk Road trade.

Baghdad Capital of the Islamic Empire under the Abbasid dynasty, founded in 762 CE (in modern-day Iraq). In the medieval period, it was a center of administration, scholarship, and cultural growth for what came to be known as the Golden Age of Islamic science.

Baghdad Pact (1955) Middle Eastern military alliance between countries friendly with America who were also willing to align themselves with the western countries against the Soviet Union.

Balam Na Stone temple and place of pilgrimage for the Mayan people of Mexico's Yucatan peninsula.

Balfour Declaration Letter (November 2, 1917) by Lord Arthur J. Balfour, British foreign secretary, that promised a homeland for the Jews in Palestine.

Bamboo Annals Shang stories and foundation myths that were written on bamboo strips and later collected.

Bantu Language first spoken by people who lived in the southeastern area of modern Nigeria around 1000 CE.

Bantu migrations Waves of rapid population movement from West Africa into eastern and southern Africa during the first millennium CE that brought advanced agricultural practices to these regions and absorbed most of the preexisting hunting-and-gathering populations.

barbarian Derogatory term used to describe pastoral nomads, painting them as enemies of civilization; the term *barbarian* used to have a more neutral meaning than it does today.

barbarian invasions Violent migration of people in the late fourth and fifth centuries into Roman territory. These migrants had long been used as non-Roman soldiers.

basilicas Early church buildings, based on old royal audience halls.

Battle of Adwa (1896) Battle in which the Ethiopians defeated Italian colonial forces; it inspired many of Africa's later national leaders.

Battle of Wounded Knee (1890) Bloody massacre of Sioux Ghost Dancers by U.S. armed forces.

Bay of Pigs (1961) Unsuccessful invasion of Cuba by Cuban exiles supported by the U.S. government. The invaders intended to incite an insurrection in Cuba and overthrow the communist regime of Fidel Castro.

Bedouins Nomadic pastoralists in the deserts of the Middle East.

Beer Hall Putsch (1923) Nazi intrusion into a meeting of Bavarian leaders in a Munich beer hall; the Nazis were attempting to force support for their cause; Adolf Hitler was imprisoned for a year after the incident.

Beghards (1500s) Eccentric European group whose members claimed to be in a state of grace that allowed them to do as they pleased—from adultery, free love, and nudity to murder; also called Brethren of Free Speech.

bell beaker Ancient drinking vessel, an artifact from Europe, so named because its shape resembles an inverted bell.

Berenice of Egypt Egyptian "queen" who helped rule over the Kingdom of the Nile from 320 to 280 BCE.

Beringia Prehistoric thousand-mile-long land bridge that linked Siberia and North America (which had not been populated by hominids). About 18,000 years ago, *Homo sapiens* edged into this landmass.

Berlin Airlift (1948) Supply of vital necessities to West Berlin by air transport primarily under U.S. auspices. It was initiated in response to a land and water blockade of the city instituted by the Soviet Union in the hope that the Allies would be forced to abandon West Berlin.

Berlin Wall Wall built by the communists in Berlin in 1961 to prevent citizens of East Germany from fleeing to West Germany; torn down in 1989.

Bhakti Religious practice that grew out of Hinduism and emphasizes personal devotion to gods.

Bhakti Hinduism Popular form of Hinduism that emerged in the seventh century. The religion stresses devotion (*bhakti*) to God and uses vernacular languages (not Sanskrit) spoken by the common people.

big men Leaders of the extended household communities that formed village settlements in African rain forests.

big whites French plantation owners in Saint Domingue (present-day Haiti) who created one of the wealthiest slave societies.

Bilad al-Sudan Arabic for "the land of the blacks"; it consisted of the land lying south of the Sahara.

bilharzia Debilitating water-borne illness. It was widespread in Egypt, where it infected peasants who worked in the irrigation canals.

Bill of Rights First ten amendments to the U.S. Constitution; ratified in 1791.

bipedalism Walking on two legs, thereby freeing hands and arms to carry objects such as weapons and tools; one of several traits that distinguished hominids.

Black Death Great epidemic of the bubonic plague that ravaged Europe, East Asia, and North Africa in the fourteenth century, killing large numbers, including perhaps as many as one-third of the European population.

Black Jacobins Nickname for the rebels in Saint Domingue, including Toussaint L'Ouverture, a former slave who led the slaves of this French colony in the world's largest and most successful slave insurrection.

Black Panthers Radical African American group in the 1960s and 1970s; they advocated black separatism and pan-Africanism.

black shirts Fascist troops of Mussolini's regime; the squads received money from Italian landowners to attack socialist leaders.

Black Tuesday (October 29, 1929) Historic day when the U.S. stock market crashed, plunging the United States and international trading systems into crisis and leading the world into the "Great Depression."

Blitzkrieg "Lightning war"; type of warfare in which the Germans, during World War II, used coordinated aerial bombing campaigns along with tanks and infantrymen in motorized vehicles.

Bodhisattvas In Mahayan Buddhism, enlightened demigods who were ready to reach *nirvana* but delayed so that they might help others attain it.

Bolívar, Simón (1783–1830) Venezuelan leader who urged his followers to become "American," to overcome their local identities. He wanted the liberated countries to form a Latin American confederation, urging Peru and Bolivia to join Venezuela, Ecuador, and Colombia in the "Gran Colombia."

Bolsheviks Former members of the Russian Social Democratic Party who advocated the destruction of capitalist political and economic institutions and started the Russian Revolution. In 1918 the Bolsheviks changed their name to the Russian Communist Party.

Book of the Dead Ancient Egyptian funerary text that contains drawings and paintings as well as spells describing how to prepare the jewelry and amulets that were buried with a person in preparation for the afterlife.

bourgeoisie The middle class. In Europe, they sought to be recognized not by birth or title, but by capital and property.

Boxer Protocol Written agreement between the victors of the Boxer Uprising and the Qing Empire in 1901 that placed western troops in Beijing and required the regime to pay exorbitant damages for foreign life and property.

Boxer Uprising (1899–1900) Chinese peasant movement that opposed foreign influence, especially that of Christian missionaries; it was put down after the Boxers were defeated by an army composed mostly of Japanese, Russians, British, French, and Americans.

Brahma One of three major deities that form a trinity in Vedic religion. Brahma signifies birth. *See also* Vishnu *and* Siva.

Brahmans Vedic priests who performed rituals and communicated with the gods. Brahmans provided guidance on how to live in balance with the forces of nature as represented by the various deities. The codification of Vedic principles into codes of law took place at the hands of the Brahmans. They memorized Vedic works and compiled commentaries on them. They also developed their own set of rules and rituals, which developed into a full-scale theology. Originally memorized and passed on orally, these may have been written down sometime after the beginning of the Common Era. Brahmanism was reborn as Hinduism sometime during the first half of the first millennium CE.

British Commonwealth of Nations Union formed in 1926 that conferred "dominion status" on Britain's white settler colonies in Canada, Australia, and New Zealand.

British East India Company *See* East India Company.

bronze Alloy of copper and tin brought into Europe from Anatolia; used to make hard-edged weapons.

brown shirts Troops of German men who advanced the Nazi cause by holding street marches, mass rallies, and confrontations and by beating Jews and anyone who opposed the Nazis.

bubonic plague Acute infectious disease caused by a bacterium that is transmitted to humans by fleas from infected rats. It ravaged Europe and parts of Asia in the fourteenth century. Sometimes referred to as the "Black Death."

Buddha (Siddhartha Gautama; 563–483 BCE) Indian ascetic who founded Buddhism.

Buddhism Major South Asian religion that aims to end human suffering through the renunciation of desire. Buddhists believe that removing the illusion of a separate identity would lead to a state of contentment (nirvana). These beliefs challenged the traditional Brahmanic teachings of the time and provided the peoples of South Asia with an alternative to established traditions.

bullion Uncoined gold or silver.

Cahokia Commercial center for regional and long-distance trade in North America. Its hinterlands produced staples for urban consumers. In return, its crafts were exported inland by porters and to North American markets in canoes. *See also* Mound people.

Calaveras Allegorical skeleton drawings by the Mexican printmaker and artist José Guadalupe Posada. The works drew on popular themes of betrayal, death, and festivity.

caliphate Institution that arose as the successor to Muhammad's leadership and became both the political and religious head of the Islamic community. Although the caliphs exercised political authority over the Muslim community and were the head of the religious community, the *ummah,* they did not inherit Muhammad's prophetic powers and were not authorities in religious doctrine.

Candomblé Yoruba-based religion in northern Brazil; it interwove African practices and beliefs with Christianity.

canton system System officially established by imperial decree in 1759 that required European traders to have Chinese guild merchants act as guarantors for their good behavior and payment of fees.

caravan cities Set of networks at long-distance trade locations where groups of merchants could assemble during their journeys. Several of these developed into full-fledged cities, especially in the deserts of Arabia.

caravans Companies of men who transported and traded goods along overland routes in North Africa and central Asia; large caravans consisted of 600–1,000 camels and as many as 400 men.

caravansarais Inns along major trade routes that accommodated large numbers of traders, their animals, and their wares.

caravel Sailing vessel suited for nosing in and out of estuaries and navigating in waters with unpredictable currents and winds.

carrack Ship used on open bodies of water, such as the Mediterranean.

Carthage City in what is modern-day Tunisia; emblematic of the trading aspirations and activities of merchants in the Mediterranean. Pottery and other archaeological remains demonstrate that trading contacts with Carthage were as far-flung as Italy, Greece, France, Iberia, and West Africa.

cartography Mapmaking.

caste system Hierarchical system of organizing people and distributing labor.

Caste War of Yucatan (1847–1901) Conflict between Mayan Indians and the Mexican state over Indian autonomy and legal equality, which resulted in the Mexican takeover of the Yucatan peninsula.

Castro, Fidel (1926–) Cuban communist leader whose forces overthrew Batista's corrupt regime in early January 1959. Castro became increasingly radical as he consolidated power, announcing a massive redistribution of land and the nationalization of foreign oil refineries; he declared himself a socialist and aligned himself with the Soviet Union in the wake of the 1961 CIA-backed Bay of Pigs invasion.

Çatal Hüyük Site in Anatolia discovered in 1958. It was a dense honeycomb of settlements filled with rooms whose walls were covered with paintings of wild bulls, hunters, and pregnant women. Çatal Hüyük symbolizes an early transition into urban dwelling and dates to the eighth millennium BCE.

Cathedra Bishop's seat, or throne, in a church.

Catholic Church Unifying institution for Christians in western Europe after the collapse of the Roman Empire. Rome became the spiritual capital of western Europe and the bishops of Rome emerged as popes, the supreme head of the church, who possessed great moral authority.

Cato the Elder (234–149 BCE) Roman statesman, often seen as emblematic of the transition from a Greek to a Roman world. Cato the Elder wrote a manual for the new economy of slave plantation agriculture, invested in shipping and trading, learned Greek rhetoric, and added the genre of history to Latin literature.

Caudillos South American local military chieftains.

cave drawings Images on cave walls. The subjects are most often large game, although a few are images of humans. Other elements are impressions made by hands dipped in paint and pressed on a wall or abstract symbols and shapes.

Celali revolts (1595–1610) Peasant and artisan uprisings against the Ottoman state.

Central powers Defined in World War I as Germany and Austria-Hungary.

Chan Chan City founded between 850 and 900 CE by the Moche people in what is now modern-day Peru. It had a core population of 30,000 inhabitants.

Chan Santa Cruz Separate Mayan community formed as part of a crusade for spiritual salvation and the complete cultural separation of the Mayan Indians; means "little holy cross."

Chandra Gupta II King who reigned in South Asia from 320 to 335 CE. He shared his name with Chandragupta, the founder of the Mauryan Empire.

Chandravamsha One of two main lineages (the lunar one) of Vedic society, each with its own creation myth, ancestors, language, and rituals. Each lineage included many clans. *See* Suryavamsha.

chapatis Flat, unleavened Indian bread.

chariots Horse-driven carriages brought by the pastoral nomadic warriors from the steppes that became the favored mode of transportation for an urban aristocratic warrior class and for other men of power in agriculture-based societies. Control of chariot forces was the foundation of the new balance of power across Afro-Eurasia during the second millennium BCE.

charismatic Person who uses personal strengths or virtues, often laced with a divine aura, to command followers.

Charlemagne Emperor of the West and heir to Rome from 764 to 814 CE.

chartered companies Firms that were awarded monopoly trading rights over vast areas by European monarchs (e.g., Virginia Company, Dutch East India Company).

Chartism (1834–1848) Mass democratic movement to pass the Peoples' Charter in Britain, granting male suffrage, secret ballot, equal electoral districts, and annual parliaments, and absolving the requirement of property ownership for members of the parliament.

chattel slavery Form of slavery that sold people as property, the rise of which coincided with the expansion of city-states. Chattel slavery was eschewed by the Spartans, who also rejected the innovation of coin money.

Chavín A people who lived in what is now northern Peru from 1400 to 200 BCE. They were united more by culture and faith than by a unified political system.

Chernobyl (1986) Site in the Soviet Union (in Ukraine) of the meltdown of a nuclear reactor.

Chiang Kai-shek (1887–1975) Leader of the Guomindang following Sun Yat-sen's death who mobilized the Chinese masses through the New Life movement. In 1949 he lost the Chinese Revolution to the communists and moved his regime to Taiwan.

Chimu Empire South America's first empire; it developed during the first century of the second millennium in the Moche Valley on the Pacific coast.

chinampas Floating gardens used by Aztecs in the 1300s and 1400s to grow crops.

China's Sorrow Name for the Yellow River, which, when it changed course or flooded, could cause mass death and waves of migration.

chinoiserie Chinese silks, teas, tableware, jewelry, and paper; popular among Europeans in the seventeenth and eighteenth centuries.

Christendom Entire portion of the world in which Christianity prevailed.

Christianity Religion that originated at the height of the Roman Empire and in a direct confrontation with Roman imperial authority: the trial of Yeshua ben Yosef (Joshua son of Joseph; we know him today by the Greek form of his name, Jesus). Jesus was condemned for sedition and crucified. His followers believed that he was resurrected and that his teachings were not that of a man, but a god who had walked among human beings. At first, the Roman Empire refused to recognize Christianity and persecuted its followers, but in the fourth century CE Christianity was officially recognized as the Roman state religion.

Church of England Established form of Christianity in England dating from the sixteenth century.

city Highly populated concentration of economic, religious, and political power. The first cities appeared in river basins, which could produce a surplus of agriculture. The abundance of food freed most city inhabitants from the need to produce their own food, which allowed them to work in specialized professions.

city-state Political organization based on the authority of a single, large city that controls outlying territories.

Civil Rights Act (1964) U.S. legislation that banned segregation in public facilities, outlawed racial discrimination in employment, and marked an important step in correcting legal inequality.

civil rights movement Powerful movement for equal rights and the end of racial segregation in the United States that began in the 1950s with court victories against school segregation and nonviolent boycotts.

civil service examinations The world's first written civil service examination system, instituted by the Tang dynasty to recruit officials and bureaucrats. Open to most males, the exams tested a candidate's literary skills and knowledge of the Confucian classics. They helped to unite the Chinese state by making knowledge of a specific language and Confucian classics the only route to power.

Civil War, American (1861–1865) Conflict between the northern and southern states of

America; this struggle led to the abolition of slavery in the United States.

clan A social group comprising many households, claiming descent from a common ancestor.

clandestine presses Small printing operations that published banned texts in the early modern era, especially in Switzerland and the Netherlands.

Clovis people Early humans in America who used basic chipped blades and pointed spears in pursuing prey. They extended the hunting traditions they had learned in Afro-Eurasia, such as establishing campsites and moving with their herds. They were known as "Clovis people" because the arrowhead point that they used was first found by archaeologists at a site near Clovis, New Mexico.

codex Early form of book, with separate pages bound together; it replaced the scroll as the main medium for written texts. The codex emerged around 300 CE.

cognitive skills Skills such as thought, memory, problem-solving, and—ultimately—language. Hominids were able to use these skills and their hands to create new adaptations, like tools, which helped them obtain food and avoid predators.

Cohong Chinese merchant guild that traded with Europeans under the Qing dynasty.

coins Form of money that replaced goods, which previously had been bartered for services and other products. Originally used mainly to hire mercenary soldiers, coins became the commonplace method of payment linking buyers and producers throughout the Mediterranean.

cold war (1945–1990) Ideological conflict in which the Soviet Union and eastern Europe opposed the United States and western Europe.

colonies Regions under the political control of another country.

Colons French settler population in Algeria.

colosseum Huge amphitheater completed by Titus and dedicated in 80 CE. Originally begun by Flavian, the structure is named after a colossal statue of Nero that formerly stood beside it.

Columbian exchange Movements between Afro-Eurasia and the Americas of previously unknown plants, animals, people, diseases, and products that followed in the wake of Columbus's voyages.

commanderies Provinces. Shi Huangdi (First August Emperor) divided China into commanderies (*jun*) to enable the Qin dynasty to rule the massive state effectively. The thirty-six commanderies were then subdivided into counties (*xian*).

Communist Manifesto Pamphlet published by Karl Marx and Friedrich Engels in 1848 at a time when political revolutions were sweeping Europe. It called on the workers of all nations to unite in overthrowing capitalism.

Compromise of 1867 Agreement between the Habsburgs and the peoples living in Hungarian parts of the empire that the Habsburg state would be officially known as the Austro-Hungarian Empire.

concession areas Territories, usually ports, where Chinese emperors allowed European merchants to trade and European people to settle.

Confucian ideals The ideals of honoring tradition, emphasizing the responsibility of the emperor, and respect for the lessons of history, promoted by Confucius, which the Han dynasty made the official doctrine of the empire by 50 BCE.

Confucianism Ethics, beliefs, and practices stipulated by the Chinese philosopher Kong Qiu, or Confucius, which served as a guide for Chinese society up to modern times.

Confucius (551–479 BCE) Influential teacher, thinker, and leader in China who developed a set of principles for ethical living. He believed that coercive laws and punishment would not be needed to maintain order in society if men following his ethics ruled. He taught his philosophy to anyone who was intelligent and willing to work, which allowed men to gain entry into the ruling through education.

cong tube Ritual object crafted by the Liangzhu. A cong tube was made of jade and was used in divination practices.

Congo Independent State Large colonial state in Africa created by Leopold II, king of Belgium, during the 1880s, and ruled by him alone. After rumors of mass slaughter and enslavement, the Belgian parliament took the land and formed a Belgian colony.

Congress of Vienna (1814–1815) International conference to reorganize Europe after the downfall of Napoleon. European monarchies agreed to respect each other's borders and to cooperate in guarding against future revolutions and war.

conquistadors Spanish military leaders who led the conquest of the New World in the sixteenth century.

Constantine Roman emperor who converted to Christianity in 312 CE. In 313, he issued a proclamation that gave Christians new freedoms in the empire. He also founded Constantinople (at first called "New Rome").

Constantinople Capital city, formerly known as Byzantium, which was founded as the New Rome by Constantine the Great.

Constitutional Convention (1787) Meeting to formulate the Constitution of the United States of America.

Contra rebels Opponents of the Sandinistas in Nicaragua; they were armed and financed by the United States and other anticommunist countries (1980).

Conversion of Constantine A significant political and religious turning point in the Roman Empire. Before the decisive battle for Rome in 312 CE, Constantine supposedly had a dream in which he was told to place a sign with the opening letters of Christ's name on his soldiers' shields. Constantine won the ensuing battle; he soon issued a proclamation giving privileges to Christian bishops. The edict spread Christianity through the institutions and across the byways of the Roman Empire.

Conversos Jewish and Muslim converts to Christianity in the Iberian Peninsula and the New World.

Coptic Form of Christianity practiced in Egypt. It was doctrinally different from Christianity elsewhere, and Coptic Christians had their own views of Christology, or the nature of Christ.

Corn Laws Laws that imposed tariffs on grain imported to Great Britain, intended to protect British farming interests. The Corn Laws were abolished in 1846 as part of a British movement in favor of free trade.

cosmology Branch of metaphysics devoted to understanding the order of the universe.

Council of Nicaea Church council convened in 325 CE by Constantine and presided over by him as well. At this council, a Christian creed was articulated and made into a formula that expressed the philosophical and technical elements of Christian belief.

Counter-Reformation Movement to counter the spread of the Reformation; initiated by the Catholic Church at the Council of Trent in 1545. The Catholic Church enacted reforms to attack clerical corruption and it placed a greater emphasis on individual spirituality. During this time, the Jesuits were founded to help revive the Catholic Church.

coup d'état Overthrow of established state by a group of conspirators, usually from the military.

creed Formal statement of faith or expression of a belief system. A Christian creed or "credo" was formulated by the Council of Nicaea in 325 CE.

creoles Persons of full-blooded European descent who were born in the Spanish American colonies.

Crimean War (1853–1856) War waged by Russia against Great Britain and France. Spurred by Russia's encroachment on Ottoman territories, the conflict revealed Russia's military weakness when Russian forces fell to British and French troops.

crossbow Innovative weapon used at the end of the Warring States period that allowed archers to shoot their enemies with accuracy, even from a distance.

Crusades Wave of attacks launched in the late eleventh century by western Europeans. The First Crusade began in 1095, when Pope Urban II appealed to the warrior nobility of France to free Jerusalem from Muslim rule. Four subsequent Crusades were fought over the next two centuries.

Cuban Missile Crisis (1962) Diplomatic standoff between the United States and the Soviet Union that was provoked by the Soviet Union's attempt to base nuclear missiles in Cuba; it brought the world close to a nuclear war.

cult Religious movement, often based on the worship of a particular god or goddess.

cultigen Organism that has diverged from its ancestors through domestication or cultivation.

cuneiform Wedge-shaped form of writing. As people combined rebus symbols with other visual marks that contained meaning, they became able to record and transmit messages over long distances by using abstract symbols or signs to denote concepts; such signs later came to represent syllables, which could be joined into words. By impressing these signs into wet clay with the cut end of a reed, scribes engaged in cuneiform.

Cyrus the Great Founder of the Persian Empire. This sixth-century ruler (559–529 BCE) conquered the Medes and unified the Iranian kingdoms.

Daimyo Ruling lords who commanded private armies in pre-Meiji Japan.

dan Fodio, Usman (1754–1817) Fulani Muslim cleric whose visions led him to challenge the Hausa ruling classes, whom he believed were insufficiently faithful to Islamic beliefs and practices. His ideas gained support among those who had suffered under the Hausa landlords. In 1804, his supporters and allies overthrew the Hausa in what is today northern Nigeria.

Daoism School of thought developed at the end of the Warring States period that focused on the importance of following the Dao, or the natural way of the cosmos. Daoism emphasized the need to accept the world as it was rather than trying to change it through politics or the government. Unlike Confucianism, Daoism scorned rigid rituals and social hierarchies.

Dar al-Islam Arabic for "the House of Islam"; it describes a sense of common identity.

Darius I (521–486 BCE) Leader who put the emerging unified Persian Empire onto solid footing after Cyrus's death.

Darwin, Charles (1809–1882) British scientist who became convinced that the species of organic life had evolved under the uniform pressure of natural laws, not by means of a special, one-time creation as described in the Bible.

D-Day (June 6, 1944) Day of the Allied invasion of Normandy under General Dwight Eisenhower to liberate western Europe from German occupation.

Dear Boy Nickname of an early human remain discovered in 1931 by a team of archaeologists named the Leakeys. They discovered an almost totally intact skull. Other objects discovered with Dear Boy demonstrated that by the time of Dear Boy, early humans had begun to fashion tools and to use them for butchering animals and possibly for hunting and killing smaller animals.

Decembrists Russian army officers who were influenced by events in revolutionary France and formed secret societies that espoused liberal governance. They were put down by Nicholas I in December 1825.

Declaration of Independence U.S. document stating the theory of government on which America was founded.

Declaration of the Rights of Man and Citizen (1789) French charter of liberties formulated by the National Assembly that marked the end of dynastic and aristocratic rule. The seventeen articles later became the preamble to the new constitution, which the assembly finished in 1791.

decolonization End of empire and emergence of new independent nation-states in Asia and Africa as a result of the defeat of Japan in World War II and weakened European influence after the war.

Delhi Sultanate (1206–1526) Turkish regime of Northern India. The regime strengthened the cultural diversity and tolerance that were a hallmark of the Indian social order, which allowed it to bring about political integration without enforcing cultural homogeneity.

democracy The idea that people, through membership in a nation, should choose their own representatives and be governed by them.

Democritus Thinker in ancient Greece who lived from 470 to 360 BCE; he deduced the existence of the atom and postulated that there was such a thing as an indivisible particle.

demotic writing The second of two basic forms of ancient Egyptian writing. Demotic was a cursive script written with ink on papyrus, on pottery, or on other absorbent objects. It was the most common and practical form of writing in Egypt and was used for administrative record keeping and in private or pseudo-private forms like letters and works of literature. *See also* Hieroglyphs.

developing world Term applied to countries collectively called the Third World during the cold war and seeking to develop viable nation-states and prosperous economies.

Devshirme System of taking non-Muslim children in place of taxes in order to educate them in Ottoman Muslim ways and prepare them for service in the sultan's bureaucracy.

Dhamma Moral code espoused by Aśoka in the Kalinga edict, which was meant to apply to all—Buddhists, Brahmans, and Greeks alike.

Dhimmis Followers of religions, other than Islam, that were permitted by Ottoman law: Armenian Christians, Greek Orthodox Christians, and Jews.

dhows Ships used by Arab seafarers; the dhow's large sails were rigged to maximize the capture of wind.

Dien Bien Phu (1954) Defining battle in the war between French colonialists and the Viet Minh that secured North Vietnam for Ho Chi Minh and his army and left the south to form its own government to be supported by France and the United States.

Din-I-llahi "House of worship" in which the Mughal emperor Akbar engaged in religious debate with Hindu, Muslim, Jain, Parsi, and Christian theologians.

Diogenes Greek philosopher who lived from 412 to 323 BCE and who espoused a doctrine of self-sufficiency and freedom from social laws and customs. He rejected cultural norms as out of tune with nature and therefore false.

Directory Temporary military committee that took over the affairs of the state of France in 1795 from the radicals and held control until the coup of Napoleon Bonaparte.

divination The interpretation of rituals used to communicate the wishes of gods or royal ancestors to foretell future events. Divination was used to legitimize royal authority and demand tribute.

Djoser Ancient Egyptian king who reigned from 2630 to 2611 BCE. He was the second king of the Third Dynasty and celebrated the Sed festival in his tomb complex at Saqqara.

domestication Bringing a wild animal or plant under human control.

Dominion in the British Commonwealth Canadian promise to keep up the country's fealty to the British crown, even after its independence in 1867. Later applied to Australia and New Zealand.

Dong Zhongshu Emperor Wu's chief minister, who advocated a more powerful view of Confucius by promoting texts that focused on Confucius as a man who possessed aspects of divinity.

double-outrigger canoes Vessels used by early Austronesians to cross the Taiwan Straits and colonize islands in the Pacific. These sturdy canoes could cover over 120 miles per day.

Duma Russian parliament.

Dutch learning Broad term for European teachings that were strictly regulated by the shoguns inside Japan.

dynastic cycle Political narrative in which influential families vied for supremacy. Upon gaining power, they legitimated their authority by claiming to be the heirs of previous grand dynasts and by preserving or revitalizing the ancestors' virtuous governing ways. This continuity conferred divine support.

dynasty Hereditary ruling family that passed control from one generation to the next.

Earth Summit (1992) Meeting in Rio de Janeiro between many of the world's governments in an effort to address international environmental problems.

East India Company (1600–1858) British charter company created to outperform Portuguese and Spanish traders in the Far East; in the eighteenth century the company became, in effect, the ruler of a large part of India.

Eastern Front Battlefront between Berlin and Moscow during World War I and World War II.

Edict of Nantes (1598) Edict issued by Henry IV to end the French Wars of Religion. The edict declared France a Catholic country but tolerated some Protestant worship.

Egyptian Middle Kingdom Period of Egyptian history lasting from about 2040 to1640 BCE, characterized by a consolidation of power and building activity in Upper Egypt.

Eiffel Tower Steel monument completed in 1889 for the Paris Exposition. It was twice the height of any other building at the time.

eight-legged essay Highly structured essay form with eight parts, required on Chinese civil service examinations.

Ekklesia Church or early gathering committed to leaders chosen by God and fellow believers.

Ekpe Powerful slave trade institution that organized the supply and purchase of slaves inland from the Gulf of Guinea in West Africa.

Elamites A people with their capital in the upland valley of modern Fars who became a cohesive polity that incorporated transhumant people of the Zagros Mountains. A group of Elamites who migrated south and west into Mesopotamia helped conquer the Third Dynasty of Ur in 2400 BCE.

empire Group of states or different ethnic groups under a single sovereign power.

Enabling Act (1933) Emergency act passed by the Reichstag (German parliament) that helped transform Hitler from Germany's chancellor, or prime minister, into a dictator following the suspicious burning of the Reichstag building and a suspension of civil liberties.

enclosure A movement in which landowners took control of lands that traditionally had been common property serving local needs.

Encomenderos Commanders of the labor services of the colonized peoples in Spanish America.

Encomiendas Grants from European Spanish governors to control the labor services of colonized people.

Endeavor Ship of Captain James Cook, whose celebrated voyages to the South Pacific in the late eighteenth century supplied Europe with information about the plants, birds, landscapes, and people of this uncharted territory.

Engels, Friedrich (1820–1895) German social and political philosopher who collaborated with Karl Marx on many publications, including *The Communist Manifesto*.

English Navigation Act of 1651 Act stipulating that only English ships could carry goods between the mother country and its colonies.

English Peasants' Revolt (1381) Uprising of serfs and free farm workers that began as a protest against a tax levied to raise money for a war on France. The revolt was suppressed but led to the gradual emergence of a free peasantry as labor shortages made it impossible to keep peasants bound to the soil.

enlightened absolutists Seventeenth- and eighteenth-century monarchs who claimed to rule rationally and in the best interests of their subjects and who hired loyal bureaucrats to implement the knowledge of the new age.

Enlightenment Intellectual movement in eighteenth-century Europe stressing natural laws and reason as the basis of authority.

entrepôts Trading stations at the borders between communities, which made exchange possible among many different partners. Long-distance traders could also replenish their supplies at these stations.

Epicurus Greek philosopher who espoused emphasis on the self. He lived from 341 to 279 BCE and founded a school in Athens called The Garden. He stressed the importance of sensation, teaching that pleasurable sensations were good and painful sensations bad. Members of his school sought to find peace and relaxation by avoiding unpleasantness or suffering.

Estates-General French quasi-parliamentary body called in 1789 to deal with the financial problems that afflicted France. It had not met since 1614.

Etruscans A dominant people on the Italian peninsula until the fourth century BCE. The Etruscan states were part of the foundation of the Roman Empire.

eunuchs Loyal and well-paid men who were surgically castrated as youths and remained in service to the caliph or emperor. Both Abbasid and Tang rulers relied for protection on a cadre of eunuchs.

Eurasia The combined area of Europe and Asia.

European Union (EU) International body organized after World War II as an attempt at reconciliation between Germany and the rest of Europe. It initially aimed to forge closer industrial cooperation. Eventually, through various treaties, many European states relinquished some of their sovereignty, and the cooperation became a full-fledged union with a single currency, the euro, and with a somewhat less powerful common European parliament.

evolution Process by which the different species of the world—its plants and animals—made changes in response to their environment that enabled them to survive and increase in numbers.

Exclusion Act of 1882 U.S. congressional act prohibiting nearly all immigration from China to the United States; fueled by animosity toward Chinese workers in the American West.

Ezo Present-day Hokkaido, Japan's fourth main island.

Fascism Mass political movement founded by Benito Mussolini that emphasized nationalism, militarism, and the omnipotence of the state.

Fascists Radical right-wing group of disaffected veterans that formed around Mussolini in 1919 and a few years later came to power in Rome.

Fatehpur Sikri Mughal emperor Akbar's temporary capital near Agra.

Fatimids Shiite dynasty that ruled parts of the Islamic Empire beginning in the tenth century CE. They were based in Egypt and founded the city of Cairo.

February Revolution (1917) The first of two uprisings of the Russian Revolution, which led to the end of the Romanov dynasty.

Federal Deposit Insurance Corporation (FDIC) Organization created in 1933 to guarantee all bank deposits up to $5,000 as part of the New Deal in the United States.

Federal Republic of Germany (1949–1990) Country formed of the areas occupied by the Allies after World War II. Also known as West Germany, this country experienced rapid demilitarization, democratization, and integration into the world economy.

Federal Reserve Act (1913) U.S. legislation that created a series of boards to monitor the supply and demand of the nation's money.

Federalists Supporters of the ratification of the U.S. Constitution, which was written to replace the Articles of Confederation.

feminist movements Movements that called for equal treatment for men and women—equal pay and equal opportunities for obtaining jobs and advancement. Feminism arose mainly in Europe and in North America in the 1960s and then became global in the 1970s.

Ferangi Arabic word meaning "Frank" that was used to describe Crusaders.

Fertile Crescent Site of the world's first agricultural revolution; an area in Southwest Asia, bounded by the Mediterranean Sea in the west and the Zagros Mountains in the east.

feudalism System instituted in medieval Europe after the collapse of the Carolingian Empire (814 CE) whereby each peasant was under the authority of a lord.

fiefdoms Medieval economic and political units.

First World Term invented during the cold war to refer to western Europe and North America (also known as the "free world" or the West); Japan later joined this group. Following the principles of liberal modernism, First World states sought to organize the world on the basis of capitalism and democracy.

Five Pillars of Islam The five tenets, or main aspects, of Islamic practice: testification or bearing witness that there is no God other than God (Allah, in Arabic) and that Muhammad is the messenger of God; praying five times a day; fasting from sunup to sundown every day during Ramadan (a month on the Islamic calendar); giving alms; and making a pilgrimage to Mecca.

Five-Year Plan Soviet effort launched under Stalin in 1928 to replace the market with a state-owned and state-managed economy, to promote rapid economic development over a five-year period of time and thereby "catch and overtake" the leading capitalist countries. The First Five-Year Plan was followed by the Second Five-Year Plan (1933–1937), and so on, until the collapse of the Soviet Union in 1991.

Flagellants European social group that came into existence during the bubonic plague in the fourteenth century; they believed that the plague was the wrath of God.

floating population Poor migrant workers in China who supplied labor under Emperor Wu.

Fluitschips Dutch shipping vessels that could carry heavy bulky cargo with relatively small crews.

flying cash Letters of exchange—early predecessors of paper cash instead of coins—first developed by guilds in the northwestern Shanxi. By the thirteenth century, paper money had eclipsed coins.

Fondûqs Complexes in caravan cities that included hostels, storage houses, offices, and temples.

Forbidden City Palace city of the Ming and Qing dynasties.

Force Publique Colonial army used to maintain order in the Belgian Congo; during the early stages of King Leopold's rule, it was responsible for bullying local communities.

Fourierism Form of utopian socialism based on the ideas of Charles Fourier (1772–1837). Fourier envisioned communes where work was made enjoyable and systems of production and distribution were run without merchants. His ideas appealed to middle-class readers, especially women, as a higher form of Christian communalism.

free labor Wage-paying rather than slave labor.

free markets Unregulated markets.

Free Officers Movement Secret organization of Egyptian junior military officers who came to power in a coup d'état in 1952, forced King Faruq to abdicate, and consolidated their own control through dissolving the parliament, banning opposing parties, and rewriting the constitution.

free trade Domestic and international trade unencumbered by tariff barriers, quotas, and fees.

Front de Libération Nationale (FLN) Algerian anticolonial, nationalist party that waged an eight-year war against French troops, beginning in 1854, that forced nearly all of the 1,000,000 colonists to leave.

Fulani Muslim group in West Africa that carried out religious revolts at the end of the eighteenth and the beginning of the nineteenth centuries in an effort to return to the pure Islam of the past.

fur trade Trading of animal pelts (especially beaver skins) by Indians for European goods in North America.

Gandhi, Mohandhas Karamchand (Mahatma) (1869–1948) Indian leader who led a nonviolent struggle for India's independence from Britain.

garrison towns Stations for soldiers originally established in strategic locations to protect territorial acquisition. Eventually, they became towns. Alexander the Great's garrison towns evolved into cities that served as centers from which Hellenistic culture was spread to his easternmost territories.

garrisons Military bases inside cities; often used for political purposes, such as protecting rulers and putting down domestic revolts or enforcing colonial rule.

gauchos Argentine, Brazilian, and Uruguayan cowboys who wanted a decentralized federation, with autonomy for their provinces and respect for their way of life.

Gdansk shipyard Site of mass strikes in Poland that led in 1980 to the formation of the first independent trade union, Solidarity, in the communist bloc.

gendered relations A relatively recent development that implies roles emerged only with the appearance of modern humans and perhaps Neanderthals. When humans began to think imaginatively and in complex symbolic ways and give voice to their insights, perhaps around 150,000 years ago, gender categories began to crystallize.

genealogy History of the descent of a person or family from a distant ancestor.

Geneva Peace Conference (1954) International conference to restore peace in Korea and Indochina. The chief participants were the United States, the Soviet Union, Great Britain, France, the People's Republic of China, North Korea, South Korea, Vietnam, the Viet Minh party, Laos, and Cambodia. The conference resulted in the division of North and South Vietnam.

Genoa One of two Italian cities (the other was Venice) that linked Europe, Africa, and Asia as nodes of commerce in 1300 CE. Genoese ships linked the Mediterranean to the coast of Flanders through consistent routes along the Atlantic coasts of Spain, Portugal, and France.

German Democratic Republic Nation founded from the Soviet zone of occupation of Germany after World War II; also known as East Germany.

German Social Democratic Party Founded in 1875, the most powerful Socialist party in Europe before 1917.

Ghana The most celebrated medieval political kingdom in West Africa.

Ghost Dance American Indian ritual performed in the nineteenth century in the hope of restoring the world to precolonial conditions.

Gilgamesh Heroic narrative written in the Babylonian dialect of Semitic Akkadian. This story and others like it were meant to circulate and unify the kingdom.

Girondins Liberal revolutionary group that supported the creation of a constitutional monarchy during the early stages of the French Revolution.

global warming Release into the air of human-made carbons that contribute to rising temperatures worldwide.

globalization Development of integrated worldwide cultural and economic structures.

Gold Coast Name that European mariners and merchants gave to that part of West Africa from which gold was exported. This area was conquered by the British in the nineteenth century and became a British colony; upon independence, it became Ghana.

Goths One of the groups of "barbarian" migrants into Roman territory in the fourth century.

government schools Schools founded by the Han dynasty to provide an adequate number of officials to fill positions in the administrative bureaucracy. The Imperial University had 30,000 members by the second century BCE.

Gracchus brothers Two tribunes, the brothers Tiberius and Gaius Gracchus, who in 133 and 123–21 BCE attempted to institute land reforms that would guarantee all of Rome's poor citizens a basic amount of land that would qualify them for army service. Both men were assassinated.

Grand Canal Created in 486 BCE, a thousand-mile-long connector between the Yellow and Yangzi rivers, linking the north and south, respectively.

grand unity Guiding political idea embraced by Qin rulers and ministers, with an eye toward joining the states of the Central Plain into one empire and centralizing administration.

"Greased cartridge" controversy Controversy spawned by the rumor that cow and pig fat had been used to grease the shotguns of the sepoys in the British army in India. Believing that this was a British attempt to defile their religion and speed their conversion to Christianity, the sepoys mutinied against the British officers.

Great Depression Worldwide depression following the U.S. stock market crash on October 29, 1929.

great divide The division between economically developed nations and less developed nations.

Great East Asia Co-Prosperity Sphere Term used by the Japanese during the 1930s and 1940s to refer to Hong Kong, Singapore, Malaya, Burma, and other states that they seized during their run for expansion.

Great Flood One of many traditional Mesopotamian stories that were transmitted orally from one generation to another before being recorded. The Sumerian King List refers to this crucial event in Sumerian memory and identity. The Great Flood was assigned responsibility for Uruk's demise to the gods.

Great Game Competition over areas such as Turkistan, Persia (present-day Iran), and Afghanistan. The British (in India) and the Russians believed that controlling these areas was crucial to preventing their enemies' expansion.

Great League of Peace and Power Iroquois Indian alliance that united previously warring communities.

Great Leap Forward (1958–1961) Plan devised by Mao Zedong to achieve rapid agricultural and industrial growth in China. The plan failed miserably and more than 20 million people died.

Great Proletarian Cultural Revolution (1966–1976) Mass mobilization of urban Chinese youth inaugurated by Mao Zedong in an attempt to reinvigorate the Chinese revolution and to prevent the development of a bureaucratized Soviet style of communism; with this movement, Mao turned against his longtime associates in the communist party.

Great Trek Afrikaner migration to the interiors of Africa after the British abolished slavery in the empire in 1833.

Great War (August 1914–November 1918) A total war involving the armies of Britain, France, and Russia (the Allies) against those of Germany, Austria-Hungary, and the Ottoman Empire (the Central Powers). Italy joined the Allies in 1915, and the United States joined them in 1917, helping tip the balance in favor of the Allies, who also drew upon the populations and material of their colonial possessions. Also known as World War I.

Greek Orthodoxy Enduring form of Christianity that used the framework of the "Roman" state inherited from Constantine and Justinian to protect itself from Roman Catholicism and Muslim forces. The Greek Orthodox capital was Constantinople and its spiritual empire included the Russian peoples, Baltic Slavs, and peoples living in southwest Asia.

Greenbacks Members of the American political party of the late nineteenth century that worked to advance the interest of farmers by promoting cheap money.

griots Counselors and other officials to the royal family in African kingships. They were also responsible for the preservation and transmission of oral histories and repositories of knowledge.

Group Areas Act (1950) Act that divided South Africa into separate racial and tribal areas and required Africans to live in their own separate communities, including the "homelands."

guerrillas Portuguese and Spanish peasant bands who resisted the revolutionary and expansionist efforts of Napoleon; after the French word *guerre.*

guest workers Migrants looking for temporary employment abroad.

Gulag Administrative name for the vast system of forced labor camps under the Soviet regime; it originated in a small monastery near the Arctic Circle and spread throughout the Soviet Union and to other Soviet-style socialist countries. Penal labor was required of both ordinary criminals (rapists, murderers, thieves) and those accused of political crimes (counterrevolution, anti-Soviet agitation).

Gulf War (1991) Armed conflict between Iraq and a coalition of thirty-two nations, including the United States, Britain, Egypt, France, and Saudi Arabia. It was started by Iraq's invasion of Kuwait, which it had long claimed, on August 2, 1990.

gunpowder Explosive powder. By 1040, the first gunpowder recipes were being written down. Over the next 200 years, Song entrepreneurs invented several incendiary devices and techniques for controlling explosions.

gunpowder empires Muslim empires of the Ottomans, Safavids, and Mughals that used cannonry and gunpowder to advance their military causes.

Guomindang Nationalist party of China, founded just before World War I by Sun Yat-sen and later led by Chiang Kai-shek.

Habsburg Empire Ruling house of Austria, which once ruled both Spain and central Europe but came to settle in lands along the Danube River; it played a prominent role in European affairs for many centuries. In 1867, the Habsburg Empire was reorganized into the Austro-Hungarian Dual Monarchy, and in 1918 it collapsed.

Hadith Sayings attributed to the Prophet Muhammad and his early converts. Used to guide the behavior of Muslim peoples.

Hagia Sophia Enormous and impressive church sponsored by Justinian and built starting in 532 CE. At the time, it was the largest church in the world.

Hajj Pilgrimage to Mecca; an obligation for Muslims.

Hammurapi's Code Legal code created by Hammurapi, the most famous of the Mesopotamian rulers, who reigned from 1792 to 1750 BCE. Hammurapi sought to create social order by centralizing state authority and creating a grand legal structure that embodied paternal justice. The code was quite stratified, dividing society into three classes: free men, dependent men, and slaves, each with distinct rights and responsibilities.

Han agrarian ideal Guiding principle for the free peasantry that made up the base of Han society. In this system, peasants were honored for their labors, while merchants were subjected to a range of controls, including regulations on luxury consumption, and were belittled for not engaging in physical labor.

Han Chinese Inhabitants of China proper who considered others to be outsiders. They felt that they were the only authentic Chinese.

Han Fei Chinese state minister who lived from 280 to 223 BCE; he was a proponent and follower of Xunzi.

Han military Like its Roman counterpart, a ruthless military machine that expanded the empire and created stable conditions that permitted the safe transit of goods by caravans. Emperor Wu heavily influenced the transformation of the military forces and reinstituted a policy that made military service compulsory.

Hangzhou City and former provincial seaport that became the political center of the Chinese people in their ongoing struggles with northern steppe nomads. It was also one of China's gateways to the rest of the world by way of the South China Sea.

Hannibal Great Roman general from Carthage whose campaigns in the third century BCE swept from Spain toward the Italian peninsula. He crossed the Pyrenees and the Alps mountain ranges with war elephants. He was unable, however, to defeat the Romans in 217 BCE.

Harappa One of two cities that, by 2500 BCE, began to take the place of villages throughout the Indus River valley (the other was Mohenjo Daro). Each covered an area of about 250 acres and probably housed 35,000 residents.

harem Secluded women's quarters in Muslim households.

Harlem Renaissance Cultural movement in the 1920s that was based in Harlem, a part of New York City with a large African American population. The movement gave voice to black novelists, poets, painters, and musicians, many of whom used their art to protest racism; also referred to as the "New Negro movement."

harnesses Tools made from wood, bone, bronze, and iron for steering and controlling chariot horses. Harnesses discovered by archaeologists reveal the evolution of headgear from simple mouth bits to full bridles with headpiece, mouthpiece, and reins.

Hatshepsut Leader known as ancient Egypt's most powerful woman ruler. Hatshepsut served as regent for her young son, Thutmosis III, whose reign began in 1479 BCE. She remained co-regent until her death.

Haussmannization Redevelopment and beautification of urban centers; named after the city planner who "modernized" mid-nineteenth-century Paris.

Hegira "Emigration" of Muhammad and his followers out of a hostile Mecca to Yathrib, a city that was later called Medina. The year in which this journey took place, 622 CE, is also year 1 of the Islamic calendar.

Heian period Period from 794 to 1185, during which began the pattern of regents ruling Japan in the name of the sacred emperor.

Hellenism Process by which the individuality of the cultures of the earlier Greek city-states gave way to a uniform culture that stressed the common identity of all who embraced Greek ways. This culture emphasized the common denominators of language, style, and politics to which anyone, anywhere in the Afro-Eurasian world, could have access.

hieroglyphs One of two basic forms of Egyptian writing that were used in conjunction throughout antiquity. Hieroglyphs are pictorial symbols; the term derives from a Greek word meaning "sacred carving"—they were employed exclusively in temple, royal, and divine contexts. *See also* Demotic writing.

Hijra Tradition of Islam, whereby one withdraws from one's community to create another, more holy, one. The practice is based on the Prophet Muhammad's withdrawal from the city of Mecca to Medina in 622 CE.

Hinayana (Lesser Vehicle) Buddhism Form of Buddhism that accepted the divinity of Buddha himself but not of demigods, or bodhisattvas.

Hinduism A refashioning of the ancient Brahmanic Vedic religion, bringing it in accord with rural life and agrarian values. It emerged as the dominant faith in Indian society in the third century CE. Believers became vegetarians and adopted rituals of self-sacrifice. Three major deities—Brahma, Vishnu, and Siva—formed a trinity representing the three phases of the universe (birth, existence, and destruction, respectively) and the three expressions of the eternal self, or *atma*.

Hindu revivalism Movement to reconfigure traditional Hinduism to be less diverse and more amenable to producing a narrowed version of Indian tradition.

Hiroshima Japanese port devastated by an atomic bomb on August 6, 1945.

Hitler, Adolf (1889–1945) German dictator and leader of the Nazi Party who seized power in Germany after its economic collapse in the Great Depression. Hitler and his Nazi regime started World War II in Europe and systematically murdered Jews and other non-Aryan groups in the name of racial purity.

Hittites One of the five great territorial states. The Hittites campaigned throughout Anatolia, then went east to northern Syria, though they eventually faced weaknesses in their own homeland. Their heyday was marked by the reign of the king Supiliulimua (1380 to 1345 BCE), who preserved the Hittites' influence on the balance of power in the region between Mesopotamia and the Nile.

Holocaust Deliberate racial extermination of the Jews by the Nazis that claimed around 6 million European Jews.

Holy Roman Empire Enormous realm that encompassed much of Europe and aspired to be the Christian successor state to the Roman Empire. In the time of the Habsburg dynasts, the empire was a loose confederation of principalities that obeyed an emperor elected by elite lower-level sovereigns. Despite its size, the empire never effectively centralized power; it was split into Austrian and Spanish factions when Charles V abdicated to his sons in 1556.

Holy Russia Name applied to Muscovy and then to the Russian Empire by Slavic Eastern Orthodox clerics who were appalled by the Muslim conquest in 1453 of Constantinople (the capital of Byzantium and of Eastern Christianity) and who were hopeful that Russia would become the new protector of the faith.

home charges Fees India was forced to pay to Britain as its colonial master; these fees included interest on railroad loans, salaries to colonial officers, and the maintenance of imperial troops outside India.

hominids Humanlike beings who walked erect and preceded modern humans.

Homo A word used by scientists to differentiate between pre-human and "true human" species.

Homo caudatus "Tailed man," believed by some European Enlightenment thinkers to be an early species of humankind.

Homo erectus Species that emerged about 1.5 million years ago and had a large brain and walked truly upright. *Homo erectus* means "Standing man."

Homo habilis Scientific term for "Skillful man." Toolmaking ability truly made *Homo habilis* the forerunners, though very distant, of modern humans.

Homo sapiens The first humans; they emerged in a small region of Africa about 200,000 years ago and migrated out of Africa about 100,000 years ago. They had bigger brains and greater dexterity than previous hominid species, whom they eventually eclipsed.

homogeneity Uniformity of the languages, customs, and religion of a particular people or place. It can also be demonstrated by a consistent calendar, set of laws, administrative practices, and rituals.

horses Animals used by full-scale nomadic communities to dominate the steppe lands in western Afro-Eurasia by the second millennium BCE. Horse-riding nomads moved their large herds across immense tracts of land within zones defined by rivers, mountains, and other natural geographical features. In the arid zones of central Eurasia, the nomadic economies made horses a crucial component of survival.

Huguenots French Protestants who endured severe persecution in the sixteenth and seventeenth centuries.

humanism The Renaissance aspiration to know more about the human experience beyond what the Christian scriptures offered by reaching back into ancient Greek and Roman texts.

Hundred Days' Reform (1898) Abortive modernizing reform program of the Qing government of China.

hunting and gathering Lifestyle in which food is acquired through hunting animals, fishing, and foraging for wild berries, nuts, fruit, and grains, rather than planting crops, vines, or trees. As late as 1500, as much as 15 percent of the world's population still lived by this method.

Hyksos A western Semitic-speaking people whose name means "Rulers of Foreign Lands"; they overthrew the unstable Thirteenth Dynasty in Egypt around 1640 BCE. The Hyksos had mastered the art of horse chariots, and with those chariots and their superior bronze axes and composite bows (made of wood, horn, and sinew), they were able to defeat the pharaoh's foot soldiers.

Ibn Sina Philosopher and physician who lived from 980 to 1037 CE. He was also schooled in the Quran, geometry, literature, and Indian and Euclidian mathematics.

ideology Dominant set of ideas of a widespread culture or movement.

Il Duce Term designating the fascist Italian leader Benito Mussolini.

Iliad Epic Greek poem about the Trojan War, composed several centuries after the events it describes. It was based on oral tales passed down for generations.

Il-khanate Mongol-founded dynasty in thirteenth-century Persia.

Imam Muslim religious leader and politico-religious descendant of Ali; believed by some to have a special relationship with Allah.

imperialism Acquisition of new territories by a state and the incorporation of these territories into a political system as subordinate colonies.

Imperium Latin word used to express Romans' power and command over their subjects. It is the basis of the English words *empire* and *imperialism.*

Inca Empire Empire of Quecha-speaking rulers in the Andean valley of Cuzco that encompassed a population of 4 to 6 million. The Incas lacked a clear inheritance system, causing an internal split that Pizarro's forces exploited in 1533.

Indian Institutes of Technology (IIT) Institutions originally designed as engineering schools to expand knowledge and to modernize India, which produced a whole generation of pioneering computer engineers, many of whom moved to the United States.

Indian National Congress Formed in 1885, a political party deeply committed to constitutional methods, industrialization, and cultural nationalism.

Indian National Muslim League Founded in 1906, an organization dedicated to advancing the political interests of Muslims in India.

Indo-Greek Fusion of Indian and Greek culture in the area under the control of the Bactrians, in the northwestern region of India, around 200 BCE.

Indu What we would today call India. Called "Indu" by Xuanzang, a Chinese Buddhist pilgrim who visited the area in the 630s and 640s CE.

indulgences Church-sponsored fund-raising mechanism that gave certification that one's sins had been forgiven in return for money.

industrial revolution Gradual accumulation and diffusion of old and new technical knowledge that led to major economic changes in Britain, northwestern Europe, and North America, catapulting these countries ahead of the rest of the world in manufacturing and agricultural output and standards of living.

industrious revolution Dramatic economic change in which households that had traditionally produced for themselves decided to work harder and longer hours in order to produce more for the market, which enabled them to increase their income and standard of living. Areas that underwent the industrious revolution shifted from peasant farming to specialized production for the market.

innovation Creation of a new method that allowed humans to make better adaptations to their environment such as the making of new tools.

Inquisition Tribunal of the Roman Catholic Church that enforced religious orthodoxy during the Protestant Reformation.

internal and external alchemy In Daoist ritual, use of trance and meditation or chemicals and drugs, respectively, to cause transformations in the self.

International Monetary Fund (IMF) Agency founded in 1944 to help restore financial order in Europe and the rest of the world, to revive international trade, and to support the financial concerns of Third World governments.

invisible hand As described in Adam Smith's *The Wealth of Nations,* the idea that the operations of a free market produce economic efficiency and economic benefits for all.

iron Malleable metal found in combined forms almost everywhere in the world; it became the most important and widely used metal in world history after the Bronze Age.

Iron Curtain Term popularized by Winston Churchill after World War II to refer to a rift, or an iron curtain, that divided western Europe, under American influence, from eastern Europe, under the domination of the Soviet Union.

irrigation Technological advance whereby water delivery systems and water sluices in floodplains or riverine areas were channeled or redirected and used to nourish soil.

Islam A religion that dates to 610 CE, when Muhammad believed God came to him in a vision. Islam ("submission"—in this case, to the will of God) requires its followers to act righteously, to submit themselves to the one and only true God, and to care for the less fortunate. Muhammad's most insistent message was the oneness of God, a belief that has remained central to the Islamic faith ever since.

Jacobins Radical French political group that came into existence during the French Revolution and executed the French king and sought to remake French culture.

Jacquerie (1358) French peasant revolt in defiance of feudal restrictions.

jade The most important precious substance in East Asia. Jade was associated with goodness, purity, luck, and virtue, and was carved into such items as ceremonial knives, blade handles, religious objects, and elaborate jewelry.

Jagat Seths Enormous trading and banking empire in eastern India.

Jainism Along with Buddhism, one of the two systems of thought developed in the seventh century BCE that set themselves up against Brahmanism. Its founder, Vardhamana Mahavira, taught that the universe obeys its own everlasting rules that no god or other supernatural being could affect. The purpose of life was to purify one's soul in order to attain a state of permanent bliss, which could be accomplished through self-denial and the avoidance of harming other creatures.

Janissaries Corps of infantry soldiers recruited as children from the Christian provinces of the Ottoman Empire and brought up with intense loyalty to the Ottoman state and its sultan. The Ottoman sultan used these forces to clip local autonomy and to serve as his personal bodyguards.

Jati Social groups as defined by Hinduism's caste system.

Jesuits Religious order founded by Ignatius Loyola to counter the inroads of the Protestant Reformation; the Jesuits, or the Society of Jesus, were active in politics, education, and missionary work.

Jihad Literally, "striving" or "struggle." This word also connotes military efforts or "striving in the way of God." It also came to mean spiritual struggles against temptation or inner demons, especially in Sufi, or mystical, usage.

Jih-pen Chinese for "Japan."

Jim Crow laws Laws that codified racial segregation and inequality in the southern part of the United States after the Civil War.

Jizya Special tax that non-Muslims were forced to pay to their Islamic rulers in return for which they were given security and property and granted cultural autonomy.

jong Large ocean-going vessels, built by Southeast Asians, which plied the regional trade routes from the fifteenth century to the early sixteenth century.

Judah The southern kingdom of David, which had been an Assyrian vassal until 612 BCE, when it became a vassal of Assyria's successor, Babylon, against whom the people of Judah rebelled, resulting in the destruction of Jerusalem in the sixth century BCE.

Julius Caesar Formidable Roman general who lived from 100 to 44 BCE. He was also a man of letters, a great orator, and a ruthless military man who boasted that his campaigns had led to the deaths of over a million people.

junks Trusty seafaring vessels used in the South China Seas after 1000 CE. These helped make shipping by sea less dangerous.

Justinian Roman or Byzantine emperor who ascended to the throne in 527 CE. In addition to his many building projects and military expeditions, he issued a new law code.

Kabuki Theater performance that combined song, dance, and skillful staging to dramatize conflicts between duty and passion in Tokogawa, Japan.

Kamikaze Japanese for "divine winds" or typhoons; such a storm saved Japan from a Mongol attack.

Kanun Highly detailed system of Ottoman administrative law that jurists developed to deal with matters not treated in the religious law of Islam.

Karim Loose confederation of shippers banding together to protect convoys.

karma Literally "fate" or "action," in Confucian thought; this is a universal principle of cause and effect.

Kassites Nomads who entered Mesopotamia from the eastern Zagros Mountains and the Iranian plateau as early as 2000 BCE. They gradually integrated into Babylonian society by officiating at temples. By 1745 BCE, they had asserted order over the region, and they controlled southern Mesopotamia for the next 350 years, creating one of the territorial states.

Keynesian Revolution Post-Depression economic ideas developed by the British economist John Maynard Keynes, wherein the state took a greater role in managing the economy, stimulating it by increasing the money supply and creating jobs.

KGB Soviet political police and spy agency, formed as the Cheka not long after the Bolshevik coup in October 1917. Grew to more than 750,000 operatives with military rank by the 1980s.

Khan Ruler who was acclaimed at an assembly of elites and supposedly descended from Chinngis Khan on the male line; those not descended from Chinggis continually faced challenges to their legitimacy.

Khanate Major political unit of the vast Mongol empire. There were four Khanates, including the Yuan Empire in China, forged by Chinggis Khan's grandson Kubilai.

Kharijites Radical sect from the early days of Islam. The Kharijites seceded from the "party of Ali" (who themselves came to be known as the Shiites) because of disagreements over succession to the role of the caliph. They were known for their strict militant piety.

Khmers A people who created the most powerful empire in Southwest Asia between the tenth and thirteenth centuries in what is modern-day Cambodia.

Khomeini, Ayatollah Ruhollah (1902–1989) Iranian religious leader who used his traditional Islamic education and his training in Muslim ethics to accuse the shah's government of gross violations of Islamic norms. He also identified the shah's ally, America, as the great Satan. The shah fled the country in 1979; in his wake, Khomeini established a theocratic state ruled by a council of Islamic clerics.

Khufu A pyramid, among those put up in the Fourth Dynasty in ancient Egypt (2575–2465 BCE), which is the largest stone structure in the world. It is in an area called Giza, just outside modern-day Cairo.

Khusro I Anoshirwan Sasanian emperor who reigned from 530 to 579 CE. He was a model ruler and was seen as the personification of justice.

Kiev City that became one of the greatest cities of Europe after the eleventh century. It was built to be a small-scale Constantinople on the Dnieper.

Kikuyu Kenya's largest ethnic group; organizers of a revolt against the British in the 1950s.

King, Martin Luther, Jr. (1929–1968) Civil rights leader who borrowed his most effective weapon—the commitment to nonviolent protest and the appeal to conscience—from Gandhi.

Kingdom of Awadh One of the most prized lands for annexation and the fertile, opulent, and traditional vestige of Mughal rule in India.

Kingdom of Jerusalem What Crusaders set out to liberate when they launched their attack.

Kizilbash Mystical, Turkish-speaking tribesmen who facilitated the Safavid rise to power.

Knossos Area in Crete where, during the second millennium BCE, a primary palace town existed.

Koine Greek Common form of Greek that became the international spoken and written language in the Hellenistic world. This was a simpler everyday form of the ancient Greek language.

Koprulu reforms Reforms named after two grand viziers who revitalized the Ottoman Empire in the seventeenth century through administrative and budget trimming as well as by rebuilding the military.

Korean War (1950–1953) Cold war conflict between Soviet-backed North Korea and U.S.- and UN-backed South Korea. The two sides seesawed back and forth over the same boundaries until 1953, when an armistice divided the country at roughly the same spot as at the start of the war. Nothing had been gained. Losses, however, included 33,000 Americans, at least 250,000 Chinese, and up to 3 million Koreans.

Koryo dynasty Leading dynasty of the northern-based Koryo kingdom in Korea. It is from this dynasty that the name "Korea" derives.

Kremlin Once synonymous with the Soviet government; refers to Moscow's walled city center.

Kshatriyas Originally the warrior caste in Vedic society, the dominant clan members and ruling caste who controlled the land.

Ku Klux Klan Racist organization that first emerged in the U.S. South after the Civil War and then gained national strength as a radically traditionalist movement during the 1920s.

Kubilai Khan (1215–1294) Mongol leader who seized southern China after 1260 and founded the Yuan dynasty.

kulak Originally a pejorative word used to designate better-off peasants, the term used in the late 1920s and early 1930s to refer to any peasant, rich or poor, perceived as an opponent of the Soviet regime. Russian for "fist."

Kumarajiva Renowned Buddhist scholar and missionary who lived from 344 to 413 CE. He was brought to China by Chinese regional forces from Kucha, modern-day Xinjiang.

Kushans Northern nomadic group that migrated into South Asia in 50 CE. They unified the tribes of the region and set up the Kushan dynasty. The Kushans' empire embraced a large and diverse territory and played a critical role in the formation of the Silk Road.

Labour Party Founded in Britain in 1900, the party that represented workers and was based on socialist principles.

laissez-faire The concept that the economy works best when it is left alone—that is, when the state does not regulate or interfere with the workings of the market.

"Land under the Yoke of Ashur" Lands not in Assyria proper, but under its authority; they had to pay the Assyrian Empire exorbitant amounts of tribute.

language System of communication reflecting cognitive abilities. Natural language is generally defined as words arranged in particular sequences to convey meaning and is unique to modern humans.

language families Related tongues with a common ancestral origin; language families contain languages that diverged from one another but share grammatical features and root vocabularies. More than a hundred language families exist.

Laozi Also known as Master Lao; perhaps a contemporary of Confucius and the person after whom Daoism is named. His thought was elaborated upon by generations of thinkers.

Latifundia Broad estates that produced goods for big urban markets, including wheat, grapes, olives, cattle, and sheep.

Laws of Manu Part of the handiwork of Brahman priests; a representative code of law that incorporated social sanctions and practices and provided guidance for living within the caste system.

League of Nations Organization founded after World War I to solve international disputes through arbitration; it was dissolved in 1946 and its assets were transferred to the United Nations.

Legalism Also called Statism, a system of thought about how to live an ordered life. It was developed by Master Xun, or Xunzi (310–237 BCE). It is based on the principle that people, being inherently inclined toward evil, require authoritarian control to regulate their behavior.

Lenin, Nikolai (1870–1924) Leader of the Bolshevik Revolution in Russia and the first leader of the Soviet Union.

Liangzhu Culture spanning centuries from the fourth to the third millennium BCE that represented the last new Stone Age culture in the Yangzi River delta. One of the Ten Thousand States, it was highly stratified and is known for its jade objects.

liberalism Political and social theory that advocates representative government, free trade, and freedom of speech and religion.

limited-liability joint-stock company Company that mobilized capital from a large number of investors, called shareholders, who were not to be held personally liable for financial losses incurred by the company.

Linear A and B Two linear scripts first discovered on Crete in 1900. On the island of Crete and on the mainland areas of Greece, documents of the palace-centered societies were written on clay tablets in these two scripts. Linear A script, apparently written in Minoan, has not yet been deciphered. Linear B was first deciphered in the early 1950s.

"Little Europes" Urban landscapes between 1100 and 1200 CE composed of castles, churches, and towns in what are today Poland, the Czech Republic, Hungary, and the Baltic States.

Liu Bang Chinese emperor from 206 to 195 BCE; after declaring himself the prince of his home area of Han, in 202 BCE, Liu declared himself the first Han emperor.

llamas Animals similar in utility and function to camels in Afro-Eurasia. Llamas could carry heavy loads for long distances.

Long March (1934–1935) Trek of over 10,000 kilometers by Mao Zedong and his communist followers to establish a new base of operations in northwestern China.

Longshan peoples Peoples who lived in small agricultural and riverine villages in East Asia at the end of the third millennium BCE. They set the stage for the Shang in terms of a centralized state, urban life, and a cohesive culture.

lord Privileged landowner who exercised authority over the people who lived on his land.

lost generation The 17 million former members of the Red Guard and other Chinese youth who were denied education from the late 1960s to the mid-1970s as part of the Chinese government's attempt to prevent political disruptions.

Louisiana Purchase (1803) American purchase of French territory from Napoleon, including much of the present-day United States between the Mississippi River and the Rocky Mountains.

Lucy Relatively intact skeleton of a young adult female australopithecine unearthed in the valley of the Awash River in 1974 by an archaeological team working at a site in present-day Hadar, Ethiopia. The researchers nicknamed the skeleton Lucy. She stood just over three feet tall and walked upright at least some of the time. Her skull contained a brain within the ape size range. Also, her jaw and teeth were humanlike. Lucy's skeleton was relatively complete and was the oldest hominid skeleton ever discovered.

Luftwaffe German air force.

Maastricht Treaty (1991) Treaty that formed the European Union, a fully integrated trading and financial bloc with its own bureaucracy and elected representatives.

Ma'at Term used in ancient Egypt to refer to stability or order, the achievement of which was the primary task of Egypt's ruling kings, the pharaohs.

Maccabees Leaders of a riot in Jerusalem in 166 BCE; the riot was a response to a Roman edict outlawing the practice of Judaism.

Madhyamika (Middle Way) Buddhism Chinese branch of Mahayana Buddhism established by Kumarajiva (344–413 CE) that used irony and paradox to show that reason was limited.

madrassas Higher schools of Muslim education that taught law, the Quran, religious sciences, and the regular sciences.

Mahayana (Greater Vehicle) Buddhism School of Buddhist theology that believed that the Buddha was a deity, unlike previous groups that had considered him a wise human being.

Mahdi The "chosen one" in Islam whose appearance was supposed to foretell the end of the world and the final day of reckoning for all people.

maize Grains, the crops that the settled agrarian communities across the Americas cultivated, along with legumes (beans) and tubers (potatoes).

Maji-Maji Revolt (early 1900s) Swahili insurrection against German colonialists; inspired by the belief that those who were anointed with specially blessed water (*maji*) would be immune to bullets. It resulted in 200,000–300,000 African deaths.

Mamluks (Arabic for "owned" or "possessed") Military men who ruled Egypt as an independent regime from 1250 until the Ottoman conquest in 1517.

Manaus Opera House Opera house built in the interior of Brazil in a lucrative rubber-growing area at the turn of the twentieth century.

Manchukuo Japanese puppet state in Manchuria in the 1930s.

Manchus Descendants of the Jurchens who helped the Ming army recapture Beijing in 1644 after its seizure by the outlaw Li Zicheng. The Manchus numbered around 1 million but controlled a domain that included perhaps 250 million people. Their rule lasted more than 250 years and became known as the Qing dynasty.

mandate of heaven Ideology established by Zhou dynasts to communicate the moral transfer of power. Originally a pact between the Zhou people and their supreme god, it evolved in the first century BCE into Chinese political doctrine.

Mande A people who lived in the area between the bend in the Senegal River and the bend in the Niger River east to west and from the Senegal River and Bandama River north to south. Also known as the Mandinka. Their civilization emerged around 1100.

Mandela, Nelson (1918–) Leader of the African National Congress (ANC) who was imprisoned for more than two decades by the apartheid regime in South Africa for his political beliefs; worldwide protests led to his release in 1990. In 1994 Mandela won the presidency in South Africa's first free mass elections.

Manifest Destiny Belief that it was God's will for the American people to expand their territory and political processes across the North American continent.

Mao Zedong (1893–1976) Chinese communist leader who rose to power during the Long March (1934). In 1949, he defeated the Nationalists and established a communist regime in China. Although many of Mao's efforts to transform China, such as the industrialization program of 1958 (known as the Great Leap Forward) and the Cultural Revolution of 1966, failed and brought great suffering to the people, he did instill a new spirit of independence in China and a sense of purpose after many decades of political and economic failure.

maroon community Sanctuary for runaway slaves in the Americas.

Marshall Plan Economic aid package given by the United States to Europe after World War II in hopes of a rapid period of reconstruction and economic gain, thereby securing the countries that received the aid from a communist takeover.

martyrs People executed by the Roman authorities for persisting in their Christian beliefs and refusing to submit to pagan ritual or belief.

Marx, Karl (1818–1883) German philosopher and economist who created Marxism and believed that a revolution of the working classes would overthrow the capitalist order and create a classless society.

Marxism Form of scientific socialism created by Karl Marx and Friedrich Engels that was rooted in a materialist theory of history: what mattered in history were the production of material goods and the ways in which society was organized into classes of producers and exploiters.

mass consumption Increased purchasing power in the early-twentieth-century prosperous and mainly middle-class societies, stemming from mass production.

mass culture Distinctive form of popular culture that arose in the wake of World War I. It reflected the tastes of the working and the middle classes, who now had more time and money to spend on entertainment, and relied on new technologies, especially film and radio, which could reach an entire nation's population and consolidate their sense of being a single state.

mass production System in which factories were set up to produce huge quantities of identical products, reflecting the early-twentieth-century world's demands for greater volume, faster speed, reduced cost, and standardized output.

Mastaba Word meaning "bench" in Arabic; it refers to a huge flat structure identical to earlier royal tombs of ancient Egypt.

Mau-Mau Revolt (1952–1957) Uprising orchestrated by a Kenyan guerrilla movement; this conflict forced the British to grant independence to the black majority in Kenya.

Mauryan Empire Dynasty extended by the Mauryans from 321 to 184 BCE, from the Indus Valley to the northwest areas of South Asia, in a region previously controlled by Persia. It was the first large-scale empire in South Asia and was to become the model for future Indian empires.

Mawali Non-Arab "clients" to Arab tribes in the early Islamic Empire. Because tribal patronage was so much a part of the Arabian cultural system, non-Arabs who converted to Islam affiliated themselves with a tribe and became clients of that tribe.

Maxim gun European weaponry that was capable of firing many bullets per second; it was used against Africans in the conquest of the continent.

Mayans Civilization that ruled over large stretches of Mesoamerica; it was composed of a series of kingdoms, each built around ritual centers rather than cities. The Mayans engaged neighboring peoples in warfare and trade and expanded borders through tributary relationships. They were not defined by a great ruler or one capital city, but by their shared religious beliefs.

McCarthyism Campaign by Republican senator Joseph McCarthy in the late 1940s and early 1950s to uncover closet communists, particularly in the State Department and in Hollywood.

Meat Inspection Act (1906) Legislation that provided for government supervision of meat-packing operations; it was part of a broader "Progressive" reform movement dedicated to correcting the negative consequences of urbanization and industrialization in the United States.

Mecca Arabian city in which Muhammad was born. Mecca was a trading center and pilgrimage destination in the pre-Islamic and Islamic periods. Exiled in 622 CE because of resistance to his message, Muhammad returned to Mecca in 630 CE and claimed the city for Islam.

Medes Rivals of the Assyrians and the Persians. The Medes inhabited the area from the Zagros Mountains to the modern city of Tehran; known as expert horsemen and archers, they were eventually defeated by the Persians.

megaliths Literally, "great stone"; the word *megalith* is used when describing structures such as Stonehenge. These massive structures are the result of cooperative planning and work.

Megarons Large buildings found in Troy (level II) that are the predecessors of the classic Greek temple.

Meiji Empire Empire created under the leadership of Mutsuhito, emperor of Japan from 1868 until 1912. During the Meiji period Japan became a world industrial and naval power.

Meiji Restoration Reign of the Meiji emperor, which was characterized by a new nationalist identity, economic advances, and political transformation.

Mencius Disciple of Confucius who lived from 372 to 289 BCE.

mercantilism Economic theory that drove European empire builders. In this economic system, the world had a fixed amount of wealth, which meant one country's wealth came at the expense of another's. Mercantilism assumed that colonies existed for the sole purpose of enriching the country that controlled the colony.

Mercosur Free-trade pact between the governments of Argentina, Brazil, Paraguay, and Uruguay.

meritocracy Rule by persons of talent.

Meroe Ancient kingdom in what is today Sudan. It flourished for nearly a thousand years, from the fifth century BCE to the fifth century CE.

mestizos Mixed-blood offspring of Spanish settlers and native Indians.

métis Mixed-blood offspring of French settlers and native Indians.

Mexican Revolution (1910) Conflict fueled by the unequal distribution of land and by disgruntled workers; it erupted when political elites split over the succession of General Porfirio Díaz after decades of his rule. The fight lasted over ten years and cost one million lives, but it resulted in a widespread reform and a new constitution.

Mfecane movement African political revolts in the first half of the nineteenth century that were caused by the expansionist methods of King Shaka of the Zulu people.

microsocieties Small-scale communities that had little interaction with others. These communities were the norm for peoples living in the Americas and islanders in the Pacific and Aegean from 2000 to 1200 BCE.

migration Long-distance travel for the purpose of resettlement. In the case of early man, the need to move was usually a response to an environmental shift, such as climate change during the Ice Age.

millenarian Convinced of the imminent coming of a just and ideal society.

millenarian movement Broad, popular upheaval calling for the restoration of a bygone moral age, often led by charismatic spiritual prophets.

Millets Minority religious communities of the Ottoman Empire.

minaret Slender tower within a mosque from which Muslims are called to prayer.

Minbar Pulpit inside a mosque from which Muslim religious speakers broadcast their message to the faithful.

Minoans A people who built a large number of elaborate, independent palace centers on Crete, at Knossos, and elsewhere around 2000 BCE. Named after the legendary King Minos, said to have ruled Crete at the time, they sailed throughout the Mediterranean and by 1600 BCE had planted colonies on many Aegean islands, which in turn became trading and mining centers.

mission civilisatrice Term French colonizers used to refer to France's form of "rationalized" colonial rule, which attempted to bring "civilization" to the "uncivilized."

mitochondrial DNA Form of DNA found outside the nucleus of cells, where it serves as cells' microscopic power packs. Examining mitochondrial DNA enables researchers to measure the genetic variation among living objects, including human beings.

Moche A people who extended their power and increased their wealth at the height of the Chimu Empire over several valleys in what is now modern-day Peru.

Model T First automobile, manufactured by the Ford Motor Company of Henry Ford, to be priced reasonably enough to be sold to the masses.

Modernists A generation of exuberant young artists, writers, and scientists in the late nineteenth century who broke with older conventions and sought new ways of seeing and describing the world.

Mohism School of thought in ancient China, named after Mo Di, or Mozi, who lived from 479 to 438 BCE. It emphasized one's obligation to society as a whole, not just to one's immediate family or social circle.

monarchy Political system in which one individual holds supreme power and passes that power on to his or her next of kin.

monasticism Christian way of life that originated in Egypt and was practiced as early as 300 CE in the Mediterranean. The word itself contains the meaning of a person "living alone" without marriage or family.

monetization An economic shift from a barter-based economy to one dependent on coin.

Mongols Combination of nomadic forest and prairie peoples who lived by hunting and livestock herding and were expert horsemen. Beginning in 1206, the Mongols launched a series of conquests that brought far-flung parts of the world together under their rule. By incorporating conquered peoples and adapting some of their customs, the Mongols created a unified empire that stretched from the Pacific Ocean to the shores of the eastern Mediterranean and the southern steppes of Eurasia.

Moors Term employed by Europeans in the medieval period to refer to Muslim occupants of North Africa, the western Sahara, and the Iberian Peninsula.

mosque Place of worship for the people of Islam.

"Mound people" Name for the people of Cahokia, since its landscape was dominated by earthen monuments in the shapes of mounds. The mounds were carefully maintained and were the loci from which Cahokians paid respect to spiritual forces. *See also* Cahokia.

Mu Chinese ruler (956–918 BCE) who put forth a formal bureaucratic system of governance, appointing officials, supervisors and military captains to whom he was not related. He also instituted a formal legal code.

muckrakers Journalists who aimed to expose political and commercial corruption in late-nineteenth- and early-twentieth-century America.

Muftis Experts on Muslim religious law.

Mughal Empire One of Islam's greatest regimes. Established in 1526, it was a vigorous, centralized state whose political authority encompassed most of modern-day India. During the sixteenth century, it had a population of between 100 and 150 million.

Muhammad (570–632 CE) Prophet and founder of the Islamic faith. Born in Mecca in Saudi Arabia and orphaned when young, Muhammad lived under the protection of his uncle. His career as a prophet began around

610 CE, with his first experience of spiritual revelation.

Muhammad Ali Ruler of Egypt between 1805 and 1848. He initiated a set of modernizing reforms that sought to make Egypt competitive with the great powers.

mullahs Religious leaders in Iran who in the 1970s led a movement opposing Shah Reza Pahlavi and denounced American materialism and secularism.

multinational corporations Corporations based in many different countries that have global investment, trading, and distribution goals.

Muscovy The principality of Moscow. Originally a mixture of Slavs, Finnish tribes, Turkic speakers, and many others, Muscovy used territorial expansion and commercial networks to consolidate a powerful state and expanded to become the Russian Empire, a huge realm that spanned parts of Europe, much of northern Asia, numerous North Pacific islands, and even—for a time—a corner of North America (Alaska).

Muslim Brotherhood Egyptian organization founded in 1938 by Hassan al-Banna. It attacked liberal democracy as a cover for middle-class, business, and landowning interests and fought for a return to a purified Islam.

Muslim League National Muslim party of India.

Mussolini, Benito (1883–1945) Italian dictator and founder of the fascist movement in Italy. During World War II, he allied Italy with Germany and Japan.

Muwahhidin Term meaning "unitarians"; these were followers of the Wahhabi movement that emerged in the Arabian Peninsula in the eighteenth century.

Mycenaeans Mainland competitors of the Minoans; they took over Crete around 1400 BCE. Migrating to Greece from central Europe, they brought their Indo-European language, horse chariots, and metalworking skills, which they used to dominate until 1200 BCE.

Nagasaki Second Japanese city to be hit by an atomic bomb near the end of World War II.

Napoleon Bonaparte (1769–1821) General who rose to power in a post-Revolutionary coup d'état, eventually proclaiming himself emperor of France. He placed security and order ahead of social reform and created a civil legal code. Napoleon expanded his empire through military action, but after his disastrous Russian campaign, the united European powers defeated Napoleon and forced him into exile. He escaped and reassumed command of his army but was later defeated at the Battle of Waterloo.

Napoleonic Code Legal code drafted by Napoleon in 1804; it distilled different legal traditions to create one uniform law. The code confirmed the abolition of feudal privileges of all kinds and set the conditions for exercising property rights.

National Assembly of France Governing body of France that succeeded the Estates-General in 1789 during the French Revolution. It was composed of, and defined by, the delegates of the Third Estate.

National Association for the Advancement of Colored People (NAACP) Founded in 1910, the U.S. civil rights organization dedicated to ending inequality and segregation for black Americans.

National Recovery Administration (NRA) New Deal agency created in 1933 to prepare codes of fair administration and to plan for public works. It was later declared unconstitutional.

nationalism The idea that members of a shared community called a "nation" should have sovereignty within the borders of their state.

nation-state Form of political organization that derived legitimacy from its inhabitants, often referred to as citizens, who in theory, if not always in practice, shared a common language, common culture, and common history.

native learning Japanese movement to promote nativist intellectual traditions and the celebration of Japanese texts.

native paramountcy British form of "rationalized" colonial rule, which attempted to bring "civilization" to the "uncivilized" by proclaiming that when the interests of European settlers in Africa clashed with those of the African population, the latter should take precedence.

natural rights Belief that emerged in eighteenth-century western Europe and North America that rights fundamental to human nature were discernible to reason and should be affirmed in human-made law.

natural selection Charles Darwin's theory that populations grew faster than the food supply, creating a "struggle for existence" among species. In later work he showed how the passing on of individual traits was also determined by what he called sexual selection—according to which the "best" mates are chosen for their strength, beauty, or talents. The outcome: the "fittest" survived to reproduce, while the less adaptable did not.

Nazis (National Socialist German Workers Party) German organization dedicated to winning workers over from socialism to nationalism; the first Nazi Party platform combined nationalism with anticapitalism and anti-Semitism.

Neanderthals Members of an early wave of hominids from Africa who settled in western Afro-Eurasia, in an area reaching from present-day Uzbekistan and Iraq to Spain, approximately 150,000 years ago.

needle compass Crucial instrument made available to navigators after 1000 CE that helped guide sailors on the high seas. It was a Chinese invention.

negritos Hunter-gatherer inhabitants of the East Asian coastal islands who migrated there around 28,000 BCE but by 2000 BCE had been replaced by new migrants.

Negritude Statement of the virtues of the black identity and the validation of African culture and the African past, even in a westernizing world. This idea was shaped by African and African American intellectuals like Senegal's first president, Léopold Sédar Senghor.

Nehemiah Jewish eunuch of the Persian court who was given permission to rebuild the fortification walls around the city of Jerusalem from 440 to 437 BCE.

Neo-Assyrian Empire Afro-Eurasian empire that dominated around 950 BCE. The Neo-Assyrians extended their control over resources and people beyond their own borders, and their empire lasted for three centuries.

Nestorian Christians Denomination of Christians whose beliefs about Christ differed from those of the official Byzantine church. Named after Nestorius, former bishop of Constantinople, they emphasized the human aspects of Jesus.

New Deal President Franklin Delano Roosevelt's package of government reforms that were enacted during the 1930s to provide jobs for the unemployed, social welfare programs for the poor, and security to the financial markets.

New Economic Policy Enacted decrees of the Bolsheviks between 1921 and 1927 that grudgingly sanctioned private trade and private property.

New Negro movement *See* Harlem Renaissance.

New World Term applied to the Americas that reflected the Europeans' view that anything previously unknown to them was "new," even if it had existed and supported societies long before European explorers arrived on its shores.

Nirvana Literally, nonexistence; nirvana is the state of complete liberation from the concerns of worldly life, as in Buddhist thought.

Nō drama Masked theater favored by Japanese bureaucrats and regional lords during the Tokugawa period.

Noble Eightfold Path Buddhist concept of a way of life by which people may rid themselves of individual desire to achieve nirvana. The path consists of wisdom, ethical behavior, and mental discipline.

Nok culture Spectacular culture that arose in what is today Nigeria, in the sixth century BCE. Iron smelting occurred there around 600 BCE. Thus the Nok people made the transition from stone to iron materials.

nomads People who move across vast distances without settling permanently in a particular place. Often pastoralists, nomads and transhumant herders introduced new forms of chariot-based warfare that transformed the Afro-Eurasian world.

non-governmental organizations (NGOs) Term used to refer to private organizations like the Red Cross that play a large role in international affairs.

nonviolent resistance (*Satyagraha*) Moral and political philosophy of resistance developed by Indian National Congress leader Mohandas Gandhi. Gandhi believed that if Indians pursued self-reliance and self-control in a nonviolent way, the British would eventually have to leave.

North American Free Trade Agreement (NAFTA) Treaty negotiated in the early 1990s to promote free trade between Canada, the United States, and Mexico.

North Atlantic Treaty Organization (NATO) International organization set up in 1949 to provide for the defense of western European countries and the United States from the perceived Soviet threat.

Northern Wei dynasty Regime founded in 386 CE by the Tuoba, a people originally from Inner Mongolia, that lasted one and a half centuries. The rulers of this dynasty adopted many practices of the earlier Chinese Han regime. At the same time, they struggled to consolidate authority over their own nomadic people. Ultimately, several decades of intense internal conflict led to the dynasty's downfall.

northwest passage Long-sought marine passageway between the Atlantic and Pacific oceans.

Oceania Collective name for the lands of Australia and New Zealand and the islands of the southwest Pacific Ocean.

Odyssey Composed in the eighth century BCE, an epic tale of the journey of Odysseus, who traveled the Mediterranean back to his home in Ithaca after the siege of Troy.

Oikos The word for "small family unit" in ancient Greece, similar to the *familia* in Rome. Its structure, with men as heads of household over women and children, embodied the fundamental power structure in Greek city-states.

oligarchy Clique of privileged rulers.

Olmecs A people who emerged around 1500 BCE and lived in Mesoamerica. The name means those who "lived in the land of the rubber." Olmec society was composed of decentralized villages. Its members spoke the same language and worshipped the same gods.

Open Door Policy Policy proposed by American Secretary of State John Hay that would give all foreign nations equal access to trade with China. As European imperial powers carved out spheres of trade in late-nineteenth-century China, American leaders worried that the United States would be excluded from trade with China. To prevent this, Hay proposed the Open Door Policy.

Opium War (1839–1842) War fought between the British and Qing China over British trade in opium; resulted in the granting to the British the right to trade in five different ports and the ceding of Hong Kong to the British.

oracle bones Animal bones used by Shang diviners. Diviners applied intense heat to the shoulder bones of cattle or to turtle shells, which caused them to crack. The diviners would then interpret the cracks as signs from the ancestors regarding royal plans and actions.

Organization of Petroleum Exporting Countries (OPEC) International association established in 1960 to coordinate price and supply policies of oil-producing states.

orientalism Genre of literature and painting that portrayed the nonwestern peoples of North Africa and Asia as exotic, sensuous, and economically backward with respect to Europeans.

orientalists Western scholars who specialized in the study of the East.

Orrorin tugenensis Predecessor to hominids that first appeared 6 million years ago.

Ottoman Empire Rulers of Anatolia, the Arab world, and much of southern and eastern Europe in the early sixteenth century. They transformed themselves from nomadic warrior bands who roamed the borderlands between Islamic and Christian worlds in Anatolia into sovereigns of a vast, bureaucratic empire. The Ottomans embraced a Sunni view of Islam. They adapted traditional Byzantine governmental practices but tried new ways of integrating the diverse peoples of their empire.

Pacific War (1879–1883) War between Chile and the alliance of Bolivia and Peru.

Pagani Pejorative word used by Christians to designate pagans.

palace Official residence of the ruler, his family, and his entourage. The palace was both a social institution and a set of buildings. It first appeared around 2500 BCE, about a millennium later than the Mesopotamian temple, and quickly joined the temple as a defining landmark of city life. Eventually, it became a source of power rivaling the temple, and palace and temple life often blurred, as did the boundary between the sacred and the secular.

Palmyra Roman trading depot in modern-day Syria; part of a network of trading cities that connected various regions of Afro-Eurasia.

pan movements Groups that sought to link people across state boundaries in new communities based on ethnicity or, in some cases, religion (e.g., pan-Germanism, pan-Islamism, pan-Slavism).

Pansophia Ideal republic of inquisitive Christians united in the search for knowledge of nature as a means of loving God.

papacy The institution of the pope; the Catholic spiritual leader in Rome.

papal Of, relating to, or issued by a pope.

Parthians Horse-riding people who pushed southward around the middle of the second century BCE and wiped out the Greek kingdoms in Iran. They then extended their power all the way to the Mediterranean, where they ran up against the Roman Empire in Anatolia and Mesopotamia.

pastoral nomadic communities Groups of people that moved their domesticated animals from place to place to meet the animals' demanding grazing requirements. Around 3500 BCE, western Afro-Eurasia witnessed the growth and spread of pastoral nomadic communities.

pastoralism Herding and breeding of sheep and goats or other animals as a primary means of subsistence.

Paterfamilias Latin for "Father of the family," which itself was the foundation of the Roman social order.

Patria Latin, meaning "fatherland."

patrons In the Roman system of patronage, men and women of wealth and high social status who protected dependents or "clients" of a lower class.

Pax Mongolica Term that refers to the political and especially the commercial stability that the vast Mongol Empire provided for the travelers and merchants of Eurasia during the thirteenth and fourteenth centuries.

Pax Romana Latin for "Roman Peace"; refers to the period between 25 BCE and 235 CE during which conditions in the Roman Empire were settled and peaceful.

Pax Sinica Period of peace (149–87 BCE) during which agriculture, commerce, and industry flourished in East Asia under the rule of the Han.

Peace Preservation Act (1925) Act instituted in Japan that specified up to ten years' hard labor for any member of an organization advocating a basic change in the political system or the abolition of private property.

Pearl Harbor American naval base in Hawaii on which the Japanese launched a surprise attack on December 7, 1941, bringing the United States into World War II.

Peloponnesian War War fought between 431 and 404 BCE between two of Greece's most powerful city-states, Athens and Sparta.

Peninsular War (1808–1814) Conflict in which the Portuguese and Spanish populations, supported by the British, resisted the French invasion under Napoleon of the Iberian Peninsula.

Peninsulars Spaniards who, although born in Spain, resided in the Spanish colonial territories. They regarded themselves as superior to Spaniards born in the colonies (Creoles).

Peoples' Charter Document calling for universal suffrage for adult males, the secret ballot, electoral districts, and annual parliamentary elections. It was signed by over 3 million British between 1839 and 1842.

periplus Book that reflected sailing knowledge; in such books captains would record landing spots and ports. The word *periplus* literally means "sailing around."

Persepolis Darius I's capital city in the highlands of Fars; a ceremonial center and expression of imperial identity as well as an important administrative hub.

Peterloo Massacre (1819) The killing of 11 and wounding of 460 following a peaceful demonstration for political reform by workers in Manchester, England.

Petra City in modern-day Jordan that was the Nabataean capital. It profited greatly by supplying provisions and water to travelers and traders. Many of its houses and shrines were cut into the rocky mountains. *Petra* means "rock."

phalanx Military formation used by Philip II of Macedonia, whereby heavily armored infantry were closely arrayed in battle formation.

Philip II of Macedonia Father of Alexander the Great, under whose rule Macedonia developed into a large ethnic and territorial state. After unifying Macedonia, Philip went on to conquer neighboring states.

philosophia Literally "love of wisdom"; this system of thought originally included speculation on the nature of the cosmos, the environment, and human existence. It eventually came to include thought about the nature of humans and life in society.

Phoenicians Known as the Canaanites in the Bible, an ethnic group in the Levant under Assyrian rule in the seventh century BCE; they provided ships and sailors for battles in the Mediterranean. The word *Phoenician* refers to the purple dye they manufactured and widely traded, along with other commercial goods and services, throughout the Mediterranean. While part of wider Mesopotamian culture, their major contribution was the alphabet, first introduced in the second millennium BCE, which made far-reaching communication possible.

phonemes Primary and distinctive sounds that are characteristic of human language.

piety Strong sense of religious duty and devoutness, often inspiring extraordinary actions.

plant domestication Process of growing plants, harvesting their seeds, and saving some of the seeds for planting in subsequent growing cycles, resulting in a steady food supply. This process occurred as far back as 5000 BCE, when plants began to naturally retain their seeds. Plant domestication was practiced first in the southern Levant and spread from there into the rest of Southwest Asia.

Plato (427–347 BCE) Disciple of the great philosopher Socrates; his works are the only record we have of Socrates' teaching. He was also the author of formative philosophical works on ethics and politics.

plebs In Rome, term that referred to the "common people." Their interests were protected by officials called tribunes.

Pochteca Archaic term for merchants of the Mexicos.

polities Politically organized communities or states.

polyglot communities Societies composed of diverse linguistic and ethnic groups.

popular culture Affordable and accessible forms of art and entertainment available to people at all levels of society.

popular sovereignty The idea that the power of the state resides in the people.

populists Members of a political movement that supported U.S. farmers in late-nineteenth-century America. The term is often used generically to refer to political groups who appeal to the majority of the population.

potassium-argon dating Major dating technique based on the changing chemical structure of objects over time, since over time potassium decays into argon. This method makes possible the dating of objects up to a million years old.

potato famine (1840s) Severe famine in Ireland that led to the rise of radical political movements and the migration of large numbers of Irish to the United States.

potter's wheel Fast wheel that enabled poeple to mass-produce vessels in many different shapes. This advance, invented at the city of Uruk, enabled potters to make significant technical breakthroughs.

pottery Vessels made of mud and later clay that were used for storing and transporting food. The development of pottery was a major breakthrough.

Prague Spring (1968) Program of liberalization under a new communist party in Czechoslovakia that strove to create a democratic and pluralist socialism.

predestinarian Belief of many sixteenth- and seventeenth-century Protestant groups that God had foreordained the lives of individuals, including their bad and good deeds.

primitivism Western art movement of the late-nineteenth and early-twentieth centuries that drew upon the so-called primitive art forms of Africa, Oceania, and pre-Columbian America.

progressive reformers Members of the U.S. reform movement in the early twentieth century that aimed to eliminate political corruption, improve working conditions, and regulate the power of large industrial and financial enterprises.

proletarians Industrial wage workers.

prophets Charismatic freelance religious men of power who found themselves in opposition to the formal power of the kings, bureaucrats, and priests.

Prophet's Town Indian village that was burned down by American forces in the early nineteenth century.

Protestant Reformation Religious movement initiated by sixteenth-century monk Martin Luther, who openly criticized the corruption in the Catholic Church and voiced his belief that Christians could speak directly to God. His doctrines gained wide support, and those who followed this new view of the Christianity rejected the authority of the papacy and the Catholic clergy, broke away from the Catholic Church, and called themselves "Protestants."

Protestantism Division of Christianity that emerged in western Europe from the Protestant Reformation.

Proto-Indo-European The parent of all the languages in the Indo-European family, which includes, among many others, English, German, Norwegian, Portuguese, French, Russian, Persian, Hindi, and Bengali.

Pullman Strike (1894) American Railway Union strike in response to wage cuts and firings.

puppet states Governments with little power in the international arena that follow the dictates of their more powerful neighbors or patrons.

Puritans Seventeenth-century reform group of the Church of England; also known as dissenters or nonconformists.

Qadiriyya Sufi order that facilitated the spread of Islam into West Africa.

Qadis Judges in the Ottoman Empire.

qanats Underground water channels, vital for irrigation, which were used in Persia. Little evaporation occurred when water was being moved through qanats.

Qing dynasty (1644–1911) Minority Manchu rule over China that incorporated new territories, experienced substantial population growth, and sustained significant economic growth.

Questions of King Milanda (Milindapunha) Name of a second-century BCE text espousing the teachings of Buddhism as set forth by Menander, a Yavana king. It featured a discussion between the king and a sophisticated Buddhist sage named Nagasena.

Quetzalcoatl Ancient deity and legendary ruler of Native American peoples living in Mexico.

Quran The scripture of the Islamic faith. Originally a verbal recitation, the Quran was eventually compiled into a book in the order in which we have it today. According to traditional Islamic interpretation, the Quran was revealed to Muhammad by the angel Gabriel over a period of twenty-three years.

radicals Widely used term in nineteenth-century Europe that referred to those individuals and political organizations that favored the total reconfiguration of Europe's old state system.

radiocarbon isotope C^{14} Isotope contained by all living things, which plants acquire directly from the atmosphere and animals acquire indirectly when they consume plants or other animals. When living things die, the C^{14} isotope they contain begins to decay into a stable nonradioactive element, C^{12}. The rate of decay is regular and measurable, making it possible to ascertain the date of fossils that leave organic remains for ages of up to 40,000 years.

raj British crown's administration of India following the end of the East India Company's rule after the Rebellion of 1857.

raja "King" in the Kshatriya period in South Asia; could also refer to the head of a family, but indicated the person who had control of land and resources in South Asian city-states.

Ramadan Ninth month of the Muslim year, during which all Muslims must fast during daylight hours.

Rape of Nanjing Attack against the Chinese in which the Japanese slaughtered at least 100,000 civilians and raped thousands of women between December 1937 and February 1938.

Rashtriya Swayamsevak Sangh (**RSS**) (1925) Campaign to organize Hindus as a militant, modern community in India; translated in English as "National Volunteer Organization."

Rebellion of 1857 Indian uprising against the East India Company to bring religious purification, an egalitarian society, and local and communal solidarity without the interference of British rule.

rebus Probably originating in Uruk, a representation that transfers meaning from the name of a thing to the sound of that name. For example, a picture of a bee can represent the sound "b." Such pictures opened the door to writing: a technology of symbols that uses marks to represent specific discrete sounds.

Reconquista Spanish reconquest of territories lost to the Islamic Empire, beginning with Toledo in 1061.

Red Guards Chinese students who were the shock troopers in the early phases of Mao's Cultural Revolution in 1966–1968.

Red Lanterns Female supporters of the Chinese Boxers who rebelled against foreign intrusions in China at the turn of the twentieth century. Most were teenage girls and unmarried women and dressed in red garments.

Red Turban movement Diverse religious movement in China during the fourteenth century that spread the belief that the world was drawing to an end as Mongol rule was collapsing.

Reds Bolsheviks.

Reich German empire composed of Denmark, Austria, and parts of western France.

Reichstag The German parliament.

Reign of Terror Campaign at the height of the French Revolution in the early 1790s that used violence, including systematic execution of opponents of the revolution, to purge France of its enemies and to extend the revolution beyond its borders; radicals executed as many as 40,000 persons who were judged enemies of the state.

Renaissance Term meaning "rebirth" that historians use to characterize the expanded cultural production of European nations between 1430 and 1550. Emphasized a break from the church-centered medieval world and a new concept of humankind as the center of the world.

republican government Government in which power and rulership rest with representatives of the people—not a king.

Res publica Literally "public thing"; this referred to the Roman republic, in which policy and rules of behavior were determined by the Senate and by popular assemblies of the citizens.

Restoration period (1815–1848) European movement after the defeat of Napoleon to restore Europe to its pre-French revolutionary status and to quash radical movements.

Rift Valley Area of northeastern Africa where some of the most important early human archaeological discoveries of fossils were found, especially one of an intact skull that is 1.8 million years old.

river basin Area drained by a river, including all its tributaries. River basins were rich in fertile soil, water for irrigation, and plant and animal life, which made them attractive for human habitation. Cultivators were able to produce surplus agriculture to support the first cities.

riverine Term denoting an area whose inhabitants depended on irrigation for their well-being and whose populations are settled near great rivers. Egypt was, in a sense, the most riverine of all these cultures, in that it had no hinterland of plains as did Mesopotamia and the Indus valley. Away from the banks of the Nile, there is only largely uninhabitable desert.

Roman army Military force of the Roman Empire. The Romans devised a military draft that could draw from a huge population. In their encounter with Hannibal, they lost up to 80,000 men in three separate encounters and still won the war.

Roman Catholicism Branch of Christianity established by 1000 CE in western Europe and led by the Roman papacy. In contrast to ancient Greek Orthodoxy, Western Catholics believed that their church was destined to expand everywhere, and they set about converting the pagan tribes of northern Europe. Western Catholics contemptuously called the East Romans "Greeks" and condemned them for their "Byzantine" cunning.

Roman law Roman legal system, under which disputes were brought to the public courts and decisions were made by judges and sometimes by large juries. Rome's legal system featured written law and institutions for settling legal disputes.

roving bandits Large bands of dispossessed and marginalized peasants who vented their anger at tax collectors in the waning years of the Ming dynasty.

Royal Road A 1,600-mile road from Sardis in Anatolia to Susa in Iran; used by messengers, traders, the army, and those taking tribute to the king.

Russification Programs to assimilate people of over 146 dialects into the Russian Empire.

S.S. (*Schutzstaffel*) Hitler's security police force.

Sack of Constantinople Rampage in 1204 by the Frankish armies on the capital city of Constantinople.

sacred kingships Institutions that marked the centralized politics of West Africa. The inhabitants of these kingships believed that their kings were descendants of the gods.

Sahel region Area of sub-Saharan Africa with wetter and more temperate locations, especially in the upland massifs and their foothills, villages, and towns.

St. Bartholomew's Day Massacre (1572) Roman Catholic massacre of French Protestants in Paris.

St. Patrick Former slave brought to Ireland from Briton who later became a missionary, or the "Apostle of Ireland." He died in 470 CE.

Salt March (1930) A 240-mile trek to the sea in India, led by Mohandas Gandhi, to gather salt for free, thus breaking the British colonial monopoly on salt.

Samurai Japanese warriors who made up the private armies of Japanese daimyos.

Sandinista coalition Left-leaning Nicaraguan coalition of the 1970s and 1980s.

Santería African-based religion, blended with Christian influences, that was first practiced by slaves in Cuba.

Sargon the Great King of Akkad, a city-state near modern Baghdad. Reigning from 2334 to 2279 BCE, Sargon helped bring the competitive era of city-states to an end and sponsored monumental works of architecture, art, and literature.

Sasanian Empire Empire that succeeded the Parthians in the mid-220s CE in Inner Eurasia. The Sasanian Empire controlled the trade crossroads of Afro-Eurasia and possessed a strong armored cavalry, which made them a powerful rival to Rome. The Sasanians were also tolerant of Judaism and Christianity, which allowed Christians to flourish.

Sati Hindu practice whereby a woman was burned to death on the pyre of her dead husband.

satrap Governor of a province in the Persian Empire. Each satrap was a relative or intimate associate of the king.

Satyagraha See nonviolent resistance.

scientific method Method of inquiry based on experimentation in nature. Many of its principles were first laid out by the philosopher Sir Francis Bacon (1561–1626), who claimed that real science entailed the formulation of hypotheses that could be tested in carefully controlled experiments.

Scramble for Africa European rush to colonize parts of Africa at the end of the nineteenth century.

scribes Those who wield writing tools; from the very beginning they were at the top of the social ladder, under the major power brokers.

Scythian ethos Warrior ethos that embodied the extremes of aggressive mounted-horse culture, c. 1000 BCE. In part the Scythian ethos was the result of the constant struggle between settlers, hunter-gatherers, and nomads on the northern frontier of Europe.

Sea Peoples Migrants from north of the Mediterranean who invaded the cities of Egypt and the Levant in the second millennium BCE. Once settled along the coast of the Levant, they became known as the Philistines and considerably disrupted the settlements of the Canaanites.

SEATO (Southeast Asia Treaty Organization) Military alliance of pro-American, anticommunist states in Southeast Asia in 1954.

Second World Term invented during the cold war to refer to the communist countries, as opposed to the West (or First World) and the former colonies (or Third World).

second-generation societies Societies that expanded old ideas and methods by incorporating new aspects of culture and grafting them onto, or using them in combination with, established norms.

Seleucus Nikator Successor of Alexander the Great who lived from 358 to 281 BCE. He controlled Mesopotamia, Syria, Persia, and parts of the Punjab.

Self-Strengthening movement In the latter half of the nineteenth century, a movement of reformist Chinese bureaucrats that attempted to adopt western elements of learning and technological skill while retaining their core Chinese culture.

Semu Term meaning "outsiders" or non-Chinese people—Mongols, Tanguts, Khitan, Jurchen, Muslims, Tibetans, Persians, Turks, Nestorians, Jews, and Armenians—who became a new ruling elite over a Han majority population in the late thirteenth century.

sepoys Hindu and Muslim recruits of the East India Company's military force.

serfs Peasants who farmed the land and paid fees to be protected and governed by lords under a system of rule called feudalism.

settled agriculture Application of human labor and tools to a fixed plot of land for more than one growing cycle. It entails the changeover from a hunting and gathering lifestyle to one based on agriculture, which requires staying in one place until the soil has been exhausted.

Seven Years' War (1756–1763) Worldwide war that ended when Prussia defeated Austria, establishing itself as a European power, and when Britain gained control of India and many of France's colonies through the Treaty of Paris.

sexual revolution Increased freedom in sexual behavior, resulting in part from the advances in contraception, notably the introduction of oral contraception in 1960, which allowed men and women to limit childbearing and to have sex with less fear of pregnancy.

shah Traditional title of Persian rulers.

shamans Certain humans whose powers supposedly enabled them to commune with the supernatural and to transform themselves wholly or partly into beasts.

Shamisen Three-stringed instrument, often played by Japanese geisha.

Shandingdong Man A *Homo sapiens* whose fossil remains and relics can be dated to about 18,000 years ago. His physical characteristics were closer to those of modern humans, and he had a similar brain size.

Shang state Dynasty in northeastern China that ruled from 1600 to 1045 BCE. Though not as well defined by borders as the territorial states in the southwest of Asia, it did have a ruling lineage. Four fundamental elements of the Shang state were a metal industry based on copper, pottery making, standardized architectural forms and walled towns, and divination using animal bones.

Shanghai School Late-nineteenth-century style of painting characterized by an emphasis on spontaneous brushwork, feeling, and the incorporation of western influences into classical Chinese pieces.

sharecropping System of farming in which tenant farmers rented land and gave over a share of their crops to the land's owners. Sometimes seen as a cheap way for the state to conduct agricultural affairs, sharecropping often resulted in the impoverishment and marginalization of the underclass.

Sharia Literally, "the way"; now used to indicate the philosophy and rulings of Islamic law.

Sharpeville Massacre (1960) Massacre of sixty-nine black Africans when police fired upon a rally against the recently passed laws requiring nonwhite South Africans to carry identity papers.

Shawnees Native American tribe that inhabited the Ohio valley during the eighteenth century.

Shays's Rebellion (1786) Uprising of armed farmers that broke out when the Massachusetts state government refused to offer them economic relief.

Shiism One of the two main branches of Islam, practiced in the Safavid Empire. Although always a minority sect in the Islamic world, Shiism contains several subsects, each of which has slightly different interpretations of theology and politics.

Shiites Group of supporters of Ali, Muhammad's cousin and son-in-law, who wanted him to be the first caliph and believed that members of the Prophet's family deserved to rule. The leaders of the Shiite community are known as "Imam," which means "leaders."

Shinto Japan's official religion; it promoted the state and the emperor's divinity. The term means "the way of the gods."

shoguns Japanese military commanders. From 1192 to 1333, the Kamakura shoguns served as military "protectors" of the ruler in the city of Heian.

Shotoku Prince in the early Japanese Yamoto state (574–622 CE) who is credited with having introduced Buddhism to Japan.

shudras Literally "small ones"; workers and slaves from outside the Vedic lineage.

Siddhartha Gautama Another name for the Buddha; the most prominent opponent of the Brahman way of life; he lived from 563 to 483 BCE.

Sikhism Islamic-inspired religion that calls on its followers to renounce the caste system and to treat all believers as equal before God.

Silicon Valley Valley between the California cities of San Francisco and San Jose, known for its innovative computer and high-technology industries.

silk Luxury textile that became a vastly popular export from China (via the Silk Road) to the cities of the Roman world.

Silk Road Trade route linking China with central Asia and the Mediterranean; it extended over 5,000 miles, land and sea included, and was so named because of the quantities of silk that were traded along it. The Silk Road was a major factor in the development of civilizations in China, Egypt, Persia, India, and even Europe.

Silla One of three independent Korean states that may have emerged as early as the third century BCE. These states lasted until 668 CE, when Silla took control over the entire peninsula.

Silver Islands Term used by European merchants in the sixteenth century to refer to Japan, because of its substantial trade in silver with China.

Sino-Japanese War (1894–1895) Conflict over the control of Korea in which China was forced to cede the province of Taiwan to Japan.

Sipahi Urdu for "soldier."

Siva The third of three Vedic deities, signifying destruction. *See also* Brahma *and* Vishnu.

slave plantations System whereby labor was used for the cultivation of crops wholly for the sake of producing surplus that was then used for profit; slave plantations were a crucial part of the growth of the Mediterranean economy.

small seal script Unified script that was used to the exclusion of other scripts under the Qin, with the aim of centralizing administration; its use led to a less complicated style of clerical writing than had been in use under the Han.

social contract The idea, drawn from the writings of British philosopher John Locke, that the law should bind both ruler and people.

Social Darwinism Belief that Charles Darwin's theory of evolution was applicable to humans and justified the right of the ruling classes or countries to dominate the weak.

social hierarchies Distinctions between the privileged and the less privileged.

Social Security Act (1935) New Deal act that instituted old-age pensions and insurance for the unemployed.

socialism Political ideology that calls for a classless society with collective ownership of all property.

Socrates (469–399 BCE) Philosopher in Athens who encouraged people to reflect on ethics and morality. He stressed the importance of honor and integrity as opposed to wealth and power. Plato was his student.

Sogdians A people who lived in central Asia's commercial centers and maintained the stability and accessibility of the Silk Road. They were crucial to the interconnectedness of the Afro-Eurasian landmass.

Solidarity The communist bloc's first independent trade union, it was established in Poland at the Gdansk shipyard.

Song dynasty Chinese dynasty that took over the mandate of heaven for three centuries starting in 976 CE. It ruled an era of many economic and political successes, but it eventually lost northern China to nomadic tribes.

Song porcelain Type of porcelain perfected during the Song period that was light, durable, and quite beautiful.

South African War (1899–1902) Conflict between the British and Dutch colonists of South Africa which resulted in bringing two Afrikaner republics under the control of the British. Often called the Boer War.

Soviet bloc International alliance that included the east European countries of the Warsaw Pact as well as the Soviet Union but also came to include Cuba.

Spanish-American War (1898) War between the United States and Spain in Cuba, Puerto Rico, and the Philippines. It ended with a treaty in which the United States took over the Philippines, Guam, and Puerto Rico; Cuba won partial independence.

speciation The formation of different species.

specie Money in coin.

species Group of animals or plants possessing one or more distinctive characteristics.

spiritual ferment Process that occurred after 300 CE in which religion touched more areas of society and culture than before and touched them in different, more demanding ways.

Spring and Autumn period Period between the eighth and fifth centuries BCE, during which China was ruled by the feudal system. Considered an anarchic and turbulent time, there were 148 different tributary states in this period.

Stalin, Joseph (1879–1953) Leader of the communist party and the Soviet Union; sought to create "socialism in one country."

steel A metal more malleable and stronger than iron that became essential for industries like shipbuilding and railways.

stoicism Widespread philosophical movement initiated by Zeno (334–262 BCE). Zeno and his followers sought to understand the role of people in relation to the cosmos. For the Stoics, everything was grounded in nature. Being in love with nature and living a good life required being in control of one's passions and thus indifferent to pleasure or pain.

Strait of Malacca Seagoing gateway to Southeast and East Asia.

Strategic Defense Initiative ("Star Wars") Master plan, championed by U.S. president Ronald Reagan in the 1980s, that envisions the deployment of satellites and space missiles to protect the United States from incoming nuclear bombs.

stupa Dome monument marking the burial site of relics of the Buddha.

Suez Canal Channel built in 1869 across the Isthmus of Suez to connect the Mediterranean Sea with the Red Sea and to lower the costs of international trade.

Sufi brotherhoods Mystics within Islam who were responsible for the expansion of Islam into many regions of the world.

Sufism Emotional and mystical form of Islam that appealed to the common people.

sultan Islamic political leader. In the Ottoman Empire, the sultan combined a warrior ethos with an unwavering devotion to Islam.

Sumerian King List Text that recounts the making of political dynasties. Recorded around 2000 BCE, it organizes the reigns of kings by dynasty, one city at a time.

Sumerian pantheon The Sumerian gods, each of whom had a home in a particular floodplain city. In the Sumerian belief system, both gods and the natural forces they controlled had to be revered.

Sumerian temples Homes of the gods and symbols of Sumerian imperial identity. Sumerian temples also represented the gods' ability to hoard wealth at sites where people exchanged goods and services. In addition, temples distinguished the urban from the rural world.

Sun Yat-sen (1866–1925) Chinese revolutionary and founder of the Nationalist Party in China.

Sunnis Orthodox Muslims. The majority sect of Islam, Sunnis originally supported the succession of Abu Bakr over Ali and supported the rule of consensus rather than family lineage for the succession to the Islamic caliphate. *See also* Shiism.

superior man In the Confucian view, a person of perfected moral character, fit to be a leader.

superpowers Label applied to the United States and the Soviet Union after World War II because of their size, their possession of the atomic bomb, and the fact that each embodied a model of civilization (capitalism or communism) applicable to the whole world.

supranational organizations International organizations such as NGOs, the World Bank, and the IMF.

survival of the fittest Charles Darwin's belief that as animal populations grew and resources became scarce, a struggle for existence arose, the outcome of which was that only the "fittest" survived.

Suryavamsha The second lineage of two (the solar) in Vedic society. *See* Chandravamsha.

Swadeshi movement Voluntary organizations in India that championed the creation of indigenous manufacturing enterprises and schools of nationalist thought, in order to gain autonomy from Britain.

Syndicalism Organization of workplace associations that included unskilled labor.

tabula rasa Term used by John Locke to describe the human mind before it begins to acquire ideas from experience; French for "clean slate."

Taiping Heavenly Kingdom (Heavenly Kingdom of Great Peace) Religious sect established by the Chinese prophet Hong Xiuquan in the mid-nineteenth century. Hong Xiuquan believed that he was Jesus's younger brother. The group struggled to rid the world of evil and "restore" the heavenly kingdom, imagined as a just and egalitarian order.

Taiping Rebellion Rebellion by followers of Hong Xiuquan and the Taiping Heavenly Kingdom against the Qing government over the economic and social turmoil caused by the Opium War. Despite raising an army of 100,000 rebels, the rebellion was crushed.

Taj Mahal Royal palace of the Mughal Empire, built by Shah Jahan in the seventeenth century in homage to his wife, Mumtaz.

Tale of Genji Japanese work written by Lady Murasaki that gives vivid accounts of Heian court life; Japan's first novel (early eleventh century).

talking cures Psychological practice developed by Sigmund Freud whereby the symptoms of neurotic and traumatized patients would decrease after regular periods of thoughtful discussion.

Talmud Huge volumes of oral commentary on Jewish law eventually compiled in two versions, the Palestinian and the Babylonian, in the fifth and sixth centuries BCE.

Talmud of Jerusalem Codified written volumes of the traditions of Judaism; produced by the rabbis of Galilee around 400 CE.

Tang dynasty (608–907 CE) Regime that promoted a cosmopolitan culture, turning China into the hub of East Asia cultural integration, while expanding the borders of their empire. In order to govern such a diverse empire, the Tang established a political culture and civil service based on Confucian teachings. Candidates for the civil service were required to take examinations, the first of their kind in the world.

Tanzimat Reorganization period of the Ottoman Empire in the mid-nineteenth century; modernizing reforms affected the military, trade, foreign relations, and civilian life.

tappers Rubber workers in Brazil, mostly either Indian or mixed-blood people.

Tarascans Mesoamerican society of the 1400s; rivals to and sometimes subjects of the Aztecs.

Tatish Ruler of Chan Santa Cruz during the Mexican Caste War. The term means "father."

Tecumseh (1768–1813) Shawnee who circulated Tenskwatawa's message of Indian renaissance among Indian villages from the Great Lakes to the Gulf Coast. He preached the need for Indian unity, insisting that Indians resist any American attempts to get them to sell more land. In response, thousands of followers renounced their ties to colonial ways and prepared to combat the expansion of the United States.

Tekkes Schools that taught devotional strategies and the religious knowledge for students to enter Sufi orders and become masters of the brotherhood.

temple Building where believers worshipped their gods and goddesses and where some peoples believed the deities had earthly residence.

Tenskwatawa (1768–1834) Shawnee prophet who urged disciples to abstain from alcohol and return to traditional customs, reducing dependence on European trade goods and severing connections to Christian missionaries. His message spread to other tribes, raising the specter of a pan-Indian confederacy.

Teotihuacán City-state in a large, mountainous valley in present-day Mexico; the first major community to emerge after the Olmecs.

territorial state Political form that emerged in the riverine cities of Mesopotamia, which was overwhelmed by the displacement of nomadic peoples. These states were kingdoms organized around charismatic rulers who headed large households; each had a defined physical border.

Third Estate The French people minus the clergy and the aristocracy; this term was popularized in the late eighteenth century and used to exalt the power of the bourgeoisie during the French Revolution.

Third Reich The German state from 1933 to 1945 under Adolf Hitler.

Third World Nations of the world, mostly in Asia, Latin America, and Africa, that were not highly industrialized like First World nations or tied to the Soviet Bloc (the Second World).

Thirty Years' War (1618–1648) Conflict begun between Protestants and Catholics in Germany that escalated into a general European war fought against the unity and power of the Holy Roman Empire.

Tiananmen Square Largest public square in the world and site of the pro-democracy movement in 1989 that resulted in the killing of as many as a thousand protesters by the Chinese army.

Tiers monde Term meaning "Third World," coined by French intellectuals to describe countries seeking a "third way" between Soviet communism and western capitalism.

Tiglath Pileser III Assyrian ruler from 745 to 728 BCE. This leader instituted reforms that changed the administrative and social structure of the empire to make it more efficient and introduced a standing army.

Tiwanaku Another name for Tihuanaco, the first great Andean polity, on the shores of Lake Titicaca.

Tlaxcalans Mesoamerican society of the 1400s; these people were enemies of the powerful Aztec Empire.

Tokugawa shogunate Hereditary military administration founded in 1603 that ruled Japan while keeping the emperor as a figurehead; it was toppled in 1868 by reformers who felt that Japan should adopt, not reject, Western influences.

Toltecs A Mesoamerican people who, by 1000 CE, had filled the political vacuum created by the decline of the city of Teotihuacán.

tomb culture Warlike group from northeast Asia who arrived by sea in the middle of the third century CE and imposed their military and social power on southern Japan. These conquerors are known today as the "Tomb culture" because of their elevated necropolises near present-day Osaka.

Topkapi Palace Political headquarters of the Ottoman Empire, located in Istanbul.

total war All-out war involving civilian populations as well as military forces, often used in reference to World War II.

transhumant migrants Nomads who entered settled territories in the second millennium BCE and moved their herds seasonally when resources became scarce.

Trans-Siberian Railroad Railroad built over very difficult terrain between 1891 and 1903 and subsequently expanded; it created an overland bridge for troops, peasant settlers, and commodities to move between Europe and the Pacific.

Treaty of Brest-Litovsk (1918) Separate peace between imperial Germany and the new Bolshevik regime in Russia. The treaty acknowledged the German victory on the Eastern Front and withdrew Russia from the war.

Treaty of Nanjing (1842) Treaty between China and Britain following the Opium War; it called for indemnities, the opening of new ports, and the cession of Hong Kong to the British.

Treaty of Tordesillas (1494) Treaty in which the pope decreed that the non-European world would be divided into spheres of trade and missionary responsibility between Spain and Portugal.

trickle trade Method by which a good is passed from one village to another, as in the case of obsidian among farming villages; the practice began around 7000 BCE. Also called "down the line trade."

Tripartite Pact (1940) Pact that stated that Germany, Italy, and Japan would act together in all future military ventures.

Triple Entente Alliance developed before World War I that eventually included Britain, France, and Russia.

Troy Important site founded around 3000 BCE in Anatolia, to the far west. Troy is legendary as the site of the war that was launched by the Greeks (the Achaeans) and that was recounted by Homer in the *Iliad*.

Truman Doctrine (1947) Declaration promising U.S. economic and military intervention, whenever and wherever needed, for the sake of preventing communist expansion.

Truth and Reconciliation Commission Quasi-judicial body established after the overthrow of the apartheid system in South Africa and the election of Nelson Mandela as the country's first black president in 1994. The commission was to gather evidence about crimes committed during the apartheid years. Those who showed remorse for their actions could appeal for clemency. The South African leaders believed that an airing of the grievances from this period would promote racial harmony and reconciliation.

truth commissions Elected officials' inquiries into human rights abuses by previous regimes. In Argentina, El Salvador, Guatemala, and South Africa, these commissions were vital for creating a new aura of legitimacy for democracies and for promising to uphold the rights of individuals.

tsar/czar Russian word derived from the Latin *Caesar* to refer to the Russian ruler of Kiev, and eventually to all rulers in Russia.

Tula Toltec capital city; a commercial hub and political and ceremonial center.

Uitlanders British populations living in Afrikaner republics; they were denied voting rights and subject to other forms of discrimination in the late nineteenth century. The term means "outsiders."

Ulama Arabic word that means "learned ones" or "scholars"; used for those who devoted themselves to knowledge of Islamic sciences.

Umayyads Family who founded the first dynasty in Islam. They established family rule and dynastic succession to the role of caliph. The first Umayyad caliph established Damascus as his capital and was named Mu'awiya ibn Abi Sufyan.

Umma Arabic word for "community"; used to refer to the "Islamic politiu" or "Islamic community."

Universal Declaration of Human Rights (1948) U.N. declaration that laid out the rights to which all human beings are entitled.

universitas Term used from the end of the twelfth century to denote scholars who came together, first in Paris. The term is borrowed from the merchant communities, where it denoted the equivalent of the modern "union."

Untouchables Caste in the Indian system whose jobs, usually in the more unsanitary aspects of urban life, rendered them "ritually and spiritually" impure.

Upanishads Vedic wisdom literature collected in the first half of the first millennium BCE. It took the form of dialogues between disciples and a sage.

urban-rural divide Division between those living in cities and those living in rural areas. One of history's most durable worldwide distinctions, the urban-rural divide eventually encompassed the globe. Where cities arose, communities adopted lifestyles based on the mass production of goods and on specialized labor. Those living in the countryside remained close to nature, cultivating the land or tending livestock. They diversified their labor and exchanged their grains and animal products for necessities available in urban centers.

utopian socialism The most visionary of all Restoration-era movements. Utopian socialists like Charles Fourier dreamed of transforming states, workplaces, and human relations and proposed plans to do so.

Vaishyas Householders or lesser clan members in Vedic society who worked the land and tended livestock.

Vardhamana Mahavira Advocate of Jainism who lived from 540 to 468 BCE; he emphasized interpretation of the Upanishads to govern and guide daily life.

Varna Caste system established by the Vedas in 600 BCE.

vassal states Subordinate states that had to pay tribute in luxury goods, raw materials, and manpower as part of a broad confederation of polities under the kings' protection.

Vedas Rhymes, hymns, and explanatory texts composed by Aryan priests; the Vedas became their most holy scripture and part of their religious rituals. They were initially passed down orally, in Sanskrit. Brahmans, priests of Vedic culture, incorporated the texts into ritual and society. The Vedas are considered the final authority of Hinduism.

Vedic people People who came from the steppes of Inner Asia around 1500 BCE and entered the fertile lowlands of the Indus River basin, gradually moving as far south as the Deccan plateau. They called themselves Aryan, which means "respected ones," and spoke Sanskrit, an Indo-European language.

veiling Practice of modest dress required of respectable women in the Assyrian Empire, introduced by Assyrian authorities in the thirteenth century BCE.

Venus figures Representations of the goddess of fertility drawn on the Chauvet Cave in southeastern France. Discovered in 1994, they are probably about 35,000 years old.

Versailles Conference (1919) Peace conference between the victors of World War I; resulted in the Treaty of Versailles, which forced Germany to pay reparations and to give up its colonies to the victors.

Viet Cong Vietnamese communist group committed to overthrowing the government of South Vietnam and reunifying North and South Vietnam.

Viet Minh Group founded in 1941 by Ho Chi Minh to oppose the Japanese occupation of Indochina; it later fought the French colonial forces for independence. Also known as the Vietnamese Independent League.

Vietnam War (1965–1975) Conflict that resulted from concern over the spread of communism in Southeast Asia. The United States intervened on the side of South Vietnam in its struggle against peasant-supported Viet Cong guerrilla forces, who wanted to reunite Vietnam under a communist regime. Faced with antiwar opposition at home and ferocious resistance from the Vietnamese, American troops withdrew in 1973; the puppet South Vietnamese government collapsed two years later.

Vikings A people from Scandinavia who replaced the Franks as the dominant warrior class in northern Europe in the ninth century. They used their superior ships to loot other seagoing peoples and sailed up the rivers of central Russia to establish a trade route that connected Scandinavia and the Baltic with Constantinople and Baghdad. The Vikings established settlements in Iceland and Greenland and, briefly, North America.

Vishnu The second of three Vedic deities, signifying existence. *See also* Brahma *and* Siva.

viziers Bureaucrats of the Ottoman Empire.

Vodun Mixed religion of African and Christian customs practiced by slaves and free blacks in the colony of Saint Domingue.

Voting Rights Act (1965) Law that granted universal suffrage in the United States.

Wafd Nationalist party that came into existence during a rebellion in Egypt in 1919 and held power sporadically after Egypt was granted limited independence from Britain in 1922.

Wahhabism Early-eighteenth-century reform movement organized by Muhammad Ibn abd al-Wahhab, who preached the absolute oneness of Allah and a return to the pure Islam of Muhammad.

Wang Mang Han minister who usurped the throne in 9 CE because he believed that the Han had lost the mandate of heaven. He ruled until 23 CE.

war ethos Strong social commitment to a continuous state of war. The Roman army constantly drafted men and engaged in annual spring military campaigns. Soldiers were taught to embrace a sense of honor that did not allow them to accept defeat and commended those who repeatedly threw themselves into battle.

War of 1812 Conflict between Britain and the United States arising from U.S. grievances over oppressive British maritime practices in the Napoleonic Wars.

War on Poverty President Lyndon Johnson's push for an increased range of social programs and increased spending on social security, health, education, and assistance for the disabled.

Warring States period Period extending from the fifth century BCE to 221 BCE, when the regional warring states were unified by the Qin dynasty.

Warsaw Pact (1955–1991) Military alliance between the Soviet Union and other communist states that was established in response to the creation of the NATO alliance.

Weimar Republic (1919–1933) Constitutional Republic of Germany that was subverted by Hitler soon after he became chancellor.

Western Front Military front that stretched from the English Channel through Belgium and France to the Alps during World War I.

White and Blue Niles The two main branches of the Nile, rising out of central Africa and Ethiopia. They come together at the present-day capital city of Sudan, Khartoum.

White Lotus Rebellion Series of uprisings in northern China (1790–1800s) inspired by mystical beliefs in folk Buddhism and, at times, the idea of restoring the Ming dynasty.

White Wolf Mysterious militia leader, depicted in popular myth as a Chinese Robin Hood whose mission was to rid the country of the injustices of Yuan Shikai's government in the early years of the Chinese Republic (1910s).

Whites "Counterrevolutionaries" of the Bolshevik Revolution (1918–1921) who fought the Bolsheviks (the "Reds"); included former supporters of the tsar, Social Democrats, and large independent peasant armies.

witnessing Dying for one's faith, or becoming a martyr.

Wokou Supposedly Japanese pirates, many of whom were actually Chinese subjects of the Ming dynasty.

Works Progress Administration (WPA) New Deal program instituted in 1935 that put nearly 3 million people to work building roads, bridges, airports, and post offices.

World Bank International agency established in 1944 to provide economic assistance to war-torn and poor countries. Its formal title is the International Bank for Reconstruction and Development.

World War II (1939–1945) Worldwide war that began in September 1939 in Europe, and even earlier in Asia, and pitted Britain, the United States, and the Soviet Union (the Allies) against Nazi Germany, Japan, and Italy (the Axis).

Wu or Wudi Chinese leader known as the "Martial Emperor" because of his many military campaigns during the Han dynasty. He reigned from 141 to 87 BCE.

Wu Zhao Chinese empress who lived from 626 to 706 CE. She began as a concubine in the court of Li Shimin and became the mother of his son's child. She eventually gained power equal to that of the emperor, and named herself regent when she finagled a place for one of her own sons after their father's death.

Xiongnu The most powerful and intrusive of the nomadic peoples; originally pastoralists from the eastern part of the Asian steppe in what is modern-day Mongolia. They appeared along the frontier with China in the late Zhou dynasty and by the third century BCE had become the most powerful of all the pastoral communities in that area.

Xunzi Confucian moralist whose ideas were influential to Qin rulers. He lived from 310 to 237 BCE and believed that rational statecraft was more reliable than fickle human nature and that strict laws and severe punishments could create stability in society.

Yalta Accords Results of the meeting between President Roosevelt, Prime Minister Churchill, and Premier Stalin that occurred in the Crimea in 1945 to plan for the postwar order.

Yavana kings Sanskrit name for Greek rulers, derived from the Greek name for the area of western Asia Minor called Ionia, a term that then extended to anyone who spoke Greek or came from the Mediterranean.

yellow press Newspapers that sought a mass circulation by featuring sensationalist reporting.

Yellow Turbans One of several local Chinese religious movements that emerged across the empire, especially under Wang Mang's officials, who considered him a usurper. The Yellow Turbans, so called because of the yellow scarves they wore around their heads, were Daoist millenarians.

Yin City that became the capital of the Shang in 1350 BCE, ushering in a golden age.

Young Egypt Antiliberal, fascist group that gained a large following in Egypt during the 1930s.

Young Italy Nationalist organization made up of young students and intellectuals, devoted to the unification and renewal of the Italian state.

Yuan dynasty Dynasty established by the Mongols after the defeat of the Song. The Yuan dynasty was strong from 1280 to 1368; its capital was at Dadu, or modern-day Beijing.

Yuan Mongols Mongol rulers of China who were overthrown by the Ming dynasty in 1368.

Yuezhi A Turkic nomadic people who roamed on pastoral lands to the west of the Xiongnu territory of central Mongolia. They had friendly relationships with the farming societies in China, but the Yuezhi detested the Xiongnu and had frequent armed clashes with them.

Zaibatsu Large-scale, family-owned corporations in Japan consisting of factories, import-export businesses, and banks that dominated the Japanese economy until 1945.

Zamindars Archaic tax system of the Mughal Empire where decentralized lords collected tribute for the emperor.

Zapatistas Group of indigenous rebels that rose up against the Mexican government in 1994 and drew inspiration from an earlier Mexican rebel, Emiliano Zapata.

Zheng King during the Qin era who defeated what was left of the Warring States between 230 and 221 BCE. He assumed the mandate of heaven from the Zhou and declared himself First August Emperor, to distinguish himself from other kings.

Zheng He (1371–1433) Ming naval leader who established tributary relations with Southeast Asia, Indian Ocean ports, the Persian Gulf, and the east coast of Africa.

Zhong Shang Administrative central complex of the Shang.

Zhongguo Term originating in the ancient period and subsequently used to emphasize the central cultural and geographical location of China in the world; means "Middle Kingdom."

ziggurat By the end of the third millennium BCE, the elevated platform base of a Sumerian temple had transformed into a stepped platform called a *ziggurat*.

Zionism Political movement advocating the reestablishment of a Jewish homeland in Palestine.

Zoroaster Sometimes known as Zarathustra, thought to have been a teacher around 1000 BCE in eastern Iran and credited with having solidified the region's religious beliefs into a unified system that moved away from animistic nomadic beliefs. The main source for his teachings is a compilation called the Avesta.

Zoroastrianism Religion based on the teachings of Zoroaster that became the dominant religion of the Persian Empire.

Zulus African tribe that, under Shaka, created a ruthless warrior state in southern Africa in the early 1800s.

Photo Credits

Dagli Orti; p. 189: Vanni/Art Resource, NY; p. 191 (left): Michael Freeman/Corbis; (right): Erich Lessing/Art Resource, NY; p. 193: Erich Lessing/ Art Resource, NY; p. 194: Peter Willi/The Bridgeman Art Library; p. 195: The Bridgeman Art Library; p. 196 (left): Erich Lessing/Art Resource, NY; (right): HIP/Art Resource, NY; p. 197: Scala/ Art Resource, NY; p. 199: Erich Lessing/Art Resource, NY.

CHAPTER 6

Pages 202–03: © The Cleveland Museum of Art; p. 208: Erich Lessing/Art Resource, NY; p. 210: Lauros/Giraudon/The Bridgeman Art Library; p. 212: Vanni/Art Resource, NY; p. 213: AKG Images/Peter Connolly; p. 215: Illustration by Jean-Claude Golvin from *L'Afrique Antique* Tallandier, Paris 2001; p. 216 (left): Bildarchiv Preussischer Kulturbesitz/Art Resource, NY; (right): Landesmuseum, Mainz, Germany; p. 217: Stapleton Collection/Corbis; p. 218 (left): Brian A. Vikander/ Corbis; (right): The Bridgeman Art Library; p. 220: Réunion des Musées Nationaux/Art Resource, NY; p. 221: (all): Courtesy of Bill Welch, "What I Like About Ancient Coins," www.forumancientcoins .com/ moonmoth/ancientcoins.html; p. 226: © The Cleveland Museum of Art; p. 227: David Gurr/Eye Ubiquitous/Corbis; p. 228 (left): The Metropolitan Museum of Art. Gift of Muneichi Nitta, 2003 (2003.593.1) Image © The Metropolitan Museum of Art/Art Resource, NY; (right): image copyright © The Metropolitan Museum of Art/Art Resource, NY; p. 233: Bruno Morandi/Robert Harding World Imagery/Corbis; p. 234: The Art Archive/Palmyra Museum Syria/Dagli Orti; p. 235: NASA/JPL; p. 237: Wikipedia.com.

CHAPTER 7

Pages 240–41: Erich Lessing/Art Resource, NY; p. 244: HIP/Art Resource, NY; p. 246: National Library of China; p. 248 (left): The Bridgeman Art Library; (right): Louis Mazzatenta/National Geographic Image Collection; p. 250: Lauros/Giraudon/ The Bridgeman Art Library; p. 253 (top): Princeton University Art Museum; (bottom): British

Museum/Art Resource, NY; p. 255: Model of House, Chinese. 1st century C.E., Eastern Han Dynasty (25–220 C.E.). Earthenware with unfired coloring, 52×33 1/2 $\times 27$ inches ($132.1 \times 85.1 \times 68.6$ cm). The Nelson-Atkins Museum of Art, Kansas City, Missouri. Purchase: Nelson Trust, 33-521. Photograph by Jamison Miller. p. 256: (clockwise from top left): Asian Art & Archaeology, Inc./Corbis; Royal Ontario Museum/Corbis; Asian Art & Archaeology, Inc./Corbis; p. 257: Erich Lessing/ Art Resource, NY; p. 258: AM Corporation/Alamy; p. 259: The Art Archive/Genius of China Exhibition; p. 260: Image copyright © The Metropolitan Museum of Art/Art Resource, NY; p. 261: Araldo de Luca/Corbis; p. 264: Vanni/Art Resource, NY; p. 265: Robert Harding Picture Library Ltd/Alamy; p. 266: The Art Archive/Museo Capitolino Rome/ Gianni Dagli Orti; p. 267: Museo Arqueológico, Sevilla, Spain; p. 269 (top): Atlantide Phototravel/ Corbis; (bottom): Giraudon/Art Resource, NY; p. 270 (left): Roger Wood/Corbis; (right): Scala/Art Resource; p. 272 (bottom): Fridmar Damm/zefa/ Corbis; (top): HIP/Art Resource, NY; p. 277: Erich Lessing/Art Resource, NY.

CHAPTER 8

Pages 280–81: Charles & Josette Lenars/Corbis; p. 286: Réunion des Musées Nationaux/ Art Resource, NY; p. 288 (left): Scala/Art Resource; (right): Granger Collection; p. 289 (left): Jewish Museum/Art Resource; (right): Uppsala University; 290: Bettmann/Corbis; 291: Scala/Art Resource, NY; p. 295 (top, both): Cameraphoto Arte, Venice/Art Resource, NY; (bottom): Yann Arthus-Bertrand/Corbis; p. 297: Scala/Art Resource, NY; p. 298: Sami Sallinen/Panos Pictures; p. 301: British Library, London, Stein Collection; p. 302 (top): British Museum/Art Resource, NY; (bottom): Dean Conger/Corbis; p. 303: British Museum; p. 304: Werner Forman/akg-images; p. 308 (left): Liu Xiaoyang/Alamy; (right): Pierre Colombel/ Corbis; p. 309: National Palace Museum, Taipei, China; p. 314 (top): Gianni Dagli Orti/Corbis; (bottom): Charles & Josette Lenars/Corbis; p. 315: Angelo Hornak/Corbis; p. 316: Werner Forman/Art Resource, NY; p. 317: Giraudon /The Bridgeman Art Library.

CHAPTER 9

Pages 320–21: Patrick Ward/Corbis; p. 324: Suhaib Salem/Reuters/Corbis; p. 326: Erich Lessing/Art Resource, NY; p. 331: Werner Forman/Art Resource, NY; p. 333 (left): Vanni Archive/Corbis; (right): Patrick Ward/Corbis; p. 334: Bettmann/ Corbis; p. 337: Gavin Hellier/JAI/Corbis; p. 338: Christine Osborne/Corbis; p. 343 (top): akg-images/ Visioars; (bottom): akg-images; p. 345: The Art Archive/British Library; p. 346: (left): Werner Forman/Art Resource, NY; (right): Kurt Scholz/ SuperStock; p. 347: Julia Waterlow/Eye Ubiquitous/ Corbis; p. 350 (left): Copyright © National Land Image Information (Color Aerial Photograph), Ministry of Land, Infrastructure and Transport; (right): Asian Art & Archaeology, Inc./Corbis; p. 351 (left): © The Trustees of the British Museum; (right): CulturalEyes-AusGS/ Alamy; p. 352: Giraudon/ Bridgeman Art Library; p. 354: akg-images; p. 356 (left): imagebroker/ Alamy; (right): Robert Harding Picture Library Ltd/Alamy; p. 357 (top): The Art Archive; (bottom): Werner Forman/ Art Resource; p. 359: Interfoto/ Alamy.

CHAPTER 10

Pages 362–63: Erich Lessing/Art Resource; p. 365: Nik Wheeler/Corbis; p. 367: Wikipedia; p. 371: (left): Werner Forman/Art Resource, NY; (right): HIP/Art Resource, NY; p. 373 (top): Colin Hoskins/Cordaiy Photo Library/Corbis; (bottom): The Art Gallery Collection/Alamy; p. 374: Peter Guttman/ Corbis; p. 380: Keren Su/Corbis; p. 381 (top): Macduff Everton/Corbis; (bottom): The Art Archive; p. 385 (left): Wikipedia; (right): Granger Collection; p. 386: akg-images/Werner Forman; p. 389: Christophe Loviny/Corbis; p. 391 (top): Erich Lessing/Art Resource, NY; (bottom): Hubert Stadler/Corbis; p. 392: akg-images/Volker Kreidler; p. 395: Snark/ Art Resource, NY; p. 396: The Art Archive; p. 398 (left): Charles & Josette Lenars/Corbis; (right): Kevin Schafer/Corbis; p. 400 (clockwise from top left): Otto Lang/Corbis; Alamy; Michael S. Lewis/ Corbis; p. 401: akg-images; p. 404: Bettmann/ Corbis; p. 405: ullstein bild/The Granger Collection; p. 406: Granger Collection.

WORLD · POLITICAL

NATIONAL BOUNDARIES

While man's impact is quite evident, and even striking, on many remotely sensed scenes, sometimes, as in the case with most political boundaries, it is invisible. State, provincial, and national boundaries can follow natural features, such as mountain ridges, rivers, or coastlines. Artificial constructs that possess no physical reality—for example, lines of latitude and longitude—can also determine political borders. The world political map (right) represents man's imaginary lines as they slice and divide Earth.

The National Geographic Society recognizes 192 independent states in the world as represented here. Of those nations, 185 are members of the United Nations.

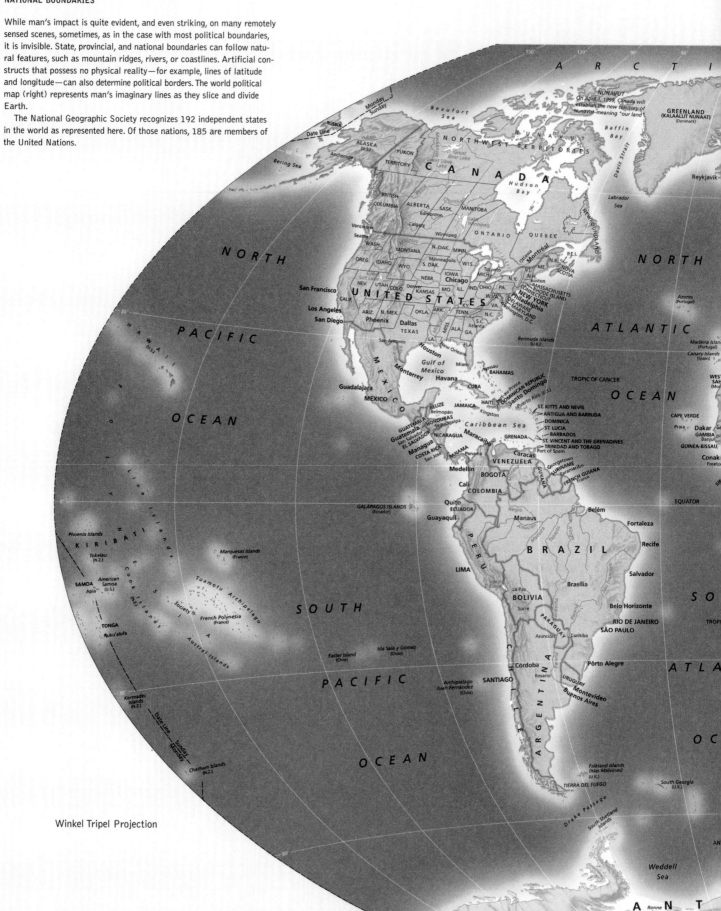

Winkel Tripel Projection